Sonic Transformations of Literary Texts

From Program Music to Musical Ekphrasis

Sonic Transformations of Literary Texts

From Program Music to Musical Ekphrasis

Nine essays edited by Siglind Bruhn

INTERPLAY: MUSIC IN INTERDISCIPLINARY DIALOGUE No. 6
Magnar Breivik and Siglind Bruhn, General Editors

PENDRAGON PRESS
Hillsdale, NY

Other Titles in the INTERPLAY Series

No. 1 *Masqued Mysteries Unmasked: Pythagoreanism and Early Modern North European Music Theater*
by Kristin Rygg

No. 2 *Musical Ekphrasis: Composers Responding to Poetry and Painting*
by Siglind Bruhn

No. 3 *Voicing the Ineffable: Musical Representations of Religious Experience.* Eleven essays edited by Siglind Bruhn

No. 4 *The Musical Order of the World: Kepler, Hesse, Hindemith*
by Siglind Bruhn

No. 5 *Neo-Mythologism in Music: From Scriabin and Schoenberg to Schnittke and Crumb*
by Victoria Adamenko

Cover design by Stuart Ross based on Francis Picabia's watercolor and gouache, *Music Is Like Painting*, from 1914-1917, Collection N. Manoukian, Paris.

Library of Congress Cataloging-in-Publication Data

Sonic transformations of literary texts : from program music to musical ekphrasis: nine essays / edited by Siglind Bruhn.
    p. cm. -- (Interplay: music in interdisciplinary dialogue; no. 6)
Includes bibliographical references and index.
ISBN 978-1-57647-140-1 (alk. paper)
1. Music and literature. 2. Program music. I. Bruhn, Siglind.
ML3849.S715 2008
780'.08--dc22

2008034678

Copyright 2008 by Siglind Bruhn

Table of Contents

Introduction
(Siglind Bruhn) 7

PART I
Fateful Couples and Symbols of Death
in Romantic Piano Music and Opera

Chopin's Preludes Op. 28 and Lamartine's *Les Préludes*
(Anatole Leikin, University of California at Santa Cruz) 13

Transposition and Transition: Berlioz's *Romeo et Juliette*
(John Neubauer, University of Amsterdam) 45

The Iagoization of Otello: A Study in Verdi's Musical Translation
of Shakespeare's Linguistic Dramaturgy
(Jeffrey Kurtzman, Washington University in Saint Louis) 69

PART II
Echoes of Anguish and Agony
in 20th-century Chamber Music

Interpreting Interpretation: Janácek's String Quartet No. 1
(William P. Dougherty, Drake University) 105

"Streicht dunkler die Geigen":
On musical renderings of Paul Celan's poetry
(Axel Englund, University of Stockholm) 119

"*Ming I – Die Verwundung des Hellen*":
Walter Steffens's Compositions about Suffering and Fate
(Siglind Bruhn, University of Michigan) 143

PART III
Intermedial Re-presentations and Reflections in Musical Expressionism

The Tone Poem: Music between Literary Criticism,
Tone Painting, and Sonata Form Plots
(Mathieu Schneider, University of Strasbourg)   173

Schoenberg's *Pierrot lunaire*:
A Musical Transformation of Art Nouveau
(Beat A. Föllmi, University of Strasbourg)   203

Amers: André Boucourechliev and Saint-John Perse,
a Missed Encounter?
(Christine Esclapez, University of Aix-Marseille)   221

Index   233

The Contributors   237

Introduction

Among the possible relationships between art forms that express themselves in different sign systems, the pairing of words and images is the one that is most thoroughly explored. One interartistic genre in particular, which was already known to the Greeks but thereafter long neglected in scholarly discourse, has experienced a significant revival in recent years: *ekphrasis* or, more specifically, ekphrastic poetry, i.e., poems inspired by paintings or other works of visual art, including etchings and drawings, sculptures and works of architecture, photographs, films, etc.

The genre is amazingly broad and varied both historically and geographically. In his three-volume study *Das Bildgedicht*, Gisbert Kranz, a German scholar of ekphrasis, lists 5764 authors of ekphrastic poetry representing 35 languages and 28 centuries, from Homer to 20th-century poets. In his huge bibliography he references altogether fifty thousand poems on visual art.[1] In addition to these poems, one finds a small number of prose works devoted to the same task: that of responding to visual representations.[2]

James Heffernan in his seminal book of 1993, *Museum of Words*, defines ekphrasis concisely as "the verbal representation of visual representation."[3]

---

[1] Gisbert Kranz, *Das Bildgedicht: Theorie, Lexikon, Bibliographie* (Cologne: Böhlau, 1981).

[2] My own favorites in the genre of ekphrastic prose are based on paintings with tragic content by Pieter Brueghel: the short story *Le massacre des Innocents* by Maurice Maeterlinck (first published in *La Pléiade* in 1886, now included in the collection *Les débris de la guerre* [Paris: Bibliothèque Charpentier, 1918]) and book-length narrative *Der Blindensturz* by Gert Hofmann (Darmstadt: Luchterhand, 1985). Maeterlinck's work constitutes a transformation: it tells of peasants near Nazareth who live through the horrific experience of child slaughter. The Belgian writer thus restores the scene portrayed in the 16th-century Dutch painting to its original geographic and historical context. By contrast, Hofmann's presentation is a critique of Brueghel's *The Parable of the Blind*, grounded not so much in the moral and spiritual message of the depiction as in the social conditions the writer imagines to have accompanied the creation of the painting. He follows a group of sightless men through their experience as models for a painter, watching their helplessness as they stumble and grope: exploited subjects who vacillate between the hope for a good meal in payment for their service and the uncomprehending horror at an artist who, for the benefit of his masterwork, requests a repeated and thus exacerbated version of the traumatic experience of blind men falling.

[3] James Heffernan, *Museum of Words: The Poetics of Ekphrasis from Homer to Ashbery* (Chicago: University of Chicago Press, 1993).

In a 1997 essay, Claus Clüver embeds ekphrasis within the broader context of semiotics by extending Heffernan's wording to "the verbal representation of a real or fictitious text composed in a non-verbal sign system"[4] and thus allowing for a wider definition of what may inspire the transmedialization.[5]

Writers, however, are not alone in seeking to cross the boundaries between the media. Just as they respond to non-verbal representations with a creative act in poetry or prose, transposing the style and structure, the message and metaphors from the visual, sonic, or kinetic to the verbal, composers, ever more frequently in the course of the 19th and 20th centuries, have also been exploring the interartistic mode of transfer. Although the musical medium is reputedly abstract, it is in fact capable of responding in myriad ways to representations created in another medium.

From the above definitions, it is only a small step to broader concepts that, in addition to the range of objects to be transmedialized, also extends the range of the agents capable of such an interartistic transfer. In an extensive study published in 2000, I have defined this application of the concept of ekphrasis to the field of music in parallel to Heffernan's wording as "the musical representation of verbal or visual representation."[6]

Taking the broader semiotic definition as a lead, one arrives at an understanding that explains musical ekphrasis more generally as "the musical representation of a text created in a non-musical sign system."

The essays in this volume examine a subset of musical representations of texts created in a non-musical sign system: sonic responses to and interpretations of literary texts, in modes ranging from programmatic tone poems and unusual music-dramatic settings to musical ekphrasis proper. The aim is to demonstrate the various aspects of music's ability to narrate or portray

---

[4]"Ekphrasis Reconsidered: On Verbal Representations of Non-Verbal Texts," in U.-B. Lagerroth, H. Lund, and E. Hedling, eds., *Interart Poetics: Essays on the Interrelations of the Arts and Media* (Amsterdam: Rodopi, 1997), 26.

[5]*Ekphrasis* and *transmedialization* are complementary terms. The former, denoting a rhetorical device, is first found in writings attributed to the Greek historian and teacher of rhetoric during the reign of Caesar Augustus, Dionysius of Halicarnassus; in the sense of the interart genre addressed here, the birth of a reflection on ekphrasis dates back to the 3rd century A.D. when Philostratus the Younger published a series of imaginative descriptions ostensibly of paintings in a gallery at Naples and spoke of this genre as "ekphrasis." By contrast, the term describing not the *result* but the *process* of the interartistic transfer, "transmedialization," is an artificial term, combining the prefix "trans-" for "crossing a border" with an emphasis on the different media represented by the artwork responded to and the one responding to it.

[6]Siglind Bruhn, *Musical Ekphrasis: Composers Responding to Poetry and Painting* (Hillsdale, NY: Pendragon Press, 2000), 28. For an in-depth discussion of the methodology, see also S. Bruhn, "A Concert of Paintings: 'Musical Ekphrasis' in the Twentieth Century," *Poetics Today* 22/3: 551-605.

extra-musical realities, along with the breadth of the various composers' attempts to reflect, comment on, or critique a literary text.

The purest cases of musical ekphrasis are unmixed transmedializations: compositions in which the responding medium does not so much *set* the literary work *to music*—as is the case in standard ways of transforming a poem into song or a drama into opera—but rather reflects or comments on aspects of the source text without including the primary medium, i.e., the words. The best-known examples are probably Schoenberg's string sextet *Verklärte Nacht* (after a poem by Richard Dehmel) and his symphonic work *Pelleas und Melisande* (after Maurice Maeterlinck's Symbolist drama); a lesser-known but exceedingly sophisticated case is Elliott Carter's *Concerto for Orchestra*, a musical ekphrasis of the long epic poem *Vents* (Winds) by Saint-John Perse.[7]

Distanced responses can also be fascinating. Thus William P. Dougherty shows that Janáček in his first string quartet, which according to its subtitle is inspired by Tolstoy's novella *The Kreutzer Sonata*, does not illustrate the story directly in music but re-interprets the tenets of the literary premise. Axel Englund in his comparison of two late 20th-century string quartets responding to poems by Paul Celan demonstrates how composers may choose either to focus on the content and structure of a specific poem or to respond more generally to aspects of contemporary music that they perceive as analogous to Celan's poetics. And Christine Esclapez's reflections on André Boucourechliev's symphonic composition *Amers* confirm that even an instrumental work whose score consists of a single huge page in graphic notation may represent an idiosyncratic reading of a literary work, in this case, Saint-John Perse's poetry collection by the same title.

The sonic response to the literary source is even more sophisticated in the parallels Anatole Leikin draws between the imagery in the French poet Alphonse de Lamartine's set of poems, *Les Preludes*, and Frédéric Chopin's musical symbolism in his Preludes op. 28, especially since Chopin finds a uniquely musical way to correspond to Lamartine's emphasis on death. And while Walter Steffens identifies his piano quartet *Ming I* as a reflection on two German poems, Siglind Bruhn substantiates that ultimately more significant for the music is the composer's unusual approach to the poet Nelly Sachs through a consultation of the Chinese oracle, on the basis of which he comprehends her life-long emphasis on human suffering as universal.

Three chapters in this collection discuss music that does, though to strikingly varying degrees and effects, include texted components. Beat A. Föllmi argues that Schoenberg's *Pierrot lunaire*, although classified as a

---

[7]For indepth analyses and interpretations of these three works, see S. Bruhn, *Musical Ekphrasis*, 141-220.

song cycle, is not a simple setting of a literary text into music but rather a kind of "instrumental music *con parole obbligate*" since the *Sprechgesang* induces a separation of the vocal field from the instrumental elements of sound or noise. Moreover, the music qualifies as a transformation of the aesthetic concept of *Jugendstil* for which the poems serve as a prototype. Jeffrey Kurtzman shows that Verdi in his opera *Otello* ingeniously recreates one of the drama's psychological effect through musical means: just as Shakespeare transmutes his protagonist from noble warrior and beloved husband to irrational murderer through the gradual displacement of Othello's eloquent language and action by Iago's vulgar and irrational modes of expression, Verdi allows the antagonist's musical style to encroach upon that of Otello. And John Neubauer expounds that Hector Berlioz's *Roméo et Juliette*, which is at once a sonic transposition of Shakespeare's play and a bold experiment in musical narration, includes textual components presented by a figure who does not stem from Shakespeare's fictional world and who comments even on music. This and other narrative aspects indicate that in purely formal terms, Berlioz's composition re-enacts unique features of literary romanticism, particularly the novel.

The romantic novel can also usefully be regarded as a model for many so-called "tone poems." While this genre—and program music in general—is distinguished from musical ekphrasis in that essential features of the extramusical inspiration stem from the composer's imagination rather than from another artist's pen or brush, Mathieu Schneider reminds us that the two categories share a significant number of the musical *means* by which composers convey extra-musical content.

The chapters originate from an exciting symposium organized under the title of this volume for the 18th Congress of the International Musicological Society in Zurich and presented there on 15 July 2007. The contributions as they appear here are much more than merely expanded versions of the symposium papers; they have grown not only in size but also in the range of their subject matter. The division of this volume into three parts additionally draws attention to the subject matter shared by many works of musical reflection on pre-existing texts: fate, agony, or death as privileged topics and structure, style, or aesthetics as prominent focal points of analogous representation.

July 2008
Siglind Bruhn

PART I

Fateful Couples and Symbols of Death in Romantic Piano Music and Opera

Chopin's Preludes Op. 28 and Lamartine's *Les Préludes*

Anatole Leikin

When Chopin's Twenty-Four Preludes, Op. 28, first appeared in 1839, many of his contemporaries did not quite know what to make of them. In some respects, Op. 28 still remains an enigma today.[1]

It was not the lack of fugues or any other subsequent pieces in Chopin's set that made a perplexed Schumann call the Preludes "strange pieces," "sketches" and "ruins," "a wild motley" containing "the morbid, the feverish, the repellent."[2] André Gide's famous bafflement is a much later development: "I admit that I do not wholly understand the title that Chopin chose to give these short pieces; *Preludes*. Preludes to what? Each of Bach's preludes is followed by its fugue; it is an integral part of it."[3] In this 20th-century view, Chopin was a trendsetter who dropped the main dish (the fugue) and kept only the appetizer, blazing a trail for the sets of preludes by Scriabin, Rachmaninov, Debussy, Shostakovich, and others. Chopin's contemporaries, however, were not bothered by the absence of fugues or any other larger compositions in Opus 28 that would follow every prelude. They knew perfectly well that Chopin's book of preludes had been preceded by dozens of prelude collections by various composers.

The concert practice of improvising short keyboard preludes before larger works was common in the 18th and early 19th centuries. Preludes were routinely improvised even on monophonic instruments, such as the flute, and even before each movement of a sonata.[4] Many contemporary concert reviews mentioned extemporaneous preludes, which Liszt, Bülow, and

---

[1] I would like to thank Leta Miller for reading an earlier draft of the article and offering numerous and immensely helpful suggestions.

[2] *Neue Zeitschrift für Musik* 41 (Nov. 19, 1839): 163, translated by Edward Lowinsky. Quoted in the critical edition of the Preludes by Thomas Higgins, Norton critical scores (New York: W. W. Norton, 1973), 91.

[3] André Gide, *Notes sur Chopin* (Paris: L'Arche, 1948), 32.

[4] See Leta Miller, "C.P.E. Bach and Friedrich Ludwig Dülon: Composition and Improvisation in late 18th-Century Germany," *Early Music* xxii/1 (February 1995): 67-68.

Anton Rubinstein played before the programmed pieces during their concerts.[5] Because of the improvisational nature of this art, however, there is little documentary evidence to tell us how these preludes sounded. One notable exception are the preludes played by Clara Schumann before most of the compositions she performed in concerts. At her daughters' request, she wrote down some of them, even though she complained that writing the preludes was difficult since she performed them differently every time.[6]

Clara Schumann's recorded preludes are short, between 8 and 40 bars. Some of them are rather all-purpose improvisational studies, with no discernible connections to presumed pieces to follow. Four preludes, however, are conceived as specific introductions to Robert Schumann's works: "Des Abends" and "Aufschwung" from Opus 12, "Schlummerlied" from Opus 124, and the slow movement of the F-minor Sonata.[7] In these four preludes Clara not only sets the key and the mood of the ensuing composition, but also anticipates the main thematic material.[8] These preludes, as well as her concert programs and published reviews of her performances, make it quite clear that improvised introductions were played not only before large-scale compositions but also as lead-ins to shorter works and even as interludes between sonata movements.

Another, rather anachronistic example of preserved improvised preludes can be found as late as 1945. In the live recordings of Josef Hofmann's Golden Jubilee Concert at the Metropolitan Opera House on November 28, 1937, and at Carnegie Hall on March 24, 1945, the pianist improvised short preludes before many of the programmed compositions. These compositions included both shorter and larger piano works, as well as Hofmann's own *Chromaticon* for piano and orchestra.[9]

In the late 18th and early 19th centuries, when the piano became immensely popular and the number of children and adults studying the

---

[5] Kenneth Hamilton, *After the Golden Age: Romantic Pianism and Modern Performance* (Oxford: Oxford University Press, 2008), 105-7; V. V. Krutov, L. V. Shvetsova-Krutova, *Mir Rakhmaninova: temy i variatsii, I* [Rachmaninov's World: Themes and Variations] (Shusharin Y. M, 2004), 402.

[6] Valerie Woodring Goertzen, "Setting the Stage: Clara Schumann's Preludes," in Bruno Nettl and Melinda Russell, eds., *In the Course of Performance: Studies in the World for Musical Improvisation* (Chicago: The University of Chicago Press, 1998), 242-43.

[7] *Ibid*, 242-44.

[8] *Ibid*, 249-51.

[9] The entire Golden Jubilee concert was released on a two LP set by I.P.A. in the 1970s, and then re-released on two compact discs in 1992 by VAI Audio (VAIA/IPA 1020-2). Only a portion of the Carnegie Hall concert has been found so far; this portion is included in the two-disc set by VAI Audio. I would like to thank my graduate student Colin Hannon for drawing my attention to the Golden Jubilee concert.

instrument grew enormously, piano methods and instructional books of piano exercises proliferated. One of the main outgrowths of the piano boom was the genre of the etude. Thousands of studies aimed at the development of piano technique at every level appeared during these decades. The prelude, related to the etude through its purpose of warming-up one's fingers as well as its predisposition for fast passage work, was another flourishing offshoot of the piano's upsurge.

In response to the public's hunger for more preludes, numerous prelude collections appeared in print. Many method books offered detailed instructions on prelude improvisation and included numerous sample preludes in various keys. Students, amateur pianists, and even professional pianists of modest improvisational abilities could either modify or memorize these preludes and then perform them publicly prior to main pieces. Carl Czerny in his instructional book on improvisation described three types of preludes. One is "quite short, as though through only a few chords, runs, passage work and transitional materials one were trying out the instrument, warming up the fingers, or arousing the attention of the listeners. These must conclude with the complete chord of the principal key of the work performed." The second type is "longer and more elaborate, just like an introduction belonging to the following piece; therefore, even the thematic materials from the latter can be introduced therein." The preludes of this kind, according to Czerny, should end on the dominant seventh chord of the following piece. Yet another style of preluding, writes Czerny, is "completely unmeasured, almost like a recitative."[10]

For further reference Czerny recommends his own *Präludien, Cadenzen und kleine Fantasien,* Op. 61; *48 Preludes in All Keys,* Op. 161; and Moscheles's *50 Preludes,* Op. 161. Collections of preludes—either in the most common keys or in all of the keys—were also composed by Clementi, Dussek, Cramer, Hummel, Kalkbrenner, and many others.[11] Some of these preludes were intended for specific companion pieces mentioned in the prelude title; these preludes usually incorporated thematic ideas from the following piece. The majority of published preludes, however, were thematically neutral. Czerny, Hummel, and others did recommend that pianists

---

[10] Carl Czerny, *A Systematic Introduction to Improvisation on the Pianoforte* (Systematische Anleitung zum Fantasieren auf dem Pianoforte), Op. 200. Transl. and ed. Alice L. Mitchell (New York: Longman, 1983), 23.

[11] For fuller lists of books of preludes published prior to Chopin's Op. 28 see Jean-Jacques Eigeldinger, "Twenty-Four Preludes Op. 28: Genre, Structure, Significance," in Jim Samson, ed., *Chopin Studies* (Cambridge: Cambridge University Press, 1988), 172, and Valerie Woodring Goertzen, "By Way of Introduction: Preluding by 18th- and Early 19th-Century Pianists," *The Journal of Musicology* xiv/3 (Summer 1996): 300-9.

individualize the preludes taken from published collections by introducing melodic ideas from the ensuing main pieces.

It was quite obvious to Chopin's contemporaries that a set of preludes in all the keys was not an innovation. Neither was Chopin's arrangement of the preludes in pairs of relative major and minor keys ascending through the sharps and descending through the flats. This particular tonal layout of twenty-four preludes was used for the first time by Hummel in 1814.

And yet, Chopin's set differed strikingly from its precursors, a fact that became apparent from the moment the preludes were presented to the public. As Liszt put it, "Chopin's Preludes are compositions of an order entirely apart; they are not merely, as the title would indicate, introductions to other *morceaux*."[12]

One extraordinary feature of Chopin's Op. 28 is that his preludes turned out to be independent, self-contained pieces rather than actual preludes to something else; after Chopin the term "prelude" has begun to indicate a short character piece.[13] This new concept of the prelude was immediately and universally recognized, for no one at that time suggested using any of Chopin's preludes as introductions to other compositions, like those of Chopin's immediate predecessors. Moreover, Chopin's notion of the prelude without a consequent became vastly popular. Indeed, a prelude leading to something that did not materialize represented a quintessential Romantic ideal, an unending longing for the unattainable, perhaps even the nonexistent.

We know of only two documented cases when two Preludes from Op. 28 were used as introductions to other pieces, and they both took place long after the composer's death. In 1885, a student at one of Liszt's master classes prefaced Chopin's C-minor Nocturne, Op. 48, with Chopin's C-minor Prelude, No. 20. A few decades later, in 1922, Busoni recorded Chopin's Etude in G♭ major, Op. 10 No. 5, placing Chopin's A-major Prelude, No. 7, before the Etude as an introduction. He also improvised a bridge between the two pieces with a short modulation from A major to G♭ major.[14]

Jeffrey Kallberg recently suggested that Chopin might have performed at least one of his preludes as an introduction to an Impromptu. The printed program from Chopin's concert in Glasgow on September 27, 1848, lists "Andante et Impromptu" as the opening number. Kallberg proposed that the "Andante" in question could have been the F♯-minor Prelude No. 8, even

---

[12] Higgins, 91-2.

[13] Jim Samson, *The Music of Chopin* (London: Routledge & Kegan Paul, 1985), 79; Jim Samson, *Chopin* (New York: Schirmer Books, 1997), 158.

[14] Hamilton, 101-2.

though the tempo of this Prelude is indicated as "Molto agitato" rather than "Andante." Kallberg argues against considering the opening "Andante" to be "Andante spianato," Op. 22, partly basing his argument on the key unity, namely, that the F♯-minor Prelude could possibly introduce the F♯-major Impromptu, Op. 36. William Atwood, however, refers to a surviving copy of the original program with opus numbers added in ink. The opus numbers were probably added by John Muir Wood (1805-1892), a Glasgow music dealer and pianist, who organized this particular concert; his son Herbert kept this annotated program. According to the notation on the program, the Impromptu was indeed Op. 36, and the "Andante" was Op. 22.[15]

In the published Op. 22, the Andante spianato is conjoined with the Grand Polonaise. Nevertheless, Chopin had no problem detaching the Andante from the Polonaise and placing it in front of other pieces. He often used the Andante spianato as a program opening that introduced another composition in a different key. The key unity was not an issue from the start, since the Andante and the Polonaise were written in two different keys—in G major and E♭ major respectively—with a short modulating bridge inserted in-between.

Thus, the program from Chopin's concert in Paris on February 21, 1842, listed the G-major Andante spianato as a preamble to the Third Ballade in A♭ major. The program of his London concert on July 7, 1848, began with "Andante Sostenuto et Scherzo (Op. 31)." If there is any question as to what piece introduced the B♭-minor Scherzo, a concert review in the *Examiner* clarified that the opening "Andante" was Op. 22, and that it had been additionally preceded by a slow, most probably improvised introduction in G minor, not mentioned in the program.[16] Chopin then repeated the Andante spianato as an introduction to the Scherzo at a concert in Manchester, on August 28, 1848.[17] Most likely, Chopin improvised a modulating bridge from the G major of the Andante spianato to the key of the subsequent piece, just the way he wrote it in the original tandem of Andante spianato and Grand Polonaise, Op. 22 (G major–E♭ major).

But if no one, including the composer, intended to take single preludes out of the collection and play them as introductions to other works, then placing single preludes into a concert program becomes problematic. Most

---

[15] William G. Atwood, *Fryderyk Chopin: Pianist from Warsaw* (New York: Columbia University Press, 1987), 179, 281.

[16] Atwood, 140, 170, and 247. Interestingly, both performances of Andante spianato and Grand Polonaise, Op. 22, by Hofmann in 1937 and 1945 also started with improvised preludes.

[17] *Ibid.*, 174, 280.

of the preludes are very short. The C-minor Prelude was originally even shorter than its final version, consisting of only the first two phrases (nine measures total). Chopin decided to repeat the second phrase as a concession to the Preludes' French publisher, Camille Pleyel, who "must have felt that the piece was outrageously short, too much so to be published."[18]

The brevity, for instance, of Cramer's, Moscheles's, or Hummel's preludes was never disputed in terms of their publishing or performance because these short introductions were not designed as self-standing pieces. Chopin's preludes, on the other hand, are self-sufficient works rather than utilitarian preambles to longer compositions. The briefness of most of the preludes is not, of course, an artistic shortcoming, despite a once common conviction that small forms were not sufficiently complex and were therefore inferior to large-scale works. This notion has been dispelled by later writers, most recently by Jeffrey Kallberg.

The terseness of Chopin's preludes presents a different kind of predicament, not aesthetic or structural but purely pragmatic. Even though Kallberg urges audiences "to accept the possibility of a work like the A-Major Prelude [...] standing alone in performance,"[19] the prospect of having the audience to settle down after applauding to a previous number, then listen to the A-major Prelude for thirty seven seconds (or to the C♯-minor Prelude for thirty seconds, or to the E♭-minor Prelude for twenty seconds) and applaud again is simply not realistic. It is indeed difficult to imagine a real-life concert program, apart from beginner student recitals, featuring a single stand-alone composition that would last a minute or less.

To be sure, like any other piece, a longer prelude may appear as a separate item on a concert program, and Chopin did write a single prelude, Op. 45. The dimensions, however, as well as the mood of this particular Prelude are comparable to a full-scale nocturne. The only attribute that distinguishes this Prelude from a nocturne is the lack of a fully developed melodic line and the incessant modulations, which impart a strong improvisatory character to the piece.

When Chopin performed Op. 28 in public concerts, he, according to the surviving program listings, played the preludes not as single pieces but in groups. One can see a few reasons why several preludes were strung together in the composer's performance. First, as mentioned above, introducing a single number that lasts less than a minute would fracture a concert program. Second, grouping several preludes together in performances serves to heighten the Romantic sense of yearning, when the opening prelude,

---

[18] Eigeldinger, "Twenty-Four Preludes," 178.

[19] Kallberg, *Chopin at the Boundaries,* 158.

without reaching its presumed goal, is followed by another prelude, then by another prelude, and so forth. How much the popular Romantic sentiment of unfulfilled yen meant for Chopin is difficult to ascertain, however, given his apparent disinterest both in lofty Romantic ideals and in much of contemporaneous music.

There is yet another, perhaps more profound, reason for Chopin to link several preludes in concerts: underlying motivic and conceptual ties joining individual preludes of Op. 28. The opinions on whether such ties exist are sharply divided. Lawrence Kramer maintains that Op. 28 is not a coherent whole but an aggregation of motley pieces, since, in his opinion, Chopin does not link different preludes motivically and "does not arrange them on the basis of any dramatic or expressive logic."[20] Similarly, Kallberg does not consider Op. 28 a set unified through either motivic or harmonic connections. He regards the preludes as self-standing concert pieces, appropriate for performance either separately or before other larger works.[21] Jeffrey Kresky concludes that motivic recurrences are lacking across the Chopin preludes. Only sometimes, writes Kresky, one can detect such a connection: for example, the gesture E-D is prominent in No. 1, finds its way into the melody of No. 2, continues on into No. 3, and is palpable in No. 4.[22]

On the other hand, Jim Samson refers to the preludes as "a unified cycle of independent pieces."[23] Another approach unites Op. 28 on the basis of tuning, i.e., "the temperament of Chopin's piano" and a melodic cell that derives from it, an ascending major sixth followed by a descending major second. As Jean-Jacques Eigeldinger suggests, "In the final analysis, what governs op. 28 and makes it a cycle is the logic of its temperament."[24]

Several writers notice that some pairs of preludes are linked by single common pitches, when the last note of one prelude serves, re-harmonized, as the opening note of the following piece. Kresky writes that Nos. 11–12 are connected by D♯ (Fig. 1), Nos. 17–18 by C, Nos. 19–20 by G, and Nos. 21–22 by B♭ in the bass.[25] Jean-Jacques Eigeldinger points out that Nos. 1–2 and 15–16 are linked by common pitch-classes (E and F, respectively).[26]

---

[20] Lawrence Kramer, *Music and Poetry: The Nineteenth Century and After* (Berkeley: University of California Press, 1984), 99-100.

[21] "Small 'Forms,'" 135-43.

[22] Jeffrey Kresky, *A Reader's Guide to the Chopin Preludes* (Westport, CT: Greenwood Press, 1994), xvii.

[23] Samson, *The Music of Chopin*, 79.

[24] Eigeldinger, "Twenty-Four Preludes," 184.

[25] Kresky, xvi.

[26] Eigeldinger, "Twenty-Four Preludes," 180.

Both Kresky and Eigeldinger mention that Nos. 3–4 are connected by the octave b–b′.[27]

FIGURES 1a and b:
Chopin, Preludes 11
(mm. 26-7)
and 12 (m.1)

Charles J. Smith gives a more extensive list of connections that includes pairs with both one and two shared pitches. Thus, the final bass note A in No. 7 becomes the first bass note in No. 8; the concluding notes in the left hand (played by the thumb) of No. 5, C♯–D, are repeated in the first bar of No. 6 in the left-hand theme, but in reverse, as D–C♯. Other two-pitch links listed by Smith include Nos. 5 (C♯–D) and 6 (D–C♯); Nos. 17 (D♭–C) and 18 (C–D♭); Nos. 21 and 22 (E♭–D in both); and Nos. 23 and 24 (A–F in both).[28]

Occasionally, Smith describes a connection that is rather tenuous and impossible to hear. For example, in Nos. 15–16 the linking role of B♭ is negligible.[29] It emerges momentarily in the right-hand part four bars before the end of No. 15 and does not return until m. 2 of No. 16 in the left hand. A far stronger tie, not mentioned by Smith, can be heard between the treble ending of No. 15 and the treble opening of No. 16 (G♭–F in both Preludes). In addition to these two-pitch connections, there are similar links between Nos. 7 (D–C♯ in the alto, mm. 14-15) and 8 (D–C♯ in the alto, then immediately repeated in the tenor in m. 1); between Nos. 11 (E–D♯ in the alto, mm. 24-25) and 12 (D♯–E in the treble, but in the same octave, m. 1); and between Nos. 15 (G♭–F in the treble, mm. 84-85 and 87-88) and 16 (G♭–F in the treble, m. 1).

The two-pitch links contain not single unconnected notes but rather short coherent motifs. Furthermore, several pairs of preludes are linked by motifs that contain more than two pitches. Thus, Nos. 13–14 are joined by a three-note motif, an elaboration on the semitone gestures listed above. This motif is notated as A♯–B–A♯ (with added neighboring tones) in the top two voices in mm. 37-38 of No. 13 and as B♭–C♭–B♭ in mm. 1-2 of No. 14.

In Preludes 9–10, one of the main thematic elements is a stepwise rise from B to E. In No. 9, this ascending motion opens each of the prelude's three

---

[27] *Ibid.* For a more detailed review of two opposing views on Op. 28 as a collection of independent pieces or as a unified cycle see Kevin Korsyn, *Decentering Music: A Critique of Contemporary Musical Research* (Oxford: Oxford University Press, 2003), 101-23.

[28] Charles J Smith, "On Hearing the Chopin Preludes as a Coherent Set," *In Theory Only*, 1/4 (1975): 8-12.

[29] *Ibid.*, 11.

phrases. At first it is introduced diatonically, as B–C♯–D♯–E in mm. 1-3. Next it appears with a chromatic variation as B–C♮–D♮–E in mm. 5-6. Then it comes back as a combination of the diatonic and chromatic versions, B–C♮–D♮–D♯–E, in mm. 9-12. The same ascending gesture concludes each phrase of Prelude 10. As B♯–C♯–D♯–E it finds its place in mm. 4, 12 and 15-18; as B–C♯–D♯–E it is stated in m. 8.

In Nos. 21–22, besides the right-hand motif E♭–D mentioned by Smith, there is also a left-hand motif B♭–A–G, which is reiterated persistently in mm. 45-54 of No. 21 and then serves as a commencement of No. 22. In the score belonging to his student Jane Stirling, Chopin highlighted this motif by adding the upward stems and moving it to the right-hand part in m. 47. In m. 49, Chopin's fingering in the same score suggests playing B♭–A–G by sliding the thumb on the first two notes, which emphasizes this gesture.[30] In addition, as the opening motif of No. 22, B♭–A–G, continues the line of the last three accented notes in the middle voice of No. 21, D—C—B♭ (Fig. 2).

FIGURES 2a and b: Chopin, Preludes 21 (mm. 45-59) and 22 (m. 1)

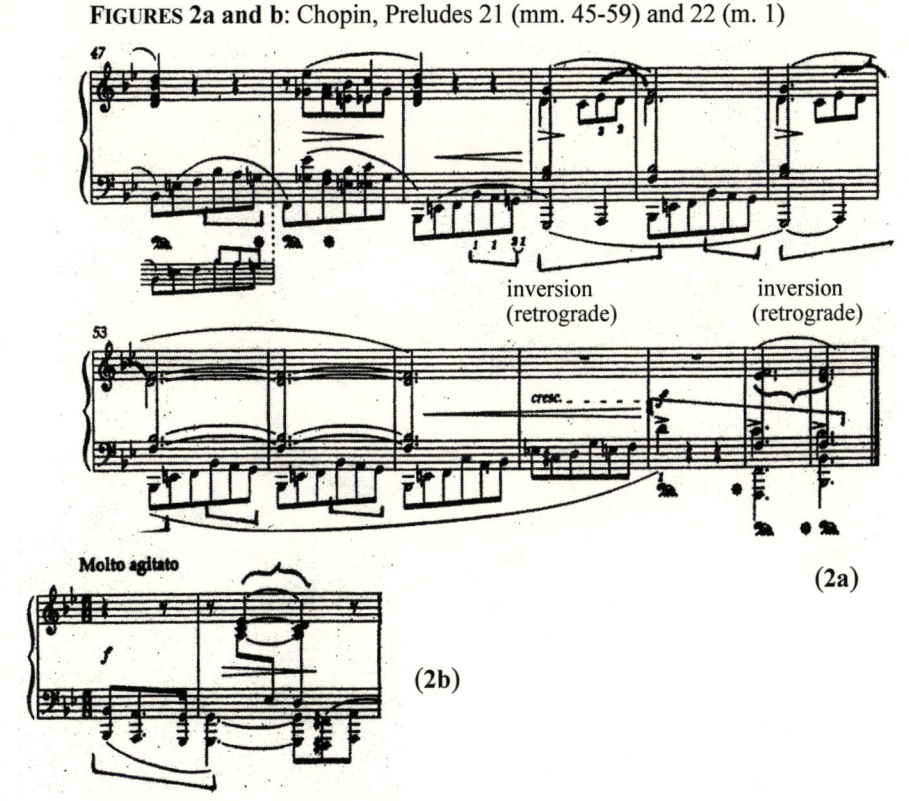

---

[30] *The Complete Chopin: A New Critical Edition,* ed. Jean-Jacques Eigeldinger (London: Edition Peters, 2003), p. 39.

22   *Anatole Leikin*

The systematic pairings of preludes in Op. 28 may shed a new light on a disputed ending of Prelude 1. In Chopin's autograph, one can discern the added E above the lowest C in the bass of the last bar (Fig. 3a). Two early impressions of the French first edition, based on Chopin's manuscript, as well as the English first edition, which derived from the second impression of the French first edition, also contain the E. The second impression of the French first edition belonging to Chopin's student Marie Scherbatoff is shown in Fig. 3b. She used this score during her lessons with the composer who added occasional markings and corrections in her copy; he did not cross out the E in the left hand.

The later editions have all discarded the left-hand E in the last bar of No. 1 as erroneous. This E, however, functions as an important connector between Nos. 1 and 2. As mentioned above, the final E in the treble of No. 1 becomes the opening E in the melody of No. 2. The lower E, which appears in the left-hand part in the last bar of No. 1 and which has been undeservedly omitted from all the later editions, likewise turns into the opening bass notes in No. 2 (Fig. 3c).

FIGURES 3a, b, and c: Chopin, Prelude 1, autograph (mm. 29-34); Prelude 1, French first edition, Scherbatoff copy (mm. 28-34); Prelude 2 (mm. 1-4)

Chopin's Preludes and Lamartine's Les Préludes 23

There is a peculiar uniformity among the motivic connectors: most of them involve half steps, one is a full step (E-D, Nos. 1-2), and one is an ascending third (F-A, Nos. 23-24). Such lack of thematic variety in the music of Chopin is rather unusual; this issue will be addressed later. For now, let us turn to another remarkable feature of Op. 28: all the connections unite the pairs of odd-numbered preludes with the following even-numbered pieces. Smith searched for pitch-identity relations between the even-numbered and the odd-numbered preludes as well (Nos. 4–5, 6–7, 8–9, 10–11, 18–19, 20–21) but concluded that in most cases such relations are non-existent. His attempts to find identical pitch connections between the other five pairs of even- to odd-numbered preludes remain unconvincing because he picks and chooses random pitches within these pairs rather than any direct links.

The links within each pair of preludes are reinforced by the preludes' endings. As Jeffrey Kallberg noted, many preludes in Op. 28 are open-ended. Specifically, eleven of them end on imperfect cadences. In addition, an accented E♭ is added to the concluding tonic in the F-major Prelude, divesting the piece of a full closure. Such uncertain endings are consistent with the nature of a prelude.[31]

Kallberg's remark can be spelled out further: some of the pieces in Op. 28 are more "preluding" than others. More specifically, most of the major-mode preludes have inconclusive endings except for Nos. 7 and 9. By contrast, all but two of the minor-mode preludes close with a perfect cadence. The only two open-ended minor endings are brought about by special circumstances. In the B-minor Prelude the bass carries the melody. After a perfect cadence in mm. 21-22, the bass outlines the tonic triad for the last time and comes to rest on the first scale degree in the final two bars (see Fig. 7 below, p. 34). The ending of the F-minor Prelude on C in the upper voice is part of a larger symmetrical design: both this and the preceding A♭-major Prelude open and close with C in the top voice, which turns out to be one of the links bonding Preludes 17 and 18.

Two questions come to mind. Why did Chopin group the preludes in pairs, tied by both open endings in the antecedent and motivic connectors between the antecedent and consequent? And why did he select the major-to-minor pairings? With regard to the second question, Smith proposes that the odd-numbered preludes are connected to the following even-numbered preludes rather than otherwise because a major tonic triad and its relative minor tonic triad have two pitch-classes in common. He immediately concedes, however, that not every even-numbered prelude begins with a minor tonic triad. The A-minor Prelude, for example, begins in E minor, and yet it

---
[31] Kallberg, *Chopin at the Boundaries*, 154-57.

has two common pitch-classes with the preceding C-major Prelude (E–D). Nos. 16 and 18 open with V^9, but each of them is nonetheless linked to the previous odd-numbered prelude by an identical two-pitch motif. Smith does not offer any explanation as to why Chopin keeps linking together the pairs of preludes, even when the minor-mode consequent does not begin in the tonic.[32] Indeed, it is impossible to answer these two questions by looking only at the internal compositional structure of Op. 28. One has to adopt a historically broader musical and literary vantage point.

Compared to the prelude collections of Chopin's immediate predecessors, the pairings in Op. 28 emerge as a remarkable innovation. Yet, one can trace a precursor of Chopin's binary grouping to a much earlier work: Bach's *Well-Tempered Clavier*. Eigeldinger argues that "Bach's influence on the Preludes, as well as on Chopin's music in general, is infinitely more powerful and subtle than that of any of the post-classical composers."[33] Ever since Chopin was introduced to—nay, brought up on—Bach's music by his first teacher, Adalbert Zywny, the baroque master remained an intrinsic part of Chopin's creative world. One of Chopin's students, Wilhelm von Lenz, wrote that when Chopin played for himself, he would play nothing but Bach. Chopin's preparation for a concert, according to Lenz, was not to practice his own compositions but rather to play Bach for a couple of weeks before the concert. Another student, Friederike Müller, mentioned that during one of her lessons Chopin played for her Bach's fourteen preludes and fugues in a row.[34] As we know, Bach's *Well-Tempered Clavier* was the only music score Chopin brought with him to Majorca, where he completed the Preludes.

Bach's set of preludes and fugues, of course, is not a unified composition but rather a series of binary subsets. Besides introducing the key of the fugue, every prelude anticipates the thematic material of the fugue, just as any well-constructed prelude should. Surprisingly, there have been only a few attempts to analyze motivic connections between preludes and the subsequent fugues in *The Well-Tempered Clavier*. The most notable endeavors were undertaken by Wilhelm Werker and Johann Nepomuk David.[35] Hermann

---

[32] *Ibid.*, 9.

[33] "Twenty-Four Preludes," 173.

[34] Jean-Jacques Eigeldinger, "Placing Chopin: Reflections on a Compositional Aesthetics," in *Chopin Studies 2*, ed. John Rink and Jim Samson (Cambridge: Cambridge University Press, 1994), 120.

[35] Wilhelm Werker, *Studien über die Symmetrie im Bau der Fugen und die motivische Zusammengehörigkeit der Präludien und Fugen des "Wohltemperierten Klaviers" von Johann Sebastian Bach* (Leipzig : Breitkopf and Härtel, 1922); Johann Nepomuk David, *Das Wohltemperierte Klavier: Der Versuch einer Synopsis* (Göttingen: Vandenhoeck & Ruprecht, 1962).

Keller remarked, however, that although both Werker and David drew attention to and clarified some previously neglected thematic relationships, their conclusions often were not always persuasive.[36]

Keller proceeded to expand on the issue of thematic links in *The Well-Tempered Clavier*, but he, too, was not always successful at discerning important thematic connections. Neither he nor his predecessors realized that the strongest, the most readily heard motivic connections occur when related motifs not only have similar intervallic structures, but are also positioned on the same pitches. Identical pitches facilitate the recognition of thematic links.

Thus, while listing and, occasionally, analyzing most of the preludes and fugues with strong thematic connections, Keller mentions a few pairs in which, as he states, motivic relationships cannot be demonstrated.[37] The links between preludes and fugues, he continues, are "even more difficult to prove in Book II than in Book I."[38] If, however, we listen carefully to pitch identities, the supposedly negligible or even absent motivic connections move to the fore and become apparent.

When Keller does find thematic correlations between preludes and fugues, he usually compares the beginning of a prelude with the fugue opening. For example, Keller correctly points out that in Prelude and Fugue in G♯ minor from Book II "the beginning notes of the prelude are also those of the fugue subject."[39] Much more significant, however, as well as more easily perceptible, are the thematic links that regularly join the conclusion of a prelude with the beginning of the following fugue. The G♯ minor prelude/fugue pair from Book II is no exception (see the corresponding braces and square brackets in Ex. 4).

FIGURES 4a and b: Bach, *The Well-Tempered Clavier*, Book II, Prelude (m. 50) and Fugue (mm. 1-2) in G♯ minor.

[36] Hermann Keller, *The Well-Tempered Clavier by Johann Sebastian Bach,* translated by Leigh Gerdine (London: George Allen & Unwin Ltd, 1976), 29.

[37] *Ibid.,* 28-29.

[38] *Ibid.,* 135.

[39] *Ibid.,* 182.

A parallel with *The Well-Tempered Clavier* is important for the understanding of Chopin's prelude pairings, even though Op. 28 has no two pieces written in the same key. Nevertheless, one has to keep in mind that in Slavic music, both folk and professional, there is a special bond between relative major and minor keys. In Russian music theory this modal pattern is known as a "parallelno-permenny lad," which can be translated as a "relative major-minor variable mode." This mode has two relative tonics that alternate on a par with each other.

Several of Chopin's Mazurkas exhibit this modal pattern. For example, in Chopin's Mazurka Op. 24, No. 2 the mode in mm. 5-12 oscillates between C major and A minor; in mm. 1-16 of the Mazurka in A minor (*Notre temps* No. 2), the configuration is reversed, starting off in A minor. Some of his other compositions are, in fact, written in two alternating relative keys; see Waltz Op. 70 No. 2 (F minor/A♭ major); Scherzo Op. 31 (B♭ minor/D♭ major); Fantaisie Op. 49 (F minor/A♭ major).

In Op. 28, preludes in relative keys form pairs akin to the same-key pairs of preludes and fugues in *The Well-Tempered Clavier*. In each pair of preludes, the odd-numbered major prelude keeps its preparatory function and outlines the thematic contents of the ensuing piece. The even-numbered minor prelude takes the place of the main work.

In comparison with Chopin's other double-key compositions, the order of relative keys in the prelude diptychs is reversed. The major-minor layout of relative keys in Op. 28 follows, of course, a traditional arrangement of a circle of fifths (with omitted enharmonic duplications of keys). This explanation is fully sufficient in the case of Hummel's Twenty-Four Preludes, in which the works are not connected to each other but rather are intended as introductions to other pieces by different composers. In Op. 28, however, the fact that each group of two preludes concludes in a minor key carries a special meaning in a broader extra-musical context.

As early as 1841, Liszt and another, anonymous critic mentioned parallels between Chopin's Twenty-Four Preludes and Alphonse de Lamartine's poem entitled *Les Préludes*. We do not know whether Liszt and the other reviewer heard these parallels in the music, learned about them from conversations with the composer, or both. Any of these scenarios, however, bolsters the case.

Lamartine's work, written in 1822 and published as part of his collection *Nouvelles Méditations poétiques*, consists of eleven sub-poems, or cantos, that have no individual titles or numbers and differ vastly in length (for convenience, I will refer to the individual sub-poems as cantos I–XI).[40]

---

[40] I am deeply indebted to Tamah Swenson for her invaluable help with the French text of Lamartine's *Les Préludes*.

The length of the sub-poems ranges from 4 (Cantos II, IV, X) to 115 lines (Canto VIII). The popularity of Lamartine in the nineteenth century was enormous, and what attracted Chopin and later Liszt to the poem is understandable.

The poem contains the most appealing Romantic images of the strange, the mysterious, and the horrifying. The reader finds in the poem bucolic scenes, various states of love from blissful passion to a "gentle smile of happiness" to overwhelming ecstasy to sorrow and tears, nocturnal visions, murmuring streams, sea water ripples, winds, and terrifying deadly storms. Perhaps this chaotic hodgepodge explicates Schumann's characteristic of Chopin's Op. 28 as "strange pieces," "sketches" and "ruins," "a wild motley" containing "the morbid, the feverish, the repellent"; although Schumann did not publicly mention the Lamartine-Chopin connection, his description fit both works perfectly.

Furthermore, the poem overflows with musical imagery. Except for Canto V, every sub-poem is replete with expressive references to instruments (a "vibrating string," the "obedient harp," a "blood-soaked string," "the joyful cymbal," a "troubled string," a "bronze bell ringing from the clock tower"). There are also references to the music of nature, music of the soul and the heavenly spheres, and other highly emotive musical impressions. Marius-François Guyard states that Lamartine's secret of success is music—that is to say, the rhythm, melody, and harmony of the verse. The poet himself defined *Les Préludes* as "une sonate de poesie"(a sonata of poetry).[41]

The organization of the cantos in *Les Préludes* can be seen as an additional stimulus for Chopin to group the preludes in twos. Lamartine ties together Cantos I and II, IV and V, VII and VIII, and, finally, X and XI. In Canto I, the protagonist calls for the divine spirit to come down and inspire him; the spirit descends in Canto II. Canto IV warns of an approaching storm at sea; in Canto V the storm rages in full force. Canto VII announces that a battle nears; Canto VIII describes a terrifying battle between multitudes of combatants. In Canto X the wind touches the hero's lyre as he retreats to his rustic homeland while the spirit ascends (Canto XI).

As Table 1 shows, Lamartine structured *Les Préludes* in such a way that Cantos I, IV, VII, and X function as introductions or "preludes" to the subsequent sub-poems. Cantos III, VI and IX, which separate the pairs, can be compared to interludes. The first two interludes, Cantos III and VI, are reflections upon the preceding pairs of sub-poems. The last interlude, Canto IX, is a plea to the spirit for a consoling song before its departure.

---

[41] Marius-François Guyard, ed., Preface to Alphonse de Lamartine, *Méditations poétiques* (Éditions Gallimard, 1981), 17.

FIGURE 5: The inner structure of Lamartine's *Les Préludes*

I/II   III   IV/V   VI   VII/VIII   IX   X/XI

Such symmetrical structure of alternating pairs and single cantos works admirably well in *Les Préludes*. The binary framework of the twenty-four major and minor keys, however, is not conducive to creating a musical analogue to the structure of *Les Préludes*. Instead of four pairs with three interludes in between, Chopin writes twelve major-minor pairs with no interludes. As mentioned earlier, the major-minor order is opposite to the succession of minor-major keys in all of Chopin's double-key compositions (Op. 70 No. 2, Op. 31, and Op. 49). The reasons for this reversal can also be gleaned from Lamartine's *Les Préludes*.

Trying to decipher tone-painting reflections of *Les Préludes* in Chopin's Op. 28 is perhaps the least rewarding undertaking, although one can hear in the preludes many of the poem's images expressed through fairly conventional means. Prelude 3 can be associated with a murmuring brook, while in Prelude 10 "the whisper of a fragrant breeze" passes over the hero's soul. Prelude 19 possibly portrays what Lamartine describes in II: 1-4 as

> La harpe obéissante
> A frémi mollement sous son vol cadencé
> Et de la corde frémissante
> Le souffle harmonieux dans mon âme a passé![42]

The rising and falling waves of the stormy sea are depicted in Prelude 24, with the ship plunging down in the end.

However these and other programmatic correspondences may be played out, they are subjective, widely open to individual interpretation, and therefore inconclusive. A much more substantial issue is the poem's heightened emotional pitch and the intensity of its expressive states: love, fear, passion, despair, futility, misery, joy, desolation, grief, exultation, melancholy. Lamartine draws sketches of one's progress through stages of wretchedness and loss: the discovery of passion and, in the end, of its ephemeral nature; the inability to hold onto the sands of time as precious life trickles through one's fingers; the horrifically destructive behavior and its consequences; and, finally, the resignation to and acceptance of death.

Death is a recurrent, nearly obsessive theme in Lamartine's *Les Préludes*. In Canto III, lines 41-45, the protagonist ruminates at the brook-side on the passing of time and vanishing of life "with each breath we take":

---

[42] "The obedient harp / Trembled indolently under its cadenced flight, / And from the vibrating string / Harmonious inspiration has entered my soul!"

> Tout naît, tout passe, tout arrive
> Au terme ignoré de son sort:
> A l'Océan l'onde plaintive,
> Aux vents la feuille fugitive,
> L'aurore au soir, l'homme à la mort.[43]

In Canto V, a storm at sea hurls a ship to the bottom of a "black abyss"; the sub-poem is filled with ominous images of drowning, the disintegration of life, and the anguish of physical suffering leading to death. Canto VIII describes (in lines 45-50) a bloody battle in which two waves of soldiers crash against each other:

> La mort vole au hasard dans l'horrible carrière :
> L'un périt tout entier; l'autre, sur la poussière,
> Comme un tronc dont la hache a coupé les rameaux,
> De ses membres épars voit voler les lambeaux,
> Et, se traînant encor sur la terre humectée,
> Marque en ruisseaux de sang sa trace ensanglantée.[44]

In Canto XI the hero escapes to the rustic homeland of his childhood before he must die.[45]

Two preludes from Op. 28 have recently been analyzed in terms of their symbolic representation of death. Carl Schachter, in an insightful analysis of Prelude 4, states the following:

> The 5–6–5 and 6–5 neighbor-tone figures in minor have a long association with the affect of grief (inherited from Phrygian compositions of the Renaissance); and minor-mode basses descending chromatically to 5 (also embodying Phrygian characteristics) have been lament figures since the seventeenth century. Semitonal intensity combined with downward motion seems an appropriate musical analogue to actions and feelings associated with loss, sadness, and death.[46]

---

[43] "All is born, all proceeds, all arrives / At the unknown hour of its fate: / To the Ocean the plaintive waves,/ To the wind fugitive leaves,/ The dawn to evening, man to death."

[44] "Death flies at random in this horrible career: / One perishes fully; the other, in the dust, / Like a trunk from which the ax has hacked off its limbs, / From its scattered members, sees the flying pieces, / And, again dragging itself on the moistened ground, / In streams of blood, marks its bloodied trail."

[45] It has been noted that Lamartine wrote *Les Préludes* two years after his happy marriage in 1820. For this reason, the poem is considered to be generally more cheerful than his previous writings. Later Lamartine returned to his habitual gloom and melancholy.

[46] Carl Schachter, "The Triad as Place and Action." *Music Theory Spectrum,* 17/2 (Fall 1995): 152.

Schachter concludes that the E-minor Prelude's motivic design and other stylistic aspects render it as "a vision of death" and relate "to countless explicitly death-oriented pieces—funeral marches, threnodies, operatic scenes, and the like."[47] In an earlier article, Eigeldinger finds an interpretational angle that strengthens Schachter's assertion. According to Eigeldinger, in the E-minor Prelude "the layout of the left hand, with its chords in close position, cloaks the descending, chromatic movement of three independent lines;" this motion "represents Chopin's response to the harmonic polyphony of the "Crucifixus" from the B-minor Mass."[48]

Eigeldinger's observation can be expanded further. The E-minor Prelude, obviously, is written in the same key as the "Crucifixus." The melodic incipits both in Prelude 4 and in the "Crucifixus" (after the orchestral introduction) are nearly identical. The ostinato figure of the "Crucifixus," a chromatic descent from E to B, finds its way into the Prelude as well. It first appears in the upper line of the left-hand part (mm. 1-8) and then is imitated, in a *stretto* fashion, in the bass (mm. 6-12). During the second half of the Prelude, this chromatic descending gesture gradually disintegrates.

In the last few bars, the "Crucifixus" modulates to G major with the concluding tonic featuring B in the top voice. Similarly, but in reverse, the E-minor Prelude is preceded by a G-major Prelude in which the concluding tonic has B in the melody; this B, as a pivot tone, connects both preludes. The key reversal actually renders the E-minor Prelude more distressing than the "Crucifixus." While the latter leads from death to life—and to the "Et resurrexit" as the next movement in the Mass—the Prelude's path proceeds in the opposite direction.

Another recently discussed example of a death-haunted piece from Op. 28 is the A-minor Prelude.[49] Throughout this Prelude both the left- and the right-hand parts contain quotations of the medieval chant Dies irae. The endings of the first three melodic phrases invoke another doleful genre: the funeral march. Yet another ecclesiastic allusion, in addition to the Dies irae, is introduced in the last two and a half bars of the Prelude. In and of itself, the character of this concluding chorale is not tragic. Its sorrowful connotations are "contextually induced":

---

[47] Ibid.

[48] Eigeldinger, "Twenty-Four Preludes," 176.

[49] Anatole Leikin, "Chopin's A-Minor Prelude and its Symbolic Language," *International Journal of Musicology* 6 (1998): 149-62.

Under the somber shadows of the Dies irae and the funeral march, this otherwise ordinary chorale becomes part of a general mournful discourse. Similarly, the semantic meaning of the swaying accompanimental figures in the reverberating lower register is contextually induced: within the given milieu, these figures evoke the funereal ringing of church bells.[50]

Finally, the nearly disintegrated tonality in the A-minor Prelude mirrors a frequent literary depiction of death as "destruction, ruin, and decay."[51] The entropic image of death is also found in the text of the Dies irae ("the world shall resolve in ashes") and is a common thread in Romantic literature.[52]

In Lamartine's poem, the subject of death appears immediately after the introductory diptych, in the first interlude (Canto III). In the subsequent pairs of the cantos—IV/V, VII/VIII, and X/XI—every ensuing unit (Cantos V, VIII, and XI) presents a different reflection on death. Liszt summarized this aspect of Lamartine's work in the program attached to his own symphonic poem *Les Préludes*: "What is life but a series of preludes to that unknown song, to which the first solemn note is intoned by Death?"

The difference between Liszt's and Chopin's treatments of the same poetic prototype is apparent. Liszt, typically, writes a programmatic composition with overt references to selected events, images, and ideas of *Les Préludes*. Chopin, just as characteristically, disguises his compositional process and conceals all the allusions and, as we will see shortly, musical quotations. Nonetheless, the major-minor pairs of preludes in Op. 28 outline the same notion: life as a prelude to death. Since there are no interludes, this conception is forcefully introduced in the opening diptych, Preludes 1 and 2. Chopin's C-major Prelude is a joyous, sensuous, hyperventilating affair, full of life and excitement. The bleak A-minor Prelude, as described earlier, is a symbol of death.

Similar relationships within the remaining pairs of major/minor preludes continue throughout the cycle, each pair ending either sorrowfully or tragically: with an elegy in Prelude 6, a funeral march in Prelude 20, and so forth. There is only a single piece of documentary evidence that shows Chopin's intentions concerning the major-minor pairings, but it is quite telling: the ascending octave pickup b-b′ in No. 4 was added later, after the Prelude had been completed. Since the preceding Prelude ends with an

---

[50] Ibid., 158.
[51] William Shakespeare, *Richard II*, Act III.
[52] Leikin, "Chopin's A-Minor Prelude," 159.

identical octave (filled in with two more notes of the G-major tonic), the added anacrusis in No. 4 strengthens the link between the two pieces.[53]

The thematic connections within Op. 28 go beyond the major/minor pairing. Jim Samson mentions a two-note "trill" motif in Preludes 1 and 5.[54] The "trill" motifs are also prominent in Preludes 4, 10, 11, 14, and 17. Moreover, there are other motifs that recur repeatedly in Op. 28. Some of them can be heard easily, such as the motif E–F♯–E–D–C♯–B in Prelude 6 (mm. 7, 15-17, and 19-20) and its transposed forms in Preludes 19 (mm. 49-53 and 57-61) and 20 (mm. 1-2, 8). Other recurrent motifs are more subtly woven into the thematic fabric of Op. 28; remarkably, as I will show, all these recurring motifs spring from a single source.

Prelude 2, the first "death" prelude in the cycle, provides a decisive clue. Chopin found perhaps the most appropriate musical reference to symbolize death and, at the same time, to unify the set: the Dies irae chant. It is the most powerful and recognizable part of the Requiem Mass, a fitting musical counterpart to Lamartine's message.

The Dies irae is also a marvelously constructed melody consisting of continually interlocking symmetries. As Fig. 6a demonstrates, there is not a single note in this tune that is not part of a symmetrical interplay. A logical extension of the multiple motivic symmetries within the Dies irae are melodic variants of these motifs based on inversions, retrogrades, inverted retrogrades, or combinations thereof (Fig. 6b).

FIGURE 6a: Dies irae (with motifs)

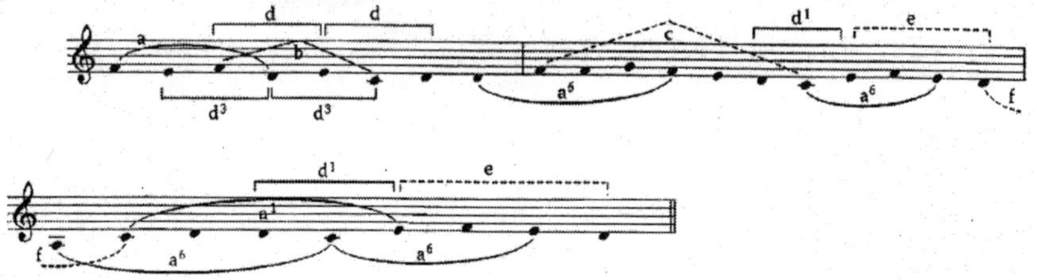

The motivic chart in Fig. 6b may seem speculative, but, astoundingly, Chopin incorporates all of the motifs listed in this chart into his preludes. Fig. 7 illustrates how Dies irae motifs are welded into the B-minor Prelude. As in the chant itself, the intricacy of intertwining symmetries, palindromic at times, is extraordinary.

---

[53] Eigeldinger, 180.
[54] Samson, *The Music of Chopin*, 74.

Chopin's Preludes and Lamartine's Les Préludes 33

FIGURE 6b: the variants of the Dies irae motifs

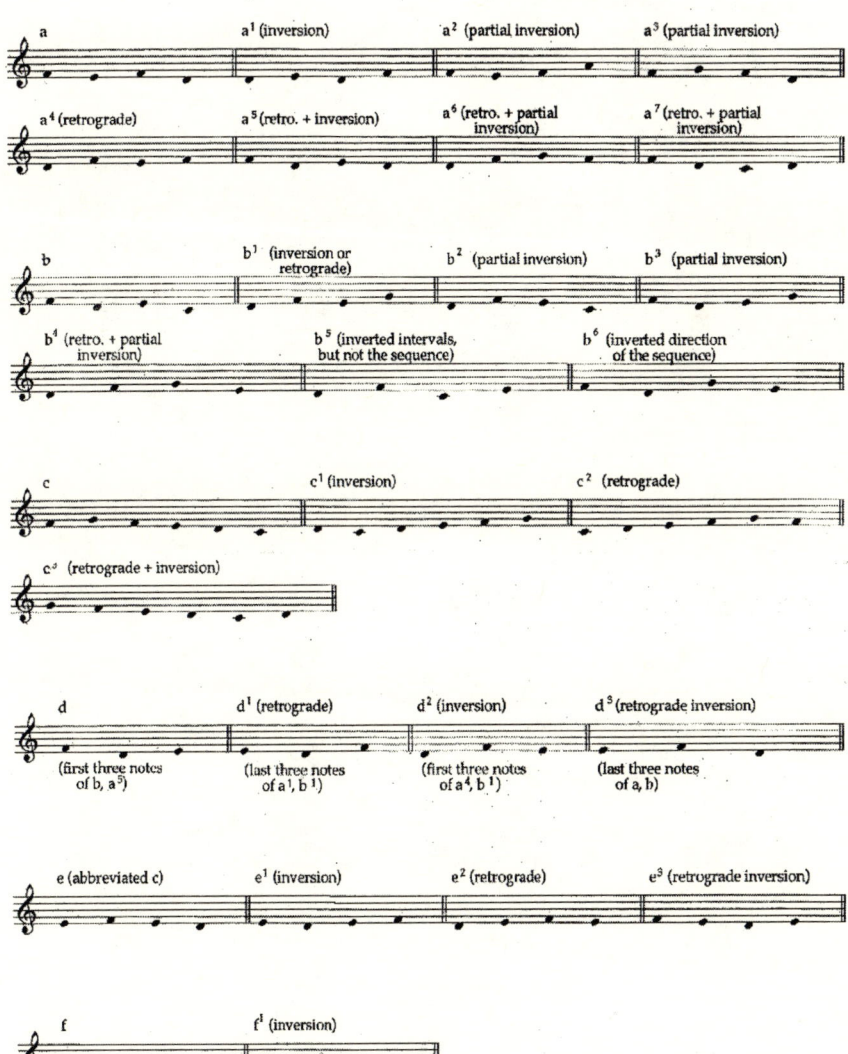

FIGURE 7: Chopin, Prelude 6

Chopin's Preludes and Lamartine's Les Préludes

The Dies irae motifs, listed in Figure 6b, imbue not only the minor-mode preludes but in fact are evidenced in every piece within Op. 28. In this regard, Chopin goes further than Lamartine in a musical portrayal of death, converting a recurrent idea into an omnipresent theme. Thus, the E♭-major Prelude, ostensibly a serene "harp" piece, includes a multitude of Dies irae motifs emerging in different parts of musical texture.

FIGURE 8: Chopin, Prelude 19

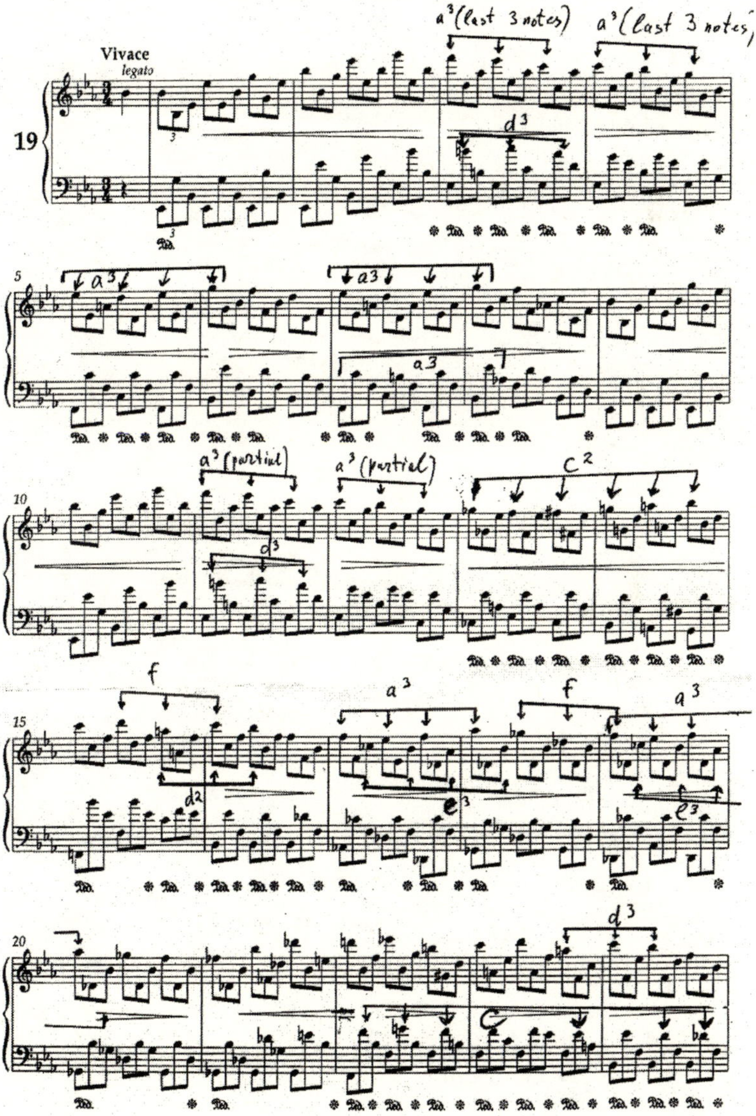

FIGURE 8 continued

The tranquility of the E♭-major Prelude is interrupted by two sudden, rather explosive crescendos (mm. 29-32 and 65-67) that reveal a disquieting undercurrent punctuated by the continual presence of Dies irae. These

FIGURE 8 continued

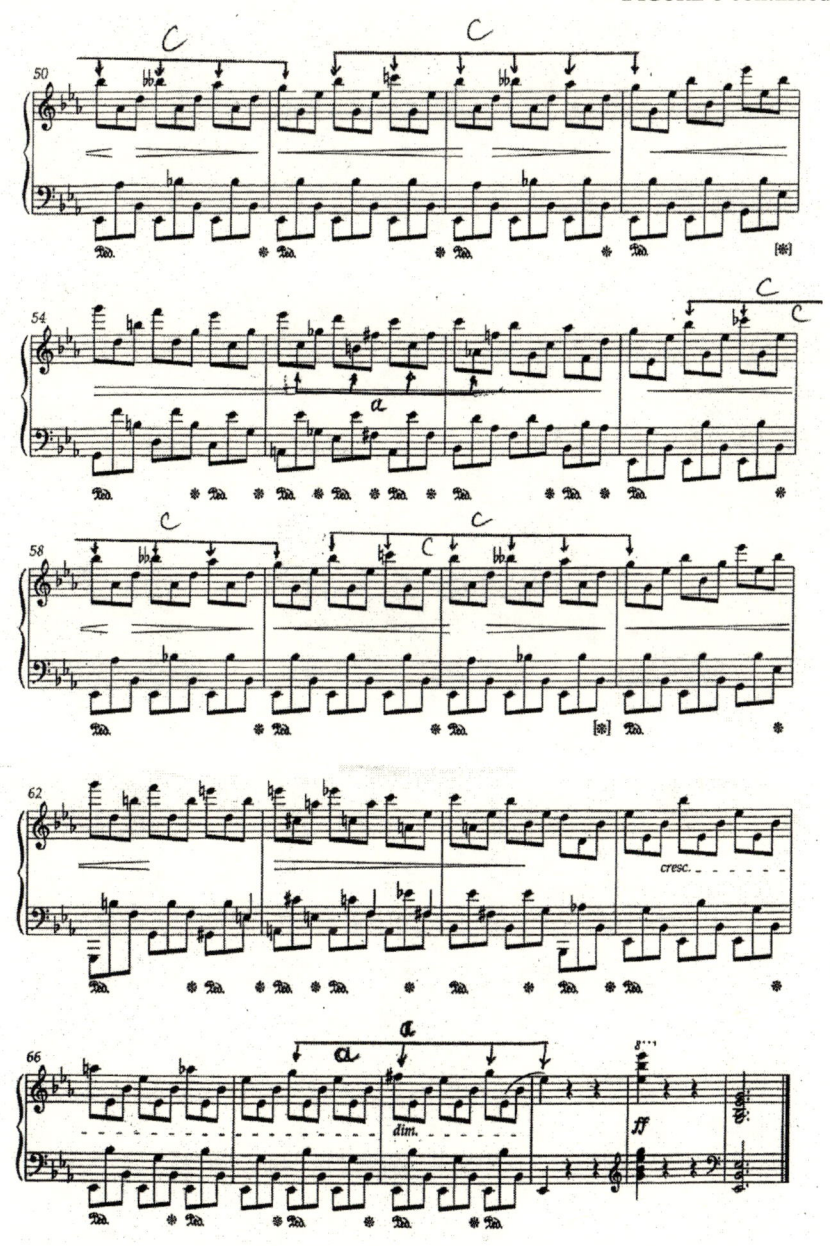

disconcerting crescendos are commonly overlooked or underplayed in performances of the Prelude.

FIGURE 9: Chopin, Prelude 12

Another frequent misinterpretation of Prelude 19 is its tempo. The indicated tempo marking is Vivace, which most modern pianists interpret as "fast" or "very fast." The traditional meaning of Vivace, however, is much slower, and Chopin, through his teacher Josef Elsner, was well steeped in musical traditions. For example, Leopold Mozart in his *Versuch einer gründlichen Violinschule* lists Vivace as the slowest of the fast tempi, slower than Allegro moderato and Allegretto. Jean-Jacques Rousseau also maintains in the *Dictionnaire de musique* that Vivace refers to the character of the work rather than its tempo.[55] Indeed, if the tempo of Prelude 19 (as well as the tempo of Prelude 11 in B major, which is also marked Vivace) adheres to the traditional guidelines, its gentle tenderness is beguiling, and it is easy for the Dies irae motifs to emerge unobstructed. In the exceedingly rapid tempo common today, Prelude 19 whizzes by in a cheerful gallop.

For the pianist, knowing which motifs of the Dies irae are used in every prelude, in what melodic form, and in which part of musical texture, is just as important as knowing the polyphonic structure of a Bach fugue. Most performers emphasize the treble in Prelude 12 as the leading voice. A far more significant part, however, is articulated by the left-hand thumb. Chopin, who considered the thumb the strongest finger, often entrusted it with carrying the main melody. In Op. 28, for example, the right-hand thumb plays an entire melodic line in Preludes 1 and 8. In Prelude 12 the left-hand thumb delivers several Dies irae motifs (see Fig. 9, previous page), which makes clear that the part played by the left-hand thumb constitutes the Hauptstimme, while the eighth-note runs in the top part form the Nebenstimme.

Even more fascinating is the placement of the Dies irae motifs in Prelude 16. Like Prelude 12, this piece is usually presented as a fast-moving melody above a light-footed oom-pah accompaniment. Many editions, including the highly influential Paderewski edition, perpetuated this approach by modifying Chopin's pedaling and introducing pedal changes every half a bar (Fig. 10).

In Chopin's autograph, the initial instructions to change the pedal every half a bar are crossed out, and the new indications direct the pianist to sustain the pedal much longer, for up to three measures at a time (Fig. 12). The new directions seem inexplicable, and I have not heard any pianist abide by Chopin's pedaling in this case. There is, nevertheless, an explanation of this unusual pedaling: the left-hand thumb plays the melodic line containing Dies irae motifs, and the pedal markings meticulously follow the individual notes in these motifs. In the recent volume of the Preludes, published as part of *The Complete Chopin—A New Critical Edition* (ed. Jean-Jacques Eigeldinger, Peters Edition, London), Chopin's pedaling is restored (see Fig. 12). Performed in this manner, with the Dies irae melodies trumpeted in the tenor against the flurries of pedaled sixteenths in the treble, the Prelude changes its character dramatically. Instead of a lighthearted dance-like affair, the Prelude turns into a terrifying, almost apocalyptic musical vision.

---

[55] See Leta E. Miller, "C.P.E. Bach's Sonatas for Solo Flute." *Journal of Musicology,* 11/2 (Spring 1993): 210.

40 *Anatole Leikin*

FIGURE 10: Chopin, Prelude 16 (the Paderewski Edition)

Space limitations do not allow me to include detailed analyses of the Dies irae motifs in the remaining Preludes. Instead, I would like to offer a catalogue of the Dies irae motifs and the preludes that incorporate them:

FIGURE 11: Dies irae motifs in Chopin's preludes

Motifs	Preludes (by numbers)	Motifs	Preludes (by numbers)
(a)	2, 3, 6, 9, 11, 12, 15, 17, 19, 20	(c)	4, 6, 8, 9, 10, 11, 12, 13, 14, 15, 16, 19, 20
(a^1)	6, 11, 12, 16, 17, 18, 24		
(a^2)	1, 6, 13, 16, 17, 18, 19, 22	(c^1)	1, 9, 10, 15, 17, 19
(a^3)	3, 5, 6, 8, 10, 11, 21, 24	(c^2)	1, 12, 15, 19
(a^4)	1, 6, 8, 12	(c^3)	3, 6, 8, 24
(a^5)	6, 8, 11, 21		
(a^6)	2, 13, 21	(d)	7, 13, 16, 17, 20, 21, 22
(a^7)	3, 4, 8, 12, 17, 19	(d^1)	15
		(d^2)	4, 5, 12, 14, 17, 18, 19, 20, 21, 23, 24
(b)	1, 7, 11, 13, 15, 17, 21, 22, 23, 24		
(b^1)	4, 5, 13, 19	(d^3)	2, 3, 7, 10, 13, 15, 17, 19, 20
(b^2)	8, 11, 15		
(b^3)	7	(e)	2, 3, 4, 7, 8, 12, 13, 15, 19
(b^4)	22	(e^1)	4, 8, 15
(b^5)	24	(e^2)	6, 15
		(e^3)	3, 12, 15, 19, 20
		(f)	2, 19, 21, 22
		(f^1)	4, 5, 9

FIGURE 12: Chopin, Prelude 16 (Peters Critical Edition)

FIGURE 12 continued

Chopin's concert-programming preferences for the preludes remain unclear. He never played the entire set in public concerts; but at the same time, as far as we know, he never publicly performed a single Prelude either. The existent concert programs and reviews mostly mention indeterminate groups of Preludes. Twice, in 1841 and 1848, the number of preludes was listed as four, but without specifying which preludes were performed.[56]

---

[56] Eigeldinger, 170; William G. Atwood, *Fryderyk Chopin: Pianist from Warsaw* (New York: Columbia University Press, 1987, 236.

Chopin's Preludes and Lamartine's Les Préludes

The fact that Chopin only performed selected groups of preludes in public concerts does not contradict the idea of Op. 28 as a unified cycle. The concert practice of the time did not treat a symphony, concerto, or sonata as an unbreakable sacrosanct whole. Selected movements from symphonies and concertos were commonly performed in public concerts in the late 18th and early 19th centuries.[57] Parisian audiences from the early 1800s into the 1830s enthusiastically applauded between the movements of an entire symphony, forcing the orchestras to repeat the individual movements. Movements of a symphony or a concerto were habitually interspersed in concerts with other, smaller works. Thus, the first three movements of the Ninth Symphony were separated from the choral finale by a few popular songs by Weber and Rossini.[58] Chopin himself, whether he performed works by others or his own compositions, frequently played only selected movements of concertos and sonatas.[59]

Consequently, even though Op. 28 forms a unified cycle, it does not necessarily have to be performed in its entirety. The intrinsic links within the diptychs of major/minor preludes, however, should be taken into consideration. Playing selected preludes in sub-sets of two, in which every major-mode prelude functions as an antecedent to the following minor-mode piece (a "prelude to death"), will maximize the dramatic effects generated by each sub-set.

In any case, whether the preludes are played as a whole or in selected sub-sets, the striking novelty and the dramatic significance of the cycle, inspired by Lamartine's *Les Préludes* and pervaded by the Dies irae, is unmistakable: Chopin's Op. 28 is essentially a piano requiem in twenty-four movements.

---

[57] Mary Sue Morrow, *Concert Life in Haydn's Vienna: Aspects of a Developing Musical and Social Institution* (Stuyvesant, NY: Pendragon Press, 1989), 153-4, 158.

[58] James H. Johnson, *Listening in Paris: A Cultural History* (Berkeley, CA: University of California Press, 1995), 199, 258-60.

[59] Atwood, 69, 83, 87, 157.

The Aftermath of Music's Emancipation from Language: Berlioz's Introduction to *Roméo et Juliette*

John Neubauer

Music and Language in the Early 19th Century

Joseph Addison still held that music was "a very agreeable Entertainment, but if it would take the entire Possession of our Ears, if it would make us incapable of hearing Sense," he would follow Plato and banish it.[1] Nietzsche, however, remarked in Section 6 of *The Birth of Tragedy*: "The poems of the lyrist can express nothing that did not already lie hidden in that vast universality and absoluteness in the music that compelled him to figurative speech. Language can never adequately render the cosmic symbolism of music."[2] I have tried to show in my book *The Emancipation of Music from Language*[3] that between these two writers, more precisely in the decades before and after 1800, an aesthetic revolution took place: if pure instrumental music had earlier been regarded as inferior, it now became a model art form, not only among the musical genres but among all the arts. From now on, as Walter Pater remarked, all the arts came to aspire to the condition of music, which meant that syntax, the articulation and combination of elements, came to dominate semantics, the content of the whole and the constituent parts of a work. For the first time in the Western history of aesthetics, abstract art assumed the pinnacle within the hierarchy of arts.

My study took the history of this transformation to about 1800, when texts by the first generation of German romantics (Wilhelm Heinrich

---

[1] *The Spectator*, March 21, 1711.

[2] "Die Dichtung des Lyrikers kann nichts aussagen, was nicht in der ungeheuersten Allgemeinheit und Allgültigkeit bereits in der Musik lag, die ihn zur Bilderrede nötigte. Der Weltsymbolik der Musik ist eben deshalb mit der Sprache auf keine Weise erschöpfend beizukommen" (Friedrich Nietzsche, *Die Geburt der Tragödie* (Munich: Hanser, 1954), 1:43).

[3] John Neubauer, *The Emancipation of Music from Language* (New Haven: Yale University Press, 1986).

Wackenroder, Novalis, E.T.A. Hoffmann) formulated a new aesthetics. I could only hint at some of the problems that extending my history into the 19th century would present. Foremost among these was that the radical revolution or paradigm shift did not eliminate texted music for good. "Do the lied, the Romantic opera, and frequent mimetic interpretations of instrumental music by Romantics not indicate that the verbal paradigm was not summarily destroyed by the revolution?"[4]—asked my imaginary interlocutor. To this I replied that the verbal tradition of music did indeed continue:

> [T]he history of music aesthetics, and intellectual history in general, is not constituted of epochs defined by a single paradigm. [...] In general the flux of ideas on any subject cannot be forced into longer cohesive periods separated by shorter revolutionary upheavals. Models of this kind, whether indebted to the notion of zeitgeist in Geistesgeschichte, Kuhn's theory of paradigms, or Foucault's notion of *epistèmes*, fabricate coherent systems by excluding or ignoring whatever resists coercion and by paying undue attention to ruptures. In a more comprehensive and accurate vision, the homogeneous and cohesive structures of history dissolve into groups of conflicting ideas, resilient competing strands of tradition that reach across the presumed revolutionary ruptures by undergoing frequent transformation but seldom, if ever, disappearing completely.[5]

Over the years I have felt with increasing urgency the need to flesh out the implications of these remarks for words/music relations in the 19th century, and I have written in the last two decades a number of articles that address specific dimensions of their new "cohabitation." Before I turn to the specific subject of my present article it may be useful to summarize the ideas I have developed, for they are relevant to my approach to Berlioz's *Roméo et Juliette*.

In writing on music's "emancipation," I was eager to show *that* a new aesthetic mode emerged at the end of the 18th century; in retrospect I think I should have explained better *what* it meant. Above all, the new aesthetics should not be understood merely as a version of formalism, as a glorification of bloodless musical forms devoid of social and historical meanings. Semantization, or meaning attribution, seems to be a fundamental human need: we wish to make sense out of the apparently most senseless events and experiences. The disappearance of verbal texts in sonatas, symphonies, variations, etudes, and a myriad of other new musical forms did not do away with language altogether. In some of them, composers started to narrate or musically imitate verbal dialogues; in others, which aspired to become

---

[4] Neubauer, *Emancipation*, 8.

[5] Neubauer, *Emancipation*, 8-9.

"absolute," listeners assumed the task that composers eschewed: where no text illuminated an a priori compositional meaning, listeners usually supplied an a posteriori content. As a result, language that disappeared from pure instrumental music returned in the 19th century in three major guises: 1) as new discourses about music, 2) as vernacular libretti in national operas, and 3) as new hybrid forms, often employing meta-reflections. National operas are not relevant to Berlioz, but I shall briefly discuss the first category, for Berlioz was a major writer in the new musical discourses, and shall then focus on the third, for which *Roméo et Juliette* is an outstanding example.

The new discourses about music emerged in large part in response to the disappearance of language from instrumental music.[6] The disappearance of texts from compositions made the hermeneutics of music interpretation much more difficult, but listeners were generally reluctant to engage in formal analyses and continued to ascribe content to pure instrumental music. They usually took recourse to the composer's alleged intentions by linking the composition to some biographical facts, or by interpreting the work in terms of some cultural-historical event. Musical analysis focused on the formal and structural features of the composition, but all kinds of metaphoric and narrative musical discourses emerged on the other end of the spectrum, in which "emancipated" listeners often gave free reign to their imagination.

Looking at this new situation from another angle, we note that a whole range of new genres of discourse emerged in the early decades of the 19th century, several of them in new institutional frameworks. They include musicology (which gained a foothold at the universities), music criticism and reviews of performances (which emerged in the new music journals), and, last but not least, fiction about music and musicians. The great composers of the previous centuries—Monteverdi, Handel, Haydn, Bach, Gluck, Beethoven, and many others—left only a handful of writings on music behind. Rameau was a great theoretician but an execrable writer, whereas Rousseau, a great writer, was only a minor composer. Mozart wrote marvelous letters, but he wrote mostly on performances and little on the principles and interpretations of music. In the 19th century, composers became prime agents in developing discursive approaches to music: the line starts with E.T.A. Hoffmann, runs through Weber, Schumann, and Berlioz, and culminates in Wagner. Writing on music, these artists fulfilled not only a personal urge to verbalize their own musical "thoughts"; they also participated in developing a cultural discourse on music that radically differed from theoretical and aesthetic treatises of the 18th century.

[6] In a perceptive recent book, *Die Literarisierung von Musik und bildender Kunst um 1800* (Munich: Fink, 2003), Corinna Caduff speaks, in my view with some exaggeration, even of a "literarization of music" around 1800.

Berlioz, the Writer

Berlioz belonged to that new breed of composers who wrote much; his livelihood depended on it, but his vivacious style reveals that he often had great pleasure with it. As one of the most gifted writers among 19th-century composers, he contributed in major ways to the emergence of a variety of discourses on music: he wrote a treatise on orchestration, he penned a great many reviews and reflections on compositions and performances, he wrote, which is less known, a number of fictional stories about musicians (some of them autobiographical), he carried on an enormous correspondence, and he wrote colorful travelogues; his *Mémoires* are, of course, a treasure house of remarks and observations on music. For our purposes, I merely wish to exemplify with a few passages his lively figural discourse on musical compositions.

At times, as in a remark on the first movement of Beethoven's Eighth Symphony, Berlioz cautiously guessed at the mental process that led to the composition of a musical passage: "Hearing this melodious caprice one could say that the composer, given to gentle emotions, had suddenly hit upon a sad idea that interrupts his joyous singing."[7] However, in the following passage on the "Lustiges Zusammensein der Landleute" of Beethoven's Sixth Symphony (which is, of course, highly mimetic), Berlioz became considerably more daring in guessing how the composition may have been created: "No doubt, Beethoven intended to characterize with it some good old German peasant. Mounted on a barrel, he is armed with a bad, dilapidated instrument, from which he barely is able to extract the two principal sounds of *F*, the dominant and the tonic."[8]

Going a step further, Berlioz gave an unashamedly romantic imaginary of how Beethoven composed the "Szene am Bach": "No doubt, the author composed this admirable adagio lying in the grass, with eyes towards the sky, ears turned to the wind, fascinated by myriads of gentle reflections of light and sound, watching, and at the same time listening, to the tiny white, scintillating waves of the brook that gently break against the pebbles of the

---

[7] "On dirait, à entendre ce caprice mélodique, que l'auteur, disposé aux douces émotions, en est détourné tout à coup par une idée triste qui vient interrompre son chant joyeux" (Hector Berlioz, *À travers chants: Études musicales, adorations, boutades et critiques* [Paris: Michel Lévy, 1882], 47).

[8] "Beethoven a sans doute voulu caractériser par là quelque bon vieux paysan allemand, monté sur un tonneau, armé d'un mauvais instrument délabré, dont il tire à peine les deux sons principaux du ton de fa, la dominante et la tonique" (*chants* 37).

bank."[9] Perhaps the force of "no doubt" here is a twinkle of the eye: "Take it with a grain of salt!"

Not all of Berlioz's metaphors focus on the composer's intentions and the external stimuli that may have inspired the composition. His "intertextual" metaphors for the first movement in Beethoven's Fifth Symphony ignore the composer and the compositional process by foreground Berlioz's own artistic experience and imagination:

> The first movement is devoted to the portrayal of confused emotions that distress a great soul prey to despair. Not that composed, calm despair that appears to be resignation, not Romeo's somber and silent pain upon learning of Juliet's death, but rather Othello's terrible fury upon listening to Iago's poisonous slanders that convince him of Desdemona's guilt. At times it is a frenzied delirium that bursts into terrible cries, at others exaggerated dejection that has only notes of regret and turns into self-pity.[10]

In my final example from the *Mémoires*, splendid erotic synaesthesia renders Berlioz's daydreams while listening to Gluck's *Armide*:

> I closed my eyes, and whilst listening to the divine gavotte with its caressing melody and its softly murmuring monotonous harmony, and to the chorus "Jamais dans ces beaux lieux," so exquisitely graceful in its expression of happiness, I seemed to be surrounded on all sides by enfolding arms, adorable, intertwining feet, floating hair, shining eyes, and intoxicating smiles. The flower of pleasure, gently stirred by the melodious breeze, expanded, and a concert of sounds, colors and perfumes poured forth from its ravishing corolla.[11]

---

[9] "L'auteur a sans doute créé cet admirable *adagio*, couché dans l'herbe, les yeux au ciel, l'oreille au vent, fasciné par mille et mille doux reflets de sons et de lumière, regardant et écoutant à la fois les petites vagues blanches, scintillantes du ruisseau, se brisant avec un léger bruit sur les cailloux du rivage" (*chants* 36).

[10] "Le premier morceau est consacré à la peinture des sentiments désordonnés qui bouleversent une grande âme en proie au désespoir; non ce désespoir concentré, calme, qui emprunte les apparences de la résignation; non pas cette douleur sombre et muette de Roméo apprenant la mort de Juliette, mais bien la fureur terrible d'Othello recevant de la bouche d'Iago les calomnies empoisonnées qui le persuadent du crime de Desdémona. C'est tantôt un délire frénétique qui éclate en cris effrayants; tantôt un abattement excessif qui n'a que des accents de regret et se prend en pitié lui-même." (*chants* 31)

[11] "Je fermais les yeux, et en entendant cette divine gavotte avec sa mélodie si caressante, et le murmure doucement monotone de son harmonie, et ce choeur: *Jamais dans ces beaux lieux*, dont le bonheur s'épanche avec tant de grâce, je voyais autour de moi s'enlacer des bras charmants, se croiser d'adorables pieds, se dérouler d'odorantes chevelures, briller des yeux diamants, et rayonner mille enivrants sourires. La fleur du plaisir, mollement agitée par la brise mélodique s'épanouissait, et de sa corolle ravissante s'échappait un concert de sons, de couleurs et de parfums" (Berlioz, *Mémoires*, ed. Pierre Citron [Paris: Garnier-Flammarion, 1969], 2:136).

Peter Kivy severely reprimands the writer: "Gluck's music simply serves as a stimulus to Berlioz' reveries. He might just as well have taken a dose of laudenum as a dose of Gluck. [...] we expect a description of *Armide*, and get, instead, a description of Berlioz' state of mind."[12] Disappointed expectations indeed. However, what Kivy rudely calls "a catalogue of spare parts"[13] may be of some interest, precisely because it reveals "Berlioz's state of mind" and suggests what music may suggest.

Roméo et Juliette: Conception, Outline, and Structure

Berlioz's *Roméo et Juliette* (1839) is both a highly ingenious transposition of Shakespeare's play and a bold experiment in musical narration that also involves some textual commentaries on music, though these function quite differently from the ones we just discussed.

When Berlioz first saw *Romeo and Juliet* in 1827, he knew no English. He learned a smattering of it in the following years, but his main source remained Pierre Letourneur's French prose translation, which, in turn, was based on David Garrick's popular revision rather than on Shakespeare's original text. Garrick granted the lovers a final, tear-jerking reunion in the Capulet monument of the churchyard.[14] Berlioz preferred the Garrick version to that of Shakespeare, though he generally hated it when actors and critics meddled with the originals.[15] He incorporated in Part 6 of his composition a reunion of the lovers, and he also followed Garrick in adding a funeral procession for Juliet (Part 5: Convoi funèbre de Juliette). Both scenes are without words.

The final impulse for writing *Roméo et Juliette* was Niccolò Paginini's generous gift of 20,000 francs, which allowed Berlioz to concentrate himself during most of 1839 on the composition. As Berlioz notes in Chapter 49 of his *Mémoires*, he had prepared a prose version that the well-known romantic writer and Shakespeare translator Émile Deschamps then put into verse.[16]

---

[12] Peter Kivy, *The Corded Shell. Reflections on Musical Expression* (Princeton: Princeton University Press, 1980), 5.

[13] For other examples of Berlioz's metaphoric music discourse and a general discussion of metaphors in early-19th-century music criticism see John Neubauer and Chris Engeler, "The Metaphors of Music Criticism in the Romantic Era," in Walter Bernhart, *The Semantics of the Musico-Literary Genres. Method and Analysis*. (Tübingen: Gunter Narr, 1994), 75-86.

[14] See Daniel Albright, *Berlioz's Semi-Operas* (Rochester: University of Rochester Press, 2001), 32-33.

[15] In Chapter 16 of the *Mémoires* (1: 121), Berlioz found Shakespeare's "dénoument" less powerful than that of Garrick. However, he had savage criticism for changes in *King Lear*.

[16] Berlioz, *Mémoires* 2:35.

The premiere of the work in 1839 was a great success, a triumph after the failure of the *Cellini* opera a year earlier. The three Parisian performances were followed by equally well-received performances in Vienna and Prague in 1846. For the latter, Berlioz introduced some important changes, which we shall discuss later. The first publication of the score appeared in 1847, and incorporated the changes he made. The final outline divides the composition into the following seven parts:

1
Introduction
Combats, Tumulte, Intervention du Prince
Prologue
    Strophes
    Scherzetto

2
Roméo seul – Tristesse – Bruits lointains de bal et de concert – Grande fête chez Capulets

3
Scène d'amour
Nuit sereine – Le Jardin de Capulet, silencieux et désert – Les jeunes Capulets sortant de la fête, passent en chantant des réminescences de la musique du bal

4
La reine Mab, ou la Fée des Songes (Scherzo)

5
Convoi funèbre de Juliette

6
Roméo au tombeau des Capulets
Invocation
Réveil de Juliette

7
Final
Air
Serment

The 1839 performance version, of which only the libretto survives, contained additional lines in the Prologue that briefly referred to the killing of Mercutio and Tybalt; it also featured a second Prologue before Part 5, which provided guidance to the orchestral parts to follow.

The outline reveals that Berlioz rearranged Shakespeare's plot and chose different points of emphasis. Friar Lawrence is the only Shakespearean character who sings, but even he enters only the seventh and last, mimetic part of the composition, which means that he must retrospectively tell how he tried to save the lovers. He then quells the renewed fighting of the Capulets and Montagues and forces them to get reconciled with each other.

Berlioz focuses more on emotional states rather than on events and the plot, but, narration is, nevertheless, prominently in his composition, both via language and music. A number of sections in the composition are texted: the Prologue, the Strophes, and the Scherzetto in Part 1, brief sections of Part 3 (the Capulet guests reminisce) and Part 5 (the Capulets mourn Juliette), and Friar Lawrence's sermon in Part 7 (with interjections from the Montagues and Capulets). The textual plot is carried mainly by the Introduction (Part 1) and the both narrative and performative function of the Friar.

The Introduction

Berlioz has subdivided the Introduction into four parts: 1) what one may call an "orchestral prelude," 2) a Prologue, 3) lyrical reflections sung by a contralto with a small choir, and 4) a fast Scherzetto that follows Mercutio's sparkling story about Queen Mab in Act I, Scene 4 of Shakespeare's play.

Shakespeare's play was Berlioz's inspiration, but it may not be the most useful foil against which to read musico-verbally Berlioz's work. Though the composer did not depart radically from the Garrick version, he enriched it with a music that has a logic and structure of its own. In contrast to Albright, who sets Berlioz's composition mainly against Shakespeare's play, I shall focus therefore on the Berlioz/Deschamps text and its relation to the music. While it is admittedly inferior to that of Shakespeare, it gives us better cues to Berlioz's musico-literary art.

The absence of mimesis, i.e., of singing by Shakespearean characters, goes beyond the muteness of Romeo and Juliet; it is a fundamental aspect of Berlioz's composition. Leaving aside brief choral passages sung by the Montagues, the Capulets, and their guests, we are left with Friar Lawrence's mentioned speech-song in the Finale. The rest of the Berlioz/Deschamps text is diegetic rather than mimetic: it is spoken by various narrators that do not

Music's Emancipation from Language: Berlioz's Roméo et Juliette 53

belong to the fictional world of Shakespeare's play. Narrators have, of course, been frequently employed in earlier texted compositions. Suffice it to mention the examples in Monteverdi's *Il combattimento de Tancredo I Clorinda* and Bach's *St. Matthew Passion*. But in these cases as well as in most other ones, the narrator assumes a consistent identity. In *Roméo et Juliette*, however, we are dealing with an assortment of different narrative voices that do not congeal: several narrators and different voices (contralto, tenor) tell the listener what happened or what is going to happen, narrators that adopt different emotional attitudes with respect to the fictional events and characters. In the Prologue, their words take on the additional function of "coding," or "tagging," musical themes, so that when these themes return in the orchestral parts of the composition, listeners can associate them with specific meanings.

The Orchestral Prelude

This is one of the most explicitly narrative and dramatic sections within the whole composition. Its program, outlined as "Fighting – riot – intervention of the Prince" is relatively easily recognized by listeners familiar with Shakespeare's play. There, these events take up the first half of the first scene in Act I. Berlioz uses purely instrumental means to render two kinds of action here: a physical combat between rival factions, and the Prince's authoritative verbal intervention that finally suppresses, however temporarily, the feud.

Berlioz constructs this imitative part of his composition with unusual musical means: he portrays the chaotic scene of "fighting" and "riot" with a fugal texture, i.e. with a musical form that is most formal and highly structured:

FIGURE 1: Allegro fugato

54   John Neubauer

When this (musically) ordered rendering of disorder reaches its climax, the Prince enters with an "instrumental recitative" that Berlioz adopted from Beethoven's Ninth.[17] The long, drawn-out base notes of the brasses in this recitative constitute a dramatic contrast to the musical scene of riot, but Berlioz seems to suggest an underlying commonality between the Prince and his subjects by using for this recitative an emphatic and vastly augmented form of the same fugato theme he used for portraying the riot:

FIGURE 2: Le Prince

As Rushton writes, the Prince's anger "is represented by tonal arbitrariness: there seems no way of predicting which key may be reinforced. [...] The dispersal of the combatants is graphically depicted by the liquidation of

---

[17] Julian Rushton, *Berlioz: Roméo et Juliette* (Cambridge: Cambridge University Press, 1994), 22-23 and 105-106.

the fugue subject onto an eventual dominant pedal." In the end, order is reestablished: "there is no room for ambiguity in the resolution, and the close, with its growing silences, is stage-clearing music, a subdued reversal of the opening."[18] The Prince's secular authority establishes, then, a symbolic musical order that represents a temporarily reestablished social order. This will be mirrored at the end of the composition, when Friar Lawrence's religious and moral authority reconciles the feuding families by means of a verbal and musical rhetoric. Note, however, that musical authority does not rule here over characteristic individuals: the musical themes have no intrinsic meaning. The fugue, for instance, can represent disorder as well as order.

Prologue[19]

According to Julian Rushton, the Prologue has two aims, "to sing, in effect, the programme of the symphony, and to introduce some of its themes."[20] In "symphonic" approaches to the Prologue the text merely codes the subsequent orchestral parts. However, the texted parts of the Prologue are not merely preparatory: they also provide emotional and perspectival images of the here and now, and they also specify what precisely went on in the prelude. Given the mimetic limitations of music, the orchestral prelude could portray only a general disorder and its suppression.[21] That these involve the Prince of Verona and the warring Capulets and Montagues becomes clear only to those who know the play and are guided by the title of the composition and Berlioz's information (combat, tumult, intervention of the Prince). To make sure that all listeners understood the initial clash, which provides the essential prehistory for the rest of the action in Shakespeare, Berlioz offers in the Prologue's initial stanza a verbal summary of what he had just narrated with orchestral means. The recapitulation is sung by a contralto and a small chorus in unison, in a recitative that monotonously remains almost at the same pitch:

> Ancient slumbering hatreds / Have risen as if from hell; / Capulets, Montagues, two warring houses, / Have crossed swords in Verona. / However, the Prince has put down / these bloody disorders, /

---

[18] Rushton, 23.

[19] In certain editions, recording booklets, and interpretations (e.g., Albright, 49) the Prologue, the Strophes, and the Scherzetto – are treated as equivalent parts. In the following, I shall regard the Strophes and the Scherzetto as subdivisions of the Prologue, because from a textual point of view they do continue, however slightly, to foreshadow of what is coming.

[20] Rushton, 23.

[21] See Berlioz's *À travers chant*, 151-52 and Albright, 43-44.

threatening with death those, who against his orders, / have recourse again to the law of steel.[22]

This verbal recall of what happened is followed by a present-tense account of current events, starting with the announcement that the Capulets give a ball in what are ominously called "moments of calm."

The rest of the Prologue constitutes, according to Jacques Chailley, "a veritable musical analysis of the score, inserted into the score itself."[23] As Berlioz himself wrote in the preface, he introduced singing at the beginning to prepare the listeners for the dramatic scenes, whose feelings and passions will be expressed by the orchestra.[24] The retrospective is thus followed by a preview of musical themes in the later orchestral parts. But this encoding of musical themes is not the only function of the remaining Prologue. Next to a plot-generating function it also provides, as I have suggested, perspectives. I mean two things by this: first, that the narrator-singers will now shift back and forth between the individual world of the protagonists (and, within that, between Roméo and Juliette), and secondly that the contralto and the Mercutio-impersonating tenor provide contrasting affective perspectives on love, this love in particular.

The first of these perspectival contrasts concerns the difference between individuals and society. Portraying the present, the "recitative harmonique" first focuses on Roméo who laments his destiny and "wanders sadly about the palace," pining away for Juliette, "the daughter/Of his family's enemies."[25] But the narratorial attention quickly shifts from Roméo's private misery to the glittering décor, the dance, and the joyous exclamations at the ball: "The noise of instruments, the melodious songs / float out of the halls where gold glitters, / rousing the dance as well as joyous peals of laughter."[26] It is at this point, that the increasingly agitated reporting gives way to a purely orchestral

---

[22] Here and in the following passages of the libretto I take the French original from Rushton (91-101). My English translations are indebted to several existing ones, including that of Rushton (91-101). "D'anciennes haines endormies / Ont surgi comme de l'enfer; / Capulets, Montagues, deux maisons ennemies, / Dans Vérone ont croisé le fer. / Pourtant, de ces sanglants désordres / Le Prince a réprimé le cours, / En menaçant de mort ceux qui, malgré ses ordres, / Aux justices du glaive auraient encore recours" (Rushton, 91).

[23] Jacques Chailley, "Roméo et Juliette," *Revue de Musicologie* 63 (1977): 117.

[24] Rushton, 87.

[25] "Le jeune Roméo, plaignant sa destinée, / Vient tristement errer à l'entour du palais; / Car il aime d'amour Juliette ... la fille / Des ennemis de sa famille!" (Rushton, 91) In Berlioz's and Garrick's versions Romeo is in love at the beginning of the action already; there is no first encounter at the ball.

[26] "Le bruit des instruments, les chants mélodieux / Partent des salons où l'or brille, / Excitant et la dans et les éclats joyeux" (Rushton, 91).

Music's Emancipation from Language: Berlioz's Roméo et Juliette 57

Allegro, a lively waltz that recurs later as a "tagged" image of sociability, for instance in Part 2 ("Roméo seul"):

FIGURE 3: Valse

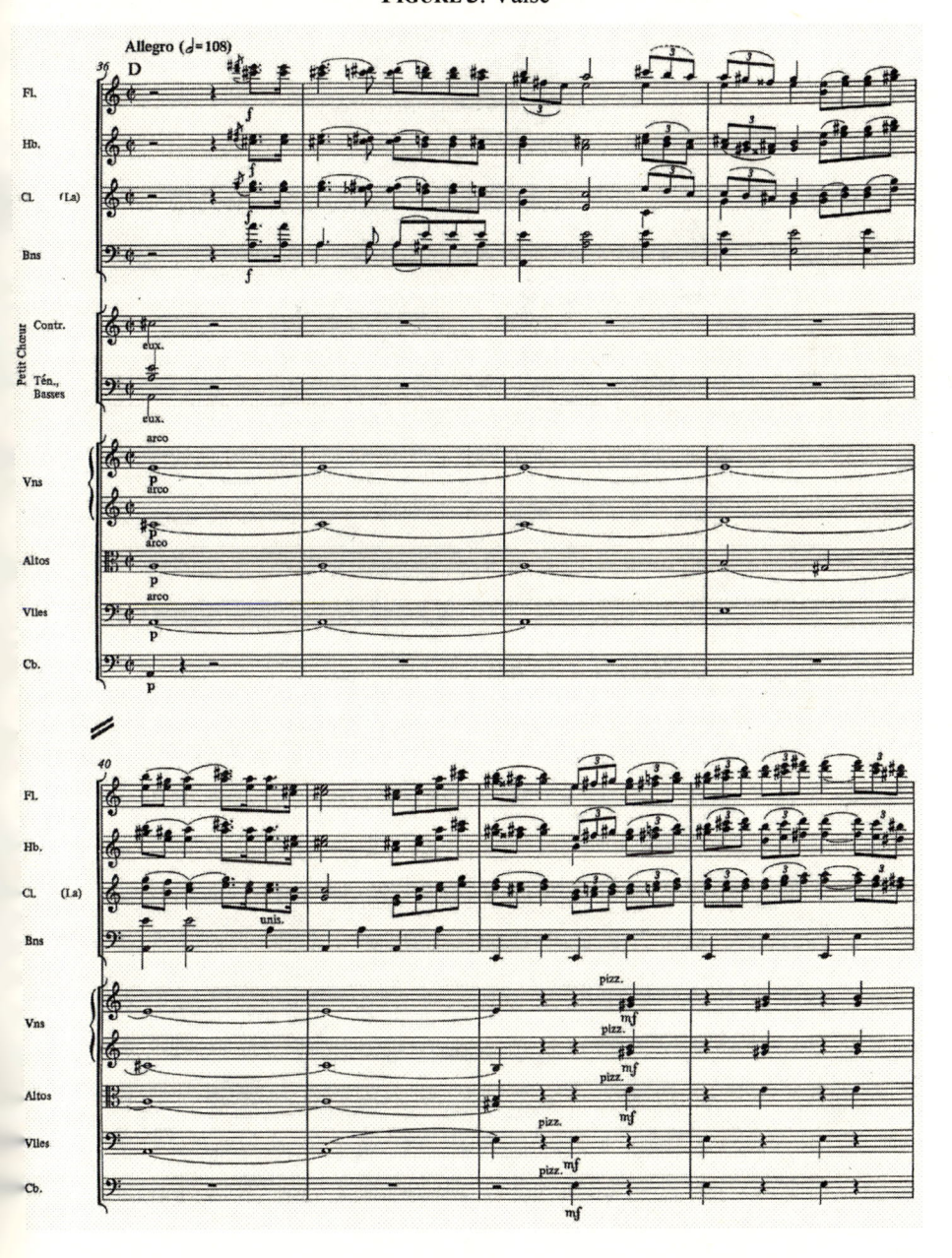

In narrative terms this shift from texted to pure music is a change from diegesis to mimesis or "scene": the narrator ceases to speak and allows the scene speak for itself in musical terms, as if this were a quotation in the diegetic discourse. The dance is not reported but directly presented as a (literal and figurative) performance. However, the dance passage is only sixteen-measures long, the music slows down in order to allow a return to the

FIGURE 4: Roméo soupire

diegetic recitative, which reports on the ending of the ball and the dispersion of the dancers: "The ball is over, and when all sound has ceased, / Under the arches can be heard / The weary dancers singing as they go off into the distance."[27]

As the societal noise subsides, the narrative voice turn to Romeo, who "sighs for he must leave Juliet" (Roméo soupire, / Car il a dû quitter Juliette!).[28] The music that accompanies these words later becomes the opening theme of Part 2, titled "Romeo seul" (measures 24-31); see Fig. 4 above:

As our hero is jolted from his passivity he assumes an increasingly active role, and the lovers engage in an increasingly passionate dialogue of gestures:: he surmounts the garden walls; she confesses her love without knowing of his presence; he reveals himself to her; and she responds with a leap of fire that recalls his leap over the wall:

> Suddenly, to breathe again the air she breathes, / He surmounts the garden walls. / Already on her balcony, white Juliet / appears …and thinking herself alone till dawn, / she Confides her love to the night. / Romeo, trembling with an anxious joy, / Reveals himself to Juliet, / And, in turn, a fire leaps from her heart.[29]

When Romeo reveals himself, the orchestral music marked "Andante con moto e appassionato assai" introduces the adagio theme of Part 3, the great orchestral love scene (see Fig. 5 below).

At this point, however, the texted music discreetly abandons reporting. The plot is interrupted; a contralto takes over (the chorus merely chimes in "ciel" at the end of each stanza), and fills the pause with lyrical-hymnic air, addressed to the lovers:

> Unforgettable first raptures, / First vows, first declarations of two lovers. Under the Italian stars; / In this hot and windless air / Perfumed with the scent of a distant orange garden, / Where the nightingale / exhausts herself with long-drawn sighs! / What art, in its chosen language, / Could do justice to your heavenly delights? / First love! Are you not / Above all poetry? / Or, in our mortal exile, are you not / That very poetry / Of which Shakespeare alone knew the secret, / And which he took with him to heaven?

---

[27] La fête est terminée, et quand tout bruit expire, / Sous les arcades on entend / Les danseurs fatigués s'éloigner en chantant" (Rushton, 92).

[28] Rushton, 92.

[29] "Soudain, / pour respirer encore cet air qu'elle respire, / Il franchit les murs du jardin. / Déjà sur son balcon la blanche Juliette / Paraît … et, se croyant seule jusques au jour, / Confie à la nuit son amour. / Roméo palpitant d'une joie inquiète, / Se découvre à Juliette, et de son coeur / Les feux éclatent à leur tour" (Rushton, 92).

FIGURE 5: se découvre à Juliette

Happy children, your hearts aflame, / Bound in love by the chance / Of a single glance / Living together in a single soul. / Hide it well in the flowery shades / This divine flame that fires you, / Such pure ecstasy / That its words are tears! / What king fancies himself equal / to your chaste ecstasy? / Happy children! And what treasures / Could buy just one of your smiles?
Ah, relish at length this honeyed cup, / Sweeter than all the chalices / From which God's angels, envious of your bliss / Drink happiness in heaven![30]

The passage contains a number of hackneyed clichés, but also some subtleties. The mention of Shakespeare is, in my opinion, not one of them. It would be grotesque if this were Shakespeare's own text, or if the voice belonged to some fictional reincarnation of it. But this is an external narrator who can speak of Shakespeare just as she can address his fictional Romeo and Juliet. And if Shakespeare has indeed taken with him to the grave the secret of poetry, if, as the text intimates, poetry must fall silent when love triumphs, music can continue to sing: the nightingale anticipates the musical representation of the love scene in Part 3 by orchestral means.

For now, this verbal glorification must come to an end, but the time of pure music has not come yet. As a tenor assumes the narration, we are back in the plot, though not at the point where it was interrupted. By an arbitrary act, which demands that listeners take an imaginative leap, we are thrown back into the social world, in which such sublime love must appear as silly madness: "Soon Romeo's pallor and distracted languor / Sets all his friends laughing: 'My dear' says elegant Mercutio, 'I bet that Queen Mab has been with you.'"[31] Of all the texted passages this one comes closest to Shakespeare's text, but this is an aside, a brilliantly evocative rendering of an imaginary being that traverses the minds of sleepers, which contributes nothing to the plot.

---

[30] "Premiers transports que nul n'oublie! / Premiers aveux, premiers serments / De deux amants / Sous les étoiles d'Italie; / Dans cet air chaud et sans zéphyrs, / Que l'oranger au loin parfume, Où se consume / Le rossignol en longs soupirs! / Quel art, dans sa langue choisie, / Rendrait vos célestes appas? / Premier amour! n'êtes-vous pas / Plus haut que toute poésie? / Ou ne seriez-vous point, dans notre exil mortel, / Cette poésie elle-même / Dont Shakespeare lui seul eut le secret suprême / Et qu'il remporta / Dans le ciel! / Heureux enfants aux coeurs de flamme! / Liés d'amour par le hasard / D'un seul regard; / Vivant tous deux d'une seule ?me! / Cachez-le bien sous l'ombre en fleurs, / Ce feu divin qui vous embrase; / Si pure extase / Que les paroles sont des pleurs! / Quel roi des vos chastes délires / Croirait égaler les transports! / Heureux enfants! ... et quels trésors / Paieraient un seul de vos sourires! / Ah! savourez longtemps cette coupe de miel, / Plus suave que les calices / Où les anges de Dieu, jaloux de vos délices, / Puisent le bonheur dans le ciel!" (Rushton, 92-93)

[31] "Bientôt de Roméo la pâle rêverie / Met tous ses amis en gaieté; / 'Mon cher, dit élégant Mercutio, je parie / Que la reine Mab t'aura visité" (Rushton, 93).

The function of the famous "Queen Mab" song is quite different here from the one it has in Act I, Scene 4 of Shakespeare's play. There, Romeo does not yet know Julia, and Mercutio's airy puff of nothingness is supposed to lift Romeo from his leaden state into which his love for Rosaline has thrown him. Queen Mab and her delicately wrought chariot of hazelnut fulfill everybody's wish, but only in a dream. If she "gallops night by night / Through lovers' brains, and then they dream of love," this is in Shakespeare an antidote or remedy for Romeo's infatuation with Rosaline that anticipates the great love still to come. There, Romeo interrupts this fantasy of "nothing," for he has ill forebodings.

In Berlioz, the quoted lines that introduce the song come after the balcony scene. If the Berlioz/Deschamps text comes close to its source in Shakespeare, its function is quite different: within the bantering of friends the songs has a sobering effect. If love was a sublime state for the contralto, for the tenor it is a temporary madness that is abruptly and sadly brought to conclusion at daybreak. The reference is to Juliet, not Romeo, and the prospective function is rather ominous: [Queen Mab] dresses up the girl, in a dream / and takes her back to the ball / But the cock crows, the day breaks, / Mab vanishes in a flash / into the air![32] Indeed, this is followed abruptly by the final lines of the Prologue, which relate the coming tragedy, or, more precisely, the reconciliation of the families: Soon Death is lord of all. / Capulets, Montagues, subdued by their sorrow, / At last approach each other to abjure the hatred / that shed so much blood, so many tears.[33]

In the original version, Berlioz inserted before these final lines a curious "address to the public" sung by the chorus that spells out all too didactically his technique: "Such are the first images and scenes that the orchestra will try to translate into music before you, exploring uncharted ways."[34] In narrative theory, this would be called an address to the "reader in the text," a device that was made famous by Laurence Sterne in *Tristram Shandy*. What is a playful trick in Sterne is here, however, an almost pedantic instruction how to listen to the coming orchestral parts. Curiously, these instructions would have followed the Queen Mab song of the Scherzetto, which does, indeed, return as an instrumental Scherzo in Part 5, albeit without reusing the musical material of its antecedent.

---

[32] [Mab] "dans un rêve, habille / La jeune fille / Et la ramène au bal. / Mais le coq chante, le jour brille, / Mab fuit comme un éclair / Dans l'air" (Rushton, 94).

[33] "Bientôt la mort est souveraine. / Capulets, Montagues, domptés par les douleurs, / Se rapprochent enfin pour abjurer la haine, / Qui fit verser tant de sang et de pleurs" (Rushton, 94).

[34] "[t]els sont les tableaux / et les scènes / Que devant vous, cherchant des routes incertaines, / L'orchestre va tenter de traduire en accords" (Rushton, 94).

Berlioz's Prologue then shifts back and forth between singing and pure instrumental music, between diegetic narration and mimesis (the imitation of character speech). It engages human voices for three main purposes: 1) to recapitulate the meaning of the combat in the instrumental opening, 2) to identify the content of the musical themes in the subsequent symphonic movements (i.e. to code the musical themes), and 3) to intimate the tragedy that will be retold by instrumental means. Berlioz assigns different narrative functions to the chorus and the soloists: the chorus focuses on the plot, on the external events, and their interrelations; the contralto primarily portrays moods and passions, and the tenor impersonates Mercutio to fill a pause in the action in another, fanciful way.

Note that the anticipatory functions of Berlioz's opening invert the method of its model, Beethoven's Ninth Symphony. In the latter, the opening of the final movement gives a survey of the themes in the preceding movements, but the only point of that review is to declare each of them inadequate for the task ahead: "Oh Freunde, nicht diese Töne" (Oh friends, not these sounds!). Berlioz, in contrast, enumerates and explains his themes *before* he elaborates on them in the orchestral sections. Looking forward in music history, his method anticipates Wagner's *leitmotif* technique, but Berlioz, in contrast to Wagner, does not have at his disposal the stage to buttress his semantization of the orchestral music. Berlioz's method has, perhaps, more in common with Mahler's technique of quoting texted music by means of instruments.

At the Fulcrum of Words and Sounds

Thus Berlioz went in *Roméo et Juliette* beyond the pure instrumental genres that emerged towards the end of the 18th century and came to be regarded as the highest form of art in general. He did hold pure instrumental music in high esteem and he admired Beethoven: music gives in his compositions "way to itself, needing no words to make its expression specific; its language then becomes quite indefinite, thanks to which it acquires still more power over *beings endowed with imagination*. Those without imagination may need words, but imaginative listeners can understand a *genre instrumental expressif*."[35] Since audiences generally include both imaginative and non-imaginative listeners, Berlioz did not grant them in *Roméo et Juliette* full interpretive freedom. Worrying about those with less imagination, he rather provided his listeners with instructions.

---

[35] Berlioz, *Le Correspondant*, October 22, 1832. Translated in Rushton, 20.

But Berlioz's position is not unequivocal. As Jacques Barzun remarks: "Berlioz expounds but a single principle: music by itself is (or can be) dramatically and psychologically expressive."[36] As Berlioz himself had emphasized, the lovers remain silent in his work:

> The duets of love and despair are confided to the orchestra ... the greatest composers have produced thousands of *vocal* duets of this kind; it seemed prudent as much as singular to try some other way of doing it. Then there is the very sublimity of this love, whose depiction by a musician is fraught with peril; his invention should be allowed the scope which the exact sense of sung words restrains, but which is possible in such circumstances with instrumental music, richer, more varied, less restricted, and thanks to its very indefiniteness, incomparably more powerful.[37]

Thus Berlioz wanted pure music to speak where language falls short of expressive means, but instrumental music did not become for him "absolute," an abstract formal structure of "tönend bewegte Formen" (shifting tonal forms)—as it did for Eduard Hanslick[38] and his later followers.

The Genre Question

These reflections lead us to the much discussed and vexed question whether *Roméo et Juliette* is symphonic or dramatic, whether it is an opera that has ingested a symphony, or a symphony that frames an opera. Both views are tenable: some see a duck where others see a rabbit. One may regard the composition as a partly "detextualized" opera[39] or as a symphony that follows Beethoven's Ninth Symphony by opening up to vocal music. Admittedly, Berlioz himself unequivocally stated in his preface that "this is neither an opera concertante, nor a cantata, but a symphony with choruses" —but this does not account for the presence of solo singers and is a problematic statement in many other respects as well.[40] Jacques Chailley followed the composer by categorically declaring that *Roméo et Juliette* was

---

[36] Jacques Barzun, "Berlioz as man and thinker," in Peter Bloom, *The Cambridge Companion to Berlioz* (Cambridge: Cambridge University Press, 2000), 11-19 [14].

[37] Rushton, 87-88.

[38] Eduard Hanslick, *Vom Musikalisch-Schönen*, 1854 (Darmstadt: Wissenschaftliche Buchgesellschaft, 1976).

[39] Albright, 64.

[40] A related passage in Chapter 49 the *Mémoires*: "Enfin, après une assez longue indécision, je m'arrêtai à l'idée d'une symphonie avec choeurs, solos de chant et récitative choral, don't le drame de Shakespeare, *Roméo et Juliette*, serait le sujet sublime et toujours nouveau" (*Mémoires* 2:35).

a symphony in five movements, though he admitted that Berlioz also characterized it as a *symphonie dramatique*.[41] Rushton rejects all such symphonic interpretations when he suggests in the final chapter of his book that the composition "is best understood as a dramatic form, albeit one without precedent and virtually, as it now appears, without prosperity."[42] I agree that *Roméo et Juliette* has an inimitable dramatic form. However, I feel compelled to add, the dramatic elements are, paradoxically, concentrated in the orchestral sections, whereas the texted sections are, as I have tried to show, diegetic, enunciated by narrators that are not part of the fictional world. Daniel Albright has recently suggested that "*Roméo and Juliette* consists of a symphony in F major embedded within an opera in B minor/major." The lovers and their "love code" are represented with a "symphonic commingling of themes," whereas the social world of Verona with its "social code" is essentially operatic.[43] This seems to me a felicitous characterization, one that fits Berlioz's composition better than the term "semi-opera" that Albright uses in the title of his book to cover both *Roméo et Juliette* and *La damnation de Faust*. Albright adopts the term from Roger North, who regarded several of Purcell's compositions as "semi-operas" because "some scenes were completely spoken, others completely sung, and still others mostly spoken, but including incidental songs."[44] However, *Roméo et Juliette* contains no scenes that are completely or mostly spoken without orchestral accompaniment.

In conclusion I prefer, rather, to follow up on a speculation that Albright adopts from David Gramit but does not work out: "*Roméo et Juliette* aspires to go beyond finite genres through the act of comprehending all at once. In this sense its analogue in the domain of literature is the novel—for the Romantic imagination, the novel was a sort of *Über*-genre, breaking down the boundaries between various types of literature.[45]

Several details in the interpretation I have given may make the novelistic approach more than just a mere speculation. We have seen that, with the exception of Friar Lawrence's words in the Finale, Berlioz's text is narrative rather than dramatic, whereby the narrators, again with the exception of Friar Lawrence, are not part of the fictional world.[46] The Prologue, the only longer

---

[41] Chailley, 115-122 [115-116].

[42] Following Jeffrey Langford, Rushton reluctantly accepts the view that due to external circumstances (Berlioz's alienation from the Parisian opera house) the composition became a "temporary substitute for opera" (Rushton, 80).

[43] Albright, 78.

[44] Albright, xi.

[45] Albright, 47

[46] Even Rushton, who suggests that *Roméo et Juliette* is a "covert opera," admits that the Prologue is "positively anti-theatrical" (84).

texted part prior to the Finale, employs three narrative voices: the "small chorus," the contralto, and the Mercutio-impersonating tenor. Each of these voices has a particular attitude and perspective on the tragedy. The abrupt transitions from one voice to another, for instance the shift from the contralto's loving admiration to the tenor's whimsical Queen Mab, have an inevitably ironic effect. Instead of assuming "the objectivity of a dramatist,"[47] Berlioz provides, I suggest, a multi-perspectival representation that is typical for novels. Not for all novels, to be sure, but particularly for those that came to be written in the second half of the 18th century in the wake of Laurence Sterne's *Tristram Shandy*: Diderot's *Jacques le fataliste*, Jean Paul's and Wilhelm Tieck's various novels, and works by several other German romantics. When the contralto in *Roméo et Juliette* addresses the lovers, or speaks of Shakespeare, when a narrative voice addresses the listener (in the eliminated second Prologue), when an unidentified narrator introduces a voice that will paraphrase Shakespeare's Mercutio, when, above all, music gives way to narration and vice versa, Berlioz engages in border crossings that violate genre definitions, very much in the manner introduced by Sterne and theoretically elaborated on by the German romantic theoretician Friedrich Schlegel. By transgressing established genre borders, Berlioz and the Sternean narrators call attention to them and problematize what seemed unproblematic. Such meta-narrative border crossings and fanciful intrusions of the narrator became crucial for Friedrich Schlegel's theory of the novel, as formulated in his "Brief über den Roman" and his famous Athenäum-Fragment 116, which defines *Progressive Universalpoesie* as an open poetic form exemplified by the novel.[48] Paradigmatic novels are for Schlegel "a mixture of narration, song, and other forms."[49] It is here, in the romantic theory and practice of the novel, that the idea of a Gesammtkunstwerk was born, way before Wagner.

Instrumental music cannot formally have a narrator,[50] but performance instructions may be regarded as meta-narrative commentaries. Berlioz makes ample use of them in *Roméo et Juliette*, as when he indicates at Part 2 m. 226 in the score: "Réunion des deux thèmes, du Larghetto et de l'Allegro"[51]

---

[47] Rushton, 80.

[48] Friedrich Schlegel, *Kritische Friedrich-Schlegel-Ausgabe*, vol. 2, ed. Ernst Behler (Paderborn: Schöhning, 1967), 329-339 and 182-183 respectively.

[49] Schlegel, 336.

[50] See John Neubauer, "Tales of Hoffmann and Others. On Narrativizations of Instrumental Music," in Ulla-Britta Lagerroth, Hans Lund, and Erik Hedling, *Interarts Poetics. Essays on the Interrelations of the Arts and Media* (Amsterdam: Rodopi, 1997), 117-136.

[51] Hector Berlioz, *Roméo et Juliette*, in D. Kern Holoman, *New Edition of the Complete Works* 18 (Kassel etc.: Bärenreiter, 1990), 98. The Allegro and the Larghetto start in measures 63 and 81 respectively.

FIGURE 6: Réunion des deux thèmes

When Berlioz shuttles between narration and reflection, between song and instrumental music, he constructs, I suggest, a uniquely Schlegelian texture. The language of the operatic sections in *Roméo et Juliette* is not only narrative and performative, but also anticipatory, critical, and reflective with respect to the performance.

Though *Roméo et Juliette* is a unique work, transgression of genre borders in music was no less frequent in the music of his time than it was in novels and novellas. The locus classicus of this intrusion of criticism into the performance was, indeed, Berlioz's ideal and model: the last movement of Beethoven's Ninth Symphony, which not only reintroduced language into orchestral music but did so in a highly critical and self-reflexive manner. The opening of the movement with a *Schreckensfanfare*[52] is followed, as I have noted, by an inventory of themes from the previous movements that is interrupted by the bass: "Oh Freunde, nicht diese Töne." This rejection of the earlier music (the recapitulated themes? The *Schreckensfanfare*? All previous movements? All instrumental music?) is what allows the subsequent introduction of the melody that accompanies Schiller's "Ode to Joy."

None of this is to suggest that *Roméo et Juliette* is a novel. I merely wanted to indicate that the composition's unique form involves structures, tendencies, and ideas that strongly resemble those employed in romantic conceptions of the novel. Working at a pivotal point in music history, Berlioz combined sounds and words in new ways, without knowing, or knowing little, about German conceptions of the novel. Berlioz, working at a pivotal point of music history, remingled sounds and words without knowing, or knowing little, about German notions of the novel. But intuitively, and perhaps constrained by circumstances, he created a work that is not out of place in a broader history of 19th-century arts. What appears within music history as a work "without precedent and virtually, as it now appears, without posterity,"[53] is from this broader perspective not atypical. *Roméo et Juliette* is, like so many 19th-century novels, a mongrel, one of those "large loose baggy monsters with their queer elements of the accidental and the arbitrary." Henry James, who coined the phrase, was puzzled by these "monsters" that he found exemplified by Tolstoy's *War and Peace* and Melville's *Moby Dick*. Not a bad company for *Roméo et Juliette*!

---

[52] Richard Wagner's much discussed term. See Stephen Hinton, "Not Which Tones? The Crux of Beethoven's Ninth," *19th-Century Music* 22.1 (1998): 61-77 [67].

[53] Rushton, 80.

The Iagoization of Otello: A Study in Verdi's Musical Translation of Shakespeare's Linguistic Dramaturgy

Jeffrey Kurtzman

No play of Shakespeare's is more about words than *Othello*. There is scarcely any action in the drama—only the aborted effort by Desdemona's father, Brabantio, to attack Othello in the streets of Venice in Act I, Cassio's drunken brawl with the captain Montano in Act II, and the final murder/suicide scene. None of these actions are instigated by politics, war, or love, but only by words, the words of Iago. Indeed the very love of Desdemona and Othello is kindled through words, the narrative of his past in the home of Brabantio. On the most fundamental level, the play is about the power of words, the ambiguity and mutability of words, the misuse of words, even words unsaid.[1] The critical literature on *Othello* has dissected the role of words in this play from a myriad of angles, but none so thoroughly and acutely as Robert Heilman's *Magic in the Web* of 1956.[2] One of the main thrusts of Heilman's analysis is the delineation of characters by means of their words and their manner of speaking. Throughout Shakespeare's *œuvre*, linguistic style is a primary means of defining personality and character, social and political position, and the fluctuations and outcome of the drama itself. Yet in no other play is the development of the title character and the outcome of that development so totally dependent on words and linguistic style. Because the use of words in *Othello* has been so thoroughly analyzed in the critical literature, I will only briefly summarize here the most important manner in which words function in the play to set the stage for

---

[1] The basis and much of the material for this article was developed in an interdisciplinary seminar at Middlebury College in 1970. I would like to acknowledge the essential contributions of Middlebury English faculty Robert Pack, David Littlefield, and Paul Cubeta to the ideas and observations presented here.

[2] Robert B. Heilman, *Magic in the Web: Action & Language in Othello* (Lexington: University of Kentucky Press, 1956).

understanding how Verdi transforms Shakespeare's dramatic process into the medium of music.

The features that characterize the speech of Iago, especially when he is expressing himself openly rather than posturing and lying to others, comprise passages in prose; broken, clipped phrases in which he utters curses; insulting epithets; bestial and other vulgar metaphors; expressions of hatred and venom; references to hell and the devil; ambiguous and nonsensical statements; illogical non sequiturs; and the emphatic negation of contemporary societal and religious values.

Shakespeare's Othello, on the other hand, establishes himself quite differently. When Brabantio and his retainers descend upon Othello in the middle of the night with torches burning and swords glistening, intent upon a brawl fomented by Iago, Othello stops them in their tracks with nothing but words, words whose eloquence is more powerful than anger and impending chaos: "Keep up your bright swords, for the dew will rust them. Good signior, you shall more command with years than with your weapons" (I.ii.58-61).[3]

When Othello subsequently appears before the Doge and Senate to respond both to the defensive needs of the state and to Brabantio's charge against him, it is once again Othello's eloquence, the magic of his speech, reiterating the words with which he had wooed Desdemona, that wins the day, impelling the Doge to respond: "I think this tale would win my daughter too" (I.iii.171). In both instances, Othello has quelled the potential chaos of a street riot and the potential chaos in his life from Brabantio's accusation, with his noble, calm demeanor and his eloquence. In Venice, he is clearly worthy of Desdemona.

The problem arises when he is outside the confines of Venice, with its elaborate governmental and judicial system, of which he was the servant. In Cyprus, he alone is in command as governor. In this context, his weaknesses and vulnerability begin to emerge. As a number of literary critics have indicated, Othello is an outsider in the world of Venetian politics and society. He is of a different race; he is a converted Christian whose obsession with the magic of the handkerchief his mother gave him reveals how superficial his Christianity actually is. He is a military man through and through, for whom ambiguity and uncertainty are foreign and intolerable conditions; his world, as he unfolded it to Desdemona, is one of violence, danger, intense suffering and hardness; he is, as Iago reminds him, unacquainted with the

---

[3] My text references in the play are from Gerald Eades Bentley, ed., *Otello* (Baltimore: Penguin Books, 1958).

customs and habits of Venetian women; and he knows nothing of love and domestic life.[4]

One of the many subjects of commentary on Shakespeare's play is how Othello is able to believe in and act on the wispy insinuations and flimsy proofs that Iago conjures up. The vulnerabilities I've just cited are the answers critics have given, for Iago clearly perceives these weaknesses in Othello and brilliantly exploits them. The result is the poisoning of Othello's mind, revealed, as everything else in the play, through language. The process begins when Iago first warns Othello "O, beware, my lord, of jealousy!" (III.iii.165). Othello's response, "O misery!" is far from the calm eloquence he displayed when in real danger in Act I, and the logical non sequiturs and bestial language of Iago quickly invade his speech. As the disintegration of Othello's language continues under Iago's onslaught, he expresses himself with short exclamations, emotional outbursts, illogical statements, epithets, curses, the word "whore," and references to animals, all characteristics of Iago's language. Ultimately, his language breaks down altogether:

> Lie with her? lie on her? We say lie on her when they belie her. Lie with her! Zounds, that's fulsome. Handkerchief—confessions—handkerchief! To confess, and be hanged for his labor—first to be hanged, and then to confess! I tremble at it. Nature would not invest herself in such shadowing passion without some instruction. It is not words that shakes me thus.—Pish! Noses, ears, and lips? Is't possible? Confess? Handkerchief?—O devil (IV.1.35-42).

After this incoherent outburst he falls silent in an epileptic fit, having lost control over every aspect of his being. This is the chaos that Othello himself predicted when he had earlier said about Desdemona, already employing an ambiguous epithet: "Excellent wretch! Perdition catch my soul But I do love thee! and when I love thee not, Chaos is come again" (III.iii.90-92). The mental chaos that induces Othello to murder is the chaos of language, the Iagoization, if you will, of Othello's own language.

When Giuseppe Verdi began composing *Otello*, he was obviously fully aware of Shakespeare's manipulation of words to achieve the goals of his drama. But with the drastic reduction of words in Arrigo Boito's libretto,

---

[4] See, for example, James L. Calderwood, *The Properties of* Othello (Amherst: University of Massachusetts Press, 1989); James Hirsch, "*Othello* and Perception," in Virginia Mason Vaughan and Kent Cartwright, eds., Othello: *New Perspectives* (Rutherford: Fairleigh Dickinson University Press; London and Toronto: Associated University Presses, 1991), 135-59; Frances Teague, "Objects in *Othello*," in Vaughan and Kent, 177-87; and Thomas Price, *Dramatic Structure and Meaning in Theatrical Productions* (San Francisco: Mellen Research University Press, 1992).

and with words being less clear when set to music, another means, a particularly musical means, was required to accomplish the same transformation in Otello as Shakespeare had achieved with words. The solution, as some scholars have gradually noted in the last thirty years, was to create a musical language for Iago, a different musical language for Otello, and then cause Iago's musical language to invade and transform that of Otello in a manner directly analogous to the way in which Shakespeare uses words.[5]

Frits Noske was the first to publish a list of the characteristics of Iago's musical language in 1977.[6] That list comprised "the downward leap of an octave with short appoggiatura, the vocal or orchestral trill, the *unisono* accompaniment, and the descending chromatic scale," triplets and "three ascending notes followed by a descending interval."[7] Noske referred to the descending chromatic scales, the triplets and the ascending motif followed by descent as Iago's "poison," borrowing Iago's own terminology—musical semiotic signs through which Iago's venom invades Otello and the other characters. More recently, Tino Drenger has also taken a semiotic approach to interpreting these and other elements of the music.[8] Both authors show valid associations, but the difficulty I find with their semiotic orientation is that the identification of indexical signs and symbols offers no explanation of how these signs and symbols originate and manage to function effectively within the context of both late 19th-century tonal language and the drama itself, i.e., how they manage to make the drama work. Their identification does not go beyond treating them any differently from merely invented conventions, and is therefore more observational than explanatory.

In a brief article, I cannot begin to cover this issue and process in detail, but would like to offer a few examples of analysis that I believe carry us further in understanding how Verdi generates musical analogues to Shakespeare's use of language. I shall begin with the oft-made observation that Iago's part is infused with chromaticism, a chromaticism that gradually infects and destroys Otello. What is meant by chromaticism? The term is frequently bandied about loosely without definition, without qualification, and without discrimination. In fact, madrigal and motet composers in the sixteenth and early seventeenth centuries had already discovered and made

---

[5] See especially Jane Hawes, *An Examination of Verdi's* Otello *and its Faithfulness to Shakespeare* (Lewiston, NY: Edward Mellen Press, 1994).

[6] Frits Noske, *The Signifier and the Signified: Studies in the Operas of Mozart and Verdi* (The Hague: Martinus Nijhoff, 1977), Chapter 7, Otello: Drama through Structure, 133-70.

[7] Nocke, 148 and 155.

[8] Tino Drenger, *Liebe und Tod in Verdis Musikdramatik: Semiotische Studien zu ausgewählten Opern*, "Hamburger Beiträge zur Musikwissenschaft," Vol. 45 (Eisenach: Verlag der Musikalienhandlung Karl Dieter Wagner, 1996), 301-55.

effective use of the many different facets of chromaticism that Verdi employs in *Otello* for very similar purposes. Much closer to Verdi, of course, Wagner had used chromaticism in quite diverse ways, as had other 19th-century composers. Chromaticism takes numerous forms in *Otello* and is used in many different contexts. And what it means within the tonal system and within the drama depends very much on those contexts.

The most obvious facet of chromaticism is the chromatic scale, most often appearing in the opera in descending form, but sometimes ascending, and on select occasions, as in Iago's Credo, as a semitonal rising sequence of musical phrases.[9] The chromatic scale, in its symmetry, is the disruptor and negator of tonality. If the tonal system generates a sense of teleological order in leading toward specific goals, the introduction of the chromatic scale in a tonal context is the introduction of potential disorder and chaos in that system. As Iago's language is the language of negation and disorder in the play, Verdi exploits the chromatic scale as the vehicle of disorder, of chaos, in his musical language. This is obvious in Verdi's great opening symbol of chaos, the storm, which numerous critics have cited as prefiguring the psychological chaos induced by Iago.

In Fig. 1, the chromatic scale in the brass, which appeared twice a short time earlier in the flutes and oboes, corresponds with the stage directions "un fulmine" (lightening) and "tuoni," (thunder) forming a musical metaphor for the lightening flash, which is, of course, irrational and unpredictable in its appearance, just as the thunder is a chaotic and unpredictable sound effect.

FIGURE 1

[9] Joseph Kerman refers to the chromatic scale and triplets as "snake-like sounds characteristic of Iago." See Kerman, *Opera as Drama* (New York: Vintage Books, 1959), p. 138.

Later, a fortissimo descending chromatic scale accompanies the cry of the crowd on shore as they witness the height of the tempest. These are only two examples from several instances of the chromatic scale as a sonic metaphor for the chaos of the storm.

FIGURE 2

Another facet of chromaticism that makes its appearance in the storm and is ubiquitous throughout it, is the diminished-seventh chord. But the diminished-seventh chord has a different function from the chromatic scale in the tonal system. Rather than introducing the same kind of chaos as the chromatic scale, it introduces dissonance and ambiguity, for the diminished-seventh chord does have a teleological function; it's goal, however, is ambiguous, since it has four natural resolutions and many times is not resolved at all. Moreover, with its two tritones, the combination of its dissonance and ambiguity brings considerable tension into the tonal system. Coupled with the chromatic scale, Verdi has powerful vehicles for generating the sense of the natural chaos and uncertainty of the storm.

But these are not the only factors contributing to that sense. Another is the frequent absence of appropriate resolution of diatonic harmonies. When harmonies do not resolve as expected, or do not resolve at all, a further sense of disorder is introduced. Corresponding to the harmonic disorder are tonal ambiguity and unexpected tonal shifts, for the cadences and tonal centers that do occur in the storm scene are unpredictable and bear no discernible tonal relationship to one another in their appearance and succession. Moreover, most of them are in the minor mode. Add to these factors the famous organ pedal point of C, C♯ and D, the rhythmic energy of many of the motifs, the frequently loud orchestration and the wind machine, and Verdi has all the elements necessary to produce this remarkable sound metaphor for the chaos of nature.

Yet another element that requires mention is the sharply articulated appoggiatura grace note, which is used in several contexts to add pungency to the attack of the principal note. In this passage from the storm it assists, with the sudden drop on the second measured note, in conveying the rough and irregular motion of the waves observed by the chorus: "treman l'onde, treman l'aure, treman basi e culmini" (the waves tremble, the winds tremble, the earth and Heaven tremble; see Fig. 3, next page).

As is often noted, Otello's salvation and first entrance put the storm and the battle with the Turks to rest with one of the most impressive entrances in all of opera. In this powerful moment, Verdi accomplishes what Shakespeare had achieved in the play's first act with his "Keep up your bright swords, for the dew will rust them" and Othello's self-defense before the Doge. Otello's musical eloquence, taming the storm and the enemy with diatonic solidity and an authentic cadence, is the analogue of Othello's verbal eloquence, and just as effectively establishes him as a noble figure of imposing stature (see Fig. 4, p. 77).[10]

---

[10] James Hepokoski comments that "The impact of 'Esultate!' ... has to be potent enough to resound in our memories throughout the rest of the work, for it is only here—and fleetingly—that we perceive an unflawed hero.... Otello crystallizes god-like out of the elements and resolves the deepest fears ... of those to whom he is responsible." See James Hepokoski, *Giuseppe Verdi:* Otello (Cambridge: Cambridge University Press, 1987), 173-74.

FIGURE 3

When we first begin to become acquainted with Iago, in his conversation with Roderigo a short time later, all the principal aspects of his musical language are revealed.[11] This conversation immediately establishes Iago as

---
[11] Parts of this passage are also discussed in Noske, 148-49.

The Iagoization of Otello

FIGURE 4

a "non-singing" role, as Verdi himself put it in a letter of November 11, 1886 to Giulio Ricordi.[12] Iago is at first unaccompanied, not only so he can be better heard and understood, but because throughout the opera he lacks substantial harmonic and orchestral support, underscoring both the insubstantiality of his discourse and the absence of human substance. His musical phrases are short and abrupt, interrupted by rests, and of irregular lengths. Iago's characteristic scornful snicker, rhetorically imitating a verbal snicker in sixteenth-note triplets, is introduced on the word "donna."

FIGURE 5

---

[12] The letter is published in Franco Abbiati, *Giuseppe Verdi*, 4 vols. (Milan: Ricordi, 1959), IV, 299. In a letter to Ricordi of May 11, 1887, Verdi says: "Iago must only declaim and snicker." See Abbiati, IV, 336-37.

78   *Jeffrey Kurtzman*

Once the strings do begin to accompany him at his first mention of Desdemona, the chords consist of a series of harmonic non sequiturs. This harmonic non-progression ends in a series of unresolved diminished-seventh chords, finally finding a cadence which is punctuated, at the end of Iago's line, with an unexpected, irrational orchestral outburst—in this instance in the form of a scalar descending fifth in octaves.

FIGURE 6

The Iagoization of Otello

As Iago speaks to Roderigo with a descending motif that regularly returns in situations where Iago is addressing someone, his line expands with the words "amico tuo sincero mi ti professo" (I profess myself your true friend) into the more lyrical expression that characterizes his lying, but in its melodious appeal makes him more convincing to his interlocutors. It is a forced lyricism that is false to Iago's native musical style, for once again, it is devoid of the substance of accompaniment and his phrase lengths are irregular.

FIGURE 7

Iago: lab - bra. Buon Ro - de - ri - go, a - mi - co tuo sin - ce - ro mi ti pro - fes - so, nè in più for - te am - ba - scia soc - cor - rer - ti po - trei. Se

Likewise irregular are the phrase lengths of his subsequent *arioso*, "se il fragil voto di femina" (if a fragile vow of a woman). Not only the fragility of the vow, but the fragility and tenuousness of Iago's words are expressed in the staccato breaks in his line and the thin, unison-and-octave doubling of the violins. What chords do support his line are soft, short, and off the main beats. In fact, Iago, when he is accompanied by the orchestra, is usually supported by no more than unison-and-octave doubling, reflecting his own lack of human substance, so effectively represented elsewhere by the richness of Verdi's triadic harmony. At the end of his twisting melodic line, as he completes the word "inferno" (hell), the orchestra interjects a repeated fortissimo diminished-seventh chord—an irrational, angry exclamation punctuating his cynical remarks. Similarly, the next phrase concludes with an orchestral outburst, this time a loud unison-and-octave drop of an octave accented by the pungent appoggiatura we already encountered in the storm scene (see Fig. 8, next page).

As Iago continues speaking to Roderigo in an aside, the strings again accompany him, beginning with an F-major triad, but as the F and the A are sustained as pedal points, the cellos and second violins move chromatically, disrupting the harmonic stability. Iago's continuation in the second system is accompanied by harmonically unstable and dissonant tremolos as his anger grows at the usurpation of his rightful station by Cassio, ending again with an orchestral outburst of unrelated chords at rehearsal W and a rapid unison-and-octave scalar punctuation at the end (see Fig. 9, p. 81).

FIGURE 8

The Iagoization of Otello

FIGURE 9

Finally, in Iago's concluding statement, we first hear his serpentine line, accompanied only by empty unison-and-octave doubling, shifting unstably from F♯ major to minor, and finally D major, concluding at the end of the first system with the famously mocking trill and another orchestral outburst comprising the sharply accented appoggiatura and unison octave leap downward we heard earlier. In the second and third systems, irregular phrases articulate Iago's warped thought, the first two interrupted by descending chromatic scales in the violins, and the conclusion punctuated by another outburst of the appoggiatura and unison octave drop.

FIGURE 10

In this passage, where we first become acquainted with Iago, Verdi has established the musical language of the villain—an unmelodious language of harmonic and tonal negation, of dissonance and tension, of ambiguity, irregularity and unpredictability, of mockery, of irrational outbursts, and the insubstantiality of no orchestral support whatsoever or thin unison-and-octave accompaniment.

The one element among all of these attributes that is expanded in its significance as Act I progresses is the descending chromatic scale that forms the conclusion of the refrain of the *brindisi*, or drinking song, leading to Cassio's brawl with Montano.

FIGURE 11

Frits Noske refers to the descending chromatic scale as Iago's "poison," while Tino Drenger identifies it as the "Todesymbolik" (death symbolism). But it is far more than an index of poison or a symbol of death. It is, more broadly, the metaphor for both potential and realized chaos, natural *and* human; but even further, what makes it so dramatically effective is that it is not merely a symbol, but the actual aural experience of the disruption of the tonal system and the resulting sonic chaos. The other musical characteristics of Iago are likewise not merely signs of his mockery and philosophy of negation, they are the musical experiences themselves of that mockery and that negation through various forms of musical disruption, irrationality, instability and insubstantiality, just as his words are in Shakespeare's play.

As I indicated previously, one of the important issues on which critics of the play have dwelt, is what makes Othello vulnerable to Iago's machinations. Some critics have gone beyond the lists of weaknesses assembled by

84   *Jeffrey Kurtzman*

various others to point out that Othello's jealousy and violent reaction are not induced by Iago, but rather that Iago taps into Othello's own latent emotions and capacities. His personal insecurities, his inability to have faith in love, his inability to trust Desdemona over Iago, his incapacity for uncertainty, and his bombastic, violent sensibility, are all his own characteristics, which are submerged just beneath the surface of his noble and calm exterior but cleverly brought to the forefront by Iago's insinuations and lies. What in Otello's music makes him vulnerable in an analogous fashion? As Sandra Corse has pointed out, in Iago's first utterance at the height of the storm, he expresses his wish that Otello be drowned by means of a descending scalar outline of a diminished-seventh chord which is itself accompanied by the same chord ambiguously notated.[13]

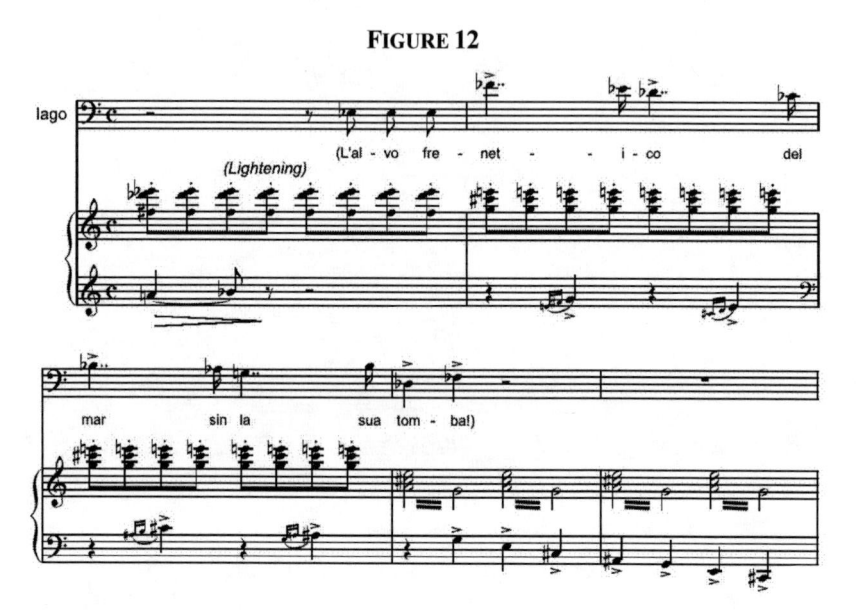

FIGURE 12

When Otello first lands triumphant on Cyprus and declares the Musselman buried in the sea by both arms and the storm, Otello sings an almost identical line, accompanied first by a C♯-major triad, but concluding in a diminished-seventh chord (refer back to Fig. 4, p. 77). The line and the

---

[13] Sandra Corse, *Opera and the Uses of Language: Mozart, Verdi, and Britten* (Rutherford, NJ: Fairleigh Dickinson University Press, 1987), 74. See the more detailed analytical commentary on this matter in Theodore Albritton Conner, "Towards an Interpretive Model of Text-Music Relations: An Analysis of Selected Scenes from Verdi's *Otello*" (Ph.D. dissertation, University of Connecticut, 1997), 87, 103, 185-97.

chord may be seen as simple "madrigalian" responses to the immediate words, but latent in the diminished-seventh chord is a momentary musical tension that emerges much more prominently the next time we encounter Otello when he puts down the brawl between the drunken Cassio and Montano instigated by Iago and Roderigo.[14]

FIGURE 13

[musical score: Otello — "Abbasso le spade! O-là! che avvien? Son io fra i Saraceni? O la turchesca rabbia è in voi tras-fu-sa da sbranar-vi l'un l'altro?"]

In this passage, Otello's short, broken phrases, without accompaniment, are interrupted by loud diminished-seventh chords, very similar already to passages in Iago's first conversation with Roderigo (see Figures 5 and 8-9, pp. 77, 80-81).[15] In the play, when Othello learns that Montano has been wounded, he declares "Now, by heaven, my blood begins my safer guides to rule, and passion, having my best judgment collied, assays to lead the way" (II.iii.195-97). Boito paraphrases Shakespeare closely at this point, and

---

[14] Conner has also drawn attention to this diminished-seventh chord as casting "a momentary shadow over Otello's entrance." See "Towards an Interpretive Model," 192.

[15] This similarity is noted by Corse, *Opera and the Uses of Language*, 74 and in the same year by Hepokoski, 173. Conner, 185-97, engages in a detailed comparative analysis of Iago's and Otello's first entrances.

Verdi's short, clipped musical phrases with intervening diminished-seventh orchestral outbursts present us with the sonorous experience of unleashed passion overwhelming the stability and order of good judgment.

At "l'ira volge l'angelo nostro," another scalar descending line similar to those we've previously heard from Iago and Otello is accompanied as before by a diminished-seventh chord, now agitated by string tremolos, punctuated at the end by a loud unison-and-octave, sharply articulated scale. Already Otello's music has begun to take on some of the characteristics of Iago's.[16]

FIGURE 14

There is not space here to trace this process through its course in the opera. Let it suffice to illustrate the point where Iago's musical language has most obviously and fully taken over that of Otello, at the moment after he has accused Desdemona of being "la vil cortigiana che è la sposa d'Otello" (the vile courtesan who is the wife of Othello). The passage begins with a descending chromatic scale in unisons and octaves in the strings, followed by a lone triplet figure in the first violins. The triplet figure originated when Iago mocked the fragility of women in his first soliloquy (see Fig. 5, p. 77), but as is well known, it becomes the principal motif of much of Act II, including its prominent appearance in Iago's Credo. Here its isolation underscores Otello's isolation; his orchestral support at this point is as thin and insubstantial as Iago's typically is. The descending chromatic scale separates each line of the text and Otello himself can no longer sing. Now

---

[16] Kerman finds that "from the time he quiets the drunken brawl, one is uneasy about his temper." See Kerman, 162.

The Iagoization of Otello 87

he can do no more than reiterate tonic and dominant pitches in A♭ minor in the same kind of irregular broken phrases that characterize Iago.[17]

FIGURE 15

---

[17] I take the opposite view from Hepokoski's comment on this passage: "Here, finally, Otello lifts himself up and provides us a glimpse of his former potential for greatness." See Hepokoski, 177.

In Shakespeare's Act III, Iago describes what has happened here:

> The Moor already changes with my poison:
> Dangerous conceits are in their natures poisons,
> Which at the first are scarce found to distaste,
> But with a little act upon the blood,
> Burn like the mines of sulphur. (III.iii.325-329)

As the act progresses, other aspects of Iago's musical style also become prominent in Otello's part and its accompaniment, such as diminished-seventh chords, appoggiaturas and trills.

Having established the general background of Iago's musical language and its impact on Otello, it is useful now to return to the question of chromaticism, with which I began, for there are other uses of chromaticism in *Otello* that play a major role in effecting Otello's downfall than just the chromatic scale and the diminished-seventh chord. In the Act I love duet, Verdi frequently employs chromatic shifts between the major and minor versions of a key or the use of ♭VI harmonies in a major key. The most prominent such shift is from an E-major triad to a C-major triad, which first appears at the conclusion of Desdemona's initial speech. Another prominent, but more complex example of third relations is in the passage (see Fig. 18, p. 94) where the two lovers first come together. The key of F major slips momentarily into F melodic minor with the introduction of the flattened 6th degree of the scale, before the ♭III chord, A♭, appears, moving directly to a C-major dominant triad. Already in the 16th century, madrigal composers had discovered that half-step chromatic inflections and chromatic harmonic shifts of a third were natural means for conveying the sense of the erotic and the exotic. The literature on eroticism rooted in chromatic melody and harmony in the 16th-century madrigal is vast. Less has been written about harmonic shifts of a third in this period. A familiar example is in Giovanni Gabrieli's well-known motet *In ecclesiis*, published posthumously in 1615, where harmonic shifts of a third are employed in the invocation *Deus, Deus* to evoke the sensation of awe at the name of God.

Now, one of the principal reasons for the downfall of Othello in Shakespeare's play is the exotic nature of the relationship between the Moor Othello and the Venetian noblewoman Desdemona, based on the eroticism aroused by his tales of war. Verdi's Act I love duet is replete with this type of erotic and exotic chromaticism, already appearing in Otello's opening gambit at the word "amplesso" (embrace) and taken up much more prominently at Desdemona's first entrance (see Figures 16 and 17, pp. 90 and 92). What makes it possible for Iago's chaotic chromaticism to invade Otello's musical style is not only Otello's own use of diminished-seventh chords, but this erotic and exotic chromaticism of Otello's and Desdemona's love, for the introduction of a few chromatic pitches to produce the sense of eroticism and exoticism requires only a few more to approach and even slip into the realm of disruption and chaos generated by the fully chromatic scale. The exotic and erotic chromaticism of the love duet thus lies somewhere between the stability of diatonicism and traditional functional harmony on the one hand, and the tension, disruption and chaos of diminished-seventh chords and chromatic scales on the other, thereby serving as the dramatic vehicle for the transition from the former to the latter. Indeed, the love duet is no pure expression of affection between Otello and Desdemona, but rather features a number of elements that provide foreboding hints of a relationship fraught with future tragedy. An analysis of these elements reveals again the sophisticated manner in which Verdi turns particular aspects of Shakespeare's dramaturgy into music.

The love duet begins after Otello has quelled the chaos of the bawl between Cassio and Montano and sent everyone home for the night. A brief orchestral interlude marks the transition to the duet as the stage clears of everyone except Otello and Desdemona. The duet itself is introduced by a muted cello quartet, which will continue as accompaniment as Otello sings his first group of lines in G♭ major, a half-step above the conclusion of the previous scene. The first exchange between Otello and Desdemona is itself rich with portent of the calamity to come. Just as Shakespeare establishes the racial difference between Otello and Desdemona as a significant factor in the collapse of their relationship, Verdi utilizes the beginning of the duet to emphasize exactly that racial difference. The cellos not only match the register of the voice, but in their dark coloring, especially in contrast to the instruments that will accompany Desdemona, serve to underscore in sound what the audience apprehends visually. Nor is the key haphazard, for G♭ is the most difficult key to play for strings built to resonate in C. None of the principal notes of the key of G♭ are in tune with the harmonics of any of the open strings and the natural resonance of the cello. As a consequence, the sound, already muted, is somewhat dull and colorless, supporting Otello with an attenuated sonority. Modern orchestras manage to generate greater richness by means of a strong vibrato, but in Verdi's day, string players did not employ a continuous vibrato, and the sound of the cellos would have been weaker.

Otello's melodic style in this passage is quite stable, relying on repeated notes and long arching phrases; its only chromatic inflection is on the word "amplesso," as noted above. The harmony, while rich with secondary dominants, remains stable with the exception of the outburst at "Tuoni la guerra e s'inabissi il mondo" (let war thunder and the earth plunge into the abyss) in the minor tonic.

FIGURE 16

When Desdemona responds, she does so only after Otello has completed his last note and with a pitch-class a fourth higher. It will be quite some time before their exchanges begin on the same pitch-class and overlap. In contrast to Otello's cellos, Desdemona, in a mid-to-high register, is accompanied by muted violins and violas also in a moderately high register, their pitch and timbre underscoring her racial difference. Moreover, her first three phrases are substantially shorter than Otello's, the melody is infused with numerous chromatic notes, and her harmony is more active and less stable, moving from G♭ through a series of unresolved chords before arriving at E♭ major at the beginning of her final phrase, only to slide chromatically upward to an E-major triad before abruptly shifting to C major a third away. Desdemona's response marks her as a very different personality from the calm stability of Otello. We hear in her vocal line and accompaniment the passionate, somewhat impetuous and willful woman who was willing to disobey her father and violate Venetian racial taboos in order to elope with Otello.[18] Verdi has powerfully impressed on us her eroticism and the exoticism of the relationship between these two contrasting individuals in their opening exchange (see Fig. 17, next page).

The next phase of the duet comprises the story of Otello's and Desdemona's courtship, taken over by Boito from Act I of Shakespeare's play (I.iii.128-259). Both characters still sing separately, with space between the end of one's passage and the beginning of another's. Desdemona leads the way with "Quando narravi l'esule tua" (when you told of your exile) in two long phrases in F major, but with a chord of B♭ minor emphasizing Otello's long sufferings ("I lunghi tuoi dolor") and the minor vi and iii chords highlighting the effect Otello's tales had on her at "coll'anima rapita" (with my soul enraptured). The passage concludes with a minor tonic triad at "quei spaventi" (your terrors), leading to a cadence in C major at "coll'estasi nel cor" (with ecstasy in my heart). The accompaniment features sustained flutes, English horn and clarinets with harps arpeggiating the chords in the bass register. The entire passage is broad and calm in its atmosphere of reminiscence. But when Otello responds with his description of arms, assaults and whistling arrows, he is clearly excited by the recollection of battles past. Beginning in C minor and concluding with a cadence in C major, the harmonies change frequently, include a prolonged diminished-seventh chord, and make use of the minor as well as major dominant. Otello's line is in the character of recitative, with frequent quick repeated notes

---

[18] Once again I disagree with the interpretation of Hepokoski, who declares of Desdemona, "In the opera we see nothing of this adventurous, bold side—the side to which Iago could insidiously refer in his 'She did deceiver her father marrying you'" (III.iii.206; cf. Hepokoski, 179).

FIGURE 17

[musical score: Desdemona vocal line with piano accompaniment]

Mio su - per-bo guer - rier! quan-ti tor-men-ti, quan-ti me-sti so - spi - ri e quan-ta spe-me ci con-dus - se ai so - a - vi ab brac - cia - men - ti! Oh! co-me è dol - ce il mor-mo-ra-re in - sie-me: te-ne-ram - men - ti!s

and several short, almost breathless phrases. As the harps increase the speed of their chordal arpeggiation that had accompanied Desdemona, all the rest of the instruments contribute to the agitation with quick, staccato repeated notes. The calm, controlled Otello has now yielded to the soldier excited by danger and violence.

Desdemona's continuation of the tale of their courtship strikes a completely different tone in recalling the desert sands of his homeland and the agonies and slavery he had suffered. Once again her accompaniment is dominated by high strings with repeated staccato notes in the violins and violas evoking the shining, wavering light of the burning desert. Desdemona's melodic line, by contrast, consists of long, soaring phrases, doubled by flute and English horn against the high string background. These phrases are suggestive of the passion aroused by Otello's war stories, and their potent effect on Desdemona is underlined by the passage shifting from the C major with which Otello had ended to A♭, turning to C minor and concluding in F minor. Once again, a key shift of a major third to ♭VI has introduced a sense of exoticism into the harmony.

Otello is clearly influenced by Desdemona's passion, for he, for the first time, overlaps her final note, beginning in the same key on the same pitch-class. But more importantly, as he describes Desdemona's reaction to his tales and how that reaction affected him, he mimics her long arching phrases. His accompaniment, though with fuller orchestration than hers, now includes the high strings in a prominent role, with the first violins doubling much of his second phrase, concluding in the key of D♭ major. The passage is brief, for Boito has been gradually bringing the lovers closer together by increasingly shorter exchanges. Just as Otello had maintained Desdemona's key and overlapped with the same pitch-class, Desdemona now does the same, overlapping Otello with the A♭ an octave higher than he had ended. And just as he had mimicked her long phrases, she now mimics his earlier recitative with rapid repeated notes, but once again with an accompaniment of harp arpeggios and doubling of her line by flutes, oboes and clarinets. Her cadence once more presents a key shift of a third, from D♭ major to F major.

The foreshortening of the verbal exchanges now leads to the first expression of emotional identity between the two lovers. They each sing the same words, taken by Boito directly from Shakespeare: "E tu m'amavi per le mie sventure, ed io t'amavo per la tua pietà" (And you loved me for the dangers I had passed, and I loved you that you did pity them—*Othello*, I.iii.167-168). Verdi follows Boito's lead in giving both the same lyrical phrase. For the first time, Otello begins simultaneously with Desdemona's conclusion of the previous passage on the same pitch-class, and Desdemona does the same in repeating Otello's music. The single phrase, accompanied by tremolo strings, is infused with an erotic chromaticism through the harmonic shifts described above. Whereas Otello's phrase is doubled only by the first violins, Desdemona's echo of the melody adds flute doubling to the violins. Reiteration of the last phrase of the text leads to a briefer imitative exchange between the two and finally a cadence in F, with the lovers for the first time singing simultaneously and closing together on the same pitch-class (see Fig. 18, next page).

This passage marks the end of the narration of their courtship and of the second phase of the love duet. It has taken Otello and Desdemona quite some time to sing the same music and to sing simultaneously, the stages of their interchanges along the way becoming shorter and shorter until they ultimately overlap, though only for a brief moment. Verdi has moved from a sharp distinction between the two at the beginning of the duet to their identity and union at the end of this phase.

FIGURE 18

The Iagoization of Otello

The next phase of the duet represents the individual reactions of Otello and Desdemona to this expression of their love. Otello begins with an exclamation about the maximum supremacy of his ecstasy, even if death should come at that moment, and the fear that "che più non mi sarà concesso quest'attimo divino nell'ignoto avvenir del mio destino" (that not again will be granted me this divine moment in the unknown future of my destiny). The thought, translated from Shakespeare's "that not another comfort like to this succeeds in unknown fate" (II.i.187-191), is, of course, ironic, since this indeed will be the height of his ecstasy, and death will follow. Otello's rapture is expressed with a lengthy lyrical phrase accompanied by the high

FIGURE 19

woodwinds previously associated with Desdemona (the strings join shortly) and an erotic succession of chromatic harmonies shifting abruptly from F major to E♭ major/minor to D♭, enharmonically to E major and finally cadencing in C major by means of the same tonal shift of a third that had concluded Desdemona's first passage at the beginning of the duet. However, at "che più non mi sarà concesso ...," Otello embarks on a systematic descent down a chromatic scale from D to F♯ before dropping a full step to its cadential E. Verdi has underscored the irony of Shakespeare's text with his own musical irony, foretelling through the chromatic scale the chaos to come in Otello's "unknown fate." That irony is magnified by the stage directions, which call for a clearing of the sky and the appearance of the moon and stars at just that moment when Otello begins the phrase culminating in the chromatic descent (see Fig. 19, previous page).

Desdemona's reaction is to pray, accompanied by arpeggiated chords in the harps, that Heaven will disperse such troubled thoughts and love will not change with the change of years. There is, however, some change in her harmony as the initial static C-major chord moves up chromatically to the minor ii, where the harps drop out, followed by harmonic changes every quarter note, including chromatic passing and neighboring tones as she herself concludes with a chromatic descent from F^4 to D^4 (much shorter than Otello's chromatic descent). Her prayer is also left open-ended by the dominant chord with which she ends, leaving Otello to finish the prayer with his own request that the heavenly hosts respond with their "Amen." His long, lyric phrase, accompanied by woodwinds and horns alone, is forcefully undercut, however, by the harmony, which, having begun in C, becomes dissonant and convoluted with seventh and diminished-seventh chords at "amen risponda," ending incompletely on a dominant of the false key of A minor. It is left up to Desdemona to complete the cadence, echoing Otello's "Amen risponda," but returning it to C major through her own clear, uncomplicated cadence. The difference between the two representations of "Amen" is striking and highlights the difference between the distortion that lurks beneath the surface in Otello's mind, and the purity of Desdemona's thoughts (see Fig. 20, next page).

The purity and simplicity of Desdemona's "Amen" so fills Otello with joy that he cannot even hold himself up, but must lean on a parapet of the embankment. As Otello sings a breathless, fragmented recitative, increasing in tempo (*stringendo poco a poco*), the strings alternate in rapid pairs of notes broken by rests, and the harmony moves from C major through two diminished-seventh chords, descending diminished and first inversion triads, and a half-diminished VII_7/V in the key of E, which serves as transition to the E major of the next section. The great soldier has been

The Iagoization of Otello 97

made weak in the knees by the ecstasy of his love, with unstable harmony, orchestral accompaniment and tempo, while he himself can barely sing (it is significant that there is no comparable reaction from Desdemona, whose expressions, though passionate, never break down in this manner).[19]

FIGURE 20

[19] Hepokoski comments, "At the climactic music leading up to and including the kiss, we are presented with the startling image of the hero physically collapsing under the impact of his emotions." On p. 34 of Verdi's *disposizione scenica*, his staging instructions for the first La Scala performance of *Otello*, the composer instructs that Desdemona must physically support Otello at this point. See Hepokoski, 175; and Hepokoski's and Mercedes Viale Ferrero's publication of the *disposizione scenica*: *Otello di Giuseppe Verdi* (Milan: Ricordi, 1990).

It is at this point that the only physical interaction between Otello and Desdemona takes place—the famous kiss.

FIGURE 21

But while this kiss expresses the height of Otello's passion, it, too, is fraught with foreboding. In the first place, the well-known motif in the oboes and clarinets, which will be repeated when Otello kisses Desdemona again in the last act as he wakens her to kill her, and once again as he himself dies, is hauntingly similar to a prominent motif from Act II and the "Liebestod" of *Tristan und Isolde* (see Fig. 22, next page).

FIGURE 22: *Tristan und Isolde,* "Liebestod"

[musical notation: Isolde's line with text: "se? Wo — ne— kla - gend, al - les— sa - gend, mild— ver - söh - nend aus— ihm— tö - nend,"]

Verdi may well have expected opera audiences to recognize the association of this motif and its connotations of death, at least on a subliminal level. But in addition to the significance of the motif, the underlying bass, beginning on an unstable six-four chord in E, descends chromatically one step in each bar from B to G (F𝄪). The height of Otello's expression of love is undermined by the very symbol and vehicle of that love's destruction.[20] Nevertheless, the connection of this moment with both Desdemona's and Otello's earlier expressions of passion is made with the E-major–C-major –E-major harmonic shifts of a third that close the passage.

James Hepokoski notes that "Boito, following Shakespeare, had originally planned to have the eavesdropping Iago vow at this point to ruin the lovers."[21] Iago's lines in *Othello* are "O, you are well tuned now! But I'll set down the pegs that make this music" (II.1.198-199). Though Iago doesn't appear in person anywhere in the love duet, Verdi has insinuated him into the scene through his musical characteristics that literally "untune" stable harmony.

The kiss merges into the conclusion of the duet in which the lovers lift their gaze from one another to the morning star Venus, the cosmological symbol of love and the city of Venice. Their voices are calmed by placing their passion in the much broader context of the heavens, and each reiterates a single pitch, E^4 and E^5 over sustained E-major and C♯-minor harmonies, before the C♯ turns enharmonically to D♭ major and the two lovers sustain a harmonious sixth while the violins, harps, flutes, and oboes shimmer in a very high register. Just as the duet had opened with an instrumental introduction, it closes with an instrumental postlude as Otello and Desdemona walk off to the castle and the curtain falls. The last sounds we hear are a repetition of the opening cello quartet, now in D♭, accompanied by a high-pitched trill in the first violins, while the harps outline the dying cadential tonic chord in

---

[20] This chromatic descent is also the inverse of the unresolved chromatic rise at the end of the first motif of the *Tristan und Isolde* prelude, which finally reaches resolution only at the very end of the "Liebestod."

[21] Hepokoski, 175. See also 30, 60.

slow descent.[22] The union of the two lovers, symbolized by the cellos on the one hand and the violins on the other, is as graphic at the end as the contrast of instruments and registers had been at the beginning of the duet.

FIGURE 23

Thus the love duet brings Otello and Desdemona together in perfect harmony, but not before a long set of interchanges and not before we have heard numerous hints at the tragedy to come, hints that derive from the substance of Iago's characterization. The love duet is a masterpiece of subtle musical innuendo at the same time it unites the two lovers with such erotic passion and rich chromatic harmony. Yet it is just this erotic and exotic chromaticism in harmony and melody that opens the door to the destructive chromaticism of Iago's descending chromatic scale.[23]

---

[22] For an earlier stage of the ending, without the reprise of the cello quartet, see Hepokoski, 61-62. Conner, 197-212, emphasizes descending melodic patterns and harmonic relationships toward the conclusion of the duet in terms of foreboding and lack of fulfillment of the couple's love, though he doesn't discuss the chromatic descents and harmonic twists. He compares the sinking of the Pleiades into the sea at the very end as parallel to Iago's opening wish that Otello be drowned in the sea.

[23] Two analyses of the love duet have been published. David Lawton's "On the 'Bacio' Theme in Otello," *19th Century Music* 1/3 (1978), 211-20 is primarily concerned with the "Kiss theme" in the tonal context of the duet and the opera as a whole. While citing the chromatic bass line of the theme in an example, Lawton's analysis is focused on the association of specific tonalities in the opera with particular characters and situations as well as the dramatic interplay and development these tonalities represent. Roger Parker and Matthew Brown in "Ancora un bacio: Three Scenes from Verdi's Otello," *19th Century Music* 9/1 (1985), 50-62 analyze the storm scene, the love duet, and the final act. They criticize the simplicity of the "semiotic" assignments of meaning by Noske and Lawton, but like Lawton, also focus on tonal structure and particular harmonic progressions, such as the diminished-7th chord on C♯ in the storm and the E-major-to-C-major harmonic shift in the duet and elsewhere in the opera. They find "no convincing sense of large-scale tonal motion" in the love duet and stress the similarities between the opening statements of Otello and Desdemona rather than the contrasts I emphasize. They do refer to chromaticism in Act II, scene 4 and Act III, scene 2 as a kind of "erotic recall" and cite the importance of chromatic descents in the last act, without, however, ascribing any dramatic significance to them. A principal objective of the article is to illustrate relationships among motifs and harmonic progressions, especially the "Kiss theme," throughout the opera.

FIGURE 24

That scale, which becomes increasingly prominent in Otello's part and his accompaniment as he falls under the influence of Iago (see Fig. 15, p. 87) has very little impact on Desdemona. It infects her only sporadically and to a very limited extent until the final scene when strangled, she revives just long enough to exculpate Otello and declare "Al mio Signor, mi raccomanda" ("recommend me to my Lord") to a descending chromatic scale. It is a moment of great poignancy and pathos.

There are many more ways in which Verdi employs the musical characteristics of Iago in the downfall of Otello, whether in Iago's seduction of Otello or in his interactions with his dupe Roderigo and with Cassio. Without painstakingly describing these, I nevertheless hope to have demonstrated the systematic manner in which Verdi has applied these musical characteristics to the progress of his drama in a manner directly analogous to the way Shakespeare utilizes language to achieve his dramatic goals. In both media the parallel processes are employed in a similar fashion and each is masterfully and profoundly effective.

PART II

Echoes of Anguish and Agony in 20th-century Chamber Music

Interpreting Interpretation: Janáček's String Quartet No. 1

William P. Dougherty

Leoš Janáček's String Quartet No. 1 is subtitled "inspired by *The Kreutzer Sonata* by L. N. Tolstoy." As such, the quartet articulates an expressive zone that hovers between strictly programmatic and strictly instrumental (or non-programmatic) modes of analysis and interpretation: to borrow a phrase from the musical *The King and I*, "'tis a puzzlement." But this particular puzzle is a telling opportunity to confront the complex issues that surround musical ekphrasis, precisely because it exemplifies how a composer might cue an interpretation of a musical work that assumes a pre-existent art work as its inspirational antecedent.

In his article on program music in *The New Grove Dictionary of Music and Musicians*, Roger Scruton notes that there are some curious examples of the relationship between music and another art form wherein "a composer declares himself to have been inspired by some literary or artistic source." He goes on to say that a "remarkable example of cross-fertilization is the quartet by Janáček composed after reading Tolstoy's novella *The Kreutzer Sonata*, itself inspired by Beethoven's violin sonata [Op. 47, "Kreutzer"]. The mere fact that Janáček's quartet was so inspired no more makes it into a programmatic narrative of the events in Tolstoy's story than it makes Tolstoy's story into a 'representation' of Beethoven's sonata."[1] Scruton's point is that Janáček's quartet is not an example of program music, as the term is generally understood, but it has, at least, a suggestive titular allegiance to an extra-musical source. To be sure, the quartet belongs to the same general species as more explicitly programmatic compositions, but there is a fundamental distinction that invites exploration. The complex and murky relationship—the puzzlement—surrounding inspiration and its role in the creation of a new musical work lies at the heart of musical ekphrasis, because it challenges notions of representation and re-presentation in music

---

[1] Roger Scruton, "Programme Music," S. Sadie and J. Tyrrell, eds., *The New Grove Dictionary of Music and Musicians*, (London: Macmillan, 2001), 26: 398.

while it simultaneously invites consideration of how the compositional strategies that a composer may use in transmedializing a pre-existent literary work can be interpreted. One of the tasks of musical ekphrasis is to ground how a musical composition might be understood in relation to the pre-existent literary work that it references, revisits, or revises, and upon which it reflects.

Janáček's String Quartet No. 1 offers both large and small parts of the puzzle. All of the pieces are tantalizing, all of them are provocative. I will show how these multi-layered pieces might be connected in ways that form a complete picture. I suspect that not all of the pieces are in their right places, and I do not claim that the puzzle has been solved. But I think I have linked the tabs and slots to form a reasonable outline that demonstrates how the local can inform a more global approach. In the process, I show how those local and global connections are fundamental to the nature of musical ekphrasis and how they tie one sign system to another through the process of interpretation.

Count Lev (Leo) Nikolayevich Tolstoy's novella, *The Kreutzer Sonata*, was published in 1889, when Tolstoy (1828-1910) was sixty-one years old. Though there is an unnamed narrator who records the tale, his participation in the novella is virtually non-existent: Apart from a few interruptions, the narrator's role is to transcribe verbatim his fellow train passenger's life story and the polemics it embeds. In essence, the novella is a monologue, a first-person narrative that erases the objectivity typically associated with a third-person setting: there is no barrier—or aesthetic distance, if you will—between the reader and the intensity of the tragic drama as it plays out.[2]

The novella tracks the fatal consequences of a self-centered character increasingly consumed by an obsessive jealousy. Pozdnyshev married for what he believed was love, but he soon realizes that his commitment was an error, and, as a result, the relationship between him and his (unnamed) wife rapidly disintegrates. Indeed, he and his wife become trapped in a loveless and increasingly virulent—and violent—relationship. His wife, formerly a pianist, returns to the piano as a means of solace and escape. She meets a

---

[2] Apparently, Tolstoy, after hearing a performance of Beethoven's Kreutzer Sonata in 1888, proposed that the artist Repin respond to the composition in painting and that he (Tolstoy) write a story that the actor Andreyev-Burlak would perform (as a monologue?) in front of the painting. Nothing came of the project, but it may have planted the seed for the novella and its monologue structure. See T. G. S. Cain, *Tolstoy* (New York: Harper and Row, 1977), 149. Eguchi argues that the predominance of a monologue creates a performance that infects the reader in a manner similar to the immediacy of a performance of Beethoven's Kreutzer Sonata. See Mahoko Eguchi, "Music and Literature as Related Infections: Beethoven's Kreutzer Sonata Op. 47 and Tolstoy's Novella 'The Kreutzer Sonata,'" *Russian Literature* 40/4 (1996): 423.

violinist named Trukhachevsky and begins performing works with him. Extra-marital relations between Pozdnyshev's wife and Trukhachevsky are never made overt in the novella, but we learn that Pozdnyshev, upon hearing the two of them perform Beethoven's Kreutzer Sonata, assumes that he will be cuckolded, based on the passionate interplay between the performers of the composition and the power of music to incite the strongest and most uncontrollable of emotions. Describing his reaction to their performance of the Beethoven, Pozdnyshev asks, "Was it not perfectly evident that the fatal step was taken by them that evening [of the performance]? Was it not perfectly evident that from that evening on, not only was there no bar between them, but that both of them—she especially—felt some sense of shame after what had happened to them?"[3]

Pozdnyshev's description of his wife's and his presumed sexual rival's performance of the "Kreutzer Sonata" works in two directions: not only does it suggest that an affair is inevitable, it also depicts a more troubling, and ultimately irrational, psychological state. In reporting the affect of the performance of the Beethoven sonata, Pozdnyshev tells us that music has the ability to excite and to inflame:

> Under the influence of music it seems to me that I feel what I do not really feel, that I understand what I do not really understand, that I can do what I can't do […] it is impossible to tell what to do in this state of mind. And that is why music is so awesome, why it sometimes has such a terrifying effect […]. Indeed, it is a terrible power to place in anyone's hands. For example, how could anyone play this *Kreutzer Sonata*, the first Presto, in a drawing room before ladies dressed in low-cut gowns? To play that Presto, then to applaud it, and then to eat ices and talk over the last bit of scandal? These things should be played only under certain grave, significant conditions, and only then when certain deeds corresponding to such music are to be accomplished: first play the music and perform that which this music was composed for. But to call forth an energy which is not consonant with the place or the time, and an impulse which does not manifest itself in anything, cannot fail to have a harmful effect. On me, at least, it had a horrible impact. It seemed to me that entirely new impulses, new possibilities, were revealed to me in myself, such as I had never dreamed of before.[4]

This bifurcation of references—first to the union of Trukhachevsky and Pozdnyshev's wife and second to the stirring of tormented emotions—makes the performance of the Kreutzer Sonata the linchpin in Tolstoy's

---

[3] Leo Tolstoy, *The Kreutzer Sonata*, trans. Isai Kamen (New York: Modern Library, 2003), 63.
[4] Tolstoy, *Kreutzer Sonata*, 60-61.

story.[5] A latent tragic fate is made patent, and what remains to be related is the *denouement* as Pozdnyshev is consumed by a state of jealous madness. At the end of the tale, Pozdnyshev unexpectedly returns from a business trip to find his wife dining with Trukhachevsky (after he had forbidden her to see him). Suspecting the worse, Pozdnyshev stabs them both, injuring Trukhachevsky and mortally wounding his wife. The story concludes as he wanders, after a short period of imprisonment, full of unresolved remorse and guilt, but without atonement. Pozdnyshev's last words to his dying wife, "forgive me," are also the last spoken words of the novella. This plea, though, rings hollow, because, as Robert Bird puts it, Pozdnyshev is "looking outside of himself [...] for forgiveness without having reached a full inner repentance."[6]

Tolstoy's novella incited instant controversy. Banned by Russian censors (even the United States Postal Service prohibited the mailing of print material that serialized the work), it found an audience only because of Tolstoy's reputation. Today, many of the polemics in the story are characterized as misogynistic screeds against marriage, sex, and procreation. Nevertheless, the novella is haunting, powerful, and disturbing. It seems slightly odd, given our contemporary hindsight, that a composer would choose to engage the novella in a musical composition, but there is little, if anything, in Janáček's string quartet that relates to the controversial diatribes in Tolstoy's novella. There is, though, a suggestive relationship between the musical composition and the literary work it reflects on—specifically, Janáček's abstraction of Tolstoy's account of a harrowing situation where remorse or, at least, a resigned acceptance, is potentially available through candid contrition—an act of self-redemption that Pozdnyshev is unable to obtain.

---

[5] Unlike other literary works that explicitly refer to a musical composition (see, e.g., Anthony Burgess, *Napoleon Symphony: A Novel in Four Movements* [New York: A. Knopf, 1974]), Tolstoy's novella does not seem to engage its referenced musical antecedent in a determined fashion. Some scholars, though, have sought to discover structural and expressive homologies between Beethoven's sonata and Tolstoy's novella: see, e.g., Dorothy Green, "The Kreutzer Sonata: Tolstoy and Beethoven," *Melbourne Slavic Studies* 1 (1967): 11-23, summarized in R.F. Christian, *Tolstoy: A Critical Introduction* (Cambridge: Cambridge University Press, 1969), 232-233; Eguchi, "Music and Literature as Related Infections," and Elizabeth Papazian, "Presto and Manifesto: The Kreutzer Sonatas of Tolstoy and Beethoven," *Russian Literature* 40/4 (1996): 491-516. These critical approaches should be compared with other attempts to view the structure of a literary work through a musical lens: see, e.g., Robert K. Wallace, "*The Murders in the Rue Morgue* and Sonata-Allegro Form," in Nancy Anne Cluck, ed., *Literature and Music* (Provo: Brigham Young University Press, 1981), 153-174, and Harold A. Basilius, "Thomas Mann's Use of Musical Structure and Techniques in *Tonio Kröger*," in Nancy Anne Cluck, ed., *Literature and Music* (Provo: Brigham Young University Press, 1981), 175-183.

[6] Robert Bird, "The Truth of the Inner Being: 'The Kreutzer Sonata' as a Tragedy of Forgiveness," *Russian Literature* 40/4 (1996): 408.

Janáček's String Quartet No. 1

Janáček (1854-1928) completed his first string quartet in 1923, when he was sixty-nine years old. The quartet was not Janáček's first attempt to cast Tolstoy's novella in a musical mold, as in 1908 he wrote a piano trio that was also based on the story. The trio is now lost and only a few fragments of it survive, but its material apparently provided a springboard for the composition of the quartet years later.[7] The quartet was first performed in 1924, about a year after its completion.

Several analyses of the composition treat the trajectory of the four quartet movements as a reflection of the characters, elements, and main outlines of Tolstoy's story. Briefly, and summarizing from several accounts,[8] the received analysis of the relationship of musical work to literary work is as follows: The first movement is the exposition of the drama that sketches a musical portrait of the wife and her passions and frustrations; the second movement evokes the cosmopolitan violinist, the seducer who eventually ignites the flames of Pozdnishev's jealousy; the third movement suggests the crisis that unleashes the passion of the wife and the jealousy of the husband (it includes what Vogel[9] identifies as subtle reference by virtue of its contour to Beethoven's Kreutzer Sonata (Figures 1a and 1b)—questionable, in my view—and a violin-and-cello duet that Zemanová believes "clearly evokes the wonderful theme of the variations in Beethoven's 'Kreutzer' Sonata"[10]—again, questionable in my view); and the fourth movement unfolds the last act of the tragedy, with Škampa hearing the musical equivalent of a cathartic atonement and "the purified awakening" of the murdering husband whose wife is dead by his hand.[11] In the bulk of most descriptions of the extra-musical content of the quartet, the wife is ultimately the heroine of Janáček's musical "story": a suffering, tormented woman whose prison house and ultimate fate are undeserved.

---

[7]See Paul Wingfield, "Janáček's 'Lost' Kreutzer Sonata," *Journal of the Royal Musical Association* 112/2 (1986-87): 229-56.

[8]I have compiled the following summary from several analyses, and although I have not included some of the more specific claims (e.g., how "foppish" viola variants portray the seducer or how the perfect fourth is a manifestation of love), my summary will suffice as a basis of contrast to the analysis presented below. The complete analyses are found in the following publications: Jaroslav Vogel, *Leoš Janáček: A Biography*. Rev. and ed. by Karel Janovický (New York: W.W. Norton, 1981), 292-294; Mirka Zemanová, *Janáček* (Boston: Northeastern University Press, 2002), 179-181; and Milan Škampa, "Preface" to the full score of Janáček's String Quartet No. 1 (n.p.: Supraphon, 1982), xii-xiv.

[9]Vogel, *Leoš Janáček*, 293.

[10]Zemanová, *Janáček*, 180.

[11]Škampa, "Preface," xiv.

FIGURE 1a: Janáček, String Quartet No. 1, I: 8-11

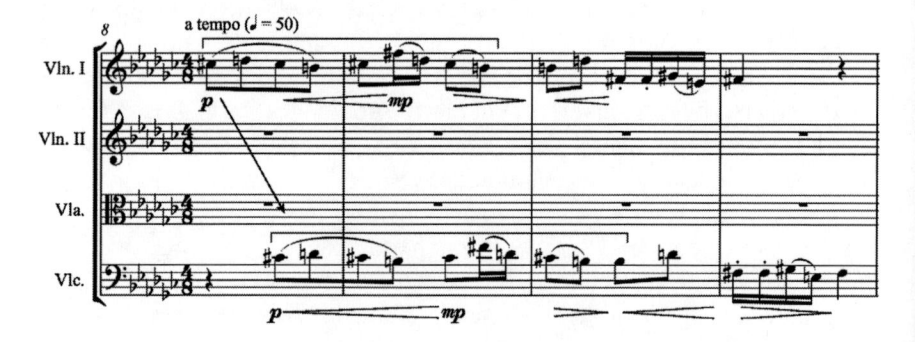

FIGURE 1b: Beethoven, Violin Sonata, Op. 47, I: 414-21

The extent to which this rendering of the quartet is bound to the composition might best be illustrated with a passage from Margriet de Moor's novel, *The Kreutzer Sonata*. In a fascinating instance of music in literature, de Moor forges another link in the Beethoven-Tolstoy-Janáček chain by incorporating an analysis of Janáček's first string quartet to serve as a microcosm of her own story of uncontrollable jealousy (a story that reworks in its own fashion the Tolstoy novella). The unnamed narrator of de Moor's story—a young musicologist—claims at one point that what Janáček had in mind when writing the quartet was "a fatal psychological drama that no earthly power could bring to a halt,"[12] and most of chapter 12 of de Moor's novel is the musicologist's analysis of the work. The relevant text is as follows:

> I'm not going to ask him [...] whether he ever again heard his wife play that quartet [String Quartet No. 1], the masterpiece composed by that sensitive skeptic, that wayward modernist Janáček, who, like many of his fellow composers, put things in his music that were meant not only for the listening ear but also for the inner eye—in

---

[12] Margriet de Moor, *The Kreutzer Sonata*, trans. Susan Massotty (New York: Arcade Publishing, 2005 [2001]), 66.

other words, the story. Consequently, in bars 1-45 of the first movement, anyone who wishes to can clearly visualize a beautiful woman. She is married. In the second movement, the *con moto*, with all those ominous tremolos, we can picture her meeting an elegant gentleman, bars 1-47, who also happens to be an excellent violinist. Flirtation: bars 48-67; suggestive remarks: bars 68-75; the encounter appears to be far from innocent: bars 185-224. Then comes the third movement, catastrophic from beginning to end, when we realize that the power of music is not always innocent, especially not when one is playing Beethoven, bars 8-10.

[...] I was still pondering the third movement, particularly the racing thirty-second notes of the *sčasovka*, a motif you run into often in Janáček. All well and good, but in this case, bars 1-34, that sweet little ditty is used to represent the demon, the evil spirit who manages, with spectacular success, to drive the husband mad. The master of the house, an inherited character who is very nasty indeed, falls into the clutches of jealousy.

[...] Increasing madness—the third movement races on. Quarrel: bar 35. Lament: bars 39-59. The andante is a breather of sorts, but there's no getting around the score, so with a heavy heart, bars 60-70, the woman admits to herself that she would be delighted if a certain fantasy, bars 73-88, were to come true. In the fourth movement one thing after another goes wrong.

[...] The composer, at the age of almost seventy, gives a new twist to the spiral of passion and fate that has gone from sonata to novella to string quartet.[13]

Even allowing for novelistic license (and, perhaps, some extravagance), the passage I have excerpted and abridged aptly describes the "inherited program" of Janáček's string quartet as it is found in several sources.[14]

There is no doubt that all of these descriptions take interpretative cues from Janáček himself. Indeed, in 1924 Janáček wrote to his late-life lover, Kamila Stösslová, that in his first string quartet he "had in mind a miserable woman, suffering, beaten, wretched, like the great Russian author Tolstoy wrote about in his *Kreutzer Sonata*."[15] Zemanová asserts that "while Tolstoy [...] marginalized the heroine's voice, Janáček—speaking on her behalf—transformed the narrative."[16] Škampa goes even further, averring that in this quartet Janáček, unlike Tolstoy, "comes forward in defense of women and their rights,"[17] and that by the end of the quartet, another of Janáček's

---

[13] de Moor, *The Kreutzer Sonata*, 117-119.

[14] de Moor (157) acknowledges Škampa as a source for the analysis of the quartet.

[15] Cited in Škampa, "Preface," xii, and (in a different translation) Zemanová, *Janáček*, 181.

[16] Zemanová, *Janáček*, 181.

[17] Škampa, "Preface," xiii.

"morally strong women-heroines has been born."[18] There is also no doubt that the "received version," as I have paraphrased it, is an overlay constructed from the general outline of the novel—the object focusing the sign, as it were (albeit with some biographical direction). But it seems that to make sense of the musical work in terms of its literary antecedent, the string quartet has been pushed through a descriptive sieve with a wide mesh, and the "program" or the "inspiration" that has been caught is largely impressionistic.

I hope to weave a finer mesh to catch more sophisticated analytic data in order to come to grips with what it might mean when composers acknowledge a pre-existent art work as a source of inspiration, and to ground as specifically as possible how we may approach those musical works when, as Siglind Bruhn puts it, "composers claim to respond to a poem or painting, a drama or sculpture, [a novel or novella,] by transforming that artwork's features and message into their own medium: musical language."[19] My goal is to capture some of these details by treating them as musical signs, correlating them to an object, and suggesting a reading of the sign-object relationship. The task is to interpret an interpretation.

Janáček's harmonic style is rooted in the late-19th and early-20th-century tonal system. To be sure, in his quartet, he employs whole-tone scales (e.g., II: 129-135), pentatonic collections (e.g., II: 172-178), quartal and quintal harmonies (e.g., I: 57-58), extended chords (e.g., I: 1-2), Moravian folk influences (e.g., I: 3-11, with its raised-fourth and natural-fourth scale degree alterations), and modality (e.g., II: 165-171). Nevertheless, the work's overall harmonic language relates to the functional chromatic tonal system as it evolved during the late 19th and early 20th centuries, and it inherits much of the expressive meaning associated with that system.

The first movement is in E minor. The form can be best described as a "truncated" sonata allegro.[20] The opening two measures (Ex. 2) begin with an ascending perfect fourth in the first violin and viola, muted and in octaves. The B-to-E interval is probably enough to suggest E as tonic, but the minor mode is not established until the second violin enters on the "and" of beat 1, with its *sforzando* G-to-B tremolo. At this juncture, E in the melodic voices gives way to an F♯ that is emphasized by its pitch height (tonic accent) and its rhythmic duration (agogic accent). The minor second formed

---

[18]Škampa, "Preface," xiv.

[19]Cf. Siglind Bruhn, "A Concert of Paintings: 'Musical Ekphrasis' in the Twentieth Century," in *Poetics Today* 22/3 (Fall 2001), 551-605 [559].

[20]Wingfield ("Janáček's 'Lost' Kreutzer Sonata, 253) suggests, correctly I believe, that the appearance of the second theme in the dominant in the quartet is a structural connection to Beethoven's Kreutzer Sonata, a minor mode work that also moves to the dominant to support the presentation of the second theme.

Janáček's String Quartet No. 1

FIGURE 2: Janáček, String Quartet No. 1, I: 1-11

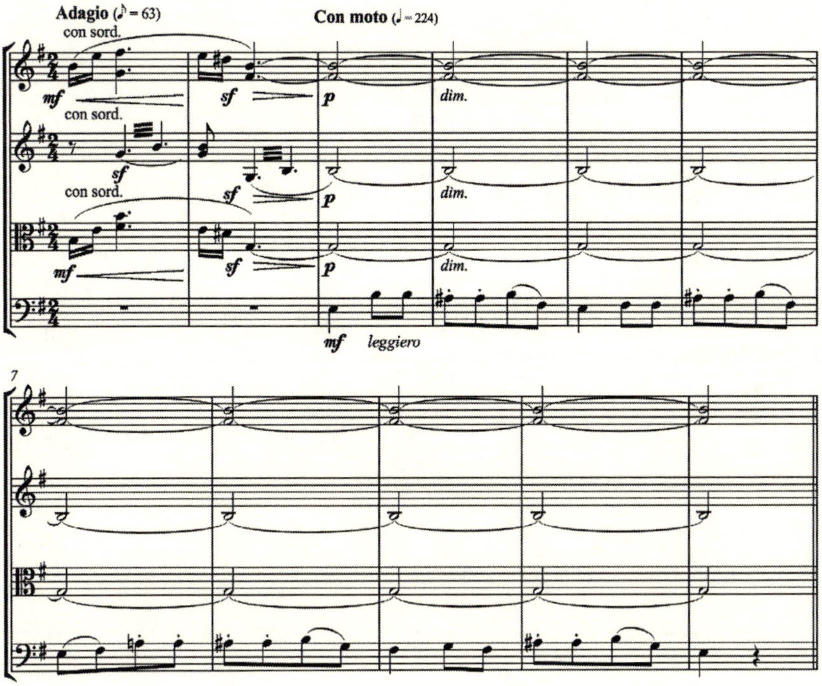

by the neighbor F♯ and the mode-defining G creates a dissonance at the apex of the melodic gesture and at the moment where mode is established. In m. 2, the melodic shape is reversed, collapsing into a sonority that still contains the F♯—an unresolved dissonance that persists for the next nine measures as part of an E-minor ninth chord. The leading-tone D♯ in the melodic reversal of m. 2 is also unresolved: Treated here as an escape tone, or échappée, it leaps in the same direction from its approach down to B. Positive ascent, or upward groping, gives way to a yielding descent. In addition, these Adagio measures are metrically ambiguous—outside of time or, perhaps, for any time. The confluence of rhythmic, dynamic, melodic, and textural events on the second eighth-note of the opening measure suggests, at least retrospectively, that the opening two sixteenth-notes may be an anacrusis. A definitive meter is not established until the con moto of m. 3.

These measures are in effect an encapsulation of the tragic pathos of the quartet. The slow tempo, metric ambiguity, non-resolution of dissonance, positive melodic ascent coupled with poignant melodic collapse, and minor mode invoke the essence of the tragic. As Robert Hatten argues, in the classical diatonic system the minor mode consistently cues the tragic and, as such, articulates a narrower range of expressive meaning than does major.[21] Even though writing in the first part of the 20th century, Janáček compositionally invokes a marked value entirely appropriate to the poignancy of his model story. But tragic as an expressive type can support many tokens—tokens that can be thematized in the particular composition. I suggest that Janáček does precisely this in the remainder of the quartet.

The first movement ends by recalling the first segment of the opening motif over a Picardy third (Ex. 3). Concluding a movement in the minor mode with a Picardy third is a standard convention in the tonal system, but I think in this case Janáček has other interpretive goals in mind that point to his comment on or reaction to the nature of tragedy in Tolstoy's novella. Most of the last thirty or so measures of the first movement are in E major. The shift in mode suggests a change from the largely tragic to a non-tragic or more positive expressive state. The end of the movement suggests a sense of a willful overcoming of a tragic fate—and for that expressive shift, I find

FIGURE 3: Janáček, String Quartet No. 1, I: 157-64

[21]Robert Hatten, *Musical Meaning in Beethoven: Markedness, Correlation, Interpretation* (Bloomington: Indiana University Press, 1994), 36.

no correlation in Tolstoy. Janáček seems to allow a glimmer of hope, and had the quartet ended here, our interpretation might have been one of detailing how the positive transcends the tragic, despite the F♯ of the last few measures that is still unresolved.

But positive is turned on its head, as it were, as G♯ is enharmonically reinterpreted as A♭ and the second movement commences in A♭ minor. In other words, the node that signified a rhetorical shift to the positive is illusory: it is, instead, a harbinger of a key area that is going to support much of the discourse of the remainder of the quartet. Janáček suggested this distant key relation—this complication—earlier in the first movement by moving quickly from E minor to A♭ minor to restate the opening motif (Ex. 4).[22] The second movement, with its scherzo-like quality, jaunty rhythms, and fits and starts, scornfully mocks, ridicules or scoffs at a positive outcome. The die is cast.

FIGURE 4: Janáček, String Quartet No. 1, I: 29-45

The issues come to a head in the fourth movement. The opening measures restate the first movement's opening motif, now in A♭ Dorian (Ex. 5).

[22]Wingfield observes that this passage also forms a direct link to the fourth movement (mm. 121-126) where the material is recalled (Wingfield, "Janáček's 'Lost' Kreutzer Sonata, 255).

FIGURE 5: Janáček, String Quartet No. 1, IV: 1-12

A plaintive solo violin line (mm. 6-12, marked, significantly, "like in tears") invokes the descending fourth chromatic tetrachord topic (here troped as descending chromatic fifth tetrachord without a C♮)—a gesture historically associated with the lament. At a critical juncture (Ex. 6), A♭ major appears, but the motif is rhythmically askew (note the cello). After two measures,

FIGURE 6: Janáček, String Quartet No. 1, IV: 78-85

A♭ minor reasserts itself, yanking the potentially earned move to the positive back into the tragic. The last page of the score offers confirmation of the duality between inexorable tragedy infused with the hope of escape—a shift that will not be realized (Ex. 7). From m. 169 to the end, the mode is A♭

Janáček's String Quartet No. 1   117

FIGURE 7: Janáček, String Quartet No. 1, IV: 166-189

Dorian. The A♭-Dorian mode, with its C♭ and G♭, is related to the minor mode; F♮, on the other hand, suggests a closer relation to the major mode. The tonic minor triad in mm. 169-171 gives way to a IV chord in mm. 172-173. A IV chord in a minor-like mode might imply that the work will end with a

Picardy third—in other words, that the raised-sixth scale degree will bring the raised-third scale degree with it. But in this case, IV moves back to i, and after a progression of VII_6 and v^9 to i, i slips back to IV (mm. 185-186) which then concludes on i in a plagal cadence that does not so much resolve as it simply finishes. Indeed, the quartet, even though ending on the tonic, has an open-ended aura about it. This sense of relative incompleteness is realized through several compositional strategies: the distant echo of the second half of the original motif in the second violin, the lack of a leading tone (indeed, G♮ was last heard in m. 168), and the (unrealized) potential of a IV chord to resolve to I.

Janáček has re-presented Tolstoy's drama in a remarkably complex way. Pozdnyshev's plea for forgiveness ("forgive me"), as noted above, rings hollow; it is not accompanied by self-realization, and, as such, it is not earned. His wife does not forgive him, the narrator does not forgive him, and we, as readers of his tale, do not forgive him. He is destined to re-live the past in the present and in the future without positive redemption. Janáček musically suggests that a willed redemption is possible, but that this growth is ultimately denied: a positive conclusion is an illusion that is not made manifest. Tolstoy crafts a tale about a person who will never escape his guilt and who will never come to terms with it. Janáček's disquieting ending appropriately responds to the tragic consequences of an empty and forlorn hope: it re-presents a failed search.

In one of his many definitions of a sign, Charles Sanders Peirce says that "a sign is something by knowing which we know something more."[23] The contextualization of musical modes, motifs, and harmonic areas are all signs wherein interpretation lurks. A focus on the sign, its correlation to an object, and how that correlation makes sense helps ground the complex interaction between music and a pre-existent literary text. I hope to have shown how an analysis of the signs in an instrumental composition can yield an interpretation that helps clarify what it means when a composer claims to have been inspired by a literary work. I also hope to have shown how a composer might abstract from the literary work in a way that re-casts the object through an interpretive web that both touches on and extends the original. To be sure, Janáček's String Quartet No. 1 is still "a puzzlement." To be sure, there are many other pieces to the puzzle. But if we already knew the answers, solving the puzzle wouldn't be any fun.

---

[23] Charles Sanders Peirce, *Semiotic and Significs: The Correspondence between Charles Sanders Peirce and Victoria Lady Welby*, edited by Charles S. Hardwick (Bloomington: Indiana University Press, 1977), 31-32.

"Streicht dunkler die Geigen": Berio and Birtwistle in Dialogue with Celan

Axel Englund

Few poets of the post-war era have inspired as many contemporary composers as the exiled Romanian Jew Paul Celan. Several hundred pieces, instrumental as well as vocal ones, have been written in reaction to his poetry.[1] There may be numerous reasons for this, one certainly being his almost incomparable position in the modernist canon, prompting Hans Egon Holthusen to ironically point out that "whenever Paul Celan is discussed, the German critic makes the face of an altar boy before the altar."[2] A more interesting reason, perhaps, is the fact that his work conveys, probably more desperately than any other poet's, the feeling of aesthetic crisis permeating the cultural climate of post-war Europe. The arguably most poignant and, at any rate, most widely known phrasing of this crisis, Adorno's caveat that writing poetry after Auschwitz is barbaric,[3] was taken by many to refer to Celan's work, and when Adorno eventually nuanced this statement, he clearly did so with Celan's poetry in mind.[4] Written in German, which was Celan's mother tongue as well as the language of those who murdered his mother and father, his poetry constantly struggles with the notion of its own impossibility in the wake of the Shoah. It is, in his own oft-quoted words, a poetry that "asserts itself at its own edge."[5] This would, arguably, appeal to the many composers of the recent decades who have, in a similar fashion, been struggling at and with the limits of their own art.

In the following, I discuss the interrelations between poetry and music in two string quartets from the last decades of the 20th century: Luciano Berio's third quartet *Notturno*, which borrows a quotation from Celan's

---

[1] Cf. Felstiner 2001, Zenck 1993, Glenn 2002.

[2] "Immer wenn Paul Celan zur Debatte steht, pflegt der deutsche Kritiker ein Gesicht zu machen wie ein Meßdiener vor dem Altar." Quoted from Mackey 1997, 1. Translations by the author unless otherwise indicated.

[3] Cf. Adorno 2003, 30.

[4] Seng 2003, 161.

[5] "... behauptet sich am Rande seiner selbst." Celan 2000 III:197.

poem "Argumentum e silentio" as its motto, and Harrison Birtwistle's "Todesfuge – Frieze 4," one of the movements of the extensive Celan-cycle *Pulse Shadows*.

Musico-literary Relations as Metaphorical Phenomena

Before moving on to the compositions themselves, I shall comment briefly on my theoretical point of departure. A recurrent notion in recent discussions on intermediality is the treatment of musico-literary relations as metaphorical phenomena. This perspective has been advocated, from different angles and with different arguments, by scholars such as Eric Prieto and Michael Spitzer.[6] Prieto holds that "there can be no literal contact between music and literature […], the only relationship that can obtain between music and literature is a metaphorical one."[7] This, according to Prieto, is an inescapable consequence of the inherent differences between the media. He stresses the need to acknowledge this inherent metaphoricity and claims that a large body of musico-literary criticism fails to do so, since it focuses on judging the appropriateness of the metaphor rather than on the interpretation of its meaning. The musico-literary critic, Prieto claims, must accept the metaphor for what it is and explicate its grounds in order to shed light on its significance.[8] This phrase might be borrowed to express the aim of the present article: to regard the juxtaposition of a verbal text (Celan) and a musical one (Berio and Birtwistle respectively) as a metaphorical constellation, and attempt to throw light on the grounds and the significance of this metaphor.

In order to do this, one must have a clear view of what is subsumed under the label "metaphor." Most present-day theories reject the traditional notion of metaphor as a substitutional trope, a figure of speech that can be explained and replaced by a literal expression for which it serves as an embellishment. Instead, metaphor is conceived of as a tension between discrete elements, giving rise to meanings that cannot be exhaustively expressed in paraphrase. This view is largely shared by, for instance, I. A. Richards, Max Black, and Paul Ricœur.[9] Although these theorists typically deal with small-scale metaphors where the metaphorical elements are words in a sentence, their thoughts can be productively applied to large-scale structures. In the present context, then, the elements involved in metaphorical

[6] Prieto 2002, Spitzer 2004.
[7] Prieto 2002, 17.
[8] Ibid., 16-18.
[9] For Richards and Black see Black 1962, 44; Ricœur 1979.

tension are the verbal paratext and the musical text of an instrumental composition. A necessary condition for this kind of interpretation, I would argue, is some sort of pretension to identity between words and music: the typical metaphor is, in essence, the claim that something is something other than it actually is. As I will show shortly, such pretension to identity is indeed present in the works to be discussed here.

In Black's view, a metaphor consists of two distinct elements, which he labels the "principal subject" and "subsidiary subject" respectively. Each of these constitutive elements of the metaphor brings with it a "system of associated implications," which might be roughly described as a set of features associated with it.[10] If the subjects are music and literature respectively, such implications might be either general commonplaces about these arts—as for instance the referential character of verbal language—or specific, material traits in the poetic and musical structures that constitute the piece. What the metaphorical interaction does, according to Black, is to restructure our conception of each element, so that the implications or features forming analogies between the elements receive a more prominent position.[11] A metaphor such as "Man is wolf"—here, the pretension to identity is rather obvious—alters our conception of man by foregrounding his animal, wolf-like qualities. In Black's view, although this metaphor is chiefly aimed at our understanding of man, metaphors are never unidirectional; thus our conception of the wolf is altered as well, its human-like qualities being foregrounded.

From this follows that if the relation between music and poetry in the works at hand is regarded as a metaphorical constellation, the interaction should be thought of as a) affecting our conception of words and music alike and b) giving the analogous implications between words and music a privileged position in our understanding of the work as a whole.

Silent Rhetoric: Luciano Berio's *Notturno*

Luciano Berio supplied his third string quartet, entitled *Notturno* (1993), with a short epigraph quoting Celan's poem "Argumentum e silentio" from the 1955 collection *Von Schwelle zu Schwelle*. The epigraph consists of only four words: "ihr das erschwiegene Wort," which John Felstiner has translated as "to her the ensilenced word."[12]

[10] Black 1962, 44.

[11] Ibid., 44f.

[12] Celan 2000, 138f. The poem is included as an appendix, along with John Felstiner's translation in Celan 2001, 78-79.

Brief and isolated as it may be, this quotation encompasses several important aspects of Celan's poetic stance. The verb "erschweigen," used participially in the quotation, is typical of Celan's predilection for polyvalent neologisms. To begin with, it functions as an implicit paronomasia on "verschweigen," which denotes the act of keeping something secret, or being silent about something. Moreover, the suppression, or perhaps silencing, of the initial letter turns the prefix into a resultative one, thus giving the impression that the action indicated by the verb entails a result or a product (as in, for instance, "erreichen" [achieve] or "erfinden" [invent]). In the quotation, this product is a word. At the same time, the prefix "er-" often indicates a deadly outcome for the direct object (as in "erschiessen" [shoot to death] or "erschlagen" [beat to death]). In the present context, this association is supported by the fact that silence could actually be thought lethal to the direct object, "Wort" [Word]. The word, if you will, is simultaneously born from and extinguished by silence.

The term "Wort" is equally typical, insofar as it is a sign for verbal self-reflection. Almost compulsively, Celan seems to return to a thematization of the material out of which his art is molded: word, language and name. This obsession must be understood in the light of Celan's complex relation to his own language, mentioned initially: the fact that he conceived of his native tongue—the only medium through which he could answer the need of communicating the experience of "das, was geschah" [that which happened][13]—as having been fundamentally damaged by its usage during the Nazi regime. Indeed, this paradox of the urge to speak and the impossibility of doing so, is apparent in the quotation itself: something needs to be communicated—a word is to be delivered to "her"—but this word can only come into existence through the act of silence.

The poem originally containing Berio's epigraph is entitled "Argumentum e silentio," a term that denotes the (fallacious) rhetorical device of drawing inference from a person's silence on a certain matter, concluding either that he or she is ignorant of the matter, or has a motive to remain silent about it. While a thorough analysis of this poem is well beyond the scope of this text and what matters for the current argument is above all the line Berio actually quotes, it seems relevant to know that the whole poem from which the quotation is taken focusses on the conflation of speech and silence. This is indeed a notion permeating a large part of Celan's work. For instance, in his most exhaustive poetological statement, the address "Der Meridian" from 1960, he maintains that "the poem unmistakably shows a strong bent toward

---

[13] Celan was in habit of referring to the Shoah in this way. Celan 2000, III:186.

falling silent."[14] This tendency has been commented on at great length, not least with reference to "Argumentum e silentio[15]," and the key position of this poem is further illustrated by its giving name to the first international symposium on Celan's poetry and poetics.[16]

As I mentioned above, some sort of pretension to identity between word and music is arguably needed to justify the reading of these as the constituent elements of a metaphor. In which way does Berio's piece claim an identity with Celan's poetry? Although not visible in the quotation itself, the dative of the epigraph actually refers to the night: "Ihr, der Nacht, [...] Ihr das erschwiegene Wort" [To her, the night, [...] to her the silenced word]. A *Notturno* is performed at night, or, in this case, even *to* the night. Berio's music, then, could be taken to *be* the word that is to be transmitted to the night, and thus an instance of language as much as of music. Also, the notion of the "erschwiegene Wort" is connected to the quietude often (though not necessarily) associated with the Notturnos of the romantic period, a fact Berio himself emphasizes in claiming that "*Notturno* is nocturnal because it is silent."[17] Moreover, an identity between language and music is suggested by "Argumentum e silentio," line 12 of which reads "Jedem das Wort, das ihm sang" [To each the word that sang to him]. Singing, then, is predicated of the word, and, by extension, music making of language. These notions all point to an identification of music with language, thus opening up the possibility of a metaphorical understanding of the interartial relations.

How, then, should we begin to interpret this metaphor? Or, phrased in Black's terms: where are the analogous implications between Celan's text and Berio's music to be found? Berio himself suggests that the silence is located at the music's rhetorical level, a notion paralleled by the rhetorical term used as the poem's title: "[*Notturno*] is silent because it is made up of unspoken words and incomplete discourse. It is silent even when it is loud, because the form itself is silent and non-argumentative."[18] This rhetorical silence manifests itself on different levels in the score. First of all, the character of the piece, established in the first few measures and more or less maintained throughout the 25 minutes of its performance, is one of stasis rather than dialectic argument. A conspicuously static gesture is seen in

[14] "zeigt – das ist unverkennbar – eine starke Neigung zum Verstummen." Celan 2000, III:197, transl. John Felstiner in Celan 2001, 409.

[15] Cf., for instance, Stewart 1972 and Olschner 1994.

[16] Colin 1987.

[17] Berio quoted in Thomas 1995, 367.

[18] Ibid., 367

ex. 1: the persistent repetition of pitch and duration. This gesture retains its dominance through a major portion of the work, sometimes measured, sometimes unmeasured, often polyrhythmic, and sometimes evolving into an oscillation between two pitches, which are never allowed to grow into a melody.[19] Another instance of such stasis can be observed in the harmonic structure of the same measures: barring the brief pickup beat in measure 5, the harmonies evolve slowly and gradually, changing only by one pitch at a time, often interrupted by halts.

FIGURE 1: *Notturno*, mm. 1-7

---

[19] Cf. Berio 1993, vla, mm. 185-192.

This static and hesitant character is not allowed to stand unquestioned throughout the entire composition. However, all attempts to create a dialogue with it collapse as soon as they have begun, giving birth to "incomplete discourse." Consider Fig. 2 below, which follows a long section of unmeasured repetitions. The determined character of these measures—marked "deciso," played forte, in common rhythmic subdivisions and with most notes in a unison of two or three instruments—can be heard as an attempt to question the stagnant mood, but after only two measures, the music returns to its prior state. The same attempt, with the same tempo, dynamics, and character is made once more in measure 366 (and, slightly varied, in several other places), but with the same result: the return to a repetitive, static mood. The long duration of the piece is a prerequisite of this effect; the outbreaks are simply too short—in comparison with the surrounding stasis—to create a dialogue. Instead, the impression is one of a voice never allowed (or inclined) to speak.

FIGURE 2: *Notturno*, mm. 99-101

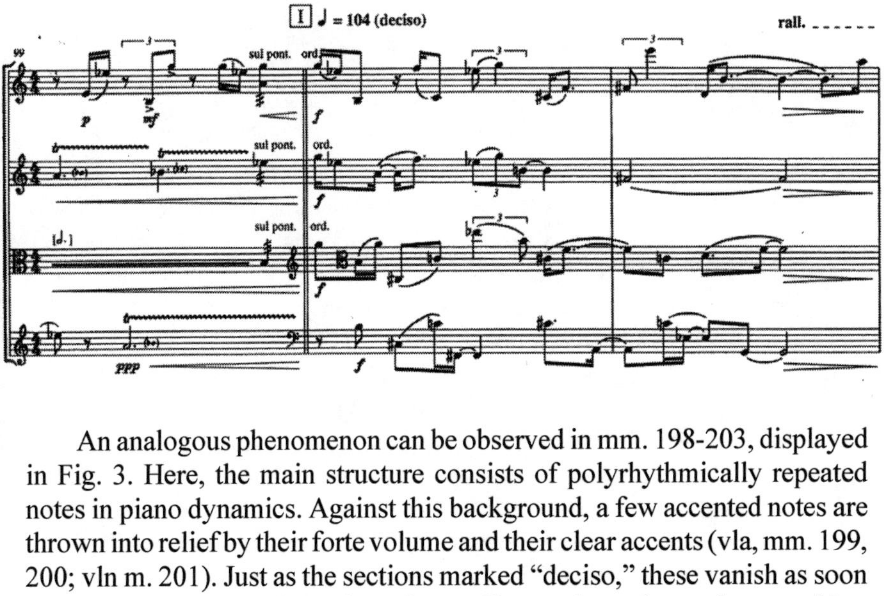

An analogous phenomenon can be observed in mm. 198-203, displayed in Fig. 3. Here, the main structure consists of polyrhythmically repeated notes in piano dynamics. Against this background, a few accented notes are thrown into relief by their forte volume and their clear accents (vla, mm. 199, 200; vln m. 201). Just as the sections marked "deciso," these vanish as soon as they have appeared. In these bars, all parts bear the curious marking "come accompagnando," and are to be played with tenuto articulation, thus producing a polyrhythmically distorted reminiscence of secondary voices in a classical quartet. Since this connotes something being accompanied, the accented notes can be heard as the attempted entries of a melody or song, which is silenced before it has begun.

FIGURE 3: *Notturno*, mm. 197-204

This, in turn, is an implication analogous to notions like "das erschwiegene Wort," "unspoken words," and "incomplete discourse," notions undergirded by the aforementioned connection between word and song established in "Argumentum e silentio": "Jedem das Wort, das ihm sang, / als die Meute ihn hinterrücks anfiel—/ Jedem das Wort, das ihm sang und erstarrte." [To each the word that sang to him / when the pack snapped at his heels – / to each the word that sang to him and froze.][20] When attacked from behind by the pack, the hitherto singing word freezes. This paralyzing attack on language—more precisely: on songful, lyric language—should doubtless be understood as the work of fascism, and the moment at which the word is transfixed by violence as the historical crisis of the Shoah. In the following stanza, the word has become "das erschwiegene Wort" referred to in Berio's epigraph, which is to be given to the night. The interrupted song and the paralyzed stasis of *Notturno* become, in the intertextual light of Celan's poem, the aesthetic answer to the historical situation of post-war Europe.

---

[20] Celan 2000, I:38. Transl. John Felstiner in Celan 2001, 79.

So far, the intermedial illumination has been described as moving in one direction only, the poetry thus affecting our perception of the music. But one of the chief merits of Black's concept is the reciprocity of the metaphorical interaction: the subsidiary subject exerts a certain influence on the perception of the principal subject, not just the other way around. Thus *Notturno*, if interpreted as an instance of metaphorical interaction between the media, potentially alters the listeners' and the readers' view of the poem serving as its epigraph, or even of the poet behind it. In the second of his Charles Eliot Norton lectures, Berio displays his acute awareness of this: "If a musical thought is to manifest itself in full relation to a text, it must be able to modify that text, to carry out an analytical transformation of it, while of course remaining conditioned by it."[21] How can one understand Berio's aesthetic stance in this *Notturno* as a comment on Celan's poetry, or on the quoted poem?

If the inclination towards falling silent is an integral part of Celan's poetic language, Berio's music might be heard as a comment on the nature of this silence: it does not, as one might initially assume, manifest itself in fragmentation or brevity, which would display a language eroded by the expanding silence which surrounds it. On the contrary: as if to actively negate such fragmentation, Berio's music extends itself in time, going on and on, thus forcing the notion of silence to be projected upon the sounds actually heard, rather than upon some cessations interrupting it, which is why the music, in Berio's words, "is silent even when it is loud." Berio's music, then, draws our attention to the fact that the silence inherent in Celan's poetry lies *in* its words and in its rhetoric gestures rather than in the blanks and white spaces surrounding them. The poem is, in the words of another Celan poem from the same collection, "ein Wort nach dem Bilde des Schweigens" [a word in the image of silence].[22] Language goes on, the poem keeps speaking, words are being uttered—but *within* these words an ever expanding silence makes itself heard.

In his influential 1980 study, *Paul Celan. Magie der Form*, Winfried Menninghaus has elegantly phrased this tendency: "The linguistic-philosophical reflection exhibits the silence not only as the muteness or failure of language vis-à-vis a certain content, but simultaneously as an implication, born from the form, of the postulated speech."[23] By very different means,

---

[21] Berio 2006, 46.

[22] The poem is called "Strähne." Celan 2000, I:92.

[23] "Die sprachphilosophische Reflexion [macht] das Schweigen nicht nur als Verstummen oder Versagen der Sprache angesichts eines bestimmten Inhalts, sondern zugleich als formgeborene Implikation des postulierten Sprechens erkennbar." Menninghaus 1980, 47.

then, Berio stresses the same point as Menninghaus: the form is a manifestation of the silence thematized in its content. Although commonly used, the dichotomy of form and content is never unproblematic. This is particularly important with respect to Celan's work: the interaction between poetry and music foregrounds the fact that, in Celan and Berio alike, form and content are entangled to the degree of inseparability, both elements aiming at the problematization of language. Strangely, the quartet carries with it the distorted echoes of Hanslick's infamous claim, that the only content of music is located at the level of form. The significant difference is that his dictum was formulated at a point in time when the notion of a language speaking by means of a fragmented or silenced form about its own inability to communicate had not yet been prompted by the historical events against the background of which Celan and Berio, albeit with very different degrees of personal involvement, engage with their respective arts.

Juxtapositional Counterpoint: Harrison Birtwistle's *Todesfuge*

In his extensive cycle *Pulse Shadows*, based on the poetry of Celan as translated by Michael Hamburger, Harrison Birtwistle intersperses the vocal pieces with instrumental ones, written for string quartet. Of the nine pieces for string quartet, only the last one has been furnished with a title—"Todesfuge." Whereas *Notturno*'s suggestion of an identity between words and music makes a metaphorical interpretation possible, Birtwistle's composition seems to make it necessary: by appropriating the name of Celan's indisputably most famous poem,[24] the music demands to be heard against the intertextual background of this literary source. In a patently metaphorical gesture, the title says: "this music is a poem" (or, more precisely, the poem "Todesfuge"). Also, the relation of the paratext to the poem from which it is borrowed is more significant in Birtwistle's case: whereas Berio's paratext has a metonymic relation to the intertext "Argumentum e silentio," Birtwistle's has a denominative relation to "Todesfuge." The latter suggests that the poem *as a whole* is actualized by the music; in Berio's case, by contrast, the music could be regarded as interacting with the quotation alone, with the poem or with Celan's poetics in general. One might also add the pragmatic point that "Todesfuge" is such a well-known poem that most listeners interested in literature are likely to be familiar with it. While this doesn't actually change the character of the musico-literary interaction, it does make it a more indispensable perspective when analyzing Birtwistle's quartet.

---

[24] Celan 2000, I:41f. The poem is included as an appendix, along with Michael Hamburger's translation in Hamburger 2002, 32-33.

For all its devastating poetic power, Celan's "Todesfuge" does not display the same sense of a threatened language that was to characterize Celan's subsequent poetry, "Argumentum e silentio" included. Rather, this poem became the focus of a controversy regarding the problems of dealing poetically with Auschwitz. Referring implicitly or explicitly to Adorno's caveat, several critics accused Celan of aestheticizing the Shoah and thus transcending the actual historical events, or even of profiting from the suffering of the Jews.[25] Apart from being gross misreadings of the poem, these accusations were all but unbearable for Celan. This in turn, as has been pointed out by Wolfgang Emmerich, indubitably contributed to the change in direction taken by Celan's poetry in the late 1950s.[26] In 1966, Celan maintained that "I do not make music any more, as I did at the time of the much-appealed-to *Todesfuge*, which has by now indeed been threshed into textbook-ripeness. I now distinguish sharply between poetry and music."[27]

Birtwistle's quartet, then, differs from Berio's in that the poem used is so clearly a case of musico-literary interaction in its own right—a poem that "makes music." This is signaled from its title. Much like Birtwistle's quartet, Celan's "Todesfuge" makes the metaphorical statement, "this poem is a fugue." In this respect, the title of Birtwistle's composition is intriguingly double-edged: if one has never encountered Celan's poem, the title would probably have to be read as an unmediated reference to the form of the work it designates (a fugue) as well as an indication of an imagined subject matter (death). Someone familiar with Celan's poem, however, must indisputably take the title to refer to this very text, which, in turn, refers to the musical form of the fugue. In other words, Birtwistle's title can be read either as a direct, musical title with an additional thematic adjective, or as twice crossing the intermedial border between music and literature. As I will show, the music itself appears to be very much aware of this ambivalence and to encourage the simultaneous presence of both readings.

So much for the title. As Celan's comment about "making music" in "Todesfuge" suggests, music is present in this poem on several other levels as well. First, one of its central images is a musical one, based on a gruesome historical fact: in the Nazi death camps Janowska and Lublin, one group of the condemned Jews were forced to perform music accompanying grave

---

[25] Cf. Emmerich 2002; Felstiner 1986; Felstiner 2001, 71, 79, 148, 225.

[26] Cf. Emmerich 2002.

[27] "Auch musiziere ich nicht mehr, wie zur Zeit der vielbeschworenen *Todesfuge*, die nachgerade schon lesebuchreif gedroschen ist. Jetzt scheide ich streng zwischen Lyrik und Tonkunst". Huppert 1988, 320.

digging, torture, or executions.[28] Second, given the context of the fugue, the line "Der Tod ist ein Meister aus Deutschland" [death is a master from Germany][29], can be understood as a reference to J. S. Bach, arguably the archetype of a German master. The implicit allusion reflects an important aspect of the poem, present already in the title, namely the close connection between death and art, particularly as an equation of mastery in these activities.[30] Third, the poem contains traces of a euphonically oriented conception of poetic musicality, with its frequent repetitions, orderly meter, and even a single rhyme on "blau" and "genau." Finally, the structure of the poem has frequently been claimed to display similarities to that of a fugue, a point to which I will return.

The fact that Birtwistle's quartet engages in an intertextual dialogue with a poem dealing openly with music has some interesting effects on the metaphorical interaction. For one thing, I submit, it makes the composer's music into a potential referent of the music thematized in the poem—particularly since Celan's poem also speaks of string instruments. Hence, the instruments of Birtwistle's quartet resound with the phrases of the poem. The open strings of subject A acquire traits of a folk music played up for a distorted dance of death, while a distinct and uninterrupted rhythm in mm. 68-82, entirely dominated by the 32nd-notes of subject D, invites association to ecstatic dancing or, for that matter, to the static rhythmic patterns of baroque counterpoint. In another semantically oriented analogy, the artificial harmonics of subject B, marked "flautando," might be interpreted as an onomatopoetic rendering of the whistling occurring in the poem "Todesfuge"—"er pfeift seine Rüden herbei / Er pfeift seine Juden hervor" [he whistles his pack out/he whistles his Jews out].[31] The playing strings could be taken to answer the orders yelled by the SS commandant: "Er ruft stecht tiefer ins Erdreich ihr einen ihr andern singet und spielt" [He calls out jab deeper into the earth you lot you others sing now and play], "spielt auf nun zum Tanz" [strike up for the dance], "Er ruft spielt süßer den Tod" [He calls out more sweetly play death], "er ruft streicht dunkler die Geigen" [He calls out more darkly now stroke your strings].[32] By way of the metaphorical interaction with this intertext, the bowing of the fiddles in the quartet is endowed with qualities

---

[28] Felstiner 2001, 28.

[29] Celan 2000, I:42. Transl. Hamburger in Celan 2002, 33.

[30] Emmerich 2002, 366.

[31] Celan 2000, I:41. Transl. Hamburger in Celan 2002, 32.

[32] Ibid., I:41-42. Transl. Hamburger in Celan 2002, 32-33.

of darkness, and their playing, as it were, summons the deadly master from Germany. On the other hand, nothing in Birtwistle's music complies with the injunction to play "more sweetly"—its rough brutality shows no interest whatsoever in sentimental beauty. Heard in the light of the accusations of over-aestheticism and beautification directed towards Celan's "Todesfuge," the quartet harshly denies any such qualities in the poem.

But these analogies are far from the only ones displayed by Birtwistle's music. I have already mentioned the conspicuously regular meter of the poem, and metrics is of course an area in which the analogies between music and literature are as obvious as historically well-trodden. In "Todesfuge," the dominant metrical units are amphibracs and dactyls, often with a certain vacillation between the two. The following line, for instance, might be heard as an upbeat, five dactyls and a trochee (i.e. a hexameter line opened by an unstressed syllable), but equally well as a line of six complete amphibracs:

FIGURE 4: metric analysis of line 34 of "Todesfuge"

er spielt mit den Schlangen und träumet der Tod ist ein Meister aus Deutschland

Keeping this figure in mind, which more or less prevails throughout the poem, some choices of Birtwistle's seem to be directly motivated by Celan's meter. As shown in Fig. 5, Birtwistle makes a point of creating repeated amphibracs, clearly emphasizing the rhythmic units by separating them with pauses, as well as by using accented downbow double stops on the second note and upbow staccato notes on the first and third. Given the prominence of the rhythm in the poem and the music alike, this is not likely to be a coincidence.

FIGURE 5: *Pulse Shadows*, "Todesfuge – Frieze 4," violin part of mm. 63-65

Furthermore, the salient exception to the dactylic/amphibrachic meter in "Todesfuge" is found in the haunting opening line, the very first words of which are actually in trochaic meter: "Schwarze Milch der Frühe wir trinken

sie abends" [Black milk of daybreak we drink it at sundown].[33] As seen in Fig. 6, Birtwistle parallels this in his first measures by introducing Subject A in two-note groupings before falling into the predominant amphibrachic rhythms.

Another possible analogy to Celan's meter, although perhaps less striking, is Birtwistle's choice of using 3/4 time throughout the composition. Obviously, one cannot equate tripartite meter in music with tripartite meter in verse, and dactyls can be just as aptly rendered within the framework of any other time signature. Nevertheless, since we are dealing with accentual rather than quantitative verse, the analogy is hardly farfetched: the sequence of one stressed metrical unit followed by two unstressed ones is an obvious common denominator between dactyls and 3/4 time. This analogy, incidentally, is made manifest in Celan's own reading of the poem, the larger part of which moves in an almost mechanical 3/4 time.[34]

The musical feature of Celan's "Todesfuge" that has attracted most attention is doubtless its putative fugal structure. How, one might ask, does this notion affect the metaphorical interaction with the actual music of Birtwistle's quartet? If one looks at this music as a potential fugue—in other words, if one interprets the title as an unmediated reference to a musical genre—four distinct subjects are readily distinguishable, as if to suggest a quadruple fugue; I have labeled them subjects A, B, C, and D in Fig. 6.[35] These are presented and polyphonically combined in different pairs and trios, with one subject appearing in one instrument at a time. It seems reasonable enough to describe this music as a modernistic, chiefly atonal, late 20th-century rendition of a fugal structure. As the music progresses, however, two or three instruments tend to play the same subject, and from measure 68 onward only one subject is played at a time, while all four instruments participate in each entrance. The piece thus gradually takes leave of the vertical, polyphonic structure in favor of a horizontal one, the climactic fortississississimo ending (*ffff*, mm. 86-94) juxtaposing rhythmically unison blocks of all four subjects, punctuated by general pauses. As I will show shortly, this development is highly interesting in relation to the purportedly contrapuntal character of Celan's poem.

---

[33] Ibid., I:41. Transl. Hamburger in Celan 2002, 32.

[34] Celan 2004.

[35] Although a more in-depth discussion of Birtwistle's composition as a fugue (asking, for instance, whether some of these subjects might be more correctly described as counter-subjects) would no doubt be interesting, it lies beyond the scope of this article.

FIGURE 6: *Pulse Shadows,* "Todesfuge – Frieze 4," fugal subjects

Subject A, mm. 1-3, viola

Subject B, mm. 1-3, cello

Subject C, mm. 5, viola

Subject D, mm. 6-7, viola.

Several attempts have been made to analyze Celan's "Todesfuge" as a verbal rendition of contrapuntal music. Some suggestions contain many pertinent points; others are rather questionable, mainly due to their over-enthusiasm.[36] Below I quote verses 4-7 of the poem and supply each line with a letter.

FIGURE 7: "Todesfuge," lines 4-7

wir schaufeln ein Grab in den Lüften da liegt man nicht eng
— A —

Ein Mann wohnt im Haus der spielt mit den Schlangen der schreibt
— B —

der schreibt wenn es dunkelt nach Deutschland dein goldenes Haar Margarete
— C —

er schreibt es und tritt vor das Haus und es blitzen die Sterne er pfeift seine Rüden herbei
— D —

---

[36] For an instance of the former, cf. Elleström 1989; for an instance of the latter, cf. Petri 1964.

The labeling is quite arbitrary; the point here is not to make yet another analysis of the poem's motivic structure, but merely to illustrate an oft-noted technique of Celan's that could metaphorically be termed verbal counterpoint. Were one, hypothetically, to consider these lines as monophonic presentations of four different motives, what follows in lines 31-32 could (again metaphorically) be said to correspond to musical counterpoint:

FIGURE 8: "Stretto" in "Todesfuge," lines 32-33

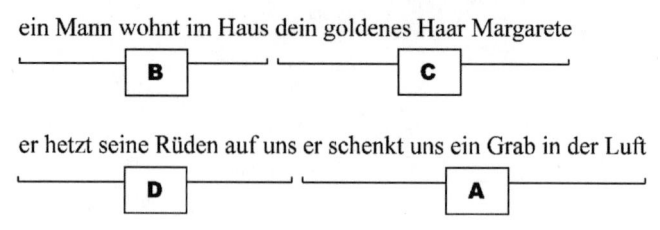

ein Mann wohnt im Haus dein goldenes Haar Margarete
⎣──── B ────⎦ ⎣──── C ────⎦

er hetzt seine Rüden auf uns er schenkt uns ein Grab in der Luft
⎣──── D ────⎦ ⎣──── A ────⎦

As a part of line C is inserted before line B is finished, line B could be heard as still sounding alongside it. Some critics have claimed that this corresponds to musical stretto, since a new entrance takes place before one has finished, thus letting the voices cut each other short. On the other hand, it might also be described as analogous to the kind of hidden two-part writing utilized by Bach and others in solo pieces for instruments unable to produce simultaneous voices, in which the music alters rapidly between the notes of two different parts, thereby creating the illusion of two independent parts sounding simultaneously. One could discuss at length to which particular contrapuntal technique these interruptions and rearrangings of textual motifs correspond; but, I submit with Prieto, that is the wrong question to ask. The proper question would be: which analogies between text and music are actualized by the interaction, and how do they alter the meaning of the composition? One answer is that by choosing to label his poem a fugue, Celan draws readers' attention to these particular aspects of his text and, if you will, invites them to hear the interrupted lines as still sounding. Just as Berio's music would hardly problematize the language of contemporary music without its meta-reflective paratexts, Celan's title does not explain an analogy to counterpoint already inherent in the text, it rather *suggests* the possibility of reading Celan's fragmented lines as metaphorically related to counterpoint, a fact underscored by the author himself: "My poem 'Todesfuge' [...] is not 'composed according to musical principles'; rather, when the poem was there, I felt it not unjustified to call it 'Todesfuge'."[37]

---

[37] "Mein Gedicht 'Todesfuge' [...] ist nicht 'nach musikalischen Prinzipen komponiert'; vielmehr habe ich es, als dieses Gedicht da war, als nicht unberechtigt empfunden, es 'Todesfuge' zu nennen." Celan 2003, 608.

Berio and Birtwistle in Dialogue with Celan 135

Turning once again to Birtwistle's quartet while keeping Celan's supposed imitation of musical counterpoint in mind, one might stop at the measures displayed in Fig. 9. Here, in a fashion very similar to what Celan does in the lines quoted in Fig. 8, Birtwistle juxtaposes short fragments of his different subjects with each other.

Whereas in the opening of the piece he creates counterpoint by traditional musical means, here Birtwistle chooses to imitate Celan's verbal imitation of counterpoint, thus reaching the concept of the fugue only metaphorically and through a double detour: by mimicking the verbal mimicking of counterpoint. As with the title of the composition, then, the trail of intertextual associations in these measures crosses the same intermedial borderline two times over: from music to literature and back to music. Once again recalling the reciprocity of the metaphoric interaction, one might observe that Birtwistle's imitation of Celan's imitation underscores the distance between the poetic structure of "Todesfuge" and an actual fugue, and thus affects our

FIGURE 9: *Pulse Shadows*, "Todesfuge – Frieze 4," mm. 40-45

understanding of the poem: the string quartet suggests that if Celan's poetic structure displays any connection to a musical style, it is much more closely related to a modernistic juxtaposition of thematically divergent fragments than to the thematic unity and uninterrupted flow of baroque polyphony.

*

By interpreting the relationship between Celan's poetry and the music of Berio and Birtwistle respectively as a large-scale metaphorical interaction, I have tried to point to some aspects of the quartets and poems discussed. In Berio's *Notturno*, a static, non-dialectic character and entrances that are interrupted before they have been articulated give rise to implications analogous to Celan's notion of a language permeated and produced by silence. This silence is not so much an absence of words and sounds. As such, it would manifest itself as a fragmentation eroding verbal and musical utterances from the outside. Rather, the metaphorical interaction suggests, it comes from the inside: the silence of which this quartet and its epigraph speak, in other words, inheres within their form. By engaging in a dialogue with Celan's poetological poetry, Berio is able to comment on the historical conditions of his own art, while at the same time reminding listeners of the intertwinement of form and content in Celan's poetry. Similarly, in Birtwistle's "Todesfuge – Frieze 4," the metaphorical interaction raises questions about relations between language and music. The quartet reflects upon the ambiguous way in which the poetic title communicates with Birtwistle's music, referring either directly to its structure and texture, or by the detour of Celan's poem. It interacts, on the one hand, with the traditional form of the fugue, and, on the other, with the musically oriented motifs as well as the metric patterning and purportedly polyphonic structure of Celan's poem.

References

Adorno, Theodor W., "Kulturkritik und Gesellschaft," in *Kulturkritik und Gesellschaft I: Prismen. Ohne Leitbild*, Frankfurt am Main: Suhrkamp, 2003, 11-30.

Berio, Luciano, *Notturno, Quartetto III*, Vienna/London/New York: Universal Edition, 1993.

—, *Remembering the Future*, Cambridge, MA: Harvard University Press, 2006.

Birtwistle, Harrison, *Pulse Shadows. Meditations on Paul Celan, for soprano, string quartet and ensemble*, London: Boosey & Hawkes, 1998.

Black, Max, "Metaphor," in *Models and Metaphors*, Ithaca: Cornell University Press, 1962.

Celan, Paul, *Gesammelte Werke in sieben Bänden*, Beda Allemann and Stefan Reichert, eds., Frankfurt am Main: Suhrkamp, 2000.

—, *Selected Poems and Prose of Paul Celan*, trans. John Felstiner, New York/ London: W. W. Norton, 2001.

—, *Poems of Paul Celan*, trans. Michael Hamburger, New York: Persea Books, 2002.

—, *Die Gedichte. Kommentierte Gesamtausgabe*, Barbara Wiedemann, ed., Frankfurt am Main: Suhrkamp, 2003.

—, *Ich hörte sagen* [CD], München: Der Hörverlag, 2004.

Colin, Amy D., ed., *Argumentum e Silentio. International Paul Celan Symposium*, Berlin/New York: Walter de Gruyter, 1987.

Elleström, Lars, "Paul Celan's 'Todesfuge'. A Title and a Poem," in William E. Grim and Michael B. Harper, eds., *Yearbook of Interdisciplinary Studies in the Fine Arts* 1 (1989): 127-153.

Emmerich, Wolfgang, "Paul Celans Weg vom 'schönen Gedicht' zur 'graueren Sprache'. Die Windschiefe Rezeption der 'Todesfuge' und ihre Folgen," in Hans Henning Hahn and Jens Stüben, eds., *Jüdische Autoren Ostmitteleuropas im 20. Jahrhundert*, Frankfurt am Main: Peter Lang, 2002, 359-383.

Felstiner, John, "Paul Celan's Todesfuge," in *Holocaust and Genocide Studies*, 1986:2. Oxford: Pergamon, 1986: 249-264.

—, *Paul Celan. Poet, Survivor, Jew*, New Haven/London: Yale University Press, 2001.

Glenn, Jerry, "Paul Celan. Eine Bibliographie der Veröffentlichten Vertonungen," in Andrei Corbea-Hoisie et al., eds., *Stundenwechsel. Neue Perspektiven zu Alfred Margul-Sperber, Rose Ausländer, Paul Celan, Immanuel Weissglas*, Konstanz: Hartung-Gorre Verlag, 2002, 455-460.

Huppert, Hugo, "Spirituell. Ein Gespräch mit Paul Celan," in Werner Hamacher and Winfried Menninghaus, eds., *Paul Celan*, Frankfurt am Main: Suhrkamp, 1988, 319-324.

Mackey, Cindy, *Dichter der Bezogenheit. A Study of Paul Celan's Poetry with Special Reference to* Die Niemandsrose, Stuttgart: Verlag Hans-Dieter Heinz, 1997.

Olschner, Leonard, "Poetic Mutations of Silence. At the Nexus of Paul Celan and Osip Mandelstam," in Aris Fioretos, ed., *Word Traces. Readings of Paul Celan*, Baltimore and London: The John Hopkins University Press, 1994, 369-385.

Petri, Horst, *Literatur und Musik. Form- und Strukturparallellen*. Göttingen: Sachse & Pohl, 1964.

Prieto, Eric, *Listening in. Music, mind, and the modernist narrative*. Lincoln: University of Nebraska Press, 2002.

Ricœur, Paul, "The Metaphorical Process as Cognition, Imagination, and Feeling," in Sheldon Sacks, ed., *On Metaphor*, Chicago: The University of Chicago Press, 1979, 141-157.

Seng, Joachim, "'Die wahre Flaschenpost'. Zur Beziehung zwischen Theodor W. Adorno und Paul Celan," in Rolf Tiedemann, ed., *Frankfurter Adorno Blätter VIII*, Munich: edition text + kritik, 2003, 151-176.

Spitzer, Michael, *Metaphor and Musical Thought*, Chicago: Chicago University Press, 2004.

Stewart, Corbet, "Paul Celan's Modes of Silence: Some Observations on 'Sprachgitter'," in *The Modern Language Review* 67 (1972): 127-142.

Thomas, Gavin, Review [untitled] in *The Musical Times* 136 (1995): 366-367.

Zenck, Martin, "...: es sind/noch Lieder zu singen jenseits/der Menschen. Vier Kompositionen des Gedichts 'Fadensonnen' aus Paul Celans 'Atemwende'," in Gerhard Buhr and Roland Reuß, eds, *Paul Celan: "Atemwende" Materialien*, Würzburg: Königshausen & Neumann, 1991, 165-172.

APPENDIX

Argumentum e silentio
Für René Char

An die Kette gelegt
zwischen Gold und Vergessen:
die Nacht.
Beide griffen nach ihr.
Beide ließ sie gewähren.

Lege,
lege auch du jetzt dorthin, was herauf-
dämmern will neben den Tagen:
das sternüberflogene Wort,
das meerübergossne.

Jedem das Wort.
Jedem das Wort, das ihm sang,
als die Meute ihn hinterrücks anfiel –
Jedem das Wort, das ihm sang
    und erstarrte.

Ihr, der Nacht,
das sternüberflogne, das meer-
    übergossne,
ihr das erschwiegne,
dem das Blut nicht gerann, als
    der Giftzahn
die Silben durchstieß.

Ihr das erschwiegene Wort.

Wider die andern, die bald,
die umhurt von den Schinderohren,
auch Zeit und Zeiten erklimmen,
zeugt es zuletzt,
zuletzt, wenn nur Ketten erklingen,
zeugt es von ihr, die dort liegt
zwischen Gold und Vergessen,
beiden verschwistert von je –

Denn wo
dämmerts denn, sag, als
    bei ihr,
die im Stromgebiet ihrer Träne
tauchenden Sonnen die
    Saat zeigt
aber und abermals?

Argumentum e silentio
For René Char

Linked in the chain
between Gold and Forgetting:
Night.
Both grasped at it.
Both had their way.

Link it,
now you too link up what
wants to dawn with each day:
the Word star-overflown,
sea-overflowed.

To each his word.
To each the word that sang to him
when the pack snapped at his heels –
to each the word that sang to him
    and froze.

To it, to night, the Word
star-overflown, sea-
    overflowed,
to it the ensilenced Word
whose blood did not clot when
    a venomed tooth
pierced its syllables.

To Night the ensilenced Word.

Against the others,
enticed by swindlers' ears,
who'll soon climb on time and seasons,
the Word at last testifies,
at last, when only chains ring out,
testifies to Night that lies
between Gold and Forgetting,
their kin for all time –

Then where's
the Word dawning, tell me, if not
    with Night
in its riverbed of tears,
Night that shows plunging suns the
    sown seed
over and over again?

Translation by John Felstiner

Todesfuge

Schwarze Milch der Frühe wir trinken sie abends
wir trinken sie mittags und morgens wir trinken sie nachts
wir trinken und trinken
wir schaufeln ein Grab in den Lüften da liegt man nicht eng
Ein Mann wohnt im Haus der spielt mit den Schlangen der schreibt
der schreibt wenn es dunkelt nach Deutschland dein goldenes Haar Margarete
er schreibt es und tritt vor das Haus und es blitzen die Sterne er pfeift
    seine Rüden herbei
er pfeift seine Juden hervor läßt schaufeln ein Grab in der Erde
er befiehlt uns spielt auf nun zum Tanz

Schwarze Milch der Frühe wir trinken dich nachts
wir trinken dich morgens und mittags wir trinken dich abends
wir trinken und trinken
Ein Mann wohnt im Haus der spielt mit den Schlangen der schreibt
der schreibt wenn es dunkelt nach Deutschland dein goldenes Haar Margarete
Dein aschenes Haar Sulamith wir schaufeln ein Grab in den Lüften
    da liegt man nicht eng

Er ruft stecht tiefer ins Erdreich ihr einen ihr andern singet und spielt
er greift nach dem Eisen im Gurt er schwingts seine Augen sind blau
stecht tiefer die Spaten ihr einen ihr andern spielt weiter zum Tanz auf

Schwarze Milch der Frühe wir trinken dich nachts
wir trinken dich mittags und morgens wir trinken dich abends
wir trinken und trinken
ein Mann wohnt im Haus dein goldenes Haar Margarete
dein aschenes Haar Sulamith er spielt mit den Schlangen
Er ruft spielt süßer den Tod der Tod ist ein Meister aus Deutschland
er ruft streicht dunkler die Geigen dann steigt ihr als Rauch
    in die Luft
dann habt ihr ein Grab in den Wolken da liegt man nicht eng

Schwarze Milch der Frühe wir trinken dich nachts
wir trinken dich mittags der Tod ist ein Meister aus Deutschland
wir trinken dich abends und morgens wir trinken und trinken
der Tod ist ein Meister aus Deutschland sein Auge ist blau
er trifft dich mit bleierner Kugel er trifft dich genau
ein Mann wohnt im Haus dein goldenes Haar Margarete
er hetzt seine Rüden auf uns er schenkt uns ein Grab in der Luft
er spielt mit den Schlangen und träumet der Tod ist ein Meister aus Deutschland

dein goldenes Haar Margarete
dein aschenes Haar Sulamith

Death Fugue

Black milk of daybreak we drink it at sundown
we drink it at noon in the morning we drink it at night
we drink and we drink it
we dig a grave in the breezes there one lies unconfined
A man lives in the house he plays with the serpents he writes
he writes when dusk falls to Germany your golden hair Margarete
he writes it and steps out of doors and the stars are flashing he whistles
    his pack out
he whistles his Jews out in earth has them dig for a grave
he commands us strike up for the dance

Black milk of daybreak we drink you at night
we drink in the morning at noon we drink you at sundown
we drink and we drink you
A man lives in the house he plays with the serpents he writes
he writes when dusk falls to Germany your golden hair Margarete
your ashen hair Shulamith we dig a grave in the breezes there
    one lies unconfined

He calls out jab deeper into the earth you lot you others sing now and play
he grabs at the iron in his belt he waves it his eyes are blue
jab deeper you lot with your spades you others play on for the dance

Black milk of daybreak we drink you at night
we drink you at noon in the morning we drink you at sundown
we drink and we drink you
a man lives in the house your golden hair Margarete
your ashen hair Shulamith he plays with the serpents
He calls out more sweetly play death death is a master from Germany
he calls out more darkly now stroke your strings then as smoke you will
    rise into air
then a grave you will have in the clouds there one lies unconfined

Black milk of daybreak we drink you at night
we drink you at noon death is a master from Germany
we drink you at sundown and in the morning we drink and we drink you
death is a master from Germany his eyes are blue
he strikes you with leaden bullets his aim is true
a man lives in the house your golden hair Margarete
he sets his pack on to us he grants us a grave in the air
he plays with the serpents and daydreams death is a master from Germany

your golden hair Margarete
your ashen hair Shulamith

Translation by Michael Hamburger

Ming I – Die Verwundung des Hellen: Walter Steffens's Compositions about Suffering and Fate

Siglind Bruhn

Among current German composers, it would be hard to find anybody as prolific in the field of musical ekphrasis as Walter Steffens. His catalogue lists more than one hundred works in the genre for which he has introduced the term *Bildvertonungen*, a term that translates as "musical settings of paintings."[1] An additional focus beside his life-long compositional response to works of visual art is his interest in literature—poetry as well as novellas and dramas—which he has alternately set and transmedialized.[2]

Born 1934 in Aachen and a child witness to the bombings during World War II, Steffens grew into adulthood with the inner need to explore three interdependent themes: human cruelty against fellow beings (the Holocaust in particular, but also other forms of extermination), the victims' relationship to the perpetrators of a crime, and the role of art as a mediator of the unspeakable. His work catalog—which is powerfully expanding since his retirement as professor of composition from the music academy of Detmold in 2000—is notable for a number of significant works addressing the agony of the Jewish people through the ages, among them *Eli*, an opera based on Nelly Sachs's mystery play on the suffering of Israel (1966); *Moses*, an orchestral work (1988); and *Die Judenbuche* [The Jew's Beech] (1993), a musical drama after the murder-mystery novella by the 19th-century German poet, Annette von Droste-Hülshoff.

---

[1] In speaking of "Bildvertonungen," the composer collates the German word for the setting of poems as songs (*Vertonung*) with the word for image or picture (*Bild*).

[2] As mentioned in the introduction, a text is considered musically "set" when it forms part of the resulting composition, as in a song, a melodrama, or an opera. For the process by which the same text is "converted into" music rather than being musically presented—sung in its original syntax, with or without some accompaniment—I have introduced the technical term "transmedialization." The emphasis is here on the interart transfer; the term combines the prefix "trans-" for "crossing a border" with a focus on the different media represented by the artwork responded to and the one responding to it.

The piano quartet discussed in this essay brings the various lines of Steffens's artistic interests together. As indicated in the work's subtitle, the composer conceived his piano quartet as a musical response to two poems—one by Elfriede Szpetecki, the other by Nelly Sachs. Moreover, he sought spiritual access to the latter poet by consulting the ancient Chinese manual for divining fate and understanding the hidden truth about life's occurrences that gained wide influence among German artists in the mid-20th century through the authoritative translation and commentary by Richard Wilhelm (1873-1930), a German Sinologist, theologian, and missionary in China.[3] The *I Ching*, as the work's title is usually transliterated in English (*Yi Jing* in modern Pinyin), is a method of throwing dice, tossing a coin or, traditionally, assembling, re-dividing, and counting yarrow stalks of different length in order to arrive at a hexagram, a six-line symbol combined from any two of eight trigrams that present the basic elements in nature. By consulting the *I Ching* about "Nelly Sachs," Steffens arrived at a hexagram with the designation "*míng í*." Struck by the way in which the ancient interpretation of this hexagram seemed to capture essential truths about the poet who had fascinated him for many years, he chose the Chinese name along with Wilhelm's German translation as a title for his quartet.[4]

In its subject matter, *Ming I – Verwundung des Hellen* reflects on three dimensions of Jewish suffering: the historic Israelites' precarious ownership of their homeland, the agony of the European Jews under Nazi atrocities, and the individual fate of the German-Jewish poet Nelly Sachs. In its inspiration by poetry transmedialized into purely instrumental music, the piano quartet belongs to the genre of musical ekphrasis. The composer's faith in oracles, in the correspondence of macro- and microcosm, and in the profound significance of magic for an intuitive understanding of deeper truths expresses itself on both the spiritual and the compositional planes.

Finally, Steffens's conviction that every tyrannical act of deliberate extermination or indifferent killing is an expression of an underlying evil aspect of human nature manifests itself in the fact that large segments of the quartet's musical material find a new context in another composition in which Steffens addresses human suffering through musical ekphrasis: *Guernica – Elegy for Viola and Orchestra* (1978). The way in which the composer matches the figures from Pablo Picasso's famous mural to the components of his music add a further interpretative layer to the poetic ekphrasis in *Ming I*.

---

[3] Richard Wilhelm, *I Ging: das Buch der Wandlungen* (Jena: Diederichs, 1924).

[4] *Ming I – Verwundung des Hellen*, op. 33, piano quartet after poems by Elfriede Szpetecki and Nelly Sachs, was commissioned by the Herford Piano Quartet, completed in September 1975, and premiered a month later in Herford, Germany. The score is self-published.

Overview of the Quartet's Structure and Main Features

The full score of *Ming I* comprises eight pages. The music falls into two sections, each of which is itself bipartite. The initial section consists of 22 measures in 4/5-time. In a slow tempo (♩ = 52) and a character defined as "sehr verinnerlicht, in ruhender Ordnung" [very internalized, in calm order], this section has a duration of a little over two minutes. In its first segment, the viola presents a two-part motif in which the upper line establishes a four-note contour that is imitated by the lower part, a minor seventh lower but in identical shape and rhythm.

FIGURE 1: the basic two-part motif

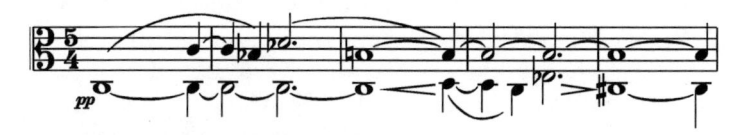

The violin (from m. 5) and the violoncello (from m. 9) follow with slightly varied imitations of the two-part unit. The piano with a slow descent draws the three entries together, and finally all instruments converge into a very soft D-major triad (mm. 11-12). In the complementary segment, the piano, playing in two-part unison, establishes a second motif, which is imitated in the unison of the three strings after 7 quarter-notes and taken back, after another 9 quarter-notes, by the piano, now also in three-part unison. This segment, too, concludes with a very soft D-major triad (strings from m. 18, joined by the piano only after a long expansion of the motif in m. 22). Both motifs are symbolically significant in several aspects; to this I will return later.

The quartet's second section, intended to arise *attacca* from the above-mentioned D-major conclusion, is contemplative in character. The music is neither metrically nor rhythmically specified. Notation is overwhelmingly in black note heads; all four instruments play their pitch sequences with relative freedom, taking their overall tempo orientation from the composer's indication of five-second units and their local cues from an occasional vertical coordination. The long section is internally structured into two corresponding but varied halves:
- In terms of the temporal organization, the measuring in seconds, initiated at the top of page 2 and discontinued (after 182 seconds) for the last third of page 4 in favor of a temporally unmarked span, restarts from 1 at the top of page 5, only to be abandoned again (this time after 181 seconds) for roughly the last third of page 8.

- In terms of the melodic material, the three string instruments develop in the first half a small number of motifs that are clearly defined in their pitch sequences as well as in their vertical placement and interrelationship, though not in their rhythm and the individual notes' octave allocation. The second half, by contrast, arising again from a D-major triad, leads from slow notes through tremolos to two spans of "wild" juxtapositions of aleatorically treated pitch groups.
- In terms of the harmony, which is determined by the piano, the first half is wholly defined by six pitches that are repeatedly struck very softly, at considerable distance and in varying sequence. Since the pedal sustains them collectively throughout the 182 seconds, the effect is that of an ethereal sound carpet. During the temporally undefined span that follows, the piano adds the remaining six semitones in a brief melodic outburst with *fz* accents. All twelve chromatic pitches then accompany the second expanse of 181 seconds. The volume is louder, swelling from *mp* (sec. 1) through *mf* (sec. 72) to *f* and *ffz* (sec. 100). The climactic heaping of all twelve pitches (at sec. 180) is topped, at the beginning of the second temporally undefined span, by a *fffz* two-forearm attack whose four-and-a-half-octave chromatic cluster then wanes gradually. Into this powerful reverberation, the three strings play utterly soft, very slow contours in vertically independent juxtaposition. The composer indicates a shifting prevalence among the instruments by means of occasional groups of white note heads.

As the total playing time of the work, given as "ca. 10 minutes," includes a first section with a little over 2 minutes as well as two contemplative stretches with a little over 180 seconds each (in other words: measured segments that add up to ca 8'10"), this leaves almost a minute for each of the temporally undetermined conclusions—a singular calm.

The Extra-musical Sources

The two poets on whose work Steffens explicitly draws for his piano quartet are of very different standing and serve strikingly different purposes in shaping the composition. Elfriede Szpetecki was born in 1921 in the borderland between Saxony and Bohemia. Losing her home during World War II like so many people from Germany's eastern provinces, she settled in Hamburg, where she was active as a writer, artist, teacher, and lecturer until shortly before her death in 2005. Szpetecki shared with Steffens both the love for ekphrasis and an interest in East Asian culture; her best-known collection is a cycle of beautiful poetry on works by the expressionist

Ming I – Die Verwundung des Hellen 147

sculptor Ernst Barlach;[5] in one of her last well-reported public appearances, she read her own adaptations of *tanka* and *haikus* to a North-German branch of the German-Japanese Society.[6] In Walter Steffens's piano quartet *Ming I*, the material and the character of the piano accompaniment in the contemplative section are determined by Szpetecki's poem "Blau."

Blau	**Blue**
Weiße Gipfel umsäumen	White peaks hem in
Gläserne Einsamkeit.	glassy loneliness.
Siehst du den Stern dort?	Do you see the star over there?
Er birgt kristallene Träume	It harbors crystal dreams
und ist ferner mir nicht	and does not feel farther from me
als der Gipfel, da sie erstarrt.	than the summit, as it congeals.[7]
Weißt du, dass man	Do you know that
in einer vergangenen Sprache	in a bygone language
für die Farbe deiner Augen	one borrowed for the color of your eyes
das Wörtchen für Himmel geliehn?	the little word for heaven?

Szpetecki's poem describes an expanse of loneliness surrounded (presumably without escape?) by snowy peaks. The impression is of something glassy—at once fragile and exposed to potential onlookers. This quality is shared by the crystal nature of the dreams projected into the star that is visible above, a source of light perceived as friendly and therefore, despite its physical distance, emotionally closer to the poet's heart than the congealed loneliness around her. In this atmosphere of desolation and fragile dreams, the turn to an addressee in the third stanza comes as a surprise. Yet the person thus gently drawn into the scene does not materialize beyond the color of the eyes. Their blue was once believed to reflect heaven—in an age when people still found comfort in religion and hoped for a blissful afterlife.

---

[5]*Und alles Sein wird Lauschen: Gedichte nach Plastiken von Ernst Barlach* (Hamburg: Christians, 1979); two other collections of Szpetecki poetry that I was able to consult are *Bau Dir ein Haus mit Wänden aus Lächeln* and *Tritt durch das Tor der Worte* (Hamburg: Christians, 1981 and 1998). Ilse Hensel, a friend and fellow poet of the late Elfriede Szpetecki, generously provided me with information and the three above-mentioned volumes. Two self-published collections, one of which is likely to contain the poem "Blau," could not be located.

[6] Szpetecki's tie to Japan was close: according to Ilse Hensel (private communication, May 2008), her Barlach poems as well as possibly another collection have been translated into Japanese and are highly esteemed in that country whose poetry she herself loved.

[7]The pronoun in the German phrase "da sie erstarrt" could grammatically refer back either to "die Träume" or to "die Einsamkeit" and would thus translate into either "as/since they (the dreams) congeal/freeze" or "as/since it (the loneliness) congeals/freezes." Steffens's poetic excerpt reveals that he chooses the latter; more on this below.

In terms of compositional technique, Steffens takes the distribution and frequency of the letters appearing in the poetic lines as a clue for the sequence and relative density of the piano's repeated pitches;[8] with regard to character, the composer excerpts four key terms from this poetic description of desolate isolation. At the very moment when his quartet progresses from its first, motivically defined and metrically settled section to the improvisatory organization of the contemplative expanse, he writes the following line above the piano part:

"gläserne", traumhafte Einsamkeit, die erstarrt
["glassy," dreamy loneliness, which congeals]

By enriching the poem's dominating image, "glassy loneliness ... which congeals," with the dreams the poet believes to be contained in the star up high, Steffens introduces a modicum of hopefulness. The music he writes for the piano part in this section—the music he generates as a kind of sonic hexagram by using the letters in Szpetecki's poem as yarrow stalks—mirrors both the primary and the secondary qualities of his poetic excerpt, both the essence of its images as introduced by the poet and the reconciliation, as introduced by the composer, of the vertically removed celestial body with the horizontally confined plane of loneliness.

The sound carpet the piano spreads below the musical meditation on "glassy loneliness" is characterized by an almost perfect vertical symmetry. The six pitches in the section's first half build a tritone + semitone-pair on either side of the central perfect fifth B-F♯; the octave displacement of the uppermost pitch endows the D♭ with the almost literal role of the star seen above. When Steffens adds the remaining six chromatic pitches for the second half of the rhythmically free expanse, he arranges them in mirror-symmetrical distances again determined by tritones and perfect fifths.

FIGURE 2: the sound carpet in the "expanse of glassy loneliness"

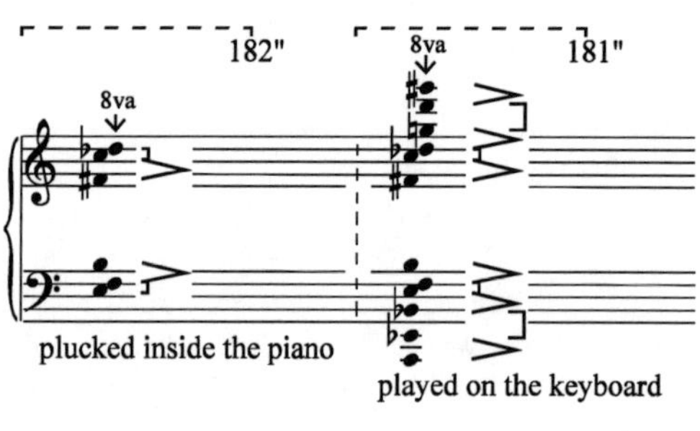

[8]The details of this method, while irrelevant to an appreciation of the result, are interesting in so far as they are reminiscent of various procedures known in oracle consultation.

Ming I – Die Verwundung des Hellen 149

The second poem mentioned in the subtitle for *Ming I* is by Nelly Sachs. Born 1891 into a Berlin family of successful Jewish merchants, Sachs lived throughout the 1930s in increasing deprivation and fear of deportation. After the renowned Swedish author Selma Lagerlöf intervened on her behalf, she and her elderly mother were granted asylum in Sweden, where she arrived in 1940, on the very last passenger flight that left Germany. Providing for herself and her mother by translating Swedish poetry—from a language she was only just learning—she lived in great poverty until her own poetry gradually gained recognition. She was awarded the Nobel prize for literature in 1966, but depression and an irrepressible fear of persecution remained with her until her death in 1970.

Sachs's poem "Israel," along with its author's personality and fate, was very obviously the primary catalyst for the piano quartet, and this in more ways than just through the one particular poem Steffens acknowledges. The composer had come in contact with her poetry when he was still in his late twenties. His *Symphonic Fragment* for large orchestra, male choir and contralto solo of 1962 is based on three poems from Sachs's collection *Flucht und Verwandlung* ("Flight and Transformation") of 1959. In this context, he exchanged several letters with the poet. A few years later, having completed the first half of an opera based on Sachs's *Eli*,[9] a commission for the opening of the new opera house in Dortmund, he learned that the poet had suffered a nervous breakdown after listening to the operatic adaptation of her mystery play made earlier by the Finnish-Jewish composer Moses Pergament. Very much alarmed, Steffens traveled to meet the poet in her exile in Stockholm. There he explained his understanding of her *Eli* and his intended aesthetic approach in the musical setting, ultimately receiving Nelly Sachs's explicit permission to proceed with the opera,[10] which was premiered on 5 March 1967 to great critical acclaim.

---

[9]*Eli: Ein Mysterienspiel vom Leiden Israels* was written in Stockholm during the final months of the Second World War and completed on 9 November 1945. It was first performed as a radio play on 23 and 26 May 1958 by the South German Broadcasting Company in its series "Radio Essays." The scenic premiere followed on 14 March 1962 at the Städtischen Bühnen Dortmund. A translation into English is available in *O the Chimneys; Selected Poems, including the verse play, Eli*; transl. by Michael Hamburger (New York: Farrar, Straus and Giroux, 1967). On the opera see Walter Steffens, "Eli – das Mysterienspiel vom Leiden Israels als Oper," in Walter A. Berendsohn, *Nelly Sachs* (Darmstadt: Agora Verlag, 1974), 177-184 [177], in particular the following statement: "*Eli* was the great artistic and human task of my current period of life, one for which I have prepared myself systematically through chamber music, an oratorio, two cantatas, and seven song cycles."

[10]The permission is confirmed in a letter written on 6 December 1965 to the Head of the Department of Cultural Affairs at the Dortmund city administration. (Carbon copy "L 90:2" in the Royal Library Stockholm.)

When, again several years later, he received the commission to write a piano quartet, Steffens decided to turn once again to Nelly Sachs's works. The poem he chose as a counterpart to Szpetecki's is taken from Sachs's second volume of poetry, *Sternverdunkelung*,[11] a title whose suggestive imagery ("star darkening" or "star eclipse") may have struck Steffens as complementary to the notion of the dream-harboring star in "Blau."

Like many other poems by Nelly Sachs, the one Steffens chose does not feature an actual title. The word "Israel" can be regarded as a refrain in two ways: As an invocation, emphasized on the printed page with capital letters, the name opens each of the individual poem's three stanzas. At the same time, the poem as a whole concludes the second section within the collection *Sternverdunkelung*, functioning both as a coda to a symmetrically structured body and as an echo to some of its internal features. As a coda, it constitutes the eleventh piece in a section entirely devoted to the people of Israel, the first ten of which are patterned as 2 + 3 + 3 + 2:
poems 1 and 2 address the founding fathers,
poems 3, 4, and 5, the prophets,
poems 6, 7, and 8, Israel's hope, self-hatred, and suffering, and
poems 9 and 10, the nation's most glorious kings.[12]
As an echo, the final poem's threefold stanza-opening invocation "Israel" picks up the twofold, refrain-like "O Israel" in the second poem and a similar, tripartite refrain "O Israel" in the sixth poem.

The poem's bipartite initial stanza tells of the gradual emergence of Israel, the transformation of an indistinct Middle Eastern tribe into God's chosen people. Sachs begins by addressing Israel as one who is only about to be born, a larva which the forces of eternity are preparing for its destiny. In this limbo-like dream state, Israel is an astrologer seeking knowledge from the signs in the sky. Then the silent heavens open and Israel is dazzled into its role, unaccustomed to this very personal encounter with the divine but not willing to yield. As the imagery changes, Sachs recasts the generic dreaminess, the state of half-awareness attributed to the forefathers, as the specific dream that becomes the people's founding event: the night-time encounter in which Jacob wrestles with God's angel, is injured, and emerges renamed: as "Israel," i.e., he who struggles with God (Gen 32: 23-28).

---

[11]Nelly Sachs, *Sternverdunkelung: Gedichte* (Amsterdam: Bermann-Fischer, 1949). This collection was preceded in 1947 by an earlier volume, *In den Wohnungen des Todes*.

[12]The symmetry extends to the choice and style of the individual poems' headings. The paired poems at either end of this ten-part body are titled with personal names ("Abraham"/ "Jakob" and "David"/"Saul" respectively), whereas in the interior threefold groupings, only one poem each has a heading (cf. "Hiob" and "Sinai").

Ming I – Die Verwundung des Hellen

ISRAEL,	ISRAEL,
namenloser einst,	nameless once,
noch von des Todes Efeu umsponnen,	still cocooned in the ivy of death,
arbeitete geheim die Ewigkeit in dir,	eternity clandestinely worked in you,
traumtief	submerged in dreams
bestiegst du	you mounted
der Mondtürme magische Spirale,	the magic spiral of moon towers,
die mit Tiermasken verhüllten Gestirne	circling
umkreisend —	the stars shrouded in animal masks —
in der Fische Mirakelstummheit	in the miraculous muteness of Pisces
oder mit des Widders anstürmender Härte.	or with Taurus's onrushing harshness.
Bis der versiegelte Himmel aufbrach	Until the sealed heaven broke open
und du,	and you,
Waghalsigster unter den Nachtwandlern,	the most daring among sleepwalkers,
getroffen von der Gotteswunde	struck by the divine wound
in den Abgrund aus Licht fielst.	fell into the abyss of light.
ISRAEL,	ISRAEL,
Zenit der Sehnsucht,	zenith of yearning,
gehäuft über deinem Haupte	heaped above your head
ist das Wunder wie Gewitter,	is the miracle like thunderstorms,
entlädt sich im Schmerzgebirge	discharging in your era's
deiner Zeit.	mountain of pain.
ISRAEL,	ISRAEL,
erst zart, wie das Lied der Vögel	only delicately, like the song of birds
und leidender Kinder Gespräche	and suffering children's conversation,
rinnt des lebendigen Gottes Quelle	does the living God's spring flow,
heimatlich aus deinem Blut —	homeland-like, from your blood —

In the second stanza, "Israel" stands neither for a person (the renamed Jacob) nor for a particular people (Jacob's descendants, committed to the covenant forged with the One God), but for the deepest form of yearning. The miracle of divine election, creating a domed ceiling above those it unites, is charged with a tension that leads to a seemingly unending pain.

In the third stanza, the fountain of divine sustenance, destined to create *Heimat*—a place as well as a sense of identity and belonging—for the founding father's blood relatives, is still only a delicate flow, beautiful but fragile ("like the song of birds and suffering children's conversation").

In his score for *Ming I*, Steffens quotes five times from this poem. As with his excerpts from Szpetecki's poem, all explicit references fall into the composition's rhythmically free second section:

- *"Israel"* (in quotation marks) is written against the motif with which the viola opens the quartet's second section;
- *Von der Gotteswunde getroffen* (without quotation marks) appears at the moment when the three strings, 25 seconds into the second section's second half, break out into tremolos and sudden accents in preparation for their first juxtaposition of aleatoric note groups;
- *Abgrund aus Licht* (without quotation marks) characterizes the contemplative section's dynamic climax, wedged between the stretto completion of the first aleatoric passage and the beginning of the second, its sudden *ff* marking the almost exact midpoint of the section's volatile second half;
- *Israel "erst zart"* informs the *pppp* beginning of the three string instruments' contribution to the final complementary segment;
- *"Quelle"* and, a little later, *"Blut"* define the composition's very last moments. As the piano's initially brutal chromatic cluster gradually wanes, the string players' notes trickle ever so softly, the violin and the viola in barely audible pizzicato meanderings, the violoncello in slow harmonics, until all music fades away completely.

The way in which Steffens matches music to the words he excerpts from the two poems invites a first reading of the "compounded" poetic subtext in the piano quartet's long second section. The whole eight-minute expanse is characterized with the words from Szpetecki's poem as a depiction of a "glassy, dreamy loneliness that congeals." During the section's first half, the piano remains within the six central pitches, which are plucked inside the piano in *ppp*. The single inscription placed against the concurrent melodic lines, the word "Israel," identifies the soft, repetitive gestures as capturing an all-encompassing experience. For the first measured segment of 182 seconds, the three string instruments move almost entirely within the confines of only four pitch sequences. Each of them is introduced by the viola and expanded in a mixture of imitation, slight modification, augmentation, and an occasional retrograde.

FIGURE 3: the melodic material in the first half of section II

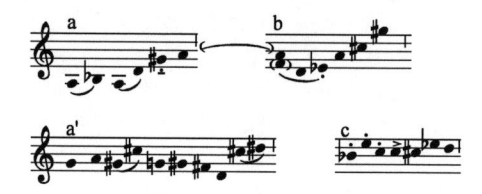

Ming I – Die Verwundung des Hellen

In a volume that fluctuates mainly between *pp* and *mf*, the three melodic voices seek a maximum of nuance by means of constant changes in sound production (*arco/pizzicato*, *con/senza sordino*, *sul ponticello*, etc.) and in single-note intensity (swift in unmarked notes / weightier in *choraliter* / harmonics drawn out for several seconds each). "Israel" as presented in Sachs's long initial half-stanza, a tribe who lives with a distinct orientation toward heaven but does not yet know the One God, is thus musically characterized as both strongly unified and individualized by much idiosyncratic variation.

During the last twenty seconds of this passage, the viola in a powerful crescendo to *ff* soars above the continuous *pp* of its partners and then uses two versions of pitch sequence b to build a splendid arch with an extended peak—Sachs' "zenith of yearning"? The piano transfers its six symmetrical pitches from inside the instrument to the keyboard and, adding the remaining six pitches in newly assertive *fz*, establishes the fully chromatic version of the vertically mirrored chord. As Sachs tells it, "the sealed heaven broke open." As Jacob-Israel is chosen and acknowledged by God in an act of valiant wrestling, the symmetric harmony takes on a quality similar chords typically have in the music of Olivier Messiaen: "as above, so below." Israel will live in the secure conviction of being created in God's image.

The strings' return to the D-major triad in *pp* suggests a new beginning. In the subsequent expanse measured as 181 seconds, all instruments sound far more emotionally charged than before. The two quotations inscribed here in the score, "Von der Gotteswunde getroffen" and "Abgrund aus Licht," are taken from the second half of the historically oriented first stanza in Sachs's poem. The drama of the Israelites' founding event, highlighted in the dual contrast of comforting and threatening forces (God / wound, light / abyss) is musically interpreted through a savage-sounding juxtaposition of aleatoric groups and a sudden *ff* outbreak.

The fall into the "abyss of light" hits rock bottom in the piano's brutal two-forearm cluster in *fffz* with which the expanse measured in seconds breaks off. This explosive attack is complemented by a seemingly shocked and disconcerted *pppp* response in the string instruments, a mixture of prescribed note sequences and aleatorically treated segments, of slower, melodically intense *arco* components and fast *pizzicato* groups in which the three almost entirely unaligned strands echo instances of what has been said before about Israel. In this final complementary segment, the number of poetic citations is denser than anywhere else in the work: Steffens writes "Israel 'erst zart'" against the first notes and "Quelle" as well as "Blut" against those shortly before the end. The reference to the living God's spring that runs only very delicately at this point is translated into a juxtaposition of swift improvisatory pizzicatos in the violin, an undetermined mixture of faster plucked and slower bowed notes in the viola, and very high, very calm harmonics in the violoncello. At "Blut," which suggests here the blood relationship of all people descending from the founding father Jacob-Israel, the piano mutes whatever is left of its waning cluster sound, while the string instruments complete their independent play in striking non-coordination. The music thus offers a vivid image of the regret one can perceive in the poem's last stanza: regret that Israel is not yet more confident, more realized, more recognized in and true to its spiritual task.

The Enlightenment from the *I Ching*

The integration of the two poems into Steffens's piano quartet actually presents a second step in the composition: these literary sources inspire above all the work's second section. The step that would prove crucial for the composition of the first section was of a very different nature. Over the years, Steffens had returned again and again to Sachs's poetry, profoundly impressed by the exiled poet's resolve to continue voicing the grief and yearnings of her fellow Jews despite her own increasingly fragile health. So unbreakable is his internal bond to Sachs that he reports to have "seen" her repeatedly since her death in 1970, encounters he has invariably interpreted as essential instigation and source of orientation for his work and spiritual outlook.

When Steffens received the commission for a piano quartet and had chosen, once again, a poem by Nelly Sachs as one of his sources of inspiration, he decided that he needed to understand her better before beginning to design his basic musical ideas. What he sought to understand was the poet's spiritual essence rather than the details of her poignant experience in fleeing the Nazis a week before she was ordered to be deported to a concentration camp.[13] To this end, he decided to undertake a formal consultation of the *I Ching*, the "Book of Changes" from ancient China.

A satisfactory introduction to the *I Ching* must remain beyond the scope of this study. Suffice it here to recall only the basic data. As Steffens knew from Richard Wilhelm's commented German translation of the work, the *I Ching* allegedly began its existence as early as 24 centuries B.C.E., when the initial trigrams and the idea of joining them to hexagrams were first conceived. Each trigram is a symbol consisting of three solid or broken lines, based on the concept of *yin* and *yang*, the universal principles which the Chinese believe to be the foundation of all existence. Solid lines stand for

---

[13] I owe these details to various conversations with Steffens, in his home on 13-15 August 2006 and by phone on 23 January 2008.

Ming I – Die Verwundung des Hellen

yang, the male or active force; broken lines represent *yin*, the female or passive aspect. The six lines, alternatively solid or broken, can form eight trigrams; placing one trigram atop another in every possible combination results in sixty-four hexagrams.

The *Book of Changes* provides clues for interpreting the hexagram as an oracular answer to the question asked. It is more than just a fortune-telling manual, since the trigrams and hexagrams became embedded in Chinese culture as a system of symbols that explained the metaphysical principles by which the universe functions. Historically, divination represented an indirect way of communicating with the divine world; the result of tossing coins or throwing dice was believed to be guided by the decisions of the gods. In a modern Western context, the suggestively enigmatic nature of the text lends itself particularly well to "deconstructivist" readings. In her introduction to the English translation of Richard Wilhelm's famous *Lectures on the I Ching*, Irene Eber observes: "Its very abstruseness suggests an intriguing richness of multiple meanings."[14]

Trigrams and hexagrams each have their assigned names, presumably hinting at major aspects of their meaning. To each hexagram is attached a brief introductory paragraph commenting on the name, a "judgment" providing a general summary of its implications, and statements explaining the significance of each of the six lines in the context. A separate volume contains a dense layer of commentaries and philosophical contemplations.[15] Confucius was long credited with having compiled the *I Ching* and written most of its extensive commentary. Today's scholars believe that the genesis was quite a bit more complex, and that Confucius's contribution is only one among several. However, the book has achieved canonization as one of the five Confucian classics.[16] "With its canonization, no later Confucian thinker can ever entirely ignore it."[17]

---

[14] Richard Wilhelm, *Lectures on the I Ching*, trans. Irene Eber (Princeton: Bollingen Series, Princeton University Press, 1979), xi.

[15] As Wilhelm explains, Chinese literature credits four sages with the authorship of the *I Ching*: Fu Hsi, King Wen, the Duke of Chou, and Confucius. Fu Hsi, a legendary cultural hero and sage from mythological times, is said to have invented the trigrams, King Wen of the Zhou (reigned 1171-1122) to have developed the hexagrams, the Duke of Zhou (died 1094) to have composed the judgments, and Confucius to have written (part of) the commentary. Both my brief summary and the subsequent comments on the hexagrams are based on *The I Ching or Book of Changes*, the Richard Wilhelm translation rendered into English by Cary F. Baynes; foreword by C.G. Jung (Princeton, NJ: Princeton University Press, 1950).

[16] In addition to the *I Ching* or "Classic of Changes," this canon comprises the Classic of Poetry, the Classic of Rites, the Classic of History, and the Spring and Autumn Annals.

[17] See Benjamin I. Schwartz, *The World of Thought in Ancient* China (Cambridge, MA: Belknap Press of Harvard University Press, 1985), 390.

The sense in which a hexagram is understood to be relevant to a given situation depends on the assumption that the complex counting process undertaken in a certain moment and state of mind reflects the unique quality of that moment. The emphasis is rarely on things as they are or will come to pass (the modern Western world's primary concern), but usually on the way in which conditions may change or be changed. The hexagrams are never read as indicators of factual circumstances but as pointers toward transformative tendencies—hence, the "book of changes." Correctly understood, each moment with its quality and propensity for change can be met with appropriate or inappropriate actions. As Wilhelm explains in his preface to the German translation of the *I Ching*, Western oracles and divination methods typically inform seekers about what they can expect to happen, whereas the *I Ching* advises them on what they might do or refrain from doing so as to strengthen a particular moment's favorable quality and weaken its inauspicious aspects. To the Chinese understanding, humans are not the passive recipients but the active co-shapers of their destiny. In every situation, *yin* and *yang* with their multifaceted significations represent not opposites but counterparts or complements. For a Western mind, this is easier to grasp in some attributes than in others. The pair light–shadow is helpful; interpretations of the *yin–yang* opposite as matter–spirit or as nature–mind also convey a sense of the mutual dependence.

To get a sense of the eight trigrams is relatively easy if one associates each of them in three ways: with an element, a family position, and various attributes. The interpretation in terms of family positions serves as a memory aid once one accepts that sons are understood to be more closely related to their mother while daughters share more with their father. The reading in terms of eight elements and their qualities or attributes provides a first step into the mystery of hexagram interpretation.

- The two basic trigrams consist of three identical lines each:
  ☰   triple *yang* (the father) stands for heaven, creativity, and strength;
  ☷   three *yin* lines (the mother) signify earth, receptivity, and yielding.

- When the mother's favorites—the sons—are born, their place in the birth order is marked by the ascending position of their single *yang* line:
  ☳   Strong *yang* below duple yielding *yin* (the first son) is an arousing and inciting force, ethereal energy as, e.g., in thunderstorms.
  ☵   Strong *yang* in the center between yielding forces (the second son) is the dangerous or abysmal force; it is water in motion, in flowing rivers, sprouting wells, plunging waterfalls, rising vapor, and falling rain.
  ☶   Strong *yang* atop two layers of yielding *yin* (the third son) is the stabilizing principle, the mountain, calm and static.

Ming I – Die Verwundung des Hellen 157

- The father's favorites—three daughters—define their attributes similarly:
- ☴ Yielding *yin* below duple *yang* (the first daughter) is wind or wood; it results in a gentle but penetrating force.
- ☲ Yielding *yin* surrounded by *yang* (the second daughter) equals fire, to the Chinese an element that never exists alone but attaches itself to matter and feeds on oxygen; it is clinging but also bright and light-giving.
- ☱ Yielding *yin* above duple strong *yang* (the third daughter) creates serenity and joyfulness; this is the lake or other quiet water.

Steffens, who had taught himself the traditional method of consulting the *I Ching*, asked the Chinese oracle for elucidation on the spiritual essence of the poet Nelly Sachs. The hexagram to which his ritual counting led him was no. 36, known by the name "Ming I."

FIGURE 4: "Ming I," hexagram no. 36 in the *I Ching*

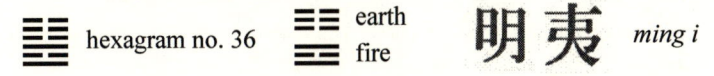

☷ hexagram no. 36   ☷ earth / ☲ fire   明夷 *ming i*

"The sun has sunk under the earth and is therefore darkened":
BRIGHTNESS WOUNDED

The explanation of the circumstance described in this hexagram is eerily fitting for the way in which Nelly Sachs's whole life was overshadowed by the Holocaust and the dark forces of evil, personified in Hitler. In Richard Wilhelm's translation and commentary on the *I Ching*, Steffens found the sentence: "Here a man of dark nature is in a position of authority and brings harm to the wise and able."[18] The "judgment" attached to the hexagram—i.e., the recommendation of beneficial behavior and action under the given circumstances—helped the composer to appreciate the poet's continuous endeavors even more fully. It reads: "In adversity it furthers one to be persevering."[19]

The Chinese name for the hexagram is *míng í*. The first character, *míng*, signifies *bright* or *brightness*; the second one, *í* (*yí* in today's Pinyin romanization) is translated in modern Chinese dictionaries as *to wound, to raze, to exterminate*.[20] Cary Baynes renders Wilhelm's explanation of the hexagram's connotation, "die Verwundung des Hellen," as "darkening of the light," an

---

[18]Wilhelm/Baynes, *The I Ching*, 139.

[19]Wilhelm/Baynes, *The I Ching*, 140.

[20]Additional translations of *ming* include *light, tomorrow, ability to discern*, and *complete*; *yí* also has secondary connotations as *ruin* or *decomposition* and as *alien* or *enemy*.

expression that seems strikingly reminiscent of the "star-darkening" in the title of Sachs's poetry collection *Sternverdunkelung*. I prefer the more literal translation Baynes offers in the course of the explanatory text, "the wounding of the bright" (or, as an even more poetic rendering, "brightness wounded"). In her dissertation on this hexagram as a representation of evil in the *I Ching*, Ariane Rump explains that the message the sages from ancient China capture in this oracular symbol is, "in view of the blows of fate as humans encounter them with particular violence in the events described by the hexagram "brightness wounded," to learn detachment and possibly develop a [creative] response."[21]

The *I Ching* chapter on hexagram no. 36 ends with a concluding statement so suggestive in the context of the fate of the Jews under the Nazis that it confirmed the composer's belief in the timeless wisdom of divination:

> The climax of the darkening is reached. The dark power at first held so high a place that it could wound all who were on the side of good and of the light. But in the end it perishes of its own darkness, for evil must itself fall at the very moment when it has wholly overcome the good, and thus consumed the energy to which it owed its duration.[22]

Thus the Chinese oracle's answer to the German composer's quest for an understanding of the poet's soul became the piano quartet's third spiritual foundation.

Symbolism in Steffens's Musical Interpretation of the Hexagram "Brightness Wounded"

The judgment for the hexagram *ming i*, "In adversity it furthers one to be persevering," can be related to the first section of Steffens's piano quartet. As briefly mentioned above, this section is characterized by a slow tempo, a steady meter in 5/4-measures, and an atmosphere the composer describes as "very internalized, in calm order." Launched from a three-octave unison C in the piano, the music soon turns to the D-major triad that serves as the tonal foundation throughout the remainder of the work. In the initial unison, the central octave is doubled in the viola—the instrument that, here as in the second section, acts as the leader among the melodic voices.

---

[21] Ariane Rump, *Die Verwundung des Hellen als Aspekt des Bösen im I Ching* (Cham, Switzerland: Gut-Druck, 1967), 87.

[22] Wilhelm/Baynes, *The I Ching*, 142.

Ming I – Die Verwundung des Hellen

Motif 1, as mentioned above, unfolds in two-part writing. Each string instrument begins with a single pitch but later adds the octave above. The added higher note then presents the melodic contour. Only when this strand has arrived and completed four beats on its target pitch does the lower strand rise a whole-tone and imitate the contour from there. When the violin joins the viola, it does so on the dominant G as would the second entry in an 18th-century fugue. It also continues the metric and rhythmic patterns.

FIGURE 5: the quartet's basic motif in quasi-fugal imitation

Ming I, mm. 1-8, viola imitated by violin: motif 1 with four entries on C, D, G, and A.

The imitative texture with six stacked entries is suggestive of the fugal style represented above all by Johann Sebastian Bach. The motif employed here as a kind of fugal subject—C-B♭-D♭-B♮ in the first entry—corroborates the assumed historical reference: its contour is a varied quotation of a very famous pitch sequence: the "head" of the third subject in the last polyphonic movement of Bach's *Art of the Fugue*, which enters "Contrapunctus XIV" at m. 193. This head, which is an acronym (based on the German system of note naming) of Bach's surname, has given rise to numerous explicit and countless unacknowledged musical bows of reverence.[23] The derivation Steffens establishes in *Ming I* can be described as a transposed permutation:

Bach's signature	= B♭-A♮-C♮-B♮
transposed up a semitone	= B♮-B♭-D♭-C♮
with beginning and end exchanged	= C♮-B♭-D♭-B♮

The continuation with which Bach expands the chromatic aggregate before he rounds off his signature motif with a cadential extension provides Steffens with the pitches for the initial imitation, which rise from the sustained foundation of the two-part voice; see Fig. 6.

The second motif in the initial section is treated quite differently: its three entries sound in unison and follow one another on D, the composition's

---

[23]In a comprehensive study published in the catalogue for the 1985 exhibition to celebrate the 300th anniversary of Johann Sebastian Bach, Ulrich Prinz lists 409 works by 330 composers from the 17th to the 20th century using the BACH motif. Cf. Ulrich Prinz, ed., *300 Jahre Johann Sebastian Bach* (Tutzing: Schneider, 1985).

home key, thus abandoning all semblance of fugal style. Melodically, however, it is related to the first motif: it picks up the pitches of the second entry and (especially in subsequent entries, where Steffens substitutes G♮ for his original final G♯) concludes on the initial pitch of the third:

FIGURE 6: the BACH theme and its modified quotation in motif 1

J. S. Bach,
The Art of the Fugue,
final theme

Walter Steffens,
Ming I, initial motif
(transposed up a semitone)

FIGURE 7: motifs 1 and 2 in their relationship

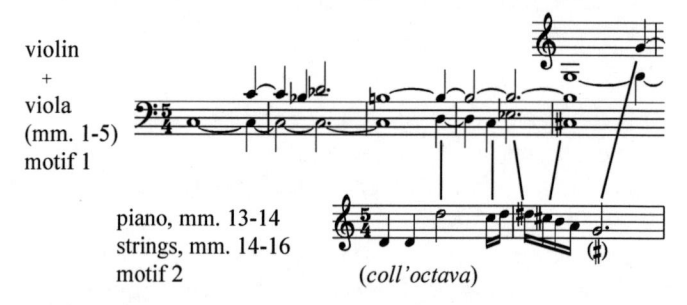

violin
+
viola
(mm. 1-5)
motif 1

piano, mm. 13-14
strings, mm. 14-16
motif 2   (*coll'octava*)

This second motif in Steffens's *Ming I* is already firmly rooted in D—the anchor of the quartet as a whole as well as of Bach's *Art of the Fugue*.

In "Contrapunctus XIV," which remained incomplete at the time of its composer's sudden death, the narrow chromatic contour is usually interpreted as an emblem of Bach's humility and spiritual modesty as well as his recognition of human smallness and insignificance. With its two descending semitones, it is evocative of the "sigh motifs" known from musical rhetoric and can be identified as a lament; owing to a contour considered to trace a cruciform shape, the sorrow expressed in the lament is associated with the suffering of Christ or, by extension, with the agony of any innocent being killed for reasons of lowly prejudice or mere indifference.

By basing the first section of his piano quartet on two motifs developed from this poignant melodic symbol, Steffens draws a musical parallel between the individual experience and affliction of Nelly Sachs, the affliction of European Jews under the holocaust, and more generally all humans whose lives are treated as unworthy of esteem and protection in view of some larger, usually gruesome political scheme.

Guernica, Elegy for Viola and Orchestra

In 1974, the year before he was to receive the commission from the Herford Piano Quartet that resulted in *Ming I*, Steffens had started sketching a work for viola and orchestra commemorating the events in the Basque town of Guernica. His subtitle describes the composition as conceived "in reflective approximation of Pablo Picasso's painting." In 1975, he interrupted this ekphrastic work to concentrate on *Ming I* and only completed the one-movement viola concerto in 1978.[24] *Guernica* was premiered in 1979 by the Northwest German Philharmonic under the baton of Janos Kulka, with Reiner Schmidt as soloist, and has since become the composer's most frequently performed work.

The entwined process of gestation has left traces in both works. The composer's preparation for music featuring a soloistic viola may explain the fact that in *Ming I*, the viola is prominently entrusted with the presentation of all new material: it introduces in mm. 1-4 the main motif of the first section, establishes in mm. 22ff the leading figure of the second section, and builds the unaccompanied expressive arch in the first unmeasured section after 182 seconds of "contemplation." At the same time, the composition on Picasso's mural shares major portions of its thematic material with the work based on poems by Elfriede Szpetecki and Nelly Sachs. In response to my question, posed some 30 years later, how a work with a distinctly different title, imagery, and source context could convey its program by means of components conceived in another context, the surprised composer declared that "emotionally and spiritually, the two works are the same."[25]

And indeed, it is the spiritual affinity between the two compositions that provides a major key to an understanding of Steffens's interpretation of Picasso's *Guernica*. "Ming I" or "brightness wounded" struck the composer as not only encapsulating Nelly Sachs's life situation after her near escape from the Nazis, but seemed to him also an appropriate description of the fate suffered by the people of Guernica.

The structure of Steffens's composition for viola and orchestra can be described as a conceptual palindrome with asymmetries. The fundamental layout is in seven sections organized around a center—A B C D C' B' A'.[26] The initial section is the only one to be fully onomatopoeic: the music

---

[24] Walter Steffens, *Guernica, Elegie für Bratsche und Orchester,* Op.32, " In reflektierender Annäherung an das Bild von Pablo Picasso" (Frankfurt: Wilhelm Hansen, 1979).

[25] From a conversation with the author, 14 August 2006.

[26] cf. A   B   C   D   C'   B'   A'
      mm. 1-22   23-47   48-88   89-93   94-118   119-143   144-183

reproduces the sound of approaching airplanes. Beginning with very soft drones in the lowest register, the orchestral pitch rises only very gradually in tone and volume. Interestingly, Steffens achieves this effect, which audiences and critics across Germany have described as chilling and profoundly disturbing, in a visually suggestive way. Taking the famous three-bomber photo shot on the fatal day by a Basque priest and using it as a collage object, the composer invites the orchestra players to "realize" the threatening shapes in aleatoric play.

FIGURE 8: Photograph of the approaching bomber squadron, taken by Padre Eusebio Arronategui in the town of Guernica

For this improvisation, Steffens specifies merely the very gradual increase through the first seventeen measures and the deafening *crescendo* through the subsequent four (see the score excerpt on the next page). Segment A must be read as a response to the devastating attack on the little town of Guernica which Picasso immortalized in his famous painting with its cries of outrage and horror. The historical facts concerning the destruction of the oldest city of the Basques and their cultural center are well documented. In democratic elections held in Spain on February 1936, the left-wing coalition Popular Front had beaten the right-wing National Front coalition. In July, endorsed by Hitler and Mussolini, fascist generals attempted a military takeover. The coup failed to topple the government and civil war (1936-39) ensued. After nearly three years of bitter struggle, Nationalist forces led by General Francisco Franco emerged victorious with the support of Nazi Germany and Italy. In the course of this war, fought on both sides with ruthless cruelty and determination, bomber planes of the German "Legion Condor" obliterated the town on 26 April 1937. Henceforth, "Guernica" became a symbol of fascist brutality—and it is this horrific slaughter of innocent civilians that an audience aware of the music's title is invited vicariously to experience.

The onomatopoeic depiction of threat in section A of Steffens's *Guernica* evokes the striking absence—or avoidance—of color in Picasso's painting. Picasso had learned of the bombardment of Guernica on 28 April 1937. On May 1 he made his first drawing; the final painting was completed

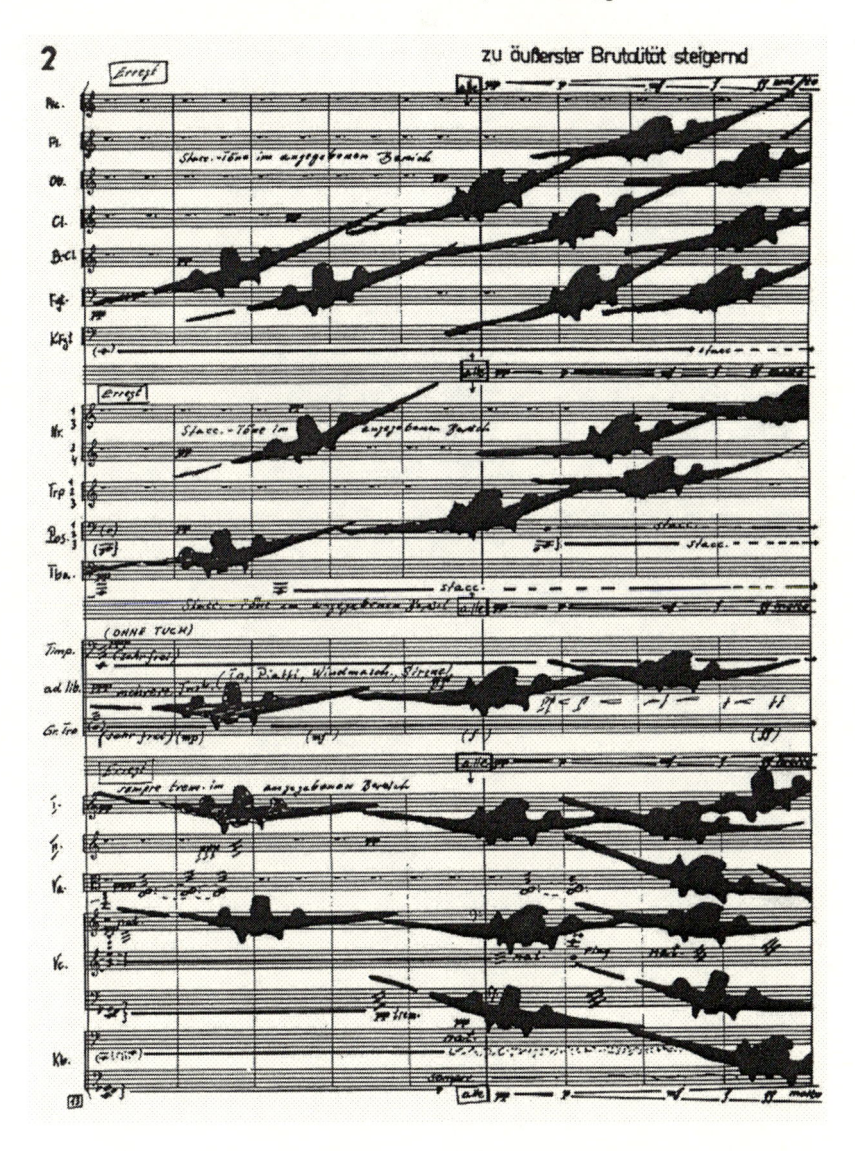

FIGURE 9: Walter Steffens, *Guernica*, p. 2

on June 4. A mural-sized canvas 11 feet 6 inches high and 25 feet 6 inches wide, it was exhibited that very month in the Paris World Exhibition's Spanish Pavilion, where it became the main attraction in the open entry hall.

With his portrayal in black, white, and gray tones, the artist spoke not only graphically but also symbolically: the starkness would have reminded his contemporaries of the black-and-white of newspaper photos and early films, thereby adding a connotation of that objectivity which the actual media coverage in France was so sadly lacking. At the same time, the choice of the palette can also be interpreted as a way to show that in the face of outrageous atrocities, the colors of the world seem to vanish into the monumentality of the black-and-white contrast. Finally, witnesses of bombings tell of the stark intensity of the light caused by each blast, an intensity blinding the unprotected eye. Visitors faced with Picasso's mural in full size and full light report a similar, lacerating sensation.[27] All this is distinctly reflected in the music's framing sections.

FIGURE 10: Pablo Picasso, *Guernica*, 1937

The music's inner segments can be summarily interpreted as portraying the victim's perspective, that of the human and animal figures filling a space Picasso does not define as exterior or interior[28] but marks only sketchily by

---

[27]Cf. Jean-Louis Ferrier, *De Picasso à Guernica. Généalogie d'un tableau* (Paris: Denoël, 1985), 11-12.

[28]Herschel B. Chipp maintains in *Picasso's Guernica: History, Transformations, Meanings* (Berkeley, CA: University of California Press, 1988), 135: "Although some writers continue to argue that this is either an interior or an exterior scene, it seems apparent that the background and foreground shapes, like a stage set, actually suggest both in different places. Thus Picasso, by indicating at one place one view and at another place another, tells us that there is no single, simple interpretation. Just as the illumination is both sun and electric (indoor) light, the time both day and night, the place both inside and outside, so the observer is not confined to a specific position in space or even a single level of reality but is imaginatively free to perceive the theme in its widest implications."

Ming I – Die Verwundung des Hellen

a backdrop of tiles on the floor and disjointed walls with windows. Steffens can be shown to be reading the painting from right to left. This agrees with the common orientation of Picasso's various figures: most bodies and all eyes are turned toward the head of the bull at the left. The sequence of the musical sections toward the center manifests itself as a progressive loss of (first tonal, then also metric) stability and order. Section B (corresponding to the principal section of *Ming I*) is written in fully determined notation. In Section C, predetermined orderliness is abandoned in favor of the improvisatory contemplations known from the second section in *Ming I*. In section D, which serves here as a short central passage (instead of constituting, as in *Ming I*, the first of two structurally analogous conclusions), Steffens allows all instruments about half a minute of completely free play with a small number of given pitches. The overlay of unrelated tempi and rhythms is briefly interrupted for a reminiscence of the first inner section's reassuring D-major chord. Sustained, this chord subsequently anchors the renewed aleatoricism.

From here on, the structural process is reversed: a rhythmically improvisatory section C' leads through a fully notated section B' (with only faint hints at the comfort of pure D major) to a final section A', which combines the two motifs Steffens derived from Bach's signature with scattered echoes of the sound of bomber planes. The fact that the conclusion gives much less space to the tone painting of an aerial assault than did its symmetrical counterpart seems appropriate; aircraft leaving a devastated town have an effect very different from the one created upon their arrival in an as yet unscarred world.

The irregularly symmetrical layout of Steffens's composition can be read as reflecting the structure of Picasso's painting. Taking into consideration the emotional charge of each section's material and considering that section B' encompasses, beside the return to fully determined notation, a self-contained segment with new and unique material (more on this below), one can couple the artist's individual images with musical sections.

Section B with its strong anchoring in tonality can be associated with the woman fleeing in panic at the extreme right of Picasso's painting. Her face with outstretched chin seems to run ahead of the rest of her body; her huge feet take giant steps despite her excessively swollen knee. She seems confident in her right to live and determined to save herself, an attitude one might see musically expressed in the repeated mooring of an otherwise atonal context on a D-major harmony. Steffens's section C with its tangible loss of security and its backdrop suggesting that no escape is possible may refer to the woman at the upper right whom Picasso paints with her arms stretched up in torment as she is burning to death in a crumbling house.

The music's oscillating middle section (cf. mm. 89-93) seems to stand for the lamp-bearing woman marking the middle axis in Picasso's painting. An overly-large female face is here seen thrusting inward through a window, while the woman's right arm, extended over her head and beyond the painting's middle axis, clutches an oil lamp that sheds light on a large area. The triangle of light borders on a stark vertical line near the center of the canvas, the backbone of the huge painting. It is reflected in the stark-white remnants of a dismembered warrior, whose severed head and lower arms with hands are scattered on the floor in the painting's lower left portion. One hand, reaching toward the women to the right, holds the handle of a broken sword and clutches a flower in its fist; the other, at the far left, is spread out in a cramp of agony. In the music, this representative of all the dead left behind as the bomber squadrons leave is oddly de-emphasized, integrated into the closing section (A') with its combination of airplane hums and emphatic melodic laments.

Section C', the improvisatory expanse with aleatoric note groups that follows the composition's central segment, can be related to Picasso's deadly wounded horse. This animal, one of the artist's favorite images, is placed very near the center of the canvas. As Rudolf Arnheim notes, the suffering horse serves Picasso as an exemplary bearer of emotion.[29] Covered with wounds, pierced by a lance, it throws back its head and emits a death-scream with a dagger-like tongue. With legs in different stages of collapse, it can no more escape death than the burning woman, a fact reflected in the music by the recurrence of the backdrop of the six statically reiterated pitches Steffens first equated with Szpetecki's "congealed loneliness."

Before turning to the interpretation of the remaining musical section in light of components in Picasso's painting, I must comment on the unique insert mentioned above. It occurs at the end of section B' and contains a striking self-quotation. Three trombones in unison play a Hebrew hymn that Steffens had first used, in the same tonality and timbre, in his opera *Eli*, composed in 1965-1967. In this musical setting of Nelly Sachs's "mystery play about the suffering of Israel," the hymn, rendered in an untexted instrumental version, surrounds the central scene. For all who know that the silently present words speak of the prophet Elijah who will soon arrive with the Messiah, the hymn in the opera tells of hope, even for victims of the Holocaust. The fact that the hymn is played by three trombones in unison— a modern sonic equivalent to the sound of the *shofar*, well-established in countless works of Western classical music as a musical signifier of God's

---

[29]Rudolf Arnheim, *The Genesis of a Painting: Picasso's Guernica* (Berkeley, CA: Univ. of California Press, 1962), 42, 44.

Ming I – Die Verwundung des Hellen

judgment[30]—opens up the perspective of divine endorsement of such hope. Transferred from the opera into *Guernica*, the musical passage also alludes to the mystery play's implicit protagonist, the innocent boy Eli whom a Nazi soldier arbitrarily clubbed to death. This allows a connection to the mother-and-child group at the far left in Picasso's painting, a bare-breasted woman crouching on the floor, holding the limp body of her dead child in her lap and crying out her loss. Her gaze and scream are directed toward the triumphant bull, the only figure in the painting that is intact, unscarred, without pain. This image can easily be recognized in section B', the context into which the *Eli* quotation is inserted. The absence of aleatoric uncertainty in the music corresponds with the bull's being above suffering, while the fact that the laments have been moved to section A' and the reassuring D-major chords of the initial B section are skirted here hints at the bull's unsympathetic sternness.

The freely symmetrical layout of the musical composition thus corresponds to the painting's macrostructure, which can be read in at least two ways. The diagonal lines rising to the tip of the woman's lamp from the dead child's broken neck on the one side and from the fleeing woman's swollen knee on the other have led many art historians to discover similarities with a Greek temple frieze. This view is endorsed by the symmetrically extended limbs: the warrior's arm and oversized hand at the bottom left and the fleeing woman's hind leg and oversized foot at the bottom right. Others discern a medieval Christian model, that of the triptych, which the grouping of the figures seems to suggest. The imaginary side panel on the right comprises three figures that are very much in motion: the burning woman, the fleeing woman and the woman thrusting her lamp through an opening. By contrast, the figures on the left—the bull, the crouching mother mourning her dead child, and the dismembered warrior—are static. The largest figure near the central axis is Picasso's allegory for the "suffering people," the mortally wounded horse. It is entwined with both side panels in that the outer groups each reach into the center with a single arm: at the top, that of the woman with the lamp, at the bottom, that of the dismembered

---

[30] In religious music, three trombones were often employed as a latter-day emblem of the angelic instruments announcing the Last Judgment, which Luther, in his translation of the Bible, had rendered as trombones; see the trombone statements with religious connotations in Mozart's edition of Handel's *Messiah* as well as in his own Requiem, in the final movement of Beethoven's Ninth Symphony, Berlioz's *Grande messe des morts*, etc. In addition to its characteristic use in church music, the triple trombone was also featured as a timbral signifier of divine pronouncements in opera: see the oracle scene of Gluck's *Alceste*, the "sacrifice" scene in Mozart's *Idomeneo*, the judgment-at-supper scene in Mozart's *Don Giovanni*, and many others.

warrior with broken sword and flower. I find it tempting to read this central portion of Picasso's "triptych" as a secular version of the Crucifixion. This somewhat daring interpretation may be supported by two components in Picasso's painting that do not find their correspondence in musical sections. One is the little bird that, close to the horse's tongue, seems nailed to the wall with a knife and calls out in agony. The other is the electric bulb in an almond-shaped lamp shade surrounded by black and white rays that, placed above the agonizing horse and bird, evokes a secularized eye of God.

The External Sources of *Ming I* and Their Role in *Guernica*

The inner correspondence between Steffens's musical and Picasso's visual components is confirmed by external interpretive information. For Picasso's painting, this information stems from his interview with Jerome Seckler published in *New Masses* in March 1945, in which the artist admits that while his paintings are normally not symbolic, the depiction in *Guernica* is indeed allegorical. The horse represents the people, he specifies; the bull is not fascism in particular so much as brutality and darkness in general— the authoritative tyrant and figure of evil in the *I Ching*'s hexagram no. 36 whose music provides some of the most oppressive sounds in this composition on the suffering at Guernica.

To pursue the spiritual bond Steffens creates musically between the suffering of Israel (as evoked on Nelly Sachs's poem) and that of the people from a small Basque town (visually commemorated in Picasso's mural), I have inserted the words found inscribed into the score of *Ming I* against the corresponding segments of Steffens's *Guernica*, with the aim of reading the composer's presumed interpretation of Picasso's painting in the light of central notions in the poems of Elfriede Szpetecki and Nelly Sachs.

The first of the quotations Steffens inscribes into the score of *Ming I* is connected with music heard at the outset of *Guernica*'s section C. In the piano quartet, Steffens writes "Israel" against the contour with which the solo viola opens this rhythmically undetermined second section. If my reading of the relationship between music and visual imagery is correct, the suffering of the people for whom the composer has such a strong empathy is thus associated with Picasso's image of a woman burning to death in a crumbling house. In the symmetrically corresponding *Guernica* section C', the first melodic contour imports from the quartet the connotation "struck by the divine wound," an imagery that seems to endorse the association between this section and Picasso's suffering horse and perhaps even my cautious interpretation of this animal as a secular version of the Crucified. Both

Ming I – Die Verwundung des Hellen

sections develop against the above-mentioned harp-and-celesta backdrop of irregularly reiterated pitches, which Steffens's inscription in *Ming I* describes as "a glassy solitude that congeals." Finally, B'_1—the first portion of the bisected section B', comprising the nine measures that precede the hymn quoted from the opera *Eli*—is based on material that, according to the composer's excerpt from Sachs's poem at this point in the piano quartet, depicts an "abyss of light." The evocation of the abyss as a metaphor of an amoral attitude can be associated with the bull, Picasso's allegory of brutality and darkness; the specification "of light" points to the lamp-bearing woman, the other figure in the painting apparently not subjected to suffering.

Together, all these readings underscore the various references to suffering people. Steffens's "elegy," heard as a multi-faceted lament over the death and destruction inflicted by the Nazis upon the population of the town of Guernica and corresponding in its intent and intensity to the desperate outcry in Picasso's painting, also echoes the large-scale experience of the Nazis' primary victim, the Jewish people. The viola, soloist in this unusual concerto, is reputed to have the most "human" voice among all orchestral instruments. Its timbral quality adds to the gripping effect produced by both compositions.

PART III

Intermedial Representations and Reflections in Musical Expressionism

Kunstkritik and *Tonmalerei* in the Tone Poems of Richard Strauss

Mathieu Schneider

How can art inspire art? How can one explain the propensity of an artist to use the work of another artist as a model for the creation of his own work? This question is not peripheral and can therefore not be eluded by theorists. In the 1980s, Gisbert Kranz published an exhaustive study in three volumes about poems and prose texts based on a pictorial model[1] in which he catalogs more than 5000 works devoted to the so-called *ekphrasis*. This term literally denotes the property of a work of art to express itself vividly or, in our case, to take a picture as a starting point for the creation of a new work in another medium.

What is, in this case, the relationship between the work and its model? Is the former just a "translation" of the latter? Or does it tell us more? The question has been answered in the case of the cross relation between music and painting by several authors, mainly by Siglind Bruhn in her articles and books on what she calls "musical ekphrasis."[2] But a similar question arises in the domain of the interface between literature and music. Unlike in the case of painting and music, many musical genres are relevant here: opera of course, lieder (mainly in the 19th century) and, after 1850, the tone poem.

This study focuses on the particular question of the exact role of the literary work in the tone poems of Richard Strauss. In 2005, I published a book that took this question as the starting point of a discussion on both the nature of the relationship between literature and music in the symphonic works of the end of the 19th century in Germany and Austria and the existence of a gap between the two main genres in orchestral music of this

---

[1] Gisbert Kranz, *Das Bildgedicht: Theorie, Lexikon, Bibliographie* (Köln: Böhlau, 1981-1987).

[2] See above all Siglind Bruhn, *Musical Ekphrasis: Composers Responding to Poetry and Painting* (Hillsdale, NY: Pendragon Press, 2000); "A Concert of Paintings: 'Musical Ekphrasis' in the Twentieth Century," *Poetics Today* 22/3 (2001): 551-605; and *Das tönende Museum* (Waldkirch: Gorz, 2004).

time: the symphony and the tone poem.[3] One of the results of this study was that the conception developed by the romantic theories of art, from Schlegel to Schopenhauer, rules out the assumption that music can only be the translation of its model into sounds. The supremacy of music among the arts, justified by its very exceptional position as a non-conceptual expressive form, does not allow it to be no more than a copy of another work of art. I use Walter Benjamin's doctoral thesis on the concept of *Kunstkritik* in German romantic theories as a model of comprehension for the relationship between the arts in general[4] and music and literature in particular. Schlegel's concept of an "universal and progressive" poetry,[5] as he develops it in his fragments and his *Windischmann-Vorlesungen*, is the frame of Benjamin's theory. Since there is no absolute form in the arts and since every form is simply a vain attempt to reach the Absolute by creating an improved "higher" form, romantic poetry may be called "progressive" and can be seen as a linear progression to still better forms and still better works. If a given work takes another work as a model, then one might regard it, says Schlegel, as a *critique* of the latter, which is taken to mean that the second work is an attempt to recast the same content in a better form. The adjective "better" is here to be understood in an objective, not in a subjective way, since the "better" form is one that is able to show or communicate more of the content than any other. The "better" form can then be interpreted as the "more accurate" one (the most accurate form would logically be the "Absolute" itself, i.e., the Truth).

Both Liszt's main essay on program music, which is actually a review of Hector Berlioz's *Harold in Italy* (its title is *Berlioz und seine Harold-Symphonie* [1855]), and Richard Strauss's commentaries on his own tone poems take up more or less this theoretical frame. Nevertheless, this discussion may not explain the musical form of all the nine tone poems Strauss composed between 1888 and 1915. If one considers that the music in the tone poems is entirely a critique of the literary work upon which it is based, one must then infer that music is a kind of sublimation of literature, a means to present the real (i.e., *true*) content of the literary work and then—as music is a non-conceptual art—its abstract or, as I will show, its "psychological" and inner content.

---

[3] Mathieu Schneider, *Destins croisés. Du rapport entre musique et littérature dans les œuvres symphoniques de Richard Strauss et de Gustav Mahler* (Waldkirch: Gorz, 2005).

[4] Walter Benjamin, *Der Begriff der Kunstkritik in der deutschen Romantik* (Frankfurt: Suhrkamp, 1973).

[5] Friedrich Schlegel, *Kritische Friedrich-Schlegel-Ausgabe*, vol. 2: "Charakteristiken und Kritiken 1 (1796-1801)," ed. Hans Eichner (Munich etc.: Schönigh; Zurich: Thomas, 1967), 182.

Kunstkritik *and* Tonmalerei *in the Tone Poems of Richard Strauss*

This argument reaches its limit where tone poems (especially Strauss's latter ones, *Don Quixote*, *Ein Heldenleben* [A Hero's Life] and *Eine Alpensinfonie* [An Alpine Symphony]) contain purely descriptive moments: the flying carpet in *Don Quixote*, the alphorn motif in *A Hero's Life*, and the cowbells in *An Alpine Symphony*. Can one argue that these elements also form part of the system of *Kunstkritik*? And if so, in which sense? Or would it mean that there are two types of tone poems, those that "criticize" (or improve on) their model and those that "describe" them by translating them into sounds?

What is at stake in this discussion is not only the relevance of an aesthetic theory, but rather a polemical debate concerning absolute music. If the descriptive elements in tone poems are external moments of the musical form, if they do not act as "critical" elements as Benjamin understands them, Hanslick's partisans would have been right to debase program music and to liken tone poems to vulgar transcriptions of literary works. In the opposite case, music would keep its autonomy and tone poems might well be regarded as "absolute" music (both in Hanslick's and in Schlegel's interpretation of the word).

This chapter is divided into two parts. In the first, the discussion focuses on the concept of *Kunstkritik*. On the theoretical level, I aim to show what makes Benjamin's and Schlegel's theory relevant for tone poems in general and for those of Richard Strauss in particular; on the practical level, I apply this theory to one specific tone poem. The second part lists all the descriptive elements contained in Strauss's tone poems in the interest of checking whether or not they may be considered as "critical" elements.

The answers to these questions are not only to be found in the works themselves, but also in the larger origins of descriptive music, especially Beethoven's. Indeed, the relatively long tradition of the concept of "tone painting" (*Tonmalerei*) had given some special features of orchestral music a more or less precise signification, so that descriptive elements gradually acquired a symbolic meaning. By studying the symbolic meanings attached to the elements I list below, it will be possible both to define their exact role in the musical form and to shed new light on the legacy of the romantic symphony in Strauss's tone poems.

The discussion on *Tonmalerei* and *Kunstkritik* will thus open new perspectives in the debate of absolute music versus program music on the one hand and the symphony versus the tone poem on the other.

Tone Poems as Critiques of their Literary Models

In his essay on *Kunstkritik*, Walter Benjamin takes Fichte's theory of science (*Wissenschaftslehre*, 1794) as his point of departure and explains how Schlegel transposes the system of reflection developed by Fichte to the domain of the arts in order to provide the theoretical framework for the so-called "progressive" poetry.[6] Indeed, Fichte asserts that knowledge results from an iterative process in which each thought on a given subject becomes itself the subject of another thought that will later become in its turn the subject of another thought. Proceeding in this way, knowledge grows continuously and increases until it reaches—but this goal is purely theoretical—"absolute" knowledge, which is in fact the Truth. In this way Fichte creates a complex system in which all the branches of science interact with each other and in which they all contribute to the improvement of general knowledge.

Schlegel takes up this conception of science, for example in his novel *Lucinde*, and transposes it to the arts, because for Schlegel and the theorists of the first German Romanticism the subject of the reflection system created by Fichte should not be the self, but Art. Since Art becomes a medium of knowledge, the iterative process of reflection may be applied to it. Schlegel thus allots a completely new function to Art, whose aim is not so much an Absolute *in general*, but an Absolute *in the Arts*. This does not mean that Schlegel denies the role of science in the process of knowledge, but rather that he admits another way of reaching the Truth, a way that starts from and goes through the arts. Each work of art is itself intended to become the subject of another work of art, and the faculty leading from one work to the other, from one form to a higher one, is *Kunstkritik*.

This theoretical system may immediately explain two important features of romantic aesthetic: fragments and progressive poetry. When Schlegel in §206 of the *Athenaeum* fragments defines the Romantic (and fragmentary) work of art as a "hedgehog," he characterizes romantic art by its lack of totality. Whereas classical art tended to present the totality of the world in its forms, romantic art acknowledges the vanity of this venture and chooses to use fragmentary forms, which point at the totality of the world like the hedgehog's spikes. The progressive poesy of which Schlegel speaks in §116 of the *Athenaeum* fragments derives from the same theoretical system, since each work of art is supposed to be sublimated in another one. *Kunstkritik* provides a concatenation of forms (what I shall call a "continuum of forms") that leads after an infinite process to the Absolute in the arts.

[6] Detailed explanations of this subject are to be found in Schneider, *Destins croisés*, 27-48.

In the 1830s and 1840s, this theoretical system became the framework of a new conception of music. Schumann is the first German composer to refer to Schlegel and his colleagues of the Jena Circle in his early works for piano, especially those from the 1830s. In the symphonic genre, Liszt theorizes a new conception of music: program music, which actually had already been used by Berlioz in his *Fantastic Symphony* and in *Harold in Italy*. In his critical essay on the latter work, especially in the second part, which deals with the program in the music,[7] the Hungarian composer refers to the romantic theory of art in general and to two of its theorists in particular: E.T.A. Hoffmann and Jean Paul.[8] Schlegel and Fichte are neither quoted nor mentioned, but as the writings of Hoffmann and Jean Paul both have their roots in the philosophy developed in and around the Jena Circle, their influence on Liszt's thought is obvious. In fact, since he was convinced that music is the only way to express the truth of a feeling *immediately*, Liszt was aware of its very strong power in comparison to the other arts. In *Berlioz und seine Harold Symphonie*, he writes:

> They [the plastic arts] are not or only approximately capable of expressing their full intensity in an immediate manner, since they are forced to do so by means of images or comparisons. Music, by contrast, renders at once *the power and the expression of the emotion*; it is embodied, tangible essence of an emotion. Perceptible to our senses, it penetrates them like an arrow, a ray, a rope, a spirit, and fills our soul.[9]

Liszt thus links music to the quest for the Absolute in the arts. But this is clearly not enough to assert that the tone poem, in Liszt's theory, can be considered as a *Kunstkritik* of the literary work on which it is based. For this to be true it is necessary to demonstrate 1) that the tone poem is an authentic creation and not just a translation of another work, 2) that the tone poem presents the same content as its model but in a "higher" form, and 3) that the relationship between the model and the tone poem is mediated by what Benjamin termed as *Kunstkritik* and what Liszt calls the "poetic idea."

---

[7] Liszt, *Schriften* (Leipzig: Breitkopf & Härtel, 1910), Vol. 4, 101-126.

[8] Liszt, *Schriften* IV, 109-110.

[9] "Ihre volle Intensität unmittelbar ausdrücken können sie [die bildenden Künste] nicht oder nur annähernd, weil sie gezwungen sind, es durch Bilder oder Vergleiche zu tun. Die Musik dagegen gibt gleichzeitig *Stärke und Ausdruck des Gefühls*; sie ist verkörperte fassbare Wesenheit des Gefühls. Unseren Sinnen wahrnehmbar durchdringt sie diese wie ein Pfeil, ein Strahl, ein Tau, ein Geist und erfüllt unsere Seele." Cf. Liszt, *Schriften* IV, 107.

The authenticity of the tone poem and its independence from its model are guaranteed by the fact that the author of the tone poem is himself an artist: for Liszt, this artist was a *Dichter* (poet), from which he derived the name *"Tondichtung"* (tone poem) and *"Tondichter"* (designating both the composer of a tone poem and the romantic composer more generally). The tone poem was thus at the center of the romantic theory of music because the composer of music was identified with a composer of tone poems. Liszt considered the tone poem as an authentic creation and not as a servile transposition of another work into sounds.

Furthermore, in his text on Berlioz's *Harold in Italy*, he underlines the difference between a "normal" composer and a *Tondichter*. Whereas the first is a servant of music who obeys the laws and rules of the masters of the past and of their theories, the latter frees himself from his debts to the past and from everything that binds him to the tradition:

> Yet there is a great difference between the tone poet and the mere musician. While the former, in order to convey his impressions and the experiences of his soul, reproduces them, the latter handles, groups, and concatenates tones following certain rules and by playfully overcoming any difficulties, reaches new and daring, unusual and complex combinations. [...] Only the *poet* among composers is endowed with the power to break the fetters hindering the free upsurge of his thought and to widen the boundaries of his art.[10]

If the composer of tone poems is not a bad artist, but on the contrary a better and finer one, how can he then manage to retain his or her freedom and simultaneously be bound by the subject of the tone poem? In other words, how can the form of the tone poem be higher than that of its model? For Liszt, the answer lies in the autonomy of program music, since the tone poem has to be understood as a pure musical genre. In a very long sentence of his essay, Liszt recalls the arguments of the detractors of program music in the conditional. He then concludes by saying that all the arguments of his opponents would be justified if the music and its literary model merely combined instead of uniting, of *building together* a new and independent form:

---

[10] "Doch ist ein großer Unterschied zwischen dem Tondichter und dem bloßen Musiker. Während der erstere, um seine Eindrücke und Seelenerlebnisse mitzuteilen, diese reproduziert, handhabt, gruppiert und verkettet der zweite Töne nach gewissen traditionellen Regeln und gelangt darin höchstens mit spielender Überwindung von Schwierigkeiten zu neuen und kühnen, ungewöhnlichen und verwickelten Kombinationen. [...] Nur dem *Dichter* unter den Komponisten ist es gegeben, die den freien Aufschwung seines Gedankens hemmenden Fesseln zu zerbrechen und die Grenzen seiner Kunst zu erweitern." Cf. Liszt, *Schriften* IV, 124-125.

> These objections would have to be acknowledged as correct if in art, two forms that are different from one another permitted merely to be *combined*, not to be *united*.[11]

The clear contrast Liszt creates between the verb *verbinden* (to combine) and *vereinen* (to unite) proves that the subject is not just the shadow of the musical work or merely integrated into the musical form, but rather that it is taken up in a new form. Further into his discussion, Liszt recognizes therefore that artistic forms constitute a kind of *continuum*, which leads from the lowest form of art to the (unreachable) "Absolute in the arts":

> Does it [art] not, like nature, produce incremental structures that bind together, by means of mediating genres—genres that are necessary and naturally, therefore, worthy of life—the remotest realms and the most converse nuances?[12]

The second point of my argument, then, is clearly established.

The third point concerns the mediation between the tone poem and its model. In his essay on *Kunstkritik*, Walter Benjamin tries to explain how two works of the so-called "continuum of forms" are bound to each other. By doing so, he fills the gaps in Schlegel's fragmentary theory, as he reconstitutes the frame into which these theory belongs. For Benjamin, the medium of the reflection of forms (i.e., the way to produce a new form) is what he calls the "Idea of Art" (*Idee der Kunst*).[13] Only ideas may be able to create something new, and a reflection may only be produced by an idea. It follows that each form is the result of the action of the Idea of Art on a previous form.

The progressive process of the "continuum of forms" is also due to the permanent action of an idea that elevates every form of art to a higher one. In program music, many composers—among them Richard Strauss, whose tone poems are the topic of this chapter—considered that the creative element in tone poems was the "poetic idea." While Liszt in his relevant essay does not provide too many details describing its faculties, Richard

---

[11] "Diese Einwendungen würden als richtig anzuerkennen sein, wenn sich in der Kunst zwei voneinander verschiedene Formen nur *verbinden,* nicht aber *vereinen* ließen." Cf. Liszt, *Schriften* IV, 111.

[12] "Produziert sie [die Kunst] nicht, wie die Natur, stufenweise Gliederungen, welche die fernliegendsten Reiche und die entgegengesetzten Abstufungen durch vermittelnde Gattungen —die notwendig und natürlich, demnach *lebensberechtigt* sind—aneinander ketten?" Cf. Liszt, *Schriften* IV, 111.

[13] Benjamin, *Begriff,* 81-82.

Strauss accords the tone poem "the potential to create forms" (*formbildende Kräfte*).[14]

A very interesting discussion of the role the poetic idea plays can be found in Carl Dahlhaus's theses on program music. The German musicologist and theorist maintains that "nothing would be more inappropriate than to identify the program [of a tone poem], i.e., the text itself as it is printed in the score, with the poetic idea whose 'sensible appearance' (in Hegel's words) is the succession of the musical events."[15] Dahlhaus agrees entirely with Richard Strauss: for both authors, the poetic idea is nothing more than the element that creates a new and authentic musical form. For this reason, it is possible to assimilate both theoretical systems, the philosophical (Schlegel) and the musical one (Liszt, Strauss); the medium of the form is in the first case the Idea of Art and in the second case, the poetic idea. The similarities are quite evident: (1) in both cases, the medium is an idea; (2) this idea is a poetic force, which does not mean that it is a "literary" idea, but rather that it is an idea that can *create* something (the term *poetic* derives from the ancient Greek verb *poiein*, "to make," "to create"); (3) the sensible appearance of the idea is the form of the new work of art; and (4) the idea is in both cases a mediator between two forms and therefore the link between all the elements of the "continuum of forms." The main difference between the Idea of Art and the poetic idea lies in the latter's particular character: each work should have its *own* poetic idea, whereas the Idea of Art is the general idea producing all works of art. It is also possible to regard the poetic idea as a particularized Idea of Art, one that is applied to a particular work.

After these explanations, it is now possible to assert that the tone poem, in the theoretical system developed by the Romantic composers—above all Liszt and Richard Strauss—is a *Kunstkritik* of its model. Concerning the theory of the tone poem, I have so far referred primarily to Liszt simply because he is the only composer to have theorized his praxis.[16] Richard Strauss took up most of Liszt's principles and applied them in his works. In fact, Strauss recognized the relevance of Liszt's conception of a "continuum

---

[14] Strauss mentioned this during a private conversation to the musicologist Willy Schuh, who reports it in his article for the leading German encyclopedia of music. See Wilhelm Pfannkuch and Willi Schuh's entry "Richard Strauß" in Friedrich Blume, ed., *Die Musik in Geschichte und Gegenwart* (Kassel etc.: Bärenreiter, 1965), Vol. 12, Col. 1487.

[15] Cf. Carl Dahlhaus's "Thesen über Programmusik" in his essay collection *Beiträge zur musikalischen Hermeneutik* (Regensburg: Gustav Bosse, 1975), 188.

[16] One should except Richard Wagner, whose theory on program music could be a very interesting starting point as well. As it is more related to his own theories on music and especially on the musical drama, I would prefer to base my discussion essentially on those composers who wrote tone poems: Franz Liszt and Richard Strauss.

of forms," the necessity of finding new forms and the importance of program music. In his *Betrachtungen and Erinnerungen*, he writes:

> New thoughts have to search for new forms: this fundamental principle of Liszt's symphonic compositions, in which the poetic idea was in fact at once the element creating the form, became from then on the code of practice for my own symphonic works.[17]

The retrospective discussion on his early works (he is speaking here of the tone poems of the 1880s and 1890s) coincides with Liszt's conception of music. This is especially pertinent in the first sentence, in which Strauss acknowledges the necessity for composers of the "New German School" like himself to renew musical forms. At the same time, he was convinced that music could not deny its past and that it had to take the forms of the classical masters into account, particularly the sonata form as Mozart and Beethoven used it. Owing to this respect for tradition, Strauss believed that his position diverged from that of the other partisans of the "New German School"—composers and theorists like Franz von Hausegger, whom he described as "musicians of the expression" and contrasted with the formalists.[18]

Many analytical books on Liszt's compositions have shown that even in his most daring works such as the *Dante-Sonata*, he never abandons sonata form completely,[19] so that Strauss's position implies an inappropriate reception of Liszt's theoretical and musical works. Strauss also puts forth his view on the relationship between the new music and the German tradition in a way that is contrary to Liszt's. For Strauss, there are two "principles" in music: the poetic and the musical. In the 1890s, the only principle that interests him is the poetic one. In a letter to his friend Johann L. Bella on the 13 March 1890 he writes:

> The representatives of our local music are divided into two groups: one for whom music is "expression" and who treat it as a language as precise as the verbal language, albeit for things whose expression is denied to the latter; the others, for whom music is "sounding form" —i.e., they underlay the work to be composed with any general atmosphere (unthinkingly retaining the classical composers' form,

---

[17] "Neue Gedanken müssen sich neue Formen suchen—dieses Lisztsche Grundprinzip seiner sinfonischen Werke, in denen tatsächlich die poetische Idee auch zugleich das formbildende Element war, wurde mir von da ab der Leitfaden für meine eigenen sinfonischen Arbeiten." Cf. Richard Strauss, *Betrachtungen und Erinnerungen*, ed. Willi Schuh (Zurich: Atlantis, 1957), 210.

[18] See a letter to Ludwig Thuille dated 19 November 1890, in Franz Trenner, ed., *Richard Strauss – Ludwig Thuille. Ein Briefwechsel* (Tutzing: Hans Schneider, 1980), 115.

[19] See Márta Grabócz, *Morphologie des œuvres pour piano de F. Liszt* (Paris: Kimé, 1996).

or rather: no longer the form but the formula) and develop the resulting themes according to an entirely external musical logic, for which I, now that I recognize a poetic logic, lack all understanding. Program music: real music! Absolute music: its solidification with the help of a certain routine and craftsmanship accessible to any merely moderately musical person. The former: true art! The latter: artistry.[20]

Conversely in another letter, written to Hans von Bülow on the 24 August 1888,[21] the Bavarian composer opines that the musical and the poetic principles have to work together in the tone poem: *Don Juan* and *Macbeth* are both composed in this manner. The contradictions between both texts can be explained by the polemical context of the 1890s in Germany, when the country was divided into the New Germans and the Formalists. The young Strauss strove for recognition and was accepted by the first group.

For my discussion, the retrospective point of view of the mature Strauss is more relevant, because at the time when he wrote his memoirs (the *Betrachtungen und Erinnerungen* already quoted), the dispute was over. In this late text, one can read that there is no musical work that is not founded on both principles, the poetic and the musical:

> Our musical savants—I mention the two foremost names: Friedrich von Hausegger ("music as expression") and Eduard Hanslick ("music as shifting tonal form") have provided formulations that have since acquired the status of adversarial contrasts. This is wrong. They are two forms of musical creation that complement one another.[22]

---

[20] "Die Vertreter der hiesigen Musik teilen sich doch in zwei Gruppen, die einen, denen Musik "Ausdruck" ist und die sie als eine ebenso präcise Sprache behandeln wie die Wortsprache, aber allerdings für Dinge, deren Ausdruck eben der letzteren versagt ist. Die anderen, denen die Musik "tönende Form" ist, d.h. sie legen dem zu componierendem Werke (die Form, d.h. nicht mehr Form, sondern Formel der Klassiker ruhig gedankenlos beibehaltend) irgend eine allgemeine Grundstimmung unter und entwickeln diese entsprungenen Themen nach einer ganz äußerlichen musikalischen Logik, für die mir heute, da ich nunmehr eine dichterische Logik anerkenne, schon jedes Verständnis fehlt. Programm-Musik: eigentliche Musik! Absolute Musik: ihre Verfestigung mit Hilfe einer gewissen Routine und Handwerkstechnik jedem nur einigermaßen musikalischen Menschen möglich. Erstere: —wahre Kunst! Zweite: Kunstfertigkeit!" Quoted after Willy Schuh, *Richard Strauss. Jugend und frühe Meisterwerke. Lebenschronik 1864–1898* (Zurich and Freiburg i. Br.: Atlantis, 1976), 154.

[21] See Willy Schuh and Franz Trenner, eds., "Hans von Bülow–Richard Strauss: Briefwechsel," *Richard-Strauss-Jahrbuch* (1954), 69.

[22] "Unsere Musikgelehrten – ich nenne die beiden Hauptnamen: Friedrich von Hausegger ("Musik als Ausdruck") und Eduard Hanslick ("Musik als tönend bewegte Form") – haben Formulierungen gegeben, die seither als feindliche Gegensätze gelten. Dies ist falsch. Es sind die beiden Formen musikalischen Gestaltens, die sich gegenseitig ergänzen." Strauss, *Betrachtungen*, 165.

For Strauss, *Kunstkritik* had to be limited by musical logic, i.e., by sonata form, as I now want to demonstrate.

The aim of this article is not to make an exhaustive analysis of all the tone poems of Richard Strauss,[23] but rather to show their theoretical background and its influence on musical form. That is why I give just a few examples of the practical application of the concept of *Kunstkritik* in Strauss's tone poems. To demonstrate that not only the tone poems based on another author's literary work but even those for which Strauss himself invented a narrative plot are influenced by the poetic and the musical principles, I will choose two tone poems that represent the two categories: *Macbeth* and *Tod und Verklärung* [Death and Transfiguration].

In the case of *Macbeth*, Strauss's first tone poem,[24] the composer states his source clearly in the title: *Macbeth* (*nach Shakespeares Drama*). There is thus no doubt that it was Shakespeare's tragedy which inspired Strauss's tone poem. How can one then see the action of *Kunstkritik* on musical form? In what way does Strauss's tone poem differ from its model? The answer to the second question is easy: as Strauss wrote a musical piece and Shakespeare a play, it is basically impossible to compare the two works.

At the same time, Strauss writes some commentaries into his score that may help beholders to compare the plot of Shakespeare's drama with the underlying "plot" of the tone poem. These commentaries or remarks contain two names: Macbeth (m. 6) and Lady Macbeth (m. 66). Beyond these names, there is no other reference to a character of the play. Strauss himself writes in his memoirs that the tone poem was to conclude with a great triumphal march of Macduff, but he ultimately chose to remove this from the final version of the score since, as he says, an overture on the subject of Egmont can end with the triumphal march of Egmont but a tone poem on Macbeth cannot close with a triumphal march of Macduff.[25] This indicates clearly that for Strauss, the tone poem is nothing other than a portrait of a very few characters. Strauss took up the model of Liszt's *Faust Symphony*, a work of which he writes:

---

[23] See Schneider, *Destins croisés*, 143-282 and 409-458.

[24] *Macbeth* is listed with the opus number 23, whereas *Don Juan* is known as opus 20, although its composition was started before that of *Macbeth*. Willy Schuh writes that the first sketches of *Macbeth* are dated 1887, whereas Walter Werbeck believes that Strauss may already have begun composing the work in 1886. See Schuh, *Jugend*, 148 and Walter Werbeck, *Die Tondichtungen von Richard Strauss* (Tutzing: Hans Schneider, 1996), 238.

[25] See Strauss, *Betrachtungen*, 211.

> The real dramatic action only takes place in "Mephisto," and only this is, after all, the "symphonic poem"; the two great characters of Faust and Gretchen, by contrast, are so complex that their *representation* along with the dramatic development was not possible in a single movement. Therefore as an exposition the two largest atmospheric pictures ever written ("Faust" actually includes a certain development), and the real dramatic embroilment in "Mephisto."[26]

In *Macbeth* there are only two main characters, whereas Strauss interprets Liszt's *Faust Symphony* as consisting of two symphonic movements on Faust and Gretchen and one "genuine" tone poem on Mephisto. The quoted letter to L. Thuille was written approximately a month after the Weimar premiere of *Macbeth* conducted by the composer himself. Is it then possible to see in this commentary a key to the form of *Macbeth*?

Strauss left another indication in the score. After the indication "Lady Macbeth" in m. 66, he quotes the fifth scene of the first act of Shakespeare's play, when Lady Macbeth says:

> Hie thee hither, that I may pour my spirits in thine ear, and chastise with the valour of my tongue, all that impedes thee from the golden round, which fate and metaphysical aid doth seem to have thee crown'd withal.

The first sentence is probably the most relevant for my argument. Why does Strauss choose to quote this particular sentence? In my opinion, he does so because the sentence emphasizes the importance of Lady Macbeth in the play, owing to her faculty to change her husband's mind and to influence him. Her tongue speaks and Macbeth's ear hears it. The subject of the tone poem is probably contained in this single quotation. It is not a translation of Shakespeare's drama scene by scene and act by act, but rather the description of the inner conflict that torments Macbeth and leads him to his own death.

The working of *Kunstkritik* is quite obvious here. The extensive form of Shakespeare's drama in five acts is reduced to a short plot that consists apparently of the conflict between Macbeth and Lady Macbeth, which is in fact Macbeth's inner conflict between his moral values and his desire to accede to the throne. A *Kunstkritik* shortens and concentrates the plot by

---

[26] "Die eigentliche dramatische Handlung geht ja erst im Mephisto vor sich und der ist ja auch erst die "sinfonische Dichtung"; die beiden großen Typen des Faust und des Gretchen sind dagegen so complicirt, dass ihre *Darstellung* nebst der dramatischen Entwicklung in einem Satze gar nicht möglich war. Daher als Exposition die beiden größten Stimmungsbilder, die je geschrieben (der Faust hat ja allerdings in sich auch eine gewisse Entwicklung), und die eigentliche dramatische Verwicklung im Mephisto." Strauss in a letter to Ludwig Thuille dated November 1890; cf. Schuh and Trenner, *Briefwechsel*, 115.

"psychologizing" it. The real subject of Strauss's tone poem, then, is the psychology of Macbeth. As in Liszt's *Faust Symphony*, there is just one character in the tone poem: Mephisto by Liszt, Macbeth by Strauss.

Liszt theorizes the "psychologization" of the plot in his essay on *Harold in Italy*, where he underlines the importance of what he called "the philosophical epos" (*die philosophische Epopöe*) in the making of a tone poem. According to Schlegel and to Liszt, the "continuum of forms" leads to a higher form, which is closest to the unreachable Absolute in the Arts and acts as a kind of "model" (although the infinite process of *Kunstkritik* excludes any form of model since the arts should be released from any canons). The higher literary form is the novel, as Schlegel asserts in the 252nd fragment of the *Athenaeum*. In music, Liszt analyses the history of vocal music since the beginning of the oratorio and of the opera and concludes that their texts belong mostly to the genre of what he calls the "antique epos" (*antikes Epos*)[27]. As the musical possibilities, mainly those of the orchestra, had increased during the classical period and the beginning of the 19th century, Liszt proposes to renew the musical forms by referring to the new kind of epos that was created by the Early Romantic writers (Goethe and Lord Byron especially) and spread throughout the whole continent in the first half of the 19th century. This new kind of epos was related to the Romantic form of the novel, and Liszt called it the "philosophical epos." The absolute models of this genre for him were Goethes's *Faust*, Byron's *Cain* and *Manfred*, and Adam Mickiewicz's *Dziady*.[28] The main difference between the antique and the new epos lies in their subject matter, which Liszt defines as follows:

> The basis and the purpose of the poem [the philosophical epos] is no longer the representation of the hero's deeds, but the representation of affects acting in his soul. The goal is to show how the hero thinks, much rather than how he behaves.[29]

One detects here a theoretical justification of the "critical" transformation of Shakespeare's drama into a psychological plot in Strauss's tone poem (the so-called "Darstellung von Affekten"). *Kunstkritik* may then be likened to a sort of "romanticization" of the original play through its musical setting. The antique epos becomes a modern epos in Strauss's work. What, one may ask, is the consequence for the musical form of the tone poem?

[27] Liszt, *Schriften* IV, 127.

[28] Liszt, *Schriften* IV, 128.

[29] "Grund und Zweck des Gedichtes [der philosophischen Epopöe] ist nicht mehr die Darstellung von Taten des Helden, sondern die Darstellung von Affekten, die in seiner Seele walten. Es gilt weit mehr zu zeigen, wie der Held denkt, als wie er sich benimmt." Cf. Liszt, *Schriften* IV, 129.

Strauss always insisted on the necessity to reconcile the musical and the poetic logics. In his first tone poem, he chooses two main themes associated with the two characters of the plot. As usual in sonata form, the first theme, the "masculine" one, is attributed to Macbeth and the second, the "feminine" one, to his wife. Had Strauss chosen more characters, thereby conserving the structure of Shakespeare's drama, he would not have had the possibility to reconcile the subject's logic with that of the music. When Schumann claimed in 1838 that sonata form was no longer able to present the (new romantic) content that composers wanted for their works, he anticipated Liszt's theories on program music and its necessity to find new rules. Liszt, however, did not abandon sonata form completely but tried to organize it in a way that allowed him to present the content of the "philosophical epos."[30] As already mentioned above, he divides his *Faust Symphony* into three movements, depicts the character of Faust and Gretchen in the two first movements and brings all the themes to a "dramatic" development in the last movement called "Mephisto."

Strauss, very much impressed by this work, adopts its principles in his *Macbeth* but integrates all the three parts of Liszt's symphony in one single movement structured in sonata form. After an introduction (mm. 1-5), he offers a musical description of Macbeth's noble and self-confident character using several motifs in 4/4 time and D minor (mm. 6-65) before turning to F major and 3/4 time to describe in sounds the duplicity and deceitfulness of Lady Macbeth (mm. 66-122). The development (mm. 123-323) is the dramatic moment of the form since it is here that he reinforces the idea of the Shakespeare quotation, namely, that the tone poem portrays nothing more than the inner conflict of Macbeth. The section shows Macbeth's reaction to his wife by continuously changing the character of Macbeth's motifs and themes.

Strauss's quotation from Shakespeare's drama contains interesting perspectives for the interpretation of the musical form. The excerpt specifies that Lady Macbeth pours her spirit through her *tongue* into Macbeth's ear. Strauss realizes this in his tone poem by giving each character a musical "framework" or "language" (i.e., in this special case, a meter and a rhythm) and by attributing motifs to them that can be transposed from one "language" to the other. More specifically, the feminine character of Lady Macbeth sounds in ternary 3/4 time, while Macbeth has motifs in a binary 4/4 meter. Macbeth's main motif, however, carries an accent that allows it to be heard in 3/4 time (see Fig. 1) since the fourth quarter-note in the first bar is stressed, so that the seven beats of this motif are divided into 3 + 3 + 1 and could therefore be integrated into 3/4 measures.

---

[30] See Grabócz, *Morphologie*, 160-162.

FIGURE 1: Macbeth's main motif (mm. 6-7) in the horns

The same feature is to be found in Lady Macbeth's main motif (Fig. 2), for which Strauss wrote a seemingly ternary music with a de facto binary stress pattern. The accent on the second eighth-note in m. 2 suggests that the first four beats may be divided as 2 + 2 and not 3 + 1, both because the tie linking the A across the bar line makes an emphasis on the first eighth-note of the second measure impossible and because the slur over the first four beats and the accent on the last eighth-note (making it sounds as if it were the anacrusis of the second part of the motif, also grouped by a slur) implies a division of the whole into 4 + 4. The only feature confirming the written 3/4 time is the half-note at the very end, which corrects the 4 + 4 division and suggests 4 + 5. The total number of beats, 9, is not divisible by 4 but by 3.

FIGURE 2: Macbeth's main motif (mm. 66-68) in the flutes and clarinets

This adaptability of both motifs is used by Strauss in the development of the sonata form, for it allows each character to speak (through his *tongue*) in the "language" of the other. The best example is certainly after bar 161, when Lady Macbeth's main motif is played by the woodwinds and the strings, *appassionato* and *forte*, in B major. The arrival of this motif after the lyric transformation of Macbeth's main motif (ex 3) in Lady Macbeth's meter (3/4)[31] is obviously the starting point of Macbeth's inner conflict, because in the following measures (173-181), one hears different motifs of Macbeth (a lyric one and another that is dark and dismal) which are played successively in 3/4 and 4/4 (Fig. 4).

---

[31] Gabriela Hanke-Knaus calls this the second theme in the exposition. This is unconvincing as it is clearly related to Macbeth's main motif, while the second theme of a movement in D minor is more likely to sound in F major. See G. Hanke-Knaus, *Aspekte der Schlußgestaltung in den sinfonischen Dichtungen und Bühnenwerken von Richard Strauss* (Tutzing: Hans Schneider, 1995), 33-35.

FIGURE 3: Macbeth's lyrical motif, derived from his main theme (mm. 123-124)

FIGURE 4: the conflict between Macbeth's two motifs in mm. 175-178[32]

[32] Richard Strauss, *Macbeth* (London etc.: Eulenburg, 1980 [1904]), 37.

These measures can be interpreted as the conflict between the ideas suggested by Lady Macbeth to her husband and symbolized by the lyric transformation of Macbeth's main motif and Macbeth's authentic, somber character as it is represented by the motif in the cellos and double basses in the 4/4 time. In this way, Strauss creates in this part of the development the proper dramatic moment of the tone poem. While the exposition of the sonata form was nothing but a description of the two characters, the development is the moment in which the conflict becomes an inner one. The intention is clearly to portray that the irruption of Lady Macbeth's *appassionato* motif destabilizes Macbeth and reinforces the opposition between his two motifs.

Strauss uses the same feature just after this section of the development, when Lady Macbeth's motif returns in m. 182 (now *furioso*), and still later in m. 202, when it sounds *sempre più furioso*.[33] Each time, these irruptions of Lady Macbeth are followed by a strong opposition from Macbeth's motif. The psychological character of the music is obvious here; it confirms my interpretation of the Shakespeare quotation in the score. The approach of *Kunstkritik* allows the tone poem to be based on a literary work without simply transposing it into sounds, but instead giving the drama a new interpretation. Not only the form of the literary model is changed, but also its content, with regard to the focus on psychological elements, as Liszt suggests in his praise of the "philosophical epos." Among all of Richard Strauss's tone poems, *Macbeth* is therefore the one in which the action of *Kunstkritik* and the necessity to reconcile the poetic logic with the musical tradition is the most obvious.

Macbeth is not, however, the only tone poem by Richard Strauss to have been composed in this Lisztian manner. Similar features can be found in each of the nine tone poems from *Macbeth* to *An Alpine Symphony*. I will give just one more example. In *Don Juan*, Strauss quotes two stanzas of a poem by Nicolaus Lenau,[34] considered by its author as *dramatisches Gedicht*. The description as a "dramatic poem" is the same as that of Lord Byron's *Manfred*, which Liszt considered as the archetype of the philosophical epos. Indeed, Lenau's poem does not tell us the story of Don Juan, as does, for instance, the libretto of Mozart's opera, but focuses entirely on the hero's feelings, impressions, and tragic fate. Furthermore, the three stanzas Strauss reproduces in the score are brought together to form a long monologue

---

[33] For more details, see Schneider, *Destins croisés*, 224-237.

[34] Reproduced in *Richard Strauss Edition* (Vienna: Verlag Dr. Richard Strauss GmbH & Co. KG, 1999), Vol. XX, 354.

spoken by Don Juan. Should one therefore interpret Strauss's tone poem as a long monologue? The poem Strauss quotes and the aesthetic context to which his tone poems belong would seem to confirm this.

Conversely, the musical form he chooses, the rondo, suggests an interpretation of the work as a "philosophical epos" in music. In fact, the rondo's two couplets (the first in B major, mm. 90-169, and the second in G major, mm. 197-312) clearly stand for two of Don Juan's beloved women owing to their very strong lyrical character. But like the irruptions of Lady Macbeth's motif in the development of *Macbeth*, these two couplets produce changes in the following refrain.[35] This means that Don Juan, whose unstable and fiery character is depicted by the impetuous music of the refrain in E major, evolves after each meeting with a new woman.

The situation is similar to that of Macbeth. Furthermore, as in the latter work, the different characters (Don Juan and the women) are musically linked to each other. For example, the theme of the first couplet is still played during the refrain (mm. 41-49), so that even the "external elements" (the women) are seen from the hero's point of view. They belong to his own inner world and appear in the couplets as an emanation of it. The fact that Strauss, in the program of his tone poem, links three stanzas of Lenau's dramatic poem, thus creating a monologue, justifies the use of a musical form in which the relationship between the couplets and the refrain also suggests a big monologue of Don Juan. Strauss's *Don Juan* must be regarded as the reduction of Lenau's work to a monologue, whereas in Lenau's own version, the story has many characters; the composition is thus a case of musical *Kunstkritik*.

The focus on the hero's feelings and the concentration of the narrative plot in the musical work are two typical features of tone poems, features one finds in all other tone poems by Richard Strauss. Even in *Don Quixote*, whose literary model is quite overtly a kind of "adventure story," Strauss chooses to describe in his music the evolution of the hero's psychology rather than the incredible adventures he endures. The musical realization of such a "poetic idea"—as Strauss would have said—implies the use of a very specific form, which allows the composer to show this evolution. Strauss's choice is the variation form (actually, it is perhaps better described as a kind of "double variation form"), which shows the evolution of both Don Quixote and his servant Sancho Pansa.

---

[35] For more details, see James Hepokoski, "Fiery-Pulsed Libertine or Domestic Hero? Strauss's *Don Juan* Reinvestigated," in: Bryan Gilliam, ed., *Richard Strauss: New Perspectives on the Composer and His Work* (Durham & Londres: Duke University Press, 1992), 135–175. See also Schneider, *Destins croisés*, 184-199.

Musical logic is thus always present in the tone poem, although it may use several forms: sonata form in *Macbeth*, rondo form in *Don Juan*, and variation form in *Don Quixote*.

I have so far considered tone poems relying on literary works written by a person other than the composer: Shakespeare, Lenau, or Cervantes. Besides these, Strauss wrote several tone poems that do *not* have a specific poem or drama as their "subject"; *Death and Transfiguration*, *A Hero's Life*, and *An Alpine Symphony* are examples of this case. Can these tone poems be considered cases of *Kunstkritik*? If so, on which work does the critique act?

I have shown that Strauss, when choosing a specific work as the "subject" of a composition, sketches for himself some kind of "second subject" (not to be mistaken for the "program" of the tone poem).[36] This "second subject" is actually nothing other than a new presentation of the "real subject" (i.e., the literary work). In the case of *Macbeth*, the "second subject" would be a sort of reduced version of Shakespeare's drama, staging two main characters (Macbeth and his wife) and showing the conflict that Lady Macbeth's arguments inflicts her husband's psychology. The "program" of the tone poem, which in this case is the quotation from Shakespeare's drama, is just an indication for the listener and the musicians of what this "second subject" might be.

If one agrees that there is an intermediate stage between the literary work (the "subject") and the tone poem and that *Kunstkritik* acts principally in this first step between the "real" and the "second" subject, one may conclude that all the tone poems lacking a literary subject should be considered as belonging to the same class as those with a "real subject," *provided that the "second subject"* (which in these cases is, in fact, the only subject) *has the characteristics of a "philosophical epos."* By saying this, I suppose that *Kunstkritik* acts exclusively in the transformation of the subject and that the musical realization is just the projection of this transformed subject on the musical form, limited by what Strauss himself called the "musical logic." The examples of *Macbeth* and *Don Juan* have shown that this latter interpretation was right.

---

[36] A discussion of this topic took place in Germany in the 1970s, involving Carl Dahlhaus (see his *Thesen*), Detlef Altenburg ("Eine Theorie der Musik der Zukunft. Zur Funktion des Programms im symphonischen Werk von Franz Liszt," *Liszt-Studien* 1 [1977], 9–25), Hans Heinrich Eggebrecht ("Dichtung, Symphonie, Programmusik. Symphonische Dichtung," *Archiv für Musikwissenschaft* XXXIX [1982], 223–233), and Constantin Floros ("Grundsätzliches über Programmusik," *Hamburger Jahrbuch für Musikwissenschaft* 6 [1983], 9–29). For me it now seems clear that one should define the "subject" as the external work or the defined theme on which the tone poem is based, and the "program" as the text inserted in the score. Therefore, the "second subject" as I define it here would be some kind of "false subject," which is the result of the transformation (through the act of *Kunstkritik*) of the genuine subject.

Returning to those of Strauss's tone poems that lack any concrete literary work as their "real subject," it is possible to check the efficacy of my "*Kunstkritik* theory" by analyzing the narrative plot on which they are based. In all of them it is quite easy to show the link to the so-called "philosophical epos." In *Death and Transfiguration*, one might think that the subject of the work is the biography of an artist, because the program of the tone poem indicates this clearly. Actually, however, Strauss specifies that the life of this artist is told in a sort of flashback just before his death. And what the agonizing person recalls is neither the concrete events of his life nor his adventures, but his feelings. Strauss writes:

> [...] his childhood flashes past him, his youth with his *striving*, his *passions*, and then, while *pain* emerged once again, there appears to him the *light of his life's path*, the idea, the ideal that he has attempted to realize, to represent through art, but which he has not been able to accomplish since it was not to be accomplished by a human being.[37]

The words that are highlighted in the above quotation clearly endorse the psychological character of this biography. Here again, *Kunstkritik* is implicitly present in the tone poem insofar as the musical work transforms a biography into emotions and feelings.

The same happens in two other tone poems by Richard Strauss using a biography. In *A Hero's Life*, the hero is presented in his complex relations to his wife, his enemies, and the world in general, but as in *Don Quixote*, Strauss tries to describe the evolution of the hero's psychology rather than his adventures.[38] In *Domestic Symphony* or, as I will demonstrate, in *An Alpine Symphony*, the principles are similar. No actions are described, only feelings or ideas. This is characteristic of Romanticism and of the literature of that time. *Kunstkritik* may then be regarded as the way to make a subject "modern," but also as the way to make its setting in music possible—since music, in the romantic theories from Schopenhauer's *The World as Will and Representation* to Liszt's critique on *Harold* and Wagner's *Opera and Drama*, is the expression of feelings and ideas. Nevertheless, one finds in Strauss's tone poems some moments where a kind of "concrete music"

---

[37] "[...] seine Kindheit zieht an ihm vorüber, seine Jünglingszeit mit seinem *Streben*, seinen *Leidenschaften* u. dann, während schon wieder *Schmerzen* sich einstellen, erscheint ihm die *Leuchte seines Lebenspfades*, die Idee, das Ideal, das er zu verwirklichen, künstlerisch darzustellen versucht hat, das er aber nicht vollenden konnte, weil es von einem Menschen nicht zu vollenden war." Cf. Werbeck, *Tondichtungen*, 538.

[38] See the analysis of Strauss's sketchbooks in Franz Trenner, *Die Skizzenbücher von Richard Strauss* (Tutzing: Hans Schneider, 1977), 10 and in Schneider, *Destins croisés*, 115-117.

appears, with elements imitating the sounds of nature (birdsong, wind, etc.). The abstraction of the plot required by the tone poem is apparently not compatible with these concrete elements. How can we then explain that Strauss integrated some of them in his last tone poems?

The Role of *Tonmalerei* in the Structure of Tone Poems

Tonmalerei, the term used for descriptive music in baroque and classical theories, is the imitation of the concrete sounds of the world (mainly of nature) in a musical composition. In his *Musikalisches Lexikon* of 1802, Heinrich Koch defined it as the musical "imitation of some sounds or phenomena of inanimate nature, such as the thunder, the roughness of the sea, the rustle of the wind, etc.." Koch agrees that the similarities between music and these sounds allow the composer to integrate them in his or her work. However, Koch argues, a composer would corrupt the music if he or she "tried to make such descriptions, since the only object of music is to depict the impulses of the heart, and not to represent inanimate things."

Koch seems to contradict himself here, asserting on the one hand that *Tonmalerei* can exist in music and on the other hand that it is not its object. The problem is partially resolved in the last part of Koch's argument, when he admits that occasionally, *Tonmalerei* is "immediately followed" by the expression of a specific mood or that it may in and of itself express the "impulses of feelings."[39] Even if Koch's musical treatise was written almost eighty years before Strauss composed his tone poems, it asserts clearly that *Tonmalerei* and musical expression were not necessarily opposite elements of the musical aesthetic of that time, but rather that there are two ways to reconcile these elements: their immediate succession or the expressive coloration of a sound that is taken up later.

When Beethoven completed his *Pastoral Symphony*, about six years after the first publication of Koch's lexicon, he tipped the balance between *Tonmalerei* and expression of feelings in favor of the latter by specifying "*Mehr Ausdruck der Empfindung als Malerey*" (expression of sentiment rather than painting) under the title. For him, both aspects might form part of a symphony (at least of *his* conception of a symphony), but only the expression of sentiments is the genuine subject of the music. He thus

---

[39] See Heinrich Koch, *Musikalisches Lexikon, welches die theoretische und praktische Tonkunst encyclopädisch bearbeitet, alle alten und neuen Kunstwörter erklärt, und die alten und neuen Instrumente beschrieben, enthält* [Musical dictionary presenting in encyclopedic fashion the theoretical and practical art of setting music, explaining all artistic terms old and new, and describing the old as well as the new instruments] (Frankfurt: Hermann, 1802), 924.

completely agrees with Koch, and particularly with the second part of Koch's argument, when he asserts that the only object of music is to depict the impulses of the heart.

Beethoven gives us a practical application of Koch's theory in the second and in the fifth movements.[40] At the end of the second movement, he imitates the song of three birds—the nightingale, the quail, and the cuckoo in the flute, the oboe, and the clarinet respectively—without any orchestral accompaniment. This moment may be interpreted as simple *Tonmalerei*, in the sense Koch defined in his treatise. But as the German theorist suggests in his article, the onomatopoeic motifs are immediately followed by the strings presenting a perfect cadence in B major, which interrupts the song of the birds in bars 132-133 and leads to the end of the movement in a very peaceful atmosphere. The external element of birdsong is thus incorporated in the form of the movement (through the conclusive cadence) and linked to the emotion expressed by the quiet string orchestration and the smooth character of B major. According to Koch, this is the first of several ways to integrate *Tonmalerei* in a musical work.

In the fifth movement of the *Pastoral Symphony*, Beethoven offers a very good example of what is, according to Koch, the second possibility of reconciling *Tonmalerei* and the expression of feelings in music by endowing onomatopoeic components with genuine expression. At the very beginning of the "Hirtengesang" movement, a so-called *ranz des vaches* is played by the solo clarinet.[41] The motif is a sort of stylization of the famous *ranz* of Rousseau, whose fourth section in a ternary 3/8 time is close to Beethoven's theme; see Fig. 5. This relationship suggests that this theme may be considered as an external element, belonging to the area of *Tonmalerei*, a hypothesis confirmed by the movement title, "Hirtengesang. Wohltätige, mit Dank an die Gottheit verbundene Gefühle nach dem Sturm" (Herdsmen's song. Beneficent feelings combined with gratitude to the godhead after the

---

[40] More about this subject in Roland Schmenner, *Die Pastorale: Beethoven, das Gewitter und der Blitzableiter* (Kassel etc.: Bärenreiter, 1998), and in David Wyn Jones, *Beethoven: Pastorale Symphony* (Cambridge: Cambridge University Press, 1995). More generally about program and characteristic symphony at Beethoven's time, see Richard James Will, *The Characteristic Symphony in the Age of Haydn and Beethoven* (Cambridge: Cambridge University Press), 2002.

[41] A *ranz des vaches*—Beethoven uses the established French term rather than the German translation *Kuhreihen*—is a simple melody traditionally played on the horn by the Swiss Alpine herdsmen as they drove their cattle to or from the pasture. Among other classical composers making use of this evocative element are Rossini (in the overture to his opera *William Tell*), Berlioz (in the *Symphonie Fantastique*), Robert Schumann (in *Manfred*) and Wagner (in Act 3 of *Tristan and Isolde*)

storm). The wording specifies that the whole movement expresses "feelings" (*Gefühle*), suggesting by implication that the *ranz* might thus be the symbolic expression of one of them.

FIGURE 5: comparison between Rousseau's ranz and Beethoven's Hirtengesang

Rousseau
Allegro

Beethoven
dolce

At the beginning of the 19th century, the *ranz* stood for the representation of an idyllic nature and the genuine expression of the "bon sauvage," the "noble savage" introduced in the context of Rousseau's philosophy.[42] For many authors, this implied natural landscape was of course inhabited by God, as one reads for example in Goethe's diary of his journeys in 1779 through the Alps and through Switzerland and in the poems he wrote there.[43] The pleasant ("wohltätig") and religious ("mit Dank an die Gottheit") feelings to which Beethoven alludes in the title are symbolized by the *ranz* ("Hirtengesang") and then developed in the whole movement by the orchestra, which takes up the *ranz* theme and highlights it as the main theme of this finale.

Beethoven's *Pastoral Symphony* may be regarded as a prototype of the romantic symphony since it integrates into its classical structure elements of *Tonmalerei* whose chief aim it is to express feelings and moods in the two manners described in Koch's treatise. The titles of all movements indicate quite unequivocally that the subject of the symphony is the expression of feelings and not primarily the presentation of onomatopoeic elements. The first movement evokes pleasant and joyful feelings ("angenehme, heitere Empfindungen"), the second a "scene at the river" (confirming the relationship between birdsong and the imagined listener's sentiments), the third a merry gathering ("lustiges Zusammensein"), the fourth a "storm" (serving as

---

[42] More to this subject in Schneider, "La Suisse vue par les compositeurs romantiques," *Analyse musicale* 54 (Nov. 2006), 65–75.

[43] A pertinent example is the poem *Gesang der Geister über den Wassern*.

a symbol for the torments of the heart), and the fifth a pastoral and religious scene ("wohltätige, mit Dank an die Gottheit verbundene Gefühle").

Moreover, the symphony's complete title reads: *Pastoral-Sinfonie oder Erinnerung an das Landleben* (Pastoral Symphony or Remembrance of life in the country).[44] This is thus a case comparable to that of Strauss's *Death and Transfiguration* or *A Hero's Life*. In each of these compositions, the music tries to "tell" us a biographical story (or a part of a biography in Beethoven's symphony), but all the composer is able (or wants) to present is remembrances ("Erinnerungen"). These remembrances are always related to the feelings associated to them. When Beethoven recalls the song of birds, he remembers the quiet atmosphere of a brook and the inner peace he experienced. When the artist in *Death and Transfiguration* remembers his youth, he associates with this memory the fiery impulses of the heart felt at that time. This similarity between Beethoven and Strauss thus allows us to consider Beethoven's use of *Tonmalerei* as a model for the interpretation of the *Tonmalerei* in Strauss's tone poems.

Richard Strauss's first tone poems contain very few motifs that might be considered as *Tonmalerei*. *Macbeth, Don Juan, Death and Transfiguration*, and *Thus Spoke Zarathustra* are practically free of onomatopoeic themes. They should therefore be regarded as genuine tone poems in the strict tradition of Liszt. Only in *Till Eulenspiegels lustrige Streiche* (Till Eulenspiegel's merry pranks) is it possible to identify motifs that aim at an imitation of concrete sounds of daily life or at otherwise suggestive expressions. In a letter of 20 October 1895 to Franz Wüllner, Strauss notes that under the motif of Till's death in mm. 613-614 (F-G♭ in the bassoons and brass) could be written the words "Der Tod" (death).[45] Does this qualify as *Tonmalerei*? The two-note figure certainly does not constitute the description of a natural phenomenon; instead, the music may be trying to imitate the sound of the falling blade; this would explain Strauss's choice of a falling seventh for this motif.

In another moment in the score of *Till Eulenspiegel*, the use of *Tonmalerei* is even more evident. In Wilhelm Mauke's *Musikführer*, Strauss indicates that he imagined Till riding a horse through a crowd of old women in the market ("Hop! Zu Pferde mitten durch die Marktweiber").[46] Correspondingly, his music introduces a "riding" motif in the flutes and bassoons (mm. 143-144, see Fig. 6).

---

[44] Ludwig van Beethoven, *Symphonie Nr. 6 F-Dur* (Kassel: Bärenreiter Urtext, 2001), XVI.
[45] See Schuh, *Jugend*, 405.
[46] See Schuh, *Jugend*, 406.

FIGURE 6: Till's riding motif

Except for these two motifs, however, *Tonmalerei* is not present in the first group of Strauss's tone poems. The situation changes in the later tone poems, after *Thus Spoke Zarathustra*; onomatopoeic sections are prominent in *Don Quixote, A Hero's Life* and *An Alpine Symphony*. In *Don Quixote*, the seventh variation (mm. 515-525) is a transposition into sound of the 41st chapter of the second book of Cervantes's novel, in which the hero thinks that he is flying on a magic carpet, while he is in fact riding blindfolded on a wooden horse.[47] Strauss chooses a unique and somewhat fanciful orchestration by introducing the wind machine and the harp. Furthermore, he gives the woodwinds very fluid chromatic motifs that recall the whistling of the wind, and the strings play a huge arpeggio over four octaves, thus reinforcing the effect of this "flying carpet" music. The only technical device suggesting the concrete sound imagined in the context of flying, however, remains the wind machine, in the baroque tradition of the French "tragédies en machineries."

All these elements belong clearly to what Strauss called the "poetic logic." Only the theme of Don Quixote in the horns is part of the "musical logic," i.e., of the variation form. The other eleven measures of this short variation reproduce the patterns of the first measure as it was just described; even the bass remains on D, while the harmony changes, progressing from the tonic D (m. 515) to A♭ (m. 518) before returning step by step to D (m. 521).[48] Strauss did not choose this movement from D to A♭ (with an A♭-major triad in second inversion) at random: the exposition of Don Quixote's theme in the introduction of the tone poem (mm. 1-13) also leaves the tonic D major and modulates suddenly to A♭ major (moving first to the second

---

[47] There is no mention in Strauss's writings that the variation corresponds to this adventure in the book. In Arthur Hahn's guide for the concert (*Richard Strauss. Don Quixote* [Leipzig: Hermann Seemann Nachfolger, without date]) as well as in Erich H. Mueller von Asow (*Richard Strauss. Thematisches Verzeichnis* [Vienna and Wiesbaden: L. Doblinger, 1959], 218-219), the relationship is clearly established.

[48] Not all the steps are diatonic. For example, after A♭ (m. 518), the harmony reaches F♯ minor (m. 519).

inversion for the cadence) before returning to D major.[49] In other words, the variation form that Strauss mentions in the work's subtitle ("Fantastische Variationen") concerns not only the various changes in the thematic surfaces, but also the harmonic structure of each variation.

This was nothing new at Strauss's time. Haydn, Mozart, and Beethoven regularly preserved the framework of a theme, its harmonic progression and cadences, in all subsequent variations. (Only in length does Strauss divert from the models of Viennese Classicism, thus apparently destroying the theme's most conspicuous external aspect.) His reason for retaining the harmonic layout seems obvious, given that the D-A♭ progression serves as the symbol of the hero's madness. A♭ is actually the "wrong" step in the harmony since listeners expect the music to move from the tonic D to the dominant A. By does not reaching A, the music misses its target, as it were. This relationship between D and A♭ can be observed in nearly all variations, so that it is possible to interpret it as Don Quixote's madness: every adventure (i.e., every variation) is just another product of the hero's insanity.

This interpretation may also shed light on the subtitle of the tone poem: each variation is "fantastic" in that it creates its own world, by doggedly reproducing the "false" progression from D to A♭ and by describing at the same time a new but equally crazy situation. Through the variations of the initial theme, Strauss does not so much describe the adventures of Don Quixote themselves as the main character's psychological evolution (or non-evolution, since he remains mad).

The correlation of form and content corresponds with what Koch called the second option for reconciling *Tonmalerei* and an expression of sentiments in music: an external element is being used for the representation of a mood or a feeling. The sound of wind incorporated in the otherwise traditional instrumental music evokes here the hallucination Don Quixote experiences on his wooden horse; at the same time, it may suggest the Castilian hero's dreaming and carefree character. The constellation is reminiscent of that found at the beginning of the last movement of Beethoven's *Pastoral Symphony*, even though the signification of the onomatopoeic element is rather different.

---

[49] Strauss had used a similar process already in *Thus Spoke Zarathustra*, with an opposition between C major and B major. For details, cf. John Williamson, *Strauss: Also sprach Zarathustra* (Cambridge: Cambridge University Press, 1993), 90-91, and Astrid Sadrieh, "Konvention und Widerspruch. Harmonische und motivische Gestaltungsprinzipien bei Richard Strauss" (Bonn: PhD dissertation, 1995), 115. On *Don Quixote*, see also Graham H. Phipps, "The Logic of Tonality in Strauss's *Don Quixote*: A Schoenbergian Evaluation," *19th Century Music* IX/3 (spring 1986), 189–205.

A Hero's Life and *Don Quixote*, two works that Strauss regarded as counterparts of one another (he spoke of "Pendants"[50]), actually have many things in common: themes[51]—especially symbolic ones—and a certain conception of the hero. In both cases, the protagonist is rather an anti-hero, whose destiny it is either to die in his conflict with the world or to flee from human life and seek refuge in a dreamlike idyll.[52] And while there is no flying carpet in *A Hero's Life* and this tone poem allegedly deals with the life of a "hero," its protagonist is also one who has to fight against his opponents and who at the end prefers to remove himself from the world. The battle scene is characterized by the irruption of a fanfare that Strauss places behind the scene ("hinter der Scene"). This is clearly a symbolically fraught external theme whose function it is to express the hero's desire to fight.

There is another theme that might be associated with *Tonmalerei*; it appears in the closing section of the work. As in Beethoven's *Pastoral Symphony*, it is a typical *ranz des vaches*, played by the English horn (mm. 827-851) over a drone (C-G) sustained in the strings. Not only the drone, but also the theme is very similar to Beethoven's (Fig. 7).

FIGURE 7: the *ranz* in *A Hero's Life*

This *ranz* emerges immediately before the last section of the tone poem begins (mm. 851-926), a section that represents for Strauss the hero's escape to the idyll. (In his sketchbooks to *A Hero's Life*, one reads: "Da erfasst ihn Ekel, er zieht sich ganz in's Idyll zurück."[53] [At this point, he feels gripped by nausea and he retreats entirely into the idyll]). The sonic reference to herdsmen's serenity is thus located in exactly the same position as the *ranz* in *Don Quixote* (mm. 657-669), and it is equally played by the English horn, though not over a string drone. Here, Strauss superimposes the varied theme of Don Quixote.

How can one explain the role of these two *ranz* themes in the light of Koch's theoretical remarks and of Beethoven's praxis? It seems obvious that in both cases, the *ranz* has a symbolic function for the narrative plot (the

---

[50] See Schuh, *Jugend*, 475.

[51] See John Michael Cooper, "The Hero Transformed: The Relationship Between *Don Quixote* and *Ein Heldenleben* reconsidered," *Richard-Strauss-Blätter* (new series) XXX (Dec. 1993), 3–18.

[52] More of this new type of hero in Schneider, *Destins croisés*, 414-419.

[53] Trenner, *Skizzenbücher*, 10.

subject of the tone poem) as well as for the musical expression. In the plot, it indicates the pastoral moment in the story. In *A Hero's Life*, this occurs when the hero leaves the human world and decides to live by himself. To find a similar correspondence between Cervantes's book and the tone poem *Don Quixote* is much more difficult, particularly since we have no authorial information that would give us a clue. But one can guess that the short evocation of the pastoral theme symbolizes a peaceful dream or thought that Don Quixote has just before his death. Anyway, whenever the composer's contemporaries heard such a *ranz* tune, they associated it necessarily with something that had to do with the pastoral and with pure nature; for that reason alone, the *ranz* has obviously an important function in the plot.

In the larger context of the 19th-century symphony in general and the tone poem in particular, a genre aimed at describing feelings and moods rather than adventures or actions, the *ranz* must also have an expressive function. One the one hand, the characteristic orchestration and the typical repetitive patterns create a peaceful and quiet atmosphere. On the other hand, ever since Beethoven, Weigl, Liszt, and Wagner, tradition linked the *ranz* to evocation of exterior or interior idylls. The two aspects of this element of *Tonmalerei* and the fact that it refers precisely to a specific mood seem to suggest that composers employed it as an essential part of *Kunstkritik*.

These considerations would be incomplete without the remark that the *ranz* of *Don Quixote* is not, of course, heard here for the first time in this tone poem. Strauss uses it already earlier, in the second variation, where the music depicts the hero fighting against a flock of sheep (mm. 227-232, woodwinds). The variation comes across as a very modern piece of music, as Strauss employs many dissonances and a pointillist orchestration. One may conjecture that doing so, he tries to imitate the bleating of the animals. In other words, this variation in itself is a master piece of *Tonmalerei*. The *ranz* has here its usual symbolic function, telling listeners that the scene is taking place in the country. The musical allusion does here not assume any expressive role, for Don Quixote is fighting and thus not at all in a quiet and peaceful mood. This is suggested by the imitation of the bleating sheep, whose dissonances and orchestration convey the fighting hero's distress. With its two elements, the *ranz* and the music of the bleating sheep, Strauss's *Tonmalerei* thus serves musical expression.

In *An Alpine Symphony*—Strauss's last tone poem, completed in 1915—onomatopoeic effects resemble those found in the earlier tone poems. Wind machine and thunder machine are used to convey the sounds of the natural phenomena. Moreover, Strauss introduces cowbells in the section he calls "Auf der Alm" (On the mountain pasture), in addition to a theme[54] that is

---

[54] Played by English horn and clarinets, three measures before cue 51.

very close to the *ranz* motifs of the German Romantic tradition. He also composes a fanfare that, as in *A Hero's Life*, is to be played off-stage; see the composer's indication between cues 18 and 19: "Jagdhörner von ferne" (hunting horns from afar). Finally, as an allusion to Beethoven's *Pastoral Symphony* and to the myriad examples of storm scenes in French baroque opera, he writes a whole section entitled "Gewitter und Sturm. Abstieg" (Thunderstorm and strong wind. Descent).

The function of all these onomatopoeic elements is exactly the same as in *A Hero's Life* or *Don Quixote*: they serve as symbols for a specific situation (mostly a pastoral one) while at the same time reinforcing the expression of a given mood (chiefly here a quiet and peaceful one). Both *Tonmalerei* and *Kunstkritik* are at work in Strauss's tone poem to express the "*Seelenzustände*" (states of the soul) that are, according to Beethoven and Liszt, the constitutive elements of Romantic instrumental music.

Conclusion

The above observations on the genuine function of symphonic music and its relation to literary "models" in tone poems answer the question asked at the outset of this chapter: how can one explain an artist's propensity to use the work of another as a starting-point for creating his own work? *Kunstkritik* theory, based mainly on Schlegel's aesthetic and on Liszt's writings about program music, enlightens the specific context of Romantic art theory. According to this theory, every work of art is intrinsically perfectible, and aesthetic canons give way to a "continuum of forms" in which every work can be improved by another artist. When a musician chooses to compose a piece "after" a work by another artist, he or she thus does not use it as a model but as a kind of starting point for a new creation. One should therefore not speak of a "model" but rather of a content that the composer aims to recast. According to Liszt's texts, the Romantic artists want to modernize masterpieces of the past like *Don Quixote* or *Macbeth* by giving them a new form. Since music is to serve the expression of moods and feelings and not the depiction of actions and adventures, Liszt beseeches his fellows to take a "philosophical epos" (by Goethe, Lord Byron, or Mickiewicz) as "subject" for their compositions and to write tone poems that may thus aspire to a kind of "musical epos." *Kunstkritik*, which generally aims at improving the form of a work of art, is transformed in Liszt's theory into a principle that removes onomatopoeic elements from a story and reduces the music to a more or less "psychological" plot. In all the tone poems of Strauss, one can show this transformation from a narrative to a psychological content.

Tonmalerei, with its forerunners in certain 18-century symphonies and in many baroque operas, is not rejected by the Romantic composers. Although Beethoven asserts that his sixth symphony is the "expression of sentiments" rather than *Tonmalerei*, he does not completely exclude the latter from his work. Neither did Strauss, who was a great admirer of Beethoven. While his first tone poems belong to the Lisztian tradition of the tone poem, the latter ones (after *Thus Spoke Zarathustra*) show an increasing use of onomatopoeic elements, invariably integrated into the "psychological" plot either because they are immediately followed by the expression of a mood related to the signification of the *Tonmalerei* or because they intrinsically convey an expression that the composer can incorporate into the musical structure. *Kunstkritik* and *Tonmalerei* are not two conflicting features, they rather complement one another.

Strauss's last three tone poems (*A Hero's Life*, *Domestic Symphony*, and *An Alpine Symphony*) are closer to the genre of the symphony than the others. They either carry the word "symphony" in their title or were once considered as such.[55] Should we see herein an indication that one possible difference between the symphony and the tone poem is the use of external elements belonging to the realm of *Tonmalerei*? Such a difference could certainly not only be explained by the mere presence of a "subject," since for instance Mahler's first symphonies have a program and are nonetheless called "symphonies." The situation is somewhat paradoxical: the tone poem is supposed to "describe" while the symphony is said to have an "absolute" form. However, if one remembers that Mahler, a contemporary of Strauss who composed mainly symphonies, conceived the symphony as a "world," it will be possible to recognize that the elements of *Tonmalerei* contribute the concrete aspect of the inner world created more generally in the work's musical structure.

The distinction between *Kunstkritik* and *Tonmalerei* in the symphonic works of the second half of the 19th century thus opens new perspectives on the differences between symphonies and tone poems by composers associated with the "New German School." May these few theoretical and practical explanations contribute to a better understanding of a very complex problem, that of the musical form and of the boundaries between different genres of instrumental music.

---

[55] Strauss often compared *Ein Heldenleben* and Beethoven's *Eroica*, so that *Ein Heldenleben* is obviously closer to the genre of the symphony, than the other tone poems (see a letter of Strauss quoted in Schuh, *Jugend*, 499).

Schoenberg's *Pierrot lunaire*: A Musical Transformation of *Jugendstil*?

Beat A. Föllmi

Arnold Schoenberg himself portrayed his artistic path from Late Romanticism via free atonality to the twelve-tone technique as a logical, indeed inevitable development. Moreover, he regarded this development as necessary in the history of music as a whole—a history he interpreted in a teleological way as an unswerving advance, propelled by a driving force that was the formulation of something new and unprecedented.[1]

From this perspective, the period of so-called free atonality must be interpreted as merely a transitional phase en route for the formulation of the "method of composing with twelve tones related only with one another": an intermediate stage, as it were, between Wagnerian or Straussian harmony taken to extremes and the complete re-ordering of pitch organization in dodecaphony.[2] Hence the "freedom" in free atonality, which refers both backwards to an emancipation from functional harmony and forwards to a hitherto unrealized ordering of the (thus emancipated) chromatic scale.

This is, of course, an interpretation *a posteriori*, which cannot do justice to the period of free atonality with its highly original responses to artistic challenges. Regarding the aesthetics of free atonality simply in terms of a "no longer" or a "not yet" would underrate the originality of many of the works created during this time. More seriously still, such an interpretation would restrict the beholder's perspective to pitch organization or the harmonic functionality of chords and intervals. In the process, as this chapter sets out to illustrate, it would overlook innumerable further aspects that might cast doubt on the historical demarcation of free atonality.

---

[1] "One has not to say something that has not been heard for a long time (as in fashion), but something that has never been said—or at any rate never this well." *Neue Musik—Meine Musik* (ca. 1930), reproduced in *Journal of the Arnold Schoenberg Institute* 1 (1976/77), 104.

[2] René Leibowitz in *L'évolution de la musique de Bach à Schoenberg* (Paris: Éditions Corrêa, 1951), for example, portrayed free atonality in this way.

With regard to Schoenberg's musical production in the period of free atonality, one can identify three central features: the relative brevity of the compositions, the prevalence of vocal genres, and finally the existence of a special aesthetic that is loosely associated with *Jugendstil*. The first of these three aspects, the terseness of the compositions, has been repeatedly remarked on, not least because it was the difficulty of writing longer works that formed the basis of the ideological justification of dodecaphony as it was subsequently presented by Berg and Webern.[3] It should, however, be noted that Schoenberg certainly succeeded in writing lengthier compositions in free atonal style; prominent examples are the monodrama *Erwartung,* op. 17 (1909), the drama *Die glückliche Hand,* op. 13 (1910-1913), and above all the monumental oratorio *Die Jakobsleiter* (1917-1922).

The second aspect, the predominance of vocal genres—or, to be more precise, the presence of the spoken or sung word—is indisputable. In his very first composition in free atonal style (i.e., the third and fourth movements of the Second String Quartet, op. 10, composed in 1908), Schoenberg used the sung word within the context of an otherwise exclusively instrumental genre. This could tempt one into describing the presence of the word as a prerequisite of the breakthrough to atonality. But here again, it must be noted that during the period in question, Schoenberg also composed purely instrumental masterworks in an atonal language (see, e.g., the Three Piano Pieces op. 11, the Six Little Piano Pieces, op. 19, and the Five Orchestral Pieces, op. 16).

The concept of *Jugendstil*, finally, is the most problematic among the three aspects listed above. But it is also the one leading, together with a dependence on the word, to the heart of the subject addressed in this essay collection: the concept of *ekphrasis*, which will be examined in the following pages with reference to Schoenberg's *Pierrot lunaire*.

Jugendstil

I'd like to begin with a few preliminary remarks on *Jugendstil*. This term originally derives from the fields of architecture and the fine arts, or arts and crafts. It has strong programmatic implications and goes back to the Munich periodical *Jugend* (Youth). The movement of the 1890s was originally pitted against the historicism and academicism of the two previous decades; it sought to break down rigid ideas and oppose conventions. The

---

[3] Cf., e.g., Anton Webern in Willi Reich, ed. *Wege zur neuen Musik* (Vienna: Universal Edition, 1960).

fact that *Jugendstil* itself increasingly turned into a "style" distanced it from its anti-traditional roots and made it the starting-point for further backward-looking movements in the 20th century.[4] Reduced to expressions characterized by myriad mannerisms, it came to be identified with similar, partly congruent and partly varying trends: with *Art Nouveau* or *Art Déco* (in which the crafts element holds pride of place), but also with the ideologically far more heavily loaded concept of *Fin de siècle*.

At the outset, *Jugendstil* was linked with literature, an association that was not unproblematic. *Jugendstil* in literature was understood as referring to certain contents and themes: materials like gold, silver, semi-transparent enamel, pearls, rubies, crystals that the crafts world so cherished; the prevalent ornaments in the visual arts, such as flowers, climbing plants, waves, young women's hair; but then also concepts like death and eros, morbid eroticism, ahistoricism, etc. All these could be translated into verbal terms or embedded in them.

It is significantly harder to transfer this many-layered but also indistinct concept to music. Interestingly, this was first attempted only much later, by Heinrich Jalowetz in the 1933 issue of the *Anbruch*. Curiously enough, the term was here related to Webern's early output and used in a disparaging way.[5] It was not until several decades had passed that interdisciplinary-minded music scholars such as Willi Schuh and Reinhard Gerlach returned to the subject.[6] For the most part these scholars were heavily dependent on conceptual definitions from the fine arts and attempted to establish parallels in structure and contents. Dahlhaus rightly points out that whereas common ground can be established for the "Anschauungsform" (mind set) or "Sehweise" (way of looking),[7] it is still an open question as to what role should be allotted to the "style" that is supposedly characteristic of *Jugendstil*.

---

[4] On *Jugendstil* in general see, for example, the anthology *Jugendstil* edited by Jost Hermand (Darmstadt: Wissenschaftliche Buchgesellschaft, 1989 [1971]).

[5] Heinrich Jalowetz, "Anton Webern wird 50 Jahre alt," *Die Musikblätter des Anbruch* 15 (1933), 135-137.

[6] Cf. Johannes Schwermer, "Jugendstil-Musik in der ästhetischen Enklave," *Neue Zeitschrift für Musik* 126/1 (1965), 2-5; Hans Hollander, *Musik und Jugendstil* (Zurich: Atlantis-Verlag, 1975); Jürg Stenzl, ed., *Art Nouveau, Jugendstil und Musik*, Zurich: Atlantis-Verlag, 1980), herein notably Carl Dahlhaus's article "Musik und Jugendstil," 73-88; Reinhold Brinkmann, "On the Problems of Establishing Jugendstil as a category in the History of Music with a negative plea," *Miscellanea Musicologica* 13 (1984), 19-48; Zoltan Roman, "From congruence to antithesis: poetic and musical Jugendstil in Webern's songs," in *Art Nouveau and Jugendstil and the music of the Early 20th Century, Miscellanea Musicologica* 13 (1984), 191-202.

[7] Carl Dahlhaus, "Musik und Jugendstil," 80.

The literary definition of the concept of *Jugendstil* permits a clearer formulation of the musical definition. If, however, musical *Jugendstil* is grasped via its conceptual and substantive affiliation with literary themes, it must be remembered that this is a relationship of the second order, because literature for its part depends on a visual concept. We are therefore presented with the possibility of constructing a kind of triangular path of influence from art via literature to music, whereby features of *Jugendstil* within any one discipline can only be defined in relation to the other two.

If musical *Jugendstil* is posited as being roughly contemporaneous with the corresponding movements in art and literature,[8] the period of the 1890s and the first decade of the 20th century must be taken into consideration. In the case of Schoenberg's œuvre, this yields the oddity that such a classification runs counter to the usual distinction between his creative periods. For shortly after 1905, there is a pronounced caesura marked by the transition to free atonality. Hand in hand with this went a change in his musical language, which affected most of the musical parameters and must thus be regarded as an actual change of paradigm. In other words: within Schoenberg's creative career, musical *Jugendstil* (ca. 1890 to 1914) does not coincide with the period of his free atonal compositions (ca. 1908 to 1920).

The situation becomes more complex if we seek to determine those works by Schoenberg which might be associated with *Jugendstil* with regard to contents and themes:

Erwartung, op. 2 No. 1 (text: Richard Dehmel)	1899
Verklärte Nacht, string sextet, op. 4 (after Richard Dehmel)	1899
Brettl-Lieder (various authors, incl. Frank Wedekind and Otto Julius Bierbaum)	1901
Pelleas und Melisande, op. 5 (after Maurice Maeterlinck)	1902-03
Ein Stelldichein (text: Richard Dehmel)	1905
Second Quartet (F♯ minor), op. 10 (*Litanei* and *Entrückung* by Stefan George)	1907-08
Three Piano Pieces, op. 11	1909
Fifteen Poems from *Das Buch der hängenden Gärten* by Stefan George, op. 15	1908-09
Erwartung, monodrama, op. 17	1909
Die glückliche Hand, drama with music, op. 18	1910-13
Six Little Piano Pieces, op. 19	1911
Herzgewächse, op. 20 (text: Maurice Maeterlinck)	1911
Pierrot lunaire, op. 21	1912

---

[8] There have been many attempts to attach the *Jugendstil* label to widely differing movements. Hollander, for example, polemically subsumed impressionism, atonality, twelve-tone music, serialism—in short, the whole of musical modernism—under this term; cf. Hollander, *Musik und Jugendstil*, 131.

In this space of this brief chapter, it is not possible to furnish detailed reasons for ascribing each of the above works to *Jugendstil*. But it is worth noticing that, except for opp. 11 and 19, every work listed comes with a text: opp. 4 and 5 are instrumental works based on a text, the remaining pieces are vocal compositions. This retrospective textual linkage makes possible a linguistic and visual fixing of the kind of *Jugendstil* motif I have already described. To be sure, the connections with *Jugendstil* and *Art Nouveau* are extremely varied; they include such different and contrasting literary worlds as the eroticism of Richard Dehmel and the Symbolism of Maurice Maeterlinck. In terms of contents, the literary motifs include flowers, waves, young women's hair, and an emphasis on arts and crafts, etc. (This is particularly notable in *Die glückliche Hand* or *Herzgewächse*).

Jugendstil as an "Anti" Stance

A salient feature of Schoenberg's *Pierrot lunaire* is its basic aesthetic stance. The dominant elements are the grotesque, parody, the playfully mannered and inauthentic, disguises, the world of the theater, cabaret or pantomime, false pathos—in short, a decidedly anti-Romantic attitude. If one compares *Pierrot lunaire* with *Verklärte Nacht* or even with the *Gurrelieder*, a work Schoenberg had just completed in 1911, it is easy to appreciates the deep gulf that separates the two creative phases. On the one hand, the *Gurrelieder* with their profoundly significant contents and enormous symphonic apparatus; on the other hand, *Pierrot lunaire* with its ironically distanced poise and its deployment of chamber-music resources.

A crucial factor is that Schoenberg became acquainted with the poems in the version by Otto Erich von Hartleben (1860-1905) and not in the original version by Giraud. In 1884, the Belgian author Albert Giraud (1860-1929, real name Marie-Émile-Albert Kayenbergh) published under the title *Pierrot lunaire* a book of fifty poems, a collection that is largely unknown today. He later brought out two further works on the Pierrot theme.[9] Otto Erich von Hartleben translated the poems of *Pierrot lunaire* into German immediately after their appearance; in 1892, Liebmann of Berlin distributed this translation in an autographed edition. Schoenberg became acquainted with them in the second edition, which was published by Georg Müller in Munich in 1911, i.e., six years after Hartleben's death.[10]

---

[9] *Pierrot narcisse* (1891) and *Héros et Pierrots* (1898).

[10] An annotated facsimile edition of Hartleben's translation (in the 1911 version, newly edited by Eckhard Fürlus) was republished in 2005 by Aisthesis in Bielefeld.

The French originals are close to Belgian Symbolism and the world of Baudelaire; they reflect the pronounced aestheticism of *l'art pour l'art*, art for art's sake. The Pierrot figure with its blasphemous and shocking behavior offered Giraud the chance of a poetic rebellion against the ideals of the group of poets known as the Parnassians, to which he himself had long belonged.[11]

Hartleben's translation was produced independently and deliberately distanced itself from its model. In Hartleben's version, the grotesque and parodistic elements were meant to predominate. Giraud's Pierrot, rebellious and shocking but at the same time shrouded in mystery, is transformed in Hartleben's version into a grotesque dandy wearing lurid make-up and showing irreverence toward anyone and everything.[12] This shift can be illustrated by comparing, for example, the last five lines of Giraud's "Supplique" with those of Hartleben's German translation, entitled "Gebet an Pierrot" (No. 9 in Schoenberg's work):

Albert Giraud "Supplique" (No. 31 in the cycle)	Otto Erich von Hartleben "Gebet an Pierrot" (No. 9 in Schoenberg)	English translation of Hartleben's German version
Quand me rendras-tu, porte-lyre	O gieb mir wieder	Oh, give me back
Guérisseur de l'esprit blessé	Rossarzt der Seele	Horse-doctor of the soul
Neige adorable du passé	Schneemann der Lyrik	Snowman of poetry
Face de Lune, blanc messire	Durchlaucht vom Monde	Highness from the Moon
O Pierrot! le ressort du rire?	Pierrot—mein Lachen!	Pierrot, my laughter!

The French text is mysterious and enigmatic; the five lines are worded as a question: "When will you give me back ... the resort of laughter?" Hartleben turns this into a direct, abrupt imperative: "Oh, give me back ... my laughter!" In Giraud, Pierrot is poetically described as a "healer of the wounded spirit," as "the lovely snow of the past," and as "moon face, pale lord." Hartleben adapted this to create such crooked, grotesquely distorted images as "Horse-doctor of the soul" and "Snowman of poetry," in which the

---

[11] On Giraud's *Pierrot lunaire* see Bryan Simms, *The Atonal Music of Arnold Schoenberg 1908-1923* (New York: Oxford University Press, 2000), 119-123.

[12] For a comparison of Giraud and Hartleben see Susan Youens, "The Text of *Pierrot lunaire*: an Allegory of Art and the Mind," in Leonard Stein, ed., *From Pierrot to Marteau: an International Cconference and Concert Celebrating the Tenth Anniversary of the Arnold Schoenberg Institute, University of Southern California School of Music, March 14-16, 1987* (Los Angeles: Arnold Schoenberg Institute, 1987), 30-32.

French original is reduced to a purely associative role, like a quarry. Even the rhyme[13] in *lyre / messire / rire*—a poetic device and Symbolist tool —has been dropped in the German version. The text has become sober, but at the same time witty and self-mocking.

Everywhere in his translation, Hartleben denounces the allegedly hollow pathos of the 19th century through poetological "insincerity." He dissolved highly charged Romantic symbols into *Jugendstil* garlands: the "whitest wonder roses," for instance, turn into "the moonlight's palest blossoms," which are shed over brown hair (No. 2 in Schoenberg's composition). Poets cut altogether comic or tragicomic figures—as in "Mondestrunken" (No. 1), where they "have become intoxicated by the holy drink," or in "Die Kreuze" (No. 14), where, like a dying Christ, they are nailed to the cross of their own verses. Romantic music is denounced as sick in "Valse de Chopin" (No. 5) or given a grotesque twist, as happens in the bizarre recital that Pierrot plays with his gigantic bow upon Cassander's bald head ("Serenade," No. 19).

From the fifty poems penned by Giraud and, after him, by Hartleben, Schoenberg selected twenty-one (3 x 7).[14] This selection does not follow the Hartleben's order. Instead, the composer devises a completely new kind of dramaturgy in three sections, which can be viewed from different perspectives. The one that may be the most plausible can be described as blending a chronological arrangement with a thematically defined sequence in which no contiguous action is discernible:

- the onset of night in the first section with the theme of the "moon" (there are frequent references to light and pallor, and a number of song titles contain the idea of the moon)
- night in the second section, with the theme of "death" (many blasphemous and ghastly events)
- a brightening in the third section, with the theme of "nostalgia" (dawn and homecoming)

Those parodistic elements featured in Hartleben's translation are not only further emphasized in Schoenberg's musical setting but constitute the very basis of the composition. In "Valse de Chopin" (No. 5), the waltz is sometimes clearly accentuated in the accompanying piano figure, while at the same time, "disruptive" elements are added (the eighth-notes repeated at the same pitch sound like "ticking"; Fig. 1).

---

[13] Giraud uses the relatively traditional rondo form with its rhyming eight-syllable lines. The three stanzas count 4, 4, and 5 lines; the rhyme scheme is: a-b-b-a / a-b-b-a / a-b-b-a-a.

[14] Schoenberg's work copy of Hartleben's book, replete with the composer's handwritten annotations, has been preserved. Cf. Christian Martin Schmidt, "Analytical remarks on Schoenberg's Pierrot lunaire," in Leonard Stein, ed., *From Pierrot to Marteau*, 41-42.

FIGURE 1: "Valse de Chopin" (Chopin Waltz),
Pierrot lunaire No. 5, m. 21

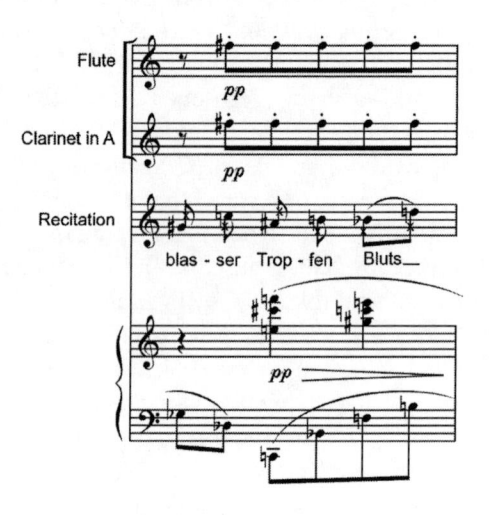

As soon as "Romantic" ideas emerge in the text, the music features anachronistic stylistic devices: the words "du nächtig todeskranker Mond" (you somber death-stricken moon) are decorated with mordents and thereby reduced to caricature; cf. the two-bar excerpt from "Der kranke Mond":

FIGURE 2: "Der kranke Mond" (The Sick Moon),
Pierrot lunaire No. 7, mm. 26-27

Similarly, the risible love of the old duenna for Pierrot in No. 17 degenerates into a veritable parody ("Parodie" being the actual heading) in which the *Sprechstimme* gives such ideas as "Liebe" and "mit Schmerzen" (mm. 12-14) a grotesque twist by means of unnatural melismas (Fig. 3), reinforced by the performance indication "sentimental" for the instruments in mm. 5-6, which can only be read as a mark of irony.

FIGURE 3: "Parodie" (Parody), *Pierrot lunaire* No. 17, mm. 13-14

False pathos also occurs in "Gebet an Pierrot" (No. 9), where the impossibly grandiloquent poetry (the "Rossarzt der Seele," the "Schneemann der Lyrik") is delivered in equally overblown *bel canto* (mm. 15-17). This anti-Romantic stance acquires a polemical note in the third section, which speaks of nostalgia for the good old days. In "Heimweh" (No. 15) the phrase "so modern sentimental" is provided with grotesque glissandi (see Fig. 4, next page), and the final song (No. 21) translates the "fragrance old from days of yore" into a spurious ecstasy of thirds (mm. 1-5, 14-15, 26-27; see Fig. 5, next page).

This anti-Romantic stance seems typical of Schoenberg's basic aesthetic outlook around 1910. A similar outlook can be discerned in Stravinsky (albeit with completely different musical results), whose famous statement "Je déteste l'Ausdruck!"[15] also shows a composer dissociating himself from Romantic pathos. In Schoenberg's *Pierrot lunaire*, however, the "anti"-stance lies at the center of the work, determining the choice of text, form, orchestration, gesture, musical rhetoric, aesthetics, etc. It is even akin to a "historical self-critique," because the "fragrance old from days of yore" had attracted Schoenberg only a few months earlier.

---

[15] See Volker Scherliess, " 'Je déteste l'Ausdruck'—Über Strawinsky als Interpreten," in Klaus Hortschansky, ed., *Traditionen—Neuansätze. Für Anna Amalie Abert (1906-1996)* (Tutzing: Schneider, 1997), 475-492.

FIGURE 4: "Heimweh" (Homesickness), *Pierrot lunaire* No. 15, mm. 8-9

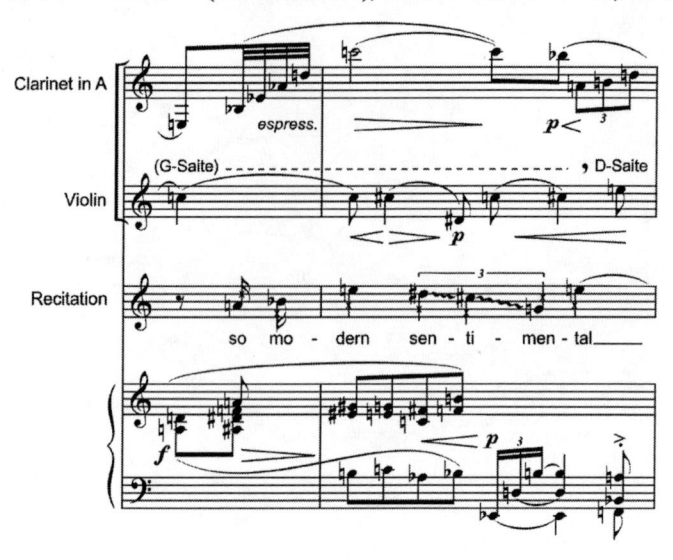

FIGURE 5: "O alter Duft" (O ancient fragrance), *Pierrot lunaire* No. 21, mm. 1-3

In *Pierrot lunaire* the composer was not, of course, concerned with just rejecting certain values, but chiefly with a reorientation. And it was precisely here—in rejection and readjustment alike—that *Jugendstil* offered a set of guidelines. The cardinal aspects for Schoenberg were as follows:
- a reduction to clear, simple lines
- a mystifying of the aesthetic element
- an emphasis on craftsmanship
- a preference for "noble and beautiful" materials
- a predilection for the ironic, grotesque, blasphemous, and ghastly.

Hartleben's translation provided Schoenberg with abundant samples for each category; see the clearly structured lines of a poem like "Galgenlied" (No. 12), the all-pervasive undulations of wind, waves, or flowers in Nos. 1, 2, 3, 4, the aesthetic self-mirroring of the "Dandy von Bergamo" in No. 3, the decadence of "Valse de Chopin" in No. 5, the glittering colors and materials in images like "des Orients Grün" (the green of the Orient) or "die krystallnen Flakons" (the crystal vials) in No. 3, "die roten, fürstlichen Rubine" (the red, princely rubies) in No. 10, "der Blendeglanz des Goldes" (the dazzling luster of gold) in No. 11, or the ghastly and blasphemous ceremonies in Nos. 6, 9, 10, 11, 14.

As these thematic and motivic links demonstrate, Schoenberg's *Pierrot lunaire* is distinctly representative of *Jugendstil* aesthetics already at its basis, i.e., with regard to its literary source and its verbal imagery. The composer found not just a thematic milieu—the *commedia dell'arte* mask of the Pierrot, Italy's ironic sweetness, the provocative and anti-bourgeois elements—but above all an opportunity to redefine his music from a structural and aesthetic standpoint.

That this was not the final answer (and there are no final answers in art) became apparent to the composer very soon. For during the First World War, a speculative element derived from theosophy gained the upper hand in Schoenberg's thinking, and by the beginning of the 1920s, he was combining the speculative with the structural. This famously led to his development of the twelve-tone method.

Pierrot lunaire: a Translation of *Jugendstil* into Music

Jugendstil as a visual and literary concept is present in Schoenberg's *Pierrot lunaire* first of all indirectly through the text, or through the objects and situations this text evokes. This situation provided the composer with a range of constructional possibilities. One of them, as already mentioned, was his division of the twenty-one chosen poems into three sets of seven; how important this numerical play was for the composer is evident in the work's original title, which reads: *Dreimal sieben Gedichte aus Albert Girauds "Pierrot lunaire"* (Three times seven poems from Albert Girauds "Pierrot lunaire").

As in Giraud, all poems in Hartleben's translation share one and the same line scheme: two four-line stanzas are followed by a stanza of five lines, with the latter stanzas picking up either lines one and two or just the first line of the initial stanza:

*A B*C D   E F*A B*   G H I K*A*

In contrast to Giraud's original, there are no rhymes in Hartleben's translation; and, again in contradistinction from Giraud's eight-syllable lines, the syllabic scheme is free, including iambuses, trochees, and even dactyls. Most lines have four accented syllables, but more or fewer feet per line also occur. This, however, regards only the poem as it might appear on the page before it is subjected to music. The declamation by the *Sprechstimme* that Schoenberg prescribed adheres neither to the syllabic pattern nor to the line-scheme. Enjambments are frequent; in addition, the repeated lines are by no means necessarily performed in the same way as when they occurred for the first time. This goes to show that Schoenberg did not use the text primarily for structural purposes, in the sense of an elementary organizing principle.

The dimension of sound in these verses is quite another matter, for great importance attaches to the sounds in Hartleben's translation (as also in Giraud's original), leading to onomatopoeia, alliteration, assonance, etc. The striking accumulation of long vowels in "Heimfahrt" (No. 20), for instance, is keenly observed and even strongly emphasized in the declamation of the Sprechgesang:

"Der Mondstrahl ist das Ruder, Seerose dient als Boot"
(The moon beam is the oar, [the] water lily serves as boat)

FIGURE 6: "Heimfahrt" (Homeward Bound), *Pierrot lunaire* No. 20, mm. 6-9

These long syllables match the elegiac tone of Pierrot's "journey home" and are taken up by the instruments designated as *Hauptstimme* in the same elegiac vein.

The grotesque scraping in Pierrot's "Serenade" (No. 19) is replicated in the accumulation of "grotesque" combinations of consonants in the words "groteskem Riesenbogen," "Kratzt," "Bratsche," "Storch," "Knipst," and "Pizzicato." Where a viola (German: Bratsche) is mentioned, Schoenberg displays a subtle sense of irony by requesting that the violist play not the instrument usually so named but a grotesquely large "viola," i.e., a cello, which for its part—just like the verbal sonority—produces "grotesque" sounds, a parody of Romantic virtuosity: bizarre flageolet tones (m. 1), frequent glissandi (mm. 2-3, 11-12, 21-22, and 35-36), extended pizzicato passages (mm. 11-13), as well as major changes of register; see Figures 7a and 7b.

Pierrot lunaire: *A Musical Transformation of* Jugendstil? 215

FIGURE 7a: "Serenade," *Pierrot lunaire* No. 19, mm. 25-26

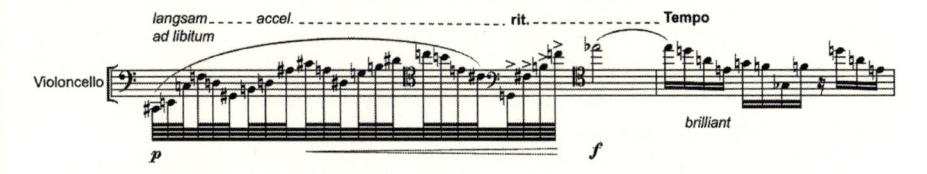

FIGURE 7b: "Serenade," *Pierrot lunaire* No. 19, mm. 35-37

The mannered behavior of the dandy of Bergamo (No. 3) is conveyed on the level of language through a cluster of the hissing and aspirating sounds "sch," "f," and "h": "phantastischen Lichtstrahl," "schwarzen, hochheiligen Waschtisch des schweigenden Dandys ..." Schoenberg's musical realization is entirely on a par with this: the vocalist switches from speaking to singing to whispering. In this way, a whole palette of human vocal expression is here displayed. Moreover, with piccolo flute and clarinet plus a piano playing mainly in the treble, the orchestration enhances the poem's sublime and delicate qualities.

Beyond mere enhancement, the music also has an independent capacity for depiction, above all in the form of an iconic reproduction of certain contents, with particular emphasis on the parodistic. In "Mondestrunken" (No. 1, mm. 35-36) the reeling ("taumelnd") poet sucks and slurps ("saugt und schlürft") the wine, sounds and gestures Schoenberg depicts by means of the triple execution of an intervallic gesture leading upwards, just as somebody inebriated will reel upstairs:

FIGURE 8: "Mondestrunken" (Moondrunk), *Pierrot lunaire* No. 1, mm. 35-36

The pale washerwoman's lack of facial coloring (No. 4) is reflected in a "pallid" orchestration of instruments in middle to low registers and a rhythmically undifferentiated delivery (mm. 1-8). The poet bleeding on the cross in "Die Kreuze" (No. 14) is portrayed in a mighty written-out *ritardando* and by freezing the music in a low register (mm. 9-12).

Such musical devices correspond more or less to traditional musical rhetoric. They are also readily comprehensible since they do not depend on tonal syntax or semantics. One novel feature is that Schoenberg does not actually pursue textual interpretation but often just realizes the "verbal sound" musically. This is certainly in keeping with the poems, which scarcely convey any contents beyond an aesthetic self-mirroring. That "taciturn dandy from Bergamo" (No. 3), for instance, who adorns himself "mit einem phantastischen Lichtstrahl" (with a fantastic lightbeam)—an embellishment perfectly conveyed in the verbal sound and the music—applies his make-up out of pure narcissism, and the poem copies him, ultimately remaining as taciturn as the dandy himself.

Jugendstil as a Formative Concept

Schoenberg's aesthetic reorientation to the aesthetics of *Jugendstil* is not only manifested on the surface of the text, the sound, or the visual concept contained in the text. It can also be detected in the very organization of the music—in material or form. The first song, "Mondestrunken," will serve to illustrate this in some detail.

As has been noted, the 3 x 7 poems are lacking in any clearly defined outward relation other than their formal stringency. They are an aesthetic self-mirroring and relate to images, sounds, colors, forms, and materials. The idea of *Fliessen* (flowing) is central to "Mondestrunken": it forms the crucial isotope of the poem.[16] Flowing is a central concept in *Jugendstil*. The idea was applied to water, waves, water-lilies, young women's hair. In "Mondestrunken," flowing is indeed omnipresent:
1. in a concrete sense, it appears as the flow of liquids in wine, waves, the spring tide, torrents, drinks, as well as sucking and slurping;
2. on a secondary level, it is implied as the flow of light (eyes, moon);
3. on a meta-level, is con be understood to be present as the flow of feelings, emotions ("desires, shivering and sweet," "verzückt")

---

[16] I am here adopting the term established in the field of textual linguistics, as it was formulated by Algirdas Julien Greimas, *Sémantique structurale* (Paris: Larousse, 1966).

In this poem, the flowing of material and immaterial phenomena (liquid and light) is combined and ultimately transcended to a flow of feelings. This in turn gives rise to a visible process, a "flowing" of the poet who is ecstatically reeling toward heaven. Whereas the wine transformed into moonlight flows down from the heavens, the poet's ecstasy (induced by the intoxication with wine) flows upwards from the ground. The image is thus doubly based on the isotope of flowing: a flowing downward and upward on the macro-level, and flowing as an all-pervasive movement on the micro-level.

Schoenberg takes this central idea as a basis for his musical realization of the poem. The all-pervasive flowing occurs right at the beginning in a motif or rather a motoric figure that has an illustrative character: a seven-part sixteenth-note figure in high register that, through its intervallic structure and descending motion, reproduces the downward flow quite literally. At the same time, the music also features an up-and-down undulating motion through the interval of a minor third in a middle register (F$\sharp^2$—D$\sharp^2$, later B$\flat^2$—G^2 as well).

FIGURE 9: "Mondestrunken" (Moondrunk), *Pierrot lunaire* No. 1, mm. 1-4

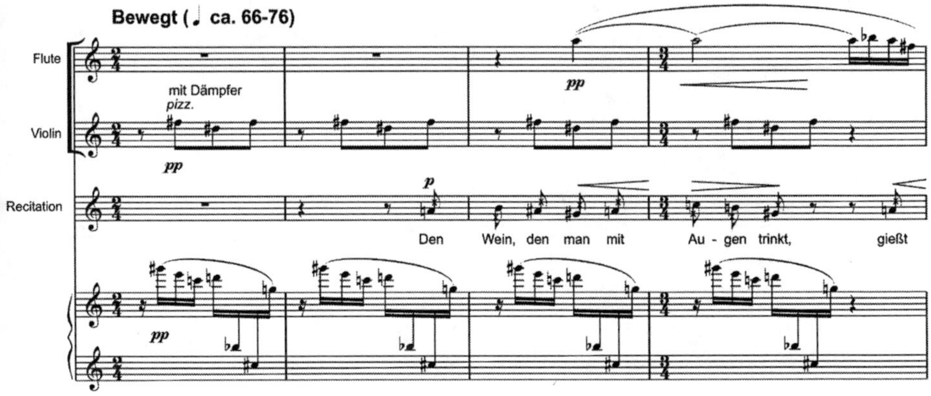

At the beginning of the song, this dual "wave motif" is repeated four times in exactly the same way, and twice in a modified form (mm. 1-4 and 5-6). It reappears one more time in a modified form after the repetition of the poem's opening lines (mm. 26-28). At the end, after the resumption of the initial line of the poem, it is heard only once, in the nature of an aborted fresh start (m. 39, with a stretto in the flute). The motif thus assumes a dual function: on the one hand, it participates in the predominant isotopy of the poem; on the other, it structures the course of the music by emerging at the caesuras prescribed by the poem and by leading back to the beginning at the close, thereby making the composition appear as an unending spiral—as a ceaseless wavy movement, to stick with the isotopic metaphor.

Schoenbergian motifs like this "wave motif" have little in common with the mechanism of Wagnerian motifs (especially leitmotifs) and indeed with the whole idea of a motif carrying a meaning. For within western classical music, a motif in the traditional sense as it was understood since the Baroque era, if not earlier, is a musical unit generally characterized by rhythmic and/or intervallic (or at least gestural) identity, thus functioning as a syntactical or semiotic marker. In *Pierrot lunaire*, admittedly, the syntactical function has initially been adopted, but only inasmuch as it is linked with the verbal text. Strictly speaking it is the *text* that articulates, the motif merely *follows*; to a certain extent, moreover, No. 1 starts again from the beginning at its close, thereby creating not linearity but circularity. In this way, the flow of the text is integrated into the musical structure.

With regard to its semiotic role, the motif in *Pierrot lunaire* also functions in a way that differs significantly from traditional leitmotifs. It is correct to say that the "wave motif" participates in the conception of that "flowing" of which the text speaks, but at no stage does it establish a semantic connection to flowing. It remains a flowing ornament itself, just as young women's hair in *Jugendstil* vignettes turns into waves or rays of light, and vice versa.

Conclusion

As was mentioned at the outset, Schoenberg's period of free atonality is generally interpreted, on the basis of his later artistic development, as a preliminary stage on his journey to dodecaphony. To be sure, the problem Schoenberg addressed around 1910 was different from the one that fascinated him during the years around 1920. When composers gave up functional harmony, they initially deprived music of two crucial functions: its syntax (i.e., the logical structuring of phrases and larger contexts) and to a large extent also its semantics.[17] With hindsight it seems logical that composers would strive to find new ways of organizing their material in such a way that musical syntax would once again become possible; Schoenberg did so with the help of the twelve-tone row.

---

[17] The fact that music from the period of free atonality is placed in the context of "fear, apprehensiveness, menace," etc. (e.g., in advertising or in films for a mass audience) is a later development.

Pierrot lunaire: *A Musical Transformation of* Jugendstil?

It is interesting to observe how Schoenberg, even when using the twelve-tone technique, produced the musical layer carrying meaning not primarily by means of structure (i.e., with the help of the chosen row), but by drawing on gestural or iconic devices.[18] Semiotics were already operative during the period of free atonality: low notes for darkness, high notes for light; a rising and falling motion for wave movement, etc.

Schoenberg availed himself of the *Pierrot lunaire* text in a number of ways. In "Mondestrunken," the poem provides a structural frame (organization of the lines, prosody, repetition of the opening lines, etc.). Moreover, the text implicitly carries the meaning—through its semantic configuration on the one hand (although one can speak of content in *Pierrot lunaire* to only a limited extent) and through its sonorous qualities on the other (the sound of the words, their rhythm, features of onomatopoeia, etc.). Schoenberg certainly did not use the text as a mere prop, i.e., as a structural framework and supplier of meaning. That would relegate the music to being just an addition that without the verbal skeleton could not exist and would only present an amorphous mass.

Instead, the composer appropriated the text of *Pierrot lunaire* in an extremely complex fashion. Since for him, music constituted the center of his creative work in any event,[19] he very rarely concentrated wholly on an interpretation of the text. Rather, the verbal text represented the basis of an aesthetic concept: *Jugendstil*. It served as a link to the visual side of this concept: to images, works of graphic art, and ornamental representations: that area where form and content are combined in an aesthetic concept. Instead of interpreting the text, the music in *Pierrot lunaire* refers to a visual dimension: a reference, however, which could only be realized by resorting to the linguistic medium of the text.[20]

---

[18] Cf. the analysis in Beat A. Föllmi, "'I cannot remember ev'rything'—Eine narratologische Analyse von Arnold Schönbergs Kantate *A Survivor from Warsaw* op. 46," in *Archiv für Musikwissenschaft* LV/1 (1998), 28-56.

[19] As he stressed in the foreword to the printed score, U.E. 5334.5336 (Vienna: Universal Edition, 1914), "Here it is the task of the performers never to create the mood and character of the individual pieces from the meaning of the words, but always solely from the music."

[20] I would like to extend my sincere thanks to Peter Palmer (Nottingham) for translating this essay.

"La poésie sans les mots"[1] in *Amers*: The Thwarted Encounter of André Boucourechliev and Saint-John Perse

Christine Esclapez

André Boucourechliev (1925–1997), the French composer of Bulgarian origin, was profoundly influenced by Saint-John Perse, a poet, *indivisible man*,[2] and French diplomat (a.k.a. Alexis Saint-Legér Léger, 1887–1975). Boucourechliev first met Perse in Washington through Edgard Varèse during his visit in the United States in 1963-1964. After this meeting, he developed plans to compose, with Perse's approval, a piece for chorus and orchestra based on *Amers* (Seamarks). This epic poem dates from the poet's American years; it was begun in 1947, during Perse's early stay on Seven Hundred Acre Island. The project was never completed, at least not in its initial form:

> Back in France, the composer tried in vain to exploit the textual fragments that he admired. Yet he gradually reached an impasse which resulted from the rhetoric of the poem itself. He claimed he felt compelled to write a *cantate à la française* and had to confess his failure to Saint-John Perse who inquired about the piece from time to time. The drafted work was never written ...[3]

Ten years after this first encounter and failed collaboration, the memory of it and a will to overcome it were still vivid. Boucourechliev dedicated a piece for orchestra to the poet. This piece without any text, entitled *Amers*, is a decontextualized and detemporalized continuation and commentary on the initial project. Because of the shared title, it bears a certain kinship with the earlier work. While Boucourechliev's *Amers* is not the double of Saint-John Perse's *Amers*, it is nonetheless undeniable that the two works are interconnected and refer to one another. Hence, my first hypothesis is that the musical piece may enlighten the poem. Yet the creative chronology of the

---

[1] "La poésie sans les mots" is the title of an article by Jean-Pierre Burgart, published in Alain Poirier, *André Boucourechliev* (Paris: Fayard, 2002), 143-155.

[2] Saint-John Perse uses this expression in his banquet speech for the Nobel Prize.

[3] Poirier, *André Boucourechliev*, 63.

piece cannot be ignored: Boucourechliev's instrumental work is in the problematic but privileged place of *what comes after*. From there I derived a second hypothesis : Boucourechliev's *Amers* represents the commentary, description and *ekphrasis* of Perse's poem.

These first observations allow me to broach the theme of this essay collection by showing how the musical work describes and, in a very detailed way, extends the poetic work, how the former exhausts itself in this description that goes *to the limits* of the described work.

But we must not lose sight of two things:

1 The initial project failed; the intended vocal work, a musico-literary commentary on the poem, was transformed into an instrumental work, i.e., into the realm where, so the conventional belief, sound refers only to itself. Boucourechliev's refusal to compose anything that would resemble a *cantate à la française* is a witticism, a rejection of the centuries-long tradition of French Baroque music in which words are painted with great care. In this tradition, setting words to music is often associated with the image of a seventeenth-century Versailles dominated by lyric tragedy, a form impetuously castigated by Rousseau who preferred the Italian vocal style and the lightness of the *opera buffa*. Boucourechliev's *Amers* comes *after*, and this *after* may not have existed. The piece is something else, another territory of meaning, an *elsewhere* that does not simply enhance the poem but goes against it while still referring to it and moving *beyond* mere commentary. Thus, Boucourechliev is not, or not in the literal sense at least, part of the pantheon of those contemporary composers who have set works by Saint-John Perse to music.[4]

2 André Boucourechliev's aesthetic positions, which are far remote from the long (too long according to him) history of the relations between music and the world, a history profoundly marked by the *ut pictura poesis*, in which only true imitation takes place. This position enslaved music and turned it into a minor art. We must not forget Boucourechliev's militancy in favor of the autonomy of music, a music free to sound and resound, his definition of form as a *system of differences*, and his desire, under Cage's influence, to let the sounds just be sounds. These two options led him unknowingly to join the group of those who, as early as the 1960s, turned to the structuralist utopia.

---

[4] Daniel Charles, "La réception de Saint-John Perse par les musiciens contemporains," *Colloque international: Postérités de Saint-John Perse*, 4–6 May 2000, Nice, Université de Nice–Sophia Antipolis; *available online at http://www.up.univ-mrs.fr/~wperse/charles.html*.

In this way, his piece *Amers* really is an *ekphrasis*; it substitutes music for language, resorting for an enhancement of the poem to the purity of instrumental music rather than the inevitably charged signification of vocal music. With such a gesture, Boucourechliev questions in his own way a secular tradition. Indeed, if the *ekphrasis* was originally the description of an object, it was rapidly given a higher function as a literary description of a work, more often of a painting, and this description eventually replaced the described work. Thus, a real impressionistic form of critique established during antiquity, which rests upon the learned exegesis of paintings and takes part in a hermeneutic enterprise aimed at the education of young people. From there derived the elaboration of commentaries on visual artworks, which combine technical analysis, exegesis of the topic at hand and a definition of the resulting emotion. From the beginning up to the *ut pictura poesis* doctrine we witness a departure from the work itself. In the realm of words and imitation, in this universe where rhetoric is sovereign, language glorifies itself promoting the disappearance of the work of art.

My hypothesis is that Boucourechliev instrumental piece *Amers* "says what it sees" in Perse's work. Denying the power of the words and their distinct performative impact, it dares put music on the same level as a literary commentary by granting it the possibility to say things by its own means, with the perspective that only the ear can have on things, closer to the realm of the perceptible.

André Boucourechliev's attitude is not surprising for those who have followed the development of his aesthetic thought in his monographs.[5] This *writer of music* as he loved to describe himself is, above all, a composer whose entire output is imbued with a view of his peers works that only a practitioner can have. Behind biographical details, he explored the creative mind. Behind the ready-made forms, the event and the departure from the tradition probe time and enable the creator to establish a dialogue with both the performers and the audience.[6] Boucourechliev's position has its point of departure in a perspective that strongly opposes the idea that music is a

---

[5] For Boucourechliev's own publications, cf. *Schumann* (1956 French, 1959 English), *Chopin: eine Bildbiographie* (1962 German, 1963 English), *Beethoven* (1963 Paris:Seuil), *Stravinsky* (1982 French, 1987 English), *Essai sur Beethoven* (1991), *Le langage musical* (1993), *Dire la musique* (1995), *Regards sur Chopin* (1996), and *Debussy. La Révolution subtile* (1998). For a discussion of his approach to essential esthetic questions cf. Christine Esclapez, *La Musique comme parole des corps: Boris de Schloezer, André Souris et André Boucourechliev* (Paris: L'Harmattan, 2007).

[6] Christine Esclapez, "Le langage musical en question", *Complexité à l'œuvre : musique, musicologie, spectacle vivant*, workshop directed by Nicolas Darbon, available online at: http://www.mcxapc.org.

means of communicating, representing, or imitating external realities or affects. From there originates his quest for a liberated music, a music that is emancipated from all subordination, that is first itself before being an empty receptacle. It is as if Boucourechliev was searching within music for a dense body, for what Gilles Deleuze in reference to Francis Bacon's paintings describes as "traversed by a wave that traces levels or thresholds in the body according to the variations of its amplitude."[7] Such a proposal resonates with the views of other 20th-century composers such as John Cage or Morton Feldman.[8] It converges with a similar urge to concentrate on the resonating matter and on the way a work sounds. For all of these composers, music belongs in principle to the realm of the perceptible, and its presence is entirely dependent upon what is perceived. According to Boucourechliev,

> We are plagued by two centuries of a vain quest for "signification," for a rational musical meaning "conveyed" by language... Yet in music, nothing is conveyed by something else.[9]

Thus the apparently thwarted encounter between Boucourechliev and Saint-John Perse takes us to the heart of the connection or disconnection between music and poetry. As Jean-Pierre Burgart noted, quoting André Boucourechliev in his outstanding article *La poésie sans les mots*,[10]

> According to Barthes, freedom is not only the power to draw oneself away from the domination of language, but also and above all to refuse to control anyone. This is "the possibility that literature (and more generally art) opens." If after many years André Boucourechliev eventually renounced the intended composition of a piece based on Saint-John Perse's works, and if with the purely instrumental piece *Amers* he paid tribute to the poet, it is because, according to him, the texts displayed such a peremptory rhetoric that there was no space left for compositional freedom.[11]

The aim of the present article is not to establish narrative or figurative connections between the two works. My hypothesis is that we are facing a failed encounter opposing an attitude of withdrawal and silence to the domination of music by language. Yet, another hypothesis would also be

---

[7] Gilles Deleuze, *Francis Bacon. The Logic of Sensation*, translated by Daniel W. Smith (Minneapolis, MN: University of Minnesota Press, 2003), 32.

[8] Morton Feldman, *Ecrits et paroles précédés d'une monographie par Jean-Yves Bosseur* (Paris: L'Harmattan, 1998).

[9] André Boucourechliev, *Le Langage musical* (Paris: Fayard, 1993), 12.

[10] Burgart, "La poésie sans les mots," 143-155.

[11] Burgart, *ibid.*, 154.

possible, suggesting that the encounter actually did take place: in the gap of a silence resounding with buried words, those of the poetic proximity that the late instrumental piece *Amers* by André Boucourechliev reveals as a musical commentary (for 19 instruments) on his own reading of Saint-John Perse's *Amers*. Silence is the space for this deferred encounter. No musical story stands for the poem; the continuation and transformation of the poetical work exist in the form of a single huge sheet of paper (see Figure 1) representing a compass rose with the cardinal points (North, East, South, West) and the intercardinal directions (NE, SE, SW and NW).

The score is suggestive of the aesthetics of the "open work," which profoundly influenced André Boucourechliev and many composers at the end of the 1960s.[12] This historically dated aesthetic takes its roots in generalized serialism and electroacoustic music. It reveals a utopian world entirely dependent on possibility and no longer on a principle of necessity. Boucourechliev's instrumental piece was composed much later, yet the principle of openness—the endless reconfiguration of the structure of the works by the performers ("the happening at the moment of mediation" evoked by Umberto Eco)—, which he had fully embraced as early as 1967 when he started composing his first *Archipel*,[13] paradoxically continued to grow during his stay in America when he first met Saint-John Perse. The Bulgarian composer did some research before abandoning the initial project. He read the poem with great care, searching around it and in it, in all directions. As Ducharme reports, "he started to lay on a big board snippets of texts jotted down on small pieces of paper.[14]" This work foreshadowed the working technique and mobility of his first open works from 1967. It was as if the impossibility of composition stemmed from a field of possibilities whose existence was not dictated by the necessity of the initial project but left in suspension.

In his article "Clefs pour l'ouverture," Jean Ducharme offers an extensive exploration of Boucourechliev's compositional techniques, and their aim to "open" a work.[15] While *Amers* is chronologically a harbinger of the *Archipels*, pieces that are emblematic of this aesthetic, the earlier composition is by no means simply a sketch. In accordance with his aesthetic principle, Boucourechliev leaves to the performers of *Amers* the freedom to determine the musical progression while imposing a few more definitely

---

[12] Jean Ducharme, "Clefs pour l'ouverture," *André Boucourechliev, ibid.*, 55-117.

[13] On the sources that led Boucourechliev to adopt the open work aesthetic see Ducharme, "Clefs pour l'ouverture,", 59-65.

[14] Ducharme, *ibid.*, 63.

[15] Cf. note 12.

FIGURE 1 : Photograph of the score for *Amers*,
Paris, Editions Musicales Alphonse Leduc, 1979

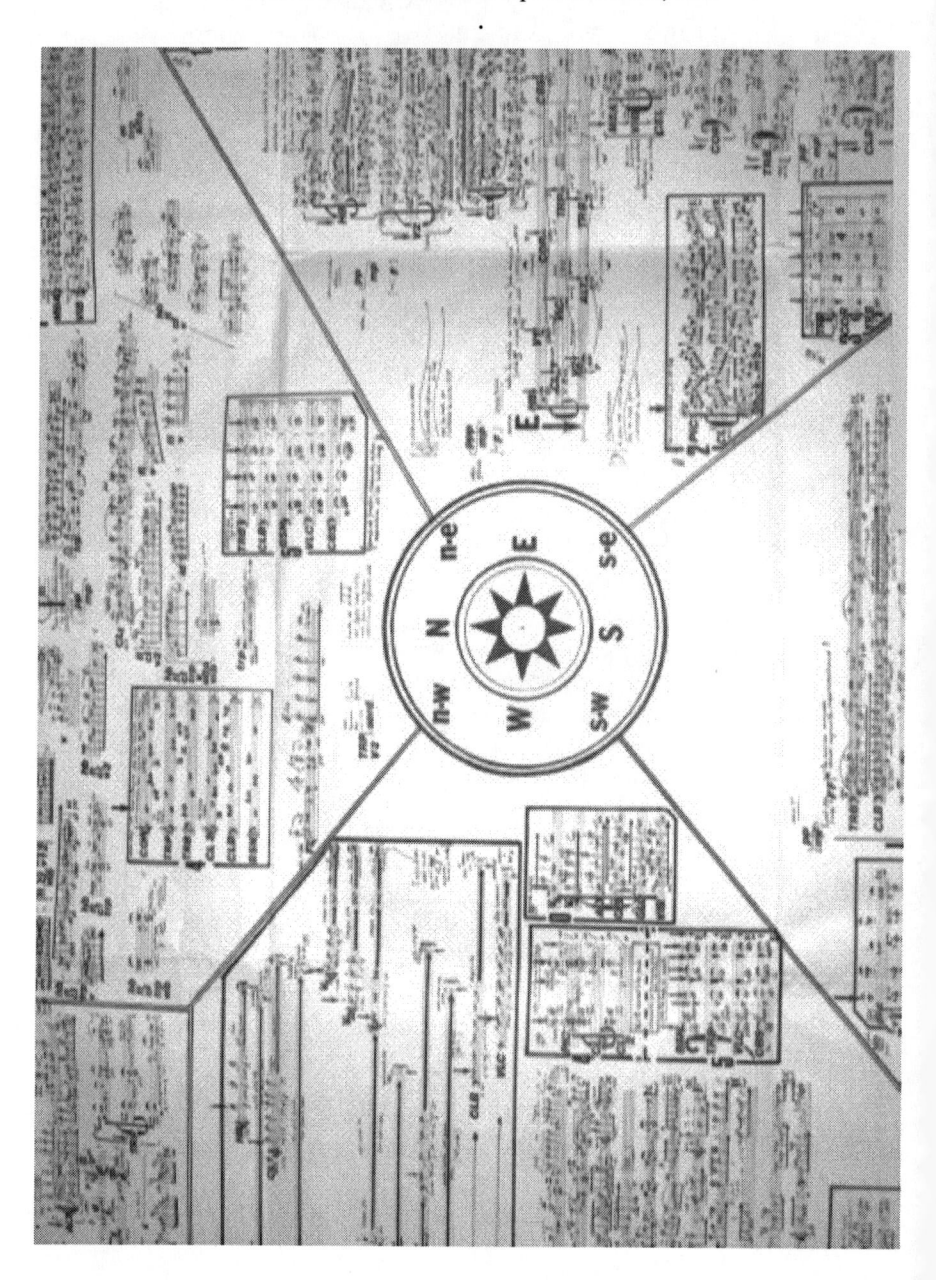

determined elements. This principle embroils the work in an everlasting oscillation between determined and undetermined, between necessity and possibility. It is as if Boucourechliev was unveiling "another world"[16] (a utopia?) by offering a material meditation on the paradox of openness: determination stems from generalized mobility. Boucourechliev's works are deemed *mobile* (open) because they urge the performers to act, setting them into motion by proposing a space of free choice during the performance.[17] At the same time, the works impose constraints on the performers, compelling them to respect certain directives and rules of execution, which in turn have an impact on both the musical material (predetermined rhythmic or melodic patterns, diffraction of melodies, indications about the reading directions: from left to right or right to left) and the overall structure of the work. The openness occurs on two levels here: one that concerns the internal structure of phrases and events and another that allows for the general recomposition of the work. In *Amers*, the composer describes the characteristics of each quadrant and intermediary point in great detail of instrumentation, intensities, etc. On a larger scale of the work's overall structure, the performer is free to start with any quadrant (North, East, South, West) but then he has to move clockwise through all the others. Moreover, he or she is not to start or finish on an intercardinal point.[18] Jean Ducharme explains what this means for the wedge between the cardinal points of conclusion and opening: "As a consequence, the composer knows that part of his work will remain unexplored."[19]

The possibility of discovering an unknown territory, enabled by the constant reconfiguration of the work, is left to the composer's good will. He even controls the virtual nature of the work-to-be. The work springs out of the predetermination of a playground (the score) in interaction with the performers' choices (conductor and instrumentalists). "Boucourechliev's schemes provide the rules for action. Each one is a principle, an abstract formula of *what can be*."[20] The open (or semi-open) work is, according to André Boucourechliev, the "reunion in a same place" of the past (the planned and composed work, subjected to norms even before being performed), the present (the moment of performance), and the future (the work-in-progress

---

[16] Daniel Charles, "Préface," *La Musique comme parole des corps. Boris de Schloezer, André Souris et André Boucourechliev* (Paris: L'Harmattan, 2007).

[17] Ducharme, "Clefs pour l'ouverture," 67.

[18] See André Boucourechliev's performance notes for *Amers* (Paris: Leduc et Cie, 1979).

[19] Ducharme, "Clefs pour l'ouverture," 103.

[20] Ducharme, *ibid.*, 79. My italics.

to be endlessly reinvented). It is therefore the "place" of a meeting,[21] in the general sense of the term, be it imaginary, virtual, or fictitious, real or thwarted. This place is apparently fictitious and unstable and it is located close to that meeting point evoked by Henri Focillon in his short work *The Life of Forms in Art*: "(...) we should stop considering form, matter, tool and hand in isolation, and we should take position at the meeting point, the geometrical place of their activity."[22]

The geometrical form is obvious on the score: a central circle from which stem constitutive quadrant-reservoirs. Yet, Boucourechliev invites us to look at what is not a simple circle but a compass rose with which he shapes his music and which establishes a connection between the bodies that come closer to it. This compass rose goes beyond the formal space to enter the performance space. It is a clue, a potential structure, a field of operations, a figure, similar to that defined by Gilles Deleuze when he described the constancy of the circle, which delimits the place where the figure stands in Francis Bacon's paintings:

> The important point is that they [the processes of isolating the Figure inside geometric forms] do not consign the Figure to immobility but, on the contrary, render sensible a progression, an exploration of the Figure within the place, or upon itself. It is an operative field. The relation of the Figure to its isolating place defines a "fact": "the fact is ...," "what takes place is ...."[23]

This compass rose, which is located in the center and towards which all attention converges, does not delimit, represent, or tell anything. It frees the musician's performance (which involves making, listening, but also seeing) and "sticks to the fact"[24] by letting the form become figure, i.e., event. In the end, nothing is impervious, neither the form nor the reservoirs. They are simply waiting for the bodies that will emerge, for the compass rose is action, mobility, meandering. Leaving aside the directives and the instructions, the eyes of the one who discovers the score can only foresee the tumult of the rhythms and vibrations, of the tone colors with such a curiosity that it becomes difficult to refrain from browsing through what can easily be seen as a canvass. This point can be pushed further by recalling that Earl Brown's

---

[21] Ducharme, *ibid.*, 86.

[22] Arnaud Macé, *La Matière* (Paris: Flammarion, 1998), 192.

[23] Deleuze, *Francis Bacon. The Logic of Sensation*, translated by Daniel W. Smith (Minneapolis, MN: University of Minnesota Press, 2005), 5-6.

[24] Deleuze, *ibid.*, 6.

graphic scores had a profound impact on Boucourechliev.[25] Yet stressing this would be tantamount to reducing the argument to the problem of influences, that is, to the problem of historical continuum. In Boucourechliev's *Amers*, following in this way Deleuze's study on Bacon, the compass rose is not a mere geometrical symbol but the figure (shape) of a body in action, a bridge between Boucourechliev and Saint-John Perse which connects their aesthetic conceptions of music and poetry, a bridge between their respective relations to the world as creators. This bridge leads towards the very place of their encounter: the West that Boucourechliev took great care to note with an ambiguous W. The introduction to the piece is clear: Boucourechliev indicates the directions in French. Yet, if the capital letters N, E, S can indiscriminately refer to the directions in French or in English, the W clearly refers to the West, to the USA, to the horizon beyond the Atlantic Ocean. It is a clue that the thwarted encounter eventually took place.

The compass rose is a figure. It puts in front of our eyes Boucourechliev's view on Perse, i.e., those aspects of the poet's life and work that make sense to the composer.

First Angle: Lands and Territories

The compass rose stands for a journey. Both Saint-John Perse and Boucourechliev are navigators and exiles: the former moved to the United States already at the beginning of Word War II and continued to share his time between France and the United States for many years after 1957; the latter sought refuge in France after the annexation of Bulgaria by the Soviet Union in 1948 and return to his homeland only just before his death. One should not, of course, draw hasty conclusions from the possible links between this remark and the respective creative output of the two authors, although many of their works repeatedly refer to the notion of passage, evoking a movement of passing—from one land to another, from one man to another, from one island to another. This emphasis also implies passing from the *Archipels* to the Island of St-Léger-les-Feuilles located off the shore of Pointe-à-Pitre where Saint-John Perse said he was born, and which echoes in part of his family name, or to the Giens peninsula where he retired at the very end of his life. It finally means passing through all these islands, which from Thomas Moore to Jules Verne represent an appetite for travel and for the discovery of remote unidentified lands, the discovery of which is also the recovery of a forgotten paradise.

---

[25] Olivier Delaigue and Alain Poirier, "La relation Boucourechliev-Brown. 'Une sorte de pont entre l'Amérique du Nord et l'Europe'," in André Poiret, *André Boucourechliev*, 119-140.

The compass rose is in this way truly a compass, for it gives direction and leads to a place. Yet this compass rose is open and replete with the gestures of the musicians. It could be said that it does not indicate a place to reach but the *passage* itself that suits Boucourechliev and Perse so well, because both were so used to interstices and in-betweens. The compass rose is the figure of their border crossing. These borders are not simply those of lands but also those of territories, of this indivisible utopian world of which both authors are, in a way, representatives: as poet and diplomat, writer and composer, Perse and Boucourechliev would not choose a side but simply cross over. It is in the life of their works that they will meet and that they will be granted the privilege to become "gardeners" who will help a "life of forms"[26] grow and flourish free from any canon. Thanks to Foucault, we know how contradictory a place a garden is. It combines in a same locale many different, sometimes incompatible spaces.[27] These heterotopical spaces permeate history and seem to best represent our era where simultaneity, juxtaposition, dispersion, and networking embody the whole field of perception and representation. As Foucault noted, "the traditional Persian garden was a sacred rectangular space within which four parts met, representing the four parts of the world (…)."[28]

Perhaps Perse and Boucourechliev were the first spokesmen of the simultaneity, dispersion, and juxtaposition of the postmodern world. They were advocating the sharing of competences after that of knowledge and a certain taste for the unclassifiable and the iconoclastic.

Second Angle: Life and Rhythm

The compass rose gives shape to their interest for life, movement, and motion. A profusion of timbres and rhythms burst out of the instrumental work, with the help of which the musicians' bodies meet the poet's body. Both Perse and Boucourechliev shared a same taste for art conceived of as a living entity, and they both considered rhythm to be revelatory of the work's life. According to Éveline Caduc,[29] rhythm is for Saint-John Perse the memory of the poet's body living in the world, and it represents the action that the poet performs on the world in order to comprehend it. Rhythm is

---

[26] Henri Focillon, *Vie des formes* (Paris: Presses Universitaires de France, 1943).

[27] Michel Foucault, "Des espaces autres," *Dits et écrits, de 1954 à 1988*, Vol. 4, 1980-1988 (Paris: Gallimard, 1994), 752-762.

[28] Foucault, *ibid.*, 758-759.

[29] Éveline Caduc, "Saint-John Perse: une philosophie au miroir de la poétique," *Noesis* 7: *La philosophie du XXe siècle et le défi poétique*, available online (15 May 2005) at http://noesis.revues.org.

"breath, blood, and muscle." Yet rhythm is also the essential agent for the enunciation, because it is perceived by the ear and makes the past and future of the text available in the present of the act of reading. Rhythm represents an experience of the text where the fusion of the subject and the act of enunciation is achieved in the poem constructed by the reader. Thus, rhythm has no meaning but creates meaning; it is consubstantial to it. As Henri Meschonnic writes, rhythm reveals a meaning of the meaning and of the unfathomable subject with the help of language as a code.[30] When reading Perse's poetry one realizes how accurate is the conception Éveline Caduc unveils. One must also recall how important rhythm is for Boucourechliev. Rhythm federates all the musical parameters in action. Without it, the very reason for musicianship ceases to exist. That rhythm became the force and life of music is one of the main conquests of musical modernity from Stravinsky to Ligeti. This sort of rhythm does not need text or words. As Boucourechliev noted:

> How can the synthesis of all parameters in action within the musical structure be obtained? Under the category of time—that is, rhythm. The moment has come to re-examine its definition.
>
> The notion of rhythm can be extended to all the parameters in action, especially if music is seen as a system of differences. Because any small change—in harmony, pitch, duration, intensity, tone color, register, attack, weight—yields a mark, an inflection on musical time, everything is rhythm.[31]

Yet again, we are dealing with a place and a figure of utopia: rhythm as the utopia *of meaning*; meaning before the said or the understood; meaning as it is, bursting out and charged with words. And beyond, the compass rose represents the open border between music and poetry where the crossing from one to the other can take place anywhere and anyhow, provided that the compass is not held too tightly, and provided one remembers that it is with a compass that the young Einstein first had the intuition of relativity.

If *ekphrasis* is a description of the absent work, moving around it and bluntly placing before us what needs to be displayed, then Boucourechliev's *Amers* truly is an *ekphrasis* of Saint-John Perse's *Amers*. Yet it is an *ekphrasis* in a state of denial. Boucourechliev's piece is a project for an emancipated music, as meaningful as poetry or, more generally, language. More profoundly, it is a *utopian* project, suggesting a realm where the

---

[30] Henri Meschonnic, *Critique du rythme. Anthropologie historique du langage* (Paris: Verdier, 1982), 715.

[31] André Boucourechliev, *Essai sur Beethoven* (Paris: Actes Sud, 1991), 43 et 46.

gathering of the arts would take place with the kind of sharing and community of perception that André Boucourechliev was advocating beyond his own poetics.

Very few composers of the time ever discussed with performers or talked about the role of the listener and the power of listening as much as Boucourechliev did. In this way, his theoretical stances placed him in the continuity of post-structuralism and of the textual pragmatics that flourished in Europe and the United States in the 1960s. Boucourechliev's inclination toward the works of Roland Barthes[32] and Umberto Eco[33] is in fact well documented. The conception of the coactoriality of the text leads to the recognition of the importance of readers (in the broad sense of the word) in the "construction—and deconstruction—of the text during the act of reading, conceived of as a necessary and effective condition for the advent of the text as such."[34]

How should we conclude? By reading or by listening? Or perhaps by making an allusion to another exile, another border-crosser, and a musician-poet who had once wanted to become a singer. I am of course talking about James Joyce and I would like to quote the first verse of a poem from *Chamber Music*[35]:

> Strings in the earth and air
> Make music sweet;
> Strings by the river where
> The willows meet.

---

[32] See Alain Poirier, *André Boucourechliev*.
[33] *Ibid.*
[34] Eco, *Les Limites de l'interprétation* (Paris: Grasset, 1992), 21-22.
[35] From James Joyce, *Chamber Music* (New York: Columbia University Press, 1954), 109.

Index

Abbiati, Franco: 77
Addison, Joseph: 45
Adorno, Theodor W.: 119, 129
Albright, Daniel: 50, 52, 55, 64
Altenburg, Detlef: 191
Arnheim, Rudolf: 166
Arronategui, Padre Eusebio: 162
Atwood, William G.: 17, 42, 43
Bach, Johann Sebastian: 13, 24-25, 39, 130, 134, 159-160, 165
Bach, Johann Sebastian: 47, 53
Bacon, Francis: 224, 228, 229
Barthes, Roland: 224, 232
Barzun, Jacques: 64
Basilius, Harold A.: 108
Baynes, Cary F.: 155, 157, 158
Beethoven, Ludwig van: 47-49, 54, 63, 64, 68, 105-112, 114, 167, 175, 181, 193-196, 198-202
Benjamin, Walter: 174-177, 179
Bentley, Gerald Eades: 70
Berg, Alban: 204
Berio, Luciano: 119-124, 126-129, 134, 136
Berlioz, Hector: 10, 45-68, 174, 177-178, 194
Bernhart, Walter: 50
Bird, Robert: 10, 108
Birtwistle, Harrison: 119-121, 128-132, 135-136
Black, Max: 120-121, 123, 127, 136
Boito, Arrigo: 71, 85, 91, 93, 99
Boucourechliev, André: 9, 221-232
Brinkmann, Reinhold: 205
Brown, Matthew: 100
Brueghel, Pieter: 7
Bruhn, Siglind: 8, 9, 112, 173

Bülow, Hans von: 13, 182
Burgart, Jean-Pierre: 221, 224
Burgess, Anthony: 108
Busoni, Federico: 16
Byron, Lord George Gordon: 185, 189, 201
Caduc, Éveline: 230
Caduff, Corinna: 47
Cain, T. G. S.: 106
Calderwood, James L.: 71
Carter, Elliott: 9
Celan, Paul: 9, 119-141
Cervantes, Miguel de: 191
Chailley, Jacques: 56, 65
Charles, Daniel: 222, 227
Chipp, Herschel B.: 164
Chopin, Frédéric: 9, 13-43
Christian, Reginald F.: 108
Clementi, Muzio: 15
Clüver, Claus: 8
Colin, Amy D.: 123
Confucius (Kung Fu-zi): 155
Conner, Theodore Albritton: 84-85, 100
Cooper, John Michael: 199
Corse, Sandra: 84, 85
Cramer, Johann Baptist: 15, 18
Cubeta, Paul: 69
Czerny, Carl: 15
Dahlhaus, Carl: 180, 191
David, Johann Nepomuk: 24-25
de Moor, Margriet: 110-111
Debussy, Claude: 13
Dehmel, Richard: 9, 206-207
Delaigue, Olivier: 229
Deleuze, Gilles: 224, 228-229
Deschamps, Émile: 50, 52, 62
Diderot, Denis: 66

Dies irae motif: 30-36, 39-40, 43
Drenger, Tino: 72, 83
Droste-Hülshoff, Annette von: 143
Ducharme, Jean: 225, 227-228
Dussek, Jan Ladislav: 15
Eber, Irene: 155
Eco, Umberto: 225, 232
Eggebrecht, Hans Heinrich: 191
Eguchi, Mahoko: 106
Eigeldinger, Jean-Jacques: 15, 18-21, 24, 30, 32, 39, 42
ekphrasis, ekphrastic: 7-10, 143, 144, 146, 173, 204, 222-223, 231
Elleström, Lars: 133
Emmerich, Wolfgang: 128, 130
Engeler, Chris: 50
Esclapez, Christine: 223
Feldman, Morton: 224
Felstiner, John: 119, 121, 123, 126, 129-130, 139
Ferrero, Mercedes Viale: 97
Ferrier, Jean-Louis: 164
Fichte, Johann Gottlieb: 176-177
Floros, Constantin: 191
Focillon, Henri: 228, 230
Föllmi, Beat A.: 219
Foucault, Michel: 230
Franco, Francisco: 162
Gabrieli, Giovanni: 88
Garrick, David: 50, 52, 56
George, Stefan: 206
Gide, André: 13
Giraud, Albert (Marie-Émile-Albert Kayenbergh: 207-209, 213-214
Glenn, Jerry: 119
Gluck, Christoph Willibald von: 47, 49, 50, 167
Goertzen, Valerie Woodring: 14, 15
Goethe, Johann Wolfgang von: 185, 195, 201
Grabócz, Márta: 181, 186
Gramit, David: 65
Green, Dorothy: 108
Greimas, Algirdas Julien: 216

Guyard, Marius-François: 27
Hahn, Arthur: 197
Hamburger, Michael ; 128, 130, 132
Hamilton, Kenneth: 14
Handel, George Frederic: 47, 167
Hanke-Knaus, Gabriela: 187
Hanslick, Eduard: 64, 128, 175, 182
Hartleben, Otto Erich von: 207-209, 213-214
Hatten, Robert: 113-114
Hawes, Jane: 72
Haydn, Joseph: 47, 198
Heffernan, James: 7-8
Hegel, Georg Wilhelm Friedrich: 180
Heilman, Robert B.: 69
Hensel, Ilse: 147
Hepokoski, James: 75, 85, 87, 91, 97, 99, 100, 190
Hermand, Jost: 205
Hinton, Stephen: 68
Hirsch, James: 71
Hitler, Adolf: 162
Hoffmann, E.T.A.: 46, 47, 177
Hofmann, Gert: 7
Hofmann, Josef : 14
Hollander, Hans: 205
Holthusen, Hans Egon: 119
Hummel, Johann Nepomuk: 15, 16, 18, 26
Huppert, Hugo: 129
I Ching: 144, 154-158
James, Henry: 68
Janáček, Leoš: 9, 105-118
Johnson, James H. Johnson: 43
Jones, David Wyn: 194
Joyce, James: 232
Jugendstil: 203-207, 209, 212, 216, 218, 219
Kalkbrenner, Frederic: 15
Kallberg, Jeffrey: 16-19, 23
Keller, Hermann: 25
Kerman, Joseph: 73, 86
Kivy, Peter: 50
Koch, Heinrich: 193-195, 198-199

Index 235

Korsyn, Kevin: 20
Kramer, Lawrence: 19
Kranz, Gisbert: 7 , 173
Kresky, Jeffrey: 19-20
Kulka, Janos: 161
Kunstkritik: 173-177, 179-180, 183-185, 189-192, 200-202
Lagerlöf, Selma: 149
Lamartine, Alphonse de: 9, 13, 26-32, 35, 43
Langford, Jeffrey: 65
Lato: 45
Lawton, David: 100
Leibowitz, René: 203
Leikin, Anatole: 30, 31
Lenau, Nicolaus: 189
Letourneur, Pierre: 50
Ligeti, György: 231
Liszt, Franz: 13, 15-16, 26-27, 31, 174, 177-181, 183-186, 189, 191, 192, 196, 200-202
Littlefield, David: 69
Mackey, Cindy: 119
Maeterlinck, Maurice: 7, 9, 206-207
Mahler, Gustav: 63
Melville, Herman: 68
Menninghaus, Winfried: 127-128
Meschonnic, Henri: 231
Messiaen, Olivier: 153
metaphor: 120-121, 123, 127-130, 132, 134-136
Mickiewicz, Adam: 185, 201
Miller, Leta: 13, 39
Monteverdi, Claudio: 47
Morrow, Mary Sue: 43
Moscheles, Ignaz: 15, 18
Mozart, Leopold: 38
Mozart, Wolfgang Amadeus: 47, 167, 181, 189, 198
Mueller von Asow, Erich H.: 197
Mussolini, Benito: 162
Neubauer, John: 45-46, 50, 66
Nietzsche, Friedrich: 45
North, Roger: 65

Noske, Trits: 72, 76, 83, 100
Novalis (Friedrich von Hardenberg): 46
Olschner, Leonard : 123
Pack, Robert: 69
Paginini, Niccolò: 50
Papazian, Elizabeth: 108
Parker, Roger: 100
Pater, Walter: 45
Paul, Jean (Jean Paul Richter): 66, 177
Peirce, Charles Sanders: 118
Pergament, Moses: 149
Perse, Saint-John: 9, 221-225, 229-231
Petri, Horst: 133
Pfannkuch, Wilhelm: 180
Phipps, Graham H.: 198
Picasso, Pablo: 144, 161, 162, 164-169
Poirier, Alain: 221, 229, 232
Price, Thomas: 71
Prieto, Eric: 120, 134
Prinz, Ulrich: 159
Rachmaninov, Sergei: 13
Rameau, Jean-Philippe: 47
ranz des vaches: 194, 199
Richards, Ivor Armstrong: 120
Ricœur, Paul: 120
Roman, Zoltan: 205
Rossini, Gioachino: 43
Rousseau, Jean-Jacques: 38, 47, 194-195
Rubinstein, Anton: 14
Rump, Ariane: 158
Rushton, Julian: 54-56, 59, 61-66, 68
Sachs, Nelly: 9, 143-144, 149-150, 153-154, 157-158, 160-161, 166, 168-169
Sadrieh, Astrid: 198
Samson, Jim: 15, 16, 19, 24, 32
Schachter, Carl: 29-30
Scherliess, Volker: 211
Schiller, Friedrich von: 68
Schlegel, Friedrich: 66, 68, 174-177, 179-180, 185, 201
Schmenner, Roland: 194
Schmidt, Christian Martin: 209

Schmidt, Reiner: 161
Schneider, Mathieu: 174, 176, 183, 189, 190, 192, 195, 199
Schoenberg, Arnold: 9, 203-220
Schopenhauer, Arthur: 192, 194
Schuh, Willi: 180-184, 196, 199, 202
Schumann, Clara: 14
Schumann, Robert: 14, 47, 177, 194
Schwartz, Benjamin I.: 155
Schwermer, Johannes: 205
Scriabin, Alexander: 13
Scruton, Roger: 105
Seckler, Jerome: 168
Seng, Joachim: 119
Shakespeare, William: 10, 31, 50, 52-53, 55, 59, 61-62, 64, 66, 69-72, 75, 83, 85, 88, 89, 91, 93, 95, 96, 99, 101, 183-186, 189, 191
Shostakovich, Dmitri: 13
Simms, Bryan: 208
Škampa, Milan: 109, 111, 112
Smith, Charles J.: 20-21, 23-24
Spitzer, Michael: 120
Steffens, Walter: 9, 143-154, 157-163, 165-166, 168-169
Sterne, Laurence: 62, 66
Stewart, Corbet: 123
Stösslová, Kamila: 111
Strauss, Richard: 173-175, 179-193, 196-202
Stravinsky, Igor: 211, 231

Szpetecki, Elfriede: 144, 146-148, 150-152, 161, 166, 168
Teague, Frances: 71
Thomas, Gavin: 123
Thuille, Ludwig: 181, 184
Tieck, Wilhelm: 66
Tolstoy, Count Lev (Leo) Nikolayevich: 9, 68, 105-111, 114, 115, 118
tone poem: 10, 173-202
Tonmalerei: 173, 175, 193-202
transmedialization: 8-9
Trenner, Franz: 181-182, 184, 192, 199
Verdi, Giuseppe: 10, 69-101
Vogel, Jaroslav: 109
Wackenroder, Wilhelm Heinrich: 45-46
Wagner, Richard: 47, 63, 66, 68, 73, 180, 192, 194, 200
Wallace, Robert K.: 108
Weber, Carl Maria von: 43, 47
Webern, Anton: 204-205
Wedekind, Frank: 206
Weigl, Joseph: 200
Werbeck, Walter: 183, 192
Werker, Wilhelm: 24-25
Wilhelm, Richard: 144, 154-158, 161
Will, Richard James: 194
Williamson, John: 198
Wingfield, Paul: 109, 112, 115
Wood, John Muir: 17
Youens, Susan: 208
Zemanová, Mirka: 109, 111
Zenck, Martin: 119

The Contributors

Siglind Bruhn is a full-time researcher in 20th-century musicology. She has been affiliated with the University of Michigan's Institute for the Humanities since 1993 and is currently also a guest researcher at the Sorbonne's Institute for the Esthetics of Contemporary Arts. She has authored more than twenty book-length monographs; among them in English most recently *Messiaen's Contemplations of Covenant and Incarnation: Musical Symbols of Faith in the Two Great Piano Cycles of the 1940s* (Pendragon 2007), *Messiaen's Explorations of Love and Death: Musico-poetic Signification in the Tristan Trilogy and Three Related Song Cycles* (Pendragon 2008), and *Messiaen's Interpretations of Holiness and Trinity: Echoes of Medieval Theology in the Oratorio, Organ Meditations, and Opera* (Pendragon 2008). In 2001 she was elected to the European Academy of Arts and Sciences; in 2008 the Swedish university of Växjö awarded her an honorary doctorate.

William P. Dougherty is the Ellis and Nelle Levitt Professor of Music at Drake University in Des Moines, Iowa, where he teaches courses in music theory and composition. He has published articles on musical semeiotic and on the relation of music and text in the art song. He is currently writing a book titled *Mignon in Music: The Art Song as Semeiotic*. The essay in this collection grows out his long-standing interest in the connections between music and literature. Also a composer, he has written works for band, orchestra, and a variety of chamber and solo combinations.

Axel Englund, a Doctoral Candidate in Literature, is currently working on a dissertation on music in and around the poetry of Paul Celan at Stockholm University, where he also teaches courses in metrics and modernist exile literature. While studying for his three previous degrees (a BA in Musicology, an MA in Comparative Literature, and an MFA in Musical Composition, all from Lund University), he taught music theory and computer notation. His music has been performed by the Helsingborg Symphony Orchestra, the Swedish National Orchestra Academy, and the Musica Vitae String Orchestra. A CD of his works was released in 2004, and in 2007 his string trio *For Sappho* represented Sweden at the UNM Festival, a showcase for young Nordic composers, in Reykjavik, Iceland.

Christine Esclapez is Associate Professor of Musicology at the University Aix-Marseille I, where she currently also serves as director of the Department of Music and Musical Sciences. Her research focuses on questions of musical temporality, aesthetics, and interpretation, on the relationship between music and language and, more generally, on the exploration of the mutual influence between musical theory and practice. In 2007, Éditions L'Harmattan in Paris published her book-length monograph on "music as language of the body," *La musique comme parole des corps. Boris de Schloezer, André Souris et André Boucourechliev.*

Beat A. Föllmi is Associate Professor of Musicology at the University of Strasbourg's Department of Protestant Theology. He completed his studies of musicology and theology at the universities of Zurich and Strasbourg with a dissertation on "Tradition as a Hermeneutic Category in the Work of Arnold Schoenberg" and has published numerous essays on Schoenberg. Concurrently, he is the editor of a critical edition of the complete works of the Swiss composer Othmar Schoeck and in this capacity has been elected to membership in the Swiss Academy of Humanities and Social Sciences. He also served on the advisory board for entries concerning Switzerland in the latest edition of the encyclopaedia *Musik in Geschichte und Gegenwart*.

Jeffrey Kurtzman is Professor of Music and former Chair of the Department of Music at Washington University in St. Louis. In 1975 he was one of the initial faculty of the newly founded Shepherd School of Music at Rice University, and was the founding President of the Society for Seventeenth-Century Music. Specializing primarily in sixteenth and seventeenth-century Italian music, he has published two books on the *Vespro della Beata Vergine* of Claudio Monteverdi, editions of the mass music of Monteverdi, editions of Vespers and Compline music of the 17th century, as well as numerous articles on Monteverdi and the repertoire of Italian Office Music in the 16th and 17th centuries. His teaching ranges across the entire history of Western music and his interest in Shakespeare's Othello and Verdi's Otello stems from his more general interest in relationships between words and music in all periods of Western music history.

Anatole Leikin is Professor of Music at the University of California, Santa Cruz. His scholarly works on such topics as Romantic performance practice, Chopin, Scriabin, Rachmaninov, Shostakovich, Granados, early tonality, and structural and hermeneutic analysis have appeared in various musicological journals and essay collections worldwide. Professor Leikin performs frequently as a solo and chamber pianist and fortepianist; he has also recorded the piano music of Scriabin, Chopin, and EMI/Cope. He currently serves as an editor for *The Complete Chopin – A New Critical Edition* (Peters Edition, London) and is writing a book on the performing style of Alexander Scriabin for Ashgate Publishing, UK.

John Neubauer is professor emeritus of Comparative Literature at the University of Amsterdam and a corresponding Fellow of the British Academy (FBA). Earlier, he taught at Princeton University, Case Western University, and the University of Pittsburgh; he was also visiting professor at Harvard, Princeton, and other universities. His publications include *Symbolismus und symbolische Logik* (1978), *Novalis* (1980), *The Emancipation of Music from Language* (1986), and *The Fin-de-siècle Culture of Adolescence* (1992), as well as substantial contributions to the "Munich edition" of Goethe's scientific works. He is a coeditor with Peter de Voogd of *The Reception of Laurence Sterne in Europe* (2004) and with Marcel Cornis-Pope of a four-volume *History of the Literary Cultures of East-Central Europe*. His recent interests include globalization, theories of literary history, and exile.

Mathieu Schneider is Associate Professor and head of the department of musicology at the University Marc Bloch in Strasbourg. A specialist of German Postromanticism, he is the author of a book-length monograph on the relationship between music and literature in the symphonic works of Gustav Mahler and Richard Strauss (*Destins croisés*, Waldkirch: Gorz, 2005). Moreover, he serves as the chief editor of the Cahiers Franz Schubert, has published essays in various scholarly journals both in France and abroad, and has contributed a number of entries to the latest edition of the leading German music encyclopaedia, *Die Musik in Geschichte und Gegenwart*. An additional field of interest is the study of representations of Switzerland in 19th-century music.

BJ 1012
H35
1988

Hazlitt, Henry, 1894–

The foundations of morality

THE FOUNDATIONS OF MORALITY

Henry Hazlitt

UNIVERSITY
PRESS OF
AMERICA

Copyright © 1988 by

University Press of America,® Inc.

4720 Boston Way
Lanham, MD 20706

All rights reserved

Printed in the United States of America

Copyright © 1964 by D. Van Nostrand Company, Inc.
Copyright © 1972 by Henry Hazlitt

This is a reprint of the 1972 Nash Publishing Company edition,
initially sponsored by the Institute for Humane Studies, Inc., California.

Library of Congress Cataloging-in-Publication Data

Hazlitt, Henry, 1894–
The foundations of morality / Henry Hazlitt.
p. cm.
Reprint. Originally published: Los Angeles : Nash Pub., 1972.
Includes bibliographical references.
1. Ethics. I. Title.
[BJ1012.H35   1988]
170—dc 19   88–18695 CIP
ISBN 0–8191–7092–5 (pbk. : alk. paper)

All University Press of America books are produced on acid-free paper.
The paper used in this publication meets the minimum requirements of American
National Standard for Information Sciences—Permanence of Paper for Printed
Library Materials, ANSI Z39.48–1984.

To preach morality is easy,
to give it a foundation is hard.
ARTHUR SCHOPENHAUER

Preface

It would be enormously presumptuous for any writer, in a subject that has engaged the earnest attention of the world's greatest minds over twenty-five centuries, to claim very much originality. Such a claim would, moreover, probably be more presumptuous in ethics than in any other subject; for as I point out in my Introduction, any ethical system that proposed a "transvaluation of all (traditional) values" would be almost certainly wrong.

Yet progress in ethics is none the less possible, and for the same reasons that it is possible and has been achieved in other branches of knowledge and thought. "A dwarf sees farther than a giant can, if he stands on the giant's shoulders." Because we stand on the shoulders of our great predecessors, and have the benefit of their insights and solutions, it is not unreasonable to hope that we can formulate more satisfactory answers to at least a few questions in ethics than the answers they were able to find. This progress is most likely to consist in achieving greater clarity, precision, logical rigor, unification, and integration with other disciplines.

I was myself originally led to write the present book by the conviction that modern economics had worked out answers to the problems of individual and social value of which most contemporary moral philosophers still seem quite unaware. These answers not only throw great light on some of the central problems of ethics, but enable us to make a better analysis of the comparative *moral* merits of capitalism, socialism, and communism than ethical specialists have hitherto been able to offer.

After I decided to write this book, however, and began to think and read more about the problems of ethics, I became increasingly impressed with the enormous amount, also, that ethical theory had to learn from what had already been discovered in jurisprudence. It is true not merely that law enforces a "minimum ethics," that "law is a circle with the same center as moral philosophy, but with a smaller circumference." It is true also that jurisprudence has worked out methods and principles for solving legal problems that can be extremely illuminating when applied to ethical problems. The legal point of view leads, among other things, to explicit recognition of the immense importance of acting in strict accordance with established *general rules*. I have sought here to present a "unified theory" of law, morals, and manners.

Finally I was increasingly struck by the falsity of the *antithesis* so commonly drawn by moral philosophers between the interests of the individual and the interests of society. When the rightly understood interests of the individual are considered *in the long run*, they are found to be in harmony with and to *coincide* (almost if not quite to the point of identity) with the long-run interests of society. And to recognize this leads us to recognize conduciveness to *social cooperation* as the great criterion of the rightness of actions, because voluntary social cooperation is the great means for the attainment not only of our collective but of nearly all our individual ends.

On the negative side, I have been depressed by the excessive preoccupation of most of the serious ethical literature of the last thirty and even sixty years (if we begin with G. E. Moore's *Principia Ethica*) with purely linguistic analysis. I have touched on this (in Sections 7 and 8 of Chapter 23) only enough to point out why most of this hair-splitting and logomachy is a digression from the true business of ethics.

In a field that has been furrowed as often as ethics, one's intellectual indebtedness to previous writers must be so extensive as to make specific acknowledgment seem haphazard and arbitrary. But the older writers from whom I have learned most are the British Utilitarians beginning with Hume, and running through Adam Smith, Bentham, Mill, and Sidgwick. And the greatest of these is Hume, whose insistence on the utility of acting strictly in accordance with *general rules* was so strangely overlooked by nearly all of his classical Utilitarian successors. Much of what is best in both Adam Smith and Bentham seems little more than an elaboration of ideas first clearly stated by Hume.

My greatest indebtedness to a living writer (as I think will be evident from my specific quotations from his works) is to Ludwig von Mises—whose ethical observations, unfortunately, have not been developed at length but appear as brief incidental passages in his great contributions to economics and "praxeology." Among contemporary moral philosophers I have learned much, even when I disagreed with them, from Sir David Ross, Stephen Toulmin, A. C. Ewing, Kurt Baier, Richard B. Brandt, J. O. Urmson, and John Hospers. And in tracing the relations between law and ethics, my chief sources have been Roscoe Pound, Sir Paul Vinogradoff, and F. A. Hayek.

I am deeply indebted both to Professor von Mises and Professor Hospers (in addition to the help I have received from their writings) for kindly reading my manuscript and offering their criticisms and suggestions. Whatever the defects of my book may still be, and however much I may have fallen short of appreciating the full force of some of their criticisms, or of making adequate correction, I am sure this is a much better book than it would have been without their generous help.

A question that may occur to some readers at the very beginning, and must haunt many a writer on ethics at some time during the course of his study and composition, is: What is the *use* of moral philosophy? A man may know what is right and still fail to do it. He may know that an action is wrong and still lack the strength of will to refrain. I can only offer for ethical theory the defense offered by John Stuart Mill in his *Autobiography* for the usefulness of his *System of Logic,* that "whatever may be the practical value of a true philosophy of these matters, it is hardly possible to exaggerate the mischiefs of a false one."

HENRY HAZLITT

December 1963

Preface to the Second Edition

I wish to express my gratitude to the Institute for Humane Studies for making this new edition possible.

No changes have been made from the original edition of 1964 except to correct a few typographical errors. This does not mean that my ideas on ethics have undergone no change whatever in the last nine years, but simply that these have not been important enough to justify rewriting and resetting.

Moral philosophers often have second thoughts. The ideas of Bertrand Russell underwent such frequent and radical changes that in 1952 he wrote to two anthologists (Sellers and Hospers) who reprinted an essay of his published in 1910: "I am not quite satisfied with any view of ethics that I have been able to arrive at, and that is why I have abstained from writing again on the subject." (Later, however, he did.)

I have no such violent reversals to report. I cannot think of a single change, for example, that I would make in my views as summarized in the final chapter. Yet if I were writing the book afresh, there would no doubt be changes in emphasis and in minor points. In discussing the ultimate goal of ethics I would use the word "happiness" less frequently and more often substitute "satisfaction" or "well-being" or even simply "good." In fact, I would give less attention to trying to specify the ultimate goal of conduct. As social cooperation is the great means of achieving nearly all our individual ends, this means can be thought of as itself the moral goal to be achieved.

If I have anywhere written a sentence which seems to imply that individuals are or should be always actuated by exclusively egocentric or eudemonic motives, I would now modify or withdraw it. I would emphasize even more strongly than I do in the section which runs from page 123 to page 127 that though the ideal rules of morality are those best calculated to serve the interest of *everyone* in the long run, there will nevertheless be occasions when these rules will call for a real sacrifice of his immediate interests by an individual, and that when they do so this sacrifice must be made because of the overriding necessity of maintaining these rules inviolate. This moral principle is no different from the universally acknowledged legal principle that a man must abide by a valid contract even when it proves costly for him to do so. The rules of morality constitute a tacit social contract.

Is the moral philosophy advocated in these pages "utilitarian" or not? In the sense that all rules of conduct must be judged by their tendency to lead to desirable rather than undesirable social results, any rational ethics whatever must be utilitarian. But when the word is used it seems most often to arouse in the minds of readers some specific nineteenth-century writer's views, if not a mere caricature of them. I found it extremely discouraging to have my ideas characterized in one so-called scholarly journal as "straight utilitarianism" (whatever that may mean) even though I had pointed out (p. 359), however facetiously, that there are probably more than thirteen "utilitarianisms," and in any case had unequivocally rejected the "classical" *ad hoc* utilitarianism implicit in Bentham, Mill and Sidgwick, and espoused instead a *"rule-*utilitism" as earlier propounded by Hume. The review just cited only reinforced the conviction I expressed (also on page 359) that the term *Utilitarianism* is beginning to outlive its usefulness in ethical discussion. I have called my own system *Cooperatism*, which seems sufficiently descriptive.

Henry Hazlitt
August, 1972.

Acknowledgments

The following publishers have kindly allowed me to quote from the works mentioned: The Bobbs-Merrill Co., *The Measure of Man*, by Joseph Wood Krutch; The Clarendon Press at Oxford, *The Law of Nations*, by J. L. Brierly; Routledge & Kegan Paul, Ltd. of London, *The Common Sense of Political Economy*, by Philip H. Wicksteed; Simon and Schuster, Inc. *Human Nature in Ethics and Politics*, by Bertrand Russell; The University of Chicago Press, *The Constitution of Liberty*, by F. A. Hayek; and the Yale University Press, *Human Action*, by Ludwig von Mises.

I have to thank the administrator of the estate of Morris Raphael Cohen for permission to quote from his *Faith of a Liberal* and *A Preface to Logic*, both published by Henry Holt and Co.

Finally, I wish to thank the Curtis Publishing Co. for permitting me to include, as an appendix, a signed editorial of mine, "Johnny and the Tiger," which appeared in the June 10, 1950 issue of *The Saturday Evening Post*.

Other acknowledgments will be found in footnotes.

H. H.

Contents

	PREFACE	vii
CHAPTER		
1	INTRODUCTION	1
2	THE MYSTERY OF MORALS	7
3	THE MORAL CRITERION	11
4	PLEASURE AS THE END	15
5	SATISFACTION AND HAPPINESS	21
6	SOCIAL COOPERATION	35
7	LONG RUN vs. SHORT RUN	44
8	THE NEED FOR GENERAL RULES	53
9	ETHICS AND LAW	62
10	TRAFFIC RULES AND MORAL RULES	70
11	MORALS AND MANNERS	75
12	PRUDENCE AND BENEVOLENCE	81
13	EGOISM, ALTRUISM, MUTUALISM	92
14	THE PROBLEM OF SELF-SACRIFICE	108
15	ENDS AND MEANS	128
16	DUTY FOR DUTY'S SAKE	139
17	ABSOLUTISM vs. RELATIVISM	150
18	THE PROBLEM OF VALUE	159
19	INTUITION AND COMMON SENSE	176
20	VOCATION AND CIRCUMSTANCE	188
21	"THE LAW OF NATURE"	203
22	ASCETICISM	207
23	ETHICAL SKEPTICISM	223

24	Justice	248
25	Equality and Inequality	262
26	Freedom	266
27	Free Will and Determinism	269
28	Rights	279
29	International Ethics	288
30	The Ethics of Capitalism	301
31	The Ethics of Socialism	325
32	Morality and Religion	342
33	Summary and Conclusion	354
	Appendix	361
	Notes	363
	Index	387

CHAPTER 1
Introduction

1. *Religion and Moral Decline*

Like many another writer, Herbert Spencer wrote his own first book on morals, *The Data of Ethics*, under a sense of urgency. In the preface to that volume, in June 1879, he told his readers that he was departing from the order originally set down for the volumes in his "System of Synthetic Philosophy" because: "Hints, repeated of late years with increasing frequency and distinctness, have shown me that health may permanently fail, even if life does not end, before I reach the last part of the task I have marked out for myself."

"This last part of the task it is," he continued, "to which I regard all the preceding parts as subsidiary." And he went on to say that ever since his first essay in 1842, on *The Proper Sphere of Government*, "my ultimate purpose, lying behind all proximate purposes, has been that of finding for the principles of right and wrong, in conduct at large, a scientific basis."

Moreover, he regarded the establishment of rules of right conduct on a scientific basis as "a pressing need. Now that moral injunctions are losing the authority given by their supposed sacred origin, the secularization of morals is becoming imperative. Few things can happen more disastrous than the decay and death of a regulative system no longer fit, before another and fitter regulative system has grown up to replace it. Most of those who reject the current creed appear to assume that the controlling agency furnished by it may safely be thrown aside, and the vacancy left unfilled by any other controlling agency. Meanwhile, those who defend the current creed allege that in the absence of the guidance it yields, no guidance can exist: divine commandments they think the only possible guides."

Spencer's fears of more than eighty years ago have been in large part realized, and at least partly for the reason he gave. Along with the decline of religious faith since his day, there has been a decline in morality. It is seen almost throughout the world in the increase of crime, in the rise of juvenile delinquency, in the increasing resort to violence for the settlement of internal economic and political disputes, in the decline of authority and discipline. Above all, and in its most extreme form, it is seen in the rise of Communism, that "religion of immoralism," [1] both as a doctrine and a world political force.

Now the contemporary decline in morality is at least in part the result of the decline in religion. There are probably millions of people who believe, with Ivan Karamazov in Dostoyevsky's novel, that under atheism "everything is permissible." And many would even say, with his half-brother Smerdyakov, who took him with tragic literalness, that "If there's no everlasting God, there's no such thing as virtue, and there's no need of it." Marxism is not only belligerently atheistic, but seeks to destroy religion precisely because it believes it to be "the opium of the people"—i.e., because it supports a "bourgeois" morality that deprecates the systematic deceit, lying, treachery, lawlessness, confiscation, violence, civil war, and murder that the Communists regard as necessary for the overthrow or conquest of capitalism.

How far religious faith may be a necessary basis of ethics we shall examine at a later point. Here I wish merely to point out that historically at least a large part of ethical rules and customs have always had a secular basis. And this is true not only of moral customs but of philosophical ethics. It is merely necessary to mention the names of such pre-Christian moralists as Confucius, Pythagoras, Heraclitus, Democritus, Socrates, Plato, Aristotle, and the Stoics and Epicureans, to recall the extent to which this is true. Even the churchmen of the Middle Ages, as represented pre-eminently by Thomas Aquinas, were indebted for more of their ethical theory to Aristotle than to Augustine.

2. *A Practical Problem*

But granted that moral custom and moral theory can have an autonomous or partly autonomous base apart from any specific religious faith, what is this base, and how is it to be found? This is the central problem of philosophic ethics. As Schopenhauer has summed it up: "To preach morality is easy, to give it a foundation is hard."

INTRODUCTION 3

It is so very hard, indeed, as to seem almost hopeless. This sense of near hopelessness has received eloquent expression from one of the great ethical leaders of our century, Albert Schweitzer:

> Is there, however, any sense in ploughing for the thousand and second time a field which has already been ploughed a thousand and one times? Has not everything which can be said about ethics already been said by Lao-tse, Confucius, the Buddha, and Zarathustra; by Amos and Isaiah; by Socrates, Plato, and Aristotle; by Epicurus and the Stoics; by Jesus and Paul; by the thinkers of the Renaissance, of the "Aufklärung," and of Rationalism; by Locke, Shaftesbury, and Hume; by Spinoza and Kant; by Fichte and Hegel; by Schopenhauer, Nietzsche, and others? Is there any possibility of getting beyond all these contradictory convictions of the past to new beliefs which will have a stronger and more lasting influence? Can the ethical kernel of the thoughts of all these men be collected into an idea of the ethical, which will unite all the energies to which they appeal? We must hope so, if we are not to despair of the fate of the human race.[2]

It would seem enormously presumptuous, after this list of great names, for anyone to write still another book on ethics, if it were not for two considerations: first, ethics is primarily a *practical* problem; and secondly, it is a problem that has not yet been satisfactorily solved.

It is no disparagement of ethics to recognize frankly that the problems it poses are primarily practical. If they were not practical we would be under no obligation to solve them. Even Kant, one of the most purely theoretical of theoreticians, recognized the essentially practical nature of ethical thinking in the very title of his chief work on ethics: *Critique of Practical Reason*. If we lose sight of this practical goal, the first danger is that we may lose ourselves in unanswerable questions such as: What are we here for? What is the purpose of the existence of the universe? What is the ultimate destiny of mankind? The second danger is that we may fall into mere triviality and dilettantism, and end up with some such conclusion as that of C. D. Broad:

> We can no more learn to act rightly by appealing to the ethical theory of right action than we can play golf well by appealing to the mathematical theory of the golf-ball. The interest of ethics is

thus almost wholly theoretical, as is the interest of the mathematical theory of golf or of billiards. . . . Salvation is not everything; and to try to understand in outline what one solves *ambulando* in detail is quite good fun for those people who like that sort of thing.[3]

Such an attitude tends toward sterility. It leads one to select the wrong problems as the most important, and it gives no standard for testing the usefulness of a conclusion. It is because so many ethical writers have taken a similar attitude that they have been so often lost in purely verbal problems and so often satisfied with merely rhetorical solutions. One can imagine how little progress would have been made in law reform, jurisprudence, or economics if they had been thought of as posing purely theoretical problems that were merely "good fun for those people who like that sort of thing."

The present fashionable disparagement of "mere practicality" was not shared by Immanuel Kant, who pointed out that: "To yield to every whim of curiosity, and to allow our passion for inquiry to be restrained by nothing but the limits of our ability, this shows an eagerness of mind not unbecoming to *scholarship*. But it is *wisdom* that has the merit of selecting, from among the innumerable problems which present themselves, those whose solution is important to mankind."[4]

But the progress of philosophical ethics has not been disappointing merely because so many writers have lost sight of its ultimately practical aims. It has been retarded also by the overhastiness of some leading writers to be "original"—to make over ethics entirely at one stroke; to be new Lawgivers, competing with Moses; to "transvalue all values" with Nietzsche; or to seize, like Bentham, on some single, oversimplified test, like Pleasure-and-Pain, or the Greatest Happiness, and to begin applying it in much too direct and sweeping a manner to all traditional ethical judgments, dismissing with short shrift all those that do not immediately seem to conform with the New Revelation.

3. *Is It a Science?*

We are likely to make more solid progress, I think, if we are not at the beginning too hasty or too ambitious. I shall not undertake in this book a lengthy discussion of the vexed question whether ethics is or can be a "science." It is enough to point out here that the word "science" is used today with a wide range of meanings, and that the struggle to apply it to every branch of inquiry or study, or to every theory, is chiefly a struggle for prestige, and an attempt to ascribe precision and certainty to one's conclusions. I will content myself here with pointing out that ethics is not a science in the sense in which that word is applied to the physical sciences—to the determination of matters of objective fact, or to the establishment of scientific laws which enable us to make exact predictions. But ethics is entitled to be called a science if we mean by this a systematic inquiry conducted by rational rules. It is not a mere chaos. It is not just a matter of opinion, in which one person's opinion is as good as another's, or in which one statement is as true or as false or as "meaningless" or as unverifiable as another; in which neither rational induction nor deduction nor the principles of investigation or logic play any part. If by science, in short, we mean simply rational inquiry aiming to arrive at a unified and systematized body of deductions and conclusions, then ethics is a science.

Ethics bears the same relation to psychology and praxeology (the general theory of human action) as medicine bears to physiology and pathology and as engineering bears to physics and mechanics. It is of little importance whether we call medicine, engineering or ethics an applied science, a normative science, or a scientific art. The function of each is to deal in a systematic way with a class of problems that need to be solved.

Whether ethics is or is not to be called a science is, as I have hinted above, largely a semantic problem, a struggle to raise or lower its prestige and the seriousness with which it should be taken. But the answer we give has important practical consequences. Those who insist on its right to the title, and use the word "science" in its narrower sense, are likely not only to claim for their conclusions an unchallengeable inflexibility and certainty, but to follow pseudo-scientific methods in an effort to imitate physics. Those who deny ethics the title in any form are likely to conclude (or have already concluded) either that ethical problems are meaningless and unanswerable and that "might is right," or, on the other hand, that they already know all the answers by "intuition," or a "moral sense," or direct revelation from God.

Let us agree, then, provisionally, that ethics is at least one of the "moral sciences" (in the sense in which John Stuart Mill used the word) and that if it is not a "science" in the exact and narrower sense it is at least a "discipline"; it is at least a branch of systematized knowledge or study; it is at least what the Germans call a *Wissenschaft*.[5]

What is the aim of this science? What is the task before us? What are the questions we are trying to answer?

Let us begin with the more modest aims and move on to the more ambitious. Our most modest aim is to find out what our unwritten moral code actually *is*, what our traditional, "spontaneous," or "common sense" moral judgments actually *are*. Our next aim must be to ask to what extent these judgments form a consistent whole. Wherever they are inconsistent, or apparently so, we must look for some principle or criterion that would harmonize them or decide between them. After twenty-five hundred years and thousands of books, it is enormously probable that no completely "original" theory of ethics is possible. Probably all the leading major principles have been at least suggested. Progress in ethics is likely to consist, rather, in more definiteness, precision, and clarification, in harmonization, in more generality and unification.

A "system" of ethics, therefore, would mean a code, or a set of principles, that formed a consistent, coherent, and integrated whole. But in order to arrive at this coherence, we must seek the ultimate criterion by which acts or rules of action have been or should be tested. We shall be inevitably led to this merely by trying to make explicit what was merely implicit, by trying to make consistent, rules that were inconsistent, by trying to make definite or precise, rules or judgments that were vague or loose, by trying to unify what was separate and to complete what was partial.

And when and if we find this basic moral criterion, this test of right and wrong, we may indeed find ourselves obliged to revise at least some of our former moral judgments, and to revalue at least some of our former values.

CHAPTER 2

The Mystery of Morals

Each of us has grown up in a world in which moral judgments already exist. These judgments are passed every day by everyone on the conduct of everyone else. Each of us not only finds himself approving or disapproving how other people act, but approving or disapproving certain actions, and even certain *rules* or *principles* of action, wholly apart from his feelings about those who perform or follow them. So deep does this go that most of us even apply these judgments to our own conduct, and approve or disapprove of our own conduct in so far as we judge it to have conformed to the principles or standards by which we judge others. When we have failed, in our own judgment, to live up to the moral code which we habitually apply to others, we feel "guilty"; our "conscience" bothers us.

Our personal moral standards may not be precisely the same in all respects as those of our friends or neighbors or countrymen, but they are remarkably similar. We find greater differences when we compare "national" standards with those of other countries, and perhaps still greater differences when we compare them with the moral standards of people in the distant past. But in spite of these greater differences, we seem to find, for the most part, a persistent core of similarity, and persistent judgments which condemn such traits as cruelty, cowardice, and treachery, or such actions as lying, theft, or murder.

None of us can remember when we first began to pass judgments of moral approval or disapproval. From infancy we found such judgments being passed upon us by our parents—"good" baby, "bad" baby—and from infancy we passed such judgments indiscriminately on persons, animals, and things—"good" playmate or "bad" playmate, "good" dog or "bad" dog, and even "bad" doorknob if we bumped our head against it. Only gradually did we begin to distinguish approval or disapproval on *moral* grounds from approval or disapproval on other grounds.

Implicit moral codes probably existed for centuries before

they were made explicit—as in the Decalogue, or the sacred law of Manu, or the code of Hammurabi. And it was long after they had first been made explicit, in speech or writing, in proverbs or commands or laws, that men began to speculate about them, and began consciously to search for a common explanation or rationale.

And then they were faced with a great mystery. How had such a code of morals come into being? Why did it consist of a certain set of commands and not others? Why did it forbid certain actions? Why only *these* actions? Why did it enjoin or command other actions? And how did men *know* that certain actions were "right" and others "wrong"?

The first theory was that certain actions were "right" and others "wrong" because God (or the gods) had so decreed. Certain actions were pleasing to God (or the gods) and certain others displeasing. Certain actions would be rewarded by God, here or hereafter, and certain other actions would be punished by God, here or hereafter.

This theory, or faith, held the field for centuries. It is still, probably, the dominant popular theory or faith. But among philosophers, even among the early Christian philosophers, it met with two difficulties. The first was this: Was this moral code, then, merely arbitrary? Were certain actions right and others wrong merely because God had so willed? Or was not the causation, rather, the other way round? God's divine nature could not will what was evil, but only what was good. He could not decree what was wrong, but only what was right. But this argument implied that Good and Evil, Right and Wrong, were independent of, and pre-existent to, God's will.

There was a second difficulty. Even if Good and Evil, Right and Wrong, were determined by God's will, how were we mortals to know God's will? The question was answered simply enough, perhaps, for the ancient Jews: God himself dictated the Ten Commandments—and hundreds of other laws and judgments—to Moses on Mount Sinai. God, in fact, wrote the Ten Commandments with his own finger on tablets of stone.

Yet numerous as the commandments and judgments were, they did not clearly distinguish in importance and degree of sinfulness between committing murder and working on the Sabbath day. They have not been and cannot consistently be a guide for Christians. Christians ignore the dietary laws prescribed by the God of Moses. The God of Moses commanded "Eye for eye, tooth for tooth, hand for hand, foot for foot, burning for burning, wound for wound, stripe for stripe" (Exodus 21:24, 25). But Jesus commanded: "Whosoever shall smite thee on thy right cheek, turn to him the other also" (Matthew 5:39); "Love your enemies, bless them that curse you, do good to them that hate you" (Matthew 5:44); "A new commandment I give unto you, that ye love one another" (John 13:34).

The problem then remains: How can we, how do we, tell right from wrong? Another answer, still offered by many ethical writers, is that we do so by a special "moral sense" or by direct "intuition." The difficulty here is not only that one man's moral sense or intuition gives different answers than another's, but that a man's moral sense or intuition often fails to provide a clear answer even when he consults it.

A third answer is that our moral code is a product of gradual social evolution, like language, or manners, or the common law, and that, like them, it has grown and evolved to meet the need for peace and order and social cooperation.

A fourth answer is that of simple ethical skepticism or nihilism which affects to regard all moral rules or judgments as the product of baseless superstition. But this nihilism is never consistent and seldom sincere. If one who professed it were knocked down, brutally beaten, and robbed, he would feel something remarkably similar to moral indignation, and he would express his feeling in words very hard to distinguish from those of moral disapproval.

A less violent way to convert the moral nihilist, however, would be simply to ask him to imagine a society in which no moral code existed, or in which it were the exact opposite of the codes we customarily find. We might ask him to imagine how long a society (or the individuals in it) could prosper or even continue to exist in which ill manners, promise-breaking, lying, cheating, stealing, robbing, beating, stabbing, shooting, ingratitude, disloyalty, treachery, violence, and chaos were the rule, and were as highly regarded as, or even more highly regarded than, their opposites—good manners, promise-keeping, truth-telling, honesty, fairness, loyalty, consideration for others, peace and order, and social cooperation.

Later we shall examine in more detail each of these four answers.

But false theories of ethics, and the number of possible fallacies in ethics, are almost infinite. We can deal only with a few of the major fallacies that have been maintained historically or that are still widely held. It would be unprofitable and uneconomic to explain in detail why each false theory is wrong or inadequate, unless we first tried to find the true foundations of morality and a reasonably satisfactory outline of a system of ethics. If we once find the right answer, it will be much easier to see and to explain why other answers are wrong or, at best, half-truths. Our analysis of errors will then be at once clearer and more economical. And we shall use such analysis of errors to sharpen our positive theory and make it more precise.

Now there are two main methods which we might use to formulate a theory of ethics. The first might be what we may call, for identification rather than accuracy, the *inductive* or *a posteriori* method. This would consist in examining what our moral judgments of various acts or characteristics actually are, and then trying to see whether they form a consistent whole, and on what common principle or criterion, if any, they rest. The second would be the *a priori* or *deductive* method. This would consist in disregarding existing moral judgments, in asking ourselves whether a moral code would serve any purpose, and if so, what that purpose would be; and then, having framed the purpose, asking ourselves what principle, criterion, or code would accomplish that purpose. In other words, we would try to *invent* a system of morality, and then test existing moral judgments by the criterion at which we had deductively arrived.

The second was essentially the method of Jeremy Bentham, the first the method of more cautious thinkers. The second, by itself, would be rash and arrogant; the first, by itself, might prove to be too timid. But as practically all fruitful thinking consists of a judicious mixture—the "inductive-deductive" method—so we shall find ourselves using now one method and now another.

Let us begin by looking for the Ultimate Moral Criterion.

CHAPTER 3

The Moral Criterion

Speculative thought comes late in the history of mankind. Men act before they philosophize about their actions. They learned to talk, and developed language, ages before they developed any interest in grammar or linguistics. They worked and saved, planted crops, fashioned tools, built homes, owned, bartered, bought and sold, and developed money, long before they formulated any explicit theories of economics. They developed forms of government and law, and even judges and courts, before they formulated theories of politics or jurisprudence. And they acted implicitly in accordance with a code of morals, rewarded or punished, approved or disapproved of the actions of their fellows in adhering to or violating that code of morals, long before it even occurred to them to inquire into the rationale of what they were doing.

It would seem at first glance both natural and logical, therefore, to begin the study of ethics with an inquiry into the history or evolution of ethical practice and judgments. Certainly we should engage in such an inquiry at some time in the course of our study. Yet ethics is perhaps the one discipline where it seems more profitable to begin at the other end. For ethics is a "normative" science. It is not a science of *de*scription, but of *pre*scription. It is not a science of what is or was, but of what *ought* to be.

True, it would have no claim to scientific validity, or even any claim to be a useful field of inquiry, unless it were based in some convincing way on what was or what is. But here we have stepped into the very center of an age-old controversy. Many ethical writers have contended during the last two centuries that "no accumulation of observed sequences, no experience of what *is*, no predictions of what *will be*, can possibly prove what *ought to be*."[1] And others have even gone on to assert that there is no way of getting from an *is* to an *ought*.

If the latter statement were true, there would be no possibility of framing a rational theory of ethics. Unless our *oughts* are to be purely arbitrary, purely dogmatic, they must somehow grow out of what *is*.

Now the connection between what is and what ought to be is always a *desire* of some kind. We recognize this in our daily decisions. When we are trying to decide on a course of action, and are asking advice, we are told, for example: "If you desire to become a doctor, you must go to medical school. If you desire to get ahead, you must be diligent in your business. If you don't want to get fat, you must watch your diet. If you want to avoid lung cancer, you must cut down on cigarettes," etc. The generalized form of such advice may be reduced to this: *If* you desire to attain a certain *end,* you *ought* to use a certain *means,* because this is the means most likely to achieve it. The *is* is the desire; the *ought* is the means of gratifying it.

So far, so good. But how far does this get us toward a theory of ethics? For if a man does not desire an end, there seems no way of convincing him that he ought to pursue the means to that end. If a man prefers the certainty of getting fat, or the risk of a heart attack, to curbing his appetite or giving up his favorite delicacies; if he prefers the risks of lung cancer to giving up smoking, any *ought* based on the assumption of a contrary preference loses its force.

A story so old that it is told as an old one even by Bentham[2] is that of the oculist and the sot: A countryman who had hurt his eyes by drinking went to a celebrated oculist for advice. He found him at table, with a glass of wine before him. "You must leave off drinking," said the oculist. "How so?" says the countryman. "*You* don't, and yet methinks your own eyes are none of the best." —"That's very true, friend," replied the oculist: "but you are to know, I love my bottle better than my eyes."

How, then, do we move from any basis of desire to any theory of ethics?

We find the solution when we take a longer and broader view. All our desires may be generalized as desires to substitute a more satisfactory state of affairs for a less satisfactory state. It is true that an individual, under the immediate influence of impulse or passion, of a moment of anger or rage, malice, vindictiveness, or the desire for revenge, or gluttony, or an overwhelming craving for a release of sexual tension, or for a smoke or a drink or a drug, may in the long run only reduce a more satisfactory state to a less satisfactory state, may make himself less happy rather than more happy. But this less satisfactory state was not his real conscious intention even at the moment of acting. He realizes, in retrospect, that his action was folly; he did not improve his condition, but made it worse; he did not act in accordance with his long-run interests, but against them. He is always willing to recognize, in his calmer moments, that he should choose the action that best promotes his own interests and maximizes his own happiness (or minimizes his own unhappiness) *in the long run*. Wise and disciplined men refuse to indulge in immediate pleasures when the indulgence seems only too likely to lead in the long run to an overbalance of misery or pain.

To repeat and to sum up: It is not true that "no amount of *is* can make an *ought*." The *ought* rests, in fact, and must rest, either upon an *is* or upon a *will be*. The sequence is simple: Every man, in his cool and rational moments, seeks his own long-run happiness. This is a *fact;* this is an *is*. Mankind has found, over the centuries, that certain rules of action best tend to promote the long-run happiness of both the individual and society. These rules of action have come to be called *moral* rules. Therefore, assuming that one seeks one's long-run happiness, these are the rules one *ought* to follow.

Certainly this is the whole basis of what is called *prudential* ethics. In fact, wisdom, or the art of living wisely, is perhaps only another name for prudential ethics.

Prudential ethics constitutes a very large part of all ethics. But the whole of ethics rests upon the same foundation. For men find that they best promote their own interests in the long run not merely by refraining from injury to their fellows, but by cooperating with them. Social cooperation is the foremost means by which the majority of us attain most of our ends. It is on the implicit if not the explicit recognition of this that our codes of morals, our rules of conduct, are ultimately based. "Justice" itself (as we shall later see more clearly) consists in observance of the rules or principles that do most, in the long run, to preserve and promote social cooperation.

We shall find also, when we have explored the subject further, that there are no irreconcilable conflicts between egoism and altruism, between selfishness and benevolence, between the long-run interests of the individual and those of society. In most cases in which such conflicts appear to exist, the appearance exists because only short-run consequences, and not consequences over the long run, are being taken into consideration.

Social cooperation is, of course, itself a means. It is a means to the never completely attainable goal of maximizing the happiness and well-being of mankind. But the great difficulty of making the latter our direct goal is the lack of unanimity in the tastes, ends, and value judgments of individuals. An activity that gives one man pleasure may be a great bore to another. "One man's meat is another man's poison." But social cooperation is the great means by which we all help each other to attain our individual ends, and so to attain the ends of "society." Moreover, we do share a great number of basic ends in common; and social cooperation is the principal means of attaining these also.

In brief, the aim of each of us to satisfy his own desires, to achieve as far as possible his own highest happiness and well-being, is best forwarded by a common means, Social Cooperation, and cannot be achieved without that means.

Here, then, is the foundation on which we may build a rational system of ethics.

CHAPTER 4

Pleasure as the End

1. *Jeremy Bentham*

The doctrine that pleasure is the sole ultimate good, and pain the sole evil, is at least as old as Epicurus (341-270 B.C.). But the doctrine, from the beginning, has been denounced as heretical by the bulk of orthodox or ascetic moralists—so much so, that it almost disappeared until it was revived in the seventeenth and eighteenth centuries. The writer who then stated it in its most uncompromising, elaborate, and systematic form was Jeremy Bentham.[1]

If we may judge by the number of references to him and his doctrines in the literature of the subject, even though most of them are critical, angry, or derisive, Bentham has been the most discussed and influential moralist of modern times. It seems profitable, therefore, to begin with an analysis of the hedonistic doctrine as he states it.

His best known (as well as his most authentic)[2] statement is in his *Principles of Morals and Legislation*. The paragraphs with which he opens that book are bold and sweeping.

> Nature has placed mankind under the governance of two sovereign masters, *pain* and *pleasure*. It is for them alone to point out what we ought to do, as well as to determine what we shall do. On the one hand the standard of right and wrong, on the other hand the chain of causes and effects, are fastened to their throne. They govern us in all we do, in all we say, in all we think: every effort we can make to throw off our subjection, will serve but to demonstrate and confirm it. In words a man may pretend to abjure their empire: but in reality he will remain subject to it all the while. The *principle of utility* recognizes this subjection, and assumes it for the foundation of that system, the object of which is to rear the fabric of felicity by the hands of reason and law. Systems which attempt to question it, deal in sounds instead of sense, in caprice instead of reason, in darkness instead of light.

It will be noticed that in the second sentence of this paragraph Bentham draws no distinction whatever between what has since come to be known as the doctrine of *psychological* hedonism (the doctrine that we always *do* take the action which we think will give us the greatest pleasure) and the doctrine that has come to be known as *ethical* hedonism (the doctrine that we *ought* to take the action which will result in the greatest pleasure or happiness). But we may leave the disentanglement of this knotty problem to a later chapter.

Bentham goes on to explain that:

> The principle of utility is the foundation of the present work. . . . By the principle of utility is meant that principle which approves or disapproves of every action whatsoever, according to the tendency which it appears to have to augment or diminish the happiness of the party whose interest is in question. . . . I say of every action whatsoever; and therefore not only of every action of a private individual, but of every measure of government.
>
> By utility is meant that property in any object, whereby it tends to produce benefit, advantage, pleasure, good, or happiness (all this in the present case comes to the same thing), or (what comes again to the same thing) to prevent the happening of mischief, pain, evil, or unhappiness to the party whose interest is considered: if that party be the community in general, then the happiness of the community: if a particular individual, then the happiness of that individual.[3]

Bentham later modified his ideas, or at least their expression. He acknowledged his debt for the "principle of utility" to Hume, but came to find the principle too vague. Utility for what end? Bentham took over from an essay on Government by Priestley in 1768 the phrase "the greatest happiness of the greatest number" but later substituted both for this and for "utility" the Greatest Happiness Principle. Increasingly, too (as revealed in the *Deontology*) he substituted "happiness" and "greatest happiness" for "pleasure," and in the *Deontology* he arrived at the definition: "Morality is the art of maximizing happiness: it gives the code of laws by which that conduct is suggested whose result will, the whole of human existence being taken into account, leave the greatest quantity of felicity."[4]

2. *The Charge of Sensuality*

It is against the statement of his theory in the form found in his *Morals and Legislation,* however (and against popular *mis-*

conceptions of what he believed or continued to believe), that the great storm of criticism has been directed.

As the primary purpose of these early chapters will be to lay the foundation for a positive theory of morals, I shall here discuss only a few of the respects in which that criticism was either valid or unjustified; and I shall discuss them, not so much as they apply to the specific doctrines of Bentham, but to hedonistic or eudaemonic doctrines in general.

The most frequent objection to hedonism or utilitarianism on the part of anti-hedonist and anti-utilitarian writers is that the "pleasure" which it makes the goal of action refers to a purely physical or *sensual* pleasure. Thus Schumpeter calls it "the shallowest of all conceivable philosophies of life," and insists that the "pleasure" it talks of is merely the pleasure epitomized in eating beefsteaks.[5] And moralists like Carlyle have not hesitated to call it a "pig philosophy." This criticism is immemorial. "Epicurean" has become a synonym for a sensualist, and the followers of Epicurus have been condemned as the "swine" of Epicurus.

Closely allied to this criticism, and sharing almost equal prominence with it, is the accusation that hedonism and utilitarianism preach essentially the philosophy of sensuality and self-indulgence, the philosophy of the voluptuary and the libertine.

Now while it is true that there are people who both practice and preach the philosophy of sensuality, it receives very little support from Bentham—or, for that matter, from any of the leading utilitarians.

So far as the charge of sensuality is concerned, no one who has ever read Bentham can have any excuse for making it.[6] For in his elaborate enumeration and classification of "pleasures," he lists not only the pleasures of sense, in which he includes the pleasure of health, and the pleasures of wealth and power, including those both of acquisition and of possession, but the pleasures of memory and imagination, or association and expectation, and the pleasures of amity, of a good name, of piety, and of benevolence or good will. (He is also realistic and candid enough to list the pleasures of malevolence or ill will.)

And when he comes to the question of how a pleasure should be measured, valued, or compared, he lists seven criteria or "circumstances": (1) Its *intensity*. (2) Its *duration*. (3) Its *certainty* or *uncertainty*. (4) Its *propinquity* or *remoteness*. (5) Its *fecundity* (or the chance it has of being followed by sensations of the *same* kind). (6) Its *purity* (or the chance it has of *not* being followed by sensations of the *opposite* kind). (7) Its *extent* (that is, the number of persons to whom it extends).[7]

The foregoing quotations do, I think, point to some of the real shortcomings in Bentham's analysis. These include his failure to construct a convincing "hedonistic calculus" (though his elaborate effort to do so was itself highly instructive). They include his tendency to treat "pleasure" or "pain" as something that can be abstracted and isolated from specific pleasures or pains and treated like a physical or chemical residue, or like a homogeneous juice that can be quantitatively measured.

I will return to these points later. Here I wish to point out that Bentham and the utilitarians generally cannot be justly accused of assigning to "pleasure" a purely sensual meaning. Nor does their emphasis on promoting pleasure and avoiding pain necessarily lead to a philosophy of self-indulgence. The critics of hedonism or utilitarianism constantly talk as if its votaries measured all pleasures merely in terms of their *intensity*. But the key words in Bentham's comparisons are *duration, fecundity*, and *purity*. And the greatest of these is *duration*. In discussing the virtue of "self-regarding prudence," Bentham constantly emphasizes the importance of not sacrificing the future to the present, the importance of giving "preference to the greater future over the less present pleasure."[8] "Is not temperance a virtue? Aye, assuredly is it. But wherefore? Because by restraining enjoyment for a time, it afterwards elevates it to that very pitch which leaves, on the whole, the largest addition to the stock of happiness."[9]

3. *Of the Greatest Number*

Bentham's views have been misunderstood in another important respect—though this is in large part his own fault. One of the phrases he is thought to have originated—which was once most often quoted with approval by his disciples but is now the most frequent target for his critics—is "the greatest happiness of the greatest number." But first, as we have seen, this was not

Bentham's original phrase, but taken by him from Priestley (who was in turn anticipated both by Hutcheson and Beccaria); and secondly, Bentham himself later abandoned it. When he did reject it he did so with a clearer and more powerful argument (so far as it goes) than any I have seen by any critic. It is quoted by Bowring in the final pages of the first volume of the posthumous *Deontology*, from which I paraphrase it:

The principle of the Greatest Happiness of the Greatest Number is questionable because it can be interpreted as ignoring the feelings or fate of the minority. And this questionableness becomes greater the greater we conceive the ratio to be of the minority to the majority.

Let us suppose a community of 4001 persons of which the "majority" numbers 2001 and the minority 2000. Suppose that, to begin with, each of the 4001 possesses an equal portion of happiness. If, now, we take his share of happiness from every one of the 2000 and divide it among the 2001, the result would be, not an augmentation, but a vast diminution of happiness. The feelings of the minority being, according to the "greatest number" principle, left out of account, the vacuum thus left, instead of remaining a vacuum, may be filled with the greatest unhappiness and suffering. The net result for a whole community would not be a gain in happiness but a great loss.

Or assume, again, that your 4001 persons are at the outset in a state of perfect equality with respect to the means to happiness, including power and opulence, with every one possessing not only equal wealth, but equal liberty and independence. Now take your 2000, or no matter how much smaller a minority, reduce them to a state of slavery, and divide them and their former property among the 2001. How many in the community will actually have their happiness increased? What would be the result for the happiness of the whole community? The questions answer themselves.

To make the application more specific, Bentham then went on to ask what would happen if, in Great Britain, the whole body of the Roman Catholics were made slaves and divided among the whole body of Protestants, or if, in Ireland, the whole body of Protestants were divided, in like manner, among the whole body of Roman Catholics.

So Bentham fell back on the Greatest Happiness Principle,

and spoke of the goal of ethics as that of maximizing the happiness of the community as a whole.

4. *"Pleasure"* vs. *"Happiness"*

This statement of the ultimate criterion of moral rules leaves many troublesome questions unanswered. We may postpone consideration of some of these to a later point, but we can hardly escape dealing with a few of them now, if our answer is to be even provisionally satisfactory. Some of these questions are perhaps purely semantic or linguistic; others are psychological or philosophical; and in some cases it is difficult to determine whether we are in fact dealing with a verbal or a psychological or a moral problem.

This applies especially to the use of the terms *pleasure* and *pain*. Bentham himself, as we have seen, who originally made the systematic use of these terms basic to his ethical system, later tended to abandon the term *pleasure* more and more for the term *happiness*. But he insisted to the end that: "Happiness is the aggregate of which pleasures are the component parts. . . . Let not the mind be led astray by any distinctions drawn between pleasures and happiness. . . . Happiness without pleasures is a chimera and a contradiction; it is a million without any units, a square yard in which there shall be no inches, a bag of guineas without an atom of gold." [10]

The conception of happiness as a mere arithmetical summation of units of pleasure and pain, however, finds little acceptance today, either by moral philosophers, psychologists, or the man in the street. And persistent difficulties are presented by the words *pleasure* and *pain*. It is in vain that some moral philosophers have warned that they should be used and understood only in a purely formal sense.[11] The popular association of these words with merely sensual and carnal pleasure is so strong that such a warning is certain to be forgotten. Meanwhile antihedonists consciously or unconsciously make full use of this association to deride and discredit the utilitarian writers who use the words.

It seems the part of practical wisdom, and the best way to minimize misunderstanding, to use the terms "pleasure" and "pain" very sparingly, if not to abandon them almost altogether in ethical discussion.

CHAPTER 5

Satisfaction and Happiness

1. *The Role of Desire*

The modern doctrine of eudaemonic ethics is differently framed. It is customarily stated, not in terms of pleasures and pains, but in terms of desires and satisfactions. Thus it bypasses some of the psychological and verbal controversies raised by the older pleasure-pain theories. As we saw in Chapter 3 (p. 12), all our desires may be generalized as desires to substitute a more satisfactory state of affairs for a less satisfactory state. A man acts, in Locke's phrase, because he feels some "uneasiness"[1] and tries as far as possible to remove this uneasiness.

I shall argue in this chapter, therefore, in defense of at least one form of the doctrine of "psychological eudaemonism." Superficially similar doctrines, under the name "psychological hedonism" or "psychological egoism," are actively opposed by many modern moral philosophers. We shall consider here the criticism offered by an older moral philosopher, Hastings Rashdall.

Rashdall, criticizing "psychological hedonism," held that it rested on a great "hysteron-proteron"—an inversion of the true order of logical dependence, a reversal of cause and effect:

> The fact that a thing is desired no doubt implies that the satisfaction of the desire will necessarily bring pleasure. There is undoubtedly pleasure in the satisfaction of all desire. But that is a very different thing from asserting that the object is desired because it is thought of as pleasant, and in proportion as it is thought of as pleasant. The hedonistic Psychology involves, according to the stock phrase, a "hysteron-proteron"; it puts the cart before the horse. In reality, the imagined pleasantness is created by the desire, not the desire by the imagined pleasantness.[2]

But in making this criticism, Rashdall was forced to concede something—the fact that men actually do seek satisfaction of their desires, whatever these desires happen to be. "The gratification of every desire necessarily gives pleasure in actual fact, and is consequently conceived of as pleasant in idea before the desire is accomplished. That is the truth which lies at the bottom of all the exaggerations and misrepresentations of the hedonistic Psychology."[3]

And here we have a firmer positive basis than the older pleasure-pain psychology on which we can build. As the German philosopher Friedrich Heinrich Jacobi (1743-1819) declared: "We originally want or desire an object not because it is agreeable or good, but we call it agreeable or good because we want or desire it; and we do this because our sensuous or supersensuous nature so requires. There is, thus, no basis for recognizing what is good and worth wishing for outside of the faculty of desiring—i.e., the original desire and the wish themselves."[4] But all this was said much earlier by Spinoza in his *Ethics* (Part III, Prop. IX): "In no case do we strive for, wish for, long for, or desire anything because we deem it to be good, but on the other hand we deem a thing to be good, because we strive for it, wish for it, long for it, or desire it."

Bertrand Russell, whose opinions on ethics have undergone many minor changes and at least one major revolution, has finally settled on this view, as revealed in two books published nearly thirty years apart. Let us begin with the earlier statement:

> There is a view, advocated, *e.g.* by Dr. G. E. Moore, that "good" is an indefinable notion, and that we know *a priori* certain general propositions about the kinds of things that are good on their own account. Such things as happiness, knowledge, appreciation of beauty, are known to be good, according to Dr. Moore; it is also known that we ought to act so as to create what is good and prevent what is bad. I formerly held this view myself, but I was led to abandon it, partly by Mr. Santayana's *Winds of Doctrine*. I now think that good and bad are derivative from desire. I do not mean quite simply that the good is the desired, because men's desires conflict, and "good" is, to my mind, mainly a social concept, designed to find issue from this conflict. The conflict, however, is not only between the desires of different men, but between incompatible desires of one man at different times, or even at the same time.[5]

Russell then goes on to ask how the desires of a single individual can be harmonized with each other, and how, if possible,

SATISFACTION AND HAPPINESS

the desires of different individuals can be harmonized with each other.

In *Human Society in Ethics and Politics,* published in 1955, he returns to the same theme:

> I mean by "right" conduct that conduct which will probably produce the greatest balance of satisfaction over dissatisfaction, or the smallest balance of dissatisfaction over satisfaction, and that, in making this estimate, the question as to who enjoys the satisfaction, or suffers the dissatisfaction, is to be considered irrelevant. . . . I say "satisfaction" rather than "pleasure" or "interest." The term "interest" as commonly employed has too narrow a connotation. . . . The term "satisfaction" is wide enough to embrace everything that comes to a man through the realization of his desires, and these desires do not necessarily have any connection with self, except that one feels them. One may, for instance, desire—I do myself—that a proof should be discovered for Fermat's last theorem, and one may be glad if a brilliant young mathematician is given a sufficient grant to enable him to seek a proof. The gratification that one would feel in this case comes under the head of satisfaction, but hardly of self-interest as commonly understood.
>
> Satisfaction, as I mean the word, is not quite the same thing as pleasure, although it is intimately connected with it. Some experiences have a satisfying quality which goes beyond their mere pleasurableness; others, on the contrary, although very pleasurable, do not have that peculiar feeling of fulfillment which I am calling satisfaction.
>
> Many philosophers have maintained that men always and invariably seek pleasure, and that even the apparently most altruistic acts have this end in view. This, I think, is a mistake. It is true, of course, that, whatever you may desire, you will get a certain pleasure when your object is achieved, but often the pleasure is due to the desire, not the desire to the expected pleasure. This applies especially to the simplest desires, such as hunger and thirst. Satisfying hunger or thirst is a pleasure, but the desire for food or drink is direct, and is not, except in a gourmet, a desire for the pleasure which they afford.
>
> It is customary among moralists to urge what is called "unselfishness" and to represent morality as consisting mainly in self-abnegation. This view, it seems to me, springs from a failure to realize the wide scope of possible desires. Few people's desires are wholly concentrated upon themselves. Of this there is abundant evidence in the prevalence of life insurance. Every man, of neces-

sity, is actuated by his own desires, whatever they may be, but there is no reason why his desires should all be self-centered. Nor is it always the case that desires concerned with other people will lead to better actions than those that are more egoistic. A painter, for example, may be led by family affection to paint potboilers, but it might be better for the world if he painted masterpieces and let his family suffer the discomforts of comparative poverty. It must be admitted, however, that the immense majority of mankind have a bias in favor of their own satisfactions, and that one of the purposes of morality is to diminish the strength of this bias.[6]

2. "Happiness" or "Well-Being"?

Thus codes of morals have their starting point in human desires, choices, preferences, valuations. But the recognition of this, important as it is, carries us only a little way towards the construction of an ethical system or even a basis for evaluating existing ethical rules and judgments.

We shall take up the next steps in succeeding chapters. But before we come to these chapters, which will be mainly concerned with the problem of *means,* let us ask whether we can frame any satisfactory answer to the question of *ends.*

It will not do to say, as some modern moral philosophers have been content to say, that ends are "pluralistic" and wholly incommensurable. This evades entirely one of the most important problems of ethics. The ethical problem as it presents itself in practice in daily life is precisely *which* course of action we "ought" to take, precisely which "end," among conflicting "ends," we ought to pursue.

It is frequently asserted by moral philosophers, for example, that though "Happiness" may be an element in the ultimate end, "Virtue" is also an ultimate end which cannot be subsumed under or resolved into "Happiness." But suppose a man is confronted with a decision in which one course of action, in his opinion, would most tend to promote happiness (and not necessarily or merely his own happiness but that of others) while only a conflicting course of action would be most "virtuous"? How can he resolve his problem? A rational decision can only be made on some common basis of comparison. Either happiness is not an ultimate end but rather a means to some further end, or virtue is not an ultimate end but rather a means to some further end. Either happiness must be valued in terms of its tendency to promote virtue or virtue must be valued in terms of its tendency to promote happiness, or both must be valued in terms of their tendency to promote some further end beyond either.

One confusion that has stood in the way of solving this problem has been the inveterate tendency of moral philosophers to draw a sharp contrast between "means" and "ends," and then to assume that whatever can be shown to be a means to some further end must be *merely* a means, and can have no value "in itself," or, as they phrase it, can have no "intrinsic" value.

Later we shall see in more detail that most things or values that are the objects of human pursuit are both means and ends; that one thing may be a means to a proximate end which in turn is a means to some further end, which in turn may be a means to some still further end; that these "means-ends" come to be valued not only as means but as ends-in-themselves—in other words, acquire not only a derivative or "instrumental" value but a quasi-"intrinsic" value.

But here we must state one of our provisional conclusions dogmatically. At any moment we do not the thing that gives us most "pleasure" (using the word in its usual connotation) but the thing that gives us most satisfaction (or least dissatisfaction). If we act under the influence of impulse or fear or anger or passion, we do the thing that gives us most momentary satisfaction, regardless of longer consequences. If we act calmly after reflection, we do the thing we think likely to give us the most satisfaction (or least dissatisfaction) in the long run. But when we judge our actions morally (and especially when we judge the actions of *others* morally), the question we ask or should ask is this: What actions or rules of action would do most to promote the health, happiness, and well-being in the long run of the individual agent, or (if there is conflict) what rules of action would do most to promote the health, happiness and well-being in the long run of the whole community, or of all mankind?

I have used the long phrase "health, happiness, and well-being" as the nearest equivalent to Aristotle's *eudaemonia*, which seems to include all three. And I have used it because some moral philosophers believe that Happiness, even if it means the long-run happiness of mankind, is too narrow or too ignoble a goal. In order to avoid barren disputes over words,

I should be willing to call the ultimate goal simply the Good, or Well-Being. There could then be no objection on the ground that this ultimate goal, this *Summum Bonum,* this criterion of all means or other ends, was not made inclusive or noble enough. I have no strong objection to the use of the term *Well-Being* to stand for this ultimate goal, though I prefer the term *Happiness,* standing by itself, as sufficiently inclusive, and yet more specific. But wherever I use the word *Happiness* standing alone, any reader may silently add *and/or Well-Being,* whereever he thinks the addition is necessary to increase the comprehensiveness or nobility of the goal.

3. *Pleasure Cannot Be Quantified*

Before leaving the subject of this chapter it seems desirable to deal with some of the objections to the eudaemonic view that it presents.

One of these has to do with the relations of desire to pleasure —the alleged "hysteron-proteron" fallacy mentioned at the beginning of the chapter. I suspect that the people who place most emphasis on this so-called fallacy are themselves guilty of a confusion of thought. Their position is sometimes stated in the form: "When I am hungry, I desire food, not pleasure." But this statement depends for its persuasiveness upon an ambiguity in the word "pleasure." If we substitute for "pleasure" the term *satisfaction* the statement becomes a form of hairsplitting: "When I am hungry I desire food, not the satisfaction of my desire." What is involved here is not a contrast between two different things, but merely between two different ways of stating the same thing. The statement: "When I am hungry, I desire food," is concrete and specific. The statement: "I desire the satisfaction of my desires," is general and abstract. There is no antithesis. Food in this example is merely the specific means of satisfying a specific desire.

Yet since the time of Bishop Butler this point has been the subject of bitter controversy. Both hedonists and anti-hedonists too commonly forget that the word "pleasure," like the word "satisfaction," is merely an *abstraction*. A pleasure or satisfaction does not exist apart from a *specific* pleasure or satisfaction. "Pleasure" cannot be separated or isolated like a sort of pure homogeneous juice from specific pleasures or sources of pleasure.

Nor can pleasure be measured or quantified. Bentham's attempt to quantify pleasure was ingenious, but a failure. How can one measure the intensity of one pleasure, for example, against the duration of another? Or the intensity of the "same" pleasure against its duration? Precisely what decrease in intensity is equal to precisely what increase in duration? If one answers that the individual decides this whenever he makes a choice, then one is saying that it is his subjective *preference* that really counts, not the "quantity" of pleasure.

Pleasures and satisfactions can be compared in terms of *more* or *less*, but they cannot be quantified. Thus we may say that they are *comparable*, but we may not go on to say that they are otherwise *commensurable*. We may say, for example, that we prefer to go to the symphony tonight to playing bridge, which is perhaps equivalent to saying that going to the symphony tonight would give us more pleasure than playing bridge. But we cannot meaningfully say that we prefer going to the symphony tonight 3.72 times as much as playing bridge (or that it would give us 3.72 times as much pleasure).

Thus even when we say that an individual is "trying to maximize his satisfactions," we must be careful to keep in mind that we are using the term "maximize" metaphorically. It is an elliptical expression for "taking in each case the action that seems to promise the most satisfying results." We cannot legitimately use the term "maximize" in this connection in the strict sense in which it is used in mathematics, to imply the largest possible *sum*. Neither satisfactions nor pleasures can be quantified. They can only be compared in terms of *more* or *less*. To put the matter another way, they can be compared ordinally, not cardinally. We can speak of our first, second, and third choice. We can say that we expect to get more satisfaction (or pleasure) from doing A than from doing B, but we can never say precisely *how much* more.[7]

4. *Socrates and the Oyster*

In comparing pleasures or satisfactions with each other, then, it is legitimate to say that one is more or less than another, but it is merely confusing to say with John Stuart Mill that one is "higher" or "lower" than another. In this respect Bentham was far more logical when he declared: "Quantity of pleasure being equal, pushpin is as good as poetry." When, trying to escape from this conclusion, Mill insisted that pleasures should be measured by "quality . . . as well as quantity,"[8] he was in effect abandoning pleasure itself as the standard of guidance in conduct and appealing to some other and not clearly specified standard. He was implying that we value states of consciousness for some other reason than their pleasantness.

If we abandon the "pleasure" as the standard and substitute *satisfaction,* it becomes clear that if the satisfaction that it yields is the standard of conduct, and John Jones gets more satisfaction from playing ping-pong than he does from reading poetry, then he is justified in playing ping-pong. One may say, if one wishes, again following Mill, that he would probably prefer poetry if he had "experience of both." But this is far from certain. It depends on what kind of person Jones is, on what his tastes are, what his physical and mental capacities are, and his mood of the moment. To insist that he should read poetry rather than play ping-pong (even though the latter gives him intense pleasure and the former would merely bore or irritate him), on the ground that if he plays ping-pong and abjures poetry he will earn your contempt, is to appeal to intellectual snobbery rather than to morality.

In fact, Mill introduced a great deal of confusion of thought into ethics when he wrote: "It is better to be a human being dissatisfied than a pig satisfied; better to be Socrates dissatisfied than a fool satisfied. And if the fool, or the pig, are of a different opinion, it is because they only know their side of the question. The other party to the comparison knows both sides."[9]

Now it may be doubted that the other party to the comparison knows both sides. An intelligent man has never been a pig, and does not know precisely how a pig feels, or how he would feel if he were a pig: he might then have a pig's preferences, whatever these should turn out to be.

In any case, Mill has simply introduced an irrelevancy. He is appealing to our snobbery, our pride, or our shame. No one who reads philosophy at all would like to admit that he prefers to be an ordinary man rather than a genius, let alone that he would prefer being a pig to being an ordinary man. The reader is expected to say, "A thousand times, *no!*"

But this does not happen to be the issue. If we stick to the issue, then, we will reply: It is better to be Socrates satisfied than Socrates dissatisfied. It is better to be a human being satisfied than a human being dissatisfied. It is better to be a fool satisfied than a fool dissatisfied. It is better even to be a pig satisfied than a pig dissatisfied.

Each of these, if dissatisfied, is usually capable of taking some action that would make him less dissatisfied. The actions that would make him least dissatisfied in the long run, assuming they were not at the expense of other persons (or pigs), would be the most appropriate actions for him to take.

The choice of such actions is a real choice. The choice implied by Mill is not. Neither a human being nor a pig, regardless of his own desires, can change his animal status to that of the other. Nor can a fool make himself into a Socrates simply by an act of choice, nor Socrates into a fool. But human beings, at least, are capable of choosing the actions that seem likely to bring them most satisfaction in the long run.

If a moron is happy gaping at television but would be miserable trying to read Plato or Mill or G. E. Moore, it would be cruel and even stupid to try to force him to do the latter simply because you think such reading would make a genius happy. It would hardly be more "moral" for a commonplace man to torture or bore himself by reading high-brow books rather than detective stories if the latter gave him real pleasure. The moral life should not be confused with the intellectual life. The moral life consists in following the course that leads to the greatest long-run happiness achievable by the individual concerned, and leads him to cooperate with others to the extent of the capacities he actually has, rather than those he might wish he had or might think he "ought" to have.

Yet this crypto-snobbish standard is appealed to again and again by moral philosophers. Bertrand Russell, in one of his many phases as a moral philosopher, once repeated, in effect, Plato's argument about the life of the oyster, having pleasure with no knowledge. Imagine such mindless pleasure, as intense and prolonged as you please, and would you choose it? Is it your good? And Santayana replied:

Here the British reader, like the blushing Greek youth, is expected to answer instinctively, No! It is an *argumentum ad hominem* (and there can be no other kind of argument in ethics); but the man who gives the required answer does so not because the answer is self-evident, which it is not, but because he is the required sort of man. He is shocked at the idea of resembling an oyster. Yet changeless pleasure, without memory or reflection, without the wearisome intermixture of arbitrary images, is just what the mystic, the voluptuary, and perhaps the oyster find to be good. . . . The impossibility which people labor under of being satisfied with pure pleasure as a goal is due to their want of imagination, or rather to their being dominated by an imagination which is exclusively human.[10]

Let us carry Santayana's argument a step further. Let us assume that the moral philosopher asked: "Suppose you could get more pleasure, both immediately and in the long run, than you now get from witnessing the plays of Shakespeare, but without ever reading, seeing, or hearing a Shakespearian play, and remaining entirely ignorant of Shakespeare's work? Would you choose this greater pleasure?" Every lover of Shakespeare would probably answer No. But isn't this simply because he would not believe in the hypothetical choice? Because he simply could not *imagine* himself getting the pleasure of Shakespeare without reading or seeing Shakespearian plays? Pleasure can hardly be conceived as a pure abstraction apart from a particular pleasure.

The antihedonist may reply in triumph that if people refuse to substitute one *kind* of pleasure for another, or one *quality* of pleasure for another, then they have made something else besides "quantity" of pleasure their test. But it should be pointed out to him that the test he applies to specific intellectual or specific "higher" pleasures could be applied, with the same kind of results, to specific sensual, carnal or "lower" pleasures. If the question were put to a voluptuary: "Suppose, by some other means, you could get more pleasure than you could get from sleeping with the most seductive woman in the world, but without having this latter privilege, would you choose this greater but disembodied pleasure?" Any lecher who was asked this question would probably also reply with an emphatic No. And the reason would be basically the same as for our Shakespeare lover. People cannot imagine or believe in a purely abstract pleasure, but only in a specific pleasure.

When a man is asked to imagine himself *feeling* pleasure, though deprived of all his present *sources* of pleasure—of all the things or activities that now *bring* him pleasure—he naturally finds himself unable to do it. It is like being asked to imagine himself in love, but not *with* anybody.

The answer becomes clearer when we abandon the word "pleasure" and substitute *satisfaction*. We do not ordinarily speak of "quantity" of satisfaction, as we are tempted to do with "pleasure," but only of *greater* or *less* satisfaction. Nor do we speak of "quality" of satisfaction. We merely ask whether this or that object or activity gives us more or less satisfaction than another. We recognize, moreover, that different people find satisfaction in different things, and that the same person who finds satisfaction in one activity today may find it in quite another tomorrow. None of us *permanently* or *always* chooses "higher" pleasures to "lower" pleasures, or even vice versa. Even the dedicated ascetic stops to eat, or to satisfy other bodily needs. And the devotee of Shakespearian tragedies may relish a good dinner just before he goes to the theater.

We will return to a fuller discussion of the "pushpin-vs.-poetry" problem in Chapter 18.

5. *Psychological Eudaemonism*

I announced at the beginning of this chapter that I would argue in defense of at least one form of the doctrine of "psychological eudaemonism."

Some antihedonists (of whom I might again cite Hastings Rashdall [11] as an outstanding example) have adopted what seems a neat way of disposing of the hedonist contention. They first seek to show that *"psychological* hedonism" cannot account for our real motives in acting. They then point out that while *"ethical* hedonism" is still possible, it is slightly ridiculous to contend that it is one's *duty* to seek solely one's own pleasure even if one doesn't always want to.

This refutation itself rests on a series of fallacies, which become particularly apparent when we abandon the word "pleasure," with its special connotations, and instead talk of "satisfaction" or "happiness."

At the cost of repetition, let us review some of the principal fallacies in the attack on psychological hedonism:

1. *The assumption that "pleasure" refers only, or primarily, to sensual or carnal pleasure.* There is hardly an antihedonist writer who does not at least tacitly make this assumption. That is why it seems advisable for eudaemonists to abandon the words "hedonist" and "pleasure" and to speak instead of "satisfaction" or "happiness." Wherever we find the word "pleasure" used we must be on guard against its ambiguity. For it may mean either: (1) sensual pleasure; or (2) a valued state of consciousness.[12]

2. *The refusal to see that the hedonist or eudaemonist position can be stated negatively.* Antihedonists accuse hedonists of contending, for example (and some ill-advised hedonists actually do) that a man voluntarily becomes a martyr because he thinks the "pleasure" of martyrdom will predominate over the pain. Rather he accepts martyrdom (where he might avoid it) because he prefers the physical agony of torture, burning, or crucifixion to the disgrace or spiritual anguish of repudiating his God or his principles or betraying his friends. He is not choosing "pleasure" of any sort; he is choosing what he regards as the lesser agony.

3. *Antihedonists (especially Rashdall, who devotes many pages to it) try to refute hedonism by referring to what they call the "hysteron-proteron" fallacy.* To quote Rashdall again: "The hedonistic Psychology explains the desire by the pleasure, whereas in fact the pleasure owes its existence entirely to the desire." [13] Or again: "[Hedonism] makes the anticipated "satisfaction" the condition of the desire, whereas the desire is really the condition of the satisfaction." [14]

The *contrast* here between "desire" and "satisfaction" is of dubious validity. It is a verbal distinction rather than a psychological one. It is merely tautological to say that what I really desire is the satisfaction of my desires. True, I will not try to satisfy a desire unless I already have the desire. But it is the satisfaction of the desire, rather than the desire itself, that I desire! Rashdall's objection comes down to the triviality that we desire a pleasure only because we desire it. To say that I seek the satisfaction of my desires is another way of saying that I desire "happiness," for my happiness consists in the satisfaction of my desires.

4. *Another objection to hedonism is that originating with Bishop Butler. It declares that what I want is not "pleasure" but some specific thing.* To quote again the sentence cited a

while back: "When I am hungry, I desire food, not pleasure." We have already pointed out that this merely emphasizes the specific *means* by which I seek the satisfaction of a specific desire. There is no real antithesis here; there is merely a choice between the concrete and the abstract statement of the situation.

5. *Antihedonists seek to discredit psychological hedonism by pointing out that a man often refuses to take the action that seems to promise the most immediate or the most intense pleasure.* But this proves nothing at all about psychological hedonism, and especially not about psychological eudaemonism. It may merely mean that the man is seeking his greatest pleasure (or satisfaction or happiness) *in the long run*. He "measures" pleasure or satisfaction or happiness by *duration* as well as by intensity.

6. *The final argument against psychological hedonism or eudaemonism is that men frequently act under the influence of mere impulse, passion, or anger and do not do the things calculated to bring them the maximum of pleasure, satisfaction, or happiness.* This is true. But it remains true that, in his cool moments, it is his long-run happiness that each man seeks.

Let us restate and summarize this. It is true that men do not seek to maximize some mere abstraction, some homogeneous juice called "pleasure." *They seek the satisfaction of their desires.* And this is what we *mean* when we say that they seek "happiness."

A man's attempted satisfaction of one of his own wishes may conflict with the satisfaction of another. If, in a moment of impulse or passion, he attempts to satisfy a merely momentary desire, he may do so only at the cost of giving up a greater and more enduring satisfaction. Therefore he must *choose* among the wishes he seeks to satisfy; he must seek to reconcile them with the conflicting wishes of others as well as with his own conflicting wishes. He must seek, in other words, to *harmonize* his desires, and to maximize his satisfactions in the long run.

And this is the reconciliation of psychological and ethical eudaemonism. A man may not always act in such a way as to maximize his own long-run happiness. He may be short-sighted or weak-willed, or the slave of his momentary passions. But he is a psychological eudaemonist none the less; for, in his cool moments, he does wish to maximize his own satisfactions or happiness in the long run. It is because of this that ethical argument may reach and convince him. If one can successfully point out to him that certain actions, satisfying some momentary passion, or appearing to promote some immediate self-interest, will reduce his total satisfactions in the long run, his reason will accept your argument, and he will seek to amend his conduct.

This is not necessarily an appeal to mere "egoism." Most people feel spontaneous sympathy with the happiness and welfare of others, particularly their family and friends, and would be incapable of finding much satisfaction or happiness for themselves unless it were shared by at least those nearest to them, if not by the community at large. They would seek their own satisfaction and happiness through acts of kindness and love. Even thoroughly "selfish" individuals can be brought to see that they can best promote their own long-run interests through social cooperation, and that they cannot get the cooperation of others unless they generously contribute their own.

Even the most self-centered individual, in fact, needing not only to be protected against the aggression of others, but wanting the active cooperation of others, finds it to his interest to defend and uphold a set of moral (as well as legal) rules that forbid breaking promises, cheating, stealing, assault, and murder, and in addition a set of moral rules that enjoin cooperation, helpfulness, and kindness.

Ethics is a means rather than an ultimate end. It has derivative or "instrumental" value rather than "intrinsic" or final value. A rational ethics cannot be built merely on what we "ought" to desire but on what we do desire. Everyone desires to substitute a more satisfactory state for a less satisfactory one. As Pascal put it: "Man's ordinary life is like that of the saints. Both seek satisfaction, and they differ only in the object in which they set it." Everyone desires his own long-run happiness. This is true if only because it is tautological. Our long-run happiness is merely another name for what we do in fact desire in the long run.

This is the basis not only of the prudential virtues but of the social virtues. It is in the long-run interest of each of us to practice the social as well as the prudential virtues and, of course, to have everyone else practice them.

Here is the answer, and the only persuasive answer, to the question: "Why should I be moral?" An *ought to* is always based upon, and derived from, an *is* or a *will be*.

CHAPTER 6

Social Cooperation

1. *Each and All*

The ultimate goal of the conduct of each of us, as an individual, is to maximize his own happiness and well-being. Therefore the effort of each of us, as a member of society, is to persuade and induce *everybody else* to act so as to maximize the long-run happiness and well-being of society as a whole and even, if necessary, forcibly to prevent anybody from acting to reduce or destroy the happiness or well-being of society as a whole. For the happiness and well-being of each is promoted by the same conduct that promotes the happiness and well-being of all. Conversely, the happiness and well-being of all is promoted by the conduct that promotes the happiness and well-being of each. In the long run the aims of the individual and "society" (considering this as the name that each of us gives to all *other* individuals) coalesce, and tend to coincide.

We may state this conclusion in another form: The aim of each of us is to maximize his own satisfaction; and each of us recognizes that his satisfaction can best be maximized by cooperating with others and having others cooperate with him. Society itself, therefore, may be defined as nothing else but the combination of individuals for cooperative effort.[1] If we keep this in mind, there is no harm in saying that, as it is the aim of each of us to maximize his satisfactions, so it is the aim of "society" to maximize the satisfactions of each of its members, or, where this cannot be completely done, to try to reconcile and harmonize as many desires as possible, and to minimize the dissatisfactions or maximize the satisfactions of as many persons as possible in the long run.

Thus our goal envisions continuously both a present state of well-being and a future state of well-being, the maximization of both present satisfactions and future satisfactions.

But this statement of the ultimate goal carries us only a little way toward a system of ethics.

2. *The Way to the Goal*

It was an error of most of the older utilitarians, as of earlier moralists, to suppose that if they could once find and state the ultimate goal of conduct, the great *Summum Bonum,* their mission was completed. They were like medieval knights devoting all their efforts to the quest of the Holy Grail, and assuming that, if they once found it, their task would be done.

Yet even if we assume that we have found, or succeeded in stating, the "ultimate" goal of conduct, we have no more finished our task than if we had decided to go to the Holy Land. We must know the way to get there. We must know the means, and the means of obtaining the means.

By what means are we to achieve the goal of conduct? How are we to know what conduct is most likely to achieve this goal?

The great problem presented by ethics is that no two people find their happiness or satisfactions in precisely the same things. Each of us has his own peculiar set of desires, his own particular valuations, his own intermediate ends. Unanimity in value judgments does not exist, and probably never will.

This seems to present a dilemma, a logical dead end, from which the older ethical writers struggled for a way of escape. Many of them thought they had found it in the doctrine that ultimate goals and ethical rules were known by "intuition." When there was disagreement about these goals or rules, they tried to resolve it by consulting their own individual consciences, and taking their own private intuitions as the guide. This was not a good way out. Yet a way of escape from the dilemma was there.

This lies in *Social Cooperation.* For each of us, social cooperation is the great means of attaining nearly all our ends. For each of us social cooperation is of course not the ultimate end but a means. It has the great advantage that no unanimity with regard to value judgments is required to make it work.[2] But it is a means so central, so universal, so indispensable to the realization of practically all our other ends, that there is little harm in regarding it as an end-in-itself, and even in treating it as if it were *the* goal of ethics. In fact, precisely because none of us knows *exactly* what would give most satisfaction or happiness to others, the best test of our actions or rules of action is the extent to which they promote a social cooperation that best enables each of us to pursue *his own* ends.

Without social cooperation modern man could not achieve the barest fraction of the ends and satisfactions that he has achieved with it. The very subsistence of the immense majority of us depends upon it. We cannot treat subsistence as basely material and beneath our moral notice. As Mises reminds us: "Even the most sublime ends cannot be sought by people who have not first satisfied the wants of their animal body." [3] And as Philip Wicksteed has more concretely put it: "A man can be neither a saint, nor a lover, nor a poet, unless he has comparatively recently had something to eat." [4]

3. *The Division of Labor*

The great means of social cooperation is the division and combination of labor. The division of labor enormously increases the productivity of each of us and therefore the productivity of all of us. This has been recognized since the very beginning of economics as a science. Its recognition is, indeed, the foundation of modern economics. It is not mere coincidence that the statement of this truth occurs in the very first sentence of the first chapter of Adam Smith's great *Wealth of Nations,* published in 1776: "The greatest improvement in the productive powers of labor, and the greater part of the skill, dexterity, and judgment with which it is any where directed, or applied, seem to have been the effects of the division of labor."

Adam Smith goes on to take an example from "a very trifling manufacture; but one in which the division of labor has been very often taken notice of, the trade of the pin-maker." He points out that "a workman not educated to this business (which the division of labor has rendered a distinct trade), nor acquainted with the use of machinery employed in it (to the invention of which the same division of labor has probably given occasion), could scarce, perhaps, with the utmost industry, make one pin a day, and certainly could not make twenty." In the way in which the work is actually carried on (in 1776), he tells us: "One man draws out the wire, another straights it, a third cuts it, a fourth points it, a fifth grinds it at the top for receiving the head" and so on, so that "the important business of making a pin is, in this manner, divided into about eighteen distinct operations." He tells how he himself has seen "a small manufactory of this kind where ten men only were employed" yet "could make among them upwards of forty-eight thousand pins in a day. Each person, therefore, making a tenth part of forty-eight thousand pins, might be considered as making four thousand eight hundred pins in a day. But if they had all wrought separately and independently, and without any of them having been educated to this peculiar business, they certainly could not each of them have made twenty, perhaps not one pin a day; that is, certainly, not the two hundred and fortieth, perhaps not the four thousand eight hundredth part of what they are at present capable of performing, in consequence of a proper division and combination of their different operations."

Smith then goes on to show, from further illustrations, how "the division of labor . . . so far as it can be introduced, occasions, in every art, a proportionable increase of the productive powers of labor"; and how "the separation of different trades and employments from one another seems to have taken place in consequences of this advantage."

This great increase in productivity he attributes to "three different circumstances; first, to the increase of dexterity in every particular workman; secondly, to the saving of the time which is commonly lost in passing from one species of work to another; and lastly, to the invention of a great number of machines which facilitate and abridge labor, and enable one man to do the work of many." These three "circumstances" are then explained in detail.

"It is the great multiplication of the productions of all the different arts, in consequence of the division of labor," Smith concludes, "which occasions, in a well-governed society, that universal opulence which extends itself to the lowest ranks of the people."

But this brings him to a further question, which he proceeds to take up in his second chapter. "This division of labor, from which so many advantages are derived, is not originally the effect of any human wisdom, which foresees and intends that general opulence to which it gives occasion. It is the necessary, though very slow and gradual, consequence of a certain propensity in human nature which has in view no such extensive utility; the propensity to truck, barter, and exchange one thing for another."

In resting the origin of the division of labor on an unexplained "propensity to truck, barter, and exchange," as he sometimes seems to do in his succeeding argument, Adam Smith was wrong. Social cooperation and the division of labor rest upon a recognition (though often implicit rather than explicit) on the part of the individual that this promotes his own self-interest— that work performed under the division of labor is more productive than isolated work. And in fact, Adam Smith's own subsequent argument in Chapter II clearly recognizes this:

> In civilized society [the individual] stands at all times in need of the co-operation and assistance of great multitudes. . . . Man has almost constant occasion for the help of his brethren, and it is in vain for him to expect it from their benevolence only. He will be more likely to prevail if he can interest their self-love in his favor, and show them that it is for their own advantage to do for him what he requires of them. Whoever offers to another a bargain of any kind, proposes to do this: Give me that which I want, and you shall have this which you want, is the meaning of every such offer; and it is in this manner that we obtain from one another the far greater part of those good offices which we stand in need of. It is not from the benevolence of the butcher, the brewer, or the baker, that we expect our dinner, but from their regard to their own interest. We address ourselves, not to their humanity but to their self-love, and never talk to them of our own necessities but of their advantages.

"Nobody but a beggar," Smith points out in extending the argument, "chooses to depend chiefly upon the benevolence of his fellow citizens," and "even a beggar does not depend upon it entirely," for "with the money which one man gives him he purchases food," etc.

"As it is by treaty, by barter, and by purchase," Adam Smith continues, "that we obtain from one another the greater part of those mutual good offices which we stand in need of, so it is this same trucking disposition which originally gives occasion to the division of labor. In a tribe of hunters or shepherds a particular person makes bows and arrows, for example, with more readiness and dexterity than any other. He frequently exchanges them for cattle or for venison with his companions; and he finds at last that he can in this manner get more cattle and venison, than if he himself went to the field to catch them. From a regard to his own interest, therefore, the making of bows and arrows grows to be his chief business, and he becomes a sort of armourer." And Smith explains how in turn other specialists develop.

In brief, each of us, in pursuing his self-interest, finds that he can do it most effectively through social cooperation. The belief that there is a basic conflict between the interests of the individual and the interests of society is untenable. Society is only another name for the combination of individuals for purposeful cooperation.

4. *The Basis of Economic Life*

Let us look a little more closely at the motivational basis of this great system of social cooperation through exchange of goods or services. I have just used the phrase "self-interest," following Adam Smith's example when he speaks of the butcher's and the baker's "own interests," "self-love," and "advantage." But we should be careful not to assume that people enter into these economic relations with each other simply because each seeks only his "selfish" or "egoistic" advantage. Let us see how an acute economist restates the essence of this economic relation.

The economic life, writes Philip Wicksteed, "consists of all that complex of relations into which we enter with other people, and lend ourselves or our resources to the furtherance of their purposes, as an indirect means of furthering our own." [5] "By direct and indirect processes of exchange, by the social alchemy of which money is the symbol, the things I have and the things I can are transmuted into the things I want and the things I would." [6] People cooperate with me in the economic relation "not primarily, or not solely, because they are interested in my purposes, but because they have certain purposes of their own; and just as I find that I can only secure the accomplishment of my purposes by securing their co-operation, so they find that they can only accomplish theirs by securing the co-operation of yet others, and they find that I am in a position, directly or indirectly, to place this co-operation at their disposal. A vast range, therefore, of our relations with others enters into a system of mutual adjustment by which we further each other's purposes simply as an indirect way of furthering our own." [7]

So far the reader may not have detected any substantial difference between Wicksteed's statement and Adam Smith's. Yet there is a very important one. I enter into an economic or business relation with you, for the exchange of goods or services for money, primarily to further *my* purposes, not yours, and you enter into it, on your side, primarily to further *your* purposes, not mine. But this does not mean that either of our purposes is necessarily selfish or self-centered. I may be hiring your services as a printer to publish a tract at my own expense pleading for more kindness to animals. A mother buying groceries in the market will go where she can get the best quality or the lowest price, and not to help any particular grocer; yet in buying her groceries she may have the needs and tastes of her husband or children in mind more than her own needs or tastes. "When Paul of Tarsus abode with Aquila and Priscilla in Corinth and wrought with them at his craft of tent-making we shall hardly say that he was inspired by egoistic motives. . . . The economic relation, then, or business nexus, is necessary alike for carrying on the life of the peasant and the prince, of the saint and the sinner, of the apostle and the shepherd, of the most altruistic and the most egoistic of men." [8]

The reader may have begun to wonder at this point whether this is a book on ethics or on economics. But I have emphasized this economic cooperation because it occupies so enormous a part of our daily life. It plays, in fact, a far larger role in our daily life than most of us are consciously aware of. The relationship of employer and employee (notwithstanding the misconceptions and propaganda of the Marxist socialists and the unions) is essentially a cooperative relationship. Each needs the other to accomplish his own purposes. The success of the employer depends upon the industriousness, skill, and loyalty of his employees; the jobs and incomes of the employees depend upon the success of the employer. Even economic competition, so commonly regarded by socialists and reformers as a form of economic warfare,[9] is part of a great system of social cooperation, which promotes continual invention and improvement of products, continual reduction of costs and prices, continual widening of the range of choice and continual increase of the welfare of consumers. The competition for workers constantly raises wages, as the competition for jobs improves performance and efficiency. True, competitors do not cooperate *directly* with each other; but each, in competing for the patronage of third parties, seeks to offer more advantages to those third parties than his rival can, and in so doing each forwards the whole system of social cooperation. Economic competition is simply the striving of individuals to attain the most favorable position in the system of social cooperation. As such, it must exist in any conceivable mode of social organization.[10]

The realm of economic cooperation, as I have said, occupies a far larger part of our daily life than most of us are commonly aware of, or even willing to admit. Marriage and the family are, among other things, a form not only of biological but of economical cooperation. In primitive societies the man hunted and fished while the woman prepared the food. In modern society the husband is still responsible for the physical protection and the food supply of his wife and children. Each member of the family gains by this cooperation, and it is largely on recognition of this mutual economic gain, and not merely of the joys of love and companionship, that the foundations of the institution of marriage are so solidly built.

But though the advantages of social cooperation are to an enormous extent economic, they are not solely economic. Through social cooperation we promote all the values, direct and indirect, material and spiritual, cultural and aesthetic, of modern civilization.

Some readers will see a similarity, and others may suspect an identity, between the ideal of Social Cooperation and Kropotkin's ideal of "Mutual Aid." [11] A similarity there surely is. But Social Cooperation seems to me not only a much more appropriate *phrase* than Mutual Aid, but a much more appropriate and precise *concept*. Typical instances of cooperation occur when two men row a boat or paddle a canoe from opposite sides, when four men move a piano or a crate by lifting opposite corners, when a carpenter hires a helper, when an orchestra plays a symphony. We would not hesitate to say that any of these were cooperative undertakings or acts of cooperation, but we should be surprised to find all of them called examples of "mutual aid." For "aid" carries the implication of *gratuitous* help—the rich aiding the poor, the strong aiding the weak, the superior, out of compassion, aiding the inferior. It also seems to carry the implication of *haphazard* and *sporadic* rather than of *systematic* and *continuous* cooperation. The phrase Social Cooperation, on the other hand, seems to cover not only everything that the phrase Mutual Aid implies but the very purpose and basis of life in society.[12]

CHAPTER 7

Long Run vs. Short Run

1. *The Voluptuary's Fallacy*

There is no irreconcilable conflict between the interests of the individual and those of society. If there were, society could not exist. Society is the great means through which individuals pursue and fulfill their ends. For society is but another name for the combination of individuals for cooperation. It is the means through which each of us furthers the purposes of others as an indirect means of furthering his own. And this cooperation is in the overwhelming main *voluntary*. It is only collectivists who assume that the interests of the individual and of society (or the State) are fundamentally opposed, and that the individual can only be led to cooperate in society by Draconian compulsions.

The real distinction we need to make for ethical clarity is not that between the individual and society, or even between "egoism" and "altruism," but between interests in the short run and those in the long run. This distinction is made constantly in modern economics.[1] It is in large part the basis for the condemnation by economists of such policies as tariffs, subsidies, price-fixing, rent control, crop supports, featherbedding, deficit-financing, and inflation. Those who say mockingly that "in the long run we are all dead"[2] are just as irresponsible as the French aristocrats whose reputed motto was *Après nous le déluge*.

The distinction between short-run interests and long-run interests has always been implicit in common-sense ethical judgments, particularly as concerns prudential ethics. But it has seldom received explicit recognition, and more seldom still in those words.[3] The classical moralist who came nearest to stating it systematically is Jeremy Bentham. He does this not in the form of comparing short-run interests with long-run interests, or short-run consequences of actions with long-run consequences, but in the form of comparing greater or smaller amounts of pleasure or happiness. Thus in his effort to judge actions by comparing the quantities or "values" of the pleasures they yield or lead to, he measures these quantities by "duration" (among seven standards) as well as by "intensity."[4] And in his *Deontology* a typical statement is: "Is not temperance a virtue? Aye, assuredly is it. But wherefore? Because by restraining enjoyment for a time, it afterwards elevates it to that very pitch which leaves, on the whole, the largest addition to the stock of happiness."[5]

The common-sense reasons for temperance and other prudential virtues are frequently misunderstood or derided by ethical skeptics:

> Let us have wine and women, mirth and laughter,
> Sermons and soda-water the day after.

So sang Byron. The implication is that the sermons and soda-water are a short and cheap price to pay for the fun. Samuel Butler, also, cynically generalized the distinction between morality and immorality as depending merely on the order of precedence between pleasure and pain: "Morality turns on whether the pleasure precedes or follows the pain. Thus it is immoral to get drunk because the headache comes after the drinking, but if the headache came first, and the drunkenness afterwards, it would be moral to get drunk."[6]

When we talk seriously, it is of course not at all a question whether the pain or the pleasure comes first, but which exceeds the other in the long run. The confusions that result from failure to understand this principle lead not only, on the one hand, to the sophisms of the ethical skeptics but, on the other, to the fallacies of anti-utilitarian writers and of ascetics. When the anti-utilitarians attack not merely the pleasure-pain calculus of the Benthamites but the Greatest Happiness Principle, or the maximization of satisfactions, it will be found that they are almost invariably assuming, tacitly or expressly, that the utilitarian standards take only immediate or short-run consequences into consideration. Their criticism is valid only as applied to crude forms of hedonistic and utilitarian theories. We shall return to a longer analysis of this later.

2. *The Ascetic's Fallacy*

The confusion in another form leads to the opposite result—to the theories and standards of asceticism. The utilitarian standard, consistently applied, merely asks whether an action (or more properly a rule of action) will tend to lead to a surplus of happiness and well-being, or a surplus of unhappiness and ill-being, for all those whom it affects, in the long run. One of Bentham's great merits was that he attempted to apply the standard thoroughly and consistently. Though he was not wholly successful, because there were several important tools of analysis that he lacked, what is remarkable is the degree of his success, and the steadiness with which he kept this standard in mind.

In the interests of the individual's long-run well-being, it is necessary for him to make certain short-run sacrifices, or apparent sacrifices. He must put certain immediate restraints on his impulses in order to prevent later regrets. He must accept a certain deprivation today either in order to reap a greater compensation in the future or to prevent an even greater deprivation in the future.

But ascetics, by a confused association, conclude that the restraint, deprivation, sacrifice, or pain that must sometimes be undergone in the present for the sake of the future, is something virtuous and praiseworthy for its own sake. Asceticism was caustically defined by Bentham as "that principle, which, like the principle of utility, approves or disapproves of any action, according to the tendency which it appears to have to augment or diminish the happiness of the party whose interest is in question; but in an inverse manner: approving of actions in as far as they tend to diminish his happiness; disapproving of them in as far as they tend to augment it." [7] And he continued: "It is evident that any one who reprobates any the least particle of pleasure, as such, from whatever source derived, is *pro tanto* a partizan of the principle of asceticism." [8]

A more favorable judgment of asceticism is possible if we give it another definition. As Bentham himself explained, it comes etymologically from a Greek word meaning *exercise*. Bentham then went on to declare that: "The practices by which

Monks sought to distinguish themselves from other men were called their Exercises. These exercises consisted in so many contrivances they had for tormenting themselves." [9]

However if, rejecting this definition, we think of asceticism as a form of *athleticism,* analogous to the discipline that athletes or soldiers undergo to harden themselves against possible adversity, or against probable trials of strength, courage, fortitude, effort, and endurance in the future, or even as a process of restraint to sharpen "the keen edge of seldom pleasure," then it is something that serves a utilitarian and even a hedonistic purpose.

Confusion of thought will continue as long as we use the same word, *asceticism,* in both of these senses. We can avoid ambiguity only by assigning separate names to each meaning.

I am going to reject the semantic temptation to take advantage of the traditional moral prestige of the ascetic ideal by using *asceticism* only in the "good" sense of a far-sighted discipline or restraint undertaken to maximize one's happiness in the long run. If I did this, I would then be obliged to use exclusively some other word, such as *flagellantism,* for the "bad" sense of mortification or self-torment. No one can presume to set himself up as a dictator of verbal usage. I can only say, therefore, that in view of traditional usage I think it would be most honest and least confusing to confine the word *asceticism* to the anti-utilitarian, antihedonist, anti-eudaemonist meaning of self-denial and self-torment for their own sakes, and to reserve another word, say *self-discipline,* or even to coin a word, like *disciplinism*[10] for the doctrine which believes in abstinence and restraint, not for their own sakes, but only in so far as they serve as means for increasing happiness in the long run.

The distinction between the consideration of short-run and long-run consequences is so basic, and applies so widely, that one might be excused for trying to make it, by itself, the whole foundation for a system of ethics, and to say, quite simply, that morality is essentially, not the subordination of the "individual" to "society" but the subordination of immediate objectives to long-term ones. Certainly the Long-Run Principle is a necessary if not a sufficient foundation for morality. Bentham did not have the concept (which has been made explicit mainly by modern economics) in just these words, but he came close to it in his constant insistence on the necessity of considering the future as well as the present consequences of any course of conduct, and in his attempt to measure and compare "quantities" of pleasure not merely in terms of "intensity" but of "duration." Many efforts have been made to define the difference between *pleasure* and *happiness*. One of them is surely that between a momentary gratification and a permanent or at least prolonged gratification, between the short run and the long run.

3. *On Undervaluing the Future*

Perhaps this is an appropriate point to warn the reader against some possible misinterpretations of the Long-Run Principle. When we are asked to take into consideration the probable consequences of a given act or rule of action in the long run, this does not mean that we must disregard, or even that we are justified in disregarding, its probable consequences in the short run. What we are really being asked to consider is the *total net* consequences of a given act or rule of action. We are justified in considering the pleasure of tonight's drinking against the pain of tomorrow's headache, the pleasure of tonight's eating against the pain of tomorrow's indigestion or unwelcome increase in weight, the pleasure of this summer's vacation in Europe against this fall's precarious bank balance. We should not be misled by the term "long run" into supposing that pleasure, satisfaction, or happiness is to be valued only in accordance with its duration: its "intensity," "certainty," "propinquity," "fecundity," "purity," and "extent" also count. In this insight Bentham was correct. In the rare cases of conflict, it is the rule of action that promises to yield the *most* satisfaction, rather than merely the *longest* satisfaction, or merely the greatest *future* satisfaction, that we should choose. We need not value probable future satisfaction *above* present satisfaction. It is only because our human nature is too prone to yield to present impulse and forget the future cost that it is necessary to make a special effort to keep this future cost before the mind at the moment of temptation. If the immediate pleasure does indeed outweigh the probable future cost, then refusal to indulge oneself in a pleasure is mere asceticism or self-deprivation for its own sake. To make this a rule of action would not increase the sum of happiness, but reduce it.

In applying the Long-Run Principle, in other words, we must apply it with a certain amount of common sense. We must confine ourselves to consideration of the *relevant* long run, the finite and reasonably *cognizable* long run. This is the grain of truth in Keynes's cynical dictum that *"In the long run* we are all dead." [11] *That* long run we may no doubt justifiably ignore. We cannot see into eternity.

Yet no future, even the next five minutes, is *certain*, and we cannot do more at any time than act on probabilities (although, as we shall see, some probabilities of a given course of conduct or rule of action are considerably more probable than others). And there are people capable of concern regarding the fate of mankind far beyond the probable length of their own lives.

The Long-Run Principle presents still another problem. This is the value that we ought to attach to future pains and pleasures as compared with present ones. In his list of the seven "circumstances" (or, as he later called them, "elements" or "dimensions") by which we should value a pain or a pleasure, Bentham lists "3. Its *certainty* or *uncertainty*," and "4. Its *propinquity* or *remoteness*." Now a remote pain or pleasure is apt to be less certain than a near one; in fact, its uncertainty is widely considered to be a function of its remoteness. But the question we are asking now is to what extent, if any, Bentham was justified in assuming that we ought to attach less value to a remote pain or pleasure than to a near one, even when the element of certainty or uncertainty is disregarded or, as in Bentham's list, treated as a separate consideration.[12]

Most of us cannot prevent ourselves from valuing a future good at less than the same present and otherwise identical good. We value today's dinner, say, more than a similar dinner a year from now. Are we "right" or "wrong" in doing so? It is impossible to answer the question in this form. All of us "undervalue" a future good as compared with a present good. This "undervaluation" is so universal that it may be asked whether it is undervaluation at all. Economically, the value of anything is what it is valued at. It is value *to* somebody. Economic value cannot be thought of apart from a valuer. Is ethical value quite different in kind? Is there such a thing as the "intrinsic" ethical value of a good (as many moralists persist in thinking) apart from anybody's valuation of that good? I shall come to a fuller discussion of this point later.[13] Here we are concerned merely with the question of how we "ought" to value future goods or satisfactions as compared with present ones.

When we look at the relative value that we actually do assign to them, we find that in the economic world the market has worked out a "rate of interest" which is, in effect, the average or composite rate of discount that the market community applies to future as compared with present goods. When the interest rate is 5 per cent, $1.05 a year from now is worth no more than $1 today, or $1 a year from now no more than about 95 cents today. If an individual (who is in desperate need) values $2 a year from now at no more than $1 today, we are perhaps entitled to say that he undervalues future as compared with present goods. But whether we are entitled to say, simply because there *is* a rate of interest or a rate of time-discount, that *the economic community as a whole* "undervalues" the future, is very dubious. Backward communities have a higher rate of future time discount than progressive communities. The poor tend to put a higher relative valuation on present goods than the rich. But can we say that the lower valuation placed on future as compared with present goods by humanity as a whole is "wrong"?

I for one will no more attempt to answer this question in the ethical than in the economic realm. At best we can judge the individual's valuation against the whole community's valuation. What we can say, however, is that any course of action based on a real underestimation or undervaluation of future consequences will result in less total happiness than one which estimates or values future consequences justly.

The distinction between short- and long-run consequences was implicitly, though not expressly, the basis of the ethical system that Bentham presented in his *Deontology,* in which he classifies all the virtues under the two main heads of Prudence and Beneficence, and further divides them, in four chapters, under the heads of Self-Regarding Prudence, Extra-Regarding Prudence, Negative Efficient Benevolence, and Positive Efficient Benevolence.

It is consideration of long-run consequences that gives Prudence a far larger role in ethics than it has been commonly assumed to have. This is suggested by Bentham's title head, "Extra-Regarding Prudence." The happiness of each of us is dependent upon his fellows. He depends upon their concurrence and cooperation. One can never disregard the happiness of others without running a risk to his own.

To sum up: The distinction between the short-run and the long-run effects of conduct is more valid than the traditional contrasts between the interests of the individual and the interests of society. When the individual acts in his own long-run interests he tends to act also in the long-run interest of the whole society. The longer the run we consider, the more likely are the interests of the individual and of society to become identical. Moral conduct is in the long-run interest of the individual.

To recognize this is to perceive the solution of a basic moral problem that otherwise seems to present a contradiction. The difficulties that arise when this is not clearly recognized can be seen from a passage in an otherwise penetrating writer:

> Moralities are systems of principles whose acceptance by everyone as overruling the dictates of self-interest is in the interest of everyone alike, though following the rules of morality is not of course identical with following self-interest. If it were, there could be no conflict between a morality and self-interest and no point in having rules overriding self-interest. . . . The answer to the question "Why be moral?" is therefore as follows. We should be moral because being moral is following rules designed to overrule self-interest whenever it is in the interest of everyone alike that everyone should set aside his interest.[14]

If we emphasize the distinction between short-run and long-run interests, however, the solution to this problem becomes much simpler and involves no paradox. Then we would rewrite the foregoing passage like this: Moralities are systems of principles whose acceptance by everyone as overruling the apparent dictates of immediate self-interest is in the long-run interest of everyone alike. We should be moral because being moral is following rules which disregard apparent self-interest in the short run and are designed to promote our own real long-run interest as well as the interest of others who are affected by our actions.

It is only from a short-sighted view that the interests of the individual appear to be in conflict with those of "society," and vice versa.

Actions or rules of action are not "right" or "wrong" in the sense in which a proposition in physics or mathematics is right or wrong, but expedient or inexpedient, advisable or inadvisable, helpful or harmful. In brief, in ethics the appropriate criterion is not "truth" but *wisdom*. To adopt this concept is, indeed, to return to the concept of the ancients. The moral appeal of Socrates is the appeal to conduct our lives with wisdom. The Proverbs of the Old Testament do not speak dominantly of Virtue or Sin, but of Wisdom and Folly. "Wisdom is the principal thing; therefore get wisdom. . . . The fear of the Lord is the beginning of wisdom. . . . A wise son maketh a glad father: but a foolish son is the heaviness of his mother. . . . As a dog returneth to his vomit, so a fool returneth to his folly."

We shall reserve until later chapters the detailed illustration and application of the Long-Run Principle. Here we are still concerned with the epistemological or theoretical foundations of ethics rather than with casuistry or detailed practical guidance. But it is now possible to take the next step from the theoretical to the practical. It is one of the most important implications of the Long-Run Principle (and one that Bentham, strangely, failed explicitly to recognize) that we must act, not by attempting separately in every case to weigh and compare the probable specific consequences of one moral decision or course of action as against another, but by acting according to some *established general rule or set of rules*. This is what is meant by acting *according to principle*. It is not the consequences (which it is impossible to know in advance) of a specific *act* that we have to consider, but the probable long-run consequences of following a given *rule* of action.

Why this is so, and how it is so, we shall examine in our next chapter.

CHAPTER 8

The Need for General Rules

1. *The Contribution of Hume*

David Hume, probably the greatest of British philosophers, made three major contributions to ethics. The first was the naming and consistent application of "the principle of utility."[1] The second was his account of sympathy. The third, no less important than the others, was to point out not only that we must adhere inflexibly to *general rules* of action, but *why* this is essential to secure the interests and happiness of the individual and of mankind.

It is a puzzling development in the history of ethical thought, however, that this third contribution has been so often overlooked not only by subsequent writers of the Utilitarian school, including Bentham, but even by historians of ethics when they are discussing Hume himself.[2] One reason for this, perhaps, is that Hume, in the discussion of Morals in his *Treatise of Human Nature* (1740) devotes only a comparatively few paragraphs to the point. And in his *Inquiry Concerning the Principles of Morals*, published twelve years later (in 1752), which in his autobiography he described as "incomparably the best" of all his writings, historical, philosophical, or literary, he gave even less space to it. Yet it is so important and so central that it can hardly receive too much emphasis and elaboration.

Let us begin with Hume's own exposition of the principle, and of the reasons for it, in the *Treatise*:

> A single act of justice is frequently contrary to *public interest;* and were it to stand alone, without being followed by other acts, may, in itself, be very prejudicial to society. When a man of merit, of a beneficent disposition, restores a great fortune to a miser, or a seditious bigot, he has acted justly and laudably; but the public is the real sufferer. Nor is every single act of justice, considered apart, more conducive to private interest than to public; and it is easily conceived how a man may impoverish himself by a single instance of integrity, and have reason to wish that, with regard

to that single act, the laws of justice were for a moment suspended in the universe. But however single acts of justice may be contrary either to public or private interest, it is certain that the whole plan or scheme is highly conductive, or indeed absolutely requisite, both to the support of society, and the well-being of every individual. It is impossible to separate the good from the ill. Property must be stable, and must be fixed by general rules. Though in one instance the public be a sufferer, this momentary ill is amply compensated by the steady prosecution of the rule, and by the peace and order which it establishes in society. And even every indivdual person must find himself a gainer on balancing the account; since, without justice, society must immediately dissolve, and every one must fall into that savage and solitary condition which is infinitely worse than the worst situation that can possibly be supposed in society. When, therefore, men have had experience enough to observe that whatever may be the consequence of any single act of justice, performed by a single person, yet the whole system of actions concurred in by the whole society is infinitely advantageous to the whole, and to every part, it is not long before justice and property take place. Every member of society is sensible of this interest: every one expresses this sense to his fellows, along with the resolution he has taken of squaring his actions by it, on condition that others will do the same. No more is requisite to induce any one of them to perform an act of justice, who has the first opportunity. This becomes an example to others; and thus justice establishes itself by a kind of convention or agreement, that is, by a sense of interest, supposed to be common to all, and where every single act is performed in expectation that others are to perform the like. Without such a convention, no one would ever have dreamed that there was such a virtue as justice, or have been induced to conform his actions to it. Taking any single act, my justice may be pernicious in every respect; and it is only upon the supposition that others are to imitate my example, that I can be induced to embrace that virtue; since nothing but this combination can render justice advantageous, or afford me any motives to conform myself to its rules.[3]

And some thirty pages further on, Hume observes: "The avidity and partiality of men would quickly bring disorder into the world, if not restrained by some general and inflexible principles. It was therefore with a view to this inconvenience that men have established those principles, and have agreed to restrain themselves by general rules, which are unchangeable by spite and favor, and by particular views of private or public interest."[4]

In his *Inquiry Concerning the Principles of Morals,* a dozen years later, Hume returns to the theme, though it is unfortunately made less central to his argument than in the earlier work. In the body of the *Inquiry* we find only one or two brief references, in a single sentence, to "the necessity of rules wherever men have any intercourse with each other."[5] It is not till we get to the Conclusion that we come to a second brief reference to the need of "homage to general rules."[6] And it is not till we get to the Appendices that we find any extended discussion, and even this is confined to two or three pages:

> The benefit resulting from [the social virtues of justice and fidelity] is not the consequence of every individual single act, but arises from the whole scheme or system concurred in by the whole or the greater part of the society. General peace and order are the attendants of justice, or a general abstinence from the possessions of others; but a particular regard to the particular right of one individual citizen may frequently, considered in itself, be productive of pernicious consequences. The result of the individual acts is here, in many instances, directly opposite to that of the whole system of actions; and the former may be extremely hurtful, while the latter is, to the highest degree, advantageous. Riches inherited from a parent are in a bad man's hand the instrument of mischief. The right of succession may, in one instance, be hurtful. Its benefit arises only from the observance of the general rule; and it is sufficient if compensation be thereby made for all the ills and inconveniences which flow from particular characters and situations.[7]

Hume then speaks of "the general, inflexible rules necessary to support general peace and order in society," and continues:

> All the laws of nature which regulate property as well as all civil laws are general and regard alone some essential circumstances of the case, without taking into consideration the characters, situations, and connections of the person concerned or any particular consequences which may result from the determination of these laws in any particular case which offers. They deprive, without scruple, a beneficent man of all his possessions if acquired by mistake, without a good title, in order to bestow them on a selfish miser who has already heaped up immense stores of superfluous riches. Public utility requires that property should

be regulated by general inflexible rules; and though such rules are adopted as best serve the same end of public utility, it is impossible for them to prevent all particular hardships or make beneficial consequences result from every individual case. It is sufficient if the whole plan or scheme be necessary to the support of civil society and if the balance of good, in the main, do thereby preponderate much above that of evil.[8]

2. *The Principle in Adam Smith*

It would be impossible to exaggerate the importance of this principle both in law and in ethics. We will find later that, among other things, it alone can reconcile what is true in some of the traditional controversies of ethics—the long-standing dispute, for example, between Benthamite Utilitarianism and Kantian formalism, between relativism and absolutism, and even between "empirical" and "intuitive" ethics.

Most commentators on Hume completely ignore the point. Even Bentham, who not only took over the principle of utility from Hume, but christened it with the cumbersome name of Utilitarianism, which stuck,[9] missed, for all practical purposes, this vital qualification.

It is only natural that we should look for some trace of the influence of Hume's General-Rules Principle in Adam Smith, his admirer and younger friend (by twelve years), and—at least in some doctrines—his disciple. (Many of the views in *The Wealth of Nations,* on commerce, money, interest, the balance and freedom of trade, taxes and public credit, are anticipated in Hume's *Essays, Literary, Moral, and Political,* published some thirty years earlier.) And we do in fact find that Adam Smith incorporated the General-Rules Principle in his *Theory of the Moral Sentiments* (1759), particularly in Part III, Chapters IV and V. He states it eloquently:

> Our continual observations upon the conduct of others insensibly lead us to form to ourselves certain general rules concerning what is fit and proper either to be done or avoided. . . .[10] The regard to those general rules of conduct is what is properly called a sense of duty, a principle of the greatest consequence in human life, and the only principle by which the bulk of mankind are capable of directing their actions. . . .[11] Without this sacred regard to general rules, there is no man whose conduct can be

THE NEED FOR GENERAL RULES 57

much depended upon. It is this which constitutes the most essential difference between a man of principle and honor, and a worthless fellow. The one adheres on all occasions steadily and resolutely to his maxims, and preserves through the whole of his life one even tenor of conduct. The other acts variously and accidently, as humour, inclination, or interest chance to be uppermost. . . .[12] Upon the tolerable observance of these duties [justice, truth, chastity, fidelity] depends the very existence of human society, which would crumble into nothing if mankind were not generally impressed with reverence for those important rules of conduct.[13]

But in spite of this emphatic statement of the principle, Adam Smith makes a doubtful qualification which is, in fact, inconsistent with it. He tells us, apparently in contradiction to Hume, that: "We do not originally approve or condemn particular actions because, upon examination, they appear to be agreeable or inconsistent with a certain general rule. The general rule, on the contrary, is formed by finding from experience that all actions of a certain kind, or circumstances in a certain manner, are approved or disapproved of." [14] He goes on to declare that "the man who first saw an inhuman murder committed" would not have to reflect, "in order to conceive how horrible such an action was" that "one of the most sacred rules of conduct" had been violated.[15] And he becomes ironic at the expense of "several very eminent authors" (Hume?) who "draw up their systems in such a manner as if they had supposed that the original judgments of mankind with regard to right and wrong were formed like the decisions of a court of judicatory—by considering first the general rule, and then, secondly, whether the particular action under consideration fell properly within its comprehension." [16]

Smith oversimplifies the problem, and does not recognize his own inconsistency. If we had always, from the beginning of time, instantly recognized, just by seeing them, hearing of them, or doing them, what actions were right and what were wrong, we would not *need* to frame general rules and resolve to abide by general rules, unless it were the general rule: Always do right and never do wrong. We would not even need to study or discuss ethics. We could dispense with all treatises on ethics or even any discussion of specific ethical problems. All ethics could be

58   THE FOUNDATIONS OF MORALITY

summed up in the foregoing rule of seven words. Even the Ten Commandments would be nine commandments too many.

3. *Rediscovery in the Twentieth Century*

The problem, unfortunately, is more complicated. It is true that our present ethical judgments of some actions are instantaneous; they seem based on abhorrence of the act itself, and not on any consideration of its consequences (apart from those that seem inherent in the act, such as the suffering of a person who is being tortured, or the death of a person who is killed), or on any judgment that they involve the violation of an abstract general rule. Nevertheless most of these instantaneous judgments may indeed be partly or mainly based on the fact that a general rule is being violated. We may look with horror on another car speeding directly toward us on *its* left side of the road, though there is nothing *inherently* wrong with driving on the left side of the road, and the whole danger comes from the violation of a general rule. And in our private moral judgments, no less than in law, we do in fact try to decide under what general rule we should act or under what general rule a given act should be classed. The courts must decide whether a given act is First-Degree Murder, or Manslaughter, or Self-Defense. If a patient's disease is hopeless a doctor who is asked for reassurance must decide whether this would be Telling a Lie, or Sparing Needless Suffering. When we are deciding (if we ever consciously do) whether or not to tell our hostess that we can't remember when we have had such a wonderful evening, we must decide whether this would be Perjury, Hypocrisy, or the Duty of Politeness.

The problem of deciding under what rule an act should be classed can sometimes present difficulties. F. H. Bradley was so impressed by these, in fact, that he even deplored any effort to solve the problem "by a reflective deduction" and insisted it must only be done "by an intuitive subsumption, which does not know that it is a subsumption." "No act in the world," he argued, "is without *some* side capable of being subsumed under a good rule; e.g. theft is economy, care for one's relations, protest against bad institutions, really doing oneself but justice, etc.," and *reasoning* about the matter leads straight to immorality. (*Ethical Studies,* pp. 196-197.) I do not think we need take

THE NEED FOR GENERAL RULES 59

this obscurantist argument very seriously. Logically followed, it would condemn all reasoning about ethics, including Bradley's. The problem of deciding under what rule of law an act should be classed is one that our courts and judges must solve a thousand times a day, and not by "intuitive subsumption" but by reasoning that will stand up on appeal. In ethics the problem may not often arise—but when it does it is precisely because our "intuitive subsumptions" conflict.

The need of adhering inflexibly to general rules is plain. Even the qualifications to rules must be drawn according to general rules. An "exception" to a rule must not be capricious, but itself capable of being stated as a rule, capable of being made *part* of a rule, of being *embodied* in a rule. Even here, in brief, we must be guided by generality, predictability, certainty, the non-disappointment of reasonable expectations.

The great principle that Hume discovered and framed was that, while conduct should be judged by its "utility," that is, by its consequences, by its tendency to promote happiness and well-being, it is not specific acts that should be so judged, but general *rules* of action. It is only the probable long-run consequences of these, and not of specific acts, that can reasonably be foreseen. As F. A. Hayek has put it:

> It is true enough that the justification of any particular rule of law must be its usefulness. . . . But, generally speaking, only the rule as a whole must be so justified, not its every application. The idea that each conflict, in law or in morals, should be so decided as would seem most expedient to somebody who could comprehend all the consequences of that decision involves the denial of the necessity of any rules. "Only a society of omniscient individuals could give each person complete liberty to weigh every particular action on general utilitarian grounds." Such an "extreme" utilitarianism leads to absurdity; and only what has been called "restricted" utilitarianism has therefore any relevance to our problem. Yet few beliefs have been more destructive of the respect for the rules of law and of morals than the idea that the the rule is binding only if the beneficial effect of observing it in the particular instance can be recognized.[17]

The principle of acting in accordance with general rules has had a most curious history in ethics. It is implicit in religious ethics (the Ten Commandments); it is implicit in "intuitive" ethics and in "common-sense" ethics—in the concept of the "man of principle" and the "man of honor"; it is explicitly stated by the first utilitist, Hume; then it is almost completely overlooked by the classical Utilitarian, Bentham, and only fitfully glimpsed by Mill; and now, practically within the last decade, it has been rediscovered by a group of writers.[18] They have given it the name *rule-utilitarianism* as contrasted with the older *act-utilitarianism* of Bentham and Mill. The former designation is excellent (though I would prefer *rule-utilitism* as a little less cumbersome), but the aptness of the latter is more questionable. In *both* cases it is the probable consequences of an *act* that are being judged, but in the first it is the probable consequences of the act *as an instance of following a rule,* and in the second it is the probable consequences of an act *considered in isolation* and apart from any general rule. Perhaps a better name for this would be *ad hoc utilitism.*

In any case, there will often be a profound difference in our moral judgment, according to which standard we apply. The standards of *direct* or *ad hoc* utilitism will not necessarily in every case be less demanding than the standards of *rule*-utilitism. In fact, to ask a man *in his every act* to do that "which will contribute more than any other act to human happiness" (as some of the older utilitarians did) is to impose upon him an oppressive as well as impossible choice. For it is impossible for any man to know what all the consequences of a given act will be when it is considered in isolation. It is not impossible for him to know, however, what the probable consequences will be of *following a generally accepted rule.* For these probable consequences are known as a result of the whole of human experience. It is the results of previous human experience that have framed our traditional moral rules. When the individual is asked merely to follow some accepted rule, the moral burdens put upon him are not impossible. The pangs of conscience that may come to him if his action does not turn out to have the most beneficent consequences are not unbearable. For not the least of the advantages of our all acting according to commonly accepted moral rules is that our actions are *predictable* by others and the actions of others are predictable by us, with the result that we are all better able to cooperate with each other in helping each other to pursue our individual ends.

THE NEED FOR GENERAL RULES 61

When we judge an act by a mere *ad hoc* utilitism, it is as if we asked: What would be the consequences of this act *if* it could be considered as an isolated act, as a *just-this-once* act, without consequences as a *precedent* or as an *example to others?* But this means that we are deliberately disregarding what may be its most important consequences.

In pursuing the further implications of the principle of acting according to general rules, we must consider the whole relationship of ethics and law.

CHAPTER 9

Ethics and Law

1. Natural Law

In primitive societies religion, morals, law, customs, manners, exist as an undifferentiated whole.[1] The boundaries between them are hazy and ill-defined. Their respective provinces are distinguished only gradually. For generations it is not only ethics that retains a theological base, but jurisprudence, which was a part of theology for two centuries prior to the Reformation.

The outstanding illustration of the fusing and separation of the provinces of ethics, law, and theology is the growth of the doctrine of Natural Law. The Greeks put a theoretical moral foundation under law by the doctrine of natural right. The Roman jurists made natural right into natural law and sought to discover the content of this natural law and to declare it. The Middle Ages put a theological foundation under natural law. The seventeenth and eighteenth centuries took out this theological foundation and replaced it or partially replaced it by a rational foundation. At the end of the eighteenth century Kant tried to replace the rational foundation by a metaphysical foundation.[2]

But what was natural law, and how did the concept arise? In the hands of Roman lawyers, the Greek theories of what was right by nature and what was right by convention or enactment gave rise to a distinction between law by nature and law by custom or enactment. Rules based on reason were law by nature. The right or the just by nature became law by nature or natural law. In this way began the identification of the legal with the moral that has been characteristic of natural-law thinkers ever since.[3]

In the Middle Ages the concept of natural law was identified with the concept of divine law. Natural law proceeded immediately from reason but ultimately from God. According to

Thomas Aquinas, it was a reflection of the "reason of the divine wisdom governing the whole universe." Later thinkers saw no conflict between natural law and divine law. According to Grotius, for example, both were based on eternal reason and on the will of God who wills only reason. This is also the view of Blackstone. It is reflected in the views of American judges, as, for example, Mr. Justice Wilson, who tells us that God "is under the glorious necessity of not contradicting himself." [4]

The concept of natural law has played a major role both in legal confusion and in legal progress. The confusion comes from its unfortunate name. When natural law is identified with the "laws of nature" it comes to be assumed that human thought can have no part in forming or creating it. It is assumed to pre-exist. It is the function of our reason merely to discover it. In fact, many writers on natural law throw out reason altogether. It is not necessary. We know—or at least *they* know—just what natural law is from direct intuition.

This aroused the wrath of Bentham. He contended that the doctrine of natural law was merely one of the "contrivances for avoiding the obligation of appealing to any external standard, and for prevailing upon the reader to accept of the author's sentiment or opinion as a reason for itself. . . . A great multitude of people are continually talking of the Law of Nature; and then they go on giving you their sentiments about what is right and what is wrong: and these sentiments, you are to understand, are so many chapters and sections of the Law of Nature. . . . The fairest and openest of them all is that sort of man who speaks out, and says, I am of the number of the Elect: now God himself takes care to inform the Elect what is right: and that with so good effect, and let them strive ever so, they cannot help not only knowing it but practising it. If therefore a man wants to know what is right and what is wrong, he has nothing to do but to come to me." [5]

If, however, we think of natural law as merely a misnomer for Ideal Law, or Law-as-It-Ought-to-Be, and if, in addition, we have the humility or scientific caution to assume that we do not intuitively or automatically know what this is, but that it is something to be discovered and formulated by experience and reason, and that we can constantly improve our concepts without ever reaching finality or perfection, then we have a powerful tool for the continuous reform of positive law. This, in fact, was the implicit assumption and method of Bentham himself.

2. *The Common Law*

Positive law and "positive" morality are both products of a long historical growth. They grew together, as part of an undifferentiated tradition and custom that included religion. But law tended to become secular and independent of theology sooner than did ethics. It also became more definite and explicit. Anglo-American common law, in particular, grew through customs of judicial decision. Individual judges realized, implicitly if not explicitly, that law and the application of law must be certain, uniform, predictable. They tried to solve individual cases upon their "merits"; but they recognized that their decision in one case must be "consistent" with their decision in another, and that the decisions of one court must be consistent with those of others, so that they would not easily be overthrown on appeal.

They therefore sought for general rules under which particular cases might be brought and decided. To find these general rules they looked for analogies both in their own previous decisions and in the previous decisions of other courts. Contending lawyers usually did not deny the existence or validity of these general rules. They did not deny that cases should be decided in accordance with established precedents. But they tried to find and to cite the analogies and precedents that favored their particular side. The attorney for one litigant would argue that his client's case was analogous to previous case Y, not X, and that it therefore came under Rule B, not Rule A, while the attorney for the opposing litigant would argue the opposite.

Thus there grew up, through precedent and analogical reasoning, the great body of the Common Law. There was in it, of course, in the beginning, much reverence for mere precedent as such, whether the precedent was rational or irrational. But there was clearly a great deal of utilic rationality in respecting precedent as such: this tended to make the application of law certain, uniform, and predictable. Moreover, there was also, even in early periods, and increasingly later, an element of utilic rationality in particular decisions. For even in trying to decide a case "upon its individual merits," a judge would probably give at least one eye to a consideration not only of the probable practical effects of that particular decision but to the probable practical effects of like decisions in other cases. Thus the Common Law was built up both through induction and deduction: in deciding particular cases judges arrived at general rules, i.e., at rules that would apply to like cases; and when a new concrete case came before them, they would look for the relevant pre-existing general rule under which it would be appropriate and just to decide it.

Thus judges both made law and applied it. But common law had the defect of a wide margin of uncertainty. Where precedents were conflicting and analogies were debatable, litigants could not know in advance by which precedent or analogy a particular judge would be guided. Where the general rule or principle had received vague or inconsistent statement, no one could know in advance which form of the rule a given judge would accept as valid or determining. How could men protect themselves from capricious or arbitrary decisions? How could they know in advance whether the actions they were taking were legal or whether the contracts and agreements they were making would be called valid? The demand arose for a more explicit written law.

But the law as a whole, common and statute law together, was a steadily growing and constantly more consistent body of general rules, and even of general-rules-for-finding-the-general-rule under which a particular case came. And the attempt to make these general rules more precise and consistent, and to find a utilitarian basis for them or reconstruct them on such a basis, led to the development of the philosophy of law and the science of jurisprudence.

Writers on jurisprudence were divided roughly into two schools, the analytical and the philosophical. "Analytical jurisprudence broke with philosophy and with ethics completely. . . . The ideal pattern of the analytical jurist was one of a logically consistent and logically interdependent system of legal precepts. . . . Assuming an exact logically defined separation of powers, the analytical jurist contended that law and morals were distinct and unrelated and that he was concerned only with law." [6] On the other hand, "Throughout the nineteenth century philosophical jurists devoted much of their attention to the relation of law to morals, the relation of jurisprudence to ethics." [7]

Yet there is an irony here. While most writers on jurisprudence have been constantly concerned with the relations of law to ethics, while they have sought to make legal rules consistent with ethical requirements, and to find what jurisprudence has to learn from ethics, moralists have not at all troubled to find what they could learn from jurisprudence. For the jurists have made the tacit assumption that while the law is something that was created and developed by man, and is to be perfected by him, ethics is something already created by God and known to man by intuition. The great majority of ethical writers have made a similar assumption. Even the evolutionary and utilitarian moralists have not troubled to see what they could learn from a study of law and jurisprudence.

And this was true, strangest of all, even of Jeremy Bentham, who made tremendous contributions both to jurisprudence and to ethics, and whose most famous book is called, significantly, *Introduction to the Principles of Morals and Legislation.* Yet he too was concerned principally with what legislation had to learn from morals, or rather with what both had to learn from the Principle of Utility or the Greatest Happiness Principle, and not with the great lesson that ethical philosophy had to learn from jurisprudence and law—the importance and necessity of general rules.

Nevertheless, Bentham has left us an illuminating simile: "Legislation is a circle with the same center as moral philosophy, but its circumference is smaller." [8] And Jellinek in 1878 subsumed law under morals in the same way by declaring that law was a minimum ethics. It was only a part of morals—the part that had to do with the indispensable conditions of the social order. The remainder of morals, desirable but not indispensable, he called "an ethical luxury." [9]

3. *The Relativism of Anatole France*

The great lesson that moral philosophy has to learn from legal philosophy is the necessity for adhering to general rules. It also has to learn the nature of these rules. They must be general, certain, uniform, regular, predictable, and equal in their application. "Rules of property, rules as to commercial transactions, the rules that maintain the security of acquisitions and the security of transactions in a society of complex economic organization—such rules may be and ought to be of general and absolute application." [10] "The very conception of law involves ideas of uniformity, regularity, predictability." [11]

The essential requirements of law have seldom been better described than by F. A. Hayek in *The Constitution of Liberty*. It must be free from arbitrariness, privilege, or discrimination. It must apply to all, and not merely to particular persons or groups. It must be certain. It must consist in the enforcement of known rules. These rules must be general and abstract rather than specific and concrete. They must be so clear that court decisions are predictable. In brief, the law must be certain, general, and equal.[12] "The true contrast to a reign of status is the reign of general and equal laws, of the rules which are the same for all." [13] "As they operate through the expectations that they create, it is essential that they be always applied, irrespective of whether or not the consequences in a particular instance seem desirable." [14] True laws must be "known and certain. . . . The essential point is that the decisions of the courts can be predicted." [15]

When these requirements are met, the requirements of liberty are met. As John Locke put it: "The end of the law is, not to abolish or restrain, but to preserve and enlarge freedom. . . . For liberty is to be free from restraint and violence from others, which cannot be where there is no law." [16]

"Freedom of men under government is to have a standing rule to live by, common to every one of that society, and made by the legislative power erected in it; a liberty to follow my own will in all things, where that rule prescribes not: and not to be subject to the inconstant, uncertain, arbitrary will of another man." [17]

When Justice is represented on court house statues as being blind, it does not mean that she is blind to the justice of the case, but blind to the wealth, social position, sex, color, looks, amiability or other qualities of the particular litigants. It means that she recognizes that justice, happiness, peace, and order can only be established, in the long run, by respect for general rules, rather than respect for the "merits" of each particular case. This is what Hume means when he insists that justice will often require that a poor good man be forced to pay money to a rich bad man—if, for example, it concerns the payment of a just debt. And this is what the advocates of an *ad hoc* "justice," a "justice" that regards only the specific "merits" of the particular case before the court, without considering what the extension of the rule of that decision would imply, have never understood. Almost the whole weight of the novelists and intellectuals of the last two centuries, in their treatment of both legal and moral questions, has been thrown in this *ad hoc* direction. Their attitude is summed up in the famous ironical jibe by Anatole France at "the majestic equality of the law that forbids the rich as well as the poor to sleep under bridges, to beg in the streets and to steal bread." [18]

But neither Anatole France nor any of those who take this *ad hoc* view have ever bothered to say what rules or guides, apart from their own immediate feelings, they would apply in place of equality before the law. Would they decide in each case of theft how much the thief "needed" the particular thing he stole, or how little its rightful owner "needed" it? Would they make it illegal only for a rich man to steal from a poor man? Legal for anybody to steal from anybody richer than himself? Would Anatole France himself, in his pose of magnanimity, have considered it all right for anyone to pirate or plagiarize from him, provided only that the plagiarist could show that he was not yet as prosperous or well-known as Anatole France?

The forthright declaration of a Thomas Huxley that it is not only illegal but immoral for a man to steal a loaf of bread even if he is starving, seems like a cruel and shocking Victorian pronouncement to all our "modern" ethical relativists, to all the *ad hoc* theoreticians who pride themselves on their peculiar "compassion." But they have never suggested what rules should be put in place of the general rules they deplore, or how the exceptions should be determined. The only general rule they do in fact seem to have in mind is one they seldom dare to utter —that each man should be a law unto himself, that each man should decide for himself, for example, whether his "need" is great enough or the "need" of his intended victim small enough to justify a particular contemplated theft.

4. *Inner and Outer Circle*

Before concluding this discussion of the relation of law to ethics, let us turn back to the simile from Bentham that law is a circle with the same center as moral philosophy but with a smaller circumference, and to the similar conclusion of Jellinek that law is a "minimum ethics." Let us try to see just where the radius of the smaller legal circle ends, and why it ends there.

We may do this by a few concrete illustrations. The first is of the schoolmaster who said: "Boys, be pure in heart or I'll flog you." [19] The point is that the law can only operate through sanctions—through punishment, redress, or forcible prevention—and therefore can only insure the outward morality of words and acts.

The second illustration is that of an athletic young man with a rope and a life-belt at hand, who sits on a bench in a park along a river bank, and quietly sees a child drown, although he could act without the least danger.[20] The law has refused to impose liability. As Ames has put it: "He took away nothing from a person in jeopardy, he simply failed to confer a benefit upon a stranger. . . . The law does not compel active benevolence between man and man. It is left to one's conscience whether he will be the good Samaritan or not." [21]

This legal reasoning is supported, also, by certain practical difficulties of proof. Suppose there is more than one man watching on the bank, and each contends that the other is in a much better position to effect the rescue? Or suppose we take the broader question raised by Dean Pound: "If John Doe is helpless and starving, shall he sue Henry Ford or John D. Rockefeller?" [22] This raises the question of the difficulty of saying upon whom the duty of being the good Samaritan should devolve.

But if we pass over these practical difficulties, and come back to our original illustration of the man who sits alone on a bank and coolly lets a child drown, knowing there is no other person from whom help can come but himself, there can be no question of what the common-sense moral judgment upon his act would be. The case is sufficient to illustrate the far wider sphere of ethics as compared with law.[23] Morality certainly calls for active benevolence beyond that called for by the law. But how far this duty extends must be the subject of a later chapter.

CHAPTER 10

Traffic Rules and Moral Rules

We may illustrate and reinforce the comparison in the last chapter between ethics and law by taking what may seem at first glance a trivial example—the necessity of framing, enforcing, and adhering to traffic rules.

A closer look will show, I think, that the illustration is not trivial. In present-day America, and even in Europe, it represents the citizen's most frequent contact with the law. It calls for the strictest daily, hourly, and even moment-to-moment observance of prescribed rules, impartially enforced on all.

It is instructive to notice that Hume, insisting even in the middle of the eighteenth century on "the necessity of rules wherever men have any intercourse with each other," went on to point out: "They cannot even pass each other on the road without rules. Wagoners, coachmen, and postilions have principles by which they give the way; and these are chiefly founded on mutual ease and convenience."[1]

Now the first thing to be observed about traffic rules is that they illustrate with special force John Locke's principle that "The end of the law is, not to abolish or restrain, but to preserve and enlarge freedom."[2] They do not exist in order to reduce or to slow up traffic, but to accelerate and maximize it to the greatest extent consistent with mutual safety. Red lights are not put up so that people will be compelled to stop in front of them. The lights and rules do not exist for their own sakes. They exist to provide the freest and smoothest flow of traffic, and to reduce conflicts, accidents, and disputes to a minimum.

True, the traffic rules rest in part on decisions that are arbitrary (though these "arbitrary" decisions usually grow out of immemorial custom). It may be originally a matter of indifference whether we decide that cars should pass each other on the right, as in the United States and most other countries, or on the left, as in England. But *once the rule is fixed,* once it is certain and known, it is of the utmost importance that everyone conform to it. In traffic-rule enforcement, as in much wider areas of law and morals, we cannot allow the right of private judgment. We cannot allow every individual to decide for himself, for example, whether it is better to drive on the right or on the left side of the road. Here is an example of a rule that must be obeyed *simply because it has already been established,* simply because it *is* the accepted rule.

And this principle has the widest bearings. We do and should obey rules, in law, manners and morals, simply because they *are* the established rules. This is their utility. We cooperate better in helping to achieve each other's ends by acting on rules *on which others can count.* We cooperate by being able to *rely* on each other, by being able to *anticipate with confidence* what the other fellow is going to do. And we can have this essential mutual confidence and reliance only if both of us act in accordance with the established rule and each knows that the other is going to act in accordance with the established rule. When two drivers are coming straight towards each other, each driving at a mile a minute near the middle of a narrow country road, each must know that the other, soon enough before the moment of passage, is going to bear toward and pass on the right (or in England on the left) as the established rule prescribes.

In short, in ethics as in law, the traditional and accepted rule is to be followed *unless there are clear and strong reasons against it.* The burden of proof is never on the established rule, but on breaking or changing the rule. And even if the rule is defective it may be unwise for the individual to ignore it or defy it unless he can hope to get it *generally* changed.

Each moral rule must be judged, of course, in accordance with its utility. But some moral rules have this utility simply because they are already accepted. In any case, this established acceptance *adds* to the utility of rules that have utility on other grounds.

It is the task of the moral philosopher, and even of the rule-utilitist, not so much to *frame* the appropriate moral rule governing a particular situation as to *find* the appropriate moral rule. In this he is similar to a judge finding and interpreting the relevant law. The fallacy of too many moral philosophers, ancient and modern, has been the assumption that we can begin *ab initio,* tear up all the existing ethical rules by the roots, or ignore them and start fresh. This would be obviously silly and impossible when dealing, for example, with language. It is no less silly, and far more dangerous, to try to do the same with established moral codes which, like languages, are the product of immemorial social evolution. The improvement or perfection of moral codes, like the improvement or perfection of languages, is to be achieved by piecemeal reforms.

It has been observed again and again how the morality of savage tribes decays and disintegrates when they are confronted by the utterly alien moral code of their "civilized" conquerors. They lose respect for their old moral code before they acquire respect for the new one. They acquire only the vices of civilization. The moral philosophers who have preached root-and-branch substitution, in accordance with some "new" ill-digested and oversimplified principle, have had the effect of undermining existing morality, of creating skepticism and indifference, and of making the rules by which the individual acts "a matter of personal taste."

The traffic-rule illustration throws light also on the philosophy of utilitarianism. Naive hedonism or crude utilitarianism would tell you to do whatever gave you most pleasure at the moment. If you could get to your destination fastest in a particular case by passing red lights without accident and without getting caught, that is what you should do. But a truly enlightened utilitism would insist that it is only by everyone's adhering strictly to general traffic rules that the smoothest and fullest traffic flow, the fewest disputes and accidents, and the maximum satisfaction of drivers, can be achieved in the long run.

We have a still further lesson to learn from the analogy of traffic rules. In general, as with moral rules, we must adhere inflexibly to them. True, expediency and even long-run utility require that there must sometimes be exceptions. *But even the exceptions must ge governed by rules.* For example, fire-engines, police cars, and ambulances are allowed to go through traffic lights. *But only under certain specified conditions.* The fire-engine must be going to a fire, not coming from it. The police car must be in hot pursuit of criminals or responding to an emergency call for help. The ambulance must also be responding to an emergency call. And even the exceptions we allow, it must be recognized, are not without their dangers—to pedestrians, to cross-street traffic, to the fire-engine, police-car, or ambulance occupants themselves.

None of these exceptions, moreover, means that anybody is free to pass a red light because he is a public official, or a Very Important Person, or considers stopping inconvenient. In the same way, and for the same reason, no one is free to flout the moral law because he considers himself a superman. If a driver were asked, "Why did you pass that red light?" and he replied, "Because I am a genius," the humor and effrontery would not be more than that of the Nietzsches and Oscar Wildes and whole droves of self-styled "Non-Conformists" with their claims to be beyond morality. If rules are not universally and inflexibly obeyed, they lose their utility. To quote Locke once more, "Liberty is to be free from restraint and violence from others, which cannot be where there is no law." [3]

Still one more lesson is to be learned from the analogy of traffic rules—or perhaps it is merely the restatement of previous lessons in another form. One of the purposes of traffic rules, like one of the purposes of all law and all morals, is to learn *how to keep out of each other's way*. In traffic each of us may have a different destination, as in life each may have a different goal. That is one reason why we must all adhere to a set of general rules which not only avert head-on collisions, but enable each other to get to our destinations sooner. Traffic rules, like legal and moral rules in general, are not adopted for their own sakes. They are not adopted primarily to restrain but to liberate. They are adopted to *minimize* frustration and suppression in the long run, and to maximize the satisfactions of all and therefore of each.

The traffic rules are, in sum, a legal system and a moral system in microcosm. Their specific purpose is to maximize traffic and to maximize safety, to enable each to reach his destination with the least interference from others. Whenever paths cross or conflict, *somebody* must yield the right of way to somebody else. I must sometimes give way to you, and you must sometimes give way to me. These times must be unambiguously and unmistakably determined by some general rule or set of general rules. (In traffic rules, traffic from the side streets must give precedence to traffic on the main avenues, or the car on the left must yield to the car on the right.) But who has the right of way is determined not by who you are, or who the other fellow is, but by the *objective situation,* or by a situation that can be objectively defined.

And so the traffic laws embody and illustrate one of the broadest principles of law and morals. As one writer on law puts it: "The problem consists in allowing such an exercise of each personal will as is compatible with the exercise of other wills. . . . [A law] is a limitation of one's freedom of action for the sake of avoiding collision with others. . . . In social life, as we know, men have not only to avoid collisions, but to arrange co-operation in all sorts of ways, and the one common feature of all these forms of co-operation is the limitation of individual wills in order to achieve a common purpose." [4]

And as Dean Pound, summarizing the view of Kant, writes: "The problem of the law is to keep conscious free-willing beings from interference with each other. It is so to order them that each shall exercise his freedom in a way consistent with the freedom of all others, since all others are to be regarded equally as ends in themselves." [5]

CHAPTER 11

Morals and Manners

Let us recall once more (as at the beginning of Chapter 9) that in primitive societies religion, morals, law, customs, manners exist as an undifferentiated whole. We cannot say with confidence which came first. They came together. It is only in comparatively modern times that they have become clearly differentiated from each other; and as they have done so, they have developed different traditions.

Nowhere is this difference in tradition more striking than in that between religious ethics and manners. Too often moral codes, especially those still largely attached to religious roots, are ascetic and grim. Codes of manners, on the other hand, usually require us to be at least outwardly cheerful, agreeable, gracious, convivial—in short, a contagious source of cheer to others. So far, in some respects, has the gap between the two traditions widened, that a frequent theme of plays and novels in the eighteenth and nineteenth centuries and even today is the *contrast* between the rough diamond, the crude proletarian or peasant with inflexible honesty and a heart of gold, and the suave, polished lady or gentleman with perfect manners but completely amoral and with a heart of ice.

The overemphasis on this contrast has been unfortunate. It has prevented most writers on ethics from recognizing that both manners and morals rest on the same underlying principle. That principle is *sympathy, kindness, consideration for others*.

It is true that a part of any code of manners is merely conventional and arbitrary, like knowing which fork to use for the salad, but the heart of every code of manners lies much deeper. Manners developed, not to make life more complicated and awkward (though elaborately ceremonial manners do), but to make it in the long-run smoother and simpler—a dance, and not a series of bumps and jolts. The extent to which it does this is the test of any code of manners.

Manners are minor morals. Manners are to morals as the final sandpapering, rubbing, and polishing on a fine piece of furniture are to the selection of the wood, the sawing, chiseling, and fitting. They are the finishing touch.

Emerson is one of the few modern writers who have explicitly recognized the ethical basis of manners. "Good manners," he wrote, "are made up of petty sacrifices."

Let us pursue this aspect of manners a little further. Manners, as we have seen, consist in consideration for others. They consist in deferring to others. One tries to deal with others with unfailing courtesy. One tries constantly to spare the feelings of others. It is bad manners to monopolize the conversation, to talk too much about oneself, to boast, because all this irritates others. It is good manners to be modest, or at least to appear so, because this pleases others. It is good manners for the strong to yield to the weak, the well to the sick, the young to the old.

Codes of manners, in fact, have set up an elaborate, unwritten, but well understood order of precedence, which serves in the realm of politeness like the traffic rules we considered in the preceding chapter. This order of precedence is, in fact, a set of "traffic rules" symbolized in the decision concerning who goes first through a doorway. The gentleman yields to the lady; the younger yields to the older; the able-bodied yield to the ill or the crippled; the host yields to the guest. Sometimes these categories are mixed, or other considerations prevail, and then the rule becomes unclear. But the unwritten code of rules laid down by good manners in the long run saves time rather than consumes it, and tends to take the minor jolts and irritations out of life.

The truth of this is most likely to be recognized whenever manners deteriorate. "My generation of radicals and breakers-down," wrote Scott Fitzgerald to his daughter, "never found anything to take the place of the old virtues of work and courage and the old graces of courtesy and politeness."

Ceremony can be overelaborate and therefore time-consuming, tiring, and boring, but without any ceremony life would be barren, graceless, and brutish. Nowhere is this truth more clearly recognized than in the moral code of Confucius: "Ceremonies and music should not for a moment be neglected by any one. . . . The instructive and transforming power of ceremonies is subtle. They check depravity before it has taken form, causing men daily to move toward what is good and to keep themselves from wrong-doing, without being conscious of it. . . . Ceremonies and music in their nature resemble Heaven and earth, penetrate the virtues of the spiritual intelligences, bring down spirits from above and lift the souls that are abased." [1]

To recognize the truth of this, we have only to imagine how bare and empty life would seem to many without marriage ceremonies, funeral ceremonies, christenings, and Sunday church services. This is the great appeal of religion to many who give a very tepid credence to the dogmas on which their religion is ostensibly founded.

In the ethics of Confucius manners play a major role, as they should. I do not know of any modern philosopher who has deliberately sought to base his ethical system on a widening and idealization of the traditional code of manners, but the effort would probably prove instructive, and prima facie less foolish than one rooted in some idealization of asceticism and self-abasement.

I have said that manners are minor ethics. But in another sense they are major ethics, because they are, in fact, the ethics of everyday life. Every day and almost every hour of our lives, those of us who are not hermits or anchorites have an opportunity to practice the minor ethics of good manners, of kindness toward and consideration for others in little things, of petty sacrifices. It is only on great and rare occasions of life that most of us have either the need or the opportunity to practice what I may call Heroic Ethics. Yet most ethical writers seem to be almost exclusively concerned with heroic ethics, with Nobility, Magnanimity, All-Embracing Love, Saintliness, Self-Sacrifice. And they despise any effort to frame or to find the rules or even to seek the rationale behind the workaday ethics for the masses of humanity.

We need to be more concerned with *everyday* morality and relatively less with *crisis* morality. If ethical treatises were more concerned with everyday morality they would stress far more than they do the importance of good manners, of politeness, of consideration for others in little things (a habit which must carry over into larger things). They would praise the day-to-day social cooperation that consists in doing one's own job conscientiously, efficiently, and cheerfully.

Most writers on ethics, however, still *contrast* manners and morals rather than treat them as complementary. There is no more frequent character in modern fiction than the man or woman with suave and polished manners and all the outward show of politeness but completely cold, calculating, selfish and even sometimes fiendish at heart. Such characters exist, but they are the exception, not the rule. They are less frequently found than their opposites—the upright, honest, and even kind-hearted person who is often unintentionally blunt or even rude, and "rubs people the wrong way." The existence of both classes of persons is in part the result of the existence in separate compartments of the tradition of morals and the tradition of good breeding. Moralists have too often tended to treat etiquette as of no particular importance, or even as irrelevant to morals. The code of good breeding, especially the code of the "gentleman," was for a long period largely a class code. The "gentleman's" code applied mainly to his relations with other gentlemen, not with his "inferiors." He paid his "debts of honor," for example—his gambling debts— but not his debts to poor tradesmen. Notwithstanding the special and far from trivial duties sometimes imposed by *noblesse oblige,* the code of good breeding, as it existed in the eighteenth and nineteenth centuries, did not necessarily exclude a sometimes cruel snobbery.

But the defects in the conventional code of morals and in the conventional code of manners are corrected when the two traditions are fused—when the code of manners is treated as, in effect, an extension of the code of morals.

It is sometimes supposed that the two codes dictate different actions. The traditional code of ethics is thought to teach that one should always tell the exact and literal truth. The tradition of good breeding, on the other hand, puts its emphasis on sparing the feelings of others, and even on pleasing them at the cost of the exact truth.

A typical example concerns the tradition of what you say to your host and hostess on leaving a dinner party. You congratulate them, say, on a wonderful dinner, and add that you do not know when you have had a more enjoyable evening. The exact and literal truth may be that the dinner was mediocre, or worse, and that the evening was only moderately enjoyable or a downright bore. Nevertheless, provided your exaggerations and protestations of pleasure are not so awkward or extreme that they sound insincere or ironic, the course you have taken is in accord with the dictates of morality no less than with those of etiquette. Nothing is gained by hurting other people's feelings, not to speak of arousing ill-will against yourself, to no purpose. Technically, you may have told an untruth. But as your parting remarks are the accepted, conventional and expected thing, they are not a lie. Your host and hostess, moreover, have not really been deceived; they know that your praise and thanks are in accordance with a conventional and practically universal code, and they have no doubt taken your words at the appropriate discount.

The same considerations apply to all the polite forms of correspondence—the dear-sir's, the yours-truly's, and yours-sincerely's, and even, until not so long ago, the your-humble-servant's. It is centuries since these forms were taken seriously and literally. But their omission would be a deliberate and unnecessary rudeness, frowned upon alike by the codes both of manners and morals.

A rational morality also recognizes that there are exceptions to the principle that one should always tell the full literal and exact truth. Should a plain girl be told that, because of her plainness, she is unlikely to find a husband? Should a pregnant mother be told at once that her eldest child has been killed in an accident? Should a man who may not know it be told that he is hopelessly dying of cancer? There are occasions when it may be necessary to utter such truths; there are occasions when they may and should be withheld or concealed. The rule of truth-telling, on utilitist grounds alone, is rightly considered one of the most rigid and inflexible of all the rules of morality. The exceptions to it should be rare and very narrowly defined. But nearly every moralist but Kant has admitted that there are such exceptions. What these are, and how the rules should be drawn that govern the exceptions, does not need to be considered in detail here. We need merely take note that the rules of morality, and the rules of good manners, can and should be harmonized with each other.

No one in modern times has more clearly recognized the importance of manners than Edmund Burke:

"Manners are of more importance than laws. Upon them, in great measure, the laws depend. The law touches us but here and there, and now and then. Manners are what vex or soothe, corrupt or purify, exalt or debase, barbarize or refine us, by a constant, steady, uniform, insensible operation, like that of the air we breathe in. They give their whole form and color to our lives. According to their quality, they aid morals, they supply them, or they totally destroy them." [2]

CHAPTER 12

Prudence and Benevolence

1. *Bentham's* Deontology

Nowhere is a more logical, better-organized, or more stimulating discussion of private ethics to be found than in the two volumes of Jeremy Bentham's *Deontology: or The Science of Morality*. Yet these two volumes have had an unfortunate history. They were published posthumously, in 1834. They do not profess to be wholly by Bentham, even on their title page. That title page is for several reasons worth quoting in full: "*Deontology: or The Science of Morality*: in which the harmony and co-incidence of Duty and Self-Interest, Virtue and Felicity, Prudence and Benevolence, are explained and exemplified. From the MSS. of Jeremy Bentham. Arranged and Edited by John Bowring."

The whole of Bentham's work, partly because of its sheer range and mass, partly because of its stylistic eccentricities, partly because of his own carelessness and indifference regarding publication, and his refusal to do his own revision and editing of most of his manuscripts, has lain in comparative neglect until recently. Though his influence has been enormous, it has been mainly indirect, through Dumont, John Austin, James Mill, and above all John Stuart Mill. Yet the neglect of the *Deontology* has exceeded even the general neglect of Bentham's work. It has been considered of doubtful authenticity. It has been suspected that much was filled in between Bentham's notes by his editor Bowring. Whatever the truth may be, the greater part of the book seems to me to show the hand of the master.

The purpose of this chapter is primarily, taking off from the presentation in Bentham's *Deontology*, to discuss the "harmony and coincidence" of Prudence and Benevolence. But because the *Deontology* has been out of print since its original edition, and because the volumes in the original are very difficult to come by, I shall give a somewhat wider summary of their contents than would otherwise be warranted merely by a discussion of the relations between Prudence and Benevolence.

The *Deontology* opens with a general statement of the utilitarian theme, seeking to emphasize "the alliance between interest and duty." "To a great extent . . . the dictates of prudence prescribe the laws of effective benevolence. . . . A man who injures himself more than he benefits others by no means serves the cause of virtue, for he diminishes the amount of happiness" (I, 177). "Prudence is man's primary virtue. Nothing is gained to happiness if prudence loses more than benevolence wins" (I, 189-90).

Bentham contends that "prudence and effective benevolence . . . being the only two intrinsically useful virtues, all other virtues must derive their value from them, and be subservient to them" (I, 201). He seeks to apply this standard systematically to the virtues mentioned by Hume—to sociability, good nature, humanity, mercy, gratitude, friendliness, generosity, beneficence, justice, discretion, industry, frugality, honesty, fidelity, truth (veracity and sincerity), caution, enterprise, assiduity, economy, sobriety, patience, constancy, perseverance, forethought, considerateness, cheerfulness, dignity, courage, tranquillity, politeness, wit, decency, cleanliness, chastity, and allegiance.

Bentham rightly points out that Hume's list of virtues is unsystematic, disorderly, and disjointed; that many of them overlap and others are merely different names for the same thing. Nor does he find that all of them deserve the name of virtue. "Courage," he declares courageously, "may be a virtue or may be a vice. . . . For a man to value himself on his courage, without any reference to the occasions on which it is exercised, is to value himself on a quality possessed in a far higher degree by a dog, especially if the dog is mad" (I, 251).

Bentham even writes a chapter on what he calls "False Virtues," among which he lists Contempt for Riches (sarcastic paragraphs directed against Socrates and Epictetus), Love of Action, Attention, Enterprise, and Dispatch. At all points he warns:

> The affections may be so engaged with one side of a question, as to interfere with a right judgment of its moral merit. A mother steals a loaf to satisfy the hunger of a starving child. How easy it would be to excite the sympathies in favor of her maternal

tenderness, so as to bury all consideration of her dishonesty in the depth of those sympathies. And, in truth, nothing but an enlarged and expansive estimate, such as would take the case out of the regions of sentimentality into the wider regions of public good, could ever lead to the formation of a right judgment in such matters [I, 259-60].

In the second volume (which is surprisingly self-contained and complete in itself) Bentham[1] opens again with an Introduction and "General Statement" of general principles. Here we find him shifting from the emphasis on "pleasures" and "pains" in his *Introduction to the Principles of Morals and Legislation* to an almost exclusive reference to the effect of conduct on "happiness" and "misery." While he still rejects "any distinctions drawn between pleasures and happiness," while he still insists that "happiness is the aggregate of which pleasures are the component parts" (II, 16), the shift is none the less significant. Bentham seems eager to prevent the accusation or misunderstanding that he is concerned purely with physical or sensual pleasures and pains.

But he retains the essentials of his "hedonistic calculus." The inquiries of the moralist, he contends, may in the abstract

> . . . be reduced to a single inquiry. At what cost of future pain or sacrifice of future pleasure is a present pleasure purchased? What repayment of future pleasure may be anticipated for a present pain? Out of this examination morality must be developed. Temptation is the present pleasure—punishment is the future pain; sacrifice is the present pain—enjoyment is the future recompense. The questions of virtue and vice are, for the most part, reduced to the weighing of that which *is*, against that which *will be*. The virtuous man has a store of happiness in coming time, the vicious man has prodigally spent his revenues of happiness. Today the vicious man seems to have a balance of pleasure in his favor; tomorrow the balance will be adjusted, and the day after it will be ascertained to be wholly in favor of the virtuous man. Vice is a spendthrift, flinging away what is far better than wealth, or health, or youth, or beauty—namely, happiness: because all of these without happiness are of little value. Virtue is a prudent economist that gets back all her outlay with interest [II, 27-8].

"Morality," continues Bentham, "is the art of maximizing happiness: it gives the code of laws by which that conduct is suggested whose result will, the whole of human existence being taken into account, leave the greatest quantity of felicity" (II, 31).

2. How Prudence Leads . . .

Bentham proceeds to reduce the virtues to two, Prudence and Effective Benevolence, but he divides each of these, respectively, into Self-Regarding Prudence and Extra-Regarding Prudence, and into Negative Efficient Benevolence and Positive Efficient Benevolence, and devotes a long separate chapter to each of these four divisions.

On these four cornerstones Bentham builds his palace of morality. He is concerned to show that each one of these virtues leads naturally and almost inevitably into the next. He begins with Self-Regarding Prudence, which refers to actions whose influences do not reach beyond the actor; he moves next to "that prudence which is demanded from him in consequence of his intercourse with others; a prudence which is closely connected with benevolence, and especially with abstential benevolence" (II, 81).

As regards external actions, "what prudence can do, and all that prudence can do, is to choose between the present and the future; and in so far as the aggregate of happiness is increased, thereby to give preference to the greater future over the lesser present pleasure" (II, 82). But, he warns, the sacrifice of an immediate pleasure that does not promise to increase our own or somebody else's future happiness to an amount greater than that immediately sacrificed "is mere asceticism; it is the very opposite of prudence; it is the offspring of delusion"; it is "folly"; it is not virtue, it is vice (II, 34).

Bentham then shows the application of the dictates of self-regarding prudence to sexual morality: "The option is often between the enjoyment of a moment and the pain of years; between the excited satisfaction of a very short period and the sacrifice of a whole existence; between the stimulation of life for an hour, and the consequent adjacency of disease and death" (II, 85).

After rejecting asceticism as applied to sexual morality, Bentham asks: "Is not chastity, then, a virtue? Most undoubtedly, and a virtue of high deserving. And why? Not because it diminishes, but because it heightens enjoyment. . . . In fact, temperance, modesty, chastity, are among the most efficient sources of delight" (II, 87-88). He proceeds to apply the same standards in discussing why intoxication, irascibility, gambling, and extravagance tend to produce in the long run more misery than happiness to the person who indulges in them.

We come next to Bentham's chapter on "Extra-Regarding Prudence."

> Of man's pleasures, a great proportion is dependent on the will of others, and can only be possessed by him with their concurrence and co-operation. There is no possibility of disregarding the happiness of others without, at the same time, risking happiness of our own. There is no possibility of avoiding those inflictions of pain with which it is in the power of others to visit us, except by conciliating their good will. Each individual is linked to his race by a tie, of all ties the strongest, the tie of self-regard [II, 132-3].
>
> Morality can be nothing but the sacrifice of a lesser for the acquisition of a greater good. The virtue of extra-regarding prudence is only limited by our intercourse with our fellow men; it may even extend far beyond the bounds of our personal communion with others, by secondary, or reflected influences. . . . Both national and international law may be said to constitute a proper ground for the introduction of that prudence which concerns others [II, 135].

In our relations with others, prudence no less than benevolence suggests the two simple precepts: "Maximize good, minimize evil" (II, 164). Hence the rules of good manners; the rule of sparing our neighbor's feelings; the rule of avoiding the ill will and cultivating the good will of others towards us.

3. *To Benevolence*

Just as self-regarding prudence must lead us to be considerate and kind to others, because our own happiness depends on their good will towards us or at least the absence of their ill will, so this extra-regarding prudence leads on in turn to "Negative Efficient Benevolence." "A due regard to the felicity of others is the best and wisest provision for our own" (II, 190). The first requirement is to avoid doing evil to others. Never do evil to any other except in so far as that may be necessary to accomplish a greater good. Never do evil to any other solely on the ground that it is "deserved," but only if this is unavoidable to accomplish a greater good. Even in sport or as a joke, say nothing and do nothing that will cause uneasiness to another. The justifications for inflicting pain on others by your discourse are seldom tenable. "Remember, on all occasions, that kind costs a man no more than unkind language" (II, 217). Blame nobody except to prevent some future cause of blame. Never do or say anything to wound or humiliate another.

Bentham comes next to his chapter on "Positive Efficient Benevolence." (He draws a frequent distinction between *benevolence,* or the disposition and desire to do good for others, and *beneficence,* which is the actual doing of such good, and insists that any truly moral action must be *both* benevolent and beneficent.) He begins by pointing out the strong prudential reasons which a man has for the exercise of benevolence:

> Over and above any present pleasure with which an act of beneficence may be accompanied to the actor, the inducement which a man has for its exercise is one of the same sort as that which the husbandman has for the sowing of his seed; as that which the frugal man has for the laying up of money. . . . By every act of virtuous beneficence which a man exercises, he contributes to a sort of fund, a savings-bank, a depository of general good-will, out of which services of all sorts may be looked for, as about to flow from other hands into his; if not positive services, at any rate negative services; services consisting in the forbearance to vex him by annoyances with which he might otherwise have been vexed [II, 259-60].

Negative beneficence is exercised in so far as mischief is *not* done to others. . . . Negative beneficience is a virtue, in so far as any mischief which without consideration might have been produced, is by consideration forborne to be produced. In so far as it is by the consideration of the effect which the mischievous action might have upon a man's own comfort, the virtue is prudence—self-regarding prudence: in so far as it is by the consideration of the effect which the mischievous action might have upon the comfort of any other person, the virtue is benevolence.

A main distinction here is, between beneficence which cannot be exercised without self-sacrifice, and beneficence which can be exercised without self-sacrifice. To that which cannot be exercised without self-sacrifice there are necessarily limits, and these comparatively very narrow ones. . . .

To the exercise of beneficence, where it is exercised without self-sacrifice, there can be no limits; and by every exercise thus made of it, a contribution is made to the good-will fund, and made without expense. . . .

Described in general terms, the inducement to positive beneficence, in all its shapes, is the contribution it makes to the man's general good-will fund; to the general good-will fund from which draughts in his favor may come to be paid: the inducement to negative beneficence is the contribution it keeps back from his general ill-will fund. . . .

He who is in possession of a [good-will] fund of this sort, and understands the value of it, will understand himself to be the richer by every act of benevolent beneficence he is known to have exercised. He is the richer, and feels that he is so, by every act of kindness he has ever done. . . .

Independently of the rewards of opinion, and the pleasures of sympathy, the acts of positive benevolence tend to the creation of the habits of benevolence. Every act adds something to the habit; the greater the number of acts, the stronger will be the habit; and the stronger the habit, the larger the recompense; and the larger the recompense, the more fruitful in producing similar acts; and the more frequent such acts, the more will there be of virtue and felicity in the world.

Employ, then, every opportunity of beneficent action, and look out for other opportunities. Do all the good you can, and seek the means of doing good [II, 259-266].

In illustrating the requirements of beneficence, Bentham applies in the ethical field the same lesson he had applied in the legal field in his *Principles of Morals and Legislation*:

In the application of evil for the production of good, never let it be applied for the gratification of mere antipathy; never but as subservient to and necessary for the only proper ends of punishment, the determent of others by example, the determent of the offenders by suffering. In the interest of the offender, reformation is the great object to be aimed at; if this cannot be accomplished, seek to disable him from inflicting the like evil on himself or others. But always bear in mind the maxim, which cannot be repeated too often:—Inflict as much and no more pain than is necessary to accomplish the purpose of benevolence. Create not evil greater than the evil you exclude [II, 266-267].

4. *No Exact Dividing Line*

Bentham returns to a discussion of the relations between prudence and benevolence:

> It is not always possible to draw the exact line between the claims of efficient benevolence, whether positive or negative, and those of prudence, self-regarding or extra-regarding; nor is it always necessary or desirable, for where the interests of the two virtues are the same, the path of duty is quite clear. But points of agreement and of difference may be easily pointed out, and a general definition may show what, in ordinary cases, is the distinction between the two qualities. As for example: you are called upon to do service to another. If he is in a condition to render you services in return, prudence as well as benevolence combine to interest you in his favor. If he is wholly removed from the occasions of serving you, your motives can be those of benevolence alone.
>
> But though in a given case it may be difficult to show that the interests of prudence demand a particular act of beneficence, it is not the less true that the self-regarding consideration does, in fact, occupy the whole ground of conduct. Whatever peculiar reasons benevolence may furnish for a given course of beneficent action, the universal principle remains, that it is in every man's *interest* to stand well in the affections of other men, and in the affections of mankind in general. A really beneficent act, which may seem to be removed from the prudential considerations—always taking for granted that the act is itself no violation of prudence, and that it is one which has the sanction of the Deontological principle, by producing a balance of good—such an act will, in its remoter consequences, serve the self-regarding interests, by helping to create, to establish, or to extend that general reputation for judicious benevolence, which it is every man's obvious interest to possess in the opinions of his fellow men [II, 268-270].

But because Bentham so often insists that the roots of benevolence are to be ultimately found in self-regarding prudence, it is a mistake to assume that he ever disparages benevolence. On the contrary, his pages are full of such passages as this:

> To give exercise, influence, and extension to efficient benevolence, is one of the great consequences of virtue. Nor let it be thought that such benevolence is to be bounded in its conse-

quences by the race of man. . . . Let men remember that happiness, *wherever* it is, and by *whomever* experienced, is the great gift confided to their charge. . . .

It has been said that "Honesty is the *best* policy." This is not exactly true. There is a policy that is better—the policy of active benevolence. Honesty is but negative: it avoids doing wrong; it will not allow intrusion into the enjoyments of others. It is, however, only an abstential, and not an active quality. The *best* policy is that which creates good; the second best is that which avoids evil [II, 272].

We need to forward virtue not merely by our actions, but through the judicious use of our approval and disapproval:

To that end we must labor, each for himself, and as far as he is able, marking out for his highest approbation in the conduct of others those actions which have produced, or are likely to produce, the greatest sum of happiness, and visiting with his loudest reprobation that conduct which leads to, or creates, the greatest amount of misery. By this means every man will do something to make the popular sanctions more useful, healthful, active, and virtuous. The alliances of true morality with the great interests of mankind, mankind will soon discover [II, 274].

It often happens that, in the anxiety to get rid of [a political] evil, a greater evil is entailed on an individual or a class, than the evil got rid of by the community; that the sufferings experienced by the few are not counterbalanced by the benefits resulting to the many. . . . "Sweep abuses away" is undoubtedly the maxim of political wisdom; but so sweep them away that as little disappointment, vexation, or pain be created as possible [II, 285].

Despotism never takes a worse shape than when it comes in the guise of benevolence. . . . Pleasures and pains, the sweets and the bitters of existence, cannot be tried by the taste of another. What is good for another cannot be estimated by the person intending to do the good, but by the person only to whom it is intended to be done. The purpose of another may be to increase my happiness, but of that happiness I alone am the keeper and the judge. . . .

Refrain, then, from doing good to any man against his will, or even without his consent. . . .

To this pretension of doing good to others in spite of themselves, may be traced the worst of religious persecutions. . . .

The most horrible of offenses, the most devastating and murderous of crimes, if followed up to their origin, will be found only a distortion of the happiness-seeking principle; the creation of a misery, intending to prevent a greater misery, but mistaking its purpose and miscalculating its means. And of such mistakes and such miscalculations none has been more prolific than the despotism of benevolent *intention* [II, 289-291].

Prudence must not allow the individual to sacrifice more happiness than he gains. Benevolence demands that, to the common stock of happiness, every man should bring the largest possible contribution [II, 292].

Let no man apprehend for himself or others, that he can produce too much good, or remove too much evil. It is not on the side of expansive benevolence that his mistakes are likely to be made. Let him do all the good he can, and wherever he can, he will never do too much for his own happiness, or the happiness of others [II, 193].

It may be laid down as a general principle, that a man becomes rich in his own stock of pleasures, in proportion to the amount he distributes to others [II, 295].

In his concluding chapter, Bentham tells us that reason and morality themselves must be made subservient to the great end of promoting human happiness. "Virtue is made up of pleasures, vice of pains, and . . . morality is but the maximization of happiness" (II, 309).

5. *The Role of Sympathy*

I have been quoting from Bentham's (out-of-print) *Deontology* at this great length, not only because of the brilliant light it throws on the necessary relations of prudence and beneficence, but because it develops the Greatest Happiness Principle with more thoroughness and logic than any other work with which I am acquainted. By identifying morality not with a pointless "will to refrain" or self-sacrifice, but with the maximization of happiness, and by emphasizing the essential harmony between self-interest and the general interest, Bentham provides a far greater incentive to morality than the conventional moralist. His detractors, from Matthew Arnold to Karl Marx, have always been fond of dismissing him as crass and vulgar, but he is as superior to them in the breadth of his sympathies as he is in analysis and logic.

This is not to say that his discussion is definitive or lacking in faults. He too often assumes, for example, that an action can be taken on a direct calculation of the happiness or misery that would follow from that action considered in isolation. He failed to grasp the full weight of Hume's principle that we must inflexibly act according to *rule,* and that it is the goodness or badness of the *rules* of moral action, the tendency of the moral *code* to produce happiness or unhappiness, that is to be judged, rather than the assumed consequences of an isolated individual act.

There is also implicit in Bentham's discussion the assumption that benevolence can *only* grow out of enlightened and farseeing prudence. Most benevolence is, in fact, direct; it is the result of an immediate and spontaneous affection, love, kindness, or *sympathy,* a fellow-feeling with others (a theme that Hume and Adam Smith had developed), and not of any conscious calculation that its benefits will redound to the future advantage of the agent himself. The Biblical injunction, "Cast thy bread upon the waters: for thou shalt find it after many days," implies, as Bentham does, that charity and other acts of benevolence will ultimately redound to the benefit of the one who performs them; but it implies, in addition, that the repayment is not necessarily dependable or proportional.

Yet Bentham was right in recognizing the essential *long-run* harmony between self-interest and the general interest, between the actions prescribed by "prudence" and the actions prescribed by "benevolence," between farsighted "egoism" and farsighted "altruism." And the recognition of this essential long-run harmony will be found to be the basis for solving one of the central problems of ethics—the true relations of "egoism" and "altruism," and the relative roles that each should properly play.

CHAPTER 13

Egoism, Altruism, Mutualism

1. *The Views of Spencer and Bentham*

The two main issues on which moral philosophers have been most deeply divided, almost from time immemorial, have been that of Hedonism versus Non-Hedonism (some supposedly broader or "higher" goal), and that of Egoism versus Altruism. These two issues overlap, so much so that they are often confused with each other. A far greater overlap, almost to the point of identity, exists between the subject of the present chapter, the proper relations between Egoism and Altruism, and that of our preceding chapter, the relations between Prudence and Benevolence. In fact, Prudence and Egoism on the one hand, and Benevolence and Altruism on the other, may seem to many to be nearly synonymous terms. In any case, the subject calls for further exploration, and the traditional terms Egoism and Altruism will emphasize different aspects of it from those we have already considered.

The division between Egoism and Altruism has seldom been so wide or deep as is generally supposed. Let us distinguish, first of all, between *psychological* theory and *ethical* theory. There have been many moral philosophers (of which the archetype is Hobbes) who have contended that men are necessarily selfish, and never act except in accordance with their own (real or imagined) self-interest. These are the *psychological* Egoists. They contend that when men *appear* to be acting unselfishly or altruistically the appearance is deceptive or a hypocritical fraud; they are merely promoting their selfish interests. But there are very few *ethical* Egoists (the only one I can think of is the contemporary Ayn Rand, if I rightly understand her), who hold that while men can and do act altruistically and self-sacrificially, they *ought* only to act selfishly.

A similar division is possible (but practically non-existent) among Altruists. A psychological Altruist might hold that men necessarily and always act unselfishly and altruistically. I know of no one who does hold or ever has held this position. A pure ethical Altruist holds that men should always act altruistically and never out of self-interest. The ethical Altruist is necessarily a psychological Altruist, however, if only in the sense that he must believe it possible for a man to act solely in the interests of others and not of himself—otherwise it would be impossible for him to do what he ought to do. Most moral philosophers have been ethical Altruists—so much so that the popular conception of ethics is action in the interest of others and the popular conception of the chief dilemma of ethics is the supposed conflict between Self-Interest and Duty.

The basic cause of the immemorial controversy over Egoism and Altruism, in fact, has been the false assumption that the two attitudes are necessarily opposed to each other. Even conscientious efforts to effect a "reconciliation" between Egoism and Altruism have been at least partly vitiated by this assumption. A notable example is that of Herbert Spencer. In his *Data of Ethics* we have first a chapter (XI) on "Egoism versus Altruism," then a chapter (XII) on "Altruism versus Egoism," then a chapter (XIII) on "Trial and Compromise," and finally a chapter (XIV) called "Conciliation."

Spencer's conceptual error is most clearly revealed at the beginning of Chapter XIII on "Trial and Compromise": "In the foregoing two chapters the case on behalf of Egoism and the case on behalf of Altruism have been stated. The two conflict; and we have now to consider what verdict ought to be given. . . . Pure egoism and pure altruism are both illegitimate. If the maxim, 'Live for self,' is wrong, so also is the maxim, 'Live for others.' Hence, a compromise is the only possibility."

Spencer might have avoided this assumption of necessary conflict if he had examined more closely the implication of his own previous arguments. He begins his chapter on "Egoism versus Altruism," for example, by maintaining that "the acts by which each mantains his own life must, speaking generally, precede in imperativeness all other acts of which he is capable. . . . Egoism comes before altruism. The acts required for continued self-preservation . . . are the first requisites to universal welfare.

Unless each duly cares for himself, his care for all others is ended by death.... The adequately egoistic individual retains those powers which make altruistic activities possible."

But what is this but an argument that the same acts that are necessary to promote egoistic ends are necessary to promote altruistic ends?

Similarly, when he comes to the chapter on "Altruism versus Egoism" Spencer argues: "In various ways the well-being of each rises and falls with the well-being of all.... Each has a private interest in public morals, and profits by improving them.... Personal well-being depends in large measure on the well-being of society," etc. What is this, again, but an argument that the actions which promote the well-being of society also promote the well-being of the individual? As Spencer himself puts it: "From the dawn of life, then, egoism has been dependent upon altruism as altruism has been dependent upon egoism."

All that Spencer succeeds in proving by his specific arguments, in fact, is that a *misconceived* or *short-sighted* pursuit of self-interest is not really in one's self-interest, and that a *misconceived* or *short-sighted* benevolence or self-sacrifice for the imagined good of others is not really beneficent, and harms, rather than promotes, the long-run good of others or the ultimate well-being of society.

This is true also of the argument of Spencer in which he seeks to reduce "pure" altruism to an absurdity:

> When, therefore, we attempt to specialize the proposal to live not for self-satisfaction but for the satisfaction of others, we meet with the difficulty that beyond a certain limit this cannot be done....
>
> Mark the consequences if all are purely altruistic. First, an impossible combination of moral attributes is implied. Each is supposed by the hypothesis to regard self so little and others so much, that he willingly sacrifices his own pleasures to give pleasures to them. But if this is a universal trait, and if action is universally congruous with it, we have to conceive each as being not only a sacrificer but also one who accepts sacrifices. While he is so unselfish as willingly to yield up the benefit for which he has labored, he is so selfish as willingly to let others yield up to him the benefits they have labored for. To make pure altruism possible for all, each must be at once extremely unegoistic and extremely egoistic. As a giver, he must have no thought for self; as a receiver, no

thought for others. Evidently, this implies an inconceivable mental constitution. The sympathy which is so solicitous for others as willingly to injure self in benefiting them, cannot at the same time be so regardless of others as to accept benefits which they injure themselves in giving.[1]

Spencer's *reductio ad absurdum,* of which the foregoing quotation is only a part, is shrewd and entirely valid. His argument, in fact, was anticipated by Bentham:

> Take any two individuals, A and B, and suppose the whole care of the happiness of A confined to the breast of B, A himself not having any part in it; and the whole care of the happiness of B confined to the breast of A, B himself not having any part in it; and this to be the case throughout. It will soon appear that in this state of things the species could not continue in existence, and that a few months, not to say weeks or days, would suffice for the annihilation of it. Of all modes in which for the governance of one and the same individual the two faculties could be conceived as placed in different seats—sensation and consequent desire in one breast, judgment and consequent action in another—this is the most simple. If, as has been said with less truth of the blind leading the blind, both would in such a state of things be continually falling into the ditch, much more frequently and more speedily fatal would be the falls supposing the separation to have place upon any more complex plan. Suppose the care and the happiness of A being taken altogether from A were divided between B and C, the happiness of B and C being provided for in the same complex manner, and so on, the greater the complication the more speedy would the destruction be, and the more flagrant the absurdity of a supposition assuming the existence of such a state of things.[2]

2. *Egoism and Altruism Interdependent*

But though egoism, in the final analysis, must have priority over altruism, it remains true, as both Bentham and Spencer contended, that they are interdependent, and that, in general and in the long run, the actions that promote the one tend also to promote the other.

In brief, to say that whatever promotes the interests of the individual promotes those of society, and vice versa, is another way of saying that society consists of, and is simply another name for, the collection of individuals and their interrelations.

The argument, however, should not be overstated. The interests of a particular individual can never be said to be *identical* with those of society (even if we consider a "long-run" period as long as that individual's life). But over the long run (and the longer the period considered the more is this true) there is a *tendency toward coalescence* in the actions, and especially the *rules* of action, that promote self-interest and the public interest respectively. For in the long run it is in the greatest interest of the individual that he should live in a society characterized by law, peace, and good-will; a society in which he can rely on the word of others; in which others keep their promises to him; in which his right peaceably to enjoy the fruits of his labor, his rights to security and property, are respected; in which he is not shoved, cheated, beaten or robbed; in which he can depend on the cooperation of his fellows in undertakings that promote their mutual benefit; in which he can even depend on their active aid should he meet with accident or misfortune through no commensurate or glaring fault of his own.

And as it is in the interest of everyone to promote such a code of conduct on the part of others, so it is in his own interest to abide rigorously and inflexibly by such a code. For every infraction on the part of any individual tends to provoke infractions on the part of others, and endangers the maintenance of the code. There must even be a *sanctity* surrounding observance of the moral rules. If this sanctity does not exist, if the code is not inflexibly preserved, it loses its utilitarian value. (This is the element of truth in the objections to crude or *ad hoc* utilitism though not to *rule*-utilitism.)

Any individual who violates the moral code not only contributes to the disintegration of the code, but the more frequently or flagrantly he does so the more likely he is to be found out, and the more likely he is, therefore, to be punished, if not by the law, then by the retaliations and reprisals not only of those whom he has directly injured, but of others who have learned of the injuries he has inflicted.

Even to emphasize the necessity for "reconciling" egoism and altruism, therefore, as Herbert Spencer does, may be misleadingly to imply that they are normally antagonistic to each other.

On the contrary, particularly when we consider the long run, the usual and *normal* situation is the *coincidence* of egoism and altruism, the tendency of their aims to coalesce. It is their apparent "*ir*reconcilability" that is unusual and exceptional. In fact, the overwhelming majority of people could be persuaded to adhere to a given code of ethics only if they were persuaded, however vaguely or even subconsciously, that adherence to such a code was in their own ultimate interest as individuals as well as in the interest of society.

We may, however, go even further than this. Not only does the code of conduct which best promotes the long-run interests of the individual tend to coincide with the code that best promotes the long-run interests of society, and vice versa, but it is much less easy than the majority of moral philosophers acknowledge to determine when an individual is acting primarily out of self-regard or out of regard for the interests of others. When a young man spends half his week's salary on a Saturday night taking his girl to dinner, the theater and a night club, is he acting "selfishly," or "altruistically"? When a rich man buys his wife a mink coat, does he do it, as Thorstein Veblen contended, merely to advertise his own wealth and success, or does he do it to please his wife? When parents make "sacrifices" to send their children to college are they doing it for the pleasure of boasting about their children (or even about their own sacrifices), or are they doing it primarily out of love for their children?

3. *Bishop Butler on Self-Love*

In contending that the same rules of conduct that tend most to promote the long-run interests of society are those that tend most also to promote the long-run interests of the individual who adheres to them, in contending that "egoism" and "altruism" tend to coincide, in contending even that "selfish" and "altruistic" motives are in practice often difficult to distinguish, I no doubt do my argument an injury in the eyes of a certain group of writers by pointing out the extent to which Herbert Spencer and particularly Jeremy Bentham supported it. For these writers have for years indicated their own superior culture, sensitiveness, and spirituality by their disdainful references to "Benthamism"; and their scorn has been effective because the prevailing conception of what Bentham thought and taught has been in fact a caricature. But perhaps these writers will be more impressed if I point out that the arguments of Bentham on this point were in turn anticipated, a full century before him, by no less a figure than the pre-Utilitarian, Bishop Butler.

The subtle mind of Butler made contributions both to ethical and psychological insight that are as valuable today as when he published his *Fifteen Sermons* in 1726. I shall confine myself here to those bearing directly on the issue between egoism and altruism.

"Self-love and benevolence, virtue and interest," he tells us in his preface,

> . . . are not to be opposed but only to be distinguished from each other. . . . Neither does there appear any reason to wish self-love were weaker in the generality of the world than it is. . . . The thing to be lamented is not that men have so great regard to their own good or interest in the present world, for they have not enough; but that they have so little to the good of others. . . . Upon the whole, if the generality of mankind were to cultivate within themselves the principle of self-love, if they were to accustom themselves often to set down and consider what was the greatest happiness they were capable of attaining for themselves in this life, and if self-love were so strong and prevalent as that they would uniformly pursue this their supposed chief temporal good, without being diverted from it by any particular passion, it would manifestly prevent numberless follies and vices.

Butler is here opposing "self-love" to "mere appetite, will, and pleasure," or "any vagrant inclination." But what he is really arguing for, in more modern terms, is the practice of the prudential virtues. He urges us to act in our true *long-run* self-interest rather than for some merely temporary advantage or under the influence of unreflecting impulse or passion.

"To aim at public and private good," Butler tells us in his First Sermon, "are so far from being inconsistent that they mutually promote each other. . . .

> I must however remind you that though benevolence and self-love are different, though the former tends most directly to public good, and the latter to private, yet they are so perfectly coincident

that the greatest satisfactions to ourselves depend upon our having benevolence in a due degree, and that self-love is one chief security of our right behavior toward society. It may be added that their mutual coinciding, so that we can scarce promote one without the other, is equally a proof that we were made for both.

Butler goes on to point out some of the psychological reasons why this is so.

> Desire of esteem from others . . . naturally leads us to regulate our behavior in such a manner as will be of service to our fellow creatures. . . . Mankind are by nature so closely united, there is such a correspondence between the inward sensations of one man and those of another,[3] that disgrace is as much avoided as bodily pain, and to be the object of esteem and love as much desired as any external goods; and in many particular cases, persons are carried on to do good to others, as the end their affection tends to and rests in, and manifest that they find real satisfaction and enjoyment in this course of behavior. . . . Men are so much one body that in a peculiar manner they feel for each other. . . . And therefore to have no restraint from, no regard to, others in our behavior is the speculative absurdity of considering ourselves as single and independent, as having nothing in our nature which has respect to our fellow creatures, reduced to action and practice. And this is the same absurdity as to suppose a hand or any part to have no natural respect to any other or to the whole body.

In his Third Sermon Butler goes even further: "Conscience and self-love, if we understand our true happiness, always lead us the same way. Duty and interest are perfectly coincident, for the most part in this world, but entirely and in every instance if we take in the future and the whole, this being implied in the notion of a good and perfect administration of things."

Though this argument depends for its full force on the Christian assumption of a life hereafter, with the rewards of heaven or the punishments of purgatory, it is enlightening to notice the similarity of the worldly part of it to that of Bentham's *Deontology,* with its subtitle: "The Science of Morality, in which the Harmony and Co-incidence of Duty and Self-Interest, Virtue and Felicity, Prudence and Benevolence, are Explained and Exemplified."

It is in his Eleventh Sermon, however, that Butler expounds at greatest length his criticism of the view that self-love and benevolence are necessarily hostile to or even inconsistent with each other:

> And since, further, there is generally thought to be some peculiar kind of contrariety between self-love and the love of our neighbor, between the pursuit of public and of private good, insomuch that when you are recommending one of these, you are supposed to be speaking against the other; and from hence arises a secret prejudice against and frequently open scorn of all talk of public spirit and real goodwill to our fellow creatures; it will be necessary to inquire what respect benevolence hath to self-love, and the pursuit of private interest to the pursuit of public; or whether they be anything of that peculiar inconsistency and contrariety between them, over and above what there is between self-love and other passions and particular affections, and their respective pursuits.

Butler's inquiry and argument show a philosophic penetration far in advance of his time; in fact, most contemporary writers on ethics have not yet caught up with it. "Every particular affection, even the love of our neighbor," he writes in his Fourth Sermon,

> . . . is as really our own affection as self-love; and the pleasure arising from its gratification is as much my own pleasure as the pleasure self-love would have from knowing I myself should be happy some time hence, would be my own pleasure. . . . Is desire of and delight in the happiness of another any more a diminution of self-love than desire of and delight in the esteem of another? . . . That others enjoy the benefit of the air and the light of the sun does not hinder but that these are as much one's private advantage now as they would be if we had the property of them exclusive of all others. So a pursuit which tends to promote the good of another, yet may have as great tendency to promote private interest as a pursuit which does not tend to the good of another at all or which is mischievous to him.

4. *What Is Egoism?*

But these quotations raise an unsettling question, which may seem to make everything I have previously said or quoted, not only in *contrasting* "egoism" and "altruism" but even in *distinguishing* them, confused and invalid. Suppose we extend

Bishop Butler's conception of "self-love" just a bit more. We have asserted that all action is action undertaken to exchange a less satisfactory state of affairs for a more satisfactory state. Isn't every action I take, therefore, taken to increase my *own* satisfaction? Don't I help my neighbor because it gives *me* satisfaction to do so? Don't I seek to increase the happiness of another only when this increases *my* satisfaction? Doesn't a doctor go to a plague spot, to inoculate others or tend the sick, even at the risk of catching the disease or dying of it, because this is the course that gives *him* most satisfaction? Doesn't the martyr willingly go to the stake rather than recant his views because this is the only choice capable of giving *him* satisfaction? But if the most famous martyrs and the greatest saints were acting just as "egoistically" as the most brutal despots and the most abandoned voluptuaries, because each was only doing what gave *him* most satisfaction, what moral meaning can we continue to attach to "egoism," and what useful purpose is served by the term?

The problem, I suspect, is chiefly a linguistic one. *My* choices and decisions are necessarily *mine*. *I* do what gives *me* satisfaction. But if we therefore extend the definition of egoism to cover every decision I make, *all* action becomes egoistic; "altruistic" action becomes impossible, and the very word egoism ceases to have any moral meaning.

We can solve the problem by returning to the common usage of the terms involved, and examining it more carefully. Because I necessarily act to satisfy my *own* desires, it does not follow that these desires merely concern my *own* state, or my own narrow personal "welfare." In a shrewd psychological analysis, Moritz Schlick concludes that "egoism" is not to be identified with a will to personal pleasure or even to self-preservation, but means, in its common usage as a term of moral disparagement, simply *inconsiderateness*. It is not because he follows his special impulses that a man is blamed, but because he does so quite untroubled by the desires or needs of others. The essence of egoism, then,—or, to use the more common term, "selfishness"—"is just inconsiderateness with respect to the interests of fellow men, the pursuit of personal ends at the cost of those of others." [4]

5. Mutualism

What we normally condemn, in brief, is not the pursuit of self-interest, but only the pursuit of self-interest at the *expense* of the interests of others.

The terms "egoistic" and "altruistic," though they are used loosely in common conversation, and are difficult if not impossible to define with precision, are still useful and even indispensable in describing the dominant *attitude* that guides a man or one of his actions.

So, returning to this loose but common usage, let us see how far we have now come in this chapter, and whether it is possible to push our analysis a little further.

Neither a society in which everybody acted on *purely* egoistic motives, nor one in which everybody acted on *purely* altruistic motives (if we can really imagine either) would be workable. A society in which each worked *exclusively* for his own interest, narrowly conceived, would be a society of constant collisions and conflicts. A society in which each worked *exclusively* for the good of others would be an absurdity. The most successful society would seem to be one in which each worked *primarily* for his own good while always *considering* the good of others whenever he suspected any incompatibility between the two.

In fact, *egoism* and *altruism* are neither mutually exclusive nor do they exhaust the possible motives of human conduct. There is a twilight zone between them. Or rather, there is an attitude and motivation that is not quite either (especially if we define them as necessarily excluding each other), but deserves a name by itself.

I would like to suggest two possible names that we might give this attitude. One is an arbitrary coinage—*egaltruism,* which we may define to mean consideration *both* of self *and* others in any action or rule of action.[5] A less artificially contrived word, however, is *mutualism*. This word has the advantage of already existing, though as a technical word in biology, meaning "a condition of symbiosis (i.e. a living together) in which two associated organisms contribute mutually to the well-being of each other." The word can with great advantage be taken over (even retaining its biological implications) by moral philosophy.

If two people, where there might otherwise be conflict, act on the principle of *egaltruism* or *mutualism,* and each considers the interests of *both,* they will necessarily act in harmony. This is in fact the attitude that prevails in harmonious families, in which husband and wife, father, mother, and children, put first, not only as the principle on which they act, but in their spontaneous feelings, the interests of the *family.* And mutualism, enlarged, becomes the sentiment or principle of Justice.

We might indicate the consequences of each of these three attitudes, in its pure state, by an illustration (in which I shall permit myself a touch of caricature). A fire breaks out in a crowded theater in which the audience consists solely of pure egoists. Each rushes immediately for the nearest or the main exit, pushing, knocking down, or trampling on anybody in his way. The result is a panic in which many people are needlessly killed or burned because of the stampede itself. The fire breaks out in a crowded theater in which the audience is made up solely of pure altruists. Each defers to the other— "After you, my dear Alfonse"—and insists on being the last to leave. The result is that all burn to death. The fire breaks out in a crowded theater in which the audience is made up solely of cooperatists or mutualists. Each seeks to get the theater emptied as quickly and with as little loss of life as possible. Therefore all act much as they would at a fire drill, and the theater is emptied with a minimum loss of life. A few, who are farthest from the exits or for other reasons, may perish in the flames; but they accept this situation, and even cooperate in it, rather than start a stampede which may cost far more lives.

I have preferred to call the ethical system outlined in this book *Cooperatism.* But it could almost as well be called *Mutualism.* The former name emphasizes the desired *actions* or rules of action and their probable consequences. But the latter name emphasizes the appropriate feeling or *attitude* that inspires the actions or rules of action. And both imply that the attitude and actions that best promote the happiness and well-being of the individual in the long run, tend to coincide with the attitude and actions that best promote the happiness and well-being of society as a whole.

The *word* Mutualism may seem new and contrived in this connection, but there is nothing new or contrived about the attitude it stands for. It may not necessarily imply a universal Christian love, but it does imply a universal sympathy and kindness, and a love of those who are nearest.

6. *How Moral Rules Are Framed*

Let us examine again the false antithesis between the "Individual" and "Society."

It is a confusion of thought to think that ethics consists of the rules that "society" imposes on the "individual." Ethics consists of the rules that we all try to impose *on each other*. It may even be thought of as the rules that each individual tries to impose on all other individuals, on "society," at least in so far as their actions are likely to affect him. The individual does not want anyone to aggress against him; therefore he seeks to establish non-aggression both as a legal and a moral rule. He feels obliged, in consistency (and for the sake of getting the rule enforced), to abide by it himself.

This is how our moral rules are continuously framed and modified. They are not framed by some abstract and disembodied collectivity called "society" and then imposed on an "individual" who is in some way separate from society. We impose them (by praise and censure, approbation and disapprobation, promise and warning, reward and punishment) on each other, and most of us consciously or unconsciously accept them for ourselves.

Each of us plays in society a constant dual role—he who acts, and he who is affected by the action, the Actor and the Affected, the Agent and the Patient, the Doer and the Done-to. Each of us may play also, at times, a third role—that of the Disinterested or Impartial Observer.

If we are to frame workable and acceptable moral rules, we must imaginatively look at each hypothetical or real situation from all three standpoints—that of the Agent, that of the Patient, and that of the Impartial Observer. It is because over the course of accumulated human thought and experience, actions have been looked at and judged from all three standpoints, that our traditional moral code, in the main, takes account of all three. Moral disputes and moral rebellions arise,

EGOISM, ALTRUISM, MUTUALISM

in large part, because one or both of the disputants looks at a situation from only one of these standpoints.

As a prospective Agent it may seem to A's short-run interest to hit his neighbor P over the head and take his money. But as the prospective Patient P will find this wholly objectionable. And either, or a third man O, will see as an Impartial Observer that such a rule of action would be disastrous to society. It is the failure to look at actions or rules of action from all three standpoints, and to put oneself imaginatively, in turn, in the role of Agent, Patient, and Disinterested Spectator, that has led to innumerable ethical fallacies—from the fallacy of short-sighted pursuit of selfish aims to the fallacy that everybody should sacrifice himself to everybody else.

It is the purpose of ethics to help us test or frame moral rules. We cannot secure objectivity in testing or framing such rules unless we imaginatively put ourselves successively in the place of each of the persons that a given rule would affect. Suppose our question is: Should a passerby undertake to rescue a drowning swimmer? Under what circumstances, and at how much risk to himself? In seeking the answer one should first put oneself in the position of the passerby, and ask how much inconvenience, risk, or danger one would think it obligatory or rational to undertake. Secondly, one should put oneself in the position of the struggling swimmer, and ask how much danger or risk on the passerby's part, if you were the man in the water, you would think it obligatory or rational for him to undertake. And if you arrived by this process at two widely differing answers, you should then ask whether an Impartial Spectator might arrive at some answer in between.

Suppose we use this method to test the Golden Rule: *Do unto others as you would have others do unto you.* The difficulty with this is that there is practically no limit to the benefits that most of us would be willing to accept from others, at whatever cost to them. But suppose now that we turn the rule around, and make it: *Do not ask or expect others to do for you more than you would be willing to do for them,* or *Accept from others only as much help as you would be willing to extend to them if you were in their position.* You would begin to set more reasonable and workable limits to the rule. (Either in the

Golden Rule or in this Converse Golden Rule, however, as thus stated, the test is too subjective. Only in one's role as an Impartial Observer can one frame the appropriate rule objectively.)

Suppose we apply the test to the Christian precept "That ye love one another." Literally, probably none of us is capable of fulfilling such a universal and indiscriminate obligation, if only because we cannot command our feelings. We can love a few people to whom we are drawn by special qualities or bound by special ties. But for the rest the most we are capable of is *outward* demeanor or action—considerateness, fairness, kindness. This constant effort to be considerate and kind in our outward attitude will, of course, affect our inward feelings. The Christian ideal, by commanding an unattainable goal, has sometimes led men, from despair or cynicism, to fall far below a reasonably attainable moral achievement. "Man is neither angel nor beast, and the mischief is that he who would play the angel plays the beast." [6] Nevertheless, because of the Christian ideal, there is probably far more loving-kindness in the world than there would have been without it.

7. *The Limits of Obligation*

Regarding the extent of our obligations to others, the opinions of different individuals are bound to vary widely. In general the strong and independent and well-off will think that relatively narrow limits should be set around the supposed extent of their obligation to others, whereas the weak and dependent and badly off will want the assumed extent of obligation to others to be considered much wider. Experience will tend to work out a compromise of such opinions in the moral tradition, because each will find himself at times in the position of one who wants help and at times in the position of one who is asked to help.

That is why this is one of the unsettled problems of ethics. There will be those who think that the only obligation of the individual is not to transgress against others; and there will be those who think that his obligation to help others is practically without limits. There will be still others who take an intermediate position, and hold that people in need or distress should be helped, but only to the extent that this does little or nothing to reduce their incentives to self-help—or to reduce the incentives to production and effort of those who are called upon to supply the help.

Probably no exact boundary can be drawn, and no exact rules can be framed, concerning the extent of our duties to others. In such duties there will always be a twilight zone, shading off from what is clearly imperative to what is clearly quixotic and in the long run harmful.

We might end this chapter, logically, with a discussion of the problem of "self-sacrifice." But this problem has occupied such a prominent and crucial role from the very beginnings of moral philosophy—and above all since the birth of Christianity—as to call for consideration in a separate chapter.

CHAPTER 14

The Problem of Self-Sacrifice

1. *"Individual" and "Society"*

Let us summarize the discussion in the two preceding chapters to see where it has brought us.

We have seen that there tends to be a *coincidence* between the actions or rules of action that best promote the interests of the individual in the long run and the rules of action that best promote the interests of society as a whole in the long run. We have seen that this coincidence tends to be greater the longer the period we take into consideration. We have seen, moreover, that it is difficult to distinguish "egoistic" actions from "altruistic" or "mutualistic" ones, because an enlightened and farsighted selfishness might often dictate precisely the same course as an enlightened and farsighted benevolence.

There is another consideration, which needs to be re-emphasized. The *antithesis* so often drawn between the "individual" and "society" is false. Society is merely the name we give to the collection of individuals and their interrelations. It would be clarifying and useful, in fact, if in sociological, economic, and ethical discussion we were most commonly to define society as *other people*. Then, in a society consisting only of three persons —A, B, and C—A, from his own point of view, is "the Individual," and B and C are "Society," whereas B, from his own point of view, is "the Individual" and A and C, "Society," etc.[1]

Now each of us sees himself sometimes as the individual and sometimes as a member of society. In the former role he is apt to emphasize the necessity of liberty and in the latter the necessity of law and order. A as a member of society is concerned that neither B nor C do anything to injure *him*. He insists that laws be passed to prevent this; and injuries that cannot satisfactorily be prevented by law he seeks to prevent by condemnation or disapproval. But he soon realizes that he cannot consistently or successfully use devices of condemnation or praise to influence the actions of others without accepting them for like actions by himself. Both to seem consistent to others and to be consistent in his own eyes (for the "rational" man tends to accept consistency as an end in itself) he feels an obligation to accept for himself the moral rules he seeks to impose on others. (This is part of the explanation of the origin and growth of conscience.)

And the moral rules that we seek, for egoistic reasons, to impose on others, do not stop at inducing them not to inflict positive injury on us. If we found ourselves on board a ship sinking at sea we would think it the moral duty of those on any vessels near by to answer our SOS signals, and to come to our rescue, even at considerable risk to themselves.

I do not mean to imply by this that all moral rules arise out of egoistic considerations. There are people who are spontaneously so moved by the suffering of others or a danger to others that they do not need to imagine themselves in the same predicament in order to think it their duty to come to the rescue of others. They will do so out of their spontaneous desire. Nearly all of us, in fact, do take spontaneous satisfaction in the happiness of others—at least of *some* others. What I am concerned to point out is that even if we were to assume, with Hobbes, that people are guided only by egoistic motives, we would probably arrive at the conclusion that they would be driven, in the end, to impose virtually the same outward code of morals on each other as if they were guided by altruistic motives as well. And because it is to the interest of each individual to live in a society characterized not only by peace and order and justice, but by social cooperation and mutual affection and aid, it is in the interest of each individual himself to help to create or preserve such a society through his own code and his own example.

We must repeat once more, then, that the *antithesis* between the interests of the Individual and the interests of Society is false. *Normally* and *usually* the actions that best promote the happiness and well-being of the individual best promote the happiness and well-being of the whole society. There is normally, to repeat, a *coincidence* between the long-run interests of the individual and the long-run interests of society. But we must frankly face the fact that there is not a complete *identity*. There will be times when the interests of the individual, even his interests in the long run, appear in his own eyes to conflict with those of society. What, then, is his duty? By what rule should he be guided? What should the moral code prescribe?

In examining this conflict, or apparent conflict, it will be profitable to move from the easier to the harder examples. What appears easiest at first glance is the establishment of a negative rule. Adam Smith states such a rule in sweeping form: "One individual must never prefer himself so much even to any other individual as to hurt or injure that other in order to benefit himself, though the benefit to the one should be much greater than the hurt or injury to the other. The poor man must neither defraud nor steal from the rich, though the acquisition might be much more beneficial to the one than the loss could be hurtful to the other." [2]

Here the specific illustration is beyond dispute, but the statement of the principle is much less so. The reason stealing is wrong under any conditions, as Adam Smith later points out, is that it is a violation of "one of those sacred rules upon the tolerable observation of which depend the whole security and peace of human society." [3]

2. *Duty* vs. *Risk*

But surely it cannot be wrong to do *anything* to benefit oneself simply because an incidental consequence may be to hurt or injure the interests of another. Should one reject the offer of a better job than one already has, simply because the present occupant, or another candidate, may then lose that particular job and may not be able to get another as good? Should a scientist refuse to publish a truthful criticism of another scientist's work because the result of that criticism may be to increase the first scientist's reputation at the cost of destroying the reputation of the scientist criticized? Evidently the rule proposed by Adam Smith would have to be carefully qualified to forbid injury to others only through coercion, violence, malice, misrepresentation, or fraud—i.e., the class of actions forbidden must be only those that tend to injure the long-run interests of society as a whole, and the class of actions prescribed must be only those that tend to benefit the long-run interests of society as a whole.

Turning to positive rules—i.e., those that enjoin help rather

THE PROBLEM OF SELF-SACRIFICE

than those which merely forbid injury—let us begin with the athletic young man with a rope and a life-belt at hand (previously referred to on p. 69), who sits on a bench in a park along a river bank, and quietly sees a child drown, although he could rescue the child without the least danger. There can be no moral defense for such inaction. As Bentham pointed out, not only should it "be made the duty of every man to save another from mischief, when it can be done without prejudicing himself," but it might well be made a duty legally enforceable upon him by punishment for nonfeasance.[4]

But what should be the rule when the risk to the would-be rescuer rises? Here the problem becomes difficult, and the answer may depend not only on the degree of the risk, but on the relationship (whether, e.g., that of parent or of stranger) of the potential rescuer to the person or persons to be rescued. (It may also depend on a numerical relation. For example, whether the situation is [1] one in which one person, say a sapper, or soldier whose job it is to get rid of enemy mines, may be asked to risk his life to save a hundred or a thousand, or [2] one in which a hundred or a thousand may be asked to risk their lives to save only one, say a king or a president who is being held as a hostage.)

The ethical problem here may be difficult to answer precisely because, for example, the degree of risk being run may be indeterminable unless the risk is actually undertaken. Many a man has been tortured by conscience all the rest of his life because he has suspected that cowardice or selfishness led him to overestimate a risk that he refused to take to save another.

If we turn for help to the answers given by traditional ethical systems and by "common-sense" ethics we find them to be in some cases not only clear but stern. There are conditions under which these traditional codes demand not only that a man risk his life for others but that he be willing, indeed, to sacrifice it. A soldier who deserts or runs away in battle, a captain who violates the rule that he should be the last to leave his ship, a doctor who refuses to enter a city where there is an epidemic or to attend a patient suffering from a contagious disease, a fireman (or father) who fails to try to rescue a child or an invalid from a fire, an armed policeman who stands idly by or runs away when an innocent citizen is being held up by a bandit at the point of a gun—all these are condemned by nearly every traditional or common-sense moral code.

And the reason for this condemnation is plain. A nation that cannot depend on the bravery and self-sacrifice of its armed forces is doomed to conquest or annihilation. The inhabitants of a city who could not depend on the willingness of their policemen to take risks would be overrun by criminals, and would not be safe in the streets. The welfare and survival of a whole community, in brief, may depend upon the willingness of certain individuals or groups to sacrifice themselves for the rest.

But the duty is not always clear. If an unarmed citizen happens to be near when another unarmed citizen is being held up at gunpoint, is it the duty of the former to try to take the gun away? If even a hundred other unarmed citizens are by when a bandit is robbing one of them at gunpoint, is it the duty of one of the bystanders to try to take the gun away? And which one? No doubt collectively they could succeed; but it is the first to try who takes the greatest risk.

The answer of common-sense ethics to this situation is far from clear. The people who read in the next day's newspapers about a thug shooting a victim and getting away because a crowd of a hundred did nothing to stop him, may be righteously indignant, and contemptuous of those who were too cowardly to act. Some of those who were in the crowd will feel secretly ashamed of their inaction, or at least a little uneasy. But most of them will argue to themselves or others that it would have been an act of sheer foolhardiness for them to take the initiative in interfering.

3. *Search for a General Rule*

Can we find the answer to the problem of self-sacrifice in any general rule or principle?

I think we can reject without any further argument the contention of a few contemporary ethical writers that it is *never* the duty of an individual to sacrifice himself for others, or that it is even "immoral" for him to do so. The examples we have cited, and the reasons why such self-sacrifice may sometimes be necessary, are sufficient and clear.

On the other hand, we do not need to give prolonged examination to the precisely opposite extreme contention that self-sacrifice is the *normal* ethical requirement and that we need not count its cost. I have already cited the arguments of Bentham and Spencer against the folly of everybody's living and sacrificing for everybody else. These arguments are accepted by most modern ethical writers. "A society in which everybody spent his life sacrificing all his pleasure for others would be even more absurd than a society whose members all lived by taking in each other's washing. In a society of such completely unselfish people who would be prepared to accept and benefit by the sacrifice?" [5]

Nevertheless, the doctrine of sacrifice for sacrifice's sake was not only held by Kant and other eminent moral philosophers, but is still found in more modern writers. "Were there no use possibly to be made of it, no happiness which could possibly be promoted, generous and self-forgetting action would be worth having in the universe." [6] This is sanctifying a means while ignoring its purpose. As E. F. Carritt rightly replies: "One cannot act generously if one can find nothing that anybody wants, and self-forgetfulness, when there was nothing else practicable to remember, would be simply self-neglecting." [7]

With these two extremes out of the way, we can try to formulate an acceptable rule. Suppose we frame and examine the rule as follows:

Self-sacrifice is only required or justified where it is necessary in order to secure for another or others a *greater* good than that sacrificed.[8]

This is substantially the rule proposed by Jeremy Bentham—except that he would have used the word "pleasure" or "happiness" rather than "good." It is the rule of all the moral philosophers who have argued, with Adam Smith, that it is the duty of the agent to act in the way that an "impartial spectator" would approve.[9] "The point is that the interests of others should be treated on just the same level as one's own, so that the antithesis between self and others is made as little prominent in one's ethical thinking as possible." [10]

Now it is at least reasonably clear that no one should sacrifice his own interests to another or others unless a *greater* good is accomplished by the sacrifice than is lost to the agent. This is clear even from the most impartial view. Any rule of action should tend to promote a net gain of good on the whole rather than a net loss.

4. *The Concept of Costs*

Here we may draw a parallel not only with what has already been said about the requirements of simple prudence, but with the whole conception of *costs* in human action. The only rational prudential reason why a man should give up a pleasure, a satisfaction, or a good is to gain a greater pleasure, satisfaction, or good. This greater good may, of course, be nothing more than the absence of the subsequent pain or suffering caused by excessive indulgence in the pleasure given up—as a man may give up excessive drinking or smoking or eating in order to feel better in the long run—to improve his health and prolong his life. Prudential sacrifices are usually sacrifices of immediate pleasures or satisfactions in order to enjoy greater future happiness or satisfactions.

This is merely an illustration in the moral field of a "law of costs" that is usually discussed only in economic textbooks, but which in fact covers the whole realm of human action. "Everything, in short, is produced at the expense of foregoing something else. Costs of production themselves, in fact, might be defined as the things that are given up (the leisure and pleasures, the raw materials with alternative potential uses) in order to create the thing that is made." [11]

Costs thus conceived in "real" terms are sometimes distinguished by economists from money costs by the special name *opportunity costs*. This means, as the name implies, that we can do one thing only at the expense of foregoing something else. We can seize one opportunity only at the cost of foregoing what we consider the next best opportunity. Mises defines the concept in its broadest form:

> Action is an attempt to substitute a more satisfactory state of affairs for a less satisfactory one. . . . What gratifies less is abandoned in order to attain something that pleases more. That which

is abandoned is called the price paid for the attainment of the end sought. The value of the price paid is called costs. Costs are equal to the value attached to the satisfaction which one must forego in order to attain the end aimed at.[12]

Or, more precisely and technically: "Costs are the value attached to the most valuable want-satisfaction which remains unsatisfied because the means required for its satisfaction are employed for that want-satisfaction the cost of which we are dealing with." [13]

This concept, unfortunately, is not very commonly understood or applied by writers on ethics. When we do apply it to the moral field, it is clear that every action we take must involve a *choice* of one value at the *expense* of other values. We cannot realize all values at once. We cannot realize more of one value without realizing less of another. We cannot give more time to learning one subject, or developing one skill, for example, without giving less time to learning some other subject or developing some other skill. We cannot achieve more of one good without achieving less of some other good. All good, all value, can be achieved only at the cost of foregoing some lesser good or value.

In brief, a "sacrifice," in the sense of a cost, is inescapable in all moral action as it is in all (narrowly conceived) "economic" action. In economics, the excess of the value gained over the value sacrificed is called a "profit." Because of the pejorative sense in which this word is commonly used by socialists and others, some readers may be shocked by its application to the realm of morality. But it is merely another way of saying that what is gained by an action should be greater than what is lost by it. In the broadest sense, "profit is the difference between the higher value of the good obtained and the lower value of the good sacrificed for its obtainment." [14]

This higher net value gained is of course the test of decisions and actions that concern oneself alone. It is the justification of the prudential virtues. But it should also be the test of actions that affect others. A man's duty cannot require that he give up any good of his own except for the *greater* good of another or others. In fact, it can reasonably be argued that it would be *immoral* for him to go beyond this—to sacrifice his own good to confer a *lesser* good on others. For the net effect of this would be to *reduce* the amount of good, to reduce the amount of happiness and well-being, in the universe.

Now what are we to say of the argument, by such moralists as Kant, and more recently by Grote, Hastings Rashdall, and G. E. Moore, that Self-Sacrifice, or Duty, or Virtue (usually spelled with a capital to impress the point) is *itself* an end, or even *the* end?

I must content myself here with saying that I consider self-sacrifice essentially a *means*—a means sometimes necessary for promoting the end of maximum happiness and well-being for the whole community. But its value is wholly *instrumental* or *derivative* (like the value, in economic life, of irksome labor, or a raw material or a capital good). To the extent that an overzealous or misdirected self-sacrifice tends to *reduce* the sum of human happiness and well-being, its value is lost or becomes negative. It is therefore a mere confusion of thought to consider Self-Sacrifice (or Duty or Virtue) an *additional* good or value *independent* of the ultimate purpose it serves.

What leads to the confusion is the difficulty, if not the impossibility, of conceiving of a society in which happiness and well-being were maximized but in which nobody ever sacrificed his short-run interests to the long-run interests of others, in which nobody ever did his duty, and in which nobody had any virtues. But the reason for the difficulty or impossibility of conceiving such a society is that is involves a self-contradiction in concept and in terms. For the same reason it would be an impossibility to conceive of an economic community in which the production of ultimate consumer goods and services was maximized without the use of labor, raw materials, factories, machines, or means of transport. What we *mean* by rational Self-Sacrifice and Duty and Virtue is performing acts that tend to promote the maximum of happiness and well-being for the whole community and refraining from acts that tend to reduce such happiness and well-being. If the effect of Self-Sacrifice were to *reduce* the sum of happiness and well-being it would not be rational to admire it, and if the effect of other alleged duties and virtues were to *reduce* the sum of human happiness and well-being, we would cease to call them duties and virtues.

Once we have straightened out the confusion of thought that regards Self-Sacrifice, Duty, or Virtue to have not merely an instrumental, subordinate, or *derived* value, but a value *additional to* and *independent of* the happiness and well-being to which they are means, a lot of imposing ethical maxims and systems, from Kant's Categorical Imperative to Hastings Rashdall's "Ideal" Utilitarianism,[15] fall to the ground.

But the questions raised here are so wide that we may later have to return to them for more extended consideration.

This may be a useful point for a semantic digression. In using the word "Self-Sacrifice," and in contending that there are occasions, however rare, when it is necessary, I am probably courting resistance from some readers to whom Self-Sacrifice means the equivalent of self-abasement and self-immolation, of asceticism and martyrdom. Many of these readers would find this view more acceptable if I used some milder term, like Self-Subordination. But the difficulty with this milder term is that it refers to a milder thing. Self-Sacrifice, as I conceive the term, is a duty that most of us are called upon to exercise only on a few rare occasions of crisis; self-subordination is a duty that most of us are called upon to exercise almost daily. We subordinate our own ego or our own immediate interests to wider interests whenever we refrain from starting to eat until everybody at the table has been served; or whenever, as part of an audience, we hear a speaker out without heckling or rushing up to the platform ourselves; or whenever we restrain a cough, at some inconvenience to ourselves, during, say, the soft bars of a symphony. Every member of a family, and especially the parents and the older children, must habitually practice self-subordination if family life is to be possible. But this self-subordination is something that each individual implicitly recognizes as necessary to the harmonious social cooperation that is in turn necessary to promote his own long-run interests.

5. *Obligations Have Limits*

Let us return, then, to the word Self-Sacrifice and to the rule which we framed on page 113 that self-sacrifice is only required or justified where it is necessary in order to secure for another or others a *greater* good than that sacrificed. This rule sets an upper limit on altruism or self-sacrifice. But may not even this often set the upper limit too high? Does it not in fact ignore the highly personal and *circumstantial* nature of our duty? Other people do not stand to me merely in the relation of fellow human beings. They may also stand to me in the relation of promiser to promisee, of creditor to debtor, of employer to employee, of doctor to patient, of client to attorney, of wife to husband, of child to parent, of friend to friend, of business colleague or of fellow countryman. As Sir David Ross points out, each of these relations may be the foundation of a prima facie duty, which is more or less incumbent on me according to the circumstances of the case.[16] Can the abstract rule as we stated it on page 113 be extended indefinitely to cover all mankind, all strangers, no matter where in the world they may be found? And does my duty to make such a sacrifice, assuming that it exists, have nothing to do with whether the sacrifice is made, say, to make it possible for a supreme genius to live and function, or merely to make conditions more comfortable for a stupid bore?

Conscience tells a man, according to Adam Smith, that he is "but one of the multitude, in no respect better than any other in it" and must act as an "impartial spectator" might decide.[17] But Smith almost immediately draws back from some of the conclusions to which this might logically lead. He refuses to associate himself with

> . . . those whining and melancholy moralists [e.g., Pascal and the poet James Thomson] who are perpetually reproaching us with our happiness, while so many of our brethren are in misery, who regard as impious the natural joy of prosperity, which does not think of the many wretches that are at every instant laboring under all sorts of calamities, in the languor of poverty, in the agony of distress, in the horrors of death, under the insults and oppression of their enemies. Commiseration for those miseries which we never saw, which we never heard of, but which we may be assured are at all times infesting such numbers of our fellow creatures, ought, they think, to damp the pleasures of the fortunate, and to render a certain melancholy dejection habitual to all men.[18]

A similar view, more violently expressed, appears in a letter to Lady Gray from Sydney Smith in 1823:

> For God's sake, do not drag me into another war. I am worn down, and worn out, with crusading and defending Europe, and protecting mankind: I must think a little of myself.

I am sorry for the Spaniards—I am sorry for the Greeks—I deplore the fate of the Jews; the people of the Sandwich Islands are groaning under the most detestable tyranny; Baghdad is oppressed: I do not like the present state of the Delta; Thibet is not comfortable.

Am I to fight for all these people? The world is bursting with sin and sorrow. Am I to be champion of the Decalogue, and to be eternally raising fleets and armies to make all men good and happy? We have just done saving Europe, and I am afraid the consequence will be, that we shall cut each other's throats.

No war, dear Lady Gray—no eloquence; but apathy, selfishness, common sense, arithmetic; I beseech you, secure Lord Gray's swords and pistols, as the housekeeper did Don Quixote's armour. If there is another war, life will not be worth having. I will go to war with the king of Denmark, if he is impertinent to you, or does any injury to Howick; but for no other cause.

Several moral strands are twisted together in both of these arguments. In the quotation from Sydney Smith the question whether the people of other countries should be helped is entangled with the question whether war is a desirable way to help them. But the implication of his plea for "apathy, selfishness, common sense, arithmetic" is that it is folly to sacrifice one's own comfort for millions of unknown foreigners. Adam Smith's chief reason, however, for dismissing "this extreme sympathy with misfortunes which we know nothing about" as "altogether absurd and unreasonable" is that, though "all men, even those at the greatest distance, are no doubt entitled to our good wishes," we are in a position in which "we can neither serve nor hurt" them.

It is precisely this argument which would today be questioned. Americans are not only being importuned by private charities, but compulsorily taxed by their own government, to give food and aid and dollars to millions all over the world whom they will never see. What is their real obligation in this field? And when can they consider it discharged?

Suppose we conclude that sacrifice is required whenever it will yield more happiness to those for whom it is made than it will cost in happiness to those who make the sacrifice? It could plausibly be argued that, when we give this an objective or material interpretation, it would require us to keep giving away our fortunes or income or food as long as we had any more of any of these than the most miserably housed or clothed or fed person alive. We should have to keep giving, in other words, down to the point of absolute world equality of income and living standards.

Such an equal distribution of income, housing, clothing, and food, quantitatively and qualitatively, would be, of course not only physically impossible, but inconceivable. The attempt to achieve it, even by "voluntary" means and through pure moral approval and disapproval, would so tremendously reduce the incentives to work and production at both ends of the economic scale as to lead toward universal impoverishment. It would enormously reduce, and not increase, the sum of human happiness and well-being. The attempt to achieve such an egalitarian altruism, the attempt to impose such practically limitless and bottomless responsibilities, would bring misery and tragedy to mankind far beyond any harm resulting from the most complete "selfishness." (In fact, as Bishop Butler pointed out, and as many have recognized since, if everyone were constantly guided by a rational, enlightened, and far-sighted "egoism," the world would be an immensely better place than it is).

But, some readers may say, I have been presenting an argument that does not really touch the rule we have been testing. By hypothesis, the sacrifices we are enjoined to make are only those that will yield *more* happiness in the long run to those for whom they are made than they will cost in *less* happiness (in the long run) to those who make them. Therefore we are asked to make *only* such sacrifices as will tend in the long run to *increase* the sum of happiness.

This is true. But even if we bypass here the crucial question whether it is possible to speak validly of a *sum* of happiness, or possible to compare the "increase" of one man's happiness with the "decrease" of another's, the preceding discussion will also show that it is very dangerous to give this principle any merely physical or short-term interpretation—or to base our duty, say, on any mathematical income comparisons. The less our active sympathies with the persons we are called upon to help, the more remote such persons are from our direct acquaintance and daily lives, the more reluctant we will be to make any sacrifice to help them, the less satisfaction we will take in any sacrifice—and, conversely, the less likely are those helped to appreciate the sacrifice on our part or to be permanently benefited by it.

The ethical problem here is complicated by the fact that certain acts of so-called "sacrifice" are not considered by those who make them to be sacrifices at all. Such are the sacrifices that a mother makes for her child. Certainly as long as the child is very young and truly helpless, most such sacrifices may directly and immediately, as well as in the long run, increase the happiness both of the one who makes the "sacrifice" and the one for whom it is made. Such sacrifices present an ethical problem of limitation only when they are carried to the point where they may either permanently impair the ability of the benefactor to continue his or her sacrifices or where they coddle or spoil or in some other way demoralize the child or other intended beneficiary.

6. *Maxima and Minima*

But the problem we are concerned with here is whether it is possible to frame a *general rule* to apply to the duty or limits of self-sacrifice—for the benefit of people, say, whom we may not know, or even for the benefit of people whom we may not like. One difficulty of such a general rule is that it cannot be simple. Our duty or non-duty may depend upon the relations, as I have previously hinted, in which we find ourselves with other people, relations which may sometimes be accidental. Thus if we are walking along a lonely road, even if we are on a temporary visit to a foreign country, and find a man who has been seriously injured by an automobile, or robbed, beaten, and left half dead, we cannot pass by "on the other side" and tell ourselves that the whole matter is none of our business, and besides we are late for an appointment. Our duty is to act as the Good Samaritan did. But this does not mean that our duty is to take all the world's burdens on our own shoulders, or to keep constantly touring around trying to find people to save, regardless of how they got into their predicament or what the long-run effect of our rescue operations would be on them.

This means that we must carefully distinguish between the special case and the general rule, or even between any single instance considered in isolation and a general rule. If you give a dollar to a beggar, or even $1,000 to a chance pauper who "needs" the money more than you do, a mathematical comparison of the supposed marginal utility of the money to him with its supposed much smaller marginal utility to you (assuming such a comparison were possible) may seem to result in a net gain of happiness for the two of you considered together. But to erect this into a general rule, to impose it as a general obligation, would result in a net loss of happiness for the community considered as a whole.

In brief, a single act of indiscriminate charity (or discriminate only in the sense of moving toward equalization of income without any other criterion) may seem to increase the happiness of the recipient more than it reduces the happiness of the donor. But if such extensive and practically limitless charity were erected into a *general moral rule* imposed on us it would lead to a great diminution of happiness because it would encourage permanent mendicancy in increasing numbers of people, who would come to regard such help as a "right," and would tend to discourage effort and industry on the part of those on whom this moral burden was imposed.

Let us now try to sum up the drift of our discussion. It may often be extremely difficult in practice to know how to apply our principle that self-sacrifice is occasionally necessary, though only when it seems likely to result in an increase in the sum of happiness and well-being. Limitless charity, or a limitless *obligation* to charity, is unlikely to achieve this result. All of us cannot sell all that we have, and give it to the poor.[19] Universalized, the idea becomes self-contradictory: there would be no one to sell to. Between never doing a charitable act, and giving away one's all, lies a wide range of possibilities for which no definite and clean-cut rule can be laid down. It may be right to contribute to a certain cause but not wrong not to.

But if the problem cannot be solved with precision, it does not follow that it cannot be solved at least within certain upper and lower limits. The upper limit, as we have seen, is that no act of self-sacrifice is justified unless it secures for another a *greater* good than the good that is sacrificed. The lower limit is, of course, that one should refrain from any positive harm to one's neighbors. In between is a twilight zone of obligation.

The problem can probably be solved within closer maxima

THE PROBLEM OF SELF-SACRIFICE

and minima than this.[20] The overriding guide to rules of ethics is social cooperation. The rules we should establish for mutual obligation are those that, when generalized, tend most to promote social cooperation.

7. *Self-Interest* vs. *Morality?*

The problem we are concerned with in this chapter may be stated in another form. In Chapter 7 we were tempted to *define* morality as "essentially, not the subordination of the 'individual' to 'society' but the subordination of immediate objectives to long-term ones."

Each of us, in his own long-run interest, is constantly called upon to make *temporary* sacrifices. But does morality require us to make *"genuine"* sacrifices—that is, sacrifices on *net balance,* sacrifices from which we cannot hope to realize any fully compensating gain even in the long run?

An enlightening but paradoxical answer to this question has been offered by Kurt Baier. I quoted part of it in Chapter 7 (p. 51). Now I should like to quote it more at length and analyze it more fully, because it poses what is perhaps the central problem of ethics:

> Moralities are systems of principles whose acceptance by everyone as overruling the dictates of self-interest is in the interest of everyone alike, though following the rules of a morality is not of course identical with following self-interest. If it were, there could be no conflict between a morality and self-interest and no point in having moral rules over-riding self-interest. . . .
>
> The answer to our question "Why should we be moral?" is therefore as follows. We should be moral because being moral is following rules designed to overrule self-interest whenever it is in the interest of everyone alike that everyone should set aside his interest. It is not self-contradictory to say this, because it may be in one's interest *not* to follow one's interest at times. We have already seen that enlightened self-interest acknowledges this point. But while enlightened self-interest does not require any genuine sacrifice from anyone, morality does. In the interest of the possibility of the good life for everyone, voluntary sacrifices are sometimes required from everybody. Thus, a person might do better for himself by following enlightened self-interest rather than morality. It is not possible, however, that *everyone* should do

better for himself by following enlightened self-interest rather than morality. The best possible life for *everyone* is possible only by everyone's following the rules of morality, that is, rules which quite frequently may require individuals to make genuine sacrifices.[21]

I have already pointed out one weakness in this ingenious statement. Its air of paradox stems from the use of the word "self-interest" in two different senses. If we distinguish immediate or short-term interest from long-run interest, much of this paradox disappears. Thus the proper statement is: Moralities are systems of principles whose acceptance by everyone as overruling the apparent dictates of immediate self-interest is in the long-run interest of everyone alike.

It *is* self-contradictory to say that "It is in the interest of everyone alike that everyone should set aside his interest." But it is *not* self-contradictory to say that it is in the long-run interest of everyone alike that everyone should set aside his mere momentary interests whenever their pursuit is incompatible with the long-run interests of others. It *is* self-contradictory to say that "it may be in one's interest *not* to follow one's interest at times." But it is *not* self-contradictory to say that it may be in one's long-run interest at times to forego some immediate interest.

Emphasis on the distinction between long-run and short-run interests solves half the problems raised by Baier's statement, but it does not solve them all. The rest exist because of possible conflict or incompatibility in the interests of different people. But is there therefore a *contrast* between the requirements of "enlightened self-interest" and the requirements of "morality"? The moral rules are precisely the rules of conduct designed to *maximize* the satisfactions, if not of everyone, then of the greatest number of persons possible. The enormous gain to everyone of adhering faithfully to these rules entirely outweighs the occasional sacrifices that this adherence involves. I am tempted to say that for 99 per cent of the people 99 per cent of the time, the actions called for by enlightened self-interest and by morality are identical.

I have said that Baier's antithesis between "self-interest" and "morality" depends for its plausibility upon the use of the word "self-interest" in two different senses—upon his failure to dis-

THE PROBLEM OF SELF-SACRIFICE

tinguish between short-run and long-run interest. It is ambiguous in another important sense also—in his conception of *self-*interest and his conception (elsewhere in his book) of "egoism." If we (implicitly or explicitly) *define* "egoism" and "self-interest" as "disregard of or indifference to the interests of *others*," then Baier's antithesis stands up. But this is because our use of words has begged the question. This is because we have implicitly defined the "egoist" as a cold calculating person who habitually regards his "self-interest" as *conflicting with* the interests of others. But such "egoists" are rare. Most people do not consciously pursue their *self-*interest but merely their *interests*. These interests do not necessarily exclude other persons. Most people feel spontaneous sympathy with others and take satisfaction in the happiness of others as well as of themselves. Most people recognize, however dimly, that their *principal* interest is to live in a moral and cooperative society.

Yet all this, it must be conceded, is only a partial answer to Baier's formulation. It is not conclusive. There remains the rare case when the individual may be called upon to make a "genuine" sacrifice. This is the occasion when a soldier, a ship-captain, a policeman, a fireman, a doctor, or perhaps a mother, father, husband, or brother, may be called upon to risk or to lose life itself, or to be maimed for life, in the fulfillment of some clear responsibility. There is then no future "long run" that can compensate for the sacrifice. Then society, or the rules of morality, say in effect: This risk you must take, this sacrifice you must make, whether or not you consider it in your own enlightened self-interest, because it is in the long-run interest of *all* of us that each abide unfalteringly by the responsibilities that the established rules of morality may lay upon him.

This is the price that any of us may be called upon some day to pay for the untold benefit that each of us derives from the existence of a code of morals and its observance by all the rest.

And this is the element of truth in Baier's formulation. Though he is wrong in implying a basic *conflict* between the requirements of "enlightened self-interest" and the requirements of "morality," where there is in fact a prevailing harmony and *coincidence,* he is right in insisting that these requirements may not *in every instance* be *identical*. As he states it elsewhere, supporting the element of truth in Kant's ethics: "Adopting the moral point of view involves acting on principle. It involves conforming to rules even when doing so is unpleasant, painful, costly, or ruinous to oneself." [22] But this is true precisely because universal and inflexible adherence to the moral rules is in the long-run interest of *everyone*. Once we allow anyone to make an exception in his own favor, we undermine the very purpose that the rules are designed to serve. But what is this but a way of saying that it is to the *self-interest* of everyone to obey the rules and to hold everyone else inflexibly to them?

Baier is wrong, in brief, in *contrasting* "morality" and "the pursuit of self-interest." Moral rules are designed precisely to promote individual interest to the maximum extent. The true contrast is between the kind of self-interest that is incompatible with the interest of others and the kind of self-interest that is compatible with the interest of others. Just as the best traffic rules are those that promote the maximum flow of safe traffic for the most cars, so the best moral rules are those that promote the maximum self-interest for the most people. It would be a contradiction in terms to say that the maximum interest of all was promoted by everyone's *restricting* the pursuit of his own interest. True, *some* must forego the pursuit of certain *apparent* or *temporary* advantages because these are of the kind that would thwart the achievement of the real interests not only of most others but even of himself. But the happiness of *all* cannot be maximized unless the happiness of *each* is maximized.

If we have a society consisting (let us say for simplicity) of only two people, A and B, then the rules of conduct they should adopt and adhere to are not those that are solely in A's interest, nor solely in B's interest, but most in the long-run interest of *both*. The rules that are most in the interest of *both* must be in the long run the rules that are most in the interest of *each*. This remains true when our hypothetical society is increased from A and B to everybody from A to Z.

This *mutualism* is the reconciliation of "self-interest" and "morality." For one best promotes one's own interest in the long run precisely by abiding by the rules that best promote the interest of *everyone*, and by cooperating with others to hold everyone *else* to those rules. If it is to *everyone's* long-run interest to adhere to and uphold the moral rules, it must therefore be to *mine*.

To sum up: The ideal moral rules are those that are most conducive to social cooperation and therefore to the realization of the greatest possible number of interests for the greatest possible number of people. The very function of morality, as Toulmin has put it, is "to correlate our feelings and behavior in such a way as to make the fulfilment of everyone's aims and desires as far as possible compatible." [23] But just as *all* interests, major and minor, long-term and short-term, cannot be realized all the time (partly because some are inherently unachievable and partly because some are incompatible with others) so not *everybody's* interests can be realized all the time. If we think of such a rare crisis example as people taking to the lifeboats of a sinking ship, then an orderly and mutualistic procedure, as contrasted with a disorderly and sordid stampede, will maximize the number of people who can be saved. But even in the "moral" procedure *some* people may have to be sacrificed. And though they will be *fewer* people than would have been sacrificed in an immoral scramble, they may none the less be *different* people. A few of those who are lost *may* have been among those who could have saved themselves by ruthlessness. The ideal moral rules, therefore, may not only sometimes oblige an individual to make some immediate or temporary sacrifice in his own long-run interest, but even (though very rarely) to sacrifice even his own long-run interest to the larger long-run interest of everybody else.

We come back once more to the conclusion that the real interests of the individual and of society nearly always *coincide,* but are not (such is our human predicament) in every case *identical.*

CHAPTER 15

Ends and Means

1. *How Means Become Ends*

All men act. They act purposefully. They employ means to achieve ends. This may seem elementary. Yet there has been no more fertile source of confusion in ethical philosophy than that concerning means and ends.

"Ends" may be "pluralistic," as many moral philosophers insist, but only if we recognize that this refers to subordinate or intermediate ends. Ends are never *irreducibly* pluralistic. In choosing between subordinate ends, as we constantly find ourselves obliged to do, we are necessarily guided by a preference of one over the other. And this preference is based on our judgment that one of these "ends" is more nearly an ultimate end for us, or at least a better means of realizing a more ultimate end, than the other.

Thus intermediate ends are at once means and ends. I am tempted to coin a new word, "means-ends," to emphasize this dual nature.

Our immediate end may always be described as a satisfaction or the removal of a dissatisfaction. Even our ultimate end may be described as the attainment of a state of affairs that suits us better than the alternatives.[1] But in achieving any end we have to use means that in turn we may come to think of as ends. A man and his wife, living in New York, may decide to take a trip to the Greek islands. They think of this as their end, though it could also be thought of as merely the means to achieve the enjoyment they expect to get out of the trip. But as they have never been abroad before, they decide that on the way they will visit London, Paris and Rome. Each of these visits then in turn becomes an end. They decide to go by boat; but this means of crossing the ocean is then also regarded as an end in itself. The man's wife, say, regards the ocean voyage as "the most enjoyable part of the trip," in which case, to her, what was originally merely a means to a more ultimate end becomes an end valued higher than the original end.

And this transformation of means into ends is illustrated in a whole life. A man not only wishes to protect himself against hunger and cold; he wishes to have a comfortable and attractive home, to marry and raise children, to send them to college. To achieve these more ulterior ends, he needs money. "Making money" then becomes both a means and a secondary end. To make money he must get a job. Getting a job is both a means and a tertiary end. Thus action and life are like a flight of steps in which each step is an end in relation to the preceding one and a means in relation to the next one.

The wise man tends to see his work, recreations, and ambitions in this dual way. He does not live wholly in the present moment. That would be to make no prudent provision for the future. He does not live wholly in the future. That would be never to enjoy the present moment. He lives in both the present and the future. He enjoys himself as he goes along, savoring life; but he also sets himself a goal or goals towards which he tries to make further progress.

The ideal balance is not easy to achieve. Our temperament or habits may lead us to err on one side or the other. One error is to think of everything merely as a means to something else; to become lost in work or duty; to be driven on, without ever savoring the fruits of past success, by a restless ambition that is never satisfied; to be, as Emerson put it, "always getting ready to live, but never living." Another error is to forget that something is primarily a means and to treat it only as an end in itself. A typical example of this perversion is the miser, constantly piling up money and working for still more, but never spending it.

2. *Dewey, Kant, and Mill*

The same confusions regarding means and ends that people fall into in practical life exist also in the theories of moral philosophers. An outstanding example of the tendency to blur entirely the distinction between means and ends—to reduce all means to ends and all ends to means, to insist that nothing, even ideals, can be regarded as constant or permanent, to demand that everything must be always moving, changing, forward-gazing—is found in John Dewey: "The end is no longer a terminus or limit to be reached. It is the active process of transforming the existent situation. . . . Growth itself is the only moral end." [2]

The question that immediately occurs to one is, Growth toward what? Should men grow twelve feet tall, and keep growing? Should population, overcrowding, noise, traffic jams, government power, delinquency, crime, filth, cancer, keep growing? If growth itself is the only moral end, then the growth of pain and misery is as much a moral end as the growth of happiness, and the growth of evil as much a moral end as the growth of good. The glorification of growth for growth's sake, change for change's sake, movement for movement's sake, reminds one of an old popular song, which went: "I don't know where I'm going, but I'm on my way!" Ethical values and ideals, as well as the distinction between means and ends, are dissolved and vaporized in such a philosophy.

But the opposite error, of regarding means as ultimate ends or ultimate ideals, is perhaps more frequent among traditional moral philosophers. This error is most conspicuous in a writer like Kant, whose concept of duty for duty's sake will be examined in our next chapter. But it is also found, in somewhat milder form, even in modern writers who call themselves "Ideal Utilitarians," such as Hastings Rashdall.[3] "The view that we have arrived at is that the morality of our actions is to be determined ultimately by its tendency to promote a universal end, which end consists of many ends, and in particular two—Morality and pleasure." [4] In other places Rashdall substitutes the words Virtue and Happiness as if they were synonymous with these, and implies that "the Good" consists of these two elements.

Now if the *Ultimate* End consists of *both* Virtue and Happiness, it becomes impossible to resolve either into terms of the other. They then become not only incommensurable, but incomparable. So when we are confronted with the problem of which of two courses to adopt, one of which is conducive to more Virtue but to less Happiness, and the other of which is conducive to more Happiness and to less Virtue, or one of which will tend to increase Virtue more than Happiness and the other to increase Happiness more than Virtue, how can we decide which course to take?

Ends need not necessarily be commensurable, but they must be comparable;[5] otherwise there is no way to choose or decide between them. This is another way of saying that we cannot have "pluralistic" or heterogeneous *ultimate* ends. When we are confronted by two or more alleged ultimate ends, or two or more alleged "parts" of an ultimate end, neither or none of which can be reduced to the other or expressed in terms of the other, we shall do well to suspect that we are dealing merely with a confusion of thought, and that one of the two "ultimate" ends is really a means to the other.

Let us examine the confusion as it occurs in Kant. Kant is usually, and rightly, regarded as the arch antihedonist and antiutilitarian; but in one remarkable passage he assigns so important a role to happiness that he seems to teeter on the verge of eudaemonism:

"*Virtue* (as worthiness to be happy) is the *supreme condition* of all that can appear to us desirable, and consequently of all our pursuit of happiness, and is therefore the *supreme* good. But it does not follow that it is the whole and perfect good as the object of the desires of rational beings; this requires happiness also. . . . Now inasmuch as virtue and happiness together constitute the possession of the *summum bonum* in a person, and the distribution of happiness in exact proportion to morality (which is the worth of the person, and his worthiness to be happy) constitutes the *summum bonum* of a possible world; hence this *summum bonum* expresses the whole, the perfect good, in which, however, virtue as the condition is always the supreme good, since it has no condition above it; whereas happiness, while it is pleasant to the possessor of it, is not of itself absolutely and in all respects good, but always presupposes morally right behavior as its condition." [6]

Kant's subsequent discussion of the relationship of Virtue and Happiness is so confused that it seems unprofitable to follow it further. He concludes, among other things, that "happiness and morality are two specifically *distinct elements of the summum bonum,* and therefore their combination *cannot* be analytically cognized." [7] In the course of his argument he states but rejects the answer of "The Epicurean": "The Epicurean maintained that happiness was the whole *summum bonum,* and virtue only the form of the maxim for its pursuit, viz. the rational use of the means for attaining it." [8]

Yet if we interpret happiness in this context as referring not merely to the short-run happiness of the agent but to the general long-run happiness of the community, then this "Epicurean" view is obviously the correct solution. The ultimate end is happiness. Virtue is a necessary long-run *means* to that end.

Bertrand Russell has put the point clearly and simply: "What is called good conduct is conduct which is a means to other things which are good on their own account." [9]

Some people will be shocked at this, because they will interpret it as a downgrading of virtue or morality to a *mere* means. But a necessary means to a great end is seldom regarded by us as a *mere* means; it becomes an (intermediate or penultimate) end in itself; it even becomes in our minds an indispensable part or ingredient of the ultimate end.

All this was clearly recognized by John Stuart Mill in his *Utilitarianism:*

> Whatever may be the opinion of utilitarian moralists as to the original conditions by which virtue is made virtue; however they may believe (as they do) that actions and dispositions are only virtuous because they promote another end than virtue; . . . they not only place virtue at the very head of the things which are good as means to the ultimate end, but they also recognize as a psychological fact the possibility of its being, to the individual, a good in itself, without looking to any end beyond it; . . . as a thing desirable in itself, even although, in the individual instance, it should not produce those other desirable consequences which it tends to produce, and on account of which it is held to be virtue.[10]

G. E. Moore later had great sport with Mill for the whole passage of which this is a part, accusing him of "glaring contradiction," and of having "broken down the distinction between means and ends." "We shall hear next," Moore went on, "that this table is really and truly the same thing as this room." [11] Mill did lapse into some contradictions, but his discussion of the relation of means and ends was psychologically correct. There *is* a distinction between means and ends, indispensable for the intelligent conduct of life. But it is not an *objective* distinction, like that between a table and a room. The distinction between means and ends is *subjective*. Means and ends have meaning only in relation to human purposes and human satisfactions, and, for each individual, in relation to *his* purposes and *his* satisfactions. An object cannot be now a table and now a room, but it may very well be now a means and now an end. It can even be *simultaneously* a means and end, *both* a means and an end, an *intermediate* end, if we so treat it and regard it in achieving our purposes and deriving our satisfactions.

3. Virtue Is Instrumental

In short, we agree to *call* Virtue and Morality precisely those actions, dispositions, and rules of action that tend in the long run to promote Happiness. Actions and dispositions that tend in the long run *not* to promote Happiness, or to promote only pain or misery, we agree to call Vice or Immorality.

Hence when a satirical writer like Mandeville writes *The Fable of the Bees, or Private Vices Made Public Benefits* (1705), and argues that it is really the "vices" (i.e., the self-regarding actions of men) that, through luxurious living and extravagance, stimulate all invention, action and progress by circulating money and capital, what he is really saying is that what we call the vices we should call the virtues, and what we call the virtues we should call the vices. Mandeville was not wrong in principle (i.e., so far as the principle of the relationship of means and ends is concerned); he was wrong in his conclusion only because his economics were wrong. (Like his later disciple Keynes, he assumed that saving led only to economic stagnation and that only extravagance in consumption stimulated industry and trade.)

Whenever we are trying to discover which is means and which end, or which of two ends is ulterior, the test is simple. We have merely to ask ourselves two main questions, such as: Would it be better to have more Virtue (or Morality) in the world at the cost of less Happiness? Or would it be better to have more Happiness at the cost of less Virtue? The moment such questions are posed, it becomes obvious that, as between these two, Happiness is the ulterior end and Virtue or Morality the means.

134   THE FOUNDATIONS OF MORALITY

Clarity on this point is so important that it is worth risking excessive repetition to achieve it. To recognize that something is primarily a means—in this case Virtue—is not to deny that it has a high value also in itself. It is merely to deny that it has a value completely *independent* of its utility or necessity as a means. We may make the relation clear by an analogy from the world of economic value. Capital goods derive their value from the consumer goods they help to produce. The value of a plow or a tractor is derived from the value of the crops that it helps to create. The value of a shoe factory and its equipment is derived from the value of the shoes it helps to produce. If the crops or the shoes ceased to be needed, or ceased to be valued, the means that helped to produce them would also lose their value. What we call morality has tremendous value because it is an indispensable means of achieving human happiness.

(Some readers may object that the phrase I have frequently been using to describe the ultimate end, "Happiness and Well-Being," really describes two ends, and that a test similar to the one I applied as between Happiness and Virtue should be applied as between Happiness and Well-Being to resolve the dualism and clarify the relationship. But when we ask: "Would it be better to have more [human] Happiness at the cost of less [human] Well-Being?"; or, "Would it be better to have more Well-Being at the cost of less Happiness?" we immediately perceive that the question cannot be meaningfully answered because we are simply dealing with synonyms that describe precisely the same thing. I have frequently been using the full phrase because this performs a double function. It emphasizes that I am using the word *happiness* in the broadest sense possible, to indicate not mere sensual or superficial pleasure no matter how prolonged, but to *mean* "everything that seems to us worth aiming at." And the full phrase emphasizes also that when I use the words "happiness" and "well-being" I am talking of precisely the same thing, and not of two different things, as Rashdall and other "Ideal Utilitarians" imagine they are).[12]

I have frequently spoken in this chapter of "ultimate ends," by which I have meant simply ends pursued solely for their own sake and not also as means to something further. I have even occasionally spoken, as above, of *"the* ultimate end," using this merely as a synonym for "long-run happiness and well-being."

But in the interests of psychological realism I am perfectly willing to accept the qualification suggested by C. L. Stevenson:

"If [a writer on normative ethics] is sensitive to the plurality of ends that people habitually have in view, he will scarcely seek to exalt some one factor as *the* end, reducing everything to the exclusive status of means. . . . If he wishes general, unifying principles, he must attend not to 'the end,' and not even to 'ends,' exclusively, but rather to focal aims. . . . A focal aim is something valued partly as an end, perhaps, but largely as the indispensable means to a multitude of other ends. It may play a unifying role in normative ethics; for once it is established, the value of a great many other things, being a means to *it,* can probably be established in their turn." [13]

That is why, though in the ethical system I am here proposing "the ultimate end" is Human Happiness, I have thought it preferable to put my emphasis on the "focal aim"—Social Cooperation.

4. *Does the End Justify the Means?*

We come now to a further problem concerning the relationship of means and ends. Does the end justify the means?

Now we can answer this question affirmatively or negatively, depending upon how we interpret the terms of the question itself. Let us begin with the negative answer, because it is the one most frequently made by moral philosophers. I cannot do better than quote Aldous Huxley:

> Good ends . . . can be achieved only by the employment of appropriate means. The end cannot justify the means, for the simple and obvious reason that the means employed determine the nature of the ends produced. . . .[14]

Our personal experience and the study of history make it abundantly clear that the means whereby we try to achieve something are at least as important as the end we wish to attain. Indeed, they are even more important. For the means employed inevitably determine the nature of the result achieved; whereas, however good the end aimed at may be, its goodness is powerless to counteract the effects of the bad means we use to reach it.[15]

These quotations make clear that what people mean when they say that "the end does *not* justify the means" is simply that *evil* means cannot be justified on the argument that they are being pursued in order to achieve a "good" end. But the reason most of us accept this adage is that we do not believe that really evil means are ever necessary or that they *can* in fact lead to a really good end.

Let us look at the argument as it is stated by A. C. Ewing:

> It is still often felt that ideal utilitarianism is not ethically satisfactory. One reason for this is because it seems to lead to the principle that "the end justifies the means," a principle commonly rejected as immoral. If the end is the greatest good possible and the means necessary to attain it include great moral evils such as deceit, injustice, gross violation of individual rights or even murder, the utilitarian will have to say that these things are morally justified, provided only their moral evil is exceeded by the goodness of the results, and this seems a downright immoral doctrine, and certainly a very dangerous one (as is shown by its applications in recent times in politics.)[16]

Ewing seems to me here to be (no doubt unconsciously) misrepresenting the position of the utilitarian, and certainly that of the *rule*-utilitist. The rule-utilitist would say that ordinarily "immoral" means could in a specific situation be justified, not only provided "their moral evil is exceeded by the goodness of the results," but provided these means were *the only possible way* to attain these good results, and provided *also* that these means led on net balance to *greater* long-run good than any other means.

This is, in fact, the answer of a rule-utilitist like John Hospers:

> Sometimes the end justifies the means and sometimes it doesn't. . . . Even when the means involves agonizing sacrifice, the end may justify it if it can be achieved in no other way and if the end is worth it.
>
> But when is the end worth the means? If the end is removal of war from the face of the earth and the means is the death of a few thousand human beings now, the utilitarian would say that the end is so supremely worthwhile that it justifies the means, *provided* that the means really involves no more evil than the statement indicates (often the evils involved in the means lead to other evils so that in the final analysis the means contains far more evil than the end does good), and *provided* that the end

really will be achieved once this means is taken (there must be no slip), and *provided* that the end can be achieved by no other means that involves *less* evil than this one. In actual practice, the end doesn't justify the means as often as one might think because these conditions are not met.[17]

We must be very slow, in brief, to adopt means that involve evil even to secure the most desirable ends. We must tolerate, for example, even major injustices and suppressions of liberty before we resort to the certain evils of armed rebellion or revolution or civil war. And especially in today's world we must tolerate national insults and serious aggressions before we let loose the appalling disaster of nuclear war.

But the exact amount of injustice or suppression or aggression it is wise to tolerate before we resort to rebellion or war is a question that abstract ethical principles alone cannot answer. We are compelled to weigh alternatives and probabilities and to fall back upon our practical judgment in a specific situation.

It is not always a question, unfortunately, of whether "evil" means can ever lead to "good"; it is too often a question, in the actual world in which we live, of whether means generally and rightly regarded as evil may not sometimes be unavoidable to terminate or prevent a still greater evil.

We may illustrate this by answering a question raised by Ewing. "Might not a lie be justified to save an invalid from death or prevent a war?" [18] Any sensible person must admit (as against Kant, for example) that there are times, however rare, when a lie can be justified. If so, a lie in such circumstances is relatively "right." The supreme example of the folly of sanctifying the means while forgetting the end is probably found in Fichte's declaration: "I would not tell a lie to save the universe from destruction." We may continue to say (as Kant and Fichte do) that lying is always an evil; but we may add that in some circumstances it may be necessary to avert a still greater evil. And we may say the same of resort to armed rebellion or to war. This principle is also the only possible justification for capital punishment.

In brief, our choice is sometimes forced. When we are reduced to a choice of evils, we must choose the lesser.

To sum up the central theme of this chapter: The *logical* distinction between ends and means is basic. To admit that men act purposively is to admit that they drive toward *ends*. They must necessarily employ *means* to achieve them. Yet certain objects or activities can become ends in themselves as well as means to other ends. A man may work at a certain job not only for the money, but also because he enjoys the work itself. The primary purpose of his work is to earn money. This may therefore be said to be his "end." But he regards the money itself chiefly as a *means* to other ends.[19]

Thus we strive for *intermediate* ends that in turn become means toward still further ends. It is therefore not always possible to say *precisely* how much we value something "instrumentally" and how much "intrinsically." But it is always possible to be clear-headed about the distinction. Morality must be valued primarily as a *means* to human happiness. Because it is an *indispensable* means, it must be valued very highly. But its value is *primarily* "instrumental" or *derivative,* and it is only confusion of thought to hold that its value is something wholly apart from, and independent of, any contribution it may make to human happiness.

CHAPTER 16

Duty for Duty's Sake

1. *Mistaking Means for Ends*

We come now to the doctrine that we ought to perform our "duty" simply because it is our "duty"—the doctrine, in other words, that morality has no other end beyond itself. Before the formulation of utilitarianism, this was the most commonly accepted view, and it still has a tremendous hold on men's minds. In its modern form, however, it was most explicitly formulated by Immanuel Kant, and it is in that form that it is most convenient to examine it.

Let us begin by trying to clear away a central ambiguity. "Duty for duty's sake" may mean that when our duty is clear—i.e., when once we recognize or acknowledge that a certain course of action is right—that is the action we ought to take, whether at the moment we like it or not. This is merely another way of saying that a man should always do his duty, that he should always act morally, regardless of his immediate inclinations.

But "duty for duty's sake" may also mean that a man should always act blindly in accordance with some rigid rule, not only without examining what the probable immediate consequences of his action will be in those particular circumstances, but without considering even the long-run consequences (for happiness or misery, good or evil) of acting in accordance with that rule. It would be hard to find a better description of irrational conduct.

Yet Kant himself appears to have been guilty of this as well as of a whole complex of other ambiguities and confusions. He held, among other things, that nothing was truly and unconditionally good except the good will. The only act that really deserved to be called moral, in his opinion, was an act done from a sense of duty, an act done because it was thought right, and for no other reason.

140   THE FOUNDATIONS OF MORALITY

This view has brought down on his head the caustic satire of Bertrand Russell:

> Kant was never tired of pouring scorn on the view that the good consists of pleasure, or of anything except virtue. And virtue consists in acting as the moral law enjoins, *because* that is what the moral law enjoins. A right action done from any other motive cannot count as virtuous. If you are kind to your brother because you are fond of him, you have no merit; but if you can hardly stand him and are nevertheless kind to him because the moral law says you should be, then you are the sort of person that Kant thinks you ought to be. [And Russell concludes that if Kant] believed what he thinks he believes, he would not regard heaven as a place where the good are happy, but as a place where they have never-ending opportunities of doing kindnesses to people whom they dislike.[1]

But if Russell is one of the most caustic critics of the Kantian view, he is not the first. He has been anticipated by scores of moral philosophers. Even Schiller, otherwise an admirer of Kant, travesties this view in lines in which he has a disciple of Kant complain:

> Gladly, I serve my friends, but alas I do it with pleasure.
> Hence I am plagued with the doubt that I am not a virtuous person.

In reply to which he gets the advice:

> Sure, your only resource is to try to despise them entirely,
> And then with aversion to do what your duty enjoins you.[2]

One reason for Kant's error is that he looked with the deepest suspicion on all desire or natural inclination itself, because he assumed that all desire was desire for pleasure, and pleasure in the narrow or carnal sense. But he slid into this error also for a more subtle reason, which it will be instructive to explore. When Kant assumed that an action, no matter how beneficent in result, was not moral if done from natural inclination but only if done *against* natural inclination, "for duty's sake," his error was the result of a confusion easily explicable on psychological grounds. When we perform a beneficent act out of love or completely spontaneous benevolence we are not *conscious* of "doing our duty." It is only when we have a *disinclination* toward an act and nevertheless "force" ourselves to do it, in the conviction that it is our duty, that we are *conscious* of "doing our duty."

This, I think, explains the psychological genesis of Kant's error. Moral action is action which is conducive to general well-being, regardless of whether it is done spontaneously or from conscious (or reluctant) adherence to duty.

The germ of truth in Kant's position is that it is always our duty to do what is right, *whether we want to do so or not*. But this comes down to the tautology that it is always our duty to do our duty.

Perhaps a slight digression may be necessary at this point. So far in this chapter (and in this book) we have been using the word *duty* without raising the question of the validity of the concept and without specifically asking: *"Why* should I do my duty?" We have simply taken the concept of duty for granted. This is because it is, in fact, implicit in all ethics. In origin, duty means what is *due,* what is *owing*—to one's family, friends, associates, employer, and other persons in general. One's duty means: what one has an *obligation* to do.

Doing one's duty is not necessarily coextensive with morality. It is something different from doing the right thing, in the sense of the best or wisest thing, or the thing that would promote the greatest good of the greatest number. Your duty, in this restricted sense, would be a special obligation or responsibility that fell specifically upon you because of your vocation or special relation. Thus it could be said of a lifeguard who saved a drowning woman's life that "He was only doing his duty"—and by implication deserved no special credit. In this sense, one's duty is merely that which would be wrong if you did *not* do it. If another swimmer who was not a lifeguard had saved the woman, however, perhaps at considerable risk to himself, then he would properly be praised for doing *more* than his duty, as soldiers are sometimes honored for "conduct beyond the call of duty." It can be said in favor of this more restricted concept of duty that it refrains from laying limitless obligations upon people. Thus Kurt Baier maintains that: "No one ever has a duty to do something simply because it would be beneficial to someone if he did it." And again: "We are morally required to do good only to those who are actually in need of our assistance. The view that we always ought to do the optimific act . . . would have the absurd result that we are doing wrong whenever we are relaxing, since on those occasions there will always be opportunities to produce greater good than we can by relaxing."[3]

But the concept of one's *duties* implies that there are certain obligations we are bound to respect, and certain rules of action we are bound to follow, at all times. Most of these rules of action have been determined in advance by human experience, thought, and tradition. They act as guides, as touchstones, relieving us from the necessity of making elaborate calculations of the probable consequences of this decision or that in every new situation that confronts us. They cannot, as Kant supposed, always give simple and certain answers. But their existence saves us from having to solve every moral problem *ab initio*. (A very instructive contribution is the concept of *"prima facie* duties" elaborated by Sir David Ross.)[4]

To return after this digression to what we have found to be the germ of truth in Kant's position: It is always our duty to do what is right, whether we like it or not. But that it is *sometimes* necessary to remind ourselves of our duty and force ourselves to do it against our inclination does not mean, as he went on to imply, that these occasions are the only ones in which we are acting morally. In fact, one of the paradoxical consequences to which Kant's doctrine leads is this. A man who spontaneously radiates good will toward other men, or who has in early life formed the habit of always acting morally, will more and more tend to act that way habitually and spontaneously, rather than from a conscious sense of duty. Therefore he will, according to Kant, be less and less frequently acting "morally"—or he will at least be accorded less moral merit than he would doing the right thing *reluctantly* from a sense of duty.

It is clear that Kant mistakes means for ends, a confusion into which moral philosophers are particularly liable to slip. As Bertrand Russell has put it: "The moralist . . . being primarily concerned with conduct, tends to become absorbed with means, to value the actions men ought to perform more than the ends which such actions serve."[5] So Kant came to think that we could judge the rightness or wrongness of acts without considering the consequences to which they led in the way of happiness or satisfaction, good or evil, to ourselves or anybody else.

But if actions or rules of action are not to be judged by their probable consequences, how are we to know what actions are right or wrong? Here Kant's position is peculiar. He does not seem to hold that we know our duty in each case *a priori* or from direct intuition, but he does hold that we can determine our duty from certain *a priori* principles, and he proceeds to try to find and to formulate these principles.

2. *The Test of Universalizability*

He puts forward first of all his famous notion of a Categorical Imperative. Duty is a categorical imperative, because when we see a thing to be right, we feel commanded to do it categorically, and absolutely, as a means to no end beyond itself. It is "objectively necessary." This is to be distinguished from a mere *hypothetical* imperative, which represents "the practical necessity of a possible action as means to something else that is willed," [6] such as keeping healthy, being happy, or going to Heaven. Now a hypothetical imperative depends on what our particular end happens to be, but "the mere conception of a categorical imperative" supplies us also with the formula for it. "There is therefore but one categorical imperative, namely, this: *Act only on that maxim whereby thou canst at the same time will that it should become a universal law.*" [7]

There is a prima facie attractiveness about this maxim, but Kant's effort to deduce a code of morals from it seems to me a complete failure. A code of morals can be deduced only by consideration of the actual or probable consequences of acts or of rules of actions, and the desirability or undesirability of those consequences. Kant tries to prove that non-observance of his maxim would involve a logical contradiction; but the examples he gives fail to do this. Thus his argument against lying is that if everybody lied nobody would be believed, so that lying would be futile and self-defeating. This does not prove, however, that there is anything *logically* contradictory about universal lying; it merely points out that one of the consequences would be bad. Kant's argument here is, in fact, an appeal to practical consequences, and not to the worst ones, which are the harm that the lying would do the victims as long as they believed it, and the breakdown of almost all social cooperation once people knew that they could not trust each other's words or promises.

Kant's test of universalizability, properly interpreted, might express a necessary but not a sufficient condition of moral rules. It would apply for example, against Aristotle's magnanimous or great-souled man, who "is fond of conferring benefits, but ashamed to receive them." [8] We can hardly imagine two of Aristotle's great-souled men getting on very well together. Each would be pressing favors on the other, which the other would spurn as insulting. Kant's maxim would also apply as against Nietzsche's superman. It is impossible for everyone to practice a master morality; to act as a master one needs at least one slave. In order to make Nietzsche's master morality workable for even half the population, the other half must accept a slave or anti-Nietzschean morality.

On the other hand, there are courses of conduct which are certainly moral, even though they cannot be universalized, and even though the person who adopts them would not wish them to be universalized. A man may decide to become a minister or a lawyer; but everybody cannot decide to become a minister or a lawyer, because we would all starve. A man may decide to learn the violin without wishing that everybody should learn to play the violin. In fact, if he expected to make his living at it, he would wish, to increase his own scarcity value and income, that as few other people as possible would become competent violinists.

It may be replied that this is mere quibbling; that Kant obviously did not intend his maxim of universalizability to apply to the adoption of a specific trade or vocation; that the universal maxim to fit such a case might be: "In the interests of division of labor, everyone should adopt *some* trade or vocation," or: "Everyone should adopt the trade or profession to which he is best suited (or in which he can be most useful)." But what, then, are the permissible rules for generality or specificity in framing a "universal" law? "Everybody else can lie, but only when caught in the particular kind of jam that I find myself in now?" Kant himself was a bachelor and a celibate. Could he have willed that everyone should be celibate? What was the wording of the universal law that permitted him to be so?

What value, finally, has the Kantian maxim? We can conclude, I think, that it does have a certain negative value. It points out that our moral rules must not be inconsistent with each other. We are not entitled to exempt our own conduct from the moral rules that we would wish to see followed by others. We are not entitled to adopt for ourselves maxims which we would be horrified to find others acting on. We are not entitled to justify our own conduct by an excuse that we would not accept from anybody else. Moral rules, in short, like legal rules, should be drafted with as much generality as possible, and should be applied to ourselves, our friends, and our enemies, *impartially,* without discrimination or favoritism. They should be no respecter of persons. They should also meet the condition of *reversibility,* i.e., they must be acceptable to a person whether he is at the giving or receiving end of an action.[9]

But none of this helps us in any substantive way to determine precisely what our moral rules should be. It might be universally possible, or nearly so, for everybody to smoke cigarettes or to drink whisky; but this is hardly sufficient ground to regard either as a duty.

There is no way, in fact, to adopt or frame moral rules except by considering the consequences of acting on those rules and the desirability or undesirability of those consequences. Kant's categorical imperative does, in fact, rest on an unacknowledged consideration of consequences. What he is saying, in effect, is: "Lying is wrong, because if everybody lied the consequences would be so-and-so." But he does not show that there is any *logical contradiction* in everybody's lying. All that he shows (and it is enough) is that the consequences would be such that we would not like them.

But this kind of argument makes the moral case against lying seem weaker than it really is. Lying would not be wrong merely if it were adopted as a universal rule. Nearly every individual lie does some harm. Of course the more widespread lying became, the more harm it would do. But lying no more than murder is to be condemned *merely* because it cannot be universalized. In fact, either *could* be universalized; we simply would not like the consequences. Murder could be universalized until only one man was left on earth, and even he would then be perfectly free to commit self-murder. Universal celibacy would also extinguish mankind; but Kant did not therefore regard his own celibacy as a crime.

At the cost of repetition, let us state the preceding argument in another form. Suppose we take Kant's categorical imperative: "Act only on that maxim which thou canst at the same time will to become a universal law," and translate it into current colloquial English. We then get: "Act only on a rule that you wish to see generally followed by everyone." This is merely saying that you have no right to treat yourself as an exception. It is saying that morality consists in a set of rules of conduct that ought to be followed by everyone; that it does harm and destroys morality for each or anyone to treat himself as an exception. But it tells us nothing of what the content of the rule or set of rules should be. *It in fact implicitly takes utilitarian criteria for granted.* For each of us would want to see universally followed the rules that would tend to maximize happiness and minimize pain and misery—his own and that of others. Kant did not see that his categorical imperative, as he stated it, rested on a basic *desire* of the individual. The rule that the individual *wills* to see universally followed is the rule he *wishes* to see universally followed, the rule he *desires* to see universally followed. Kant was a crypto-rule-utilitarian.

3. *Kant's Other Maxims*

So much, then, for Kant's most famous maxim. But the categorical imperative is supposed to yield two other rules of action, and while we are dealing with Kant we may just as well examine them. The first of them is: *"So act as to treat humanity, whether in thine own person or in that of any other, in every case as an end withal, never as a means only."* [10]

Ewing tells us that:

> These words of Kant have had as much influence as perhaps any sentence written by a philosopher; they serve indeed as a slogan of the whole liberal and democratic movement of recent times. They rule out slavery, exploitation, lack of respect for another's dignity and personality, the making of the individual a mere tool of the State, violations of rights. They formulate the

greatest moral idea of the day, perhaps one might add the greatest moral (as distinct from "religious") idea of Christianity.[11]

Kant himself tells us that his maxim rules out lying promises to others and attacks on the freedom or property of others.

But two questions obtrude themselves. The first is whether we need this maxim to establish the immorality of lying, stealing, or coercion. Are the rules against lying, stealing, coercion, violations of rights, etc., in other words, mere *corollaries* of Kant's maxim? Or can they be established independently of this maxim?

The second question is whether Kant's maxim taken in isolation is definite, adequate, or even true. We are constantly using each other merely as means. This is practically the essence of all "business relations." We use the porter to carry our bags from the station; we use the taxicab driver to take us to our hotel; we use the waiter to bring us our food and the chef to prepare it. And the porter, taxicab driver, waiter, and chef, in turn, use us merely as a means of getting the income by which they in turn are enabled to use people to furnish them with what they want. We all use each other as "mere" means to secure our wants. In turn, we all lend ourselves or our resources to the furtherance of other people's purposes as an indirect means of furthering our own.[12] This is the basis of social cooperation.

Of course we do treat our close friends and the members of our immediate family as "ends" as well as means. We may even be said to treat trades people as ends when we inquire about their health or their children. We do owe it to others, even (and especially) when they are in the position of servants or subordinates, to treat them always with civility, politeness, and respect for their human dignity. And, of course, we should always acknowledge and respect each other's rights. The world could have arrived, and did arrive, at these acknowledged duties and rules largely without the benefit of Kant's maxim. But perhaps the maxim does help to clarify and unify them.

Kant's third maxim, or third form of the categorical imperative, "Act as a member of a kingdom of ends," seems to be little more than another form of the second maxim. We should treat ourselves and others as ends; we should regard every human being as having equal rights; we should regard the good of others as equal to our own. This seems to be merely another way of framing the requirements of justice and of equality before the law.

The truth is, to repeat, that the mere capability of a rule's being consistently or universally followed is not in itself a test of the goodness or badness of the rule. That can be determined only by considering the consequences of following it and the desirability or undesirability of those consequences. Morality is primarily a means—a necessary means to human happiness. If we declare that duty should be done merely for duty's sake, without regard to the ends that are served by doing our duty, we leave ourselves with no way of deciding what our duty, in any particular situation, really is or ought to be.

In addition to mistaking means for ends, Kant tremendously oversimplified the moral problem. That is why he held, for example, that a lie was *never* justified, even, say, to avert a murder. He refused to recognize that situations could arise in which two or more ordinarily sound rules or principles could conflict, or in which we might be forced to choose, not absolute good, but the least of two or more evils. But this is our human predicament.

If I may summarize the conclusions of this chapter, I cannot do so better than in the words of F. H. Bradley, taken from his own essay with the same title. Bradley's essay takes off, by his own confession, from Hegel, and like most of what he wrote on ethical theory, it is by turns perverse, unintelligible, and stuffed with paradoxes and self-contradictions. But its final paragraphs emerge into a brilliant sunlight of common sense:

> Is duty for duty's sake a valid formula, in the sense that we are to act always on a law and nothing but a law, and that a law can have no exceptions, in the sense of particular cases where it is overruled? No, this takes for granted that life is so simple that we never have to consider more than one duty at a time; whereas we really have to do with conflicting duties, which as a rule escape conflict simply because it is understood which have to give way. It is a mistake to suppose that collision of duties is uncommon. . . .
>
> To put the question plainly—It is clear that in a given case I

may have several duties, and that I may be able to do only one. I must then break some "categorical" law, and the question the ordinary man puts to himself is, Which duty am I to do? He would say, "All duties have their limits and are subordinated one to another. You can not put them all in the form of your 'categorical imperative' (in the shape of a law absolute and dependent on nothing besides itself) without such exceptions and modifications that, in many cases, you might as well have left it alone altogether. . . ."

All that [the categorical imperative] comes to is this (and it is, we must remember, a very important truth), that you must never break a law of duty to please yourself, never for the sake of an end not duty, but only for the sake of a superior and overruling duty. . . .

So we see "duty for duty's sake" says only, "do the right for the sake of the right"; it does not tell us what right is. . . .[13]

CHAPTER 17

Absolutism vs. Relativism

1. *The Dilemma of Hume and Spencer*

One of the central problems of ethics is the extent to which its rules and imperatives are absolute or merely relative. The chief reason why this problem still lacks a satisfactory solution is that its very existence is so seldom explicitly recognized. On the one hand are absolutists like Kant, with his Categorical Imperative, and his tacit assumption that our duties are always simple, clear, and never in conflict. On the other hand are the ethical anarchists or *ad hoc* utilitarians who contend that general rules are unnecessary, impracticable, or absurd, and that every ethical decision must be based entirely on the particular circumstances of the moment and the specific "merits of the case." That our duties may be absolute in some respects, and relative in others, is a possibility that is too seldom considered —still less the problem of the precise limits of absolutism and relativism respectively.

One of the few moral philosophers who gave specific and extensive consideration to the problem is Herbert Spencer; and though his discussion is unsatisfactory in many respects, it states some important truths, and can still serve as a profitable starting point for consideration.

Spencer begins[1] by criticizing an early sentence (later apparently omitted) in the first edition of Henry Sidgwick's *Methods of Ethics:* "That there is in any given circumstances some one thing which ought to be done, and that this can be known, is a fundamental assumption made not only by philosophers only, but by all who perform any processes of moral reasoning." Spencer answers: "Instead of admitting that there is in every case a right and a wrong, it may be contended that in multitudinous cases no right, properly so called, can be alleged, but only a least wrong." And further, "in many of these cases . . . it is not possible to ascertain with any precision which is the least wrong."

He proceeds to give a number of illustrations. For example: "The transgressions or shortcomings of a servant vary from the trivial to the grave, and the evils which discharge may bring range through countless degrees from slight to serious. The penalty may be inflicted for a very small offense, and then there is wrong done, or, after numerous grave offenses, it may not be inflicted, and again there is wrong done. How shall be determined the degree of transgression beyond which to discharge is less wrong than not to discharge?"

He proceeds to other illustrations: Under what conditions is a merchant justified in borrowing to save himself from bankruptcy, when he is also risking the funds of the friend from whom he borrows? To what extent can a man neglect his duty to his family in fulfilling what appears to be a peremptory public duty?

The illustrations that Spencer gives of conflicting considerations and conflicting duties are all real and all valid, though perhaps comparatively trivial. This conflict may exist in the most crucial human decisions. War is a dreadful recourse. It has usually brought far greater evils in its train than those that provoked the resort to war even by those originally on the "defensive." Does this mean that no nation should ever resort to war under any provocation whatever—that it should submit to dishonor, humiliation, tribute, subservience, invasion, servility, enslavement, even annihilation? Is there any wisdom in propitiation, non-resistance, appeasement? Or does this only encourage the aggressor? At just what point is resort to war justifiable? The same questions may be asked in regard to submitting to despotism and deprivation of property or liberty, or starting a revolt or revolution of uncertain outcome or consequence. Here indeed we are confronted by choices in which there is no absolutely right but only a relatively right decision —in which, in fact, there may seem to be no solution at all that is "right" but only one that is least wrong.

Then Spencer turns to another but similar problem. He argues that the coexistence of a perfect man and an imperfect society is impossible:

> Ideal conduct, such as ethical theory is concerned with, is not possible for the ideal man in the midst of men otherwise constituted. An absolutely just or perfectly sympathetic person could

not live and act according to his nature in a tribe of cannibals. Among people who are treacherous and utterly without scruple, entire truthfulness and openness must bring ruin. If all around recognize only the law of the strongest; one whose nature will not allow him to inflict pain on others must go to the wall. There requires a certain congruity between the conduct of each member of a society and others' conduct. A mode of action entirely alien to the prevailing modes of action cannot be successfully persisted in—must eventuate in death of self, or posterity, or both.

Spencer, of course, was not the first to pose this problem. It had been raised more than a century before, with even greater force, by David Hume:

> Suppose, likewise, that it should be a virtuous man's fate to fall into the society of ruffians, remote from the protection of laws and government, what conduct must he embrace in that melancholy situation? He sees such a desperate rapaciousness prevail, such a disregard to equity, such contempt of order, such stupid blindness to future consequences, as must immediately have the most tragical conclusion and must terminate in destruction to the greater number and in a total dissolution of society to the rest. He, meanwhile, can have no other expedient than to arm himself, to whomever the sword he seizes, or the buckler, may belong; to make provision of all means of defense and security. And his particular regard to justice being no longer of *use* to his own safety or that of others, he must consult the dictates of self-preservation alone, without concern for those who no longer merit his care and attention.[2]

2. *The Mirage of Perfection*

Before examining some of the conclusions that Hume and Spencer respectively draw from this hypothetical situation, I should like to go on to examine some of the further and possibly even more basic difficulties in the conception of Absolute Ethics.

These difficulties, it seems to me, center around the concept of the Absolute and the concept of *Perfection*. I do not wish to get bogged down in the interminable discussions of the nature of the Absolute as found in metaphysical literature,[3] so I will confine myself to a discussion of the concept of Perfection.

Spencer, as we have seen, concludes that the "perfect man" can exist only in the "perfect society." If we carry his logic a step further, the perfect society can be conceived to exist only in a perfect world.

Now to attempt to frame a conception of *perfection* seems to me to involve us in insoluble problems and contradictions. Let us begin with the concept of a perfect world.

A perfect world would be one in which all our desires were instantly and completely satisfied.[4] But in such a world desire itself could not come into existence. Desire is always a desire for change of some kind—for changing a less satisfactory state of affairs into a more satisfactory (or less unsatisfactory) one. The existence of a desire presupposes, in other words, that the existing state of affairs is not completely satisfactory. All thinking is primarily problem-solving. How could thinking exist with no problems to be solved? All activity or action is a striving for something, for a change or alteration in the existing state of affairs. Why should there be any striving, any action, when conditions are already perfect? Why should I sleep or waken, dress or undress, eat or diet, work or play, smoke or drink or abstain, think or talk or move, why should I raise my hand, or let it fall, why should I desire any action or change of any kind, when everything is perfect just as it is?

Our difficulties do not appreciably decrease when we try to imagine a perfect society or a perfect man in this perfect world. There would be no place for many of the ethical qualities that most moralists admire—effort, striving, persistence, self-denial, courage, and compassion. Those who believe that the great ethical goal of each of us should be to improve others, to incite them to more virtue, would find nothing to do. He who was already perfect would not have to struggle to improve or perfect himself.

"Self-perfection" is frequently laid down as a man's only true moral goal. But those who make it the goal dodge the difficulties by tacitly assuming that it is unattainable. They suggest that a man should strive to cultivate all his faculties, ignoring the fact that he can cultivate some only by relative neglect of others. By treating "self-perfection" as an end in itself, they avoid asking themselves what a man is going to do with his perfect character after he has achieved it. For the *perfectly* moral man not only must never do the slightest amount of harm but must *always* be doing positive good—otherwise he is less than perfect.

He cannot make perfectly wise decisions unless he has infinite knowledge and clairvoyance, and can forsee all the consequences of his acts. The perfect man must exercise *unceasing* benevolence; but in a society of perfect men no one would have any opportunity or need to exercise benevolence.

In brief, it is the effort to conceive of an *absolute* ethics or a *perfect* world and society that has landed ethics, historically, into so much rhetoric and sterility. We are more likely to make sense by talking in the relative terms of *better* and *worse*. It is when we try to say what would be *worst* and what would be *best* that our difficulties mount. For to determine what is *best* is often to make a choice among an infinite number of possibilities. But if we ask, more modestly—What actions or rules of action would make things worse? What actions or rules of action would make things better?—we are often more likely to make progress. We would do well to dwell on the meaning and the important element of truth in Voltaire's aphorism: "The best is the enemy of the good."

But when we state the case against absolutism in ethics, we must be extremely careful not to overstate it, and so land in the bottomless swamp of relativism or moral anarchy. We must avoid, I think, some of the sweeping conclusions of Spencer, who decided that all present-day ethics must be Relative Ethics, and that the rules of Absolute Ethics, which contemplate only "the ideal man . . . in the ideal social state" would be framable or applicable only in some indefinite future when pain had ceased to exist and everybody was perfectly adjusted to a perfect environment. For in Spencer's "ideal" society populated only by "ideal" men there is, *ex hypothesi, no ethical problem at all*.

I have said that the instances Spencer cited of conflicting ethical duties or decisions posed real and valid problems; but I do not think they justify his conclusion that "throughout a considerable part of conduct, no guiding principle, no method of estimation, enables us to say whether a proposed course is even relatively right; as causing, proximately and remotely, specially and generally, the greatest surplus of good over evil."

Real ethical problems arise; real conflicts arise; but they are comparatively rare, and they are not insoluble. It is often difficult to say with confidence what is the *best* solution, but it is seldom difficult to say what is the worse and what is the *better* solution. Humanity has, over the generations, worked out moral traditions, rules, principles, which have survived, and are daily reinforced anew, precisely because they do solve the great majority of our moral problems, precisely because it has been found that, by adhering to them, we best achieve justice, social cooperation, and the long-run maximization of happiness or minimization of misery. We do not have to solve our daily moral problems, or make our daily moral decisions, by a fresh and special calculus of the probable total consequences of each act or decision over an infinity of time. The traditional moral rules save us from this. Only where they conflict, or are patently inadequate or inapplicable, are we thrown back on the necessity of thinking out our problem afresh, without any "guiding principle" or "method of estimation."

And even when we are thrown into the situation envisioned by Hume and Spencer we are not entirely without guiding principles. A completely moral man is not forced to be as savage and ruthless as the most savage and ruthless ruffian or scoundrel in the society, or even as savage and ruthless as the average. He is forced to defend himself and his family and his property; he must be constantly on guard against being robbed or swindled or betrayed; but he does not need himself to slaughter (except in self-defense) or rob or swindle or betray. His duty and salvation is to try to raise the average level of behavior both by setting an example and by letting others see that they do not need to fear him if they act decently.

The Hume-Spencer dilemma does show how tremendously threatening it is to individual ethics when the *general level* of ethics in a community deteriorates. The ethical standards and practices of the individual and the prevailing ethical standards and practices of the whole community are clearly *interdependent*. But if the ethical standards of the community help to determine the ethical standard of the individual, so do those of the individual help to determine those of the community. Criminals and scoundrels everywhere, invariably use as an excuse to themselves and others, that "everybody" does the crimes that they do, or "would if they had the nerve." In order to assure themselves that they are no worse than anybody else, they contend that nobody else is any better than they are. But the moral man, the man of honor, will never be satisfied to tell himself that he is as good as the average. He will recognize that his own long-run happiness, and the long-run happiness of the community, can only be furthered by *raising* the average. And this he will tend to do by his own example.

In fact, even in a "completely" demoralized community, the fear by each individual of assaults, depredations, and betrayals by others will incite individual and, finally, general efforts to restore peace and order and morality and mutual trust. Hence, when the moral "equilibrium" has been violently upset, the general unacceptability or intolerableness of the resulting situation may itself finally set in motion forces tending to restore the equilibrium. Yet irreparable harm may be done before this restoration can be brought about.

The morality of each is enormously influenced by the morality of all, and the morality of all by the morality of each. When everyone is moral, it is much easier for me to be so, and the pressure on me to be so (through the approval and disapproval of others) is also greater. But where everyone else is immoral I must fight, cheat, lie, betray, to survive—or at least I may tell myself that I must. And though self-corrective forces will doubtless finally set in, the misfortune is that an immoral social environment will probably incite immorality in the individual quicker than a moral social environment will encourage morality in him. That is why the general level of morality is never completely secure, and can be raised or even maintained only by the constant vigilance and effort of each of us.

3. Obligatory and Optional Ethics

So far in our discussion of absolute and relative ethics I have been using these terms in a different sense than that found in most contemporary discussion. Ethical "relativism" is frequently defined as meaning that morality is wholly relative to a particular place, time, or person. Sometimes it is used as a name for the doctrine that conflicting ethical opinions can be equally valid. We must reject relativism in either of these senses. There are basic moral principles that are valid for all ages and all peoples, for the simple reason that without them social life would be impossible.

This need not mean, however, that we must all be ethical

absolutists in the rigid sense, say, that Kant was. Morality is primarily a means rather than an end in itself. It exists to serve human needs—which means the needs of man as he is or can become. A society of angels would not need a moral code. We should distinguish, therefore, between a minimum acceptable ethics, to which we can insist that everybody conform, and an ethics of supererogation—conduct which we do not expect of each other, but which we applaud and marvel at when it occurs.

And do we not find, in fact, such a distinction between a minimum and a supererogatory standard implicit in our traditional commonsense ethics? For whereas that ethics *insists* on a set of *duties*, it praises a morality that goes beyond duty. As Mill points out in his *Utilitarianism*:

> It is a part of the notion of Duty in every one of its forms, that a person may rightfully be compelled to fulfill it. Duty is a thing which may be *exacted* from a person, as one exacts a debt. Unless we think that it may be exacted from him, we do not call it a duty. . . . There are other things, on the contrary, which we wish that people should do, which we like or admire them for doing, . . . but yet admit they are not bound to do.

And as J. O. Urmson writes in supplementing this:

> The trichotomy of duties, indifferent actions, and wrongdoing is inadequate. There are many kinds of action that involve going beyond duty proper, saintly and heroic actions being conspicuous examples of such kinds of action. We may look upon our duties as basic requirements to be universally demanded as providing the only tolerable basis of social life. The highest flights of morality can then be regarded as more positive contributions that go beyond what is universally to be exacted; but while not exacted publicly they are clearly equally pressing *in foro interno* on those who are not content merely to avoid the intolerable.[5]

The general moral code, in brief, should not impose excessive positive duties on us, so that we cannot even play, enjoy ourselves, or relax without a guilty conscience. Unless the code prescribes a level of conduct that most of us can reasonably hope to achieve, it will simply be disregarded. There must be definite limits to our duties. People must be allowed a moral breathing spell once in a while. The greatest happiness is promoted by rules that do not make the requirements of morality ubiquitous and oppressive. That is one reason why the negative Golden Rule: "Do not do unto others as you would not want others to do unto you" is a better rule of thumb, in most circumstances. than the positive Golden Rule.

CHAPTER 18

The Problem of Value

1. *The Value of Value*

Aldous Huxley, in his book *Ends and Means* (1937) and in some of his essays, was greatly troubled by what he thought was the verdict of "Science" regarding the existence of "Value." "Science," he thought, denied "value" and "meaning" in the Universe; yet "Science" must be wrong: life, he asserted, does have "value" and "meaning."

Huxley was completely right in declaring that life does have value and meaning, but wrong in supposing that Science proclaimed the absence of such value and meaning. Only the bad metaphysical assumptions of materialism or panphysicalism did that.

It is merely a confusion of thought to assume that Science denies value. The *physical* sciences *abstract* from value, simply because *that is not the problem with which they are concerned*. Every science abstracts from a total situation or an infinity of facts simply the particular facts or the particular aspects of the situation with which it is concerned. This abstraction is merely a methodological device, a necessary simplification. For physics, chemistry, astronomy, meteorology, mathematics, etc., human valuations, human hopes and fears, are *irrelevant*. But when human values are our *subject matter,* the case is different. And in all the "social sciences," in "praxeology," in the "sciences of human action"[1] human valuations—human actions, decisions, choices, preferences, ends and means—are precisely our subject matter.

Yet there is another possible course of confusion. Ever since Max Weber[2] it has been an established maxim that even the social sciences must be *"wertfrei,"* i.e., free from judgments of value. But this means that no writer on these subjects is entitled to impose or smuggle in *his own* valuations. If he is an economist, for example, he must deal with the valuations that he finds in the market place as his ultimate data, or "givens." He studies how market prices and values are formed. He studies the consequences of given actions and given policies. But he takes the ends of people for granted, and asks only whether the means they adopt are appropriate or likely to achieve their ends. He does not, *qua* economist, either praise or condemn their ends, and he does not undertake to substitute his own scale of values for theirs.[3]

When we come to aesthetic values or moral values, however, the matter becomes more complicated. It seems to be precisely the function of the moral philosopher to *evaluate* moral judgments and moral values. For ethics seems to be not only a study of how people do value actions, means and ends, but of how they *ought* to value actions, means and ends. It may be true that there can be no dispute about *ultimate* ends. But this does not mean that there can be no dispute concerning what *are* "ultimate" ends and what are merely means or intermediate ends, and how appropriate or efficacious these means or intermediate ends are in achieving ultimate ends.

Putting the matter another way: Economics is concerned with the actual valuations that people make; ethics with the valuations they *would* make if they always had benevolence and foresight and wisdom. It is the function of the ethical philosopher to determine what some of these valuations would be.

In any case we need have no misgivings about the value of value itself. Values are, by definition, the *only* things *worth while!* There need be no apology for them, no uneasy effort to "justify" them. The function of science is to discover the objective truth about the universe, or some particular aspect of it. But the sciences exist only because men have already decided that the objective truth is *worth* discovering. Men have recognized that it is *important*—i.e., *valuable*—to know the objective truth. That is why they think it important that science, including the sciences of human action, should be "value-free." They insist on value-free science, in brief, because they find it more valuable than argument into which an author has insinuated his own personal prejudices or value-judgments. And though men are seeking for *objective* facts or truths, they are constantly deciding *which* facts or propositions, out of an infinite possible number, are *worth* finding or proving; and *what* objective knowledge, out of infinite possible knowledge, will best serve some human purpose.

The case has been eloquently put by Santayana:

> Philosophers would do a great discourtesy to estimation if they sought to justify it. It is all other acts that need justification by this one. The good greets us initially in every experience and in every object. Remove from anything its share of excellence and you have made it utterly insignificant, irrelevant to human discourse, and unworthy of even theoretic consideration. Value is the principle of perspective in science, no less than of rightness in life. The hierarchy of goods, the architecture of values, is the subject that concerns man most. Wisdom is the first philosophy, both in time and in authority; and to collect facts or to chop logic would be idle and would add no dignity to the mind, unless that mind possessed a clear humanity and could discern what facts and logic are good for and what not. The facts would remain facts and the truths truths; for of course values, accruing on account of animal souls and their affections, cannot possibly create the universe those animals inhabit. But both facts and truths would remain trivial, fit to awaken no pang, no interest, and no rapture. The first philosophers were accordingly sages. They were statesmen and poets who knew the world and cast a speculative glance at the heavens, the better to understand the conditions and limits of human happiness. Before their day, too, wisdom had spoken in proverbs. *It is better,* every adage began: *Better this than that.* Images or symbols, mythical or homely events, of course furnished subjects and provocations for these judgments; but the residuum of all observation was a settled estimation of things, a direction chosen in thought and in life because it was better. Such was philosophy in the beginning and such is philosophy still.[4]

In sum, for human beings value not only "exists"; it is all important. It is the very standard by which we judge importance. All men act. All men seek to substitute a more satisfactory state of affairs for a less satisfactory state. All men strive for definite ends. They wish to choose the most effective or appropriate means to achieve their ends. This is why they need knowledge—knowledge of factual truth, knowledge of physical cause and effect, knowledge of science. All such knowledge helps them to choose the most effective or appropriate means for achieving their ends. Science, knowledge, logic, reason, are *means* to the achievement of ends. The value of science is primarily *instrumental* (though knowledge and the pursuit of knowledge are also valued "intrinsically" and for their own sake). But men's ultimate ends need not be justified by science; the pursuit of scientific knowledge is justified, for the greater part, as a means for the pursuit of ends beyond itself. Science must be justified by value, not value by science.

It is not Science, in any case, that denies value. It is only an arbitrary and unprovable metaphysical theory, it is only a philosophy of materialism, panphysicalism or logical positivism that attempts to deny value.[5]

2. *Subjectivism* vs. *Objectivism*

We come now to a problem that has been a source of immemorial perplexity and division of opinion in ethics. Is value "subjective" or "objective"? More often the problem has been framed in a somewhat different way: Is ethics (or are ethical rules) "subjective" or "objective"?

This dispute has proved so persistent, I think, partly because the answers have been oversimplified, and partly because the wrong questions have been asked (or, what is almost the same thing, because the wrong vocabulary has been used).

All valuation is in origin necessarily subjective. Value, like beauty, is in the eye of the beholder. All valuation implies a valuer. Valuation expresses a relation between the valuer and the thing valued. This relation depends upon the valuer's own needs, wants, desires, preferences, as well as upon his judgment regarding the extent, if any, to which the object valued will help him to realize his desires.

Objects or activities may be valued as means, or subordinate ends, or final ends. Activities or states of consciousness that are valued "purely for their own sake," as ultimate ends, are said by ethical writers to have "intrinsic" value. Though the term is widely used by ethical philosophers, it is troublesome to anyone trained in economics. Applied to an object, it implies that the value is *in the object itself,* rather than in the mind of the valuer, or in a relation between the valuer and the object. It is difficult, however, to find a satisfactory substitute for the term and the distinction it emphasizes. Objects or activities that are valued merely as means to ends may be said to have merely *instrumental* or *derivative* value. But many things—promise-keeping, truth-telling, freedom, justice, social cooperation—have both "instrumental" and "intrinsic" value.

The distinction between the two types of value in ethics is analogous to the distinction in economics between the value of consumers' goods and the value of producers' goods or capital goods. The value of capital goods is ultimately derived from the value of the consumers' goods they help to produce. Nevertheless, capital goods have the same kind of exchange value, the same kind of market value, as consumers' goods. A home, a dwelling, is a consumers' good: it is wanted for its own sake, for the direct needs it meets and the direct satisfactions it yields. A factory is a producers' good: its value is derivative: it is valued because of the value of the consumers' goods that it helps to produce, and therefore because of the monetary profit that it yields its owner. But though the value of the dwelling may be direct and "final" and "intrinsic," and the value of the factory is indirect, instrumental, and derivative, the factory has a value in the market just as the dwelling has, and may be saleable at a much higher monetary price. A final and "intrinsic" value, in brief, in the ethical as in the economic realm, is not necessarily a higher or *greater* value than a derivative or instrumental value. And many things, in the ethical as well as in the economic realm, can have both kinds of value.[6]

Let us return to the problem of subjectivity and objectivity in value. All valuation, to repeat, is in *origin* subjective. But here a major difficulty develops. *My* (subjective) opinions, estimates, valuations, and purposes are *objective* for *you*. And *your* (subjective) valuations and purposes are *objective* for *me*. That is, to me, your valuations are external facts with which I must deal (say in trying to sell something to you or buy something from you) as I am forced to deal with any other "objective" facts. And *my* valuations are "objective" facts which you must take into account as you would any other objective fact.

And just as you and I must deal with the valuations and attitudes of each other as objective facts, so each of us must deal, as objective facts, with the valuations and attitudes of all other people, or "society" as a whole. Prices in the market place are formed by the diverse valuations of individuals. They are the composite result of these diverse individual valuations. Our individual valuations have been, in turn, "socially" formed. And the market price is to each of us an objective fact by which he must guide his own actions. If the price of a house that you would dearly love to own is $25,000, this is the hard "objective" fact with which you must deal (even though this market price can be traced back to other people's subjective valuations). Unless you have or can get the $25,000, and unless you yourself (subjectively) value the house more than you (subjectively) value $25,000, you cannot or will not buy it.

And so, again, when the housewife goes to the supermarket to make her purchases, she is confronted with an enormous number of (to her) "objective" prices of different foods, different grades, and different brands, about which she must make her subjective decisions to buy or not to buy. But her own subjective decisions of yesterday (by resulting in objective actions) have helped to form today's objective prices, as her subjective decisions today will help to form tomorrow's objective prices.

So far we have been drawing our illustrations purely from the economic realm. But what is true of market prices and economic values is also true, though in a less precise way, of aesthetic, cultural, and moral values. The individual, in the whole range of his life and thought and activity, finds himself confronting and dealing with an infinitely complex set of *social* values. These are, of course, ultimately the valuations of other people; but the mutual relationship and causation are complex. Just as, in the economic realm, the infinitely diverse valuations of other people do not result in an infinite number of market prices, but, at a given time and place, just one market price for a given (homogeneous) commodity, a price that is the composite result of individual valuations, so in the political, aesthetic, cultural and moral realms we find ourselves dealing also with such *composite* valuations, which seem to have a life and existence of their own, and to stand apart from the valuations of any one individual. Thus we speak, and seem to be warranted in speaking, of *the* reputation of Beethoven, Michelangelo, or Shakespeare, of *the* sentiment of the community, of *public* opinion, of *the* moral tradition, or *the* prevailing moral code.

And this is certainly more, and something different from, a

mere "average" of everybody's opinion or valuation. Each of us individually grows up, in fact, in a world of such *social* valuations, with a *social* moral code, which, like our language, had an existence prior to any of the individuals now living, and seems to have determined their thought and opinions rather than been determined by them.

Thus value, which is in origin individual and *subjective*, becomes social, and so in this sense *objective*. This is true both of economic and of moral values. The objective heating power of coal, for example, gives it "objective" value on the market. And the rules of ethics, of course, are objective in the sense that they must be acknowledged and followed by everybody. We cannot have an ethics for one man alone that is not also the ethics of other people. The rules of ethics demand *general* acceptance and conformity. Without this there would be complete ethical disorder, anarchy, and confusion. Thus moral values are subjective from one aspect and objective from another.

3. *The Social Mind*

There is nothing inexplicable or mysterious in all this. All mental processes are in the minds of individuals. There is no social "oversoul" which transcends individual minds. There is no social "consciousness" which stands outside of and above the consciousness of individuals. Yet social moral values are a product of the interplay of many minds—including the minds of our long-dead ancestors. The individual is born into a world in which there already exists a Moral Law, which seems to stand above him, demanding the sacrifice of many of his impulses and immediate desires. There is, in brief, a realm of Social Objectivity, which seems to be set above the individual's own will and purpose.

This "social mind" is completely accounted for when all individuals (past as well as present) are completely accounted for. But it cannot be accounted for by considering these individuals *separately*. No individual is completely, or primarily, accounted for until his *relations* with the rest of society are analyzed. The individuals are *in* society, but society is more than the mere *sum* of the individuals. It is also their interrelations and *interfluences*. Men's minds *function* together, in a cooperative unity. Morality is the product of a cooperating society, the product of the interplay of many minds.

How this works out in the economic as well as in the moral realm has been brilliantly explained by the late Benjamin Anderson:

> Economic value is not intrinsic in goods, independent of the minds of men. But it is a fact which is in large degree independent of the mind of any given man. To a given individual in the market, the economic value of a good is a fact as external, as objective, as opaque and stubborn, as is the weight of the object, or the law against murder. There are individual values, marginal utilities, of goods which may differ in magnitude and in quality from man to man, but there is, over and above these, influenced by them in part, influencing them much more than they influence it, a social value for each commodity, a product of a complex social psychology, which includes individual values, but includes very much more as well.
>
> Our theory puts law, moral values, and economic values in the same general class, *species* of the *genus,* social value. . . . They are the *social forces,* which govern, in a social scheme, the actions of men.
>
> It may be well to suggest rough *differentiae* which mark off these values from one another. Legal values are social values which will be enforced, if need be, by the organized *physical* force of the group, through the government. Moral values are social values which the group enforces by approbation and disapprobation, by cold shoulders and ostracism or by honor and praise. Economic values are values which the group enforces under a system of free enterprise, by means of profits and losses, by riches or bankruptcy.[7]

The only statement in the preceding quoted paragraphs which I might seriously question is that maintaining that social value influences individual values *more than* they influence it. But I would certainly agree that social value is more than a mere average or composite, and more than a mere resultant, of individual values. There is a two-way interaction, a two-way causation.

I hope the reader will forgive me if I stress once more the complex relation of the "individual" to "society." Society is not merely a collection of individuals. Their interrelations in society make them quite different from what they would be in isolation. Brass is not merely copper and zinc; it is a third thing. Water is not merely hydrogen and oxygen, but something quite different from either. What an individual would be like if he had lived completely isolated from birth (assuming he could have survived at all) we can hardly even imagine. If we did not have some experience of hydrogen and oxygen in their pure state, we could certainly not have deduced their nature from looking at water. We can hope to solve many social problems not by looking at them exclusively from either an "individualist" or a "collective" aspect, but by looking at each aspect alternately.

The complex two-way interaction of the individual and society is most impressively illustrated by the example of language. Language is a social product. It was not a gift to man from heaven. It did not suddenly spring into existence in a Tower of Babel. All its words and structure and meaning were contributed by individuals—though very few, proportionately, by individuals in the present generation. Each of us now living grew up "into" a language already existing and functioning. That language has shaped each individual's concepts and values. Without it the individual could hardly think or reason at all. We think in words and in sentences—in inherited, socially-given, words and sentence structures. We improve and develop our thought by mutual exchange, by listening to words and sentences, talking words and sentences, reading each other's words and sentences. Language not only enables us to think as we do but, by the concepts that its words and sentences embody or suggest, almost *forces* us to think as we do. The individual is almost completely dependent on language.

And yet language is—ultimately—the product of the interplay and "interfluence" of individual minds. It would certainly be true to say that language has influenced any given individual more than that individual has influenced language. It might even be true to say that language has influenced the present generation more than the present generation has influenced language. But it would not be valid to say that language has influenced *all* individuals, past and present, more than they have influenced language. For it is they who created it.

And this applies also when we are discussing the moral tradition and moral values. The moral tradition in which we grow up exercises so powerful an influence that it is accepted by many people as "objective." And for any given individual it *is* objective, however subjective it may be in the sense that it originally developed and was formed by the interplay of individual human minds. Moral judgments do have objective binding force on the individual. And moral rules are objective not only in the sense that they call for objective actions but that they call for objective adherence by *everybody*.

4. *The Solipsistic and the Shared*

In brief, there is an element of truth on both sides of the subjectivist-objectivist controversy—and an element of error on both sides. Subjectivists are right in contending that all moral judgments are in one sense subjective. But they are wrong when they go on to draw disparaging inferences from this— to imply, for example, that they are "merely" subjective. For there is a profound difference between a subjective judgment, as any judgment is bound to be, and a *solitary* or *solipsistic* judgment confined to a single individual. The latter might be merely the passing hallucination of an unbalanced mind. But a subjective judgment may be *socially shared;* it may be a judgment that is held in only slightly different form by the majority in a community, or even a judgment that is held generally and almost universally.

The Objectivists are right, on the other hand, in pointing out that all human acts have objective consequences. But they are wrong in assuming that these consequences are *objectively* "good" or "bad." They can only be good or bad in somebody's opinion.

The controversy between Objectivists and Subjectivists may take another form. There are "objectivists" who, like Kant, view morality as a matter of categorical obligation, independent of the human will, independent of consequences, inherent in the nature of things. And there are "subjectivists" for whom morality is merely the arbitrary opinion, emotion, or approval of some individual, not necessarily binding or valid for anybody else. We have already, in substance, examined both of these views. Neither can stand analysis.

To sum up: The individual's moral values are necessarily

subjective, however he may have come by them. The moral values of others are for him necessarily *objective* facts to which he must adjust himself or with which he must deal. And there is a body of *social* moral values, of moral values accepted and shared by most of the people in the community (and even existing prior to those now living), which for each individual in the community is an objective fact that exercises tremendous influence on his own thought and conduct, and which he in turn may apply to influence the thought and conduct of others. Finally, moral rules require *objective* adherence from everybody.

Perhaps the confusion on this subject may be due to a deficiency in the traditional concepts and vocabulary. Moralists and scientists have assumed that whatever is not objective must be subjective, and vice versa. But may this not be equivalent to the assumption that whatever is not day must be night, or whatever is not black must be white? Just as there is a twilight zone between day and night (which cannot, except arbitrarily, be said to be either), and just as there are an infinite number of possible shades and colors between black and white, may there not be a twilight zone, or even a third category, between the objective and the subjective?

Behaviorists and logical positivists disparage or deny the subjective completely, and try to resolve everything into the objective—or at least think it a waste of time to deal with anything except the objective. On the other hand, in the idealistic philosophy of Berkeley and others, the objective is absorbed entirely into the subjective. Even modern scientists recognize that the "objective" can only be known (or inferred) from the subjective senses, so that one of our most eminent contemporary authorities on scientific method refers to "verification" or "falsification" through laboratory experiments as an "inter-subjective" verification.[8]

5. *The Multifaceted Nature of Value*

The difficulties in which we seem to have become involved are, I suggest, the result of inadequate analysis. Nearly all philosophical discussion has hitherto assumed that whatever is not "objective" must be "subjective," and vice versa; that these categories are exhaustive, and that they are also mutually exclusive.

But must values necessarily be either "objective" or "subjective?" Must value, in other words, either be "in the object" or "in the subject"? Stephen Toulmin has shrewdly suggested that such an assumption may involve the merely "figurative use" of the word "in," and that this may be no more than a "spatial metaphor," valuable enough in its own place, but not to be taken "too literally." [9]

There is a third possibility—that value refers to a *relation* between an "object" and a "subject." This I take to be the view not only of a moral philosopher like R. B. Perry,[10] but of modern economics. Economists have traditionally divided value into "use value" and "exchange value." The Austrian school distinguished "*subjective*-use value" from "*objective*-exchange value." Though this latter correspondence, as Böhm-Bawerk[11] has pointed out, does not invariably hold, economic value reflects a *relation* between certain objective qualities of an object and human needs. It is because coal has the objective quality of giving heat, and that apples have the "objective" quality of edibleness and nutritiveness, that both have "subjective" value.

In brief, because values are relational, they can be either objective or subjective, individual or social, depending on the point of view from which they are regarded. There is no contradiction in this, any more than there is in saying that the same object may be to the left or to the right, above or below, depending on the position of the observer.

And this is the reconciliation of Objectivism and Subjectivism, not only as regards economic values, but as regards moral values and moral principles. Moral values are subjective from one point of view, objective from another. Ethics is valid for everybody, for all ages and for all peoples—if only because (as Hume put it) of "the absolute necessity of these principles to the existence of society." [12]

The reader must keep in mind, however, that when we call value "objective" we are using that predicate in a special sense. We mean that a valuation is not necessarily peculiar to one individual, but that it can be shared by others—even, in effect, by a whole society. But an "objective" value in this sense is not a *physical* property. Value, in fact, is not a *property* of an object at all. Nor are *good* and *bad* properties of objects or actions. They are relational predicates. They express valuations in the same way as do such words as *valuable* and *valueless*. They express a *relation* between the valuer and the thing valued. If the valuer is an individual they express a "subjective" value. If the valuer, by implication, is society as a whole, they express an "objective" value. The tacit assumption that *good* referred to a *property* of a thing or that *right* referred to a *property* of an action—the failure to recognize that these words simply expressed valuations—was the basic fallacy of G. E. Moore and the early Bertrand Russell. Moral philosophers have been taking half a century to grope their way out of that fallacy.

6. *Can Value be Measured?*

We come now to the final major problem of value in ethics. Each of us is constantly seeking to bring about what he regards as a more satisfactory state of affairs (or a less unsatisfactory state of affairs). This is another way of saying that each of us constantly seeks to maximize his satisfactions. And this again is but another way of saying that each of us is constantly seeking to get the maximum *value* out of life.

Now the word "maximum" or "maximize" implies that values or satisfactions can be increased or added together to make a sum—in other words, that values or satisfactions can be *measured,* can be *quantified*. And *in a sense* they can be. But we must be careful to keep in mind that it is only in a special and limited sense that we can legitimately speak of adding, measuring, or quantifying values or satisfactions.

It may help to clarify the question if we begin by considering merely economic values, which seem most nearly to lend themselves to measurement. Economic value is a quality which *we* attach to commodities and services. It is subjective. But in our unphilosophic moments we are apt to regard it as a quality inhering in the commodities and services themselves. So regarded, it would belong to that class of qualities that can be greater or less, and can mount or descend a scale without ceasing to be the same quality—like heat or weight or length.[13] Such qualities could be measured and quantified.

And probably most economists today still think, like the man in the street, that economic values are in fact "measured" by monetary prices. But this is an error. Economic values—or at least market values—are *expressed* in money; but this does not mean that they are measured by it. For the value of the monetary unit itself may change from day to day. A measure of weight or length, like a pound or a foot, is always objectively the same;[14] but the value of the monetary unit may constantly vary. And it is not even possible to say, in *absolute* terms, how much it has varied. We can only "measure" the value of money itself by its "purchasing power": it is the reciprocal of the price "level." But what we are "measuring" is merely a *ratio of exchange*. And a change in such a ratio—e.g., a change in a money price—can be the result *either* of a change in the market value of a commodity *or* of a change in the market value of the monetary unit, or both. And though we may guess, we can never know which value changed, or whether both changed, or precisely by how much each changed.

Even more, we can never measure *precisely* how much a given individual (even if he is ourself) values an object in terms of money. When a man buys something, it means that he values the object he buys *more than* he values the money he pays for it. When he refuses to buy something, it means that he values the money asked for it more than he values the object.[15]

Even when we are talking of exchange values, or of the *relative* valuations of an individual, in short, we can never know these more than approximately. We can know when an individual values sum-of-money A *less than* commodity B; it is when he actually pays that much for it. We can know when he values sum-of-money A *more than* commodity B; it is when he refuses to pay that much for it. If a man refuses $475 for a painting but accepts $500, we know that he values the painting (or valued it) somewhere between $475 and $500. But we don't know exactly where. He never values it at *precisely* the price he accepts; he values it at *less:* otherwise he would not have sold. (Of course he may believe that the "real" value of the painting is considerably more than what he is "forced" to accept; but this does not change the fact that at the moment of sale he values [for whatever reason] the sum received more than the painting he parts with.)

Psychic values can never be measured in any absolute sense,

even when they are "purely economic." To the unsophisticated layman it may seem obvious that a man will value $200 twice as much as $100, and $300 three times at much. But a little study of economics, and particularly of "the law of diminishing marginal utility," will probably change his mind. For it is not merely true that a man who will pay, say, $1 for a lunch will probably refuse to pay $2 for double portions. The law of diminishing marginal utility works, though not so quickly and sharply, even with the generalized or "abstract" good called money. The diminishing marginal utility of added monetary income will be reflected in practice by a man's refusal to make proportionate sacrifices—e.g., to work proportionately longer hours (though these of course will have an *increasing* marginal *disutility*)—to earn it.

When we turn from the realm of strictly "economic" or "catallactic" values (or the realm of exchangeable goods) to the broader realm that comprises all values, including the moral, the difficulties of measurement obviously become greater rather than less. And this has posed a serious problem for all conscientious and realistic moral philosophers. In order for us to make the correct moral decision, it has been thought necessary that we be able to make a correct "hedonistic calculus" or at least that all values be "commensurable." In other words, it has been thought necessary that we be able to measure "pleasure" or "happiness" or "satisfaction" or "value" or "goodness" *quantitatively*.[16]

But this is not really necessary. The fact of *preference* decides. Values do not have to be (and are not) precisely *commensurable*. But they do have to be (and are) *comparable*. In order to choose between taking action A and taking action B, we do not have to decide that action A will give us, say, 3.14 times as much satisfaction as action B. All we have to ask ourselves is whether action A is likely to give us *more* satisfaction than action B. We can answer questions of *more* or *less*. We can say whether we *prefer* A to B, or vice versa, even if we can never say by exactly *how much*. We can know our own order of preferences at any given moment among many ends, though we can never measure exactly the quantitative differences that separate these choices on our scale of values.[17]

Those who think that we can make an exact "hedonistic calculus" are mistaken, but they are at least dealing with a real problem which those who talk vaguely of "higher" and "lower" pleasures, or who insist that values or ends are "irreducibly pluralistic," refuse to face. For when it comes to choosing between a "large amount" of a "lower" pleasure and a "small amount" of a "higher" pleasure, or among "irreducibly pluralistic" ends, how do we make our choice? Either these pleasures or ends must be commensurable, or they must at least be comparable in such a way that we can say which is greater and which less.

And the only common "measure" or basis of comparison is our actual *preference*. This is why some economists hold that our choices in the economic realm (and the same would of course apply in the moral realm) can be *ranked* but not *measured*, that they can be expressed in *ordinal* but not in *cardinal* numbers.[18] Thus, in deciding how to spend an evening, you may ask yourself whether you prefer staying at home and reading, going to the theater, or calling up some friends and playing bridge. You may have no trouble in deciding on your order of preference, though you would be hard put to it to say by *exactly how much* you prefer one to the other.

In the moral realm, both hedonists and antihedonists get into insuperable difficulties when they talk of "pleasures" and try to measure or compare them in any other sense than what I have called the purely formal or philosophic sense of "desired or valued states of consciousness."[19] But when we define "pleasure" in this formal sense, we see that it is identical with "satisfaction" or "value." And we see also that it is always possible to compare satisfactions or values in terms of *more* or *less*.

When we say, in short, that our aim is always to "maximize" satisfactions or values, we mean merely that we are constantly striving to get the *most* satisfaction or value or the *least* dissatisfaction or "disvalue"—though we can never measure this in exact quantitative terms.

And this brings us back again to the great goal of social cooperation. Each of us finds his "pleasure," his happiness, his satisfactions, his values, in different objects, activities, or ways of life. And social cooperation is the common means by which we all forward each other's purposes as an indirect means of forwarding our own, and help each other to achieve our individual and separate goals and to "maximize" our individual values.

7. *The Pushpin-vs.-Poetry Problem*

We are now in a position to solve more fully a problem that we touched on in Chapter 5.

Bentham's famous dictum: "Quantity of pleasure being equal, pushpin is as good as poetry," was deliberately written as a shocker. One of those it shocked was John Stuart Mill, who tried to rescue Utilitarianism from its supposed philistinism by insisting on a *qualitative* difference between "higher" and "lower" pleasures.

What troubled Mill in ethics was the same "paradox of value" that baffled the classical economists. Why was "gold" so much more valued in the market than "bread," or "platinum" than "water," when bread and water had an infinitely higher "usefulness"? The classical economists were confused because they were unconsciously comparing "gold" and "bread" *in general,* and forgetting that what was exchanged on the market was *definite quantities, specific units* of gold and bread. When something of vital importance, like water, is abundant, the *marginal* value of a small unit is very low; when something of much less total importance to humanity, like platinum, is very scarce, the *marginal* value of a small unit is very high.

This discovery of marginal-utility economics supplies the key to the solution of the value problem in ethics. A man does not choose between pushpin-in-general and poetry-in-general. He is not forced to choose between *abstract classes* of activities at all. And certainly he is not forced to make any *exclusive* or *permanent* choice among activities. When he is satiated with poetry he can turn for a moment to pushpin. When he has had his fill of golf he can turn to Goethe, and vice versa. So Bentham's dictum becomes defensible if amended to read: "Marginal satisfaction being equal, a unit of pushpin is as good as a unit of poetry." A man need not lose intellectual or moral stature if he occasionally turns to something trivial. Marginal value being equal, an hour of tennis is worth an hour of Tennyson.

CHAPTER 19

Intuition and Common Sense

1. *When Intuitions Conflict*

The ethical doctrine known as Intuitionism is perhaps the oldest known to man. It existed as a tacit assumption long before it made any appearance as an explicit philosophical tenet. It is the theory that we know immediately, without consideration of their consequences, what acts are "right" and what acts are "wrong."

When they come to saying *how* we know this, the Intuitionists give a wide variety of answers. Some say we know it by a special "moral sense" implanted in each of us by God. Some say we know it through the Inner Voice of our "conscience." Some (e.g., Alfred C. Ewing) say we know it by immediate perception, or "direct cognition." Sir David Ross tells us that at least certain acts ("fulfilling a promise . . . effecting a just distribution of good . . . returning services rendered . . . promoting the good of others . . . promoting the virtue or insight of the agent") are *"prima facie* duties," and that their prima facie rightness is "self-evident . . . just as a mathematical axiom, or the validity of a form of inference, is evident." [1]

Sidgwick defines Intuitionism as the theory that regards "rightness as a quality belonging to actions independently of their conduciveness to any ulterior end." [2] The presence of that quality is presumably ascertained simply by "looking at" the actions themselves, without considering their consequences. But Sidgwick goes on to point out that "no morality ever existed which did not consider consequences" [3]—at least sometimes and to some extent. Prudence (or forethought), for example, has always been considered a virtue. All modern lists of virtues "have included Benevolence, which aims generally at the happiness of others, and therefore necessarily takes into consideration even remote effects of actions." [4] It is difficult,

INTUITION AND COMMON SENSE 177

also, to draw the line between an act and its consequences. A consequence of beating a dog is that it suffers; a consequence of shooting a man is that he dies. Such consequences are usually thought of as part of the act itself. The distinction between an act and its consequences is in part arbitrary. In a sense *all* inevitable or reasonably foreseeable consequences may be considered as part of the act itself.

I shall not enter here into any lengthy refutation of Intuitionism. That has already been amply supplied by other writers.[5] It is no more rational to judge an act without some consideration of its consequences than it would be to perform the act without some consideration of its consequences. And the moral notions that have seemed equally innate, self-evident, or authoritative to those who held them have varied enormously with different races, nations, periods, and individuals. Cannibalism, slavery, polygamy, incest, prostitution, have all seemed morally acceptable to some tribes or peoples at some time. Our concepts of chastity, decency, propriety, modesty, pornography, are constantly undergoing subtle changes. Our judgments on what constitutes sexual morality and immorality have altered enormously even in our own generation. Even within the Bible itself we find the most direct conflicts between moral injunctions. The Mosaic Law tells us to repay injury with its like: "Eye for eye, tooth for tooth, hand for hand, foot for foot; burning for burning, wound for wound, stripe for stripe" (Exod. 21:24-25). But Jesus tells us: "Ye have heard that it hath been said, An eye for an eye, and a tooth for a tooth: But I say unto you, that ye resist not evil: but whosoever shall smite thee on thy right cheek, turn to him the other also" (Matt. 5:38-39).

I need not go further into the differences and conflicts between the moral "intuitions" that have been regarded as "self-evident" in different times and places. Overwhelming documentation of these can be found in the works of John Locke, Herbert Spencer, W. E. H. Lecky, William Graham Sumner, L. T. Hobhouse, Robert Briffault, etc.

When we decide whether or not to act in accordance with any given moral rule, we do in fact give some consideration to the probable consequences of acting on it or failing to act on it. This is especially true when two established moral rules conflict—e.g., the rule that we should always tell the truth with the rule that we should not cause avoidable humiliation, distress, or pain to others. There is still no "self-evident" answer to the question whether a doctor should tell his patient that she is dying of cancer.

2. *Morals Built into Language*

But if there are no moral "intuitions," how have so many philosophers, and so many other intelligent persons, come to think that there are? The reason is that most of our moral judgments *seem* immediate, *seem* to be instantaneous and made without consideration of the probable consequences of an act. But this is so because these judgments have been, as it were, built into us by the social traditions and conventions, and from our earliest infancy. They are built into the language. From its earliest days an infant hears the words "good baby" or "bad baby," "good doggie" or "bad doggie." Moral judgment is embodied in description, and confused with it. We absorb our moral judgments with our language. They are both parts of our social inheritance. The reason we know that *lying* is wicked and *being mistaken* is not necessarily so; that *theft* is wrong but *transfer* not necessarily so; that *murder* is monstrous but *killing in self defense* is justified, is that these judgments *are embodied in the words themselves,* by the judgments of our fellows and the generations that have gone before us.

Now no philosopher, to my knowledge, has held or holds that we know the meaning of words—of *black* and *white, dog* and *cat, table* and *chair, high* and *low*—by intuition. But some philosophers do seem to maintain that we know the meaning of *good* and *bad, right* and *wrong,* by some sort of intuition. They are held to be "indefinable" in some much more mysterious and "nonnatural" way than *blue* and *yellow, up* and *down, right* and *left,* are indefinable.[6]

Now the ethical tradition in which we have grown up, and the ethical valuations and judgments that go with it, impregnate and color all our thought. We pick them up in the same way as we do our language. Like our language, they *condition* our thought. They do not do so to quite the same extent as our language (for without the social inheritance of language it is doubtful that the individual could think, in any civilized sense of the term, at all); but our social ethical conventions and valuations condition our individual thought and attitudes to an enormous extent. It is because they are so habitual, immediate, and instantaneous that they are so often mistaken for "intuitions."

A writer like Henry Sidgwick[7] does sometimes confuse them with intuitions. Nevertheless, one of the great contributions that Sidgwick made to ethics was to examine and try to spell out the ethical tradition of his time and place with more care and in more detail than any of his predecessors had done. He did not call it the ethical tradition but the Morality of Common Sense. As he explains in the preface to the second edition of his *Methods of Ethics*: "The Morality that I examine in Book III is my own morality as much as it is any man's: it is, as I say, the 'Morality of Common Sense,' which I only attempt to represent in so far as I share it; I only place myself outside it either (1) temporarily, for the purpose of impartial criticism, or (2) in so far as I am forced beyond it by a practical consciousness of its incompleteness. I have certainly criticized this morality unsparingly. . . ."[8]

As a Benthamite (i.e., a direct and *ad hoc*) Utilitarian, Sidgwick sometimes criticizes "common sense" morality too hastily and cavalierly; but he is for the most part far more cautious and respectful in doing so than Bentham was. At one point, indeed, he pays eloquent tribute to it:

> If, then, we are to regard the morality of Common Sense as a machinery of rules, habits, and sentiments, roughly and generally but not precisely or completely adapted to the production of the greatest possible happiness for sentient beings generally; and if, on the other hand, we have to accept it as the actually established machinery for attaining this end, which we cannot replace at once by any other, but can only gradually modify; it remains to consider the practical effects of the complex and balanced relation in which a scientific Utilitarian thus seems to stand to the Positive Morality of his age and country.
>
> Generally speaking, he will clearly conform to it, and endeavor to promote its development in others. For, though the imperfection that we find in all the actual conditions of human existence —we may even say in the universe at large as judged from a

human point of view—is ultimately found even in Morality itself, in so far as this is contemplated as Positive; still, practically, we are much less concerned with correcting and improving than we are with realizing and enforcing it. The Utilitarian must repudiate altogether that temper of rebellion against the established morality as something purely external and conventional, into which the reflective mind is always apt to fall when it is first convinced that its rules are not intrinsically reasonable. He must, of course, also repudiate as superstitious that awe of it as an absolute Divine Code which Intuitional moralists inculcate. Still, he will naturally contemplate it with reverence and wonder as a marvellous product of nature, the result of long centuries of growth, showing in many parts the same fine adaptation of means to complex exigencies as the most elaborate structures of physical organisms exhibit: he will handle it with respectful delicacy as a mechanism, constructed of the fluid element of opinions and dispositions, by the indispensable aid of which the actual *quantum* of human happiness is continually being produced: a mechanism which no "politicians or philosophers" could create, yet without which the harder and coarser machinery of Positive Law could not be permanently maintained, and the life of man would become— as Hobbes forcibly expresses it—"solitary, poor, nasty, brutish, and short." [9]

Sidgwick goes on to say: "Still, as this actual moral order is admittedly imperfect, it will be the Utilitarian's duty to aid in improving it; just as the most orderly, law-abiding, member of a modern civilized society includes the reform of laws in his conception of political duty." [10]

This is all excellent as far as it goes. Still, it is not quite as easy to reform and improve traditional or common-sense[11] morality as Sidgwick and other classical Utilitarians too often seemed to suppose. Certainly I cannot agree, with Sidgwick, that "the only possible method" of modifying or supplementing common-sense morality is that of "pure empirical Hedonism." [12]

It is of cardinal importance that we recognize why we must treat the existing positive moral code not only with as much respect as we do our country's laws but with a great deal more —with something very close to reverence and awe. This moral code grew up spontaneously, like language, religion, manners, law. It is the product of the experience of immemorial generations, of the interrelations of millions of people and the interplay of millions of minds. The morality of common sense is a sort of common law, with an indefinitely wider jurisdiction than ordinary common law, and based on a practically infinite number of particular cases. We are not required to perform the optimum act—the specific act that would do most to increase the sum of human happiness—because we can never know precisely what that act is. But we do know what the traditional moral rules prescribe. These rules crystallize the experience and moral wisdom of the race.

The morality of common sense cannot be put beyond criticism, of course, for then there would be no ethical progress. But this criticism should never be made impatiently, arrogantly, condescendingly, or frivolously (after the fashion of so many philosophers, from Thrasymachus to Bentham, and from Nietzsche to Bertrand Russell and other Logical Positivists), but with great care and caution, and only after every effort has been made to see the possible utility or need of some traditional moral rule whenever such utility or need is not immediately obvious.

3. *The Importance of Precedent*

We have elsewhere discussed at length the need to be guided in ethics by the utility of general rules, rather than by the estimated consequences of particular acts considered in isolation. Common-sense morality has always implicitly recognized the need of abiding by such general rules. It has also recognized the need of allowing very few exceptions, even when such exceptions would in themselves be harmless, for the reason that such exceptions, once admitted, would tend to become too wide and numerous. The whole social code that restricts the time, place, and circumstances of social intercourse between men and women is based on this principle.[13] Common and statute law embody the same principle: one is supposed to stop at the red light even at a deserted intersection. But this principle is usually ignored or overlooked by hasty critics of common-sense morality.

Another consideration that these critics commonly overlook is the importance of precedent. Precedent is at least as important in ethics as in law. Rules should be changed slowly, individually, after careful thought. An attempt at any sudden "transvaluation of all values" can merely create confusion and chaos.

Precedent is of the first importance in law for the protection of individual rights. The law must be certain—i.e., not only must the law be reasonably precise but decisions of the courts must be reasonably predictable, so that people may know when they are acting within their rights, and may embark on a course of action with reasonable assurance that the rules will not be changed in the middle of the game. This is no less true of ethical laws. The standards of right and wrong, of praise and blame, should change only gradually, slowly, piecemeal, so that people can become accustomed to the new rules. This gradualness assures the maximum of social cooperation and even of progress. This is the element of truth in conservatism, in so far as this reflects a philosophy of gradualism. New rules and standards must be tested by a minority before they are adopted by or enforced on everyone.

Let us put this in still another form. Why is devotion to duty important? Because it means following a recognized and established rule. Why is following an established rule important? Because these rules are the product of millions of individual decisions in millions of situations and embody the accumulated experience and wisdom of the race. Because following these established rules has been found to have the consequence in the long run of maximizing human harmony, cooperation, and well-being (or of minimizing human discord and strife). And finally, because it is necessary that we should be able to depend on each other's reactions and responses. If we stopped before each act or decision to make a fresh calculation of the probable consequences of action A, B, C, or N, if we decided to "judge each case on its merits" without regard to any established rule or principle of action, others could not depend on our actions or responses. The primary basis of human cooperation, which is mutual dependence on each of us playing his expected role, would be undermined or destroyed.

In a symphony, every player and instrument has his or its assigned role in carrying the theme or producing the harmony. Any false or untimely note from any instrument, any failure

INTUITION AND COMMON SENSE

in tempo or synchronization, would spoil the cooperative result. So with the symphony of life.

This brings us to a still further corollary. Even a rather poor ethical rule is better than no rule at all. This is again because we need to know in our daily actions what to expect of each other, because we are obliged to rely on each other's conduct, and must be reasonably able to count in advance on what the action of others is going to be.

Perhaps an analogy with traffic laws will make this clearer. A rule that *permits* you to turn right at a red light may be better or worse than a rule that *forbids* you to turn right at a red light. A rule that one must drive on the right side of the road may be better or worse than a rule that one must drive on the left side. But it is much more important that we adopt and abide by even the inferior rule (whichever it is) than that we adopt no rule at all. For in the former case each driver knows what to expect of the other drivers; in the latter case he does not know what to expect, and the number of arguments, snarls, and accidents is bound to increase.

Let us summarize the conclusions at which we have arrived. The existing Common Law and the existing Moral Tradition deserve tremendous respect from each of us because of the process by which they have come into being. The Common Law is the product of the hundreds of thousands of decisions by thousands of judges passing on specific cases, trying not only to settle each of them but to settle it on the basis of established precedents and principles acceptable to both sides. (Scientists and "advanced thinkers" often ridicule the law and lawyers for their "blind" deference to precedents. But this is what gives *certainty* to the law. This is what allows people to know that they have certain rights that others are bound to respect; to know what it is that they have a right to expect from others and can reasonably depend on from others when they make their own plans.) And what applies to the Common Law applies to the Moral Tradition (or "common-sense" morality, or the moral consensus) multiplied a hundredfold. From the beginning of time, all of us have experienced daily conflicts, disputes, problems of division, precedence, priority, and "fairness," and in seeking to resolve these have sought to do so on the basis of consistent or accepted principles that would also appeal to others. Our "common-sense" morality is the composite product of these immemorial millions of judgments and decisions.

4. *"Always Follow the Rule—Unless"*

The practical course to which all this leads is clear. We should abide by the morality of common sense, we should abide by the conventional rules of conduct of our time and place, whatever they happen to be, unless in some particular case we have strong reasons for departing from the rule. We should never refuse to abide by an established moral rule merely because we cannot understand the purpose of it. No single person can be in a position to know all the experiences, decisions, and considerations that have caused a moral rule to take some particular form.

This is the great element of practical truth (though not of "self-evidence") in the injunction of Sir David Ross that we should always abide by what he calls our *"prima facie* duties" even when we cannot see in some particular case precisely how this will promote our own individual well-being or even the well-being of our community in the long run. Our general maxim should be this: *Always follow the established moral rule, always abide by our prima facie duty, unless there is a clear reason for not doing so.*

This is little more than the general form of Mark Twain's sarcastic admonition: "When in doubt, tell the truth." When in doubt, follow the established moral rule.

The burden of proof must be upon the exception, or upon the alleged moral innovation. In fact, it should be a large part of the aim of the moral philosopher to *discover* the reasons for an existing moral rule, or the function that it serves.[14] If each of us were free to change or to ignore the traditional moral code at whatever point it did not suit him, or even at whatever point he did not fully understand the reason for its application, the code would lose all its authority.

There is truth, then, in the conclusion of Hegel: "Virtue is not a troubling oneself about a peculiar and isolated morality of one's own. The striving for a positive morality of one's own

INTUITION AND COMMON SENSE

is futile, and in its very nature impossible of attainment. In respect of morality the saying of the wisest men of antiquity is the only one which is true, that to be moral is to live in accordance with the moral tradition of one's country." [15]

This, however, overstates the matter. Unless a few had the courage to depart from the prevailing moral code of their country or time in this or that particular, for some carefully considered reason, there would be no moral progress. We must never allow the existing moral code to become petrified and immutable, for then even the reasons behind it would be forgotten, and it would tend to become meaningless. "The letter killeth, but the spirit giveth life." Each of us may and must cooperate in its continuous improvement and perfection.

Fortunately, each of us daily has this opportunity. For the prevailing moral code, or the Morality of Common Sense, when closely examined, consists for the most part of generalities which, when it comes to detailed application, lack a great deal in clarity and precision. Common-Sense Morality prescribes such virtues as Prudence, Temperance, Self-Control, Good Faith, Veracity, Justice, Courage, Benevolence, etc.; but these concepts are often vague, and sometimes even mutually contradictory. They do not tell us, for example, precisely how, where they conflict, we can reconcile the claims of Prudence with the claims of Benevolence, or precisely at what point Courage becomes Foolhardiness. Yet each of us, in his praise and blame, his advice, and above all in his own conduct and in his own decisions, can help to make these ideas more exact. The function of the moral philosopher is constantly to look for some unifying principle that can explain the origin and necessity of most of the traditional virtues and duties, can help to give them a more precise form, and can reconcile them in a more coherent system.[16]

Meanwhile, however, the existing morality seems quite adequate, and is certainly indispensable, for practical guidance for most people in most circumstances. Without a profound general respect for and deference to the traditional moral code, there would be no morality at all, but moral chaos. And in our age this is a far greater danger than that of an imperfect and inflexible code held in superstitious awe.

5. *The Moral Contract*

Before we leave this consideration of the traditional moral code, a word should be said about one significant element in its nature. The chief function that the common morality serves is to reduce social conflict and to promote social cooperation. And it is important to notice in this morality the role played by *tacit agreement.* Since the days of Rousseau, a great deal has been said in political theorizing about the "Social Contract." Now there is no evidence that there ever was an explicit historical social contract. Nevertheless, men have acted, from time immemorial, politically and morally, *as if* there were a social contract. This has been a tacit, unformulated, unexplicit, but none the less real *agreement,* an agreement reflected in our actions and in our rules of action. It takes the general form: I will do this if you do that; I will refrain from this if you refrain from that. I will not attack you if you do not attack me. I will respect your person and family and property and other established rights if you respect mine. I will keep my word if you keep yours. I will tell the truth if you do. I will take my place on line and wait my turn if you will do the same. Those who violate these tacitly-agreed-upon rules not only do direct and immediate harm, but also imperil general adherence to the rules. Individual respect for law and general respect for law, individual morality and general social morality, are interdependent. They are, in fact, two names for the same thing.

6. *Are Maxims "Self-Evident"?*

We come now to a final question. Granted that there are no such things as moral "intuitions"—or granted, at least, that the word should not be used because of its misleading mystical connotations—do we have "direct moral cognitions"? Are there any moral "axioms" that are "self-evident"?

Euclidian geometry, and all deductive reasoning, rest on "axioms" or postulates, the truth of which is assumed to be self-evident, or is at least taken for granted. Let us see how this applies to ethical reasoning.

Ethical reasoning, as we have seen in Chapter 15, deals with ends and means. This reasoning may be hypothetical or factual. It may take the hypothetical form: *If* you want to maximize your own happiness in the long run, *then* you ought to adopt the rules of conduct that will tend to maximize your happiness in the long run; and those rules are these. . . . Or it may take the factual form: You want to substitute a more satisfactory state of affairs for a less satisfactory state. You want to maximize your happiness in the long run; therefore you should adopt the rules of action that will tend to maximize your happiness in the long run. Or: We want to achieve the maximum happiness for each of us. Therefore we should adopt for ourselves, and impose (by censure or praise) on each other, the rules of action most likely to achieve the maximum happiness for each of us.

We may say, therefore, that moral rules tend to become self-evident when they tend to become tautologous, or when our goal is self-evident for the reason that we *see* it to be in fact our goal.

We need not go here into the question of how far this realm of "self-evident morality" extends. Many moral rules—such as the rule that we should not torture a child—are self-evident in the sense that no person of normal feelings would ever ask the reason or the justification for the rule. Henry Sidgwick held that "in the principles of Prudence, Justice and Rational Benevolence as commonly recognized there is at least a self-evident element, immediately cognizable by abstract intuition.[17] Other ethical writers have contended that this "self-evidence" extends over a much wider field. As a practical matter, however, the ethical philosopher will be well advised to adhere in his reasoning to something like the equivalent of Occam's razor, and not multiply alleged intuitions or direct cognitions unnecessarily, but reduce them to the minimum, or try to get along without them altogether if he can.

CHAPTER 20

Vocation and Circumstance

1. *Duties—Universal or Special?*

Just as, in our economic life, there is a necessary division and specialization of labor, so in our moral life there is a necessary division and specialization of duty. Failure to recognize this has led to a great deal of confusion in ethical thought. It is commonly assumed that what is a duty for one must be a duty for all, and that what is not a duty for most of us cannot be made a duty for anyone. It is commonly assumed, in other words, that a duty must either be universal or it is not a duty at all. This is the common interpretation of Kant's rule: "Make the maxim of thy action that which thou wouldst at the same time to be universal law."

A little reflection will show, however, that each of us has special moral duties just as each of us has a special vocation and a special job. In fact, a large number of these special duties grow directly out of our special vocation and our special job. Just as it is the moral duty of each of us to fulfill the conditions of an economic contract, so it is the moral duty of each of us to fulfill the implied duties of any job we have accepted. And often, precisely because we have accepted these special duties, they are not the necessary duties of others.

Let us illustrate this by a few special situations. If you are walking alone along a deserted beach, and someone in the water is drowning and cries for help, and the distance from the shore, the waves and tide, your own swimming ability and other conditions are such that you can probably save him without excessive risk to your own life, then it is your duty to try.

But suppose, now, under the same conditions, a hundred people are on that beach? Your duty to undertake the rescue does not altogether disappear—*somebody* must be the rescuer —but it is considerably attenuated. The duty is heavier on the stronger swimmers than on the weaker ones—because their chances for success are higher and their risks to themselves are lower. And if there is on the beach a professional lifesaver specifically employed to watch that beach, then the duty is clearly his. If the lifeguard were absent, or ill, or drunk, or had just announced that he had gone on strike, then it would become the duty of someone else on the beach to undertake the rescue—but neither the law nor the rules of morality could say specifically *whose* duty. All one is entitled to say is that if no one at all undertook the rescue, and the victim drowned, everyone on that beach *capable* of having made the rescue would share the guilt of nonfeasance and would have good reason to feel ashamed of himself.

Clear specific vocation and specific assignment of duties solves many a moral problem of this sort. If you know that a helpless little girl or a woman invalid is in a burning building, is it your duty to try to save her? The answer depends on many circumstances—on the possibility of a successful attempt or the apparent hopelessness of it; on your particular relationship to the victim; on whether other possible rescuers, better equipped, are present. But if professional firemen have arrived, with proper equipment, then the question whose duty it is—if the rescue is feasible at all—is practically settled.

Suppose a bandit on the street is holding someone up at the point of a gun. You happen to be there and are unarmed. Is it your duty to try to stop him, in spite of the huge risk? Suppose he starts to beat the victim with the butt of his gun? Does your duty to intervene become stronger? Or suppose—a situation that sometimes occurs—an armed bandit is robbing or shooting someone and a crowd of people are present? It is, most people would say, the crowd's duty to stop him. But one essential part of the question is usually left unanswered. Whose duty is it to make the first move—to try to take the gun away from the bandit?

Again, the answer to these questions must depend to some extent on special circumstances—for instance, on whether the object of the bandit's attack is your wife, say, or a stranger. But one circumstance would definitely settle the question, in most people's opinion. If an armed policeman were on the scene, it would be *his* duty to take the risks of intervention.

Thus certain duties become clear and unequivocal for the

simple reason that they have already been accepted either explicitly or implicitly by the adoption of a vocation or the acceptance of a particular job or assignment. We often speak of the "duties" of a particular job when referring merely to the routine requirements of it. But whenever failure to perform these requirements would do appreciable harm, these are moral duties also. No man who has no intention of assuming the risks necessary to the vocation he has voluntarily chosen—whether that of a policeman, soldier, ship captain, airplane pilot, fireman, lifeguard, night watchman, or doctor—has any right to adopt such a vocation.

"Common-sense" ethics suggests, as we have seen in the course of this discussion, that we have certain duties which might almost be called *duties of accident*. If we happen to be the only person on a beach when someone calls for help in the water, if we are in the first car to arrive when someone has met an accident or some pedestrian lies groaning on the road, we cannot tell ourselves that it is a mere accident that we, and we alone, happen to be at this precise spot at this precise moment, that rescue or help by us would be inconvenient, that we are somewhat in a hurry, that this is none of our business, and that someone else will probably be along a little later. A duty has fallen upon us—by accident, it is true—but it is none the less a duty. So of the three people who came upon the man who went down from Jerusalem to Jericho, and fell among thieves, the two who passed by on the other side were ignoring the plainest duty of compassion, and only the good Samaritan was acting morally (Luke 10:30-33).

The rationale of this duty is clear enough. Any one of us would expect this of a passer-by if we were the man who had been beaten and robbed. And a world in which passers-by did not accept such a duty is one that no one could envisage as a truly moral world.

2. *The Limits of Responsibility*

Yet we would greatly underrate the importance of such duties if we called them "duties of accident." A much better term would be *duties of circumstance* or *duties of relation*. And the latter term would cover not only the duties that fall to us because of our *blood* relation to some other person or persons —the duties of consanguinity—but the duties that fall to us because of our relationships of all kinds, sometimes even spatial, to other persons—the duties of *proximity*.

None of us is an abstract or disembodied spirit. Each of us is a citizen of a particular country, a resident of a particular city or a particular neighborhood, a son or daughter, a father or mother, a brother or sister, a husband or wife, a friend or acquaintance, an employer or employee, a business colleague, or fellow worker, a neighbor, a tradesman or his customer, a doctor or his patient, a lawyer or his client, or, temporarily, a fellow traveler with others in the same boat or the same bus. And in each of these capacities he has assumed certain explicit or implied duties to other specific persons. It is a man's duty to support and defend his own wife but not necessarily anybody else's. It is a man's duty to provide for the education of his own children but not necessarily for other peope's children. If a man is driving his car along a lonely road and comes upon a motorist who has had a serious accident, it is his duty, even if he happens to be in a foreign country, or is on that road by the merest chance, to stop and do what he reasonably can to help.

But it is precisely because each of us has so many special duties of vocation, relation, or proximity that he cannot and does not have limitless duties in all directions. If we come upon someone in distress, and we are the only source of help available to him at the moment, it is our duty to do what we reasonably can to relieve him. But it is not therefore our duty to go around *looking* for people to help. It is not our duty to meddle in other people's affairs or to force our assistance on them. In the world today, someone is dying with almost every tick of the clock. In the United States alone three people die every minute. Somewhere, we may be sure, perhaps in Korea or in Paraguay, some people must be suffering or starving. But it does not follow that it is our duty to drop whatever we are doing and help; or even to let ourselves be endlessly taxed for bottomless "foreign aid" distributed by well-paid bureaucrats who constantly search for possible aid-recipients and derive a sense of immense self-righteousness from their vicarious generosity. Nor does it follow that, because of our abstract knowledge of death and suffering *somewhere,* we must develop a guilt-complex because we happen at the moment to be enjoying ourselves.

The conclusion that each of us has special duties, in brief, peculiar to his vocation, relation, or circumstances, must have as its corollary and obverse the conclusion that the duty of each of us has certain definite limits.

But the problem of defining the exact sphere and limits of our individual duties is one of the most difficult in ethics. I do not remember reading anywhere any fully satisfactory solution. In fact, few moral philosophers seem even to have been aware of the problem. One of those who has, and who has framed at least a partial criterion of the limits of individual responsibility, is F. A. Hayek:

> The sense of responsibility has been weakened in modern times as much by overextending the range of an individual's responsibilities as by exculpating him from the actual consequences of his actions. . . . To be effective, responsibility must be both definite and limited, adapted both emotionally and intellectually to human capacities. It is quite as destructive to any sense of responsibility to be taught that one is responsible for everything as to be taught that one cannot be responsible for anything. . . .
>
> Responsibility, to be effective, must be individual responsibility. . . . As everybody's property in effect is nobody's property, so everybody's responsibility is nobody's responsibility. . . .
>
> The essential condition of responsibility is that it refer to circumstances that the individual can judge, to problems that, without too much strain of the imagination, [a] man can make his own. . . .
>
> We cannot expect the sense of responsibility for the known and familiar to be replaced by a similar feeling about the remote and the theoretically known. While we can feel genuine concern for the fate of our familiar neighbors and usually will know how to help them when help is needed, we cannot feel in the same way about the thousands or millions of unfortunates whom we know to exist in the world but whose individual circumstances we do not know. However moved we may be by accounts of their misery, we cannot make the abstract knowledge of the numbers of suffering people guide our everyday action. If what we do is to be useful and effective, our objectives must be limited, adapted to the capacities of our mind and our compassions. To be constantly reminded of our "social" responsibilities to all the needy or unfortunate

in our community, in our country, or in the world, must have the effect of attenuating our feelings until the distinctions between those responsibilities which call for our action and those which do not disappear. In order to be effective, then, responsibility must be so confined as to enable the individual to rely on his own concrete knowledge in deciding on the importance of the different tasks, to apply his moral principles to circumstances he knows, and to help to mitigate evils voluntarily.[1]

Professor Hayek was writing primarily a political book; but we need merely substitute the word "duty" in the foregoing passage for the word "responsibility" to recognize that it applies equally in the ethical realm. The individual's duties are not limitless.

3. "All Mankind"—or Your Neighbor?

Yet the typical utilitarian tells us that, "We have in each case to compare all the pleasures and pains that can be foreseen as probable results of the different alternatives of conduct presented to us, and to adopt the alternative which seems likely to lead to the greatest happiness on the whole." [2] Or that, "The criterion of an action—what constitutes it right or wrong—is its tendency to promote for all mankind a greatest quantity of good on the whole." [3]

Now it is one thing to concede that this criterion may be a legitimate test for a system of moral rules considered as a whole. But it does not follow that each individual must make this a direct criterion to guide his own actions. For it may turn out (as I believe it does) that the most promising way to maximize the happiness of humanity as a whole is not by each individual's trying to achieve that result directly but, on the contrary, by each individual's acting in accordance with appropriate *general rules,* by doing his own special job well, and by cooperating with his immediate family and associates.

Some utilitarians tell us that each of us, on the basis of the goal of maximizing human happiness, should be willing by a benevolent action to sacrifice his own happiness at least up to the point where his action reduces it less than it can increase the happiness of another. Common-sense morality would reply, I think, that much depends on *what* the sacrifice is and on *who* this "other" is. If he or she is one's wife or daughter or other loved one, the rule seems acceptable enough: in such a case, in fact, it may be doubtful that one is really sacrificing any of his own happiness at all. But if the person for whom one is asked to make this sacrifice is a complete stranger, or someone that one knows but detests, I doubt that common-sense morality would accept any such mathematical calculation for "maximizing human happiness," even if it were in fact possible to measure the decrease in one's own happiness against the increase of the stranger's.

Is it possible to solve this problem in abstract terms or by definite general rules? Let us at least try; and let us begin by looking at the implicit but rather nebulous rules that have been worked out by common-sense morality, to see whether they can furnish us with any clue.

The spirit of that morality leads us to be properly suspicious, I think, of the modern reformer, typified by Rousseau or Marx, whose professed love for all mankind is so often accompanied by neglect of or callousness toward his own family and friends. "For the social courtesies and minor loyalties of life," once wrote Albert Jay Nock, "give me the old fogy every time in preference to radicals . . . or indeed most of us. We are so taken up with our general love for humanity that we don't have time to be decent to anybody." [4]

And perhaps this result is not accidental. I suspect that the classical utilitarians slipped into a confusion of thought, which can have, and has already had, some pernicious consequences. It is one thing, and correct, to say that our moral rules should be such as to promote the maximum happiness for all humanity. But it is a questionable corollary that it is therefore the duty of each individual himself to attempt to promote directly the maximum general happiness for all humanity. For the best way to promote this maximum general happiness may be for each individual to cooperate with, and perform his duties toward, his immediate family, neighbors, and associates.

I hope I may be forgiven if I attempt to clarify and illustrate the point by a graphic illustration. In the chart (Fig. 1) A has direct ties of family, friendship, business, or neighborhood with B, C, D, and E, and corresponding (reciprocal) obligations and duties. If A takes care of these, and B, C, D, and E

VOCATION AND CIRCUMSTANCE

respectively take care of *their* direct ties and duties, and so throughout, then *total* social cooperation and mutual helpfulness is assured. But if A is told or believes that he not only has direct duties toward B, C, D, and E, but *equal* duties and ob-

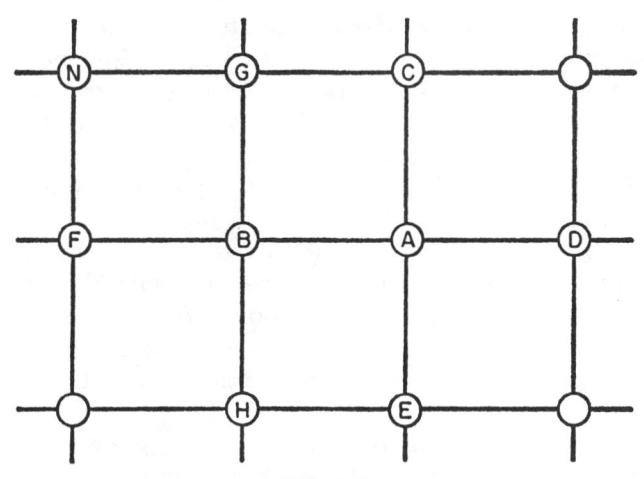

Figure 1

ligations toward N, and toward a practically infinite number of N's, the sheer impossibility of fulfilling any such duties and obligations may cause him to slight or abandon his direct duties to those near him. If his duty to N, a stranger (he may unconsciously reason), is no less than that to B, his brother, then his duty to B is no greater than his duty to N—and he may therefore neglect both, or give them both mere lip-service. But if A fulfills his direct duties to B, etc., and B fulfills his direct duties to A, H, F, and G, then F and G can be depended on to cooperate with N, etc.

It may, perhaps, never be possible to reduce to any precise rule the strength and urgency of A's duty to B as compared with his remote and indirect duty to N, etc. Possibly one day some law may be formulated that is equivalent in the moral realm to the law of gravitation in the physical, according to which one's duties to others decrease, say, as the square of the "distance" (or increase inversely as the square of the "distance").

Meanwhile, we can only be guided by the rather nebulous

rules that have been worked out by common-sense morality. But these nebulous rules do, I think, implicitly follow some such Principle of Proximity as the one I have here outlined—a duty of person-to-person rather than of person-to-people, of each-to-each rather than of each-to-all or each-to-humanity, which the classical utilitarians too hastily adopted. For there is much wisdom in the proverb: "What's everybody's business is nobody's business." And a corollary is: What's everybody's vague "responsibility" tends to be nobody's real responsibility.

But here we are brought to a major problem that has received astonishingly little discussion by moral philosophers. We have recognized validity in Kant's precept: "Act as if the law of thy action were to become by thy will law universal." Many have drawn from this the corollary that *all* moral rules should be "universalizable." But now we seem to be saying the opposite: that the duties of each of us are particular, depending upon our vocation, our "station," or our special relations with others.

Is there really a contradiction here? Or is there some way in which we can reconcile the necessary *universality* with the necessary *particularity* of duties? Such a reconciliation is possible, I think, if we state each person's duty correctly. Then we would say, for example, that every mother has duties toward her *own* children, every husband toward his *own* wife, every man toward his *own* job and his *own* employer, every employer toward his *own* employees, etc. Thus we can state the rule or the duty so that it is at once particular and of universal application.

Another way of reconciling the necessary universality with the necessary particularity of duties is to say that a man's duty depends *on the particular circumstances* in which he finds himself or in which he is asked to act; and that *his* duty in *those* circumstances would be *any*one's or *every*one's duty in the *same* circumstances. The difficulty with this solution is that no two people ever do find themselves in *exactly* the same circumstances, and that some circumstances are *morally relevant* and others are not.

But the only way we can decide which circumstances are morally relevant is to ask ourselves what would be the *consequences* of embodying those circumstances *in a general rule*.

Thus we can relevantly say that it is the duty not only of A, but of *anybody* in the same comfortable circumstances, to pay for a college education for his own son. But we cannot relevantly say that it is not only the duty of A, but of *anybody else* in the soap business, to pay for a college education of his own son. We can relevantly say that it is right not only for A, but for everyone, to tell a lie *if he has to do so to save a life;* but we cannot relevantly say that it is right not only for A, but for everyone, to tell a lie on Thursday night.[5]

In brief, the extent to which a moral rule or a duty should be generalized or particularized can only be determined by the social consequences that generalization or particularization would tend to have. And this once more points to the unsatisfactoriness of Kant's formulation of the principle of universalizibility. It is valid (in so far as it insists that no one is entitled to treat himself as an exception), but it is not of much use. It tells us only that what is a moral rule for A is a moral rule for B or for anybody, that what is a duty for A is a duty for B or for anybody else *in those circumstances*. But it gives us no hint of how we are to test the validity or expediency of one moral rule as against another, or of what our particular duty *is* in particular circumstances.

A practical problem for which it is even more difficult to draw specific rules is: When someone fails, for any reason, to perform his or her specific duty, *whose* duty is it to substitute? If a mother and father fail in their duties to their own children, and allow them to go hungry or carelessly expose them to some contagious disease, whose duty is it to try to rectify the situation? The common law finds no solution to this problem, and common-sense morality gives no definite answer.

4. *The Choice of Vocation*

But it is clear from the foregoing discussion that our special duties of relation and circumstance tend to merge with our special duties of vocation. Let us therefore return to our consideration of the latter.

Once we have adopted a vocation, we have either implicitly or explicitly adopted the special duties and risks that attend it. But this brings us to the problem: Have we any duty to adopt one vocation rather than another? Does each of us have one "true" vocation? Are we obliged to follow it? And how are we to determine what it is?

Obviously within a very wide range the choice of a trade or profession (when it is not more or less forced on us, as it often is) is a decision to be made mainly on economic grounds and on grounds of personal taste and preference. Within this wide range moral considerations cannot be said to enter. Yet the "duty" of choosing a profession has been called by one writer "the most important of all duties." [6] Certainly it is one of the most important *decisions*, and sometimes the most important, that each of us makes in his life. To what extent do or should moral considerations enter into this decision?

It is obvious that they must certainly enter in a negative sense. Nobody can excuse himself for a life of crime by declaring that he decided to adopt it because he thought this the quickest way to make a living, or because he had a special taste or talent for that kind of life. And even when we come to occupations that are within the law, many men will refuse even to consider going into a business that they feel to be ignoble or disreputable. Other men will feel that they have a positive "calling" or a positive duty to take up, say, the ministry or medicine.

We have said enough to indicate that the choice of a profession or vocation, though within certain limits it may be morally indifferent, must often involve a moral choice. Most of us recognize, in our judgments on our friends or on public figures, that a man owes a special obligation to his own gifts. Of the men whom we find throwing away their lives in drunkenness and dissipation, we condemn far more strongly a man whom we consider to be a great potential artist, scientist or writer, than one who has never shown any particular talent at all. We say of the former that he has sinned against his own talents. We are apt to be intolerant even of a mild laziness in him.

This may seem unjust and paradoxical. But common-sense morality is right in recognizing that special talents do impose special duties. For it recognizes that when such talents are unused, humanity loses far more than it does from the idleness or dissipation of mediocrities.

A man, then, has a duty to his own talents. He has a duty not to underestimate them, if this underestimate leads him to set his sights too low. "A man's reach should exceed his grasp." But only slightly. It is almost an equal sin for a man to overestimate his talents when it leads him into ambitious projects at which he cannot succeed rather than into a more modest but more useful career. It is the latter possibility that is today more often forgotten or neglected. If one were to judge from the bulk of novels and plays on this theme in the last generation, the world is full of men who would have made great novelists or artists but were forced by their in-laws to go into the advertising business instead. Yet the real truth seems to be that America has a surplus of incompetent novelists and painters who, given the true nature and level of their talents, might at least have made useful and successful advertising-copy writers or illustrators.

If a man does have a duty to his talents, however (and I am assuming he does), this implies that special talents impose special duties. These duties rest on two grounds. We assume that a man who does not fully employ his talents will be unhappy. And if it is a duty of all of us to maximize the *general* happiness, then those whose powers enable them to make a greater contribution must have a greater obligation.

But does this not also have its reverse side? Does the genius who is the slave of his talent not have in compensation certain immunities from the duties of ordinary men? Does he have the right, for example, to abandon his wife and children to pursue his chosen work—or is he bound, like the rest of us, to the obligations he assumed by his earlier choice?

I shall not attempt here to answer this question, which has fascinated many novelists and dramatists (Somerset Maugham in *The Moon and Sixpence*, Bernard Shaw in *The Doctor's Dilemma*, Joyce Cary in *Herself Surprised*, *The Horse's Mouth*, etc.), but I can make one generalization. We have said that the great test of the morality of actions is their tendency to promote or contribute toward social cooperation. But an individual can sometimes cooperate best in the long run by declining all but the most imperative family duties and appeals for cooperation in specific "good causes" in order to concentrate all his time and energies on something that he alone can do, or at least on something that he can do superlatively well—writing, painting, composing, scientific research, or whatnot. The moral judgment that we pass on him will depend both on whether his neglect of the ordinary duties and decencies was really necessary to his end, and whether we decide that he really was a genius, or only a mediocrity afflicted with megalomania.

5. *A Moral Aristocracy?*

One further question may be raised under the heading of Vocation. Can there be or should there be a specific Moral Vocation? As it is necessary to have policemen, but not necessary that everyone be a policeman, may it not be necessary to have saints and heroes, even though not everyone can be a saint or a hero? [8]

There are masters in all lines, whether in sports or games, like golf, tennis, swimming, chess, and bridge, or in industry, in science, in music, and in art. These masters in each line— not only by what they have specifically learned and taught but by the inspiration of their very existence—raise the level of performance in their line. Is there not similarly a need for an ethical elite, a moral aristocracy? And is there not similarly a need for this moral leadership not only in the ministry, the priesthood, or in religious orders, but in business and the professions? Where millions have been inspired by the example of Jesus of Nazareth and of the Christian saints, and other millions by the example of a Confucius or a Buddha, thousands also have found moral inspiration in the example of a Socrates, a Spinoza, a Washington, a Jenner, a Pasteur, a Lincoln, a Darwin, a John Stuart Mill, a Charles Lindbergh, an Albert Schweitzer. (I am speaking now, not of anyone in his capacity as a moral *philosopher,* but as a moral exemplar or *character,* distinguished by outstanding dedication, courage, singleness of purpose, compassion, or nobility.)

And if there is a need for such a moral elite, to serve as an inspiration to the rest of us, upon whose shoulders does the duty fall? Here we can only reply, I think, that the duty, if there is one, must be self-assumed. We can welcome, applaud, and admire it, but we cannot demand it. It probably requires, in fact, an inborn moral genius, as scientific or artistic mastery requires an inborn intellectual or artistic genius.

From the holders of certain positions, however, like a minister or a priest, a public official, a teacher, or a college president, we have a right to expect a much better than average conduct because of the greater good that its existence could do or the greater harm that its absence could do to the parishioners, the citizens, or the students who look to them for guidance.

6. *Summary*

To sum up, then: A large part of human duty consists of acts that are not the duty of everybody. There is and must be a division and specialization of duty as there is and must be division and specialization of labor. This is not merely an analogy: the one implies the other. Because we have to assume the full duties and responsibilities of our particular job, we are unable to take over the duties or responsibilities of other jobs. Most of an educator's duties are confined not merely to education, but to the education of his particular students in his particular subject, and not to other students or even to his own students in other subjects. A policeman cannot be held responsible for the efficiency of the police department even in another precinct, let alone for the efficiency of the fire department, or the efficiency of the fire department in another city.

And apart from the division and specialization of duty as the result of the division and specialization of labor, our duty is also limited and defined by our special talents, and by the vicinity, the relation, the particular circumstances, place, or "station" in which we find ourselves. It is because some of us have these special duties that others are relieved of them. This is precisely what we mean when we say that everyone has his own inescapable *personal* responsibilities, which he cannot foist on others.

This does not mean, of course, that there are *no* universal duties. *Everyone* has a duty to speak the truth, to keep his promises and agreements, to act honorably. And even much particularity of duties (as we saw on page 196) can be reconciled with universality. But *every* act does not depend for justification on its universalizability. Some courses (such as voluntary celibacy) can quite properly, in fact, only be chosen by some on condition of their not being chosen by all.[7]

And if we ask how we are to know our special duties, apart from those that inhere in the special vocation we have chosen, we are brought back for answer to two very old maxims, which may profitably be combined into one: Know thyself and Be thyself.

From our discovery of the necessary specialization of many duties we can come to a further conclusion. Our duties are not bottomless and endless. If the duties of each of us are specialized, they are also limited. No man is required to take the burdens of all mankind on his shoulders.

Many moral writers tell us that, "A man's duty under all circumstances is to do what is most conducive to the general good."[9] But this should not be interpreted as imposing on us the duty of trying to relieve the distress of everybody in the world, whether in India, China, or Upper Chad. The weight of such limitless duties, if we assumed we had them, would make us all feel constantly inadequate, guilty, and miserable. It would distract us from properly fulfilling our duties to ourselves and our immediate family, friends, and neighbors. These limited duties are as much as we can reasonably call upon most men to perform. Any generosity or dedication beyond that is optional, to be admired but not exacted. The professional do-gooders now rushing about the world, meddling in everybody's affairs, and constantly exhorting the rest of us that we are forgetting the wretchedness and poverty in Bolivia, Burma, or Brazil, and are relaxing, playing or laughing when somebody is suffering or dying somewhere, make a very dubious contribution to the betterment of the human lot.

The principal real duties of the average man are, after all, not excessively onerous or demanding. They are to do his own job well, to treat his family with love, his intimates with kindness, and everyone with courtesy, and apart from that not to meddle in other people's affairs. A man who does this much is in fact cooperating with his fellows, and very effectively. If everyone did as much, the lot of man might still be far from perfect, but it would show infinite improvement over its present state.

CHAPTER 21

"The Law of Nature"

From time immemorial, many philosophers and poets have held that the sufficient ethical guide for man was to "follow the laws of nature."

Taken literally, the advice is unnecessary and absurd. It is impossible to violate the laws of nature; man cannot help obeying them.

The definitive word on the theory that man "ought" to follow the laws of nature, or that he should take whatever happens in "nature" as his moral guide, was said by John Stuart Mill in his essay on *Nature* (written in 1854 but not published until 1874, after his death).

The word Nature, Mill points out, has two principal meanings: it either denotes the entire system of things, with the aggregate of all their properties, including the relations of cause and effect, or it denotes things as they would be if there were no human intervention.

In the first sense, the doctrine that man ought to follow nature is meaningless. Man has no power to do anything else. All his actions are necessarily in conformity with or "obedience" to one or more of nature's physical or mental laws. The other sense of the term, the doctrine that man ought to follow nature —i.e., ought to make the spontaneous course of things the model of his own voluntary actions—Mill held to be not only irrational but immoral.

It is irrational because all human action whatever consists in altering the spontaneous course of nature, and all useful action consists in improving it. It is immoral because nature can be wanton, destructive, and cruel:

> In sober truth, nearly all the things which men are hanged or imprisoned for doing to one another, are nature's every day performances. Killing, the most criminal act recognized by human laws, Nature does once to every being that lives; and in a large proportion of cases, after protracted tortures such as only the

greatest monsters whom we read of ever purposely inflicted on their living fellow-creatures. If, by an arbitrary reservation, we refuse to account anything murder but what abridges a certain term supposed to be allotted to human life, nature also does this to all but a small percentage of lives, and does it in all the modes, violent or insidious, in which the worst human beings take the lives of one another. Nature impales men, breaks them as if on the wheel, casts them to be devoured by wild beasts, burns them to death, crushes them with stones like the first Christian martyr, starves them with hunger, freezes them with cold, poisons them by the quick or slow venom of her exhalations, and has hundreds of other hideous deaths in reserve, such as the ingenious cruelty of a Nabis or a Domitian never surpassed. All this Nature does with the most supercilious disregard both of mercy and of justice, emptying her shafts upon the best and noblest indifferently with the meanest and worst; upon those who are engaged in the highest and worthiest enterprises, and often as the direct consequence of the noblest acts; and it might almost be imagined as a punishment for them. She mows down those on whose existence hangs the well-being of a whole people, perhaps the prospects of the human race for generations to come, with as little compunction as those whose death is a relief to themselves, or a blessing to those under their noxious influence.

Such are Nature's dealings with life. Even when she does not intend to kill, she inflicts the same tortures in apparent wantonness. In the clumsy provision which she has made for that perpetual renewal of animal life, rendered necessary by the prompt termination she puts to it in every individual instance, no human being ever comes into the world but another human being is literally stretched on the rack for hours or days, not unfrequently issuing in death. Next to taking life (equal to it according to a high authority) is taking the means by which we live; and Nature does this too on the largest scale and with the most callous indifference. A single hurricane destroys the hopes of a season; a flight of locusts, or an inundation, desolates a district; a trifling chemical change in an edible root starves a million of people. The waves of the sea, like banditti, seize and appropriate the wealth of the rich and the little all of the poor with the same accompaniments of stripping, wounding, and killing as their human antitypes. Everything, in short, which the worst men commit either against life or property, is perpetrated on a larger scale by natural agents. Nature has Noyades more fatal than those of Carrier; her explosions of fire damp are as destructive as human artillery; her plague and cholera far surpass the poison cups of the Borgias. Even the love of "order" which is thought to be a following of the ways of Nature, is in fact a contradiction of them. All which people are accustomed to deprecate as "disorder" and its consequences, is precisely a counterpart of Nature's ways. Anarchy and the Reign of Terror are overmatched in injustice, ruin, and death, by a hurricane and a pestilence. . . .

Nature cannot be a proper model for us to imitate. Either it is right that we should kill because nature kills; torture because nature tortures; ruin and devastate because nature does the like; or we ought not to consider at all what nature does, but what it is good to do. If there is such a thing as a *reductio ad absurdum,* this surely amounts to one. If it is a sufficient reason for doing one thing, that nature does it, why not another thing? If not all things, why anything? . . .

Conformity to nature has no connection whatever with right and wrong.

The point is sufficiently made. Perhaps it is over-made, and I need to call attention to some reservations. If we see nature as the source of all evil, we must not overlook that it is also the source of all good. If it wounds and kills us, it also gives us health and life. Nature may someday destroy Man, but it is Nature that has made Man possible. And as Bacon reminded us, "Nature is not governed except by obeying her." We cannot "improve" on nature, we cannot use her to forward our own purposes, unless we study her and learn her laws. We must make use of one or more of her laws to help us to overcome the obstacles presented to our aims by one or more of her other laws. "That art which you say adds to nature, is an art that nature makes. . . . The art itself is nature."[1] The study of the ways of nature is the first law of intelligence, of prudence, and even of survival.

But all this does not mean, as Cicero thought, that "Whatever befalls in the course of nature should be considered good." The identification or confusion of the idea of Nature with the idea of Reason or the idea of Good has, in fact, almost hopelessly confused legal thought for almost twenty centuries. This is illustrated by the history of the doctrine of *Jus Naturale,* or natural law in the legal sense, which has for the most part been advocated and rejected for the wrong reasons. The concept is right, and indispensable to all legal reform; but the terminology is misleading. The ancient Romans came by both "naturally" enough. All legal rules, they thought, should be reasonable and "natural." The Stoics saw and worshiped the "rule of nature" in the world at large. They were convinced that Reason and Right were the voice of Nature. But what was really meant by the Law of Nature was the Law of Reason or Ideal Law. "The law of nature," as one writer has put it, "is an appeal from Caesar to a better informed Caesar. It is an appeal by society at large, not against single decisions or rules, but against entire systems of positive law."[2] The plea for Natural Law, in brief, is a plea for the purification and reform of positive law, an appeal from positive law to justice, an appeal from reality to ideals, an appeal, so to speak, from the highest existing human court to a still Higher Court.

All improvement in positive law depends on the retention of that ideal, as all improvement in positive morality depends on the retention, and the purification and perfection, of our ethical ideals.

CHAPTER 22

Asceticism

1. *The Cult of Self-Torture*

Deeply embedded in the Christian ethical tradition—in fact, deeply embedded in nearly every ethical tradition that rests on a religious foundation, is a broad vein of asceticism. So deep does this go that even today a "moralist" is usually thought of as a killjoy, and most writers on ethics are at best rather patronizing toward pleasure and seem fearful of repudiating the ascetic principle except in its more extreme forms.

Jeremy Bentham scandalized most of his contemporaries by his open derision of the principle of asceticism. He defined it as "that principle which, like the principle of utility, approves or disapproves of any action according to the tendency which it appears to have to augment or diminish the happiness of the party whose interest is in question; but in an inverse manner: approving of actions in as far as they tend to diminish his happiness; disapproving of them in as far as they tend to augment it. It is evident that any one who reprobates any the least particle of pleasure, as such, from whatever source derived, is *pro tanto* a partisan of the principle of asceticism." [1]

And he went on to ridicule its logical basis:

> Ascetic is a term that has been sometimes applied to Monks. It comes from a Greek word which signified *exercise*. The practices by which Monks sought to distinguish themselves from other men were called Exercises. These exercises consisted in so many contrivances they had for tormenting themselves. By this they thought to ingratiate themselves with the Deity. For the Deity, said they, is a Being of infinite benevolence: now a Being of the most ordinary benevolence is pleased to see others make themselves as happy as they can: therefore to make ourselves as unhappy as we can is the way to please the Deity. If any body asked them, what motive they could find for doing all this? Oh! said they, you are not to imagine that we are punishing ourselves for nothing: we know very well what we are about. You are to know,

that for every grain of pain it costs us now, we are to have a hundred grains of pleasure by and by. The case is, that God loves to see us torment ourselves at present: indeed he has as good as told us so. But this is done only to try us, in order just to see how we should behave: which it is plain he could not know, without making the experiment. Now then, from the satisfaction it gives him to see us make ourselves as unhappy as we can make ourselves in this present life, we have a sure proof of the satisfaction it will give him to see us as happy as he can make us in a life to come.[2]

Asceticism, when it is carried to its logical conclusion, can only result in suicide, or voluntary death. No man can suppress *all* his desires. Unless he keeps at least the desire for food and drink, or "consents" to take them, he can survive only a few days. The ascetic who constantly flagellates himself renders himself even unfit for work, by exhausting his body and mind. He must then depend for survival upon the generosity of others who consent to give him alms. But this means that the ascetic can survive only because asceticism is not obligatory upon everybody. Others must work productively so that he may live on part of what they produce. And as the ascetic must not only tolerate but even depend on nonascetics for survival, asceticism must develop a dual morality, one for saints and one for worldlings, that splits ethics in two. If ascetics suppress all sexual desires, they must depend on others to keep the human race from dying out.[3]

But though only a few have been able to carry the ascetic principle to its logical conclusion, and then only in the last week of their lives, many have succeeded in carrying it to fantastic and incredible lengths. Let us listen to the account that Lecky gives of the "ascetic epidemic" that swept over the Christian world during the fourth and fifth centuries:

> There is, perhaps, no phase in the moral history of mankind of a deeper or more painful interest than this ascetic epidemic. A hideous, sordid, and emaciated maniac, without knowledge, without patriotism, without natural affection, passing his life in a long routine of useless and atrocious self-torture, and quailing before the ghastly phantoms of his delirious brain, had become the ideal of the nations which had known the writings of Plato and Cicero and the lives of Socrates and Cato. For about two centuries, the

hideous maceration of the body was regarded as the highest proof of excellence. St. Jerome declares, with a thrill of admiration, how he had seen a monk, who for thirty years had lived exclusively on a small portion of barley bread and of muddy water; another, who lived in a hole and never ate more than five figs for his daily repast; a third, who cut his hair only on Easter Sunday, who never washed his clothes, who never changed his tunic till it fell to pieces, who starved himself till his eyes grew dim, and his skin "like a pumice stone," and whose merits, shown by these austerities, Homer himself would be unable to recount. For six months, it is said, St. Macarius of Alexandria slept in a marsh, and exposed his body naked to the stings of venomous flies. He was accustomed to carry about with him eighty pounds of iron. His disciple, St. Eusebius, carried one hundred and fifty pounds of iron, and lived for three years in a dried-up well. St. Sabinus would only eat corn that had become rotten by remaining for a month in water. St. Besarion spent forty days and nights in the middle of thorn-bushes, and for forty years never lay down when he slept, which last penance was also during fifteen years practised by St. Pachomius. Some saints, like St. Marcian, restricted themselves to one meal a day, so small that they continually suffered the pangs of hunger. Of one of them it is related that his daily food was six ounces of bread and a few herbs; that he was never seen to recline on a mat or bed, or even to place his limbs easily for sleep; but that sometimes, from excess of weariness, his eyes would close at his meals, and the food would drop from his mouth. Other saints, however, ate only every second day; while many, if we could believe the monkish historian, abstained for whole weeks from all nourishment. St. Macarius of Alexandria is said during an entire week to have never lain down, or eaten anything but a few uncooked herbs on Sunday. Of another famous saint, named John, it is asserted that for three whole years he stood in prayer, leaning upon a rock; that during all that time he never sat or lay down, and that his only nourishment was the Sacrament, which was brought him on Sundays. Some of the hermits lived in deserted dens of wild beasts, others in dried-up wells, while others found a congenial resting-place among the tombs. Some disdained all clothes, and crawled abroad like the wild beasts, covered only by their matted hair. In Mesopotamia, and part of Syria, there existed a sect known by the name of "Grazers," who never lived under a roof, who ate neither flesh nor bread, but who spent their time for ever on the mountain side, and ate grass like cattle. The cleanliness of the body was regarded as a pollution of the soul. And the saints who were most admired had become one hideous mass of clotted filth. St. Athanasius relates with enthusiasm how St. Antony, the patriarch of monachism, had never, to extreme old age, been guilty of washing his feet. The less constant St. Poemen fell into this habit for the first time when a very old man, and, with a glimmering of common sense, defended himself against the astonished monks by saying that he had "learnt to kill not his body, but his passions." St. Abraham the hermit, however, who lived for fifty years after his conversion, rigidly refused from that date to wash either his face or his feet. He was, it is said, a person of singular beauty, and his biographer somewhat strangely remarks that "his face reflected the purity of his soul." St. Ammon had never seen himself naked. A famous virgin named Silvia, though she was sixty years old and though bodily sickness was a consequence of her habits, resolutely refused, on religious principles, to wash any part of her body except her fingers. St. Euphraxia joined a convent of one hundred and thirty nuns, who never washed their feet, and who shuddered at the mention of a bath. An anchorite once imagined that he was mocked by an illusion of the devil, as he saw gliding before him through the desert a naked creature black with filth and years of exposure, and with white hair floating to the wind. It was a once beautiful woman, St. Mary of Egypt, who had thus, during forty-seven years, been expiating her sins. The occasional decadence of the monks into habits of decency was a subject of much reproach. "Our fathers," said the abbot Alexander, looking mournfully back to the past, "never washed their faces, but we frequent the public baths." It was related of one monastery in the desert, that the monks suffered greatly from want of water to drink; but at the prayer of the abbot Theodosius a copious stream was produced. But soon some monks, tempted by the abundant supply, diverged from their old austerity, and persuaded the abbot to avail himself of the stream for the construction of a bath. The bath was made. Once, and once only, did the monks enjoy their ablutions, when the stream ceased to flow. Prayers, tears, and fastings were in vain. A whole year passed. At last the abbot destroyed the bath, which was the object of the Divine displeasure, and the waters flowed afresh. But of all the evidences of the loathsome excesses to which this spirit was carried, the life of St. Simeon Stylites is probably the most remarkable. It would be difficult to conceive a more horrible or disgusting picture than is given of the penances by which that saint commenced his ascetic career. He had bound a rope around him so that it became imbedded in his flesh, which putrefied around it. "A horrible stench, intolerable to the bystanders, exhaled from his body, and worms dropped from him whenever he moved, and they filled his bed. Sometimes he left the monastery and slept in a dry well, inhabited, it is said, by demons. He built successively three pillars, the last being sixty feet high and scarcely two cubits in circumference, and on this pillar, during thirty years, he remained exposed to every change of climate, ceaselessly and rapidly bending his body in prayer almost to the level of his feet. A spectator attempted to number these rapid motions, but desisted from weariness when he had counted 1,244. For a whole year, we are told, St. Simeon stood upon one leg, the other being covered with hideous ulcers, while his biographer was commissioned to stand by his side, to pick up the worms that fell from his body, and to replace them in the sores, the saint saying to the worm, "Eat what God has given you." From every quarter pilgrims of every degree thronged to do him homage. A crowd of prelates followed him to the grave. A brilliant star is said to have shone miraculously over his pillar; the general voice of mankind pronounced him to be the highest model of a Christian saint; and several other anchorites imitated or emulated his penances.[4]

Lecky goes on to tell us that

> . . . self-torture was for some centuries regarded as the chief measure of human excellence. . . . The hermit's cell was the scene of perpetual mourning. Tears and sobs, and frantic strugglings with imaginary daemons, and paroxysms of religious despair, were the texture of his life. . . . The solace of intellectual occupations was rarely resorted to. "The duty," said St. Jerome, "of a monk is not to teach, but to weep." . . . The great majority of the early monks appear to have been men who were not only absolutely ignorant themselves, but who also looked upon learning with positive disfavor. . . .
> Most terrible of all were the struggles of young and ardent men. . . . With many of the hermits it was a rule never to look upon the face of any woman. . . . [In the fourth and fifth centuries] the cardinal virtue of the religious type was not [Christian] love, but chastity. And this chastity, which was regarded as the ideal state, was not the purity of an undefiled marriage. It was the absolute suppression of the whole sensual side of our nature. . . . The business of the saint was to eradicate a natural appetite. . . . The consequence of this was first of all a very deep sense of the habitual and innate depravity of human nature; and, in the next place, a very strong association of the idea of pleasure with that of vice. All this necessarily flowed from the supreme value placed upon virginity. . . .

Severance from the interests and affections of all around him was the chief object of the anchorite, and the first consequence of the prominence of asceticism was a profound discredit thrown upon the domestic virtues.

The extent to which this discredit was carried, the intense hardness of heart and ingratitude manifested by the saints towards those who were bound to them by the closest of earthly ties, is known to few who have not studied the original literature on the subject. These things are commonly thrown into the shade by those modern sentimentalists who delight in idealizing the devotees of the past. To break by his ingratitude the heart of the mother who had borne him, to persuade the wife who adored him that it was her duty to separate from him for ever, to abandon his children, uncared for and beggars, to the mercies of the world, was regarded by the true hermit as the most acceptable offering he could make to his God. His business was to save his own soul.

The effect of the mortification of the domestic affections upon the general character [concludes Lecky] was probably very pernicious. The family circle is the appointed sphere, not only for the performance of manifest duties, but also for the cultivation of the affections; and the extreme ferocity which so often characterized the ascetic was the natural consequence of the discipline he imposed upon himself.[5]

2. *William James for the Defense*

In William James's *Varieties of Religious Experience* (1902) we find further examples of asceticism, drawn, for the most part, from much later periods. James is almost as severe as Lecky in condemning self-torture in its more extreme forms. "Catholic teachers," he points out, "have always professed the rule that, since health is needed for efficiency in God's service, health must not be sacrificed to mortification." And he adds: "We can no longer sympathize with cruel deities, and the notion that God can take delight in the spectacle of sufferings self-inflicted in his honor is abhorrent."[6] But James defends asceticism in its milder forms, and it may be instructive to examine his arguments.

His first defense rests chiefly on psychological grounds. The saint may find "positive pleasure in sacrifice and asceticism."[7] He later cites a striking example:

ASCETICISM

> Of the founder of the Sacred Heart order . . . we read that: "Her love of pain and suffering was insatiable. . . . She said that she could cheerfully live till the day of judgment, provided she might always have matter for suffering for God; but that to live a single day without suffering would be intolerable. She said again that she was devoured with two unassuageable fevers, one for the holy communion, the other for suffering, humiliation, and annihilation. 'Nothing but pain,' she continually said in her letters, 'makes my life supportable.' "[8]

It is true that James treats this case as "perverse" and "pathological," but he does strongly commend a more "healthy-minded" asceticism:

> Asceticism may be a mere expression of organic hardihood, disgusted with too much ease. . . .
> Quite apart from the immediate pleasure which any sensible experience may give us, our own general moral attitude in procuring or undergoing the experience brings with it a secondary satisfaction or distaste. Some men and women, indeed, there are who can live on smiles and the word "yes" forever. But for others (indeed for most), this is too tepid and relaxed a moral climate. Passive happiness is slack and insipid, and soon grows mawkish and intolerable. Some austerity and wintry negativity, some roughness, danger, stringency, and effort, some "no! no!" must be mixed in, to produce the sense of an existence with character and texture and power.[9]

No one can deny that this is psychologically true. But it is not, on examination, an argument in favor of *real* asceticism. It merely points out that men find their happiness in different ways. It is an argument only against a shallow and shortsighted hedonism that identifies "pleasure" with a mere sensual indulgence or foam-rubber comfort. It might even be considered a refined *hedonistic* argument for "asceticism," which counsels "austerity" in order to sharpen "the keen edge of seldom pleasure." It assumes, in other words, that one can maximize one's satisfactions and one's long-run happiness by some temporary deprivation, toughening, or struggle, or else what is gained, in James's own words, "comes too cheap and has no zest."

It is surprising to find how many of the ostensibly "antihedonist" arguments that fill the ethical textbooks really turn out, on examination, to be arguments in favor of more subtle, intelligent, and far-sighted ways of maximizing pleasure or happiness than those that the so-called "hedonists" are supposed to recommend.

But in addition to this psychological defense of "asceticism," James does undertake an ethical justification, which I think is worth quoting at some length:

> Yet I believe that a more careful consideration of the whole matter, distinguishing between the general good intention of asceticism and the uselessness of some of the particular acts of which it may be guilty, ought to rehabilitate it in our esteem. For in its spiritual meaning asceticism stands for nothing less than for the essence of the twice-born philosophy. It symbolizes, lamely enough no doubt, but sincerely, the belief that there is an element of real wrongness in this world, which is neither to be ignored nor evaded, but which must be squarely met and overcome by an appeal to the soul's heroic resources, and neutralized and cleansed away by suffering. . . .
>
> Does not . . . the worship of material luxury and wealth, which constitutes so large a portion of the "spirit" of our age, make somewhat for effeminacy and unmanliness? Is not the exclusively sympathetic and facetious way in which most children are brought up today—so different from the education of a hundred years ago, especially in evangelical circles—in danger, in spite of its many advantages, of developing a certain trashiness of fibre? Are there not hereabouts some points of application for a renovated and revised ascetic discipline? . . .
>
> One hears of the mechanical equivalent of heat. What we now need to discover in the social realm is the moral equivalent of war: something heroic that will speak to men as universally as war does, and yet will be as compatible with their spiritual selves as war has proved itself to be incompatible. I have often thought that in the old monkish poverty-worship, in spite of the pedantry which infested it, there might be something like that moral equivalent of war which we are seeking. May not voluntarily accepted poverty be "the strenuous life," without the need of crushing weaker peoples?
>
> Poverty indeed *is* the strenuous life,—without brass bands or uniforms or hysteric popular applause or lies or circumlocutions; and when one sees the way in which wealth-getting enters as an ideal into the very bone and marrow of our generation, one won-

ders whether a revival of the belief that poverty is a worthy religious vocation may not be "the transformation of military courage," and the spiritual reform which our time stands most in need of.

Among us English-speaking peoples especially do the praises of poverty need once more to be boldly sung. We have grown literally afraid to be poor. We despise any one who elects to be poor in order to simplify and save his inner life. If he does not join the general scramble and pant with the money-making street, we deem him spiritless and lacking in ambition. We have lost the power even of imagining what the ancient idealization of poverty could have meant: the liberation from material attachments, the unbribed soul, the manlier indifference, the paying our way by what we are or do and not by what we have, the right to fling away our life at any moment irresponsibly,—the more athletic trim, in short, the moral fighting shape. When we of the so-called better classes are scared as men were never scared in history at material ugliness and hardship; when we put off marriage until our house can be artistic, and quake at the thought of having a child without a bank-account and doomed to manual labor, it is time for thinking men to protest against so unmanly and irreligious a state of opinion.[10]

Most readers will find it difficult not to feel a great deal of sympathy with this eloquent exhortation, though they may suspect that James has temporarily deserted the role of moral philosopher for that of preacher. When we examine his plea critically, we find a certain ambiguity in his use of the word "poverty" as well as in his use of the word "asceticism." Certainly it is hard to admire mere acquisitiveness, the pursuit of wealth simply for wealth's sake, or for the sake of mere comfort or, worse, of mere ostentation. But does this apply to the pursuit of wealth—at least of a competence—as a means to other ends? Is James advocating *real* poverty—the kind of poverty that means the constant pangs of hunger or actual starvation, lack of proper education or even proper nutrition for one's children, the inability to secure medical help for oneself or one's family when suffering pain or wasting away from some grave disease? Would this kind of poverty really "simplify and save" one's "inner life"? Or would it not tend rather to make the enrichment of one's inner life almost impossible?

A person with this kind of "voluntarily accepted poverty,"

moreover, is not in a very good position to be of much help to others; he is likely, on the contrary, when it comes to a crisis, to find himself dependent on the wealth-seeking neighbors whom he despises.

What James overlooked is that all honestly acquired wealth tends to be achieved in direct proportion to what a man contributes to production—to the production, that is, of the goods and services that his neighbors need or want. The phrase "money-making" is a misleading metaphor. What people (except counterfeiters) "make" or produce is not money, but goods and services that are sufficiently desired so that people are willing to pay money for them. The phrase "money-making" is apt to be applied to activities that one does not admire—perhaps because one does not understand the function they serve or the need for them. Good doctors, dentists, and surgeons all "make money"—usually in proportion to how good they are. This money is voluntarily paid. Would James have disapproved of such careers—or of the efforts of a man to make himself a better doctor, dentist, or surgeon in order to "make more money"?

In the cultural field, eminent pianists, violinists, opera singers, orchestra leaders, painters, architects, actors, playwrights, novelists, even psychologists, philosophers, and professors, "make money." But this does not mean that they are *primarily* engaged in money-making. And all of them make their money by rendering a service to others that others are willing to pay for. For many of them, as for a Henry Ford or a Thomas Edison, the money they make is merely a by-product of what they add to the community's amenities, satisfactions and progress. True, most people in our civilization never achieve eminence, and most of them are in humbler occupations that contribute nothing to "culture" but a good deal to the material basis without which culture would not be possible. A sensible man does not despise the baker, the butcher, the dairyman, the grocer, the trucker, or farmers because their activities have been undertaken to make money. In making money for themselves these people have been rendering essential services to *him*. So money-making, in the disparaging sense, is apt to be applied to activities of which the speaker does not approve, such as brewing or distilling, or of which he does not quite understand the economic purpose, such as stockbroking or advertising. The disparagers are apt to forget, also, that callings that seem dull to them are often intensely interesting to those who engage in them, and help to give excitement, color, and flavor to their lives.

Finally, it seems inconsistent of James to praise "voluntarily accepted poverty" because it involves "the strenuous life" and to condemn money-making because it involves "scrambling" and "panting." This is really to condemn money-making as entailing much *too* strenuous a life. Could it not be that many people do in fact find in production and intense business rivalry the exercise for their talents, the outlet for their energies, the strengthening of their faculties, and the testing of their nerve, grit, and stamina that become for them "the moral equivalent of war"?

The moral philosopher should not attempt to impose his own merely personal preferences and values on others. None of us has the right to insist that other people must lead the kind of lives or pursue the special ends that would appeal to *us*. What the moral philosopher *can* do, *qua* moral philosopher, is to suggest that people ask themselves whether the kind of lives they are leading and the objectives they are pursuing are really most likely to promote their own happiness in the long run or the happiness of the community of which they are a part. Within these limits, everyone must decide for himself what kind of life or what objectives would be most likely to promote his own happiness. This is the realm of *chacun à son goût*.

3. *Self-Restraint, and Self-Discipline*

The ascetic ideal, however, is still reflected in most contemporary ethical theories. Let us see how it makes its appearance, for example, in the ethics of Irving Babbitt.[11] The whole emphasis of Babbitt is on the virtues of decorum, moderation, restraint, self-conquest, "the inner check," "the Will to Refrain." [12] But very little is said in answer to the natural question: To refrain from *what?* From doing good? From painting a great picture, composing a great symphony, discovering a cure for some dread disease?

The ideal of Virtue summed up in "the will to refrain," like the monkish and ascetic ideals of the Dark Ages, is essentially negative. Virtue is to consist in *refraining* from something. But virtue is positive. Virtue is not the mere absence of vice, any more than vice is the mere absence of virtue. When a man is asleep (unless he is a sentry on duty or otherwise in a position where he should *not* be sleeping) he cannot be said to be either virtuous or vicious. If, as Aristotle once put it, "The greatest virtues are those which are most useful to other persons," [13] your "will to refrain" is only negatively useful to them.

The element of truth in Babbitt's theory is an element that has been recognized, if not by Rousseauistic romanticists and the apostles of self-indulgence, at least by every intelligent utilitarian since Bentham. We must refrain from impulsive acts that may give us momentary pleasure at the cost of a more than offsetting disappointment, pain, and misery in the long run. Each of us, in brief, must practice *self-discipline*. This is unexpectedly but eloquently affirmed even by Bertrand Russell in a sketch of his friend Joseph Conrad:

> He thought of civilized and morally tolerable human life as a dangerous walk on a thin crust of barely cooled lava which at any moment might break and let the unwary sink into fiery depths. He was very conscious of the various forms of passionate madness to which men are prone, and it was this that gave him such a profound belief in the importance of discipline. His point of view, one might perhaps say, was the antithesis of Rousseau's: "Man is born in chains, but he can become free." He becomes free, so I believe Conrad would have said, not by letting loose his impulses, not by being casual and uncontrolled, but by subduing wayward impulse to a dominant purpose. . . .
> Conrad's point of view was far from modern. In the modern world there are two philosophies: the one, which stems from Rousseau, and sweeps aside discipline as unnecessary; the other, which finds its fullest expression in totalitarianism, which thinks of discipline as essentially imposed from without. Conrad adhered to the older tradition, that discipline should come from within. He despised indiscipline, and hated discipline that was merely external.[14]

Self-discipline is certainly a major virtue, and a necessary means for most of the other virtues. But self-discipline is essentially a *means*. It is a confusion of thought to treat it as the end itself. Its value is largely *instrumental* rather than "intrinsic," *derivative* rather than independent. One refrains from sexual excesses, or excesses in smoking, drinking, or eating, in the interests of one's long-run health and happiness.

Anything that is so important as a means tends of course to be regarded also as an end in itself. And provided the primarily instrumental function of self-restraint or self-discipline is kept in mind, this does no harm. But when self-discipline is regarded as *the* virtue, when its pursuit becomes obsessive, it is in danger of being perverted into a form of asceticism.

There is, however, a twilight zone in which practical decision may be difficult. William James, in a famous passage of his *Psychology*, urged his readers to practice self-restraint in little "unnecessary" things to develop the moral strength and the habit:

> *Keep the faculty of effort alive in you by a little gratuitous exercise every day.* That is, be systematically ascetic or heroic in little unnecessary points, do every day or two something for no other reason than that you would rather not do it, so that when the hour of dire need draws nigh, it may find you not unnerved and untrained to stand the test. Asceticism of this sort is like the insurance which a man pays on his house and goods. The tax does him no good at the time, and possibly may never bring him a return. But if the fire *does* come, his having paid it will be his salvation from ruin. So with the man who has daily inured himself to habits of concentrated attention, energetic volition, and self-denial in unnecessary things. He will stand like a tower when everything rocks around him, and when his softer fellow-mortals are winnowed like chaff in the blast.[15]

This is bracing and altogether admirable advice for the young, and probably essential to a good moral education. But when the character has been formed, and one has reached middle age, I doubt the necessity of being ascetic or heroic in "unnecessary" points. If one gets up every morning early enough to catch the 8:05, showers, shaves, and does one's other necessary morning chores, puts in a full day's work at a job sufficiently arduous to be lucrative, keeps one's appointments and other promises, keeps regular hours, doesn't indulge excessively in drinking or smoking, eats moderately, stays away from foods that one can't digest or that lead to overweight or excessive cholesterol, does enough exercise to keep fit and prevent flabbiness, one is doing a good deal. The Lord will not blame you too much for not looking around for little "unnecessary" deprivations simply in order to develop your moral muscles.

We may agree with William James, in brief, in regarding self-discipline as, so to speak, a form of moral insurance, but this is no reason for paying an excessive insurance premium. James frequently used the word "asceticism" when he did not mean *real* asceticism but only self-discipline or self-toughening —what might better be called *athleticism*. Let us say, for clarity of concept and definition, that any voluntary deprivation or exertion that *undermines* one's health and strength is *really* asceticism, but any voluntary deprivation, exercise, or exertion that *increases* one's health, strength and hardihood is *not* asceticism but athleticism or self-discipline.

In sum: We practice self-restraint, we refuse to yield to every impulse or passion or animal appetite, not for the sake of sacrifice itself, but only in the interests of our health, happiness, and well-being in the long run.

As Ludwig von Mises has put it:

> To act reasonably means to sacrifice the less important to the more important. We make temporary sacrifices when we give up small things to obtain bigger things, as when we cease to indulge in alcohol to avoid its physiological after-effects. Men submit to the effort of labor in order that they may not starve.
>
> Moral behavior is the name we give to the temporary sacrifices made in the interests of social cooperation, which is the chief means by which human wants and human life generally may be supplied. All ethics are social ethics. . . . To behave morally, means to sacrifice the less important to the more important by making social co-operation possible.
>
> The fundamental defect of most of the anti-utilitarian systems of ethics lies in the misconstruction of the meaning of the temporary sacrifices which duty demands. They do not see the purpose of sacrifice and foregoing of pleasure, and they construct the absurd hypothesis that sacrifice and renunciation are morally valuable in themselves. They elevate unselfishness and self-sacrifice and the love or compassion which lead to them, to absolute moral values. The pain that at first accompanies the sacrifice is defined as moral because it is painful—which is very near asserting that all action painful to the performer is moral.

From the discovery of this confusion we can see why various sentiments and actions which are socially neutral or even harmful come to be called moral. . . .

Man is not evil merely because he wants to enjoy pleasure and avoid pain—in other words, to live. Renunciation, abnegation, and self-sacrifice are not good in themselves. . . .[16]

4. *Erecting Means into Ends*

But the immemorial persistence of this moral confusion, of this erection of temporary means into absolute ends, has tended to make the dominant philosophies of morals dismal and grim. All theories that insist on Virtue and Duty for their own sake are almost necessarily dreary and joyless. They place their emphasis always on self-denial, self-deprivation, self-sacrifice for their own sake, and tend to lead to the fallacy that suffering, mortification, and flagellation are pleasing to God. But theories that emphasize Virtue and the performance of Duty as primarily means to the reduction of human misery and the promotion of human happiness not only have the enormous advantage of making Virtue attractive rather than unpalatable to the mass of mankind, and are not only cheering in themselves, but imply that Cheerfulness is itself one of the Virtues, because it makes those who adopt it a source of cheer and joy to others, by example and contagion rather than by solemn (and inconsistent) admonition.

Both asceticism and self-sacrifice, as moral *ideals,* can be a perversion of true morality. Both confuse means with ends, and erect a means into an end. The *readiness* to undergo hardships or to make sacrifices, if they should prove necessary, is one thing; the *insistence* on undergoing hardships and making sacrifices (and making the extent of the hardships and sacrifices rather than the good achieved the test of the "morality" of an action) is quite another.

Yet this moral confusion, this exaltation of means above ends, persists in modern moral judgments. A chemist who develops a new drug that cures millions (but whose work may involve no particular risk to himself and may even bring him a profit), is not regarded as an outstanding exemplar of "morality," whereas a Western doctor who goes to Africa to cure a comparative handful of savages, and perhaps administer this same drug to them, gets a worldwide reputation as a "saint" because his actions, while quantitatively far less beneficial to mankind, involve great hardships and self-sacrifice.

It may be argued that while this doctor has not perhaps conferred as much direct and immediate good on humanity as the discoverer of the new drug, he has nevertheless earned greater *moral* merit, and that in the long run his inspiring personal example may confer a benefit upon mankind not to be measured merely by the immediate physical suffering that the doctor has relieved by his work. Perhaps. Yet it is hard to escape the suspicion that much of the idolatry of the doctor in Africa is the result of regarding asceticism, sacrifice, "morality," "self-perfection," as *the* end in itself, wholly apart from what it may or may not contribute to relieving human misery. The medieval saint, symbolized by Simeon Stylites, performed prodigious feats of asceticism, but was of very little use to anybody else, whereas a modern medical researcher, who injects himself with the germs or virus of a dread disease, in order that he may test his remedy, may confer a priceless benefit on mankind. *His* risk or self-sacrifice is not sacrifice for its own sake, but for the sake of a goal which gives meaning and value to the sacrifice.

In sum, morality is a means. The striving for "morality" or "self-perfection" for its own sake is a perversion of true morality.

CHAPTER 23

Ethical Skepticism

1. *One-Sided Skepticism*

Hume begins his *Inquiry Concerning the Principles of Morals* by dismissing "those who have denied the reality of moral distinctions" as "disingenuous disputants" who "really do not believe in the opinions they defend, but engage in the controversy from affectation, from a spirit of opposition, or from a desire of showing wit and ingenuity superior to the rest of mankind." And he contemptuously suggests that "the only way . . . of converting an antagonist of this kind is to leave him to himself."

Hume may be right in assuming that the professed ethical nihilist is not sincere. But one can think of more persuasive refutations than a mere refusal to answer him. One could point out to him, for example, that if he were set upon by a gang of thugs, and savagely beaten and robbed, he would feel, in addition to his physical pain, something very close to moral indignation.

It is hard, in fact, to find consistent ethical nihilists. When they boldly profess their nihilism, they are thinking of only one side of the problem. They do not see why *they* should be bound by any of the traditional moral rules. But cross-examination, or their own unguarded statements, will quickly reveal that they expect *others* to be. And in this respect they perhaps differ from the rest of us only in degree. In fact, morality might be cynically defined as the conduct that each of us desires *others* to observe toward himself. We do not want others to kill us, beat us, rob us, cheat us, lie to us, break their promises to us, or even to be carelessly late for an appointment with us. And the best way to assure that these things are not done to us, we recognize (when they are not acts that can be forbidden by enforceable law), is not to do them ourselves. In addition to this directly utilitarian consideration, most of us feel the need of intellectual consistency in the standards we apply to ourselves as well as to others.

We might not be going too far wrong, in fact, if we thought of this as the origin and basis of common-sense ethics. I do not mean to suggest that this type of reasoning arose at some particular historic time in the past, but rather that it has gradually evolved, and is a consideration that is continually occurring to each of us anew, half-consciously if not explicitly. Ethics may be thought of as a code of rules that we first try to impose on each other and then—recognizing the need for consistency, the importance of our own example, and the force of the retort: "How about *you?*"—agree to accept also for ourselves.

In brief, people may profess to be ethical skeptics when asked to abide by some moral rule, but no one is an ethical skeptic about the rules he thinks *others* should adopt in *their* conduct towards *him*. And out of this consideration grow both the Confucian or negative Golden Rule: "Do not do unto others what you would not wish others to do unto you," and the Golden Rule itself: "Do unto others as ye would have others do unto you." (Both of these rules are too subjective in form, however, for a scientific ethics. The objective statement would be: It is right to act toward others as it would be right for them to act toward you.)

2. *"Might Is Right"*

Now the professed ethical skeptic or nihilist will nearly always be found to be either insincere or inconsistent—when he is not merely being ironical. This applies to the first such skeptic we meet in systematic ethical literature—the Thrasymachus of the Platonic dialogues, who proclaims that "justice is nothing else than the interest of the stronger." [1]

It soon becomes clear, however, as the dialogue progresses, that Thrasymachus does not believe that this is really justice, but merely what commonly passes as such. His actual belief, as his argument reveals, is that *injustice* is the interest of the stronger. At the back of his mind he believes, as Socrates does, that the true rules of justice are the rules that are in the interest of the whole community. Perhaps Socrates does not make the best possible refutation, but he does make a very good one. Its most effective point, in fact, is that justice tends to increase social cooperation, whereas injustice tends to destroy it: "Injustice creates divisions and hatreds and fighting and justice imparts harmony and friendship. . . . The just are clearly wiser and better and abler than the unjust. . . . The unjust are incapable of common action." [2] Unfortunately Socrates did not recognize the full importance or develop the full utilitarian implications of this point. If he had, he would have made an even greater contribution to philosophical ethics.

One of these implications, for example, is that even criminals must have a code of ethics among themselves if they are to be reasonably successful when they operate as a gang. Recognition of this requirement is embodied in proverbial wisdom. "When thieves quarrel, robberies are discovered." "When thieves fall out, honest men come by their own." Hence there must be "honor" even among thieves. They must agree to and abide by a "fair" division of the loot. They must not betray each other. The bribed official must "stay bought." The same transgressions that are condemned by the law-abiding community are denounced as "double-crossing" by criminals themselves when practiced against them by their fellow-criminals. This underworld code is the homage that criminals must pay to virtue.

In Thrasymachus we have the original form of the theory that Might makes Right. We have an anticipation of the later ethical cynicism of Mandeville as well as the germ of Nietzsche's master-morality and Marx's theory of class-ethics. But in all these theories we find either a lack of sincerity or a lack of consistency, or a lack of both.

How many people sincerely believe, for example, that Might *is* Right? In the mouth of the conqueror, the tyrant, or the bully, it is merely the shortest way of saying: "What I say goes! Do this—or else!" Or, "What are you going to do about it?" In the mouth of the conquered, the victim, or the cynical philospher, it is the shortest way of saying, "The strong will always act solely in their own interest, and impose their will upon the weak. It is vain to expect anything better." But neither the tyrant nor the victim really means: "This is the way things ought to be. The rules laid down by the strong are always the best rules. This is the system that would work out, in the long run, to the best interests of humanity." And if the tyrant really thinks he means this when he is on top, he changes his mind as soon as somebody stronger comes along and deposes him.

Bernard Mandeville's *Fable of the Bees, or Private Vices Made Public Benefits* (1724), while marked by great penetration, suffers from this very lack of sincerity or consistency. Mandeville's thesis is that naturally egoistic man was tricked by clever politicians into relinquishing his own individual interests and subordinating them to the good of the community. But Mandeville never seems quite certain whether this outcome has been good or bad for humanity.

3. *Nietzsche's "Master-Morality"*

Nietzsche's "master-morality" is merely another form of the Thrasymachus doctrine that "justice is nothing else than the interest of the stronger." But the master-morality is inconsistent and self-destructive. In order that some may be masters, others must be slaves. Nietzsche recognizes this, but he does not recognize its implications. For he does not *advocate* slave-morality; he despises it. The master-morality is for the "superior," the slave-morality for the "inferior." But who is to separate the "superiors" from the "inferiors" and assign them their respective roles?

Perhaps Nietzsche thought himself capable of doing this, but he was vague concerning the criterion he would apply. Would it be comparative intelligence, or craftiness and cunning (a quite different thing), or physical courage, or moral courage, or will to dominate others, or physical strength? Or would it be some weighted average of these qualities? In any case, what he (or his disciple) would undoubtedly find is that if he arranged men in this order they would form, not two classes with a definite break or gap between them, but a continuous series, running from the tallest to the shortest (in the quality or amalgam of qualities specified), with an almost infinitesimal difference between each man and the next, so that the line would look like the smooth "demand curves" drawn by the economist. The dividing point would be arbitrary. The borderline cases would present insoluble problems. For men in the "inferior" class would be growing into maturity and strength, and men in the "superior" class would be sinking into weakness and senility.

Is each man then himself to decide whether he belongs in the "superior" or "inferior" class? Then, as each man seeks to be admired and not to be despised, all will seek to belong to the master class—which is impossible. But if each seeks to enslave all the others, then there is a mutually destructive war of each against all, until one "superman" has enslaved all the rest.

Nietzsche does at times seem to favor this ideal. At other times he seems to favor an ideal under which a small class of masters owe certain vaguely specified obligations to their "equals," but none at all to their "inferiors." But who is to decide which are one's "equals" and which are one's "inferiors"? How does one convince or compel anyone else to acquiesce in the role of "inferior"? And if all have the mentality and the "will to power" that Nietzsche admires, if none will ever passively or permanently accept the role of slave, then the only alternative is a war of mutual destruction until only the top superman is left—after which even he cannot function as a master because there is no one left to enslave.

Possibly this is being unfair to Nietzsche, but this is the best I can make of him. True, his work is full of acute insights. But it is impossible to fit them into a coherent system. His philosophy is made up of rhetoric, rhapsody, and rant; and the only way a coherent philosophy can be made out of this is for the interpreter or the commentator to ask the reader to select this statement or that one and forget all the rest.

The theory that man not only is but *ought* to be entirely selfish, and give no consideration to others, has certain similarities to Nietzscheanism, and might be thought to require discussion here. I doubt, however, that this can be properly regarded as ethical skepticism or nihilism. It is rather to be classed as a definite moral—or immoral—theory. In any case, I have said what little needs to be said about it in Chapter 13.

4. *The Class Theory of Marx*

But I do believe that a discussion of the Marxist theory of morals belongs here, even though I have a separate chapter (31) on "Socialism and Communism." For the Marxist theory is something quite different from socialist and communist practice.

Marx's ethical theory is simply part of his general social theory. This is that economic forces determine the course of history. "The material conditions of production" determine the entire "superstructure" of society—political organization, laws, ideology, culture, art, philosophy, religion and, of course, morals. And since all societies have hitherto been class societies, the morality prevailing at any time has been a code devised to serve the interests of the ruling class.

The reader will perceive that we have here merely another and not very different form of the doctrine of Thrasymachus that "justice is nothing else than the interest of the stronger." The difference consists merely in the greater and more complex elaboration of the theory.

The defects of the theory are quickly apparent (though generations of pious Marxists have been blind to them). It explains the current morality as a mere "result" of the "material productive forces." But it never explains the origin of the "material productive forces" themselves, or how or why one "mode of production" is superseded by another. Obviously the changes in "modes of production" are brought about by human thought,[3] but this never seems to have occurred to Marx. It is true, of course, that once one man has improved a productive method or process, other people see the improvement and this leads to further improvements and further ideas. It is likewise true that our physical environment affects our ideas: a child who grows up in a world of telephones and electric lights, automobiles and airplanes, radio and television, intercontinental missiles and space probes, computers and automation, will not have precisely the same outlook on life as a child who grew up in a world of windmills and ox-carts. But this is an entirely different thing from saying that there is a merely one-way causation from an (uncaused?) "material productive force" to human thought or a definite set of ideas. Man determines and creates his technological environment far more than that environment, in turn, influences him. But Marx was himself deeply influenced by the fashionable philosophic "materialism" of his time.

Another difficulty with the Marxist moral theory (which is

much less a moral theory than a theory of how moral theories originate) is the whole Marxist concept of an economic "class." In the Marxian schematism, slavery, feudalism, and capitalism form an ascending economic and moral series which will culminate in socialism. The first three are all called "class" systems; only the last is the "classless" society. This schematism is not only arbitrary, but palpably unreal. Slavery and feudalism are, indeed, class systems, even caste systems. But what distinguishes the system that Marx labeled capitalism (i.e., the system of private property, free markets, and freedom of contract) is precisely that it broke up the old system of status and introduced mobility and fluidity into economic and other human relations. In a word, it moved toward the *classless* society. The transition was slow; but nobody could any longer be counted upon to stay put, to "know his place," to aspire to nothing beyond the status and occupation to which he was born. It is rather the socialist society, with its ruling bureaucracy, and its assignment of each individual by a monopolistic employer, the state, to his specific job and role and rank, as in an army, that marks a return toward a class society.

Marx's class theory faces the same schematic difficulty as Nietzsche's Superman theory. If you arrange men in a series on the basis either of wealth or income, from the lowest income receiver to the highest, then the line would run in a smooth curve with a barely perceptible difference between each man and the next. Just where would the dividing line between "classes" be drawn? Who would be the richest proletarian and who would be the poorest capitalist? And would not today's class division have to be changed tomorrow? The problem is not escaped by Marx's customary division of "capitalists" and "workers," employer and employed, "exploiters" and "exploited." For, on the one hand, the highly-paid motion picture star or president of a big airline may be merely an employee, and hence, by definition, an exploited wage slave, while a barber in business for himself, who hired one additional barber (providing him with a customer's chair and a pair of scissors), would be a "capitalist" and an "exploiter." To speak of a "proletariat" in the Marxist sense in modern-day America has become so ridiculous, with its 80,000,000 automobiles and its 75,000,000 telephones, that even Communists blush to do it.

But even if one could find such a class division, the interflow between them is so great that it is absurd to speak of a moral ideology peculiar to each class.

A further reply to be made to the Marxist moral theory is almost identical with that made by Socrates to the theory of Thrasymachus. When the latter declared that "justice is nothing else than the interest of the stronger" he tacitly assumed that the stronger always infallibly knew what their true interests were. Socrates simply pointed out that they could be mistaken. So Marx's class theory of morals tacitly assumed that the bourgeoisie infallibly know precisely what moral code is in their own interest as a class. He never learned that people, whether "bourgeoisie" or "proletarians," do not act in accordance with their interests, but in accordance with what they *think* is their interests—which may be merely in accordance with their illusions.

One further aspect of Marx's ethical theory deserves mention. It is only another form of "moral positivism"—the theory that there is no moral standard but the one that exists. But as an "historicist" moral theory, it does not hold, like ordinary moral positivism, simply that *might is right,* but rather that COMING *might is right.* The future is substituted for the present. Popper calls this theory a kind of "moral futurism."[4]

It is hard to refrain, finally, from one or two *ad hominem* arguments, for in this case they are slightly more than that. Marx and Engels held that the bourgeoisie could not escape from their "class" ideology. But they were themselves both members of the bourgeoisie. (Engels was the son of a wealthy cotton-spinner; Marx the son of a lawyer, and university educated). Neither was a proletarian. How, then, were they not only able to escape from their predestined bourgeois ideology, but actually to formulate the proletarian ideology that the proletarians had been unable to formulate for themselves?[5]

A final point. When Marx and Engels denounce the "greed," the "cynicism," the "callousness," the "ruthless exploitation" practiced by the employers, the capitalists, and the bourgeoisie, they do not appeal to any new proletarian code of morality. They base their moral indignation and rest their case against capitalism on moral standards and moral judgments assumed to be already common to all classes.[6]

5. *The Freudian Ethic*

There is some question whether "the Freudian ethic" should be regarded as a special ethical system or as an anti-ethical system. I am referring here not to the ethical views explicitly propounded by Freud himself at various times, but to the ethics implied in popular "Freudianism," with its hostility to self-restraint and self-discipline in all forms and its tolerance of self-indulgence and irresponsibility. An examination of this would carry me to excessive length, and I will content myself with referring the reader to the instructive analysis by Richard LaPiere in *The Freudian Ethic*.[7]

Professor LaPiere defines "the Freudian ethic" as the idea that man cannot and should not be expected to be provident, self-reliant, and venturesome, but that he must and should be supported, protected, and socially maintained. He contends that this ethic is being spread in America through "the permissive home" and "the progressive school," that it stresses "adjustment" and security, and that it is used to condone crime and social incompetence. In this view the criminal is merely "sick"; he invariably requires psychiatric "treatment" and never punishment; he is not personally responsible for his actions; he is the victim of "society," with the stresses and strains and repressions that its rigorous moral code puts upon him; and any attempt to make him live in accordance with this moral code will turn him into a complex-ridden, guilt-ridden neurotic. There can be little doubt that this "ethic" has encouraged the spread of lawlessness and juvenile delinquency.

While leaving the detailed examination of this attitude to Professor LaPiere, I should like to say a word of my own about a somewhat related "ethic," that of the celebrated Dr. Alfred C. Kinsey, the author (with W. B. Pomeroy and C. E. Martin) of *Sexual Behavior in the Human Male*[8] and *Sexual Behavior in the Human Female*.[9] These books gave everybody an opportunity to satisfy his prurient curiosity under the comforting assurance that he was not reading pornography but "science." This is not the place to ask just how "scientific" the Kinsey report actually was, or how trustworthy its statistical methods and conclusions. I wish here merely to examine its implied moral philosophy, which I shall call the Statistical Theory of ethics. Much sexual conduct is considered "immoral," declared many admirers of Dr. Kinsey's work, because people did not know, prior to this study, just how widely practiced it was, but now that we have found out, it is obvious that we can no longer call it immoral.

Suppose we extend this reasoning into other fields than sexual conduct. If we found that the amount of lying, cheating, stealing, vandalism, assault, mugging, and murder were greater than we had previously supposed, or if those forms of conduct were to become more frequent or prevalent, would that make them less immoral? Whether any form of conduct is to be called moral or immoral does not depend upon its frequency, but upon its tendency to lead to good or bad results for the individual and the community.

6. *Haphazard Skepticism*

While skeptical and cynical statements are constantly being made about morality, few of them form part of a coherent and consistent philosophy. I shall call these *random* or *haphazard* skepticism. Precisely because such skepticism is not systematically developed, it is hard to refute. It may be asked, indeed, whether it is worth trying to refute it. To analyze every such random remark would be an endless task, and an appallingly repetitious one. Yet this haphazard ethical skepticism is so frequently met in our era, and is so widely regarded as evidence of profound wisdom, insight, or originality, that it may be useful to take one or two samples for examination.

This random skepticism is commonly found, not among professional philosophers, but among literary men. Every eminent literary man today is expected to be not only a good storyteller, and a wit and a stylist, but to have his own special "philosophy of life." Sooner or later he is tempted to set up shop as a philosopher, and often (e.g., Jean-Paul Sartre) as head of a new philosophic cult or "school."

One such home-made philosopher was the late Theodore Dreiser. His philosophy was typified by his frequent remark that "Man is a chemism." Now if this meant merely that man's body is made up of chemical constituents, and that the nature and changes of these constituents in some way, still only fragmentarily understood, affect his energy, actions, thoughts, emotions, character, and whether he lives or dies, he would have been saying what was true but also what was commonly known. But if he meant, as he seemed to, that man is *nothing but* a "chemism," he was saying something that he did not know to be true. He was guilty of what logicians would call the fallacy of reduction, and the fallacy of simplism or pseudo-simplicity.[10] Even some logical positivists might point out that no conceivable series of experiments could conclusively *prove* that man is *nothing but* an aggregation of chemicals, and therefore by their logic they would have to call Dreiser's contention meaningless or nonsensical. This applies to all materialism or panphysicalism which, as we have already seen,[11] is a metaphysical dogma and not a "verdict of science."

I turn now to a writer far more sophisticated than Dreiser, one who has a background of philosophic reading and who writes a prose of rare lucidity and charm—W. Somerset Maugham. I shall take a few samples of his philosophy as they appear in that fascinating book, *The Summing Up*.[12]

"There is no reason for life," we find Maugham writing (on page 276), "and life has no meaning." What does this sentence mean? How does Maugham know that there is no "reason" for life? How would he go about proving this? How would anyone, for that matter, go about disproving it? What would be the "reason" for life if there were one? And what, in turn, would be the reason for the reason, and so *ad infinitum?*

Maugham apparently here uses the word *reason* as a synonym for *purpose*. But purpose is a purely anthropomorphic concept. Purpose applies only to the use of means to attain ends. The means we employ are explained in terms of the end we have in view. Human beings can have a purpose; *means* have a purpose; but *ends* cannot have a purpose, precisely because they are ends. An omniscient and omnipotent Being, the Creator of the Universe, would not have to use means to attain ends. He need have no purpose. He would certainly not have to use elaborate means to attain some far-off end; He would not require millions of years, He would not even require time at all, to achieve his end; He could simply will it immediately. To demand a reason for life is like demanding a reason for happiness. Life no more needs a reason than health or happiness or satisfaction needs a reason.

The same kind of comment must be made about the second half of Maugham's statement: "Life has no meaning." What does Maugham *mean* by "meaning" in this context? This word too seems to be used here as a synonym for *purpose*. What would life need, in Maugham's view, to *give* it a "meaning"? What experiments, procedures, or tests could be devised to prove that life has a "meaning" or that it doesn't have? Why does life *need* a "meaning" beyond itself? I am tempted to say, with the logical positivists, that the sentence "Life has no meaning" is itself meaningless.

Maugham goes on in this vein and writes again of "the senselessness of life" [13] and "the meaninglessness of life." [14] But I call this *random* skepticism because there is no attempt to follow it out consistently. On the very next page we are told that "the wisdom of the ages" has selected three values as "most worthy," and: "These three values are Truth, Beauty and Goodness." [15] How such values can exist in a meaningless and senseless world we are not told. But in an especially interesting section, in discussing Platonism and Christianity, Maugham makes an instructive distinction between "love" (in the sense of sexual love) and "loving-kindness." "Loving-kindness," he tells us, "is the better part of goodness. . . . Goodness is the only value that seems in this world of appearances to have any claim to be an end in itself. Virtue is its own reward. I am ashamed to have reached so commonplace a conclusion." [16] This seems to place him definitely among the moralists, almost among the Kantian moralists. But two pages farther on he is back again among the Skeptics: "But goodness is shown in right action and who can tell in this meaningless world what right action is? It is not action that aims at happiness; it is a happy chance if happiness results." [17] This is dismissing utilitarianism rather summarily. Right action can be action made in accordance with rules that experience has shown to be *most likely* (though not certain) to promote the happiness of the individual or society in the long run—or, to put it negatively, that are *most likely* to minimize the unhappiness of the individual or society in the long run. One of Maugham's fallacies here is a frequent fallacy of opponents of utilitarianism—that of forgetting its negative corollary. Right action is *necessary* to the attainment of happiness but not *sufficient*.

7. *Logical Positivism*

I have reserved until last consideration of the most plausible and influential attack on ethics in our time—that of the logical positivists. This attack has been made by a number of writers and in many forms; but the most slashing onslaught in English has come from Alfred J. Ayer in *Language, Truth and Logic*.[18] This attack was made nearly thirty years ago. The controversy stimulated by it has continued ever since, and has given rise to a formidable literature. But precisely because Ayer's attack was so unqualified and unequivocal, I think we can do most to clarify the issues it raises by first examining it in the form in which he originally made it.

The contention of Ayer is not that the propositions of ethics are untrue, but that they are meaningless—that they are literally nonsense. They are mere "ejaculations," commands, shouts, squeals, or noises which do nothing but express the emotions of the speaker, his approval or disapproval. They "are simply expressions of emotion which can be neither true nor false. . . . They are mere pseudo-concepts. . . . If now I . . . say, 'Stealing money is wrong,' I produce a sentence which has no factual meaning. . . ."[19]

> We can now see why it is impossible to find a criterion for determining the validity of ethical judgments. It is not because they have an "absolute" validity which is mysteriously independent of ordinary sense-experience, but because they have no objective validity whatsoever. If a sentence makes no statement at all, there is obviously no sense in asking whether what it says is true or false. And we have seen that sentences which simply express moral judgments do not say anything. They are pure expressions of feeling and as such do not come under the category of truth or falsehood. They are unverifiable for the same reason as a cry of pain or a word of command is unverifiable—because they do not express genuine propositions. . . . Ethical judgments have no validity.[20]

Before we deal with these specific statements, it is perhaps necessary to say a few words about the philosophy of logical positivism in general. As this has been elaborated in many and often lengthy books, it would be obviously a little difficult to refute it satisfactorily in a few paragraphs. Fortunately, however, the task of refutation has already been done, and out of several excellent refutations I should like to refer the reader to the late Morris R. Cohen's *Preface to Logic*,[21] and to Karl R. Popper's *The Logic of Scientific Discovery*.[22]

I shall not even undertake to summarize Cohen's argument here, but I shall indicate its general lines. The central thesis of logical positivism is that no statement that is not "verifiable" (outside of a "tautology") can have any meaning at all. Cohen's argument deals with the theory as elaborated by Rudolph Carnap, on whose writings Ayer's attack on ethics is based. I quote a few scattered sentences from Cohen's comments:

> Carnap and others deny that any unverifiable proposition has meaning. This seems at the outset a violent *tour de force*. We do not ordinarily think the meaning of anything is identical with its verifiable consequences. . . . Thus Carnap's assertion that unverifiable statements are meaningless is not itself verifiable. . . .
>
> The fundamental error of the positivists arises from the fact that they view the world solely under the categories of determinate existence and nonexistence, losing sight of the twilight zones in which most of our statements are made. They paint the world exclusively black or white to the utter neglect of the grays or other intermediate colors. . . .
>
> We may conclude that the realm of meaning is broader than the realm of propositions. . . . It is not true that without verification propositions are utterly meaningless. . . .
>
> You may identify the words *meaningful* and *physical* by an arbitrary definition or resolution. But the difference between what is ordinarily meant by *meaning* and by *physical existence* cannot thereby be wiped out. . . .
>
> Logical analysis, as practiced by Carnap, seems to be another term for what used to be called the fallacy of division. Thus Carnap tries to do away with the possibility of metaphysics or ethics by trying to show that they are neither empirical, nor *a priori*, nor tautologous, nor instances of logical analysis. In point of fact, even the wildest metaphysics contains many empirical elements as well as purely logical propositions. . . .
>
> There is no conclusive reason why ethics may not follow the ideal of rigorous scientific method—systematizing not only judgments of existence but also judgments as to what is desirable if certain ends are to be attained.[23]

ETHICAL SKEPTICISM

I do not think much needs to be added to the argument of Morris Cohen or Karl Popper in its full form. If it is necessary to add anything, it might be a few words concerning the necessary role of judgments of *relevance* and the necessary role of judgments of *importance* in all scientific procedure. Judgments of relevance and judgments of importance are not only necessarily involved in selecting, out of an infinity of "facts" and possible propositions, the facts and propositions bearing on the particular problem to be solved; they are necessarily involved *in selecting the problem itself* out of an infinity of possible problems. But the word *importance* is a value-word, and the concept of *importance* is a value-concept. And value-words and value-concepts, according to the logical positivists, have no place in scientific procedure or in philosophical analysis!

I should like to add just one short quotation from Karl Popper's discussion:

> The positivist dislikes the idea that there should be meaningful problems outside the field of "positive" empirical science. . . . [And] nothing is easier than to unmask a problem as "meaningless" or "pseudo." All you have to do is to fix upon a conveniently narrow meaning for "meaning," and you will soon be bound to say of any inconvenient question that you are unable to detect any meaning in it. Moreover, if you admit as meaningful none except problems in natural science, any debate about the concept of "meaning" will also turn out to be meaningless.[24]

The first logical positivist in the realm of ethics, in fact, was not Ayer, or Carnap, or Moritz Schlick, or Wittgenstein, or even Comte or Saint-Simon, but Falstaff. Falstaff showed by linguistic analysis that "honor" was a meaningless sound:

> Can honour set to a leg? no: or an arm? no: or take away the grief of a wound? no. Honour hath no skill in surgery, then? no. What is honour? a word. What is in that word honour; what is that honour? air. A trim reckoning! Who hath it? he that died o' Wednesday. Doth he feel it? no. Doth he hear it? no. It is insensible, then? yea, to the dead. But will it not live with the living? no. Why? detraction will not suffer it. Therefore I'll none of it. Honour is a mere scutcheon. And so ends my catechism.[25]

In one point, of course, the logical positivists are right. You can only verify or refute a proposition, or an alleged statement of fact. You cannot verify or refute a *value*. You can only recognize a value, or feel it, or tacitly accept or assume it, or explicitly reject it. You cannot *prove* that a beautiful world is better than an ugly world. You cannot *prove* that a life that is shared, rich, happy, civilized, and long is any better than a life that is "solitary, poor, nasty, brutish, and short."

Extreme logical positivism would leave no room for, and attach no meaning to, beauty or ugliness, health or sickness, pleasure or pain, happiness or misery, good or bad, right or wrong, better or worse. These concepts or categories are not tautologies; they cannot be measured or weighed; there are no physical experiments that can prove or disprove their existence. True, you can show that if you tear a child's arm from its socket, the child will scream or faint or die. But you cannot prove that there is anything "cruel" or "horrible" or "wrong" or even "harmful" or "undesirable" in this, because these words are mere value-judgments, i.e., "ejaculations," nonsensical expressions of disapproval, meaningless noises.

The extreme logical positivists talk as if the only purpose of life is to verify or refute propositions, and as if everything else is to be tested or judged by science. But they forget to ask themselves: What is the *purpose* of verifying propositions? What is the *purpose* of science? What is the *purpose* of learning the truth about anything? What is the *use* of it? In a word, what is the *value* of it?

The answer to this question is tacitly *taken for granted* by the logical positivists. The answer is in their minds, but never mentioned, never explicitly uttered. No, I am wrong; it *is* sometimes uttered, but absentmindedly, and without recognizing the implication of the answer. It is uttered by Ayer, who explicitly recognizes its crucial importance. "Actually," writes Ayer, at one point in *Language, Truth and Logic,* "we shall see that the only test to which a form of scientific procedure which satisfies the necessary condition of self-consistency is subject, is the test of its success in practice." [26]

But what, if anything, does this sentence *mean*? What is the *meaning* of the word "success"? How do you *prove* that something is a "success" or a "failure"? What are the *physical* characteristics of "success"? How long, wide, and thick is it; how hard is it; how much does it weigh? Ayer has committed the cardinal positivist sin. He has used a mere value-word, and used it as if it actually meant something.

But, says Ayer, "success" enables us to "predict future experience, and so to control our environment." We answer, like a more consistent positivist: So what? What is the purpose of "controlling our environment" if not to make conditions more satisfactory to ourselves, if not to fulfill more human desires, if not to produce an environment that more nearly meets our approval? Even our "mere" approval?

So even Ayer, after having ostentatiously thrown out "value" because we cannot establish its "truth," finally admits, inadvertently, that we seek Truth itself primarily because it has Value for us. Truth-seeking is a means to an end, as ethics is a means to an end. And the end is to substitute a more satisfactory state of affairs for a less satisfactory state.

The reader who has prior knowledge of this controversy may ask at this point why I have confined my answer to the logical positivists' attack on ethical judgments in the very vulnerable form in which it was made by A. J. Ayer in 1936. Not only has Ayer himself since substantially modified his position, it may be urged, but a full-length and far more formidable presentation of the "emotivist" argument has since been made by Charles L. Stevenson in *Ethics and Language*,[27] not to speak of Paul Edwards in *The Logic of Moral Discourse*[28] and scores of presentations of still other forms of the theory.

My answer would be that this chapter is devoted to ethical skepticism. I have centered my discussion on Ayer's 1936 attack because that was so extremely skeptical and even derisive. But though I have no wish to take up at great length a linguistic problem that seems to me already to have received such disproportionate attention in the ethical literature of the last thirty years,[29] I suppose I must in justice, now that I have gone this far, say something of Ayer's later writing and of the theory in the form presented by C. L. Stevenson.

Ayer returned to the subject in an essay "On the Analysis of Moral Judgments" in his *Philosophical Essays*.[30] In this he concedes at one point that: "To say, as I once did, that these moral judgments are merely expressive of certain feelings, feelings of approval or disapproval, is an over-simplification." [31]

But he fails to make clear either the nature or extent of that "over-simplification." And he still goes on to assert that his theory of moral judgments "is neutral as regards all moral principles" [32]—a lily that needs no gilding by me.

"Does not the promulgation of such a theory," he goes on to ask, "encourage moral laxity? Has not its effect been to destroy people's confidence in accepted moral standards? And will not the result of this be that something mischievous will take their place?" [33] I think we must answer: "To the extent that his theory is taken seriously, Yes."

Ayer cannot see that this answer follows. "My own observations," he protests, "for what they are worth, do not suggest that those who accept the 'positivist' analysis of moral judgments conduct themselves very differently as a class from those who reject it." [34]

I am willing to believe that this is true. I do believe that it is true. I am not accusing the logical positivists of moral turpitude but of intellectual error. But I suggest that the reason they are just as moral as most of the rest of us is that they do not take their own analysis too seriously. In this respect they are the analogues in the moral realm of the philosophical idealists in the physical realm. The idealist solemnly affirms that only minds or mental events exist, and that the furniture in his room, for example, "exists" only because and to the extent that he perceives it. Nevertheless, if he has to get up in the middle of the night in pitch dark, he will grope his way as cautiously as the crudest materialist, for fear of stubbing his toe or bumping his shins against an unperceived chair. For he cannot (fortunately for him) get rid of his "animal faith" that the unperceived furniture "really" exists and can hurt him. Just so, the logical positivists, in the moral realm, cannot quite shed the results of their upbringing or shrug off the disapprobation by their fellows (or even the disapprobation by themselves) that would be certain to follow the commission of an immoral act. But if they took their skeptical views with entire seriousness, and if they persuaded a sufficient number of others to do the same, morality would undoubtedly be undermined and irreparable mischief would be done. Ethical theorizing must be serious and responsible. It is not a philosopher's plaything.

ETHICAL SKEPTICISM 241

And Ayer, by a glaring inconsistency in his final paragraph, reveals that he does not take his own theory with entire seriousness. "If it could be shown," he writes, "as I believe it could not, that the general acceptance of the sort of analysis of moral judgments that I have been putting forward would have unhappy social consequences, the conclusion drawn by illiberal persons might be that the doctrine ought to be kept secret. For my part I think that I should dispute this conclusion on moral grounds." [35]

Moral grounds? *What* moral grounds? *Whose* moral grounds? Isn't this the same A. J. Ayer who has been telling us that moral judgments are "mere ejaculations"? That they are unverifiable and hence "meaningless"? And who has just told us in the preceding paragraph that his theory is "neutral as regards all moral principles"? What could his "moral" argument possibly be? Would he merely resort to the same kind of meaningless ejaculations he has just been deriding?

With this *non sequitur* Ayer throws away his entire case.

8. *Mr. Stevenson's Empiricism*

When we turn to Charles L. Stevenson, we find a writer far more guarded in reasoning and far more conciliatory in tone. His *Ethics and Language* is a real contribution.[36] Though we must reject its central thesis and its underlying "empiricist" philosophy, we owe a great deal to many of its shrewd analyses. Stevenson repudiates the simplism of Ayer, and regards the term emotive "as a tool for use in careful study, not as a device for relegating the nondescriptive aspects of language to limbo." [37] He even concedes that "persuasive methods, cautiously used, have a legitimacy that is scarcely open to question." [38]

Nevertheless, Stevenson is rightly classed as an "emotivist," and preaches an empiricism that would make true ethical understanding and progress impossible. He talks as if nothing had yet been firmly established in ethics, and as if it must be left to future writers whose "slow results will be cumulative," to contribute "to an ethics that will progressively come to grips with the issues of practical life." [39] He talks, in fact, in the final paragraphs of his book, as if the establishment of firm ethical principles were something that must wait for a distant future, if it is possible at all:

"Ethical theory is given to the age-old quest for ultimate principles, definitively established. This not only hides the full complexity of moral issues, but puts static, other-worldly norms in the place of flexible, realistic ones. It is the writer's hope that the present study, attentive to the role of science in ethics, but attentive also to the way in which ethical issues differ from scientific ones, will help to make illusory conceptions of certitude give place to conceptions which are commensurate with the problems that they seek to resolve.

"The demand for a final proof springs less from hopes than from fears. When the basic nature of a subject is poorly understood, one must conceal his insecurity, from himself as much as from others, by consoling pretenses. . . . Living questions are too rich in their complexity to be answered by a formula." [40]

The foregoing paragraphs seem to me to make use of the very kind of "emotive" terms and "persuasive definitions" that Mr. Stevenson has spent most of his book in deploring. How can he be so certain, one is tempted to ask, that we can never be certain? In any case, I suggest that contemporary confidence that at least certain broad moral principles have been "definitively established" is not altogether misplaced. We do not have to wait until *future* writers "come to grips with the issues of practical life." Older writers have already done so. It has *already* been reasonably well established that promise-breaking, lying, cheating, mugging, and murder do not lead to very satisfactory social results, and that promise-keeping, truthfulness, non-violence, fair-dealing, and kindness do in general lead to much more satisfactory social results. To say this, of course, is not to disparage efforts toward *further* progress in both practical and theoretical ethics; it is merely to remind ourselves that we do not have to begin from scratch.

Stevenson's difficulty, I suspect, lies in his special brand of empiricism, with its assumption that only empirical methods are scientifically valid. This assumption must be rejected. In ethics these empirical methods, standing alone, would be frustrating and sterile. In ethics we are dealing with human action, with human purposes, with human wishes and desires, with human choices and preferences, with the conscious use of means to attain chosen ends. Ethics is not a branch of physics, and the methods appropriate to it are not the experimental, statistical, and empiric methods appropriate to physics. Ethics is *sui generis*, with methods peculiarly its own. But it is, among other things, based on "praxeology," which, like logic and mathematics, is deductive and aprioristic.[41]

9. *Ethics Is Not Linguistics*

Three-fourths of the recent literature on ethics seems to treat ethical problems as if they were primarily linguistic or semantic problems. This is revealed in the very titles of some of the outstanding books—Charles L. Stevenson's *Ethics and Language* (1944), and R. M. Hare's *The Language of Morals* (1952). Mr. Hare tells us in his Preface, for example, that, "Ethics, as I conceive it, is the logical study of the *language* of morals." (My italics.) I do not wish to deny that there is something to be learned from this approach. But I do confess that, with a few notable exceptions, I find most of this literature sterile and dreary. Are ethical statements and judgments merely "emotive"? Is it their sole function to have a "magnetic effect" on attitudes? Are they essentially commands, requests, orders? Or are they recipes or prescriptions? Or is ethical language "multifunctional"?

The answer to the last question is surely Yes. As P. H. Nowell-Smith puts it: "[Ethical terms] are used to express tastes and preferences, to express decisions and choices, to criticize, grade, and evaluate, to advise, admonish, warn, persuade and dissuade, to praise, encourage and reprove, to promulgate and draw attention to rules; and doubtless for other purposes also." [42]

But it has taken thousands of words and scores of volumes to get around to this conclusion; and the "emotivists" haven't got there yet. I cannot refrain from quoting Karl Popper once more: "These philosophers who had started by denouncing philosophy as merely verbal and who had demanded that, instead of attempting to solve them, we should turn away from the verbal problems to those that are real and empirical, found themselves bogged in the thankless and apparently endless task of analyzing and unmasking verbal pseudo problems." [43]

I do not want to say that *all* this linguistic discussion, this hair-splitting and logomachy, has been futile and worthless. It became, perhaps, unavoidable once the challenge was raised. And some of it has, in fact, been clarifying and illuminating. But I do suggest that the discussion of these verbal "meta-ethical" problems has been grossly *disproportionate* compared with other and genuinely ethical problems. "Moral" philosophers have become excessively preoccupied, not to say obsessed, with purely linguistic problems. A great part of the ethical literature of the last sixty years has been like an enormous detour in which the drivers have become so fascinated by the strange and unexpected scenery that they have forgotten to get back on the main road and have even forgotten their original destination.

The Great Digression started in 1903, when G. E. Moore published his celebrated *Principia Ethica*,[44] in which he contended that the word "good" was "indefinable" and "unanalyzable." This became the most widely discussed book on ethics of the twentieth century. Then, in 1930, the digression was carried even further by the publication of *The Meaning of Meaning*, by C. K. Ogden and I. A. Richards.[45]

" 'Good,' " wrote these authors, "is alleged to stand for a unique, unanalyzable concept. This concept, it is said, is the subject matter of Ethics. This peculiar ethical use of 'good' is, we suggest, a purely emotive use. When so used the word stands for nothing whatever, and has no symbolic function." [46] And then in a footnote, specifically referring to Moore's *Principia Ethica*, they added: "Of course, if we define 'the good' as 'that of which we approve of approving,' or give any such definition when we say 'This is good,' we shall be making an assertion. It is only the indefinable 'good' which we suggest to be a purely emotive sign. The 'something more' or 'something else' which, it is alleged, is not covered by any definition of 'good' is the emotional aura of the word.[47]

And then the Thirty Years War broke out.

The "emotivists," I think, slipped into two main fallacies. Their first mistake was not in asserting that ethical language had an "emotive" function, but in denying that it had any other. And their second mistake was to try to dispose of ethics by calling it names. For the word "emotive" is a derogatory word. Those who use "emotive" language, it suggests, are using merely emotional language; and may even be pretending to be stating a fact when they are simply giving vent to their personal feelings.

If, instead of asserting that all ethical statements and judgments were "emotive," the positivists had merely insisted that they were *valuative*,[48] they would have been saying what was true, but what few moral philosophers have ever ventured to deny. But the fact that ethical statements are valuative does not mean that they cannot *also* state facts.

Ethical judgments and decisions do, after all, deal with facts. They deal with actions, which are facts. They deal with the consequences of actions, which are facts. They deal with the ends that people wish to achieve (and it is a fact that people do have these ends) and with the means they employ (and these means are facts) to achieve those ends. True, *in addition* to dealing with facts, or to stating facts—"John stole the money" —ethical statements imply judgments and contain value-words. They are valuative. But this seems a strange reason for objecting to them, or trying to dismiss them as meaningless. They judge the efficacy of means, and the reasonableness or desirability, from the social standpoint, of the intermediate if not the ultimate ends of individuals.

It is not only ethical language that is valuative. *All* practical language is valuative. All human action implies valuation. All human action is purposeful: which means that it employs means to achieve ends: which means that it must evaluate the comparative desirability of ends and the comparative efficacy of means.

10. *What Is the Best Thing to Do?*

The prescriptions of the moral philosopher need be no more "emotive" (in the disparaging sense in which that term is commonly used) than the prescriptions of the engineer. Both are trying to answer the question: *What is the best thing to do?* The answer of the moral philosopher need be no more emotional [49] than the answer of the engineer. Suppose the problem set before an engineer is: What is the best way to connect Staten Island with the mainland? Should it be by a bridge or a tunnel? If a bridge, what type of bridge? How should it be designed? What materials should be used? How thick should the cables be, how wide the arch, how high the towers? What kind of design would look best? Of course not all of these are strictly engineering problems, though on all of them the engineer must be consulted. Some of them are political problems. Some are economic problems—problems of relative costs. Some are traffic problems. Some are aesthetic problems. But they can all be subsumed under the overriding question: What is the best thing to do? And this, of course, is a *value* problem.

It may be objected that the moral philosopher does not ask, "What is the best thing to do?" in the same sense that the engineer does, but that his predominant question is, rather, "What is the *right* thing to do?" The real difference, however, is that the moral philosopher's question must take account of much wider considerations (than, say, the engineer's)—not merely what is the best thing to do from the standpoint of the long-run good of the agent, but what is the best thing to do— what are the best rules to make—from the standpoint of the long-run good of society. But when these wider considerations are kept in mind, the best thing to do and the right thing to do become identical.

To sum up: Ethical propositions are not true or false in the sense that existential propositions are true or false. Ethical rules are not *de*scriptive but *pre*scriptive. But though not true or false in the existential sense, ethical propositions can be *valid* or *invalid*, consistent or inconsistent, logical or illogical, rational or irrational, justified or unjustified, expedient or inexpedient, intelligent or unintelligent, *wise* or *unwise*. True, ethical judgments or propositions, though they must always take facts into consideration, are not themselves purely factual but *valuative*. But this does not mean that they are arbitrary or merely "emotive" (in the derogatory sense in which that adjective is used by positivists and, indeed, for which it seems to have been coined). Ethical rules, judgments, and propositions are attempts to answer the question: What is the best thing to do?

And should it be so astonishing that "What is the best thing to do?" should be a different kind of question from the factual and descriptive one, "What is the present situation?" It is the latter, the "scientific" question, that is the *derivative* one: the answer to it is the *means* to the answer to the first. The chief thing we are interested in regarding cancer is *how to cure it.* To answer that, we must *first* answer such questions as "Exactly what is it?" and "What causes it?" But no one in his senses says or implies that the latter questions are the only "real" ones, because the only "scientific" ones, or that the question "How can we cure it?" is merely "emotive" or "merely" valuative. Yet this is the kind of thing that is being said constantly today, by positivists and others, concerning ethical questions.

The overriding problem of man, from the beginning of time, has been "How can I improve my condition?" (As the individual, in society, finds that his condition is inextricably bound up with that of his fellows, the problem evolves into "How can *we* improve *our* condition?") Mankind finds that to answer this question it must first increase its knowledge of what existing conditions actually *are,* its knowledge of facts, of the operation of cause and effect, of the distinction between reality and illusion—in brief, its mastery of positive science.

Thus the study of fact and science is, to repeat, a *means* to the solution of the problem of how to improve man's condition. Ethics is the attempt to deal with one broad aspect of this problem; the individual sciences are a relatively roundabout means of dealing with specific aspects of the problem. But along come the positivists and prove triumphantly that ethics is *not* a description of existing fact or the discovery of scientific laws; and they therefore dismiss it as "purely emotive" or "meaningless."

This is the exaltation of means over end. The end, how to improve our condition, is treated as meaningless or unimportant; the means, scientific knowledge, is treated as all-important, as *solely* important. The instrumental and derivative value is rated above the intrinsic value from which it is derived.

To hold this inverted view is to be completely at sea in moral philosophy.

CHAPTER 24

Justice

1. *Justice and Freedom*

The key terms used by moral philosophers—"good," "right," "ought," etc.—all seem to be indefinable except in other terms that already imply the same notion. Such a term is Justice. Ask the average man what he means by justice and he will probably reply that what is just is what is "equitable" or what is "fair." To the Institutes of Justinian we owe the famous definition that justice is the constant and continual purpose which gives to everyone his own. But if we ask how we determine what *is* a man's "own," we are told that his own is what is "rightfully" his own, and if we ask how we are to determine what is rightfully his own, we are likely to be brought back to the answer that this is determined in accordance with the dictates of justice.

One difficulty is that the terms Justice and Just are used in many different senses in many different settings. As Roscoe Pound has written:

> In different theories which have been urged justice has been regarded as an individual virtue, or as a moral idea, or as a regime of social control, or as the end or purpose of social control and so of law, or as the ideal relation among men which we seek to promote and maintain in civilized society and toward which we direct social control and law as the most specialized form of social control. Definitions of justice depend upon which of these approaches is taken.[1]

The problem is difficult, and perhaps the best procedure is to clear the ground by examining at least two famous definitions or formulas of justice to see whether they are satisfactory.

The first of these is the formula of justice originally enunciated by Kant and later (independently, as he thought) by Herbert Spencer. The Kantian idea of justice was the external liberty of each limited by the like liberty of all others: "The

JUSTICE 249

universal Law of Right may then be expressed thus: 'Act externally in such a manner that the free exercise of thy Will may be able to co-exist with the Freedom of all others, according to a universal Law!'" The rule as formulated by Herbert Spencer is very close to this: "Every man is free to do that which he wills, provided he infringes not the equal freedom of any other man." [2]

The first thing to be said about this is that it sounds much more like a formula for Liberty than a formula for Justice. And it does not appear, on examination, to be a very satisfactory formula for either. Interpreted literally, it implies that a thug should have the freedom to stand behind a street corner and hit everyone who rounds the corner on the head with a club provided he concedes the equal freedom of anybody else to do the same thing. If it be answered that such action would infringe the freedom of others to do the same thing because it would incapacitate them from doing so, the formula still seems to give a license for all sorts of mutual injuries and annoyances that are not actually crippling or fatal.

The curious fact is that (probably as a result of prior criticisms) Spencer recognized this objection and attempted to answer it:

> A possible misapprehension must be guarded against. There are acts of aggression which the formula is presumably intended to exclude, which apparently it does not exclude. It may be said that if A strikes B, then, so long as B is not debarred from striking A in return, no greater freedom is claimed by the one than by the other; or it may be said that if A has trespassed on B's property, the requirement of the formula has not been broken so long as B can trespass on A's property. Such interpretations, however, mistake the essential meaning of the formula. . . . Instead of justifying aggression and counter-aggression, the intention of the formula is to fix a bound which may not be exceeded on either side.[3]

But this is a strange defense. A philosopher cannot set forth an explicit formula, and then say that it does not mean exactly what it appears to mean, because it is *intended* to mean something else. What it "really" means and what it does not "really" mean must be explicitly embodied in the formula itself. If it is not, the formula must be restated, or another formula must be substituted that does in fact say what it is intended to say, no more and no less.

His formula "does not countenance," Spencer explains, "a *superfluous* interference with another's life [my italics]." [4] But he does not define what he means by "superfluous," or which interferences are superfluous and which are not. He is compelled, in fact, in his later explanations, to fall back upon a utilitarian justification of his formula as tending to promote the maximum of freedom, happiness, and life; but elsewhere he declares that the principle of utility presupposes the anterior principle of justice, and that the principle of justice rests on an *a priori* cognition.

It is very doubtful, in fact, that any autonomous formula can be framed for either Liberty or Justice. Any satisfactory formula will be found to depend upon or to imply teleological or utilitist considerations. But before passing on to the justification of this conclusion, we must consider further the difficulties of any independent formula.

The difficulty is excellently summed up (if I may anticipate the discussion of Chapter 26) by Henry Sidgwick in connection with freedom:

> The term Freedom is ambiguous. If we interpret it strictly, as meaning Freedom of Action alone, the principle seems to allow any amount of mutual annoyance except constraint. But obviously no one would be satisfied with such Freedom as this. If, however, we include in the idea freedom from pain and annoyance inflicted by others, the right of freedom itself seems to prevent us from accepting the principle in all its breadth. For there is scarcely any gratification of a man's natural impulses which may not cause some annoyance to others: and we cannot prohibit all such annoyances without restraining freedom of action to a degree that would be intolerable: and yet it is hard to lay down any principle for distinguishing intuitively those that ought to be allowed from those that must be prohibited.[5]

2. *The Golden Rule*

Suppose we try a different formula altogether. The Golden Rule in its positive form enjoins one to "Do unto others as you would have others do unto you." This is intended as much more than a formula of Justice; it is a formula of Benevolence.

Even as such it raises many problems. I may wish my uncle to leave me his fortune. Should I, therefore, turn over my own wealth to my uncle? Even if we dismiss all such extreme interpretations, the Rule seems to ignore differences in preference and taste. You may wish your friend to give you a set of Shakespeare for Christmas. Should you, therefore, give him a set? He may prefer a case of whiskey. You may wish a girl to give you her love; but she may prefer not to have yours.

Most of these difficulties are avoided by the Golden Rule in its negative form (which also appears to be historically much older): "Do not do unto others," as Confucius put it, "what you would not wish others to do unto you." This is certainly a good practical rule of thumb both in ethics and in law. Its political utility is well explained by Bruno Leoni:

> In any society feelings and convictions relating to actions that should *not* be done are much more homogeneous and easily identifiable than any other kind of feelings and convictions. Legislation protecting people against what they do not want other people to do to them is likely to be much more easily determinable and more generally successful than any kind of legislation based on other "positive" desires of the same individuals. In fact, such desires are not only usually much less homogeneous and compatible with one another than the "negative" ones, but are also often very difficult to ascertain.[6]

Yet though the negative form of the Golden Rule is a rough working formula of justice, it is not, any more than the positive form of the Rule, a precise guide that can be applied with complete literalness. A man may not like to be haled into court for nonpayment even of a just debt. But this does not mean that he should never sue anybody else to collect a just debt.

3. *"Every One to Count for One"*

One of the principal difficulties in the concept of justice is that, though almost everyone uses the word with assurance, its meaning varies widely in different contexts. At times it seems to call for Equality and at other times for Inequality. This is recognized at the beginning of a long discussion by Hastings Rashdall:

Now, when we ask "What is Justice?", we are at once met by two conflicting ideals, each of which on the face of it seems entitled to respect. In the first place the principle that every human being is of equal intrinsic value, and is therefore entitled to equal respect, is one which commends itself to common sense, a principle which may naturally claim to be the exacter expression of the Christian ideal of Brotherhood. On the other hand, the principle that the good ought to be preferred to the bad, that men ought to be rewarded according to their goodness or according to their work, is one which no less commends itself to the unsophisticated moral consciousness. We shall perhaps best arrive at some true idea of the nature of Justice by examining the claims of these two rival and *prima facie* inconsistent ideals—the ideal of equality, considered in the sense of equality of consideration, and the ideal of just recompense or reward—and we shall perhaps do well to start with the suspicion that there will be a considerable presumption against any solution of the problem which does not recognize some meaning or element of truth in each of them.[7]

Though I find Rashdall's subsequent discussion of Justice somewhat disappointing, the procedure he suggests, of examining "these two rival and *prima facie* inconsistent ideals" of Justice, cannot fail to be enlightening, so I propose to follow him a little further.

He begins by examining the Benthamite maxim "Every one to count for one and nobody to count for more than one." This maxim, Rashdall continues, was put forward by Bentham "as a canon for the distribution of happiness. He saw clearly enough that his 'greatest happiness' principle, or the principle of greatest good (however good may be interpreted), stands in need of this or some supplementary canon before it can be available for practical application."[8]

Rashdall then considers the alleged mathematical problem of "distributing" maximum happiness as among, say, a hundred people, and adds: "The principle which Bentham adopted as a solution of such problems is the maxim 'Every one to count for one and nobody for more than one.' He failed to see how impossible it is to establish such a principle by experience or to rest it upon anything but an *a priori* judgment."[9]

Rashdall then goes on to consider in what sense the maxim properly applies. He rejects the formula of equality of material rewards or "equality of opportunity" and concludes that "there is only one sort of equality that is always practicable and always right, and that is *equality of consideration.*" [10] (My italics.) He then proceeds to argue that the Benthamite maxim is acceptable only if it is interpreted to mean: "Every man's good to count as equal to the *like good* of every other man." [11]

Let us return to Rashdall's contention that the Benthamite maxim could not possibly have been established by experience but must rest upon "an *a priori* judgment." This is the contention not only of Rashdall, but of many other ethical writers. It is found, for example, even in Herbert Spencer:

> Already I have referred to Bentham's rule—"Everybody to count for one, nobody for more than one," joined with Mr. Mill's comment that the greatest happiness principle is meaningless unless "One person's happiness . . . is counted for exactly as much as another's." Hence the Benthamite theory of morals and politics posits this as a fundamental, self-evident truth. . . . For this assumption no warrant is given, or can be given, other than alleged intuitive perception. It is an *a priori* cognition.[12]

Now I think it can be shown that this principle is not "intuitive" or *a priori*, but was developed out of human experience. It is the ethical parallel of the juridical principle of *equality before the law*. If this principle is intuitive or *a priori*, it would become enormously difficult to explain why moral and legal philosophy took so long to get around to recognizing it, or why it is still so difficult to formulate the principle with satisfactory precision. In examining this question we shall be incidentally examining the whole problem of intuitionism in ethics.

Bentham, of course, did not invent or *discover* the principle. He merely gave explicit verbal formulation to a principle already implicit in existing social customs, conventions, tacit rules and understandings, and working arrangements. How did such tacit rules and arrangements come into being?

We can clarify our understanding of the process if we begin by imagining a minimum society consisting solely of A and B.[13] If A and B are of equal strength and ability, or approximately so, A will not be able to keep the product of their joint effort entirely for himself, or even to appropriate a grossly disproportionate share of it, for the simple reason that B will not let him. After a certain number of squabbles they will, for the sake of economizing effort, minimizing annoyance, and keeping the peace, probably arrive at a tacit or even explicit *modus vivendi* by which each will agree to accept approximately equal shares of their joint product or will agree to certain uniform rules of division of work, division of product, priority, etc.

And such a *modus vivendi* of rules and division becomes more and more likely as we expand our imaginary society to three, four, five or n persons. For then no individual will be strong enough to grab for himself what the rest regard as an excessive share, and there will grow up a tacit and even an explicit set of rules embodied in laws which will force equality of consideration and "fairness" in "ownership" or "distribution" simply because this will be recognized as the best if not the only way of minimizing disputes and of *keeping the peace*.

But suppose, coming back to our minimum society of two, that A is much stronger than B? Then A may try to grab everything for himself, to let B starve, or even to kill her. Then that society is over and sets no precedent. But if, as is more likely and more frequent, A recognizes that he needs or prefers B's company and cooperation, he will have to release to B at least enough to assure the continuance of that cooperation, and, in proportion as he is wise, he will release enough to *maximize* that cooperation. This means that it is in A's interest to maximize the incentives of B as it is in B's interest to maximize those of A. And this also is true as we enlarge our imaginary society. No matter how unequal the respective members are in talents or abilities, it is in the interest of each that the contributions of all the others should be maximized. And each will eventually discover (after perhaps having tried slaughter, robbery, pillage, slavery, coercion, chicanery, or exploitation) that the best way to assure this maximum contribution by others is to provide those others with maximum incentives.

Let us, at the risk of excessive repetition, state this in another way. The "Benthamite" rule, "Every one to count for one and no one to count for more than one," is merely another way of stating the rule of equality before the law. It is not an "axiom" in the sense that its truth is immediately self-evident or that a contrary rule is inconceivable or self-contradictory. It is not based, as Spencer and Sidgwick and Rashdall seemed to as-

JUSTICE   255

sume, on an "intuition." It evolved because *it was the only rule on which it was possible to secure agreement.* It was, in origin, empirically determined. It doubtless developed gradually out of thousands of decisions by courts and tribunals. Its acceptance was, at the beginning, *ad hoc* in particular cases. It was vague, not definite; implied, not explicit. It was not at first consciously generalized. When generalized, in fact, it is still resisted by some writers. The rule was established in thousands of legal decisions and millions of private agreements and understandings because it was the only rule that could peaceably resolve disputes. Disputants or acting individuals came to accept it for much the same reasons that the impartial spectator now accepts it. It is now a rule that is basic to a thousand other rules.

Here we begin to glimpse the origins of our modern concept of justice both in the economic and in the legal and moral realm. The concepts of equality before the law, and equality of consideration, develop because the majority see the danger to themselves, as well as to the public peace, of more arbitrary or discriminatory rules.

And here we see, also, the reconciliation of the two apparently inconsistent rules of equality of consideration and inequality of rewards for inequality of contribution, that puzzled Rashdall in his search for some absolute rule of Justice. For the secret of both of these apparently inconsistent rules is that they tend to preserve the public peace, to satisfy most individuals, and to maximize the incentives of each for production and social cooperation.

4. *Rules to Promote Cooperation*

So we are brought back once more to the promotion of Social Cooperation as the key to the problem of Justice as well as other major ethical problems. "The ultimate yardstick of justice is conduciveness to the preservation of social cooperation. . . . Social cooperation becomes for almost every man the great means for the attainment of all ends. . . . In ethics a common ground for the choice of rules of conduct is given so far as people agree in considering the preservation of social cooperation the foremost means for attaining all their ends." [14]

Now if we adopt this explanation, we recognize that Justice is not the ultimate ethical end, existing purely for its own sake, but is primarily a means, and even a means to a means. Justice and Freedom are the great means to the promotion of Social Cooperation, which in turn is the great means to the realization of each individual's ends and therefore to the realization of the ends of "society."

The subordination of Justice to a "mere" means, however important that means is regarded to be, may come as a shock to many moral philosophers, who have been accustomed to regard it as the supreme ethical end, at least in the social field. The extreme form of this view is epitomized in the famous phrase: *fiat justitia, ruat caelum,* or even *fiat justitia, pereat mundus.* Let justice be done though the heavens fall, let justice be done even if it destroys the world. Common sense draws back from any such frightful conclusion. But the answer to such slogans is not that we should be satisfied with a little less than Absolute Justice, in order to hold things together; the answer is that there is something wrong in the conception of justice embodied in such slogans. Justice was made for man, not man for justice.

Let us see what happens when we reject the notion of justice as a means to the promotion of social cooperation and hence to the maximization of happiness and well-being, and treat Justice as *the* supreme end in itself. Even Herbert Spencer came near doing this in his section on Justice in the second volume of his *Principles of Ethics.* We have already seen that he regarded the Benthamite rule "Everybody to count for one, nobody for more than one" as "an *a priori* cognition." [15] He quoted Sir Henry Maine in support of putting the Law of Nature, or Justice, above the goal of human happiness, and went on: "Since Roman times there has continued to be this contrast between the narrow recognition of happiness as an end, and the wide recognition of natural equity as an end." And he concluded that we must accept "the law of equal freedom [his formula for Justice] as an ultimate ethical principle, having an authority transcending every other." [16]

Now if we want to decide the relative claims of Happiness and Justice as the ultimate ethical goal we can hardly do better than adopt the same type of argument that Spencer himself used in the *Data of Ethics* (§ 15) when ridiculing Carlyle's attempt to substitute "blessedness" for happiness as the end of mankind. Are Happiness and Justice antithetical? Then would we prefer more Justice at the cost of less Happiness and of more pain and misery? Would we fight hard and persistently for more Justice even though we knew this would have no effect whatever in increasing Happiness or reducing Misery? Or would we not be tempted to insist on an actual reduction of Justice if we found that to reduce Justice was the best means of reducing misery and increasing Happiness? Which would we prefer: Happiness without Justice or Justice without Happiness?

It is obvious that to treat Justice as an *alternative* to Happiness, or as *preferable* to Happiness, gets us into absurd contradictions. Once we accept Justice as a *means* to the increase as well as the "better distribution" of Happiness, however, these contradictions disappear.

One could apply the same method in deciding between Justice and Social Cooperation as end or means. Social Cooperation is the great means of maximizing the happiness and well-being of each and therefore of all; and Justice is the name we give to the set of rules, relationships, and arrangements that do most to promote voluntary Social Cooperation. The most just rules are those rules governing distribution, ownership, rewards, and penalties that, while minimizing the temptations to antisocial behavior, maximize the encouragements and incentives to effort, production, and mutual helpfulness.

I have in this chapter several times criticized some of Herbert Spencer's ideas regarding Justice; but it would be unfair as well as ungenerous not to pay tribute to one of his greatest contributions to the subject. It is strange, in fact, that his definition and concept finally went wrong after they came so close to being right. For I find in Spencer a clearer anticipation of the central importance of Social Cooperation as the great means to all our ends than in any other writer up to his time. He again and again uses the phrase. Already in the *Data of Ethics*, published in 1879, we find him writing:

> Harmonious co-operation, by which alone in any [society] the greatest happiness can be attained, is, as we saw, made possible only by respect for one another's claims: there must be neither

those direct aggressions which we class as crimes against person and property, nor must there be those indirect aggressions constituted by breaches of contracts. So that maintenance of equitable relations between men is the condition to attainment of greatest happiness in all societies, however much the greatest happiness attainable in each may differ in nature, or amount, or both.[17]

This is an isolated reference. But in the section on *Justice*, which did not appear until 1891, and was embodied in Volume II of *The Principles of Ethics*, we find Spencer repeatedly returning to the phrase and the concept: "Active co-operation" (p. 11). "The *a priori* condition to harmonious cooperation comes to be tacitly recognized as something like a law" (p. 13). "The advantages of co-operation can be had only by conformity to certain requirements which association imposes" (p. 20). "This pro-altruistic sentiment of justice serves temporarily to cause respect for one another's claims, and so to make social co-operation possible" (p. 31). "As fast as voluntary co-operation which characterizes the industrial type of society, becomes more general than compulsory co-operation which characterizes the militant type of society" (p. 33). "The equality concerns the mutually-limited spheres of action which must be maintained if associated men are to co-operate harmoniously. . . . But here we have only to do with those claims and those limits which have to be maintained as conditions to harmonious co-operation" (p. 43). "Amicable social co-operation" (p. 56). "Peaceful co-operation" (p. 61).

How did it happen, after coming so near to the truth in his preliminary argument, that Spencer ended by offering, not an adequate explanation of the nature and purpose of Justice, but an (unsatisfactory) formula for Freedom? The reason, I think, is that, in spite of his new insights, he could not bring himself to abandon the chief concepts and conclusions at which he had arrived in his *Social Statics* in 1850.

Before we leave this subject, it will be profitable to return for a moment to the slogan: *fiat justitia, ruat caelum*. It is extravagant and absurd, but there is a grain of truth in it. We should not lightly abandon the established rules of equity, fairness, and justice in a particular case because we may feel that in that particular case their application may do more harm than good. For the established rules of justice must have a

JUSTICE

certain sanctity or near-sanctity. They are the product of mankind's reason applied to its accumulated experience. They are to be tested by their long-run consequences in the overwhelming majority of cases rather than by their short-run consequences in particular cases. The dangers of breaking an established rule of justice or equity in a particular case are not to be underestimated. The harm that the strict application of these rules may do in particular cases is enormously less than the harm that would follow from applying the rules discriminately or capriciously, from making constant exceptions in the alleged interest of the "merits of the particular case."

But all this has been pointed out by Hume. I need merely refer the reader again to the extensive quotations I made from Hume in Chapter 8, on "The Need for General Rules," in which Hume points out that just laws may sometimes "deprive, without scruple, a beneficent man of all his possessions if acquired by mistake, without a good title, in order to bestow them on a selfish miser who has already heaped up immense stores of superfluous riches." [18] Nevertheless, in the interests of long-run public good, it is essential that established general rules of justice be applied without arbitrary exceptions.

So, to come back once more to *fiat justitia, ruat caelum,* the demand that "justice be done, though the heavens fall" is indeed preposterous; but it is not preposterous to demand—on the contrary, it is essential to demand—that justice be done (i.e., that the established rules of justice be applied) even though it causes some temporary inconvenience or regrettable result in this or that particular case.

5. *Justice as a Means*

That justice is primarily a means to social cooperation, that social cooperation is primarily a means to promote the maximum happiness and well-being of each and all, does not reduce the importance of either justice or social cooperation. For both are the necessary means, the *indispensable* means to the desired goal. And therefore both of them are to be valued and cherished as ends-in-themselves. For a means can also be an end, if not *the* ultimate end. It can even seem to form an integral part of the ultimate end. The happiness and well-being of men simply cannot be achieved, and hardly imagined, without Justice and Social Cooperation.

Among the older writers the one who seems to me, second only to Hume, to have most clearly recognized the true basis, nature, and importance of Justice is John Stuart Mill. His discussion occurs in Chapter V (the final chapter) of his essay on *Utilitarianism*. It is probably the excellence of this section that is responsible for that essay's high reputation and continued appeal, in spite of some inconsistencies and logical weaknesses in the earlier chapters. I cannot refrain from quoting a page or two from this chapter, "On the Connection Between Justice and Utility":

> While I dispute the pretensions of any theory which sets up an imaginary standard of justice not grounded on utility, I account the justice which is grounded on utility to be the chief part, and incomparably the most sacred and binding part, of all morality. Justice is a name for certain classes of moral rules which concern the essentials of human well-being more nearly, and are therefore of more absolute obligation, than any other rules for the guidance of life; and the notion which we have found to be of the essence of the idea of justice—that of a right residing in an individual—implies and testifies to this more binding obligation.
>
> The moral rules which forbid mankind to hurt one another (in which we must never forget to include wrongful interference with each other's freedom) are more vital to human well-being than any maxims, however important, which only point out the best mode of managing some department of human affairs. They have also the peculiarity that they are the main element in determining the whole of the social feelings of mankind. It is their observance which alone preserves peace among human beings: if obedience to them were not the rule, and disobedience the exception, every one would see in every one else an enemy against whom he must be perpetually guarding himself. What is hardly less important, these are the precepts which mankind have the strongest and the most direct inducements for impressing upon one another. By merely giving to each other prudential instruction or exhortation, they may gain, or think they gain, nothing: in inculcating on each other the duty of positive beneficence they have an unmistakable interest, but far less in degree: a person may possibly not need the benefits of others; but he always needs that they should not do him hurt. Thus the moralities which protect every individual from being harmed by others, either directly

or by being hindered in his freedom of pursuing his own good, are at once those which he himself has most at heart and those which he has the strongest interest in publishing and enforcing by word and deed. It is by a person's observance of these that his fitness to exist as one of the fellowship of human beings is tested and decided; for on that depends his being a nuisance or not to those with whom he is in contact. Now it is these moralities primarily which compose the obligations of justice. The most marked cases of injustice, and those which give the tone to the feeling of repugnance which characterizes the sentiment, are acts of wrongful aggression or wrongful exercise of power over some one; the next are those which consist in wrongfully withholding from him something which is his due—in both cases, inflicting on him a positive hurt, either in the form of direct suffering or of the privation of some good which he had reasonable ground, either of a physical or of a social kind, for counting upon.[19]

CHAPTER 25
Equality and Inequality

The problem of equality vs. inequality has been touched upon in the preceding chapter on Justice, and will be dealt with again when we come to compare the ethical merits of capitalism and socialism. But it may be instructive to consider it briefly in a chapter by itself.

The problem may be stated thus: Why does "justice" sometimes seem to call for *equality* of treatment, and sometimes for *inequality* of treatment? Is this as inconsistent as it seems on its face? Or are we here applying the terms *equality* and *inequality* in two different senses—or in two different frames of reference?

Let us begin with the biological field. It is simply not established, *biologically,* that "all men are created equal." On the contrary, the preponderant opinion of biologists and biochemists today is that all men are created *unequal*. All men are born with a unique combination of genes and chromosomes; with different physical potentialities that will lead to different fingerprints, different faces, different heights and bodily structures, different degrees of energy, health, immunity or susceptibility to disease, and longevity; with different intellectual and moral potentialities, gifts and deficiencies.[1]

Differences in environment, nutrition, education, and experience will determine the direction that potentialities take, and may increase or decrease the potential differences that existed at birth. It is the impossibility of scientifically separating or isolating innate from acquired characteristics—or at least failure to do so up to now—that has made it impossible to say with confidence which characteristics of an adult are the result of inborn and which of environmental factors, or precisely how much influence to attribute to each. But the dogma of innate *equality* cannot be established, and the presumption of innate *inequality* is enormously strong.[2] Even Karl Marx admitted "the inequality of individual endowment and therefore productive capacity" and "unequal individuals (and they would not be different individuals if they were not unequal)." [3]

A number of highly important practical consequences follow from this recognition of unequal endowments. One of them is inequality of treatment in many respects. It is not "just," but foolish, to try to give the same education to mentally retarded children and to exceptionally gifted children. We may be wasting our time on the former and failing to develop the potentialities of the latter. We may be hurting both. In that case we are being unjust to both. Similarly, we are wasting time and energy (our own and that of others), as well as being unjust, when, ignoring natural endowments or propensities, we try to force a potential scientist to be an artist or a potential artist to be a scientist.

There is a second corollary which follows from either innate or acquired inequality. If two men have different endowments or different productivity, if one turns out either a greater product or a better product than another, then it is both foolish and unjust to insist that they should be paid the same amount. They should be paid, as the free market tends to pay them, in *proportion* to their productivity. Justice in this case consists in proportionality rather than equality. To give equal pay for unequal product is not only immediately unjust, but foolish because it deprives *both* the superior worker *and* the inferior worker of his incentive to produce more or better. It is therefore in the long run unjust to both, and unjust to society.[4]

So much for the necessity, and the appropriate sphere, of *inequality* of treatment. We come now to the necessity, and the appropriate sphere, of *equality* of treatment, or at least of consideration. All men are not born biologically equal, but in a just society they are born, or should be born, equal *in rights*. To say this is to say that all men are, or should be, *equal before the law*. And to say this, in turn, is to say that the law should be *general* in application, and should never allow arbitrary exceptions.

That in a theater fire *I* (whoever I am) should be allowed to be the first to get to the exit; that in a sea disaster *I* should be in the first lifeboat; that at a street crossing *I* should be allowed right of way regardless of lights or rules; that at a buffet dinner *I* should always be the first to help myself—this is what the moral rule of equality cannot permit. The common interests requires that order and precedence in these matters must be governed by general rules applied to and enforced on everyone. We cannot allow exceptions. Or rather, whatever exceptions are permitted (e.g., in traffic, to fire engines, ambulances, police cars) must be exceptions made by rule in the general interest, not merely in the special interest of the persons excepted. If everybody were to treat himself as an exception there would be a mad rush for the fire exits, a furious scramble for the lifeboats, a traffic jam and constant accidents, a disorderly, ill-mannered, and degrading rush to the buffet table, which would make things worse for everybody.

Equality in this sense means the refusal to allow exceptions, or to allow exceptions for any other than the general interest, and never merely for the interest of the exception himself. Equality in this sense means not only the rule of justice; it means the rule of law and order. It is merely another way of insisting on the strict adherence to general rules. The exceptions must be permitted only for reasons *relevant* to this purpose, and never for irrelevant reasons either of social rank or individual superiority.

In other words, to say that we should be subject to *general* laws is to say that these laws should apply *equally* to everybody. "Equality before the law" can perhaps be a misleading phrase. It is the *laws* that are equal in application. There is no implication that the persons subject to the law are equal in any other respect than their right to equality of treatment in the application of the law. There is no implication in this that "all men are born equal." This dubious premise is not needed to establish the utility and justice of equal treatment *by* the law.

Equality before the law might be stated in still another way. It is symbolized in the statues which show Justice blindfolded, holding a pair of scales. This does not mean that Justice is blind to everything else *but* the merits of the case. It means that everything else is to be ignored but compliance or noncompliance with a general abstract law, or abstract considerations of equity in a particular case. It means that race, color, religion, and all other qualities or differences in status or wealth or ability of the litigants are to be dismissed as *irrele-*

vant. Such differences are never to be recognized or seen by Justice.

In brief, there is no inconsistency in pointing out that justice sometimes demands Equality and sometime Inequality, provided we keep clearly in mind *in what respect* treatment, consideration, or reward should be equal or unequal. Everything depends upon the frame of reference.

CHAPTER 26

Freedom

Varied and multitudinous as are the conceptions of "justice," they are as nothing compared with the variety and number of the conceptions of "freedom." Entire books have been devoted to an analysis of what the word means to various writers or in various settings.[1] My purpose here is to discuss only a few of these meanings.

The words *liberty* and *freedom* are used both in the legal-political and in the moral realm. In the legal and political realm the truest, or at least the most useful and fruitful concept, seems to me to be the one set forth by John Locke in *The Second Treatise of Civil Government* (sec. 57):

> The end of law is not to abolish or restrain, but to preserve and enlarge freedom. For in all the states of created beings, capable of laws, where there is no law there is no freedom. For liberty is to be free from restraint and violence from others, which cannot be where there is no law; and is not, as we are told, "a liberty for every man to do what he lists." For who could be free, when every other man's humour might domineer over him? But a liberty to dispose and order freely as he lists his person, actions, possessions, and his whole property within the allowance of those laws under which he is, and therein not to be subject to the arbitrary will of another, but freely follow his own.

The fullest and best modern restatement of this view is found in F. A. Hayek's *The Constitution of Liberty*.[2] The purpose of law, and the chief function of the state, should be to maximize security and liberty and to minimize coercion. Liberty for the individual means that he is free to act in accordance with his own decisions and plans, in contrast to one who is subject to the arbitrary will of another. Coercion, of course, cannot be altogether avoided. The only way to prevent the coercion of one man by another is by the threat of coercion against any would-be coercer. This is the function of the law, the law-enforcing officials, and the State. The State must have a monopoly of coercion if coercion is to be minimized. And coercion by the State itself can be minimized only if it is exercised without arbitrariness or caprice, and solely in accordance with known, general rules which constitute the law.

This concept of freedom as the absence of constraint (which includes the qualification that "there are cases in which people have to be constrained if one wants to preserve the freedom of other people")[3] is the oldest political conception of freedom. It is also, fortunately, still the common property of many jurists, economists, and political scientists.[4] True, it may be called a "merely negative" concept. But this is so only "in the sense that peace is also a negative concept or that security or quiet or the absence of any particular impediment or evil is negative."[5] It will be found that most of the "positive" concepts of liberty identify liberty with the power to satisfy all our wishes or even with "the freedom to constrain other people."[6]

Now when we apply this political conception of freedom in the moral realm we see that it is both an end-in-itself and the necessary means to most of our other ends. All men and all animals rebel at physical restraint just because it is restraint. Hold a baby's arms, and it will begin to struggle, cry, and scream. Put a puppy on a leash, and it will have to be dragged along by the neck with all four paws scraping the ground. Release a dog that has been tied up, and he will leap and bound and tear around in circles of frenzied joy. Prisoners, schoolboys, soldiers or sailors will show unrestrained glee in the first moments or hours of release from jail or school or barracks or shipboard. The value attached to liberty is never more clearly seen than when men have been deprived of it, or when it has been even mildly restricted. Liberty is so precious an end in itself that Lord Acton was moved to declare that it is "not a means to a higher political end. It is itself the highest political end."

Yet though liberty is beyond doubt an end-in-itself, it is also of the highest value, to repeat, as a means to most of our other ends. We can pursue not only our economic but our intellectual and spiritual goals only if we are free to do so. Only when we are free do we have the power to choose. And only when we have the power to choose can our choice be called right or moral. Morality cannot be predicated of the act of a slave, or of any act done because one has been coerced into doing it. (The same does not apply, of course, to *immorality*. If a man flogs someone else because he fears that he will otherwise be flogged himself, or murders someone else, under orders, to save his own life, his act is still immoral.)

Liberty is the essential basis, the *sine qua non,* of morality. Morality can exist only in a free society; it can exist to the extent that freedom exists. Only to the extent that men have the power of choice can they be said to choose the good.

CHAPTER 27
Free Will and Determinism

1. *The Fallacies of Materialism*

It is possible to write a book on ethics without referring to the immemorial problem of Free Will *vs.* Determinism. Many modern books on ethics omit any discussion of it. I should myself be happy to do so, if it were not for a still widespread belief that the answer we make to the question may have crucial practical importance. "If all a man's actions are determined," ask those who hold this belief, "and if his will is not free, how can he be held responsible for his actions? And if he cannot be held responsible for them, what justification can there be for reward or punishment, praise or blame? Is there any point at all in the study of ethics?"

I have put the question in this crude and extreme form because it may help to emphasize some of the more frequent confusions and fallacies that occur in its discussion.

As such confusions and fallacies have existed on both sides of the controversy, we need to examine carefully what is right and what is wrong in the arguments both of those who call themselves Determinists and those who call themselves Libertarians.

Let us begin with the Determinists. They are right in asserting the omnipresence of Cause and Effect. They are right in asserting that everything that happens is a necessary outcome of a preceding state of things. This is not merely the discovery and conclusion of the whole body of modern science. It is an inescapable necessity of thought itself. As Henri Poincaré put it: "Science is determinist; it is so *a priori;* it postulates determinism, because without this postulate science could not exist." [1]

By the same reasoning, the Libertarian concept of a person or "self" or an individual "will" that stands outside the chain of causation, uninfluenced by the previous state of affairs, is wholly untenable.

But there is a common confusion of Determinism with Materialism. The Materialistic Determinists press on from the inescapable assumption that every effect has a cause to the arbitrary assumption that all causation, even in human action, must be *physical* or *chemical* causation. They assume that all thoughts, values, volitions, decisions, acts, are the product of physical, chemical, or physiological processes going on in the human body. In such a view the human mind or will can *originate* nothing. It transforms outward pressures and forces, or inward chemical changes, into ideas or acts, or the *illusion* of "volition" or "free will," much as a dynamo automatically transforms motion into electricity or an engine automatically transforms steam, electricity, or gasoline into motion in a fixed determinate ratio. In this view, moreover, the "self" or the human "will" hardly has even as much physical existence as the dynamo or the engine. The "will" is merely the name for an automatic and predictable process. Everything acting on it is a cause, but *it* itself seems to be a cause of nothing. A man acts for the same reason that a mechanical doll may walk. The mechanism in the former case is merely more complicated.

Now there is doubtless *some* connection between body and mind or, say, between chemicals and drugs, on the one hand, and human actions on the other. This has been shown in recent times by the effects on mind and action of a multiplicity of drugs. Men have, in fact, known from time immemorial about the effects on mind and action of alcohol. It has yet to be shown, however, that these effects will ever be completely measurable, determinate, and predictable.

The chain of causation may also run the other way round. Worry, anxiety, disappointment, despair, may precipitate heart attacks and other diseases (possibly cancer), while hope and faith seem in at least some cases to have remarkable curative powers.

But though we know there is *some* connection between body and mind, between chemistry and consciousness, we still do not know the precise nature of that connection or how it operates. Certainly we do not know enough about the relations of mind and body to leap into the assumptions of panphysicalism. We know very little even about the process by which new ideas arise out of previous ideas. We know practically nothing about the way in which ideas arise out of chemical or physiological processes. The gap between chemistry and consciousness remains unbridged. We still have not the slightest knowledge of how the one world is or can be transformed into the other.[2]

This is the view that is now being accepted by modern biologists. As Julian Huxley puts it in *Evolution in Action*:

> The impulses which travel up to the brain along the nerves are of an electrical nature and differ only in their time relations, such as their frequency, and in their intensity. But in the brain, these purely quantitative differences in electrical pattern are translated into wholly different qualities of sensation. The miracle of mind is that it can transmute quantity into quality. The property of mind is something given: it is just so. It cannot be explained; it can only be accepted. . . .[3]
>
> For a biologist, much the easiest way is to think of mind and matter as two aspects of a single, underlying reality—shall we call it world substance, the stuff out of which the world is made . . . ?[4]

The point is further developed by Joseph Wood Krutch in *The Measure of Man*. In the debate during the second half of the nineteenth century between the mechanists and the humanists, he writes, the humanists made the "egregious tactical error" of permitting the issue to depend on the existence of the "soul" instead of on the existence of consciousness: This

> permitted the chemists to say, "I cannot find the soul in my test tube," without exposing clearly the fallacy of his argument. If he had been compelled to say, instead, "I cannot find consciousness in my test tube," the reply would be simple: "I don't care whether you can find it there or not. I can find it in my head. Chemistry, by failing to find it, demonstrates nothing except the limitations of its methods. I am conscious, and until you show me a machine which is also conscious I shall continue to believe that the difference between me and a mechanism is probably very significant; even perhaps that what I find in that consciousness is better evidence concerning things to which consciousness is relevant than the things which you find in a test tube. . . ."

Actually, of course, consciousness is the *only* thing of which we have direct evidence, and to say "I *think* therefore I am" is a statement which rests more firmly on direct evidence than the behaviorists' formula "I *act* therefore I am." After all, it is only because man is conscious that he can know or think he knows that he acts. What he minimizes really comes first and on it everything else rests. What the mechanist disparagingly calls "the subjective" is not that of which we are least, but rather that of which we are *most* certain. . . .

The problem of the apparent discontinuity between the two realms still remains. How a material body can be aware of sensations is perhaps the thorniest of all metaphysical problems. It is as hard to imagine how we get from one realm to the other, what is the connection between the world of things and that of thoughts and emotions—as it is to imagine how one might manage to enter the mathematician's world of the fourth dimension. But . . . the physical body does think and feel. Much as the physical scientist may hate to admit what he cannot account for, this fact he can hardly deny. The seemingly impossible is the most indisputably true.[5]

2. *The Confusions of Fatalism*

Of even greater practical importance than the fallacy of Materialism is the fallacy that confuses Determinism with Fatalism. The doctrine of Determinism merely asserts that nothing happens without a cause, that every state of affairs is the outcome of a preceding state of affairs. Without this assumption all prediction would be impossible and all reasoning would be futile. But the doctrine of Determinism, while it does necessarily assert that the past was (in one sense) inevitable, given the physical, social, and individual forces, actions, choices, and decisions that actually took place, and while it also asserts that the future will be determined in the same way, does not assert that this future can necessarily be *known in advance*. Nor does it assert that a given event will take place *regardless of what you or I may do to promote or prevent it*. Yet this is the assumption implicit in Fatalism.

People slip into this fallacy either through confused theological assumptions or confused causal assumptions. Their theological argument runs something like this: "God must have existed before the Universe that He created. He must be both omnipotent and omniscient. If He is both omnipotent

FREE WILL AND DETERMINISM 273

and omniscient, He must have both foreseen and intended everything that has happened from the beginning of time and everything that will happen into eternity. It is all written in the Book of Fate. Nothing that I can do can change it."

The Materialist Fatalist argument is curiously similar to this. "Because everything that happens has a cause, and because everything is interconnected with everything else, the future is necessarily already contained in the present. Whatever will be, will be. Even my own 'Will' is an illusion. My choices and decisions are as foreordained as anything else."

Into all the fallacies in both of these arguments I shall not attempt to enter here.[6] Dissecting most of them would be an exercise in the realm of Metaphysics or Logic. But one fallacy they share in common is to take into account every force and cause and factor *except the wishes, choices, and decisions—in brief, the will—of the agent himself.* Either this is left out, as if it counted for nothing, or it is assumed that every other force and factor is active, and only a man's will is nonexistent or passive—something that is acted upon, but that acts upon nothing.

The fatalistic philosophy can do immense harm. Fortunately nobody acts on it consistently. We are told of the Turk who will sit down and calmly watch his house burn without making any effort to extinguish the fire, because, if it is the will of Allah that it shall be burned down, it is useless for him to struggle against it; while if Allah wills that it shall be saved, Allah does not want his assistance.[7]

No doubt there have been and still are a few cases as extreme as this, but not many. Few persons would need a more rational Determinist to point out to them that the question whether or not the fire was extinguished would depend at least in part upon whether or not they turned a hose on it, and that this in turn would depend upon what sort of person they were—and perhaps especially upon whether or not they were fatalists! For the quiescent Turk is in fact assuming that it is the will of Allah that his house *shall* burn down, and not the will or expectation of Allah that the Turk himself will put forth his utmost effort to save it. For somewhere in the expectations of most Fatalists there lurks the assumption that they are somehow privy to the intentions of Fate. Their own passivity and inaction help to bring about the very misfortunes they fear. This is revealed in many of their pronouncements. " 'Tis vain to quarrel with our destiny." [8] "The event is never in the power of man." [9] "Who can control his fate?" [10] "We are little better than straws upon the water: we may flatter ourselves that we swim, when the current carries us along." [11] "The age, the actions, the wealth, the knowledge, and even the death, of everyone is determined in his mother's womb." [12] "Before a child comes into the world, it has its lot assigned already, and it is ordained and determined what and how much it shall have." [13]

The tendency of all such pronouncements, if they were taken seriously, would be to make us all quietists and inactivists, rejecting and despising all ambition, all determination, all struggle and striving, all exertion and effort. Fatalism may be harmless enough as a *retrospective* philosophy; it will never do as a *prospective* philosophy.

But fortunately, as I pointed out earlier, no one acts on this doctrine with complete consistency. Even the legendary Turk who calmly watches his house burn down with no attempt to put out the fire would never have lived beyond infancy if (on the assumption that if any of these things were the will of Allah, Allah would do them for him) he never bothered to get up in the morning, to dress himself, to work for a living, to build himself a fire for warmth, to jump out of the way of a falling rock or a speeding car, to take his meals, or to lift his food from his plate to his mouth. Those who profess to hold the doctrine of Fatalism seem to reserve it only for special crises in life. In the day-to-day routine of living, they in fact assume that the future is for the most part in our hands, that we help to shape our own destinies and that how we live and what we become depends upon what we will and what we do.

It is of the first importance, therefore, to distinguish between Activistic Determinism and Fatalistic Determinism. Activistic Determinism, though recognizing that every change is the result of a cause, "is a call to action and the utmost exertion of a man's physical and mental capacities," whereas fatalistic determinism "paralyzes the will and engenders passivity and lethargy." [14]

3. *Causation Is Not Compulsion*

If we ask, now, whether the will can be free, the answer depends upon what we mean by "free" in this context. Free from what? Certainly not free from causation. In this sense Spinoza is correct when he declares: "There is no free will in the human mind: it is moved to this or that volition by some cause, and this cause has been determined by some other cause, and that again by another, and so *ad infinitum*." [15]

But what is relevant for practical ethics is not an impossible freedom from causation, but freedom to act, freedom to aim at definite ends, freedom to choose between alternatives, freedom to choose good from evil, freedom to act in accordance with the pronouncements of our reason, and not as the mere slave of our immediate passions and appetites. And what is both ethically and politically relevant is freedom from outside coercion, freedom to act "according to one's own will instead of another's." [16] And these two kinds of freedom—from compulsion by momentary appetite and from outside coercion—most of us can have.

Determinism in the true sense does not exempt anyone from moral responsibility. It is precisely because we do not decide or act without cause that ethical judgments serve a purpose. We are all influenced by the reasoning of others, by their praise or blame, by the prospect of reward or punishment. The knowledge that we will be held "responsible" for our acts by others, or even that we will be responsible in our own eyes for the consequences of our acts, must influence those acts, and must tend to influence them in the direction of moral opinion.

The *practical* consequences of a belief in Determinism or in Free Will, respectively, depend on how we understand these terms. Practically we do act, in our social life, on the assumption that the actions of *others* are predictable because of their pre-established habits and character: "The life of man in society involves daily a mass of minute forecasts of the actions of other men." [17] To that extent we are all Determinists. And to the extent that we are Determinists, also, we will tend to regard punishment as preventive rather than retributive.[18]

In fact, it is possible to reverse the common argument of

the Libertarians and to contend that *only* on the assumptions of Determinism can moral responsibility have any meaning. This was the position of Hume:

> Nay, I shall go further, and assert that this kind of necessity [Determinism] is so essential to religion and morality that without it there must ensue an absolute subversion of both, and that every other supposition is entirely destructive of all laws, both divine and human. It is indeed certain that as all human laws are founded on rewards and punishments, it is supposed as a fundamental principle that these motives have an influence on the mind, and both produce the good and prevent the evil actions. . . .
>
> But according to the doctrine of liberty or chance . . . [an] action itself may be blamable; it may be contrary to all the rules of morality and religion: but the person is not responsible for it; and as it proceeded from nothing in him that is durable or constant, and leaves nothing of that nature behind it, it is impossible he can, upon its account, become the object of punishment or vengeance. According to the hypothesis of liberty [Free Will], therefore, a man is as pure and untainted, after having committed the most horrid crimes, as at the first moment of his birth. . . . It is only upon the principles of necessity [Determinism] that a person acquires any merit or demerit from his actions, however the common opinion may incline to the contrary.[19]

And nearly a century even before Hume, Hobbes had also seen with brilliant clarity that there was no inherent contradiction between Free Will and Determinism—or, in the older vocabulary, between Liberty and Necessity—when the meaning of both was clearly understood:

> *Liberty,* or *Freedom,* signifieth, properly, the absence of opposition . . . [of] external impediments. . . .
>
> *A Free man is he, that in those things, which by his strength and wit he is able to do, is not hindered to do what he has a will to.* . . . From the use of the word *free-will,* no liberty can be inferred of the will, desire, or inclination, but the liberty of the man; which consisteth in this, that he finds no stop, in doing what he has the will, desire, or inclination to do. . . .
>
> *Liberty* and *necessity* are consistent: as in the water, that hath not only *liberty* but a necessity of descending by the channel; so likewise in the actions which men voluntarily do: which, because they proceed from their will, proceed from *liberty;* and yet, be-

cause every act of man's will, and every desire, and inclination proceedeth from some cause, and that from another cause, in a continual chain . . . proceed from *necessity*. So that to him that could see the connexion of those causes, the *necessity* of all men's voluntary actions would appear manifest.[20] [His italics.]

I hope I may be forgiven if I supplement these by at least one modern quotation, for it seems to me that there has been a convergence of the best modern philosophic thought toward the conclusion that, when both terms are correctly understood, it is perfectly possible to reconcile determinism with freedom of the will. The quotation is from A. J. Ayer's *Philosophical Essays* (1954): "That my actions should be capable of being explained is all that is required by the postulate of determinism. . . . It is not . . . causality that freedom is to be contrasted with, but constraint." [21]

The question should be raised, indeed, whether the whole immemorial dispute between Determinism and Free Will does not rest on a misunderstanding—a simple confusion between natural laws, in the sense of rules of universal validity, and legal laws, in the sense of laws that impose a compulsion—*des*criptive laws versus *pres*criptive laws. All science presupposes the principle of causation. Freedom in the moral sense does not mean freedom from *causation*, but freedom from *compulsion*. A man is free from compulsion when he is not restrained or coerced by forces or persons *outside* of himself. He is free when he can follow his *own* desires, his *own* will, regardless of how that will may itself have come to be what it is. And in *this* sense, it is true, freedom is the presupposition of moral responsibility. When we ask who is *responsible* for an act, we mean in practice who is to be rewarded or punished for it, who is to be praised or blamed for it. And as we reward or punish, praise or blame, in order to improve moral conduct, the problem of determining moral responsibility is practical rather than metaphysical.

To sum up: There is no irreconcilable antithesis between Determinism and Free Will when both are rightly understood. Determinism simply assumes that everything, including our every act and decision, has a prior cause. But it does not assert or assume that every cause or force acting on us is *outside* of us. On the contrary, it assumes that our own character, *which we ourselves have helped to form,* our own past habits, resolutions and decisions, help to determine our present acts and decisions, and that these in turn will help to determine our future acts and decisions. And Free Will, rightly understood, means that we are not necessarily the slaves of our immediate appetites, but are free to make the choice among alternatives of conduct that we consider most rational. We are free to choose our ends. We are free, within limits, to choose what we consider to be the most appropriate means to our ends.

What more freedom do we really need?

CHAPTER 28

Rights

1. Legal Rights

The concept of Rights is in origin a legal concept. In fact, in most European languages the term for Law is identical with the term for Right. The Latin *jus*, the French *droit*, the Italian *diritto*, the Spanish *derecho*, the German *Recht* signify both the legal rule that binds a person and the legal right that every person claims as his own. These coincidences are no mere accident. Law and Right are correlative terms. They are two sides of the same coin. All private rights are derived from the legal order, while the legal order involves the aggregate of all the rights coordinated by it. As one legal writer puts it: "We can hardly define a right better than by saying that it is the *range of action assigned to a particular will within the social order established by law.*" [1]

In other words, just because every person under the rule of law is divested of an unlimited liberty of action, a certain liberty of action *within* the legal limits is conceded and guaranteed to him by right.

When a man claims something as a right, he claims it as *his own* or as *due to him*. The very conception of a legal right for one man implies an *obligation* on the part of somebody else or of everybody else. If a creditor has a right to a sum of money owed to him on a certain day, the debtor has an obligation to pay it. If you have a right to freedom of speech, to privacy, or to the ownership of a house, every one else has an *obligation* to respect it. A legal right for me implies a legal duty of others not to interfere with my free exercise of it.

Among legal rights almost universally recognized and protected today are the right to freedom from assault, or from arbitrary arrest or imprisonment; the right to be protected from arbitrary intrusion into one's home; the right to freedom of speech and publication (within certain established limits); the right to hold property; the right to compensation for damages inflicted by trespassers; the right to demand fulfillment of a contract; and many others.

The notion of legal right has its counterpart in legal duty. In their legal relations men either *claim* or *owe*. If A exerts an acknowledged right, he has the legal power to require that B (or that B, C, D, etc.) shall act or forbear to act in a certain way—shall do something or abstain from doing something.

Neither legally nor morally can "property rights" be properly contrasted with "human rights":

> The right of ownership is, strictly speaking, quite as much a personal right—the right of one person against other persons—as a right to service, or a lease. It may be convenient for certain purposes to speak of rights over things, but in reality there can only be rights *in respect of* things *against* persons. . . . Relations and intercourse arise exclusively between live beings; but goods as well as ideas are the object and the material of such relations; and when a right of ownership in a watch or a piece of land is granted to me by law, this means not only that the seller has entered into a personal obligation to deliver those things to me, but also that every person will be bound to recognize them as mine.[2]

"Every single legal rule may be thought of as one of the bulwarks or boundaries erected by society in order that its members shall not collide with each other in their actions."[3] As every legal rule appears as a necessary adjunct to some relation of social intercourse, it is often difficult to say whether the rule precedes the rights and duties involved in the relation, or vice versa. Both of these sides of law stand in constant cross-relations with each other.

In the last three centuries there has been an expansion of legal rights and an increasingly explicit recognition of their existence and importance. To protect the individual against abuses in statute law or by law-enforcement officials, "bills of rights" have been incorporated into written constitutions. The most famous of these is the Bill of Rights adopted in 1790 in the American Constitution.

The Bill of Rights is another name for the first Ten Amendments. It guarantees freedom of worship, of speech, and of the press; the right of the people peaceably to assemble, and to petition the government for a redress of grievances; the right of the people to be secure in their persons, houses, papers, and effects, against unreasonable searches and seizures; the right of every person not to be compelled in any criminal case to be a witness against himself; nor to be deprived of life, liberty, or property, without due process of law; nor to have his property taken for public use, without just compensation; the right of the accused, in all criminal prosecutions, to a speedy and public trial by an impartial jury; the right to be protected against excessive bail and excessive fines, and cruel and unusual punishments.

This list is not complete. To the rights specified in the first Ten Amendments, additional rights were later added in the Fourteenth Amendment. Some rights, in fact, are specified in the original Constitution. The privilege of the writ of *habeas corpus* cannot be suspended unless in cases of rebellion or invasion the public safety may require it. Congress is prohibited from passing any bill of attainder or *ex post facto* law. Any State also is prohibited from passing any bill of attainder, *ex post facto* law, or law impairing the obligation of contracts.

We shall return later to fuller consideration of some of these rights, and of their scope and limitations.

2. *Natural Rights*

Especially in the last two centuries, there has been a broadening of the concept of legal rights to the notion of "natural" rights. This was already implicit and sometimes explicit, however, in the thought of Plato and Aristotle, of Cicero and the Roman jurists, and becomes more explicit and detailed in the writings of Locke, Rousseau, Burke, and Jefferson.[4]

The term *Natural Rights,* like the term *Natural Law,* is in some respects unfortunate. It has helped to perpetuate a *mystique* which regards such rights as having existed since the beginning of time; as having been handed down from heaven; as being simple, self-evident, and easily stated; as even being independent of the human will, independent of consequences, inherent in the nature of things. This concept is reflected in the Declaration of Independence: "We hold these truths to be self-evident, that all men are created equal, that they are endowed by their Creator with certain unalienable Rights, that among these are Life, Liberty, and the pursuit of Happiness."

Yet though the term *Natural Rights* easily lends itself to misinterpretation, the *concept* is indispensable; and it will do no harm to keep the term as long as we clearly understand it to mean *ideal* rights, the legal rights that every man *ought* to enjoy. The historic function of the doctrine of Natural Rights has been, in fact, to insist that the individual be guaranteed legal rights that he did not have, or held only uncertainly and precariously.

By a further extension, we are justified in talking not only of "natural" *legal* rights but of *moral* rights. Yet clarity of thought demands that we hold fast to at least one part of the *legal* meaning of "rights." We have seen that every right of one man implies a corresponding *obligation* of others to do something or refrain from doing something so that he may be protected in and even *guaranteed* that right. If we abandon this two-sided concept the term *right* becomes a mere rhetorical flourish without definite meaning.

3. *Pseudo-Rights*

Before we examine the real nature and function of "natural" or moral rights it will clarify our ideas to look at some illegitimate extensions of the concept.

These have been rife for the last generation. An outstanding example is the Four Freedoms announced by President Franklin D. Roosevelt in 1941. The first two of these—"freedom of speech and expression," and "freedom of every person to worship God in his own way"—are legitimate freedoms and legitimate rights. They were, in fact, already guaranteed in the Constitution. But the last two—"freedom from want . . . everywhere in the world" and "freedom from fear . . . anywhere in the world" are illegitimate extensions of the concept of freedom or the concept of rights.

It will be noticed that the first two are freedoms *of* (or *to*), and the second two are freedoms *from*. Had Roosevelt used the synonym "liberty," he would still have been able to promise "liberty *to*," but English idiom would hardly have allowed him to promise "liberty *from*."[5] "Freedom to" is a guaranty that no one, including the government, will be allowed to *interfere* with one's freedom of thought and expression; but "freedom *from"* means that it is considered the duty of *someone else* to *supply* one's wants or to *remove* one's fears. Aside from the fact that this is a demand impossible of fulfillment (in a world of daily dangers and in a world in which we have not collectively produced enough to meet all our wants), just how does it become someone else's duty to supply my wants or to banish my fears? And how do I decide just *whose* duty it is?

Another outstanding example of a demand for pseudo-rights is found in the Universal Declaration of Human Rights adopted by the General Assembly of the United Nations in 1948. This declaration states, for example, that "everyone has the right to rest and leisure, including reasonable limitation of working hours and periodic holidays with pay." Assuming that this is even possible for *everyone* (in South America, Asia, Africa, and in the present state of civilization), whose obligation is it to provide all this? And how far does each provider's alleged obligation extend?

The same questions may be asked of all the rhetorical demands for alleged rights that we now hear almost daily—"the right to a minimum standard of living"; "the right to a decent wage"; "the right to a job"; "the right to an education"; and even "the right to a *comfortable* living"; "the right to a *satisfactory* job," or "the right to a *good* education." It is not only that all these alleged rights have vague quantitative boundaries —that they do not specify how high a wage is considered "decent" or *how much* education "the right to an education" implies. What makes them pseudo-rights is that they imply that it is somebody else's *obligation* to supply those things. But they do not usually tell us *whose* obligation, or precisely how it comes to be *his*. My "right to a job" implies that it is somebody's else's *duty* to give me a job, apparently regardless of my qualifications or even whether I would do more damage than good on the job.

4. *Absolute* vs. *Prima Facie Rights*

Unfortunately, disposing of some of the more obviously pseudo rights does only a little to simplify our problem. Natural rights or moral rights are not always self-evident, are not necessarily simple, and are seldom if ever absolute. If legal rights are the correlates of legal rules, moral rights are the correlates of moral rules. And as moral duties may sometimes conflict with each other, so may moral rights. My legal and moral rights are limited by your legal and moral rights. My right to freedom of speech, for example, is limited by your right not to be slandered. And "your right to swing your arm ends where my nose begins."

The temptation to simplify moral rights is great. One moral philosopher, Hastings Rashdall, tried to reduce them all to one single right—the right to equality of consideration:

> Not only does the principle of equal consideration not necessarily prescribe any actual equality of Well-being or of the material conditions of Well-being: when properly understood, it does not favor the attempt to draw up *a priori* any detailed list of the "rights of man." It is impossible to discover any tangible concrete thing, or even any specific "liberty of action or acquisition," to which it can be contended that every individual or human being has a right under all circumstances. There are circumstances under which the satisfaction of any and every such right is a physical impossibility. And if every assertion of right is to be conditioned by the clause "if it be possible," we might as well boldly say that every man, woman, and child on the earth's surface has a right to £1000 a year. There is every bit as much reason for such an assertion as for maintaining that every one has a right to the means of subsistence, or to three acres and a cow, or to life, or to liberty, or to the Parliamentary franchise, or to propagate his species, or the like. There are conditions under which none of these rights can be given to one man without prejudice to the equal rights of others. There seems, then, to be no "right of man" which is unconditional, except the right to consideration—that is to say, the right to have his true Well-being (whatever that true Well-being be) regarded as of equal importance in all social arrangements with the Well-being of everybody else. Elaborate expositions of the rights of man are, at best, attempts to formulate the most important actual or legal rights which an application of the principle of equality would require to be conceded to the generality of men at a particular state of social development. They are all ultimately resolvable into the one supreme and unconditional right—*the right to consideration;* and all particular applications of that principle must be dependent upon circumstances of time and place.[6]

In its negative contention—in emphasizing how many devoutly-to-be-wished-for conditions may be falsely called rights—this passage is highly instructive. But in its affirmative contention—in its effort to prove that all rights may be subsumed under equality of consideration—the passage cannot be called successful. No doubt "equality of consideration" is *one* moral right. But it is a very vague one. Suppose we think of it for a moment as a claimed *legal* right. Suppose a chair of philosophy falls vacant at Harvard and M, N, and O are among those who secretly aspire to be appointed to the post. And suppose, instead, that A gets the appointment and M, N, and O discover that A was, in fact, the only man even *considered* for the post? How could any one of the unsuccessful hopefuls go about legally *proving* that he did not get equality of consideration? (And in just what would "equality of consideration" have consisted?) He could say that the appointing group was influenced by *irrelevant* considerations—by considerations apart from what were strictly A's qualifications for the post—or that his, M's, qualifications for the post were not even considered. But could the appointing group reasonably be expected to consider equally *everybody's* qualifications for the post? Or is Rashdall's criterion merely another form of Bentham's "everybody to count for one, nobody to count for more than one"? And just how would either criterion help a man to decide a specific moral problem—such as, in a shipwreck at sea, whether to save his wife or a stranger? Or even (if conditions made this the only alternative) whether to save his wife or *two* strangers?

We must try to think of moral rights with at least as much care and precision as legislators, judges, and jurists are compelled to think of legal rights. We cannot be satisfied with any vague and easy rhetorical solutions. Legal rights actually constitute an intricate and interrelated structure of rights worked out by centuries of judicial reasoning applied to centuries of human experience. Contrary to Justice Holmes's facile epigram: "The life of the law has not been logic; it has been experience," [7] the life of the law has been *both* logic and experience. The law is the product of logic and reason *brought to bear* on experience.

As everyone's rights are conditioned by the equal rights of others, as the rights of each must be harmonized and coordinated with the equal rights of all, and as one right may not always and everywhere be compatible with another, there are few if any *absolute* rights. Even the right to life and the right to freedom of speech are not absolute. John Locke often wrote as if the rights to life, liberty, and property *were* absolute, but he made exceptions and qualifications in the course of his discussion: "Every one as he is bound to preserve himself . . . so by the like reason, *when his own preservation comes not in competition,* ought he as much as he can to preserve the rest of mankind, and not *unless it be to do justice on an offender,* take away or impair the life, or what tends to the preservation of the life, the liberty, health, limb, or goods of another." [8] (My italics.)

Even the right to freedom of speech does not extend to libel, slander, or obscenity (though there may be difficult problems of definition concerning the latter). And nearly everyone will concede the limits to free speech as defined by Justice Holmes in a celebrated opinion:

> The most stringent protection of free speech would not protect a man in falsely shouting fire in a theatre, and causing a panic. It does not even protect a man from injunction against uttering words that may have all the effect of force. The question in every case is whether the words are used in such circumstances and are of such a nature as to create a clear and present danger that they will bring about the substantive evils that Congress has a right to prevent. It is a question of proximity and degree.[9]

The suggestion has been made, following the analogy of the concept of *"prima facie* duties" (which we owe to Sir David Ross), that though we have no *absolute* rights, we do have *prima facie* rights. That is, we have a *prima facie* right to life, liberty, property, etc., which must be respected in the absence of some conflicting right or other consideration. But just as the law must be more precise than this, so must moral philosophy. Legal rights are of course subject to certain conditions and qualifications. But *within* those necessary qualifications, legal rights are or ought to be *inviolable.* And so, of course, should moral rights be.

This inviolability does not rest on some mystical yet self-evident "law of nature." It rests ultimately (though it will shock many to hear this) on utilitarian considerations. But it rests, not on *ad hoc* utilitism, on expediency in any narrow sense, but on *rule*-utilitism, on the recognition that the highest and only permanent utility comes from an unyielding adherence to *principle*. Only by the most scrupulous respect for each other's imprescriptible rights can we maximize social peace, order, and cooperation.

CHAPTER 29

International Ethics

1. *Cooperation Again*

In a world that is not only haunted by the specter of Communism but lives in the shadow of the nuclear bomb, a book on ethics that omitted these topics would be omitting precisely the ethical problems that trouble us most. For problems of personal ethics, after all, custom and tradition have worked out fairly satisfactory answers, and prescribe reasonably adequate guides for day-to-day conduct even if their philosophical basis is uncertain or obscure. But in the international realm the world today confronts some problems (at least of urgency and scale) that it has never confronted before, and to which no accepted or ready-made solutions have been worked out.

And yet there is no basic difference between the requirements of interpersonal ethics and those of international ethics. The key to both is the principle of cooperation.

In a small closed society the worst situation is one of mutual hostility, the war of each against all, "of every man against every man," under which everybody suffers and no one has any security in pursuing his aims. The second-best situation is one of refraint[1] or abstention from mutual aggression, which at least provides an atmosphere of peace. But by far the best situation, as we have repeatedly seen, is social cooperation, which enables each of us to attain his ends and satisfactions most fully.

The case is no different in the international field. The worst situation is one of mutual hostility, mutual aggression, war. The second-best is one of "isolationism," or refraint from mutual aggression. But the ideal situation is one of international *cooperation*.

This has long been recognized by the philosophy of liberalism (in the traditional eighteenth- and nineteenth-century sense). It expressed itself in the doctrine of free trade. Free trade rested on the recognition that the international division of labor, made possible by free exchange, tended to maximize the productivity of labor and capital and so to raise standards of living everywhere. The doctrine of free trade included, of course, freedom of cultural exchange.

But liberalism did not merely espouse freedom of import and export. It also espoused freedom of travel, of immigration and emigration, and freedom of capital movements. To make these freedoms possible, there had to be security of life and property, including international respect for copyright, patents, and private property of every kind.

This security and these freedoms not only tended to maximize material welfare in all countries, but also promoted world peace. Protectionism is not only an economic fallacy, but a cause of international hostility and war. All barriers to imports and exports make the efficiency of world production less than it would otherwise be. They increase costs and prices, lower quality, and reduce abundance. Protectionism is an absurdity, because each country practicing it wants to decrease its imports but at the same time to increase its exports. It cannot do so even if it is the sole culprit, because other countries can pay for their imports from it only out of the proceeds of their exports to it. When the practice is attempted all around the circle, the absurdity becomes evident even to the most stupid. Each country that makes the attempt to put it into effect arouses the resentment of its neighbors and causes them to adopt measures of retaliation. Nationalist policies that begin by efforts to beggar one's neighbor must end in the ruin of all.

I have been speaking, in the conventional way, of "countries," of "nations," and of "international" cooperation. But it is important to keep in mind that what we really mean by "international" cooperation is cooperation between *individuals* in one nation and individuals in another. An individual importer in the United States buys from an individual exporter in Great Britain. An individual investor in the United States invests in an individual company in Canada. Apart from protecting life and property within their own countries, and insuring the integrity of their own currencies, the proper role of governments is simply *to keep hands off*, to let this "international" cooperation among individuals take place. It was the cry for this in France in the eighteenth century that gave birth to the now much misunderstood slogans: *Laissez passer, laissez faire;* which should be translated: Let goods pass. Allow goods to be produced. Allow trade to go on.

The great economist David Ricardo was the first to demonstrate (in 1817) in his Law of Comparative Costs that it is advantageous for a country to produce only those goods that it can produce at a *relatively* lower cost than other countries, and to buy from those countries even goods that it could itself produce at a lower *absolute* cost. In other words, exchange may beneficially take place even when one nation is superior in all lines of production. This is also sometimes called the Law of Association or the Law of Comparative Advantage. To many the law has seemed paradoxical, but it applies between persons as well as between nations. It is profitable for a skilled surgeon to employ a nurse to sterilize his instruments and a cleaning woman to clean up after him, even though he might be able to do both operations quicker and better himself. It is advantageous, for the same reasons, for rich and technologically advanced nations to trade and cooperate with poor and technologically backward nations.

But this is not a work on economics, and I shall not further dilate on this particular point. I shall content myself with quotations from two economists, both of which emphasize the ethical as well as the economic implications of free trade. The first is from a contemporary, Ludwig von Mises: "It is first necessary for the nations of the world to realize that their interests do not stand in mutual opposition and that every nation best serves its own cause when it is intent on promoting the development of all nations and scrupulously abstains from every attempt to use violence against other nations or parts of other nations." [2]

The second quotation is from David Hume, whose three essays, "Of Commerce," "Of the Balance of Trade," and "Of the Jealousy of Trade," which appeared a quarter of a century before Adam Smith's *Wealth of Nations*, stated the economic, cultural, and moral advantages of international trade, and the folly of interfering with it, as powerfully as any subsequent explanation. Here is the final paragraph of "The Jealousy of Trade":

> Were our narrow and malignant politics to meet with success, we should reduce all our neighboring nations to the same state

of sloth and ignorance that prevails in Morocco and the coast of Barbary. But what would be the consequence? They could send us no commodities: they could take none from us: our domestic commerce itself would languish from want of emulation, example, and instruction: and we ourselves should soon fall into the same abject condition to which we had reduced them. I shall therefore venture to acknowledge that not only as a man, but as a British subject, I pray for the flourishing commerce of Germany, Spain, Italy, and even France itself. I am at least certain that Great Britain, and all those nations, would flourish more, did their sovereigns and their ministers adopt such enlarged and benevolent sentiments toward each other.[3]

2. *Not Machinery but Attitude*

To sum up the argument thus far: International ethics, like interpersonal ethics, must be based on the recognition that the citizens of each nation gain more by *cooperation* than by mutual hostility, nonintercourse, or non-cooperation. In most cases, when we say that "nations" cooperate, we mean merely that their governments permit their own citizens to cooperate with the citizens of other nations, by allowing freedom of travel, trade, and mutual investment.

But governments must also play a more positive role. They must provide security of life and property not only for their own citizens at home, but for foreigners visiting their countries, or residing in them, and security for the property of those foreigners. Hence they must give foreigners copyright protection, patent protection, and the like.

This has required the growth of international law and of international agreements and institutions to organize cooperation among national governments. It is surprising how recent some of these agreements and institutions are. Even the practice of maintaining standing legations in other countries did not become general until about the sixteenth and seventeenth ceturies. The first Geneva Convention for ameliorating the condition of the sick and wounded, which set up the Red Cross, did not take place until 1864. The International Telegraphic Union was formed in 1865, the Universal Postal Union in 1874, the Copyright Union in 1886, the International Institute of Agriculture in 1905, the Radio Telegraphic Union in 1906.

In the last century, however, international legislation and organization has developed at an accelerative rate. One writer[4] has estimated that during the half-century 1864-1914, 257 international conventions of a legislative kind were entered into, and that during the years 1919-1929 there were no fewer than 229. Of all the new institutions, perhaps the most significant and promising were the Permanent Court of Arbitration (the Hague Tribunal) established in 1899, and the Permanent Court of International Justice set up in 1921, and now replaced by the International Court of Justice under the United Nations charter.

The questions must be raised, however, whether there is not now an overmultiplication of international institutions, whether they are the right kind of institutions, and whether some of them are not doing immensely more harm than good to the cause of international cooperation, justice, and peace. Tennyson's dream of the day when

> the war drum throbbed no longer
> and the battle flags were furled
> In the Parliament of Man, the Federation
> of the world . . .

is an inspiring ideal, but some of its too zealous advocates are the victims of confusion of thought. They refuse to see that an organization like the United Nations is at best a means to an end; that it should not be treated as if it were the end itself; that it should be judged by its fruits, and not merely by the good intentions of some of its founders. Does the United Nations, as it stands, actually promote international cooperation, international justice, and world peace? Or does it merely blow up what would otherwise be small controversies into great ones? Is it merely a propaganda forum, which the free capitalist nations have helped to create and finance, from which the Communist nations launch their hate campaigns against the capitalist nations, and through which Asian and African delegates express their envy and resentment of the Western nations and demand increasing "aid"?

These are questions that the overzealous partisans of the United Nations not only never ask themselves, but berate others for asking. But such questions go to the heart of the problem. The American, British, and other governments are denounced within their own countries for not submitting every dispute to arbitration, or to the International Court, or to the United Nations, and for not agreeing in advance to accept any decision or award, whatever it may be. But the real problem is twofold. It is not only that individual nations *will* not agree in advance to submit every dispute to "judicial" settlement, but that they (in many cases rightly) do not and *cannot* trust the impartiality of the decision. Their distrust is not irrational. It is the result of bitter experience. One has merely to look at the voting record of the Assembly of the United Nations. When a country like the United States has become the richest and most powerful in the world, it arouses the envy of all other nations, and particularly of the poor and "undeveloped" nations, who can be almost counted upon to outvote it.

This does not mean that the prospects for the growth of international law, of peaceful arbitration, and of judicial settlement, are hopeless. It does mean that what is of primary importance is international *sentiment* and *attitudes* rather than the mere international *machinery* of organization. Where the right international attitudes exist, the appropriate machinery to implement them can easily follow. An outstanding example is the Universal Postal Union. It came into existence because every party to the convention of 1874 recognized that in order to have its own stamps honored in foreign countries it must honor their stamps in its country. This was the only way in which letters mailed from foreign countries could be assured of delivery to their specific address *within* the country of their destination.

But any attempt to push organization ahead of sentiment must court failure.

3. *The Right of Self-Defense*

This brings us to the fallacies of extreme pacificism. A growing number of people in the world are not content with denouncing war, but seek to put themselves on a higher moral plane, "above the battle," by denouncing *both* sides to every dispute or every war. I travestied this attitude in an article in 1950, called "Johnny and the Tiger." [5] What it overlooks or denies is the moral and legal right and necessity of self-defense.

The right of a state, as of an individual, to protect itself against an attack, actual or threatened, is beyond dispute. It is expressly affirmed in the Charter of the United Nations, Article 51 of which provides that "Nothing in the present Charter shall impair the inherent right of individual or collective self-defense if an armed attack occurs against a Member of the United Nations, until the Security Council has taken measures necessary to maintain international peace and security."

The formulation of the principle of self-defense by Daniel Webster in 1837, when he was the American Secretary of State, has met, a British writer on international law tells us, "with general acceptance." [6] There must be shown, said Webster, "a necessity of self-defense, instant, overwhelming, leaving no choice of means and no moment of deliberation"; and further, the action must involve "nothing unreasonable or excessive, since the act justified by the necessity of self-defense must be limited by that necessity and kept clearly within it." [7]

We come now to a more difficult problem. Is there, in addition to the right of self-defense, in a strictly limited sense, a much wider right, that of self-preservation? Here writers on international law differ, and their differences reflect a moral difference. W. E. Hall declares: "Even with individuals living in well-ordered communities the right of self-preservation is absolute in the last resort. *A fortiori* it is so with states, which have in all cases to protect themselves." [8] "In the last resort almost the whole of the duties of states are subordinated to the right of self-preservation." [9]

These pronouncements are vigorously disputed by J. L. Brierly: "Such statements would destroy the imperative character of any system of law of which they were true, for they make all obligation to observe the law merely conditional; and there is hardly any act of international lawlessness which, taken literally, they would not excuse." [10]

Brierly goes on to cite both international examples and personal examples. One paragraph is especially impressive:

> Lord Bacon once imagined the case of two men who seized the same plank in a shipwreck, and because the plank could not bear the weight of both, one pushed the other off and he was drowned. There is no doubt that in English law that action would be murder. Indeed, when two men and a boy were cast away at sea in

an open boat, and the men, after their food and water had been exhausted for many days, killed and ate the boy, they were actually convicted of murder, although the jury found that in all probability all three would have died unless one had been killed for the others to eat.[11] An American case is to the same effect.[12] The Ship *William Brown* struck an iceberg, and some of the crew and passengers took to the boats. The boat was leaking and overloaded, and, in order to lighten it, the prisoner helped to throw some of the passengers overboard. He was convicted of murder. In both these cases a right of self-preservation, if any such right were known to the law, would have justified the acts committed, but it is equally clear that in neither were the acts truly defensive, for they were directed against persons from whom danger was not even apprehended. National law, indeed, is so far from recognizing an absolute right in the individual to preserve himself at all costs, that it sometimes even places on him, without any fault of his own, a legal duty to sacrifice his own life; compulsory military service is an obvious case in point.[13]

Both cases cited by Brierly, however, were cases in which self-preservation was secured only at the cost of the murder or destruction of others. In both cases self-preservation was achieved only by an act of aggression. Suppose the second case had been slightly changed: that the life-boat had been filled to capacity, and that, in order to save the people already in it, the man in charge had simply refused to take on any more, in spite of their pleas?

Or suppose the case to be one of what we may call *anticipatory* self-defense. Two men are snowbound in a one-room cabin and one of them has good reason to suspect that the other means to murder him in his sleep. He cannot keep awake all night indefinitely. What is he to do? Decide to kill the other first? If he did so, a jury would presumably decide such a case on the basis of whatever objective facts it could discover concerning how real the threat was that the actual killer would otherwise have been the victim. But suppose a whole nation is in this situation, or thinks itself to be, and there is no impartial jury to which the case can be submitted, and to which submission would be in any case too late? This is the appalling problem—the problem of the "first strike"—presented by the existence of the nuclear bomb, and above all by its possession by a Communist government that has openly announced its intention to "bury" capitalist nations and that has shown itself to be utterly without moral scruples.

I do not know the answer to this problem; but it is of the first importance that we face it frankly and state it clearly, and not try to evade it by some piece of high-sounding and irrelevant rhetoric; and particularly that we not assume a sham-moral attitude "above the battle" by piously declaring that everybody else is "suicidal" and all that is necessary is sanity and trust and brotherly love on both sides. I shall at least spare the reader such a pseudo-solution.[14]

Even before the inventions of the atomic and nuclear bombs, international ethics presented far more difficult problems than interpersonal ethics—or at least far more confusions of thought. Traditional ethical judgments are judgments made from the standpoint of the interests of "the group." The individual's conduct is judged from its effect on the welfare of "the group." But conduct that is conducive to the welfare of one group may be destructive of the welfare of another. Hence the mixed-up "ethics of war." It is virtuous for *our* soldiers to kill *their* soldiers, vicious for their soldiers to kill ours. That is the "naive" idea. But then a "sophisticated" morality arises. Courage is praised as a virtue both in our soldiers and in the enemy's soldiers. "A gallant foe" is admired, even though his gallantry is not in our interest. Treason is thought despicable, even if it is the treason of one of our enemies to his own country, which redounds to our benefit.

This points to what we may call "the paradox of virtues." Most of the old-fashioned books on ethics used to make a list of the "virtues" and deliver a little sermon on each of them. Among these virtues were nearly always included (and are still included) such traits as courage, pertinacity, dedication, industry, sobriety, temperance, prudence. But then we recognize that these characteristics may be used either for good or bad ends. When they are used for bad ends do we still call them virtues? Washington is praised for his courage and dedication in fighting for the freedom of his country. Should Napoleon be praised for his courage and dedication in conquering other countries? Is the kind of courage that enables a man to be a successful gangster or bandit a "virtue"? Yet it is the same trait that enables him to become a good policeman, or fireman, or a good soldier on our side.

Part of this problem comes from the use of the word *virtue* in a double sense: as describing a trait that serves only "good" ends and as describing a trait that helps its possessor to serve *any* end, good or bad.

4. *Self-Defense* vs. *Nonresistance*

But perhaps some of these are verbal problems rather than moral problems. We can at least answer with reasonable definiteness a few central problems concerning the ethics of war. War is of course an "unethical," indeed a monstrous method of settling disputes. But this does not mean that any of us are entitled in all cases self-righteously to denounce everyone who participates in a war, or to declare "a plague on both your houses." Both sides in a war *may* be wrong; one side *must* be; but one side may be right, and defending one's country may not only be justified, but an inevasible moral duty. I should like to quote an excellent passage on this by Herbert Spencer:

> Unquestionably war is immoral. But so likewise is the violence used in the execution of justice; so is all coercion. . . . There is, in principle, no difference whatever between the blow of a policeman's baton and the thrust of a soldier's bayonet. . . . Policemen are soldiers who act alone; soldiers are policemen who act in concert. Government employs the first to attack in detail ten thousand criminals who separately make war on society; and it calls on the last when threatened by a like number of criminals in the shape of drilled troops. Resistance to foreign foes and resistance to native ones having consequently the same object— the maintenance of men's rights, and being effected by the same means—force, are in their nature identical; and no greater condemnation can be passed on the one than on the other. . . .
> Defensive warfare (and of course it is solely to this that the foregoing argument applies) must therefore be tolerated as the least of two evils. There are indeed some who unconditionally condemn it, and would meet invasion by non-resistance. To such there are several replies.
> First, consistency requires them to behave in like fashion to their fellow-citizens. They must not only allow themselves to be cheated, assaulted, robbed, wounded, without offering active opposition, but must refuse help from the civil power; seeing that they who employ force by proxy are as much responsible for it as though they employed it themselves.

Again, such a theory makes pacific relationships between men and nations look needlessly Utopian. If all agree not to aggress, they must as certainly be at peace with each other as though they had all agreed not to resist. So that, while it sets up so difficult a standard of behavior, the rule of non-resistance is not one whit more efficient as a preventive of war, than the rule of non-aggression. . . .

Lastly, it can be shown that non-resistance is also absolutely wrong. We may not carelessly abandon our rights. We may not give away our birthright for the sake of peace. If it be a duty to respect other men's claims, so also is it a duty to maintain our own.[15]

Yes, some readers may say, this is all very well for the mid-nineteenth century. But we are now past the mid-twentieth century. We are in the age of the nuclear bomb, when, without notice, any nation with such bombs may wipe out whole cities and tens of millions of people within an hour. Nuclear war means the end of civilization, if not the end of humanity itself. "Self-defense" is now an obsolete concept, another name for world suicide. It is a luxury we can no longer afford. We now have only a choice of two evils, and we must take the lesser. We must tolerate provocations, insults, indignities, affronts, threats, aggression, domination, conquest, tyranny, oppression, a reign of terror, inquisitions, atrocities, torture, slavery, *anything* rather than resist; for resistance means atomic war, and atomic war means mutual annihilation—whereas, if we can keep the nuclear bomb from being used, we can at least nourish the hope that our conquerors will in time soften and relent, and man, and civilization, and even a certain amount of liberty, will survive.

If this were indeed the dreadful alternative, many of us would choose annihilation as the lesser evil. The cry for survival *at any price* is craven and ignominious. As Santayana once put it: "Nothing can be meaner than the anxiety to live on, to live on anyhow and in any shape; a spirit with any honor is not willing to live except in its own way." [16]

But the alternative is false. Appeasement on the part of the West, in the face of Soviet threats, merely increases the danger to the West. If the masters of the Kremlin can throw the bomb without risk to themselves, they may do it *just for sport,* a possibility that does not seem to have occurred to the later Bertrand

Russell, though in some of his earlier books he lists plenty of instances of mass murder and torture for sport from Nero to Hitler.

5. *Appeasement as a Threat to Peace*

The choice before us is the exact opposite of what the Appeasers assume. It has been stated powerfully and eloquently by Wilhelm Röpke:

> The terrible lessons which the two world wars have taught us confirm the very important fact that, as a rule, war will only break out if the aggressor considers that the risk involved is a slight one. Every disagreement among the peace-loving nations, every inclination to weakness, every marked difference in the degree of armament are therefore factors which favor the outbreak of war, whereas the danger is lessened by everything which induces even the most determined aggressor to reflect upon the enormous risk he would be taking in defying the organized defensive forces. . . .
>
> The danger to peace is enhanced the more the will to war on one side grows in inverse proportion to pacificism on the other. Since however in our day the aggressively disposed country will always be a collectivistic-totalitarian one, whose almighty dictatorship always suppresses any expression of opinion which does not suit the government and whose all-encompassing propaganda shapes the opinion of the masses in the way the government desires, the tension between the unrestrained military preparedness, both actual and psychological, of the aggressor, and the defensive power of his victim, weakened by pacificism, will be very great and very dangerous.
>
> This is the real source of the policy of Appeasement, which contributed so fatefully to the outbreak of the second world war, and which since the end of the war has once again created a highly dangerous situation with regard to the totalitarian imperium of Communism with Russia at its head. . . .
>
> Once more the world looks on at the repulsive and lying drama in which the totalitarian center of aggression in the world raises its own war potential to the maximum, and by means of an unscrupulous propaganda of hate, fear and ideology develops a condition of war-preparedness in the minds of its own population, while at the same time abusing as warmongers all those in the West who admonish resistance, and putting the whole machinery of its psychological warfare into operation in order to cripple resistance by a campaign for pacifism and in order to deceive sim-

ple souls with the fata morgana of neutralism. It has up to now succeeded to a disastrous degree.

This experience brings us to the distressing conclusion that pacifism, merely as an attitude of mind which rejects war, is not only sterile but indeed dangerous to a tragic degree, since at the very moment when the danger of war is greatest it further increases that danger immeasurably by encouraging the attacker. . . . In the case of a war of aggression . . . that is to say in practically all cases today, [pacifism] not only fails but actually becomes one of the fatal links in the chain of causes which trigger off the war and possibly effect the triumph of the aggressor. . . .

The conclusion to be drawn from all this is that the chief task of war-prevention is to make it plain to every potential aggressor, beforehand and in a completely indubitable way, that the risk is overwhelming.[17]

Even if the Western powers follow the course that Röpke recommends, they have no absolute assurance that a nuclear war can be prevented. Does this mean that the problem is insoluble? Perhaps. But man can live and act only as long as he can hope. He must act on the assumption that his practical problems are solvable. Perhaps none of them are solvable permanently and absolutely. But he must act on the assumption that every problem is solvable temporarily and relatively. He can at least, in most cases, put off the evil day. If he does not know precisely what is the right thing to do, he can usually know enough to avoid doing most of the wrong things. Man solves his moral problems as he does nearly all his practical problems—not by finding perfect solutions, but by finding solutions that make his state a little better instead of a little worse.

CHAPTER 30

The Ethics of Capitalism

1. *A Socialist Smear Word*

It is commonly assumed that there is little relation between the ethical and the economic point of view, or between Ethics and Economics. But they are, in fact, intimately related. Both are concerned with human action,[1] human conduct,[2] human decision, human choice. Economics is a *description, explanation,* or *analysis* of the determinants, consequences, and implications of human action and human choice. But the moment we come to the *justification* of human actions and decisions, or to the question of what an action or decision *ought* to be, or to the question whether the consequences of this or that action or rule of action would be more *desirable* in the long run for the individual or the community, we have entered the realm of Ethics. This is also true the moment we begin to discuss the desirability of one economic *policy* as compared with another.

Ethical conclusions, in brief, cannot be arrived at independently of, or in isolation from, analysis of the economic consequences of institutions, principles, or rules of action. The economic ignorance of most ethical philosophers, and the common failure even of those who have understood economic principles to apply them to ethical problems (on the assumption that economic principles are either irrelevant or too materialistic and mundane to apply to such a lofty and spiritual discipline as Ethics), have stood in the way of progress in ethical analysis, and account in part for the sterility of so much of it.

There is hardly an ethical problem, in fact, without its economic aspect. Our daily ethical decisions are in the main economic decisions, and nearly all our daily economic decisions have, in turn, an ethical aspect.

Moreover, it is precisely around questions of economic organization that most ethical controversy turns today. The main challenge to our traditional "bourgeois" ethical standards and values comes from the Marxists, the socialists, and the Communists. What is under attack is the capitalist system; and it is attacked mainly on ethical grounds, as being materialistic, selfish, unjust, immoral, savagely competitive, callous, cruel, destructive. If the capitalistic system is really worth preserving, it is futile today to defend it merely on technical grounds (as being more productive, for example) unless we can show also that the socialist attacks on ethical grounds are false and baseless.

We find ourselves confronted at the very beginning of such a discussion with a serious semantic handicap. The very name of the system was given to it by its enemies. It was intended as a smear word. The name is comparatively recent. It does not appear in *The Communist Manifesto* of 1848 because Marx and Engels had not yet thought of it. It was not until half a dozen years later that either they or one of their followers had the happy idea of coining the word. It exactly suited their purposes. Capitalism was meant to designate an economic system that was run exclusively by and for the capitalists. It still keeps that built-in connotation. Hence it stands self-condemned. It is this name that has made capitalism so hard to defend in popular argument. The almost complete success of this semantic trick is a major explanation of why many people have been willing to die for Communism but so few have been willing to die for "capitalism."

There are at least half-a-dozen names for this system, any one of which would be more appropriate and more truly descriptive: the System of Private Ownership of the Means of Production, the Market Economy, the Competitive System, the Profit-and-Loss System, Free Enterprise, the System of Economic Freedom. Yet to try at this late date to discard the word Capitalism may not only be futile but quite unnecessary. For this intended smear word does at least unintentionally call attention to the fact that all economic improvement, progress, and growth is dependent upon capital accumulation—upon constant increase in the quantity and improvement in the quality of the tools of production—machinery, plant, and equipment. Now the capitalistic system does more to promote this growth than any alternative.

2. Private Property and Free Markets

Let us see what the basic institutions of this system are. We may subdivide them for convenience of discussion into (1) private property, (2) free markets, (3) competition, (4) division and combination of labor, and (5) social cooperation. As we shall see, these are not separate institutions. They are mutually dependent: each implies the other, and makes it possible.

Let us begin with private property. It is neither a recent nor an arbitrary institution, as some socialist writers would have us believe. Its roots go as far back as human history itself. Every child reveals a sense of property with regard to his own toys. Scientists are just beginning to realize the astonishing extent to which some sense or system of property rights or territorial rights prevails even in the animal world.

The question that concerns us here, however, is not the antiquity of the institution, but its utility. When a man's property rights are protected, it means that he is able to retain and enjoy in peace the fruits of his labor. This security is his main incentive, if not his only incentive, to labor itself. If anyone were free to seize what the farmer had sown, cultivated, and raised, the farmer would no longer have any incentive to sow or to raise it. If anyone were free to seize your house after you had built it, you would not build it in the first place. All production, all civilization, rests on recognition of and respect for property rights. A free enterprise system is impossible without security of property as well as security of life. Free enterprise is possible only within a framework of law and order and morality. This means that free enterprise presupposes morality; but, as we shall later see, it also helps to preserve and promote it.

The second basic institution of a capitalist economy is the free market. The free market means the freedom of everybody to dispose of his property, to exchange it for other property or for money, or to employ it for further production, on whatever terms he finds acceptable. This freedom is of course a corollary of private property. Private property necessarily implies the right of use for consumption or for further production, and the right of free disposal or exchange.

It is important to insist that private property and free markets are not separable institutions. A number of socialists, for example, think they can duplicate the functions and efficiencies of the free market by imitating the free market in a socialist system —that is, in a system in which the means of production are in the hands of the State.

Such a view rests on mere confusion of thought. If I am a government commissar selling something I don't really own, and you are another commissar buying it with money that really isn't yours, then neither of us really cares what the price is. When, as in a socialist or communist country, the heads of mines and factories, of stores and collective farms, are mere salaried government bureaucrats, who buy foodstuffs or raw materials from other bureaucrats and sell their finished products to still other bureaucrats, the so-called prices at which they buy and sell are mere bookkeeping fictions. Such bureaucrats are merely playing an artificial game called "free market." They cannot make a socialist system work like a free-enterprise system merely by imitating the so-called free-market feature while ignoring private property.

This imitation of a free-price system actually exists, in fact, in Soviet Russia and in practically every other socialist or communist country. But insofar as this mock-market economy works— that is, insofar as it helps a socialist economy to function at all— it does so because its bureaucratic managers closely watch what commodities are selling for on free world markets, and artificially price their own in conformity. Whenever they find it difficult or impossible to do this, or neglect to do it, their plans begin to go more seriously wrong. Stalin himself once chided the managers of the Soviet economy because some of their artificially-fixed prices were out of line with those on the free world market.

I should like to emphasize that in referring to private property I am not referring merely to personal property in consumption goods, like a man's food, toothbrush, shirt, piano, home, or car. In the modern market economy private ownership of *the means of production* is no less fundamental. Such ownership is from one point of view a privilege; but it also imposes on the owners a heavy social responsibility. The private owners of the means of production cannot employ their property merely for their own satisfaction; they are forced to employ it in ways that will promote the best possible satisfaction of consumers. If they do this well, they are rewarded by profits, and a further increase in their ownership; if they are inept or inefficient, they are penalized by losses. Their investments are never safe indefinitely. In a free-market economy the consumers, by their purchases or refusals to purchase, daily decide afresh who shall own productive property and how much he shall own. The owners of productive capital are compelled to employ it for the satisfaction of other people's wants.[3] A privately owned railway is as much "dedicated to a public purpose" as a government-owned railway. It is likely in fact to achieve such a purpose far more successfully, not only because of the rewards it will receive for performing its task well, but even more because of the heavy penalties it will suffer if it fails to meet the needs of shippers or travelers at competitive costs and prices.

3. *Competition*

The foregoing discussion already implies the third integral institution in the capitalist system—competition. Every competitor in a private-enterprise system must meet the market price. He must keep his unit production costs below this market price if he is to survive. The further he can keep his costs below the market price the greater his profit margin. The greater his profit margin the more he will be able to expand his business and his output. If he is faced with losses for more than a short period he cannot survive. The effect of competition, therefore, is to take production constantly out of the hands of the less competent managers and put it more and more into the hands of the more efficient managers. Putting the matter in another way, free competition constantly promotes more and more efficient methods of production: it tends constantly to reduce production costs. As the lowest-cost producers expand their output they cause a reduction of prices and so force the highest-cost producers to sell their product at a lower price, and ultimately either to reduce their costs or to transfer their activities to other lines.

But capitalistic or free-market competition is seldom merely competition in lowering the cost of producing a homogeneous product. It is almost always competition in improving a specific product. And in the last century it has been competition in introducing and perfecting entirely new products or means of production—the railroad, the dynamo, the electric light, the motor car, the airplane, the telegraph, the telephone, the phonograph, the camera, motion pictures, radio, television, refrigerators, air conditioning, an endless variety of plastics, synthetics, and other new materials. The effect has been enormously to increase the amenities of life and the material welfare of the masses.

Capitalistic competition, in brief, is the great spur to improvement and innovation, the chief stimulant to research, the principal incentive to cost reduction, to the development of new and better products, and to improved efficiency of every kind. It has conferred incalculable blessings on mankind.

And yet, in the last century, capitalistic competition has been under constant attack by socialists and anti-capitalists. It has been denounced as savage, selfish, cutthroat, and cruel. Some writers, of whom Bertrand Russell is typical, constantly talk of business competition as if it were a form of "warfare," and practically the same thing as the competition of war. Nothing could be more false or absurd—unless we think it reasonable to compare competition in mutual slaughter with competition in providing consumers with new or better goods and services at cheaper prices.

The critics of business competition not only shed tears over the penalties it imposes on inefficient producers but are indignant at the "excessive" profits it grants to the most successful and efficient. This weeping and resentment exist because the critics either do not understand or refuse to understand the function that competition performs for the consumer and therefore for the national welfare. Of course there are isolated instances in which competition seems to work unjustly. It sometimes penalizes amiable or cultivated people and rewards churlish or vulgar ones. No matter how good our system of rules and laws, isolated cases of injustice can never be entirely eliminated. But the beneficence or harmfulness, the justice or injustice, of institutions must be judged by their effect in the great majority of cases—by their over-all result. We shall return to this point later.

What those who indiscriminately deplore "competition" overlook is that everything depends upon *what* the competition is in, and the nature of the means it employs. Competition *per se* is neither moral nor immoral. It is neither necessarily beneficial nor necessarily harmful. Competition in swindling or in mutual slaughter is one thing; but competition in philanthropy or in excellence—the competition between a Leonardo da Vinci and a Michelangelo, between a Shakespeare and a Ben Jonson, a Haydn and a Mozart, a Verdi and a Wagner, a Newton and a Leibnitz, is quite another. Competition does not necessarily imply relations of enmity, but relations of rivalry, of mutual emulation and mutual stimulation. Beneficial competition is indirectly a form of cooperation.

Now what the critics of economic competition overlook is that —when it is conducted under a good system of laws and a high standard of morals—it is itself a form of economic cooperation, or rather, that it is an integral and necessary part of a system of economic cooperation. If we look at competition in isolation, this statement may seem paradoxical, but it becomes evident when we step back and look at it in its wider setting. General Motors and Ford are not cooperating directly with each other; but each is trying to cooperate with the consumer, with the potential car buyer. Each is trying to convince him that it can offer him a better car than its competitor, or as good a car at a lower price. Each is "compelling" the other—or, to state it more accurately, each is stimulating the other—to reduce its production costs and to improve its car. Each, in other words, is "compelling" the other to cooperate more effectively with the buying public. And so, *indirectly,—triangularly,* so to speak—General Motors and Ford cooperate. Each makes the other more efficient.

Of course this is true of all competition, even the grim competition of war. As Edmund Burke put it: "He that wrestles with us strengthens our nerves and sharpens our skill. Our antagonist is our helper." But in free-market competition, this mutual help is also beneficial to the whole community.

For those who still think this conclusion paradoxical, it is merely necessary to consider the artificial competition of games and sport. Bridge is a competitive card game, but it requires the cooperation of four people in consenting to play with each other; a man who refuses to sit in to make a fourth is considered non-cooperative rather than noncompetitive. To have a football game requires the cooperation not only of eleven men on each side but the cooperation of each side with the other—in agreeing to play, in agreeing on a given date, hour, and place, in agreeing on a referee, and in agreeing to abide by a common set of rules. The Olympic games would not be possible without the cooperation of the participating nations. There have been some very dubious analogies in the economic literature of recent years between economic life and "the theory of games"; but the analogy which recognizes that in both fields competition exists within a larger setting of cooperation (and that desirable results follow), is valid and instructive.

4. *The Division of Labor*

I come now to the fourth institution I have mentioned as part of the capitalist system—the division and combination of labor. The necessity and beneficence of this was sufficiently emphasized by the founder of political economy, Adam Smith, who made it the subject of the first chapter of his great work, *The Wealth of Nations*. In the very first sentence of that great work, indeed, we find Adam Smith declaring: "The greatest improvement in the productive powers of labor, and the greater part of the skill, dexterity, and judgment with which it is anywhere directed or applied, seem to have been the effects of the division of labor." [4]

Smith goes on to explain how the division and subdivision of labor leads to improved dexterity on the part of individual workers, in the saving of time commonly lost in passing from one sort of work to another, and in the invention and application of specialized machinery. "It is the great multiplication of the productions of all the different arts, in consequence of the division of labor," he concludes, "which occasions, in a well-governed society, that universal opulence which extends itself to the lowest ranks of the people." [5]

Nearly two centuries of economic study have only intensified this recognition. "The division of labor extends by the realization that the more labor is divided the more productive it is." [6] "The fundamental facts that brought about cooperation, society, and civilization and transformed the animal man into a human being are the facts that work performed under the division of labor is more productive than isolated work and that man's reason is capable of recognizing this truth." [7]

5. Social Cooperation

Though I have put division of labor ahead of social cooperation, it is obvious that they cannot be considered apart. Each implies the other. No can can specialize if he lives alone and must provide for all his own needs. Division and combination of labor already imply social cooperation. They imply that each exchanges part of the special product of his labor for the special product of the labor of others. But division of labor, in turn, increases and intensifies social cooperation. As Adam Smith put it: "The most dissimilar geniuses are of use to one another; the different produces of their respective talents, by the general disposition to truck, barter, and exchange, being brought, as it were, into a common stock, where every man may purchase whatever part of the produce of other men's talents he has occasion for." [8]

Modern economists make the interdependence of division of labor and social cooperation more explicit: "Society is concerted action, cooperation. . . . It substitutes collaboration for the—at least conceivable—isolated life of individuals. Society is division of labor and combination of labor. . . . Society is nothing but the combination of individuals for cooperative effort." [9]

Adam Smith also recognized this clearly:

> In civilized society [Man] stands at all times in need of the co-operation and assistance of great multitudes, while his whole life is scarce sufficient to gain the friendship of a few persons. . . . Man has almost constant occasion for the help of his brethren, and it is in vain for him to expect it from their benevolence only. He will be more likely to prevail if he can interest their self-love in his favor, and show them it is for their own advantage to do for him what he requires of them. Whoever offers to another a bargain of any kind, proposes to do this: Give me that which I want, and you shall have this which you want, is the meaning of every such offer; and it is in this manner that we obtain from one another the far greater part of those good offices which we stand in need of. It is not from the benevolence of the butcher, the brewer, or the baker, that we expect our dinner, but from their regard to their own interest. We address ourselves, not to their humanity but to their self-love, and never talk to them of our own necessities but of their advantages.[10]

What Adam Smith was pointing out in this and other passages is that the market economy is as successful as it is because it takes advantage of self-love and self-interest and harnesses them to production and exchange. In an even more famous passage, Smith pressed the point further:

> The annual revenue of every society is always precisely equal to the exchangeable value of the whole annual produce of the industry, or rather is precisely the same thing with that exchangeable value. As every individual, therefore, endeavors as much as he can both to employ his capital in the support of domestic industry, and so to direct that industry that its produce may be of the greatest value; every individual necessarily labors to render the annual revenue of the society as great as he can. He generally, indeed, neither intends to promote the public interest, nor knows how much he is promoting it. By preferring the support of domestic to that of foreign industry, he intends only his own security; and by directing that industry in such a manner as its produce may be of the greatest value, he intends only his own gain, and he is in this, as in many other cases, led by an invisible hand to promote an end which was no part of his intention. Nor is it always the worse for the society that it was no part of it. By pursuing his own interest he frequently promotes that of the society more efficiently than when he really intends to promote it.[11]

This passage has become almost too famous for Smith's own good. Scores of writers who have heard nothing but the metaphor "an invisible hand" have misinterpreted or perverted its meaning. They have taken it (though he used it only once) as the essence of the whole doctrine of *The Wealth of Nations*. They have interpreted it as meaning that Adam Smith, as a Deist, believed that the Almighty interfered in some mysterious way to insure that all self-regarding actions would lead to socially beneficial ends. This is clearly a misinterpretation. "The fact that the market provides for the welfare of each individual participating in it is a *conclusion* based on scientific analysis, not an assumption upon which the analysis is based." [12]

Other writers have interpreted the "invisible hand" passage as a defense of selfishness, and still others as a confession that a free-market economy is not only built on selfishness but rewards selfishness alone. And Smith was at least partly to blame for this latter interpretation. He failed to make explicit that only insofar as people earned their livings *in legal and moral ways* did they promote the general interest. People who try to improve their own fortunes by chicanery, swindling, robbery, blackmail, or murder do not increase the national income. Producers increase the national welfare by competing to satisfy the needs of consumers at the cheapest price. A free economy can function properly only within an appropriate legal and moral framework.

And it is a profound mistake to regard the actions and motivations of people in a market economy as necessarily and narrowly selfish. Though Adam Smith's exposition was brilliant, it could easily be misinterpreted. Fortunately, at least a few modern economists have further clarified the process and the motivation: "The economic life . . . consists of all that complex of relations into which we enter with other people, and lend ourselves or our resources to the furtherance of their purposes, as an indirect means of furthering our own."[13] Our own purposes are necessarily our *own;* but they are not necessarily purely *selfish* purposes. "The economic relation . . . or business nexus, is necessary alike for carrying on the life of the peasant and the prince, of the saint and the sinner, of the apostle and the shepherd, of the most altruistic and the most egoistic of men. . . . Our complex system of economic relations puts us in command of the co-operation necessary to accomplish our purposes."[14]

"The specific characteristic of an economic relation," according to Wicksteed, "is not its 'egoism,' but its 'non-tuism.'"[15] He explains:

> If you and I are conducting a transaction which on my side is purely economic, I am furthering your purposes, partly or wholly perhaps for my own sake, perhaps entirely for the sake of others, but certainly not for your sake. What makes it an economic transaction is that I am not considering you except as a link in the chain, or considering your desires except as the means by which I may gratify those of some one else—not necessarily myself. The economic relation does not exclude from my mind everyone but me, it potentially includes every one but you.[16]

There is a certain element of arbitrariness in making "non-tuism" the essence of "the economic relation."[17] The element of truth in this position is merely that a "strictly economic" relation is *by definition* an "impersonal" relation. But one of Wicksteed's great contributions was to dispose of the persistent idea that economic activity is exclusively egoistic or self-regarding.[18] The real basis of all economic activity is *cooperation*. As Mises has put it:

> Within the frame of social cooperation there can emerge between members of society feelings of sympathy and friendship and a sense of belonging together. These feelings are the source of man's most delightful and most sublime experiences. . . . However, they are not, as some have asserted, the agents that have brought about social relationships. They are fruits of social cooperation, they thrive only within its frame; they did not precede the establishment of social relations and are not the seed from which they spring. . . .
>
> The characteristic feature of human society is purposeful cooperation. . . . Human society . . . is the outcome of a purposeful utilization of a universal law determining cosmic becoming, viz., the higher productivity of the division of labor. . . .
>
> Every step by which an individual substitutes concerted action for isolated action results in an immediate and recognizable improvement in his conditions. The advantages derived from peaceful cooperation and division of labor are universal. They immediately benefit every generation, and not only later descendants. For what the individual must sacrifice for the sake of society he is amply compensated by greater advantages. His sacrifice is only apparent and temporary; he foregoes a smaller gain in order to reap a greater one later. . . . When social cooperation is intensified by enlarging the field in which there is division of labor or when legal protection and the safeguarding of peace are strengthened, the incentive is the desire of all those concerned to improve their own conditions. In striving after his own—rightly understood—interests the individual works toward an intensification of social cooperation and peaceful intercourse. . . .
>
> The historical role of the theory of the division of labor as elaborated by British political economy from Hume to Ricardo consisted in the complete demolition of all metaphysical doctrines concerning the origin and operation of social cooperation. It consummated the spiritual, moral and intellectual emancipation of mankind inaugurated by the philosophy of Epicureanism. It substituted an autonomous rational morality for the heteronomous and intuitionist ethics of older days. Law and legality, the moral code and social institutions are no longer revered as un-

fathomable decrees of Heaven. They are of human origin, and the only yardstick that must be applied to them is that of expediency with regard to human welfare. The utilitarian economist does not say: Fiat justitia, pereat mundus. He says: Fiat justitia, *ne* pereat mundus. He does not ask a man to renounce his well-being for the benefit of society. He advises him to recognize what his rightly understood interest are.[19]

Mises expounded the same point of view in his earlier book, *Socialism*. Here also, and in contradiction to the Kantian thesis that it is wrong ever to treat others merely as means, he emphasizes the same theme that we have seen in Wicksteed:

Liberal social theory proves that each single man sees in all others, first of all, only means to the realization of his purposes, while he himself is to all others a means to the realization of their purposes; that finally, by this reciprocal action, in which each is simultaneously means and end, the highest aim of social life is attained—the achievement of a better existence for everyone. As society is only possible if everyone, while living his own life, at the same time helps others to live, if every individual is simultaneously means and end; if each individual's well-being is simultaneously the condition necessary to the well-being of the others, it is evident that the contrast between I and thou, means and end, automatically is overcome.[20]

Once we have recognized the fundamental principle of social cooperation, we find the true reconcilation of "egoism" and "altruism." Even if we assume that everyone lives and wishes to live primarily for himself, we can see that this does not disturb social life but promotes it, because the higher fulfilment of the individual's life is possible only in and through society. In this sense egoism could be accepted as the basic law of society. But the basic fallacy is that of assuming a necessary incompatibility between "egoistic" and "altruistic" motives, or even of insisting on a sharp distinction between them. As Mises puts it:

This attempt to contrast egoistic and altruistic action springs from a misconception of the social interdependence of individuals. The power to choose whether my actions and conduct shall serve myself or my fellow beings is not given to me—which perhaps may be regarded as fortunate. If it were, human society would not be possible. In the society based on division of labor and co-operation, the interests of all members are in harmony, and it follows from this basic fact of social life that ultimately action in the interests of myself and action in the interests of others do not conflict, since the interests of individuals come together in the end. Thus the famous scientific dispute as to the possibility of deriving the altruistic from the egoistic motives of action may be regarded as definitely disposed of.

There is no contrast between moral duty and selfish interests. What the individual gives to society to preserve it as society, he gives, not for the sake of aims alien to himself, but in his own interest.[21]

This social cooperation runs throughout the free-market system. It exists between producer and consumer, buyer and seller. Both gain from the transaction, and that is why they make it. The consumer gets the bread he needs; the baker gets the monetary profit which is both his stimulus to bake the bread and the necessary means to enable him to bake more. In spite of the enormous labor-union and socialist propaganda to the contrary, the relation of employer and employed is basically a cooperative relation. Each needs the other. The more efficient the employer, the more workers he can hire and the more he can offer them. The more efficient the workers, the more each can earn, and the more successful the employer. It is in the interest of the employer that his workers should be healthy and vigorous, well fed and well housed, that they should feel they are being justly treated, that they will be rewarded in proportion to their efficiency and that they will therefore strive to be efficient. It is in the interest of the worker that the firm for which he works can do so at a profit, and preferably at a profit that both encourages and enables it to expand.

On the "microeconomic" scale, every firm is a cooperative enterprise. A magazine or a newspaper (and as one who has been associated with newspapers and magazines all his working life I can speak with immediate knowledge of this) is a great cooperative organization in which every reporter, every editorial writer, every advertising solicitor, every printer, every delivery-truck driver, every newsdealer, cooperates to play his assigned part, in the same way as an orchestra is a great cooperative enterprise in which each player cooperates in an exact way with his particular instrument to produce the final harmony. A great industrial company, such as General Motors, or the U.S. Steel

Corporation, or General Electric—or, for that matter, any of a thousand others—is a marvel of continuous cooperation. And on a "macroeconomic" scale, the whole free world is bound together in a system of international cooperation through mutual trade, in which each nation supplies the needs of others cheaper and better than the others could supply their own needs acting in isolation. And this cooperation takes place, both on the smallest and on the widest scale, because each of us finds that forwarding the purposes of others is (though indirectly) the most effective of all means for achieving his own.

Thus, though we may call the chief drive "egoism," we certainly cannot call this a purely egoistic or "selfish" system. It is the system by which each of us tries to achieve his purposes whether those purposes are "egoistic" or "altruistic." The system certainly cannot be called dominantly "altruistic," because each of us is cooperating with others, not primarily to forward the purposes of those others, but primarily to forward his own. The system might most appropriately be called "mutualistic." (See Chapter 13.) In any case its primary requirement is cooperation.

6. *Is Capitalism Unjust?*

Let us turn now to another consideration. Is the free-market system, the "capitalist" system, just or unjust? Virtually the whole burden of the socialist attack on the "capitalist" system is its alleged injustice—its alleged "exploitation" of the worker. A book on ethics is not the place to examine that contention fully. Such an examination is a task of economics. I hope the reader will forgive me, therefore, if, instead of examining this socialist argument directly, I merely accept the conclusion of John Bates Clark, in his epoch-making work, *The Distribution of Wealth* (1899), and refer the reader to that and other works on economics[22] for the supporting arguments for his conclusion.

The general thesis of Clark's work is that, "Free competition tends to give to labor what labor creates, to capitalists what capital creates, and to entrepreneurs what the coordinating function creates. . . . [It tends] to give to each producer the amount of wealth that he specifically brings into existence." [23]

Clark argues, in fact, that the tendency of a free competitive system is to give "to each what he creates." If this is true, he continues, it not only disposes of the exploitation theory, that "workmen are regularly robbed of what they produce," but it means that the capitalist system is essentially a just system, and that our effort should be, not to destroy it and substitute another utterly different in kind, but to perfect it so that exceptions to its prevalent rule of distribution may be less frequent and less considerable.[24]

Certain qualifications must be made in these conclusions. As Clark himself points out, this principle of "distribution"[25] in the free market represents a *tendency*. It does not follow that *in every instance* everyone gets exactly the value of what he has produced or helped to produce. And the value of his contribution that he gets is the *market* value—i.e., the value of that contribution *as measured by others*.

But whatever the shortcomings of this system may be from the requirements of perfect "justice," no superior system has yet been conceived. Certainly, as we shall see in our next chapter, that system is not socialism.

But before we come to our final moral evaluation of this marvelous free-market system, we must notice one other great virtue. It is not merely that it tends constantly to reward individuals in accordance with their specific contribution to production. By the constant play in the market of prices, wages, rents, interest rates, and other costs, relative profit margins or losses, the market tends constantly to achieve not only maximum production but optimum production. That is to say, through the incentives and deterrents provided by these ever-changing relationships of prices and costs, the production of thousands of different commodities and services is synchronized, and a dynamic balance is maintained in the volume of production of each of these thousands of different goods in relation to each other. This balance does not necessarily reflect the wishes of any one individual. It does not necessarily correspond with the utopian ideal of any economic planner. But it does tend to reflect the composite wishes of the whole existing body of producers and consumers. For each consumer, by his purchases or abstentions from purchase, daily casts his vote for the production of more of this commodity and less of that; and the producer is forced to abide by the consumers' decisions.[26]

Having seen what this system does, let us now look at the

justice of it a little more closely. It is commonly regarded as "unjust" because the unthinking ideal of "social justice," from time immemorial, has been absolute equality of income. Socialists are never tired of condemning "poverty in the midst of plenty." They cannot rid themselves of the idea that the wealth of the rich is the cause of the poverty of the poor. Yet this idea is completely false. The wealth of the rich makes the poor less poor, not more. The rich are those who have something to offer in return for the services of the poor. And only the rich can provide the poor with the capital, with the tools of production, to increase the output and hence the marginal value of the labor of the poor. When the rich grow richer, the poor grow, not poorer, but richer. This, in fact, is the history of economic progress.

Any serious effort to enforce the ideal of equality of income, regardless of what anyone does or fails to do to earn or create income—regardless of whether he works or not, produces or not —would lead to universal impoverishment. Not only would it remove any incentive for the unskilled or incompetent to improve themselves, and any incentive for the lazy to work at all; it would remove even the incentive of the naturally talented and industrious to work or to improve themselves.

We come back once more to the conclusions we reached in the chapter on Justice. Justice is not purely as an end in itself. It is not an ideal that can be isolated from its consequences. Though admittedly an intermediate end, it is primarily a means. Justice, in brief, consists of the social arrangements and rules that are most conducive to social cooperation—which means, in the economic field, most conducive to maximizing production. And the justice of these arrangements and rules, in turn, is not to be judged purely by their effect in this or that isolated instance, but (in accordance with the principle first pointed out by Hume) by their over-all effect in the long run.

Practically all arguments for the equal distribution of income tacitly assume that such an equal division would do nothing to reduce the average income; that total income and wealth would remain at least as great as they would have been in a free-market system in which everyone was paid in accordance with his own production or his own contribution to production. This assumption is one of unsurpassable naïveté. Such an enforced equal division—and it could only be achieved by force—would cause a violent and disastrous drop in production and impoverish the nation that adopted it. Communist Russia was quickly forced to abandon this equalitarian idea; and to the extent that communist countries have tried to adhere to it, their people have paid dearly. But this is to anticipate the discussion in our next chapter.

It may be supposed—and it is everywhere popularly supposed today—that there is some "third" system, some "middle-of-the-road" system, that could combine the enormous productivity of a free-market system with the "justice" of a socialist system—or that could, at least, bring a nearer equality of income and welfare than that produced in a completely free economic system. I can only state here my own conclusion that this is a delusion. If any such middle-of-the-road system did remedy a few specific injustices, it would do so only by creating many more—and incidentally by reducing total production compared with what a free-market system would achieve. For the basis of this conclusion I must refer the reader to treatises on economics.[27]

7. Is the Market "Ethically Indifferent"?

We come now, however, to a position very frequently taken by economists in recent decades, a position for which Philip H. Wicksteed, in his *Common Sense of Political Economy* (1910) may have helped to set the fashion. This is that the economic system is an "ethically indifferent instrument." Wicksteed argues for this position in a passage of great eloquence and penetration, from which I quote a substantial portion:

> We have now seen that the taint of inherent sordidness which attaches itself in many minds to the economic relation, or even to the study of it, is derived from a faulty conception of its nature. But, on the other hand, the easy optimism that expects the economic forces, if only we give them free play, spontaneously to secure the best possible conditions of life, is equally fallacious, and even more pernicious. It is, indeed, easy to present the working of the economic forces as wholly beneficent. Have we not seen that they automatically organize a vast system of co-operation, by which men who have never seen or heard of each other, and who scarcely realize each other's existence or desires even in imagina-

tion, nevertheless support each other at every turn, and enlarge the realization each of the other's purposes? Do they not embrace all the world in one huge mutual benefit society? That London is fed day by day, although no one sees to it, is itself a fact so stupendous as to excuse, if it does not justify, the most exultant paeans that were ever sung in honor of the *laissez-faire laissez-passer* theory of social organization. What a testimony to the efficiency of the economic nexus is borne by the very fact that we regard it as abnormal that any man should perish for want of any one of a thousand things, no one of which he can either make or do for himself. When we see the world, in virtue of its millions of mutual adjustments, carrying itself on from day to day, and ask, "Who sees to it all?" and receive no answer, we can well understand the religious awe and enthusiasm with which an earlier generation of economists contemplated those "economic harmonies," in virtue of which each individual, in serving himself, of necessity serves his neighbor, and by simply obeying the pressures about him, and following the path that opens before him, weaves himself into the pattern of "purposes he cannot measure."

But we must look at the picture more closely. The very process of intelligently seeking my own ends makes me further those of others? Quite so. But what are my purposes, immediate and ultimate? And what are the purposes of others which I serve, as a means of accomplishing my own? And what views have I and they as to the suitable means of accomplishing those ends? These are the questions on which the health and vigor of a community depend, and the economic forces, as such, take no count of them. Division of labor and exchange, on which the economic organization of society is based, enlarge our means of accomplishing our ends, but they have no direct influence upon the ends themselves, and have no tendency to beget scrupulousness in the use of the means. It is idle to assume that ethically desirable results will necessarily be produced by an ethically indifferent instrument, and it is as foolish to make the economic relation an idol as it is to make it a bogey.

The world has many things that I want for myself and others, and that I can get only by some kind of exchange. What, then, have I, or what can I do or make, that the world wants? Or what can I make it want, or persuade it that it wants, or make it believe that I can give it better than others can? The things I want, if measured by an ideal standard, may be good or bad for me to have or for others to give; and so with the things I give them, the desires I stimulate in them, and the means I employ to gratify them. When we draw the seductive picture of "economic harmony" in which every one is "helping" some one else and making himself "useful" to him, we insensibly allow the idea of "help" to smuggle in with it ethical or sentimental associations that are strictly contraband. We forget that the "help" may be impartially extended to destructive and pernicious or to constructive and beneficent ends, and moreover that it may employ all sorts of means. We have only to think of the huge industries of war, of the floating of bubble companies, of the efforts of one business or firm to choke others in the birth, of the poppy culture in China and India, of the gin-palaces and distilleries at home, in order to realize how often the immediate purpose of one man or of one community is to thwart or hold in check the purpose of another, or to delude men, or to corrupt their tastes and to minister to them when corrupted.[28]

I have quoted Wicksteed at such great length because his is the most powerful statement I have ever encountered of the thesis that the free market system is "ethically indifferent" or ethically neutral. The thesis, nevertheless, seems to me open to serious question.

Let us begin by confronting it with one or two statements of the rival thesis that the free market economy does have a positive moral value. The reader will recall the passage from Ludwig von Mises already quoted on page 312, in which he contends that "feelings of sympathy and friendship and a sense of belonging together . . . are fruits of social cooperation" and *not* the seed from which social cooperation springs. A similar contention is put forward by Murray N. Rothbard:

In explaining the origins of society, there is no need to conjure up any mystic communion or "sense of belonging" among individuals. Individuals recognize, through the use of reason, the advantages of exchange resulting from the higher productivity of the division of labor, and they proceed to follow this advantageous course. In fact, it is far more likely that feelings of friendship and communion are the *effects* of a regime of (contractual) social co-operation rather than the cause. Suppose, for example, that the division of labor were not productive, or that men had failed to recognize its productivity. In that case, there would be little or no opportunity for exchange, and each man would try to obtain his goods in autistic independence. The result would undoubtedly be a fierce struggle to gain possession of the scarce goods, since, in such a world, each man's gain of useful goods would be some other man's loss. It would be almost inevitable for such an autistic world to be strongly marked by violence and perpetual war. Since each man could gain from his fellows only at their expense, violence would be prevalent, and it seems highly likely that feelings of mutual hostility would be dominant. As in the case of animals quarreling over bones, such a warring world could cause only hatred and hostility between man and man. Life would be a bitter "struggle for survival." On the other hand, in a world of voluntary social co-operation through mutually beneficial exchanges, where one man's gain is another man's *gain*, it is obvious that great scope is provided for the development of social sympathy and human friendships. It is the peaceful, co-operative society that creates favorable conditions for feelings of friendship among men.

The mutual benefits yielded by exchange provide a major incentive . . . to would-be *aggressors* (initiators of violent action against others) to restrain their aggression and co-operate peacefully with their fellows. Individuals then decide that the advantages of engaging in specialization and exchange outweigh the advantages that war might bring.[29]

Let us now look a little more closely at Wicksteed's thesis. It is true, as he so eloquently points out, that capitalism, as it functioned in his time and today, is not yet a heaven filled with cooperating saints. But this does not prove that the system is responsible for our individual shortcomings and sins, or even that it is ethically "indifferent" or neutral. Wicksteed *took for granted* not only the economic but the ethical merits of the capitalism of his day because that was the system that he saw all round him, and therefore he did not visualize the alternative. What he forgot when he wrote the passage quoted above is that modern capitalism is not an inevitable or inescapable system but one that has been chosen by the men and women who live under it. It is a *system of freedom*. London is not fed "although no one sees to it." London is fed precisely because almost *everybody* in London sees to it. The housewife shops every day for food, and brings it home by car or on foot. The butcher and grocer know that she will shop, and stock what they expect her to buy. The meats and vegetables are brought to their shops in their own trucks or the trucks of wholesalers, who in turn order from shippers, who in turn order from farmers and order railroads to transport the food, and the railroads exist precisely to do that. All that is lacking in this system is a single dictator who ostentatiously issues commands for the whole thing and claims all the credit for it.

True, this system of freedom, this free-market system, presupposes an appropriate legal system and an appropriate morality. It could not exist and function without them. But once this system exists and functions it raises the moral level of the community still further.

8. *The Function of Freedom*

Wicksteed does not quite seem to have realized that in describing a market economy he was describing a system of economic *freedom*, and freedom is not "ethically indifferent," but a necessary condition of morality. As F. A. Hayek has put it:

> It is . . . an old discovery that morals and moral values will grow only in an environment of freedom, and that, in general, moral standards of people and classes are high only where they have long enjoyed freedom—and proportional to the amount of freedom they have possessed. . . . That freedom is the matrix required for the growth of moral values—indeed not merely one value among many but the source of all values—is almost self-evident. It is only where the individual has choice, and its inherent responsibility, that he has occasion to affirm existing values, to contribute to their further growth, and to earn moral merit.[30]

If the morality of a given free-market system falls short of perfection, this is no proof that the free-market system is ethically indifferent or ethically neutral. If a prior morality is necessary for it to come into existence, its existence none the less promotes a wider and more sustained morality. The habit of voluntary economic cooperation tends to make a mutualistic attitude habitual. And a system that provides us better than any other with our material needs and wants can never be dismissed as ethically negligible or ethically irrelevant. Morality depends upon the prior satisfaction of material needs. As Wicksteed himself so memorably put it in another context: "A man can be neither a saint, nor a lover, nor a poet, unless he has comparatively recently had something to eat." [31]

THE ETHICS OF CAPITALISM

Ironically, precisely because capitalism does make it possible for men to meet their material needs, and often amply, it has been deplored as a "materialistic" system. To this an excellent answer has been given by F. A. Hayek: "Surely it is unjust to blame a system as more materialistic because it leaves it to the individual to decide whether he prefers material gain to other kinds of excellence, instead of having this decided for him. . . . If [a free enterprise society] gives individuals much more scope to serve their fellows by the pursuit of purely materialistic aims, it also gives them the opportunity to pursue any other aim they regard as more important." [32]

To which I may add that in a free economy everyone is free to practice generosity toward others to any extent he sees fit—and better able to.

As voluntary economic cooperation makes us more interdependent, the consequences of breaches of cooperation or a breakdown of the system become more serious for all of us; and to the extent that we recognize this we will become less indifferent to failure or violation of cooperation in ourselves or in others. Therefore the tendency will be for the moral level of the whole community to be kept high or to be raised.

The way to appreciate the true moral value of the free-market economy is to ask ourselves: *If this freedom did not exist, what then?* We undervalue it, not only economically but morally, only because we have it and think it secure. As Shakespeare has put it:

> For it so falls out
> That what we have we prize not to the worth
> Whiles we enjoy it, but being lack'd and lost,
> Why, then we rack the value; then we find
> The virtue that possession would not show us
> Whiles it was ours.[33]

Writing in 1910, Wicksteed had an excuse which we do not have for regarding the capitalist system as morally indifferent. He did not have the stark alternatives before him. He had not been reading or experiencing daily, for years, the results of statism, of government economic planning, of socialism, of fascism, of communism. We will examine in our next chapter the morality, or rather the immorality, of these alternatives.

To sum up: The system of capitalism, of the market economy, is a system of freedom, of justice, of productivity. In all these respects it is infinitely superior to its coercive alternatives. But these three virtues cannot be separated. Each flows out of the other. Only when men are free can they be moral. Only when they are free to choose can they be said to choose right from wrong. When they are free to choose, when they are free to get and to keep the fruits of their labor, they feel that they are being treated justly. As they recognize that their reward depends on their own efforts and output (and in effect *is* their output) each has the maximum incentive to maximize his output, and all have the maximum incentive to cooperate in helping each other to do so. The justice of the system grows out of the freedom it insures, and the productivity of the system grows out of the justice of the rewards that it provides.

CHAPTER 31

The Ethics of Socialism

1. *The Alternative to Freedom*

In the preceding chapter we tried to confine ourselves to a discussion of the positive ethical values of "capitalism"—i.e., of the system of economic freedom. We did this because these values are so seldom appreciated or even considered. For more than a century the system has been under constant attack from numberless detractors (including those who owe most to it), and even the majority of its defenders have been apologetic about it, contenting themselves with pointing out that it is more productive than its alternatives.

This is a valid defense. It has, indeed, an ethical as well as a "merely material" validity. Capitalism has enormously raised the level of the masses. It has wiped out whole areas of poverty. It has greatly reduced infant mortality, and made it possible to cure disease and prolong life. It has reduced human suffering. Because of capitalism, millions live today who would otherwise have not even been born. If these facts have no ethical relevance, then it is impossible to say in what ethical relevance consists.

But though a defense of capitalism solely because of its productivity is valid and even ethically valid, it is not ethically sufficient. We cannot fully appreciate the positive ethical values of a system of economic freedom until we compare it with its alternatives.

So let us compare it now with its only real alternative—socialism. Some readers may object that there are any number of alternatives, a whole spectrum ranging from various degrees of interventionism and statism to communism. But to avoid getting into purely economic issues, I am going to be dogmatic at this point and say that all so-called middle-of-the-road systems are unstable and transitional in nature, and in the long run either break down or lead toward a complete socialism. For the argument in support of this conclusion, I must refer the reader to the relevant economic literature.¹ Here I will content myself with calling attention to the difference between a general undiscriminatory system of laws against force and fraud, on the one hand, and specific interventions in the market economy on the other. Some of these specific interventions may indeed "remedy" this or that specific "evil" in the short run, but they can do so only at the cost of producing more and worse evils in the long run.²

I should also warn the reader that in most of this discussion we shall be treating "socialism" and "communism" as practically synonymous. This was the practice of Marx and Engels. It is true that the words have come to have different connotations today; later in this chapter we shall recognize these. But in most of this discussion we shall assume, with Bernard Shaw, that "A communist is nothing but a socialist with the courage of his convictions." The parties and programs in present-day Europe that call themselves "socialist" in fact advocate merely a *partial* socialism—the nationalization of railroads, various public utilities, and heavy industry—but not usually of light industries, the service trades, or agriculture. When socialism becomes complete, it becomes what is generally called *communism*.

An additional distinction: the parties that call themselves Communist believe in getting into power, if necessary, through violent revolution, and in spreading their power by infiltration, hate-propaganda, subversion and war against other nations; whereas the parties that call themselves Socialist profess (for the most part sincerely) to wish to come into power only through persuasion and "democratic means." But we can leave a discussion of such differences until later.

2. Utopian Socialism

Let us begin by considering the ethical assumptions of utopian (or pre-Marxist) socialism. The utopian socialists have always deplored the alleged cruelty and savagery of economic competition, and have pleaded for the substitution of a regime of "cooperation" or "mutual aid." This plea rests, as we have seen in the preceding chapter, on a failure to understand that a free-market system is in fact a marvelous system of social cooperation, both on a "microeconomic" and on a "macroeconomic" scale. It rests on a failure to recognize, in addition, that economic competition is an integral and indispensable part of this system of economic cooperation, and enormously increases its effectiveness.

Utopian socialists constantly talk of the "wastefulness" of competition. They fail to understand that the apparent "wastes" of competition are short-term and transitional wastes necessary to increasing economies in the long run. One does not get any comparable long-run economies under monopolies. Above all, one does not get them under governmental monopolies: witness the post-office.

In *Looking Backward* (1888), the most famous utopian-socialist novel of the late nineteenth century, Edward Bellamy portrayed what he considered an ideal society. And one of the features that made it ideal was that it eliminated the

> interminable rows of stores [in Boston] . . . ten thousand stores to distribute the goods needed by this one city, which in my [utopian-socialist] dream had been supplied with all things from a single warehouse, as they were ordered through one great store in every quarter, where the buyer, without waste of time or labor, found under one roof the world's assortment in whatever line he desired. There the labor of distribution had been so slight as to add a scarcely perceptible fraction to the cost of commodities to the user. The cost of production was virtually all he paid. But here the mere distribution of the goods, their handling alone, added a fourth, a third, a half and more, to the cost. All these ten thousand plants must be paid for, their rent, their staffs of superintendence, their platoons of salesmen, their ten thousand sets of accountants, jobbers, and business dependents, with all they spent in advertising themselves and fighting one another, and the consumers must do the paying. What a famous process for beggaring a nation! [3]

What Bellamy failed to see in this incredibly naive picture was that he was putting all the costs and inconveniences of "distribution" *on the buyer, on the consumer.* In his utopia it was the buyers who had to walk or take a trolley or drive their carriages to the "one great store." They could not go just around the corner to pick up groceries, or a loaf of bread or a bottle of milk; or a medicine; or a pad and pencil; or a screwdriver; or a pair of socks or stockings. No: for the most trivial item they had to walk or ride to the "one great store," no matter how far away it might happen to be. And then, because the one great nationalized store would not have any competition to meet, it would not put on enough salesmen, and the customers would have to queue up for indefinite waits (as in Russia or most government-run "services" anywhere). And, because of the same lack of competition, the goods would be poor and of limited variety. They would not be what the customers wanted, but what the government bureaucrats thought were plenty good enough for them.

Among the things that Bellamy overlooked was that all real costs must be paid for; and if the one great government store does not put the cost of "distribution" on the price, because it does not assume that cost, it is only because it forces the consumers to assume that cost, not only in money, but in time and inconvenience and even personal hardship. The "wastes" of the kind of system that Bellamy dreamed of would be enormously greater than those of the competitive system he derided.

But these were comparatively minor errors. The major error of Bellamy's picture lay in his complete failure to recognize the role of competition in constantly reducing costs of production, in improving products as well as means of production, and in developing wholly new products. He did not foresee the thousand inventions, improvements, and new discoveries that capitalistic competition has brought to the world in the seventy-six years since he wrote in 1888. Though he was supposed to be writing about conditions in the year 2000 (in his dream), he did not foresee the airplane or even the automobile; or radio or television or high-fidelity and stereophonic systems, or even the phonograph; or "automation," or a thousand miracles of the modern world. He did foresee music being piped into homes from central government stations by telephone; but this was because the telephone had already been *privately* invented by Alexander Graham Bell in 1876 and 1877 (ten years before Bellamy wrote), and had been privately improved since then.

Nor did he foresee the enormous economies that were to be effected in distribution. He did not foresee the enormous growth that was to develop in the size of the privately-owned department store and in the varieties of goods it was to offer. He did not foresee that these stores would open branches in the suburbs or in other cities to serve their customers better. He did not foresee the development of the modern mail-order house, which would enable people to order goods from huge catalogs and save them the trouble of driving in to the "one great store" in the hope that it might carry what they wanted. He did not foresee the development of the modern supermarket, not only with its immense increase in the varieties of goods offered, but with its enormous economies in the size of sales staffs. And the reason he did not foresee these things is that he failed to recognize the enormous pressures that the competition which he deplored put on each individual store or firm constantly to increase its economies and reduce its costs.

And for the same reason he did not foresee the immense economies that were to be brought about by mechanized bookkeeping and accounting. In fact, his comments show that he hardly understood the need for bookkeeping or accounting at all. To him it was merely a way in which private merchants counted up their inexcusable profits. He knew nothing of one of the main functions of accounting. That a chief purpose of bookkeeping and accounting is precisely to know what costs are, and where they occur, so that wastes can be traced, pinpointed, and eliminated, and costs reduced, never occurred to him. He was against competition because he took all its beneficent results for granted.

I had not meant to get into economic considerations to this extent, but it seems necessary in order to show what is wrong with the implicit ethics of socialist or anti-capitalist writers.

3. "Equal Distribution" vs. Production

What socialist writers fail to understand is that only through the institution of the free market, with competition and private ownership of the means of production, and only through the interplay of prices, wages, costs, profits and losses is it possible to determine what consumers want, and in what relative proportions, and therefore what is to be produced, and in what relative proportions. Under a system of capitalism, the interplay of millions of prices and wages and trillions of price and wage and profit interrelationships produce the infinitely varied incentives and deterrents that direct production as by "an invisible hand" into thousands of different commodities and services. What socialists fail to understand is that socialism cannot solve the problem of "economic calculation." "Even angels, if they were endowed only with human reason, could not form a socialistic community." [4]

Now by any utilitarian standard (and the socialists themselves constantly appeal to a utilitarian standard) any system that cannot solve the problem of production, that cannot maximize production and cannot direct it into the proper channels, any system that would grossly reduce (compared with what is possible) the material basis for social life, the satisfaction of human wants, cannot be called a "moral" system.

We have already seen that a free-market system tends to give to every social group, and to every individual within each group, the value of what it or he has contributed to production. The working motto of such a system is: *To each what he creates.* Now Marxian socialism denies that capitalism tends to do this. It holds that under capitalism the worker is systematically "exploited" and robbed of the full produce of his labor. We have already seen in the preceding chapter that this Marxian contention is untenable.[5] But in any case the Marxists do not propose this for their own motto for distribution. Their motto is: *From each according to his ability; to each according to his need.*

The two parts of this slogan are incompatible. Human nature is such that unless each is paid and rewarded according to his ability and effort and contribution he will not exert himself to apply and develop his full potential ability, to put forth his maximum effort, or to make his maximum contribution. And the general reduction of effort will of course reduce the production out of which everybody's needs are to be supplied. And that each will have "according to his need" is an empty boast— unless need is to be interpreted as meaning just enough to keep alive. (Even this, as the history of famines in Soviet Russia and Communist China has shown, is not always achieved.) But if "needs" are to be interpreted in the sense of wants and desires, in the sense of what each of us would like to have, it is a goal never to be fully achieved as long as there is an acknowledged shortage or scarcity of anything at all. If "need" is interpreted simply as *other people's* need as estimated by a Socialist bureaucrat, then no doubt the socialist goal can be sometimes achieved.

The most common ideal of "just" distribution espoused by utopian socialists is equal division of goods or income per head of the population.[6] Applied literally, this would violate the motto of distribution according to need by giving as much to infants as to adults in their prime. But the central objection to the ideal is of a quite different nature. It would destroy production.

We have already seen (Chapter 30, pp. 317-18) why this is so. Suppose at present (or at the time that the experiment of guaranteed equality of income per head is started) the statistical average income per capita is $2,500 a year. Then nobody who had been getting less than that would work harder to increase his income, because the difference would be guaranteed to him. In fact, as the whole amount would be guaranteed to him, he would see no reason to continue to work at all—except insofar as he was coerced into doing so by slavery, the whip, a tyrannical public opinion, or the intermittent and uncertain promptings of his own conscience. As, moreover, the new guaranteed *equality* of income at $2,500 a year could only be realized by seizing everything above that amount earned by anybody, those who had previously been earning more than that amount would no longer have any incentive to do so. In fact, they would no longer have any incentive to earn *even* that amount; because it would be guaranteed to them whether they earned it or not. The result would be general poverty and starvation.

It may be replied that this would be a suicidal thing for men to do, and that the inhabitants of such a society would surely be intelligent enough to see this; that they would be intelligent enough, in fact, to see that the more each produced the more there would be for all. This is in fact the argument of all socialists and of all socialist governments. What those who put forward the argument overlook is that what is true for the collectivity is not necessarily true for the individual. The individual is told by the managers of the socialist society that if he increases *his* output he will, other things being equal, increase *total* output. Mathematically he recognizes that this is so. But mathematically he recognizes, also, that under a system of *equal* division his own contribution can have only an infinitesimal relationship to his *own* income and welfare. He knows that even if he personally worked like a galley slave, and *nobody else* worked, he would still starve. And he knows, also, on the other hand, that if *everybody else* worked like a galley slave, and *he* did *nothing*, or only went through the motions of working when somebody was watching him, he would live very well on what *everybody else* had produced.

Suppose a man lives in a socialist country with a population of 200 million. By backbreaking work, say, he *doubles* his production. If his previous production was average, he has increased the total national production by only *one-two-hundred-millionth*. This means that he personally, assuming equal distribution, increases his income or consumption by only one-two-hundred-millionth, in spite of his terrific effort. He would never notice the infinitesimal difference in his material welfare. Suppose, on the other hand, that without getting caught he does not work at all. Then he gets only one-two-hundred-millionth less to eat. The deprivation is so infinitesimal that again he would be unable to notice it. But he would save himself from any work whatever.

In brief, under conditions of equal distribution regardless of individual production, a man's output, or the intensity of his effort, will be determined not by some abstract, over-all, collectivist consideration but mainly by his assumption regarding what *everybody else* is doing or is going to do. He may be willing to "do his share"; but he'll be hanged before he'll break his back to produce while others are loafing, because he knows that it will get him nowhere. And he will probably be a little generous in measuring how hard he himself is working and a little cynical in estimating how hard everybody else is working. He will be apt to cite the very worst among his co-workers as typical of what "others" do while he slaves.[7]

That this is what actually happens in a completely socialized economy is proved by the necessity the managers of such an economy are under to maintain a constant propaganda in favor of *More Work, More Production*. It is proved by the mass starvation that immediately followed the collectivization of the farms in Soviet Russia and in Communist China. But no more impressive illustration can be found anywhere than in the very beginnings of American history.

Most of us have forgotten that when the Pilgrim Fathers landed on the shores of Massachusetts they established a communist system. Out of their common product and storehouse they set up a system of rationing, though it came to "but a quarter of a pound of bread a day to each person." Even when harvest came, "it arose to but a little." A vicious circle seemed to set in. The people complained that they were too weak from want of food to tend the crops as they should. Deeply religious though they were, they took to stealing from each other. "So as it well appeared," writes Governor Bradford, in his contemporary account, "that famine must still insue the next year allso, if not some way prevented."

So the colonists, he continues,

> begane to thinke how they might raise as much corne as they could, and obtaine a beter crope than they had done, that they might not still thus languish in miserie. At length [in 1623] after much debate of things, the Gov. (with the advise of the cheefest amongest them) gave way that they should set corne every man for his owne perticuler, and in that regard trust to them selves.... And so assigned to every family a parcell of land....
>
> This had very good success; for it made all hands very industrious, so as much more corne was planted than other waise would have bene by any means the Gov. or any other could use, and saved him a great deall of trouble, and gave farr better contente.
>
> The women now wente willingly into the feild, and tooke their litle-ons with them to set corne, which before would aledg weakness, and inabilitie; whom to have compelled would have bene thought great tiranie and oppression.
>
> The experience that was had in this commone course and condition, tried sundrie years, and that amongst godly and sober men, may well evince the vanitie of that conceite of Platos and other ancients, applauded by some of later times;—that the taking away of propertie, and bringing in communitie into a comone wealth, would make them happy and flourishing; as if they were wiser than God. For this comunitie (so farr as it was) was found to breed much confusion and discontent, and retard much imployment that would have been to their benefite and comforte.
>
> For the yong-men that were most able and fitte for labour and service did repine that they should spend their time and streingth to worke for other mens wives and children, with out any recompense. The strong, or man of parts, had no more in devission of victails and cloaths, than he that was weake and not able to doe a quarter the other could; this was thought injuestice....
>
> And for men's wives to be commanded to doe service for other

men, as dressing their meate, washing their cloaths, etc., they deemd it a kind of slaverie, neither could many husbands well brooke it. . . .

By this time harvest was come, and instead of famine, now God gave them plentie, and the face of things was changed, to the rejoysing of the harts of many, for which they blessed God. And the effect of their particuler [private] planting was well seene, for all had, one way and other, pretty well to bring the year aboute, and some of the abler sorte and more industrious had to spare, and sell to others, so as any generall wante or famine hath not been amongest them since to this day.[8]

Such are the results when an attempt is made, in the name of "justice," to substitute a system of equal division per capita for a system of allowing each to get and keep what he creates. The fallacy of all schemes for (a *necessarily coercive*) equal division of wealth or income is that *they take production for granted*. The sponsors of such schemes tacitly assume that in spite of such equal division production will be the same; a few even explicitly argue that it will be greater. We can imagine a modern Socrates questioning such a Leveler:

Socrates: Which is more just—an equal division of goods or an unequal one?

Leveler: Obviously an equal division.

Socrates: No matter who produced the goods or how much was produced?

Leveler: Under all circumstances an equal division would be clearly more just than an unequal division.

Socrates: Let us see. Suppose in a poor isolated village of a hundred people, each were allotted a small bowl of rice a day, while in another isolated village of a hundred, ten people got only one bowl of rice a day, ten others two bowls, seventy others three bowls of rice a day, while one-tenth of the group lived very well indeed, with a rich varied diet. Which village would be better off—the first or the second?

Leveler: The second, of course. But—

Socrates: But according to your own definition, there would be less "justice" in the second village.

Leveler: But you are simply changing the terms of the problem. Obviously if the greater supply of goods produced in the second village were evenly divided, the second village would be better off than before, because the division would be more just.

Socrates: But suppose it was precisely because of the coercive equal division that the first village had been reduced to a production of only one bowl of rice per person per day? Suppose the production and distribution in the first village would be the same as that in the second if, as in the second, each person were allowed to keep his own contribution to production? For I have not really been talking about two different villages at all; but about what might happen in the same village under two different systems of "distribution"—one, a forced equal distribution of the total production, and the other a system in which each person was paid for what he produced, or was allowed to keep or exchange what he produced and protected in his right to do so.

Leveler: But isn't equal division under all circumstances more just than unequal division?

Socrates: Under certain circumstances it might be, as in the food allotment to an army, or to the people of a city under siege. But it is never more just when its result is substantially to diminish the output or product to be divided.

4. *Again: What Is Justice?*

But perhaps we have already put too many opinions in the mouth of even a modernized Socrates. We must never lose sight of the fact that Justice, like Virtue, is primarily a means; and though it is also an end, it is never the ultimate end, but must be judged by its results. Whatever produces bad results, whatever reduces material welfare or human happiness, cannot be Justice. We call Justice (as we have already seen in Chapter 24) the system of rules and arrangements that increase human peace, cooperation, production, and happiness, and Injustice whatever rules and arrangements stand in the way of these consequences. All *a priori* concepts of Justice must be revised accordingly.

The system of "to each what he produces," and the system of equal division regardless of what each produces, cannot, insofar as they are legal or governmental systems, be reconciled. It is commonly thought that while enforced equal division would be impracticable, precisely because it would discourage production,

336   THE FOUNDATIONS OF MORALITY

it is at least possible to mitigate the "injustices" and inequalities in wealth and income by various devices, the most popular of which in our day is the graduated income tax. The blessings of this tax in bringing about greatly increased "social justice" are constantly extolled. It is commonly assumed today, even by most academic economists, that personal incomes can be taxed up to 91 per cent[9] without significantly reducing incentives or the capital accumulation upon which all improvement in economic conditions depends. It is just as commonly assumed that unemployment compensation and social security benefits can be increased or extended indefinitely without reducing the incentives to work and production. This is not the place to enter into a technical discussion of the economic effect of "progressive" income taxes and of welfare-state payments, or of a combination of the two. The reader may be referred for this to other sources.[10] Here it is sufficient to point out that whatever forced transfer of income from Peter to Paul reduces the total "social dividend" is a dubious gain for "justice."

So there was wisdom as well as wit in the old Victorian jingle:

> What is a Communist?
> A man who has yearnings,
> For equal division
> Of unequal earnings

We are brought back once more to the question, What is the proper conception of Justice? A system under which the talented and skilled and industrious received no more than the incompetent and shiftless and lazy, and which equalized material rewards irrespective of effort, would certainly be unproductive; and to most of us, I think, it would also be unjust. Surely most of us would prefer, if we thought that were the only alternative, an enormously productive if not ideally "just" system to one which provided a perfectly "just" distribution of scarcity and poverty—"splendidly equalized destitution." [11] This does not mean that we prefer Abundance at the expense of Justice. It means that the term Just, as applied to material rewards, must be conceived as that system of distribution that tends in the long run to maximize everybody's incentives and so to maximize production and social cooperation.

There is one more principle of economic distribution, supported by some socialists, to be discussed. This is distribution or payment on the basis of "merit." This is a less naive principle than equal division per capita, and it is peculiarly likely to appeal to literary men, artists, poets, and intellectuals in other disciplines than economics. What a scandal, some of them say, that a vulgar and ill-mannered brewer or oil prospector, or the writer of a trashy novel, should make a fortune, while a fine modern poet almost starves because his volume sells only a few hundred copies or perhaps is not published at all. People should be rewarded in accordance with their true moral worth, or at least in accordance with their "real" contribution to our cultural life.

This proposed solution leaves the central question unanswered: Who is going to decide on people's true moral worth or "real" merit? Some of us may secretly believe that *we* would be competent to decide each person's true merits, and would reward them in proper proportion with absolute impartiality and justice, once we knew "the facts." But a little thought would convince most of us that only someone with the omniscience and impartiality of God would be able to decide on the relative merit and deserts of each of us. Where the solution is attempted in practice, as in Soviet Russia, we know the nightmarish results. The nearest approach to a practical answer has been the token solutions in contemporary England, with its annual awards of knighthoods and other titles, in France with election to the Academy, and in the United States with the distribution by its colleges of honorary degrees. But people have been known to question the justice or wisdom even of some of these.

5. *Socialism Means Coercion*

The solution of the free market is not perfect, but it is superior to any alternative that has been devised or seems likely to be devised. Under it material rewards correspond to the value that a man's particular services have to his fellows. The others reveal their valuations by what they are willing to pay for his contribution. The best-paid writers or manufacturers are those who offer the public what it wants, rather than what is good for it. What it wants will correspond with what is good for it only as the general level of taste and wisdom and morality rises. But whatever the defects of this system, any coercive or arbitrary substitute will surely be a great deal worse.

The central issue between capitalism and socialism is liberty: "It is of the essence of a free society that we should be materially rewarded not for doing what others order us to do, but for giving them what they want." [12] This does not mean that capitalism is more "materialistic" than socialism. "Free enterprise has developed the only kind of society which while it provides us with ample material means, if that is what we mainly want, still leaves the individual free to choose between material and nonmaterial reward. . . . Surely it is unjust to blame a system as more materialistic because it leaves it to the individual to decide whether he prefers material gain to other kinds of excellence, instead of having this decided for him." [13]

What is not seen by those who are proposing other systems of material rewards than those provided by capitalism is that their systems can be imposed only by coercion. And coercion is the essence of socialism and communism. Under socialism there can be no free choice of occupation. Everyone must take the job to which he is assigned. He must go where he is sent. He must remain there until he gets orders to move elsewhere. His promotion or demotion depends upon the will of a superior, upon a single chain of command.

Economic life under socialism, in short, is organized on a military model. Each is assigned his task and platoon, as in an army. This is clear even in the utopian visions of a Bellamy: his people had to take their turns in the "army of labor," working in the mines, cleaning the streets, waiting on table—only, for some unexplained reason, all these tasks had suddenly become incomparably easier and more delightful. Engels assured his followers that: "Socialism will abolish both architecture and barrow-pushing as professions, and the man who has given half an hour to architecture will also push the cart a little until his work as an architect is again in demand. It would be a pretty sort of socialism which perpetuated the business of barrow-pushing." [14] In Bebel's Utopia only physical labor is recognized by society, and art and science are relegated to leisure hours.

What is implied but never clearly stated in these utopian visions is that everything will be done by coercion, by orders from the top. The press will be nationalized, intellectual life will be nationalized, freedom of speech will disappear.

The grim reality is shown today in the Russian slave camps and in Communist China. When economic liberty has been destroyed, all other liberty disappears with it. Alexander Hamilton recognized this clearly: "Power over a man's subsistence is power over his will." And as one of the masters of modern Russia—Leon Trotsky—pointed out even more clearly: "In a country where the sole employer is the State, opposition means death by slow starvation: The old principle: who does not work shall not eat, has been replaced by a new one: who does not obey shall not eat."

So complete socialism means the complete disappearance of liberty. And, contrary to the Marxist propaganda of a century, it is socialism rather than capitalism that tends to lead to war. Capitalist countries have, it is true, gone to war with each other; but those who have been most strongly imbued with the philosophy of the free market and free trade have been the leaders of public opinion in opposition to war. Capitalism depends on the division of labor and on social cooperation. It therefore depends on the principle of peace, because the wider the field of social cooperation the greater the need for peace. The maximum of trade between nations (which all true liberals recognize to be mutually advantageous) requires the constant maintenance of peace. As recalled in our chapter on International Ethics, it was one of the first great liberals, David Hume, who wrote in his essay "Of the Jealousy of Trade" in 1740: "I shall therefore venture to acknowledge that, not only as a man, but as a British subject, I pray for the flourishing commerce of Germany, Spain, Italy, and even France itself. I am at least certain that Great Britain, and all those nations, would flourish more, did their sovereigns and their ministers adopt such enlarged and benevolent sentiments towards each other."

It is socialist governments, on the contrary, notwithstanding their denunciations of the Imperialist Warmongers, that blame their almost inevitable failures on the machinations of capitalist countries, and that have been the greatest source of modern wars. We need not rehearse here in detail the war record of the National Socialists in Germany (more popularly known today by their abbreviated name, the Nazis).[15] Nor need we rehearse the constant record of aggression, subversion, and conquest of Soviet Russia and Communist China—whether the conquest was only partly successful, as in Finland, South Korea, India, and Quemoy, or completely successful as in Lithuania, Latvia, Estonia, Czechoslovakia, Hungary, Rumania, Bulgaria, Albania, etc. We have in any case, as daily reminders, Khrushchev's constant threats to bury us.

6. *A Religion of Immoralism*

We are brought back, in fact, to the pervasive immorality of Marxism from its very beginnings to the present day. The noble end of socialism was thought to justify any means. As Max Eastman writes:

> Marx hated deity, and regarded high moral aspirations as an obstacle. The power on which he rested his faith in the coming paradise was the harsh, fierce, bloody evolution of a "material," and yet mysteriously "upward-going," world. And he convinced himself that, in order to get in step with such a world, we must set aside moral principles and go in for fratricidal war. Although buried under a mountain of economic rationalizations pretending to be science, that mystical and anti-moral faith is the one wholly original contribution of Karl Marx to man's heritage of ideas.[16]

Marx expelled people from his Communist party for mentioning programmatically such things as "love," "Justice," "humanity," even "morality" itself. When he founded the First International, he wrote privately to Engels: "I was obliged to insert in the preamble two phrases about 'duty and right,' ditto 'truth, morality, and justice.' " But these lamentable phrases, he assured Engels, "are placed in such a way that they can do no harm." [17]

Lenin, a faithful follower, declared that in order to bring nearer the earthly socialist paradise: "We must be ready to employ trickery, deceit, law-breaking, withholding and concealing truth. We can and must write in a language which sows among the masses hate, revulsion, scorn, and the like, toward those who disagree with us." [18]

Addressing an all-Russian Congress of Youth, Lenin declared:

THE ETHICS OF SOCIALISM

"For us morality is subordinated completely to the interests of the class struggle of the proletariat." [19]

Stalin, when young, was an organizer of bank robberies and holdups. When he came into power he became one of the greatest mass murderers in history.

The motto of the Bolsheviks was simple: "Everything which promotes the success of the revolution is moral, everything which hinders it is immoral."

As Max Eastman exclaims, reviewing the record of this "religion of immoralism": "The notion of an earthly paradise in which men shall dwell together in millennial brotherhood is used to justify crimes and depravities surpassing anything the modern world has seen. . . . Such a disaster never happened to humanity before." [20]

CHAPTER 32

Morality and Religion

1. "If There's No God"—

Is religion necessary to the discovery of the specific moral rules that should guide us? And is a belief in the chief traditional doctrines of religion—such as the existence of a personal God, a life after death, a Heaven and a Hell—necessary in order to secure human observance of moral rules?

The belief that morality is impossible without religion has dominated the thought of the Western world for nearly twenty centuries. In its crudest form, it is put into the mouth of Smerdyakov Karamazov, in the terrible scene in which he confesses to his half-brother Ivan, a philosophical atheist, that he has murdered and robbed their father: "I was only your instrument," says Smerdyakov, "your faithful servant, and it was following your words I did it. . . . 'All things are lawful.' That was quite right what you taught me. . . . For if there's no everlasting God, there's no such thing as virtue, and there's no need of it." [1]

And Santayana satirizes the same type of argument: "It is a curious assumption of religious moralists that their precepts would never be adopted unless people were persuaded by external evidence that God had positively established them. Were it not for divine injunction and threats everyone would like nothing better than to kill and to steal and to bear false witness." [2]

2. The Indictment

Perhaps we can best arrive at an answer to the two questions that led off this chapter by reviewing the principal arguments on both sides.

Let us begin with the argument of those who have denied that religious faith is necessary for the maintenance of morality. Perhaps the fullest statement of this is that made by John Stuart

Mill in his essay on "The Utility of Religion." [3] Mill begins by contending that religion has always received excessive credit for maintaining morality because, whenever morality is formally taught, especially to children, it is almost invariably taught *as* religion. Children are not taught to distinguish between the commands of God and the commands of their parents. The major motive to morality, Mill argues, is the good opinion of our fellows. The threat of punishment for our sins in a Hereafter exercises only a dubious and uncertain force: "Even the worst malefactor is hardly able to think that any crime he has had it in his power to commit, any evil he can have inflicted in this short space of existence, can have deserved torture extending through an eternity." In any case, "the value of religion as a supplement to human laws, a more cunning sort of police, an auxiliary to the thief-catcher and the hangman, is not that part of its claims which the more highminded of its votaries are fondest of insisting on."

There is a real evil, too, in ascribing a supernatural origin to the received maxims of morality. "That origin consecrates the whole of them, and protects them from being discussed or criticized." The result is that the morality becomes "stereotyped"; it is not improved and perfected, and dubious precepts are preserved along with the noblest and most necessary.

Even the morality that men have achieved through the fear or the love of God, Mill maintains, can also be achieved by those of us who seek, not only the approbation of those whom we respect, but the imagined approbation of

> all those, dead or living, whom we admire or venerate. . . . The thought that our dead parents or friends would have approved our conduct is a scarcely less powerful motive than the knowledge that our living ones do approve it: and the idea that Socrates, or Howard, or Washington, or Antoninus, or Christ, would have sympathized with us, or that we are attempting to do our part in the spirit in which they did theirs, has operated on the very best minds, as a strong incentive to act up to their highest feelings and convictions.

On the other hand,

> the religions which deal in promises and threats regarding a future life . . . fasten down the thoughts to the person's own

posthumous interests; they tempt him to regard the performance of his duties to others mainly as a means to his own personal salvation; and are one of the most serious obstacles to the great purpose of moral culture, the strengthening of the unselfish and weakening of the selfish element in our nature. . . . The habit of expecting to be rewarded in another life for our conduct in this, makes even virtue itself no longer an exercise of the unselfish feelings.

Mill makes further remarks regarding what he considers the elements of positive immorality in the Judean and Christian religions, but an even more bitter and unqualified indictment is made by Morris R. Cohen:

> The absolute character of religious morality has made it emphasize the sanctions of fear—the terrifying consequences of disobedience. I do not wish to ignore the fact that the greatest religious teachers have laid more stress on the love of the good for its own sake. But in the latter respect they have not been different from such great philosophers as Democritus, Aristotle, or Spinoza, who regarded morality as its own reward. . . .
>
> Religion has made a virtue of cruelty. Bloody sacrifices of human beings to appease the gods fill the pages of history. In ancient Mexico we have the wholesale sacrifice of prisoners of war as a form of national cultus. In the ancient East we have the sacrifice of children to Moloch. Even the Greeks were not entirely free from this religious custom. Let us note that while the Old Testament prohibits the ancient Oriental sacrifice of the first-born, it does not deny its efficacy in the case of the King of Moab (II Kings 3:2) nor is there any revulsion at the readiness with which Abraham was willing to sacrifice his son Isaac. In India it was the religious duty of the widow to be burned on the funeral pyre of her late husband. And while Christianity formally condemned human sacrifice, it revived it in fact under the guise of burning heretics. I pass over the many thousands burned by order of the Inquisition, and the record of the hundreds of people burned by rulers like Queen Mary for not believing in the Pope or in transubstantiation. The Protestant Calvin burned the scholarly Servetus for holding that Jesus was "the son of the eternal God" rather than "the eternal son of God." And in our own Colonial America heresy was a capital offense.
>
> Cruelty is a much more integral part of religion than most people nowadays realize. The Mosaic law commands the Israelites, whenever attacking a city, to kill all the males, and all females

who have known men. The religious force of this is shown when Saul is cursed and his whole dynasty is destroyed for leaving one prisoner, King Agag, alive. Consider that tender psalm, "By the rivers of Babylon." After voicing the pathetic cry "How can we sing the songs of Jehovah in a foreign land?" it goes on to curse Edom, and ends "Happy shall he be, that taketh and dasheth thy little ones against the rock." Has there been any religious movement to expurgate this from the religious service of Jews and Christians? Something of the spirit of this intense hatred for the enemies of God (i.e., those not of our own religion) has invented and developed the terrors of Hell, and condemned almost all of mankind to suffer them eternally—all, that is, except a few members of our own particular religion. Worst of all, it has regarded these torments as adding to the beatitude of the saints. The doctrine of a loving and all-merciful God professed by Christianity or Islam has not prevented either one from preaching and practicing the duty to hate and persecute those who do not believe. Nay, it has not prevented fierce wars between diverse sects of these religions, such as the wars between Shiites, Sunnites, and Wahabites, between Greek Orthodox, Roman Catholics, and Protestants.

The fierce spirit of war and hatred is not of course entirely due to religion. But religion *has* made a *duty* of hatred. It preached crusades against Mohammedans and forgave atrocious sins to encourage indiscriminate slaughter of Greek Orthodox as well as of Mohammedan populations. . . .

Cruel persecution and intolerance are not accidents, but grow out of the very essence of religion, namely, its absolute claims. So long as each religion claims to have absolute, supernaturally revealed truth, all other religions are sinful errors. . . . There is no drearier chapter in the history of human misery than the unusually bloody internecine religious or sectarian wars which have drenched in blood so much of Europe, Northern Africa, and Western Asia. . . .

The complacent assumption which identifies religion with higher morality ignores the historic fact that there is not a single loathsome human practice that has not at some time or other been regarded as a religious duty. I have already mentioned the breaking of promises to heretics. But assassination and thuggery (as the words themselves indicate), sacred prostitution (in Babylonia and India), diverse forms of self-torture, and the verminous uncleanliness of saints like Thomas à Becket, have all been part of religion. The religious conception of morality has been a legalistic one. Moral rules are the commands of the gods. But the latter are sovereigns and not themselves subject to the rules which they lay down for others according to their own sweet wills.[4]

3. *The Defense*

In the face of such sweeping indictments, what have the defenders of religion as an indispensable basis of morality had to say? Rather strangely, it is not easy to find among recent writers on ethics uncompromising and powerful exponents of this traditional view. If we turn, for example, to the Reverend Hastings Rashdall, where we might expect to find such a view, we are surprised at the modesty of his claims. His ideas are presented at length in his well-known two-volume work, *The Theory of Good and Evil* (1907), in the two chapters on "Metaphysics and Morality" and "Religion and Morality." But in a little volume of less than a hundred pages, written a few years later, which he describes in a preface as "necessarily little more than a condensation of my *Theory of Good and Evil*," he has himself formally summarized his views on the subject. It seems to me best to quote his own summary almost in full:

> 1. Morality cannot be based upon or deduced from any metaphysical or theological proposition whatever. The moral judgment is ultimate and immediate. Putting this into more popular language, the immediate recognition that I ought to act in a certain way supplies a sufficient reason for so acting entirely apart from anything else that I may believe about the ultimate nature of things.
>
> 2. But the recognition of the validity of Moral Obligation in general or of any particular moral judgment logically implies the belief in a permanent spiritual self which is really the cause of its own actions. Such a belief is in the strictest sense a postulate of Morality.
>
> 3. The belief in God is not a postulate of Morality in such a sense that the rejection of it involves a denial of all meaning or validity to our moral judgments, but the acceptance or rejection of this belief does materially affect the sense which we give to the idea of obligation. The belief in the objectivity of moral judgments implies that the moral law is recognized as no merely accidental element in the construction of the human mind, but as an ultimate fact about the Universe. This rational demand cannot be met by any merely materialistic or naturalistic Metaphysic,

and is best satisfied by a theory which explains the world as an expression of an intrinsically righteous rational Will, and the moral consciousness as an imperfect revelation of the ideal towards which that will is directed. The belief in God may be described as a postulate of Morality in a less strict or secondary sense.

4. So far from Ethics being based upon or deduced from Theology, a rational Theology is largely based upon Ethics: since the moral Consciousness supplies us with all the knowledge we possess as to the action, character, and direction of the supreme Will, and forms an important element in the argument for the existence of such a Will.

5. We must peremptorily reject the view that the obligation of Morality depends upon sanctions, *i.e.* reward and punishment, in this life or any other. But, as the belief in an objective moral law naturally leads up to and requires for its full justification the idea of God, so the idea of God involves the belief in Immortality if the present life seems an inadequate fulfillment of the moral ideal. In ways which need not be recapitulated, we have seen that it is practically a belief eminently favorable to the maximum influence of the moral ideal on life.

The whole position may perhaps be still more simply summed up. It is possible for a man to know his duty, and to achieve considerable success in doing it, without any belief in God or Immortality or any of the other beliefs commonly spoken of as religious; but he is likely to know and do it better if he accepts a view of the Universe which includes as its most fundamental articles these two beliefs.[5]

4. *Ethics of the Old Testament*

After this brief glance at some of the conflicting arguments, what should our own answer be to the two questions with which this chapter began? Let us begin with the first.

It is hard to see how religious beliefs by themselves can give any guidance to the specific moral rules that should guide us. We are brought back to the old theologic problem: Religion tells us that we ought to act in accordance with the will of God. But is an action right simply because God wills it? Or does God will it because it is right? We cannot conceive of God's arbitrarily commanding us to do anything but the Right, or forbidding us to do anything but the Wrong. Are actions moral because God wills them, or does God will them because they are moral? Which, logically or temporally, comes first: God's will, or morality?

There is a further theologic problem. If God is omnipotent, how can his will fail to be realized, whether we do right or wrong?

Then there is the practical ethical problem. Assuming that it is our duty to follow God's will, how can we know what God does will, either in general or in any particular case? Who is privy to God's will? Who is presumptuous enough to assume that he knows the will of God? How do we determine God's will? By intuition? By special revelation? By reason? In the latter case, are we to assume that God desires the happiness of men? Then we are brought back to the position of utilitarianism. Are we to assume that he desires the "perfection" of men, or their "self-realization," or that they live "according to nature"? Then we are brought back to one of these traditional ethical philosophies—but purely by our own assumptions, and not by direct or unmistakable knowledge of God's will.

A hundred different religions give a hundred different accounts or interpretations of God's will in the moral realm. Most Christians assume that it is found in the Bible. But when we turn to the Bible we find hundreds of moral commandments, laws, judgments, injunctions, teachings, precepts. Often these preachments flatly contradict each other. How are we to reconcile the Mosaic "Eye for eye, tooth for tooth, hand for hand, foot for foot, burning for burning, wound for wound, stripe for stripe" [6] with the direct contradiction of it in Christ's Sermon on the Mount: "Ye have heard that it hath been said, An eye for an eye, and a tooth for a tooth: But I say unto you, That ye resist not evil: but whosoever shall smite thee on thy right cheek, turn to him the other also. . . .

"Ye have heard that it hath been said, Thou shalt love thy neighbor, and hate thine enemy. But I say unto you, Love your enemies, bless them that curse you, do good to them that hate you, and pray for them which despitefully use you, and persecute you." [7]

Broadly speaking, the ethical precepts of the Old and New Testaments are not only in contradiction with each other in detail, but even in their general spirit. The Old Testament commands obedience to God through fear; the New Testament pleads for obedience to God through love.

Some people are fond of saying, unthinkingly, that all the moral guidance we need is to be found in the Ten Commandments. They forget that the Ten Commandments are not specifically limited to ten in the Bible itself, but are immediately followed by more than a hundred other commandments (called, however, "judgments"). They forget also that Christ himself insisted on the need for supplementing them. "A new commandment I give unto you, That ye love one another." [8] And Jesus put more emphasis on this commandment, in his life and in his teachings, than on any other.

When we take the Ten Commandments simply by themselves, we find that, if it were not for their supposed sacred origin, we would regard them as a rather strange and unbalanced assortment of moral rules. Working on the sabbath day, if we judge by the relative emphasis given to it (94 words), is regarded as a much more serious sin or crime than committing murder (four words). Nor is there any indication, for that matter, that adultery, stealing, or bearing false witness is any less serious a sin or crime than murder. It is apparently no greater sin to steal something than merely to covet it; and the reason it is a sin to covet your neighbor's wife is apparently because she is, like his house, his manservant, his maidservant, his ox or his ass, part of your neighbor's property. Finally, the God of the Ten Commandments is not only, by his own confession, "a jealous God," but an incredibly vindictive one, "visiting the iniquity of the fathers upon the children unto the third and fourth generation of them that hate me."

Immediately following the Ten Commandments God ordered Moses to set before the children of Israel more than a hundred judgments or laws. The first one orders that if anyone buy a Hebrew slave, the slave shall serve six years and be set free in the seventh. Whoever strikes a man so that he dies is to be put to death—but so is whoever curses his father or mother. And "Thou shalt not suffer a witch to live." [9]

But enough has already been said here (and in the quotation in this chapter from Morris R. Cohen) to establish without further evidence at least the negative conclusion that the ethics of the Old Testament, explicit and implied, are not a reliable guide to conduct for twentieth-century man.[10]

5. *Ethics of the New Testament*

In the New Testament we find a strikingly different ethic. In place of the God of vengeance, to be feared, we find the God of Mercy, to be loved. The new commandment, "that ye love one another," and the example of the personal life and preaching of Jesus of Nazareth, have had a more profound influence on our moral aspirations and ideals than any other rule or Person in history.

But the ethical doctrines of Jesus present serious difficulties. We can, in large part, command our actions; but we cannot command our feelings. We cannot love all our fellow men simply because we think we ought to. Love for a few (usually members of our immediate family), affection and friendship for some, initial goodwill toward a wider circle, and the attempt constantly to discourage and suppress within ourselves incipient anger, resentment, jealousy, envy, or hatred, are the most that all but a very small number of us seem able to achieve. We may give lip-service to turning the other cheek, to loving our enemies, blessing those that curse us, doing good to those that hate us, but we cannot bring ourselves, except on the rarest occasions, to take these injunctions literally. (I am speaking here not of our duty to be just, or even outwardly kind, toward all, but of our ability to *command our inner feelings* toward all.)

Notwithstanding Matthew 7:1, "Judge not, that ye be not judged," all modern nations have policemen, courts, and judges. Most of us, whether or not we occasionally consider the beam in our own eye, cannot refrain from pointing out the mote in our brother's eye. The overwhelming majority of us are no more capable than the rich young man who came to Jesus (Matthew 19:20-22) of trying to be perfect by selling all that we have and giving the proceeds to the poor. Though it is all but impossible for a rich man to enter the kingdom of heaven (Matthew 19:24-25) most of us try to become as rich as we can and hope for the best hereafter. In spite of Matthew 6:25-28, we do take thought of our life, what we shall eat, what we shall drink, and wherewithal we shall be clothed. We do sow and reap and gather into barns, we do work and save, we do take care of ourselves in the hope of adding to our span of life.

The problem is not merely that we are incapable of reaching moral perfection. That we cannot achieve perfection is no reason why we should not set our conception of it before us as a shining ideal. The question goes deeper than this. Are some of the ideals of Jesus' teaching practicable? Would the life of the individual, or would the lives of the mass of mankind, be more satisfactory or less satisfactory if we tried literally to follow some of these precepts?

The morality taught by Jesus was apparently based on the assumption that "the time is fulfilled, and the kingdom of God is at hand: repent ye, and believe the gospel." [11]

> Jesus regards himself as the prophet of the approaching Kingdom of God, the Kingdom which according to ancient prophecy shall bring redemption from all earthly insufficiency, and with it all economic cares. His followers have nothing to do but to prepare themselves for this Day. The time for worrying about earthly matters is past, for now, in expectation of the Kingdom, men must attend to more important things. Jesus offers no rules for earthly action and struggle; his Kingdom is not of this world. Such rules of conduct as he gives his followers are valid only for the short interval of time which has still to be lived while waiting for the great things to come. In the Kingdom of God there will be no economic cares.[12]

Whether this interpretation is correct or not, practically all but the earliest Christians abandoned this notion and the "transitional" morality based upon it. As Santayana has put it: "If a religious morality is to become that of society at large—which original Christian morality was never meant to be—it must adapt its maxims to a possible system of worldly economy." [13]

6. Conclusion

We must come, then, to this conclusion. Ethics is autonomous. It is not dependent upon any specific religious doctrine. And the great body of ethical rules, even those laid down by the Fathers of the Church, have no necessary connection with any religious premises. We need merely point, in illustration, to the great ethical system of Thomas Aquinas. As Henry Sidgwick tells us,

> The moral philosophy of Thomas Aquinas is, in the main, Aristotelianism with a Neo-Platonic tinge, interpreted and supplemented by a view of Christian doctrine derived chiefly from Augustine. . . . When . . . among moral virtues he distinguishes Justice, manifested in actions by which others receive their due, from the virtues that primarily relate to the passions of the agent himself, he is giving his interpretation of Aristotle's doctrine; and his list of the latter virtues, to the number of ten, is taken *en bloc* from the *Nicomachean Ethics*.[14]

This great similarity in the ethical code of persons of profound differences in religious belief should not be surprising. In human history religion and morality are like two streams that sometimes run parallel, sometimes merge, sometimes separate, sometimes seem independent and sometimes interdependent. But morality is older than any living religion and probably older than all religion. We find a kind of moral code—or at least what, if we found it in human beings, we would call moral behavior—even among the lower animals.[15]

Let us return now to the second question with which this chapter opened. Even if religion cannot tell us anything about what the specific moral rules ought to be, is it necessary in order to secure observance of the moral code? The best answer we can make, I think, is that while religious faith is not indispensable to such observance, it must be recognized in the present state of civilization as a powerful force in securing the observance that exists. I am not speaking primarily of the effect of a belief in a future life, in a Heaven or a Hell, though this is by no means unimportant. Doing good deeds in the hope of reward in a future life, or refraining from evil in the fear of punishment in such a future life, has been shrewdly called religious utilitarianism; but though the motive is purely self-regarding, the result may be so far beneficent, like the result of what Bentham calls extra-regarding prudence.

The most powerful religious belief supporting morality, however, seems to me of a much different nature. This is the belief in a God who sees and knows our every action, our every impulse and our every thought, who judges us with exact justice, and who, whether or not He rewards us for our good deeds and punishes us for our evil ones, approves of our good deeds and disapproves of our evil ones. Perhaps, as Mill suggests, for this conception of God as the all-seeing and all-judging Witness there can be effectively substituted, as there is in many agnostics, an almost equally effective thought of what our parents or friends, or some great human figure, living or dead, whom we deeply admire or revere, would think of our action or secret thought if they or he knew of it. Still, the belief in an all-knowing and all-judging God remains a tremendous force in ethical conduct today.

There is no doubt that decay of religious faith tends to let loose license and immorality. This is what has been happening in our own generation. Yet it is not the function of the moral philosopher, as such, to proclaim the truth of this religious faith or to try to maintain it. His function is, rather, to insist on the rational basis of all morality, to point out that it does not need any supernatural assumptions, and to show that the rules of morality are or ought to be those rules of conduct that tend most to increase human cooperation, happiness and well-being in this our present life.[16]

CHAPTER 33
Summary and Conclusion

1. *Summary*

Let us see whether we can summarize briefly some of the main propositions of the ethical system at which we have arrived.

1. Morality is not an end we pursue purely for its own sake. It is a means to ends beyond itself. But because it is an *indispensable* means we value it also for its own sake.

2. All human action is undertaken in order to substitute a more satisfactory state of affairs for a less satisfactory state. The conduct we call moral is the conduct we consider likely to lead to the most satisfactory situation *in the long run*.

3. To say that we seek to maximize our satisfactions in the long run is only another way of saying that we seek to maximize our happiness and well-being.

4. Though actions must be judged by their tendency to promote long-run happiness and well-being, it is a mistake to apply this utilitarian criterion *directly* to an act or decision *considered in isolation*. It is impossible for anyone to foresee all the consequences of a particular act. But we *are* capable of judging the consequences of following established *general rules* of action—of acting *on principle*.

5. There are several reasons why we should abide by established general rules rather than attempt to make an *ad hoc* decision in each case. We must abide by an accepted code of rules (even if these are not the best imaginable) so that others may be able to depend on our actions and so that we may be able to depend on the actions of others. Only when each can guide his own course by this mutual expectation can we achieve adequate social cooperation. Moreover, the particular set of rules of conduct embodied in our existing moral tradition, the morality of "common sense," is based on thousands of years of human experience and millions of individual judgments and decisions. This traditional moral code may not be perfect, or

adequate to deal with every new situation that can arise. Some of its rules may be vague or otherwise defective, but it is on the whole a marvelous spontaneous social growth, like language, a consensus arrived at by humanity over the centuries, that the individual may justly regard with feelings approaching reverence and awe. His general rule of conduct should be always to abide by the established moral rule unless he has a good reason to depart from it. He should not refuse to follow it merely because he cannot clearly understand the reason for it.

6. Ethical progress depends not merely on adherence to existing moral rules, however, but on the constant refinement, improvement, and perfection of such rules. Yet any wholesale attempt to "transvalue all values" would be presumptuous and foolish. The best any individual (or perhaps even a whole generation) can hope to do is to modify the moral code and moral values in a few comparatively minor particulars.

7. Philosophical ethics has much to learn from a study of the principles of law and jurisprudence on the one hand, and of the rationale of manners on the other. It has also much to learn from theoretical economics. Both ethics and economics study human actions, choices, and valuations, though from different points of view.

8. Philosophical ethics is an effort to understand the rationale behind the existing moral code and to discover the broad principles or criteria by which existing moral rules can be tested or better moral rules framed. What are some of these principles of criteria? Should moral rules be framed primarily to promote the long-run happiness of the *individual* or the long-run happiness of *society?* The question assumes a false antithesis. Only a rule that would do the first would do the second, and vice versa. The society *is* the individuals that compose it. If each achieves happiness, then the happiness of society is necessarily achieved.

9. Of course if each seeks his happiness *at the expense of others,* then each must frustrate the achievement of happiness by others, and so each must frustrate the achievement of happiness by all, *including himself.* It follows from this that no man should be allowed to treat himself as an exception. All moral rules must be *universalizable,* and applied impartially to all.

10. This *universalizability* can and should be reconciled with

considerable *particularity*. This follows not only from the necessary division and specialization of labor, and the fact that each person has a particular vocation and job, but from the fact that each person is a citizen of a particular country, a resident of a particular neighborhood, a member of a particular family, and so on. So a "universal" rule may often take the particularized form that every man has a duty to his *own* job, his *own* wife, his *own* son, etc., and not necessarily to other jobs, wives, or sons.

11. The minimum purpose of moral rules is to prevent *conflict* and *collision* between individuals. The broader purpose is to harmonize our attitudes and actions so as to make the achievement of everyone's aims as far as possible compatible. This purpose can be realized when these rules are not only such as to enable us to anticipate and to depend upon each other's behavior, but when they promote and intensify our positive *cooperation* with each other. Thus *Social Cooperation* is the heart of morality, and the means by which each of us can most effectively supply his own wants and maximize his own satisfactions. It is only the division and combination of labor that has made possible the enormous increase in production, and hence in want-satisfaction, in the modern world. Society is based on an economic system in which each of us devotes himself to furthering the purposes of others as an indirect means of furthering his own.

12. Thus "egoism" and "altruism" coalesce, and the antithesis between the "individual" and "society" disappears. In fact, the appropriate moral attitude (and perhaps the dominant attitude of the typical moral man) is neither pure egoism nor pure altruism but *mutualism,* consideration both for others *and* for oneself, and often the failure to make any distinction between one's own interests and the interests of his family or loved ones, or of some particular group of which he feels himself to be an integral part.

13. Because *social cooperation* is the great means of achieving nearly all our ends, this means can be thought of as itself the moral goal to be achieved. Our dominant moral rules can therefore be aimed at achieving or intensifying this social cooperation rather than aimed directly at achieving happiness. As no two people find their happiness or satisfactions in precisely

SUMMARY AND CONCLUSION 357

the same things, social cooperation has the great advantage that no unanimity with regard to value judgments is required to make it work.

14. The so-called "sacrifices" that the moral rules sometimes call for are in the overwhelming main merely temporary or apparent sacrifices that the individual makes in the present in order to secure a greater gain in the future. The occasions on which the rules call for a real sacrifice by the individual are so rare that for most of us they never arise at all—say, the risk or actual surrender of his life. They are mainly confined to persons in certain special positions or vocations—soldiers, policemen, doctors, the captain of a sinking ship, etc. The sacrifices that a mother makes for her child, or any of us for our loved ones, are seldom regarded as sacrifices at all.

15. Immoral action is nearly always short-sighted action. If it occasionally helps an individual to achieve some immediate particular end that he might not have achieved without it, it is usually at the cost, even to him, of some more important or enduring end. And immorality can achieve even these minor successes only to the extent that it is rare and exceptional, and confined to a tiny minority. A corrupt or immoral society is ultimately an unhappy or dying society.

16. Asceticism (but not self-discipline) is a perversion of morality. The distinction between asceticism and self-discipline is that the first tends to undermine our health, shorten our life, and destroy our happiness, while the second tends to build up our health, prolong our life, and increase our happiness. Self-discipline and self-restraint are not practiced as ends in themselves, but as means to increase one's happiness in the long run and to promote social cooperation.

17. Ethical propositions are not true or false in the sense that existential propositions are true or false. Ethical rules are not *de*scriptive, but *pre*scriptive. But though not true or false in the existential sense, ethical propositions can be valid or invalid, consistent or inconsistent, logical or illogical, rational or irrational, intelligent or unintelligent, justified or unjustified, expedient or inexpedient, *wise* or *unwise*. True, ethical judgments or propositions, though they must always take facts into consideration, are not themselves purely factual but *valuative*. But this does not mean that they are arbitrary or merely "emo-

tive" (in the derogatory sense in which that adjective is used by positivists and, indeed, for which it seems to have been coined). Ethical rules, judgments, and propositions are attempts to answer the question: What is the best thing to do?

18. Morality is autonomous. While religion often serves as a force that strengthens adherence to moral rules, the appropriate moral rules themselves, and the nature of our duties and obligations, have no necessary dependence on any theological doctrine or religious belief.

This list of propositions does not, of course, aim to be complete. It is set down only to remind the reader of the general outlines of the system; the propositions are numbered merely for convenience of reference.

2. *Cooperatism*

It will be convenient to give the system of ethics set forth in this book a distinctive name. It can, of course, be fitted into several very broad existing classifications. It is *eudaemonic,* because it regards the end of action as the promotion of the greatest happiness and well-being in the long run. And it conceives of happiness in its broadest sense, as synonymous with the greatest possible harmonization and satisfaction of human desires. But many ethical systems, from the time of Epicurus and Aristotle, have been eudaemonic in their end. We need a term to describe this one more specifically.

This system is also *teleotic,*[1] because it judges actions or rules of action by the ends they tend to bring about, and defines "right" actions as actions that tend to promote "good" ends. But the majority of modern ethical systems (with a few exceptions such as Kant's doctrine of the Categorical Imperative and duty-for-duty's sake) are more or less teleotic.

The system outlined in the previous chapters is also a form of *Utilitarianism,* insofar as it holds that actions or rules of action are to be judged by their consequences and their tendency to promote human happiness. But to apply this term to our system could easily be misleading. This is not only because it has become in some quarters a term of disparagement (because of its supposed purely sensual hedonism, or because early Utili-

SUMMARY AND CONCLUSION 359

tarianism made the tendency to produce pleasure or happiness the test of an *act* rather than of a *rule* of action) but because the term is applied indiscriminately to so wide a variety of diverse systems. Any rational ethical system must be in some respects utilitarian, if we take the term merely to mean that it judges rules of action by the ends they tend to promote. A philosophical critic has enumerated "Thirteen Pragmatisms." [2] An acute analysis would probably distinguish at least as many utilitarianisms. There are "hedonistic" utilitarianism, "eudaemonic" utilitarianism, "ideal" or "pluralistic" utilitarianism, "agathistic" utilitarianism, *direct* or *ad hoc* utilitarianism, *indirect* or *rule* utilitarianism—and various combinations of these. If the system set forth here is to be called utilitarianism, then it would have to be called eudaemonic-mutualistic-rule-utilitarianism to distinguish it from other brands. But this would be hopelessly cumbrous and not too enlightening.

I should like to suggest, in fact, that the word *Utilitarianism* itself is beginning to outlive its usefulness.[3]

There are two possible names for the system of ethics outlined in this book. One is *Mutualism*. This underlines the dominant *attitude* that it suggests, as contrasted with pure "egoism" or pure "altruism." But the name which I think on the whole preferable is *Cooperatism*, which underlines the type of *actions* or rules of action that it prescribes, and so emphasizes its most distinctive feature.

It may be thought that logically a name should describe the ultimate *goal* of the system, or of the conduct that it prescribes, which is to maximize human happiness and well-being. But this *felicitism* or *eudaemonism*, as I have already pointed out, has been an implicit or explicit element of many ethical systems since the days of Epicurus. What has hitherto been insufficiently recognized [4] is that *social cooperation* is the indispensable and foremost means to the realization of all our individual ends.

Thus social cooperation is the essence of morality. And morality, as we should constantly remind ourselves, is a daily affair, even an hourly affair, not just something we need to think about only in a few high and heroic moments. The moral code by which we live is shown every day, not necessarily in great acts of renunciation, but in refraining from little slights and meannesses, and in practicing little courtesies and kindnesses. Few of us are capable of rising to the Christian commandment to *"love* one another," but most of us can at least learn to be *kind* to one another— and for most earthly purposes this will do almost as well.

Appendix[1]

Johnny was walking through the woods on a lovely day. Suddenly a tiger sprang out of the underbrush and leaped at his throat.

It was at this point that Johnny composed his great essay on the folly of fighting tigers. Continuous warfare between men and tigers, he pointed out, serves no constructive purpose whatever, and only can lead, in time, to the destruction of one side or the other.

His essay emphasized the seamy aspect of this warfare. Leaving to others admiration for the big-game guns and the colorful hunting costumes, he dwelt on the blood, the muck, the fatigue, the tedium and the absence of modern conveniences in the jungle. With bitter satire he ridiculed the belligerent instincts of men and tigers, and the war hysteria whipped up by anti-tiger propaganda. His essay was, however, balanced and impartial, sometimes condemning the aggressive tendencies of tigers as well as those of men.

But if we are ever to hope for everlasting peace, Johnny went on, men must stop sowing suspicion of tigers. Many of the things said and written about tigers, he pointed out, are actually contrary to fact. He cited many amusing examples of prejudice and misinformation. He proposed a four-point solution:

Point One. A conference, alone in the woods, between the head man and the head tiger.

Point Two. A disarmament treaty to outlaw the newer weapons. Under this treaty either side could continue to use, for example, its bare claws or bare teeth. But firearms by either side would be prohibited. These weapons were too destructive, and gave an undue advantage to the side vicious enough to resort to them.

Point Three. Formation of a United Animals Association—excluding only Spanish animals—in which all future differences could be ironed out before they arose.

Point Four. A loan of 50,000,000,000 pounds of mixed vegetables a year from the men to the tigers. If the tigers' economic conditions could be improved, Johnny was convinced, they would change their carnivorous ideology and cease attacking live men.

The tiger was now upon him. But Johnny disdained to retaliate under any trumped-up excuse of "self-defense." He urged, instead, a new peace conference, and pointed out to the tiger that this was exactly the sort of judicable problem suitable for submission to the Assembly of the proposed United Animals Association.

Unfortunately, Johnny was not given time to put these thoughts into permanent form. He had barely completed the essay in his mind when the tiger's fangs closed on his throat.

That is why the senseless warfare between men and tigers continues.

Notes

CHAPTER ONE

1. See Max Eastman's chapter with that title in his *Reflections on the Failure of Socialism* (New York: Devin-Adair, 1955).
2. *The Philosophy of Civilization* (New York: Macmillan, 1957), p. 103.
3. *Five Types of Ethical Theory* (New York, Harcourt Brace, 1930), p. 285.
4. *Dreams of a Ghost Seer,* Part II, Chap. III (*Werke,* ed. E. Cassirer, Vol. II, p. 385). See also Karl R. Popper, *The Poverty of Historicism* (Boston: Beacon Press, 1957), pp. 55-58.
5. See Fritz Machlup, "The Inferiority Complex of the Social Sciences" in *On Freedom and Free Enterprise,* ed. Mary Sennholz (Princeton: Van Nostrand, 1956). Morris R. Cohen, *Reason and Nature* (New York: Harcourt Brace, 1931; Glencoe, Ill.: Free Press, 1953), p. 89. John Stuart Mill, "On the Logic of the Moral Sciences," *A System of Logic,* Vol. II, Book VI.

CHAPTER THREE

1. Hastings Rashdall, *The Theory of Good and Evil* (London: Oxford University Press, 1907), I, 53.
2. Jeremy Bentham, *An Introduction to the Principles of Morals and Legislation* (Oxford: Clarendon Press, 1823), p. 319n.

CHAPTER FOUR

1. Bentham's ethical theories are presented chiefly in *A Fragment on Government* (1776), *An Introduction to the Principles of Morals and Legislation* (printed in 1780 but not published until 1789), and the posthumous *Deontology,* edited from manuscripts by Bowring in 1834. For a full exposition and critique of Bentham's ethical writings, as well as a history of his reputation, see David Baumgardt, *Bentham and the Ethics of Today* (Princeton University Press, 1952).
2. In the posthumous *Deontology,* which Bowring claims to have "put together" from "disjointed fragments, written on small scraps of paper, on the spur of the moment, at times remote from one another, and delivered into my hands without order or arrangement of any sort" it is difficult to tell what is Bentham's from what is Bowring's.
3. *Morals and Legislation,* p. 2.
4. *Deontology,* II, 31.

5. Joseph A. Schumpeter, *History of Economic Analysis* (New York: Oxford University Press, 1954), p. 131 et al.

6. John Hospers has shown that the charge is unjust even as directed against the actual doctrines of Epicurus. See "Epicureanism," *Human Conduct* (Harcourt, Brace, 1961), pp. 49-59.

7. *Morals and Legislation*, p. 30.

8. *Deontology*, II, 82.

9. *Deontology*, II, 89.

10. *Deontology*, II, 16.

11. See Ludwig von Mises, *Human Action* (New Haven: Yale University Press, 1949), pp. 14-15, and *Theory and History* (Yale, 1957), pp. 12-13n. Also Ludwig Feuerbach, *Eudämonismus*, in "Sämmtliche Werke," ed. Bolin and Jodl (Stuttgart, 1907, *10*, 230-93. Further sources of confusion are pointed out by John Hospers in *Human Conduct*, esp. pp. 111-116. These include the confusion of "pleasure" in the sense of a *source* of pleasure, such as a pleasurable *sensation*, with pleasure in the sense of a pleasant state of consciousness. It is the opposite of the first only that can properly be described as "pain," whereas the true opposite of the second is *displeasure*. The failure to make this distinction was a major source of confusion in Bentham and Mill.

CHAPTER FIVE

1. John Locke, *Essay on Toleration*, Book II, Chap. XXI, sec. 40.

2. Hastings Rashdall, *The Theory of Good and Evil* (London: Oxford University Press, 1907), I, 15.

3. *Ibid.*, I, 31.

4. Quoted by Ludwig von Mises, *Epistemological Problems of Economics* (Princeton: Van Nostrand, 1960), p. 151. Mises' own footnote reference reads: "According to Fr. A. Schmid, quoted by Jodl, *Geschichte der Ethik* (2nd ed.), II, 661."

5. Bertrand Russell, *Philosophy* (New York: Norton, 1927), p. 230.

6. Bertrand Russell, *Human Society in Ethics and Politics* (New York: Simon and Schuster, 1955), pp. 128-130.

7. On "maximization" see Ludwig von Mises, *Human Action*, pp. 241-244. On the possibility of *ranking* satisfactions, but the impossibility of *measuring* increases or decreases in happiness or satisfaction, or comparing changes in the satisfaction of different people, see Murray N. Rothbard, *Man, Economy, and State* (Princeton: Van Nostrand, 1962), I, 14-17, and I, 436.

8. *Utilitarianism* (1863), Chap. II.

9. *Loc. cit.*

10. George Santayana, *Winds of Doctrine* (New York: Scribner's, 1913, 1926), p. 147.

11. *The Theory of Good and Evil*. See especially I, 7ff.

12. John Hospers (in *Human Conduct*, pp. 111-121) distinguishes between: "pleasure$_1$—in the sense of a pleasurable state of consciousness," and pleasure$_2$, "the pleasure derived from bodily *sensations*."

13. *Op. cit.*, I, 28.
14. *Ibid.*, I, 40.

CHAPTER SIX

1. Cf. Ludwig von Mises, *Human Action*, p. 143.
2. Cf. Ludwig von Mises, *Theory and History* (New Haven: Yale University Press, 1957), pp. 55-61.
3. *Ibid.*, p. 57.
4. *The Common Sense of Political Economy* (London: Macmillan, 1910), p. 154.
5. *Ibid.*, p. 158.
6. *Ibid.*, p. 166.
7. *Ibid.*, p. 166.
8. *Ibid.*, pp. 170-171.
9. E.g., Bertrand Russell, *passim*.
10. Cf. Ludwig von Mises, *Human Action*, p. 274.
11. Prince Kropotkin, *Ethics: Origin and Development* (New York: The Dial Press, 1924), pp. 30-31 and *passim*. Also, *Mutual Aid, A Factor of Evolution* (London: Heineman, 1915). Kropotkin's ethical ideas were based in large part on biological theories. As against Nietzsche (and in part Spencer) he contended that not the "struggle for existence" but Mutual Aid is "the predominant fact of nature," the prevailing practice within the species, and "the chief factor of progressive evolution."
12. The phrase "social cooperation," in this chapter and throughout the book, is of course to be interpreted only in its most comprehensive meaning. It is not intended to refer to "cooperation" between individuals or groups *against* other individuals or groups—as when we speak of cooperation with the Nazis, or the Communists, or the enemy. Nor is it intended to refer to that kind of compulsory "cooperation" that superiors sometimes insist on from subordinates—unless this is compatible with a comprehensive cooperation with the aims of society as a whole. Nor is it, for the same reason, intended to apply to cooperation with a mere temporary or local majority, when this is incompatible with a broader cooperation for the achievement of human aims.

CHAPTER SEVEN

1. The theme of the present author's *Economics in One Lesson* (New York, Harpers, 1946), is summed up on page 5 as follows: "From this aspect . . . the whole of economics can be reduced to a single lesson, and that lesson can be reduced to a single sentence. *The art of economics consists in looking not merely at the immediate but at the longer effects of any act or policy; it consists in tracing the consequences of that policy not merely for one group but for all groups.*" It is clear that this generalization may be widened to apply to conduct and policy in every field. As applied to ethics it might be stated thus: *Ethics must take into consideration not merely the immediate but the longer effects of any act or rule of action; it must consider the consequences of that act or rule of action not merely*

for the agent or any particular group but for everybody likely to be affected, presently or in the future, by that act or rule of action.

2. John Maynard Keynes, *Monetary Reform* (New York: Harcourt Brace, 1924), p. 88.

3. See, however, Ludwig von Mises, *Theory and History* (New Haven: Yale, 1957), pp. 32, 55, 57.

4. *Morals and Legislation,* Chap. IV, pp. 29-30.

5. *Deontology,* II, 87.

6. *Note-Books.*

7. *Morals and Legislation,* p. 9.

8. *Loc. cit.*

9. *Morals and Legislation,* p. 8.

10. *Discipline* is also, unfortunately, used in several senses. Thus one meaning given in the *Shorter Oxford English Dictionary* is: "7. Correction; chastisement; in religious use, the mortification of the flesh by penance; also, a beating, or the like." And in *Webster's New International Dictionary* one finds: "7. R.C.Ch.: self-inflicted and voluntary corporal punishment, specif., a penitential scourge." But one also finds, in, say, *Webster's Collegiate Dictionary:* "Training which corrects, molds, strengthens, or perfects." This last definition, I think, represents dominant present-day usage.

11. John Maynard Keynes, *Monetary Reform* (New York: Harcourt Brace, 1924), p. 88. As one who has written a whole book in criticism of Lord Keynes's economic theories (*The Failure of the "New Economics"* [Princeton: Van Nostrand, 1959]), I am bound to point out in justice that this dictum, which is the one for which Lord Keynes is most frequently criticized, was not without warrant in the particular context in which he used it. It is immediately followed by the sentence: "Economists set themselves too easy, too useless a task if in tempestuous seasons they can only tell us that when the storm is long past the ocean is flat again." This is a perfectly valid argument against the neglect of short-run problems and short-run considerations. But the whole trend of Keynes's thinking, as reflected not only in *Monetary Reform* but in his most famous work, *The General Theory of Employment, Interest and Money,* is to consider only short-run and neglect far more important long-run consequences of the policies he proposed.

12. I think I am warranted, from the whole context of his list, in assuming that Bentham is thinking of what value "the legislater" *ought* to attach to these seven "dimensions" rather than the value that any given person actually does or that "all" persons actually do attach to them.

13. See *infra,* Chap. 18.

14. Kurt Baier, *The Moral Point of View* (Ithaca, N.Y.: Cornell University Press, 1958), p. 314.

CHAPTER EIGHT

1. Some of Hume's doctrines were anticipated by Shaftesbury (1671-1713) and still more clearly by Hutcheson (1694-1747), the real author of

the "Benthamite" dictum that "that action is best which procures the greatest happiness for the greatest numbers." But Hume was the first to name the principle of "utility" and to make it the basis of his system. Though, unlike Bentham, he seldom gave an explicitly hedonistic implication to "utility," he wrote one paragraph, beginning: "The chief spring or actuating principle of the human mind is pleasure or pain" (*Treatise of Human Nature*, Book III, Part III, sec. 1), that may have been the inspiration of the famous opening paragraph of Bentham's *Morals and Legislation*.

2. It is even more ironic that contemporary philosophers who have rediscovered or adopted the principle, under the name of *rule-utilitarianism,* seem to be unaware of Hume's explicit statement of it. Thus John Hospers writes (in *Human Conduct* [1961], p. 318): "*Rule-utilitarianism* is a distinctively twentieth-century amendment of the utilitarianism of Bentham and Mill." And Richard B. Brandt (in *Ethical Theory* [1959], p. 396) writes: "This theory, a product of the last decade, is not a novel one. We find statements of it in J. S. Mill and John Austin in the nineteenth century; and indeed we find at least traces of it much earlier, in discussions of the nature and function of law by the early Greeks." But he does not mention Hume.

3. David Hume, *A Treatise of Human Nature* (1740), Book III, Part II, sec. 2.

4. *Ibid.*, Book III, Part II, sec. 6.

5. David Hume, "Of Political Society," *An Inquiry Concerning the Principles of Morals* (Library of Liberal Arts), Sec. IV, p. 40.

6. *Ibid.*, p. 95n.

7. *Ibid.*, "Some Further Considerations with Regard to Justice," Appendix III, p. 121.

8. *Ibid.*, p. 122.

9. Bentham plays an immense role in the history of ideas since the eighteenth century, and his numerous verbal coinages made permanent additions to the language without which modern discussion could hardly get along. His most famous coinage was *international*. But he also gave us *codification, maximize* and *minimize,* and many words of more limited usefulness, like *cognoscible* and *cognoscibility*. But he did an ill service to mankind when he invented *Utilitarian* and *Utilitarianism,* which simply pile up needless and inexcusable syllables.

Everything began, quietly enough, with Hume, with the English adjective *useful* and the English abstract noun *utility,* derived respectively from the Latin *utilis* and *utilitas* through the French *utilité*. Why not, then, simply *Utilist* as the adjective for the doctrine, and the noun for the writer holding the doctrine, and simply *Utilism,* or at most *Utilitism,* as the name of the doctrine? But no. Instead of beginning with the adjective, Bentham began with the longer abstract Latin noun made from the adjective. Then he added three syllables—*arian*—to the noun to turn it back into an adjective. Then he added another syllable—*ism*—to turn the inflated adjective made from an abstract noun back into another abstract noun. Now behold the eight-syllabled sesquipedalian monstrosity, *Util-*

tarianism. Then John Stuart Mill came along and nailed the thing down by making the name the title of his famous essay. So as the name for the doctrine as it has existed historically, posterity is stuck with the word. But perhaps from now on, when we are describing doctrines not identical with historic Utilitarianism, as developed by Bentham and Mill, but involving the doctrine that duty and virtue are means to an end rather than sufficient ends in themselves, we can use the word *Teleology* or *Teleotism* or the simpler words *utilic*, *Utilist* and *Utilitism*. Thus we save three syllables, and escape from some confusing and outmoded associations.

10. *Adam Smith's Moral and Political Philosophy*, ed. Herbert W. Schneider (New York: Hafner Publishing Co., 1948), p. 185.

11. *Ibid.*, p. 189.
12. *Ibid.*, p. 190.
13. *Ibid.*, p. 191.
14. *Ibid.*, p. 186.
15. *Loc. cit.*
16. *Ibid.*, p. 187.
17. *The Constitution of Liberty* (University of Chicago Press, 1960), p. 159.
18. E.g., Richard Brandt, *Ethical Theory* (Englewood Cliffs, N.J.: Prentice-Hall, 1959) and John Hospers, *Human Conduct* (New York: Harcourt, Brace & World, 1961). See the bibliographical references in the latter (pp. 342-343) to others.

CHAPTER NINE

1. See Roscoe Pound, *Law and Morals* (Chapel Hill: University of North Carolina Press, 1926), pp. 26, 85, and *passim*. This is an especially valuable discussion not only for its analysis but for its scholarship. It contains a bibliography of 24 pages.

2. *Ibid.*, p. 12.
3. *Ibid.*, pp. 6-7.
4. *Ibid.*, pp. 8-9.
5. Jeremy Bentham, *The Theory of Morals and Legislation*, pp. 17 and 18n.
6. Roscoe Pound, *Law and Morals*, pp. 40, 41, 43.
7. *Ibid.*, p. 85.
8. I find this quoted in Albert Schweitzer, *The Philosophy of Civilization* (New York: MacMillan, 1957), p. 157, but have been unable to trace it down, in these words, in either Bentham's *Morals and Legislation*, the *Deontology*, or *A Fragment on Government*.
9. Jellinek, *Die sozialethische Bedeutung von Recht, Unrecht und der Strafe*, 1878 (2nd ed., 1908), Chaps. 1 and 2. See also Pound, *Law and Morals*, p. 103.
10. Roscoe Pound, *Law and Morals*, p. 71.
11. *Ibid.*, p. 79.
12. (Chicago University Press, 1960), Chaps. 10, 11, and 12.
13. *Ibid.*, p. 154.

14. *Ibid.*, p. 158.
15. *Ibid.*, p. 208.
16. *Second Treatise of Civil Government*, Sec. 57.
17. *Ibid.*, Sec. 21. See also *infra*, Chap. 26.
18. *Le Lys rouge* (Paris, 1894), p. 117.
19. Pollock, *First Book of Jurisprudence*, (4th ed.), p. 47n.
20. Roscoe Pound, *Law and Morals*, pp. 68-69.
21. Ames, "Law and Morals," 22 Harv. Law Rev. 97, 112.
22. *Op. cit.*, p. 68.
23. But Bentham asks, in his *Principles of Morals and Legislation* (1780), p. 323: "Why should it not be made the duty of every man to save another from mischief, when it can be done without prejudicing himself, as well as to abstain from bringing it on to him?" And he adds in a footnote: "A woman's head-dress catches fire: water is at hand: a man, instead of assisting to quench the fire, looks on, and laughs at it. A drunken man, falling with his face downwards into a puddle, is in danger of suffocation: lifting his head a little on one side would save him: another man sees this and lets him lie. A quantity of gunpowder is scattered about a room: a man is going into it with a lighted candle: another, knowing this, lets him go in without warning. Who is there that in any of these cases would think punishment misapplied?"

CHAPTER TEN

1. David Hume, *Inquiry Concerning the Principles of Morals* (1752), Sec. IV (Library of Liberal Arts), p. 40.
2. *Second Treatise of Civil Government*, Sec. 57.
3. *Loc. cit.*
4. Paul Vinogradoff, *Common-Sense in Law* (New York: Henry Holt, 1914), pp. 46-47.
5. Roscoe Pound, *Law and Morals*, p. 97.

CHAPTER ELEVEN

1. *The Wisdom of Confucius*, ed. Miles Menander Dawson, LL.D. (Boston: International Pocket Library, 1932), pp. 57-58. See also *The Ethics of Confucius* by the same author (Putnam's).
2. *Letters on a Regicide Peace*, I, 1796.

CHAPTER TWELVE

1. Perhaps I should write Bentham-Bowring; for Bowring tells us, in a separate preface of three pages, that: "The materials out of which this volume has been put together are, for the most part, disjointed fragments, written on small scraps of paper, on the spur of the moment, at times remote from one another, and delivered into my hands without order or arrangement of any sort." The book, then, is probably at least a sort of collaboration; yet as the greater part of the reasoning and phrasing seem

to me to be authentically Bentham's, I think we are justified in referring the work to him if he were the sole author.

In this second volume, even more than in the first, it is instructive to notice that Bentham shies away a little from the name Utilitarianism that he himself coined to describe his doctrine in its original form. At several points he gives reasons for regarding the term as inadequate and too vague. Though he does not suggest a substitute name (except, occasionally, "the Greatest Happiness Principle"), I think he would have finally come to call his doctrine *Felicitism*.

CHAPTER THIRTEEN

1. *Data of Ethics,* Chap. XIII, pp. 268 and 270.
2. Jeremy Bentham, "The Constitutional Code," *Works* (1843), Part XVII, pp. 5b, 6a, written in 1821, 1827, first published in 1830. I am indebted for the quotation to David Baumgardt, *Bentham and the Ethics of Today* (Princeton University Press, 1952), p. 420. Bentham repeated the argument, in another part of "The Constitutional Code" (using as examples Adam and Eve instead of A and B) and in *The Book of Fallacies* (1824), pp. 393f.
3. This anticipates the emphasis that Hume and Adam Smith were later to put on Sympathy.
4. Moritz Schlick, *Problems of Ethics* (New York: Dover Publications, 1962), Chap. III, p. 77.
5. The word is formed by combining *ego* and *altru*ism. If the first two syllables seem to suggest the *egal* in *egalitarianism,* that is no disadvantage, for they imply *equal* consideration of self and others.
6. "*L'homme n'est ni ange ni bête, et le malheur veut que qui fait l'ange fait la bête.*"—Pascal's *Pensées,* with an English translation, brief notes and introduction by H. F. Stewart, D.D. (Pantheon Books, 1950), p. 90.

CHAPTER FOURTEEN

1. One of the most helpful methods of ethics (as of economics) is the use of simplifying imaginary constructions, or "models." Problems of the relation of the "individual" to "society" might in many cases be clarified by: (1) imagining the necessary prudential ethics of a Crusoe on a desert island; (2) imagining the ideal ethical relations (including the necessary extent of mutual cooperation and acceptance of mutual obligation) appropriate in an isolated society of two, in which for each individual "society" is merely *the other person;* and (3) finally, imagining the ethics most appropriate in a society of three or more.
2. *The Theory of the Moral Sentiments* (1759), Sect. III, Chap. III.
3. *Loc. cit.*
4. *Principles of Morals and Legislation,* p. 323.
5. A. C. Ewing, *Ethics* (New York: Macmillan, 1953), pp. 31-32.
6. J. Grote, *Treatise on the Moral Ideals,* Chap. VI, p. 76.

7. *The Theory of Morals* (Oxford University Press, 1928), p. 54.
8. This is a paraphrase of a rule suggested (but suspected by him of being a little too exact and niggardly) by A. C. Ewing, *Ethics*, p. 32.
9. *The Theory of the Moral Sentiments*, Sec. III, Chap. III.
10. A. C. Ewing, *Ethics*, p. 33.
11. Henry Hazlitt, *Economics in One Lesson* (New York: Harper & Bros., 1946), p. 114.
12. Ludwig von Mises, *Human Action* (New Haven: Yale University Press, 1949), p. 97.
13. *Ibid.*, p. 393.
14. Ludwig von Mises, *Theory and History* (Yale University Press, 1957), p. 210.
15. *The Theory of Good and Evil* (Oxford University Press, 1907), Chap. VII.
16. *The Right and the Good* (Oxford: Clarendon Press, 1930), p. 19.
17. *Theory of the Moral Sentiments*, Sec. III, Chap. III.
18. *Loc. cit.*
19. Some theologians argue that Jesus did not intend this advice for everybody. It was given explicitly only to a rich young man who aspired to be one of his disciples: "If thou wilt be perfect, go and sell that thou hast, and give to the poor, and thou shalt have treasure in heaven" (Matthew 19:21). Other theologians, while arguing that such advice was intended for all of Christ's followers, contend that it was based on the assumption that "the Kingdom of God is at hand" (Mark 1:15), and not on the assumption of a permanent life for man in this world.
20. It seems probable that we would make greater progress in the social sciences generally (including political science, economic policy, and jurisprudence as well as ethics) if we abandoned the preconception that every problem could be solved with precision according to some single and simple abstract principle, and resigned ourselves to recognizing that some social problems can be solved only within a certain "twilight" *zone*, only within certain upper and lower limits, certain maxima and minima. This may apply to such problems as the proper sphere and limits of state power, levels and types of taxation, the laws governing libel, obscenity, boycotts, and picketing, as well as the extent and limits of mutual obigation, aid, or cooperation.
21. Kurt Baier, *The Moral Point of View* (Cornell University Press, 1958), pp. 314-315.
22. *The Moral Point of View*, p. 191.
23. Stephen Toulmin, *An Examination of the Place of Reason in Ethics* (Cambridge University Press, 1950), p. 137.

CHAPTER FIFTEEN

1. See Ludwig von Mises, *Epistemological Problems of Economics* (Van Nostrand, 1960), pp. 31-33; *Theory and History* (Yale University Press, 1957), p. 12 and *passim*.
2. Quoted by Alban G. Widgery in his additional chapter to Henry

Sidgwick's *Outlines of the History of Ethics* (London: Macmillan, 1949), p. 327.

3. Rashdall actually coined this term to describe his own position. G. E. Moore also used it. See Rashdall's *Theory of Good and Evil* (Oxford University Press, 1907), I, Chap. VII, p. 217.

4. *Ibid.*, p. 219.

5. An elaboration of this distinction will be found in Chapter 18, pp. 171-175.

6. *Kant's Critique of Pratical Reason, and Other Works on the Theory of Ethics,* translated by T. K. Abbott (6th ed.; Longmans, Green, 1909), Book II, Chap. II, pp. 206-207.

7. *Ibid.*, p. 209.

8. *Ibid.*, p. 208.

9. *Readings in Ethical Theory,* selected and edited by Wilfred Sellars and John Hospers (New York: Appleton-Century-Crofts, 1952), p. 2. From a 1910 essay by Bertrand Russell.

10. Everyman's Edition, p. 44. The reader will notice the similarity of this reasoning to that of Hume regarding Justice.

11. *Principia Ethica* (Cambridge University Press, 1903, 1959), pp. 71-72.

12. E.g.: "Morality consists in the promotion of true human good, but a good of which pleasure is only an element."—Hastings Rashdall, *The Theory of Good and Evil* (Oxford University Press, 1907), I, 217. Such a conclusion is possible only when "pleasure" is conceived in the sensual or superficial sense of the word. The whole case of the Ideal Utilitarians rests on this narrow definition.

13. Charles L. Stevenson, *Ethics and Language* (Yale University Press, 1944), pp. 329-330.

14. *Ends and Means* (Harper, 1937), p. 10.

15. *Ibid.*, pp. 59-60.

16. *Ethics* (New York: Macmillan, 1953), p. 74.

17. *Human Conduct* (New York: Harcourt, Brace & World, 1961), p. 213.

18. *Ethics*, p. 74.

19. Cf. Murray N. Rothbard, *Man, Economy, and State*, p. 66.

CHAPTER SIXTEEN

1. *Human Society in Ethics and Politics* (Simon and Schuster, 1955), pp. 28-29.

2. From *Die Philosophen.*

3. *The Moral Point of View,* p. 228, and pp. 203-204. See also J. Urmson, "Saints and Heroes," in *Essays in Moral Philosophy,* ed. A. I. Melden (Seattle: University of Washington Press, 1958), pp. 198-216.

4. Cf. his *Foundations of Ethics* and *The Right and the Good.*

5. Essay, "The Elements of Ethics," in *Readings in Ethical Theory,* ed. Wilfrid Sellars and John Hospers (Appleton-Century-Crofts, 1952).

6. *Kant's Critique of Practical Reason, and Other Works on the Theory*

of Ethics, translated by T. K. Abbott (Longmans, Green, 1873, 1948 etc.), p. 31.

7. *Ibid.,* p. 38.
8. *Nicomachean Ethics,* IV, iii, 24 (Loeb Classical Library), p. 221.
9. This is a qualification to Kant's criterion of universalizability suggested by Kurt Baier. See *The Moral Point of View* (Cornell University Press, 1958), p. 202.
10. *Op. cit.,* p. 47.
11. A. C. Ewing, *Ethics* (Macmillan, 1953), p. 62.
12. Cf. Philip H. Wicksteed, "Business and the Economic Nexus," *The Common Sense of Political Economy* (Macmillan, 1910), Chap. V. And see *infra,* Chap 30.
13. F. H. Bradley, "Duty for Duty's Sake," *Ethical Studies* (2nd ed.; Oxford: Clarendon Press, 1927), Essay IV, pp. 156-159. Kant's Categorical Imperative and his doctrine of duty for duty's sake have been subjected to almost as much criticism (though usually more deferential in tone) as Bentham's brand of Utilitarianism. Instructive discussions, to which this chapter is indebted, can be found in Hastings Rashdall's *Theory of Good and Evil,* E. F. Carritt's *The Theory of Morals,* A. C. Ewing's *Ethics,* and John Hospers' *Human Conduct.* In addition there are the classic discussions by Hegel and Schopenhauer.

CHAPTER SEVENTEEN

1. All the subsequent quotations are from the chapter "Absolute and Relative Ethics" in Spencer's *Data of Ethics.*
2. *An Inquiry Concerning the Principles of Morals* [1752] (Library of Liberal Arts), p. 18.
3. E.g., F. H. Bradley, *Appearance and Reality.*
4. A friendly critic has objected that this cannot apply to *all* our desires but only to all our *good* desires—for half the people, for instance, might desire the annihilation of all the rest. I think the suggested amendment superfluous, however; first, because a perfect world would be occupied only by perfect people, who would by definition have only good desires; and secondly, because *all* our desires could not be satisfied unless they were *all* compatible with each other.
5. "Saints and Heroes," in *Essays in Moral Philosophy,* ed. A. I. Melden (Seattle: University of Washington Press, 1958), pp. 215-216. I wish to express my indebtedness to Urmson's entire essay.

CHAPTER EIGHTEEN

1. Cf. Ludwig von Mises, *Human Action* (1949), *The Ultimate Foundation of Economic Science* (1962), etc.
2. He was not the first, but he was the most influential exponent of this view.
3. As do J. K. Galbraith, for example, in *The Affluent Society,* and untold numbers of utopian and socialist writers.

4. George Santayana, *Reason in Science*, Vol. V in *The Life of Reason* (New York: Charles Scribner's Sons, 1905), pp. 216-217.

5. Cf. Ludwig von Mises, *The Ultimate Foundation of Economic Science* (Princeton, N.J.: Van Nostrand, 1962).

6. E.g., in the economic realm, an automobile that a salesman uses both to make his calls and for pleasure trips on his days off.

7. *The Value of Money* (New York: Macmillan, 1917, 1936), pp. 25-26. The two paragraphs preceding the quotation are also in the main a summary from the same source. See also the same author's *Social Value* (Boston: Houghton Mifflin, 1911). While my own direct indebtedness is chiefly to the concept of "social value" as embodied in Anderson's writing, he in turn acknowledges heavy indebtedness for it to C. H. Cooley and to John Bates Clark.

8. Karl R. Popper, *The Logic of Scientific Discovery* (London: Hutchinson, 1959), *passim*.

9. *The Place of Reason in Ethics* (Cambridge University Press, 1950), p. 115 and p. 117.

10. Cf. *General Theory of Value* (Longmans, Green. 1926; Harvard University Press, 1950), in which Perry refers to value as a "relational predicate": "We have thus been led to define value as the peculiar relation between any interest and its object; or that special character of an object which consists in the fact that interest is taken in it" Sec. 52.

11. Cf. Eugen von Böhm-Bawerk, *Capital and Interest* (South Holland, Ill.: Libertarian Press, 1959), Vol. II, *Positive Theory of Capital*, pp. 159-160.

12. David Hume, *Natural History of Religion*, 1755, Sec. xiii.

13. Cf. Benjamin M. Anderson, Jr., *The Value of Money* (1917, 1936), p. 5.

14. Anyway, for practical purposes, and for "molar" physics, whatever may be true of atomic or microscopic physics.

15. From the assumption that all but the "marginal" consumer would, if forced, be willing to pay a little more for an object than the actual market price at any time, the economist Alfred Marshall deduced his famous doctrine of "consumers' surplus." The doctrine, however, confronts serious difficulties. It might be valid for any commodity or service considered in isolation, but it can hardly be valid for all commodities and services considered together. A consumer who spends his whole income for his total purchases of goods and services has no net (psychic) "consumer's surplus" left over, for there is nothing he *could* have paid in addition for any one good without being forced to forego some other. Of course both consumers *and* producers, both buyers *and* sellers, reap a net psychological advantage, or "psychic income" from the whole cooperative process of specialized production followed by exchange. But there is no meaningful way in which this gain can be quantitatively measured.

16. Cf. Hastings Rashdall, "The Hedonistic Calculus" and "The Commensurability of All Values," Chaps. I and II in *The Theory of Good and Evil*, II.

17. Sometimes we can come pretty close. Thus a man before attending

an auction may decide in advance that he will bid up to $500 for a given painting but no more. This means that he values the painting at *only slightly more than* $500, perhaps only $1 or $2 more! If he valued it at *exactly* $500, of course, it would be a matter of complete indifference to him whether he got the painting at that price or not.

Of course the market *prices* of goods are "social" valuations (though constantly fluctuating in relation to each other) and do bear exact quantitative relations to each other (as expressed in money); but these valuations and relations are never exactly the same as those in the mind of any specific individual.

18. Cf., for example, Ludwig von Mises, *Human Action,* and Murray N. Rothbard, *Man, Economy, and State.*

19. For an example of the difficulties into which an honest and conscientious writer can get when he tries to discuss and compare "pleasures" in accordance with the vague and vacillating common usage of the term, see Hastings Rashdall, *The Theory of Good and Evil,* especially the two leading chapters of Volume II: "The Hedonistic Calculus" and "The Commensurability of All Values." Rashdall avoids the vulgar error of antihedonists who insist on identifying the word "pleasure" with purely physical, animal, carnal, or sensual pleasures, but gets bogged down in confusion by failing to define "pleasure" formally as any desired state of consciousness and "displeasure" as any undesired state of consciousness.

CHAPTER NINETEEN

1. *The Right and the Good* (Oxford University Press, 1930), p. 29.
2. Henry Sidgwick, *The Methods of Ethics,* p. 85.
3. *Loc. cit.*
4. *Loc. cit.*
5. An excellent one is to be found, for example, in Chap. IV of Rashdall's *Theory of Good and Evil,* all the more effective because patient and conciliatory in tone.
6. A whole literature has grown around this alleged "problem." I shall content myself here with referring the reader only to Santayana's refutation of G. E. Moore and the early Bertrand Russell in *Winds of Doctrine* (Scribner's, 1913), pp. 138-154.
7. *The Methods of Ethics* (1874).
8. *Ibid.,* p. xi.
9. *Ibid.,* pp. 435-436.
10. *Loc. cit.*
11. I have taken over this phrase from Sidgwick because it seems to me a very useful one. We should be careful, however, not to interpret the term "common sense" here as necessarily implying *good* sense, as it usually does in English usage, but rather as referring to the sense of appropriateness that most of us hold in common—the existing moral *consensus.* I should be tempted, in fact, to call this Consensus Morality had not the term used by Sidgwick become so well established.
12. *Loc. cit.*

NOTES TO PAGES 181-206

13. Cf. Hastings Rashdall, *The Theory of Good and Evil*, p. 89.
14. Cf. F. A. Hayek, *The Constitution of Liberty*, p. 157.
15. "Philosophische Abhandlungen," *Werke* (1832), I, pp. 399-400. The translation is from F. H. Bradley's *Ethical Studies*, p. 173.
16. For a more detailed examination of the Morality of Common Sense see Henry Sidgwick, *The Methods of Ethics*, particularly Book III, Chap. XI.
17. *The Methods of Ethics*, p. 356.

CHAPTER TWENTY

1. F. A. Hayek, *The Constitution of Liberty*, pp. 83-84.
2. Henry Sidgwick, *The Methods of Ethics* (1874), p. 425. It is only fair to add that Sidgwick goes on to point out some of the practical difficulties that follow from any direct effort to "take into account all the effects of our actions, on all the sentient beings who may be affected by them."
3. Hastings Rashdall, *The Theory of Good and Evil*, II, 1. Of Rashdall, too, it must in fairness be said that he was so far aware of the problems here under discussion that he devoted a special chapter to "Vocation"—one of the few ethical writers to do so. Yet many utilitarian moralists and others do try to apply directly the kind of sweeping criteria I have just quoted.
4. *Selected Letters of Albert Jay Nock*, collected and edited by Francis J. Nock (Caxton, 1962).
5. See John Hospers' discussion of "The Principle of Relevant Specificity," *Human Conduct* (New York: Harcourt, Brace & World, 1961), pp. 320-322.
6. Hastings Rashdall, who endorses the statement, attributes it to Sir John Seeley. *The Theory of Good and Evil*, II, 113.
7. Paul Janet, as quoted by Hastings Rashdall, *The Theory of Good and Evil*, II, 136.
8. I again refer the reader to J. O. Urmson's fascinating essay, "Saints and Heroes," in A. I. Melden's *Essays in Moral Philosophy* (Seattle: University of Washington Press, 1958).
9. E.g., Hastings Rashdall, *The Theory of Good and Evil*, II. 135.

CHAPTER TWENTY ONE

1. Shakespeare, *A Winter's Tale*, Act IV, scene 4, line 90.
2. Paul Vinogradoff, *Common-Sense in Law* (Home University Library), p. 244. I am not competent to prescribe a satisfactory selective bibliography on the enormous literature, pro and con, on Natural Law. But no reference should omit the classic discussion by Sir Henry Maine in his chapter, "The Modern History of the Law of Nature" in *Ancient Law* (1861). A selective bibliography (which, surprisingly, omits Maine) can be found in Morris Cohen's *Reason and Nature* (1931), pp. 401-402.

CHAPTER TWENTY-TWO

1. *An Introduction to the Principles of Morals and Legislation,* p. 9.
2. *Ibid.,* p. 8n.
3. Cf. Ludwig von Mises, *Socialism,* pp. 404-408.
4. W. E. H. Lecky, *History of European Morals* (1869), II, 107-112.
5. *Ibid.,* II, 113-137.
6. *The Varieties of Religious Experience* (Mentor, 1958), p. 280.
7. *Ibid.,* p. 217.
8. *Ibid.,* p. 244. James gives the source of his quotation as: Bougaud: *Hist. de la bienheureuse Marguerite Marie,* Paris, 1894, pp. 265, 171.
9. *Ibid.,* pp. 234-236.
10. *Ibid.,* pp. 280-284.
11. Cf. *Democracy and Leadership, Rousseau and Romanticism, The New Laokoön.*
12. The phrase calls attention to a curious gap in the English language. The verb *restrain* has the noun-form *restraint,* but the verb *refrain* (though similar in origin through the Latin and the French) has no noun-form *refraint.* For the noun we are obliged to fall back, confusingly, on *restraint* (which implies coercion by *others*) or, unsymmetrically, on *self-restraint* or *abstention.* The noun *refraint* would serve a useful purpose.
13. *Rhetoric.*
14. Bertrand Russell, *Portraits From Memory,* pp. 87, 89. The passage is quoted in an article by Milton Hindus, "The Achievement of Irving Babbitt," in *The University Bookman,* August 1961.
15. *The Principles of Psychology* (New York: Henry Holt, 1890), chapter on "Habit."
16. *Socialism,* pp. 452-453.

CHAPTER TWENTY-THREE

1. Plato, *The Republic,* Book I, 338-C .
2. *Ibid.,* Book I, 351-D and 352-B.
3. Cf. Ludwig von Mises, *Socialism,* p. 353.
4. K. R. Popper, *The Open Society and Its Enemies* (London: Routledge, 1945), II, 194.
5. Marx and Engels must have been troubled by this question, for they attempted an answer in the *Communist Manifesto.* "Just as in former days part of the nobility went over to the bourgeoisie, so now part of the bourgeoisie goes over to the proletariat. Especially does this happen in the case of some of the bourgeoisie ideologists, who have achieved a theoretical understanding of the historical movement as a whole."

This answer may have been flattering to the vanity of Marx and Engels, but it was made at the cost of consistency. For if a few rare spirits can escape from their "class" ideology, why not others?

6. See the article by H. B. Mayo on "The Marxist Theory of Morals," in the *Encyclopedia of Morals* (Philosophical Library, 1956).

7. (New York: Duell, Sloan and Pearce, 1959).
8. 1948.
9. 1953.
10. Cf., for example, Morris R. Cohen and Ernest Nagel, *An Introduction to Logic and Scientific Method* (New York: Harcourt, Brace, 1934), pp. 382-388.
11. Chap. 18, pp. 211-215.
12. (Doubleday, Doran, 1943.)
13. *The Summing Up*, p. 293.
14. *Ibid.*, p. 294.
15. *Ibid.*, 294-295.
16. *Ibid.*, p. 307.
17. *Ibid.*, p. 309.
18. (Oxford University Press, 1936.) Specifically in Chap. VI, "Critique of Ethics and Theology," from which my quotations are taken.
19. *Language, Truth and Logic*, pp. 150, 158.
20. *Ibid.*, pp. 161, 163.
21. (New York: Henry Holt, 1944.) See especially the section on "Meaning and Verifiability" in Chap. III, and Chap. VIII on "Values, Norms and Science."
22. (London: Hutchinson, 1934, 1959; New York: Science Editions, 1961).
23. *Ibid.* All the above quotations are from the section, "Meaning and Verifiability," pp. 55-56.
24. *The Logic of Scientific Discovery*, p. 51.
25. Shakespeare, *King Henry IV*, Part I, Act V, scene 1. I do not really wish to accuse the logical positivists of immorality (or of sharing the motives of Falstaff) but merely of errors in reasoning. Other moral philosophers have learnt much from them, and have been forced to clarify their own ideas in attempting to answer them. All this has made for progress. I admire the lucidity of Ayer's style and the keen edges of his thinking. But his understandable wish for precision and simplification, with which I am sympathetic, led him into the fallacies of oversimplification, of reduction, and of either-or.
26. Pages 47-48.
27. (Yale University Press, 1944, 1960.)
28. (Glencoe, Ill.: The Free Press, 1955.)
29. I refer the reader who wishes to find a summary of the present state of the question to the admirable chapter on "Noncognitivism" in Richard B. Brandt's *Ethical Theory* (Englewood Cliffs, N.J.: Prentice-Hall, 1959). There the reader will also find a full list of authors, books, and articles pro and con on the controversy.
30. (London: Macmillan, 1954). This essay had appeared earlier, however, in *Horizon*, vol. xx, no. 117, 1949.
31. *Ibid.*, p. 238.
32. *Ibid.*, p. 248.
33. *Ibid.*, p. 248.
34. *Ibid.*, p. 249.
35. *Ibid.*, p. 249.

36. (Yale University Press, 1944.)
37. *Ibid.*, p. 79.
38. *Ibid.*, p. 332.
39. *Ibid.*, p. 332.
40. *Ibid.*, p. 336.
41. This methodological problem is too large to go into extensively here. For a fuller discussion I refer the reader to Ludwig von Mises in *Human Action* (Yale University Press, 1949), Chap. II, "The Epistomological Problems of the Sciences of Human Action," pp. 30-71.
42. *Ethics* (Baltimore: Penguin Books, 1954), p. 98.
43. Karl R. Popper, "What Can Logic Do for Philosophy?" (Aristotelian Society, Supplementary Vol. XXII, 1948), p. 143.
44. (Cambridge University Press.)
45. (New York: Harcourt, Brace.)
46. *Ibid.*, p. 125.
47. *Loc. cit.*
48. I was about to apologize for this as a neologism, when I thought to look it up in the *Oxford English Dictionary* and found it listed as an "obsolete" word dating from 1566. But the meaning was given as "expressive of value," which is the exact sense that I intend. The existing adjective *evaluative* suggests an explicit weighing or appraisal, and not also values that are merely implied or taken for granted.
49. The word "emotive" *does* inevitably suggest emotional, and most of the positivists who use it must be perfectly conscious of this. Though they affect to be using "emotive" as a purely descriptive term, it is not difficult to detect the derision that lurks behind it. "Emotive," in brief, is itself an emotive word, designed to influence the reader's attitude. If the word *valuative* were substituted for it, two-thirds of the apparent force of the emotivists' argument would be lost. They would then be reduced to the contention that all value-words, even in ethics, are illegitimate or "meaningless."

CHAPTER TWENTY-FOUR

1. *Justice According to Law* (Yale University Press, 1951), p. 2.
2. *The Principles of Ethics* (Appleton, 1898), II, 46.
3. *Ibid.*, II, 46-47.
4. *Loc. cit.*
5. *The Methods of Ethics* (Macmillan, 1877), pp. 246-247.
6. *Freedom and the Law* (Princeton: Van Nostrand, 1961), p. 15.
7. *Theory of Good and Evil* (Oxford University Press, 1907), I p. 223.
8. *Loc. cit.*
9. *Ibid.*, p. 224.
10. *Ibid.*, p. 233.
11. *Ibid.*, p. 240.
12. *The Principles of Ethics*, II, 58-59.
13. Students of economics will recognize that the method I am here adopting is analogous to the use of the Robinson Crusoe, or isolated indi-

vidual, hypothesis in economics. This simplifying hypothesis has frequently been ridiculed by Karl Marx and others, but seems to me essential, not only for teaching the basic principles of economics to beginners, but for the clarification of the sophisticated economist's own thinking on many problems. One of the reasons so much nonsense is written in modern economics is precisely because this method is neglected. Ethics would be in a more advanced stage than it is if moral philosophers had begun more often with the postulate of the isolated individual and then moved, for many problems, to the postulate of a society of two, three, etc. before jumping immediately to The Great Society. I believe this applies also in the other social sciences, such as economics and sociology. The careful use of this method would have avoided some of the major fallacies, for example, of so-called "aggregative" or "macroeconomics."

14. Ludwig von Mises, *Theory and History* (Yale University Press, 1957), pp. 54, 56, 61.
15. *Principles of Ethics*, II, 58-59.
16. *Principles of Ethics*, II, 60, 61.
17. § 62.
18. David Hume, *An Inquiry Concerning the Principles of Morals*, p. 122.
19. *Utilitarianism* (many editions), Chap. V (pp. 73-75).

CHAPTER TWENTY-FIVE

1. The literature on this is of course enormous. The interested reader may consult, for example, *Free and Unequal*, by Roger J. Williams, director of the Biochemical Institute of the University of Texas (University of Texas Press, 1953).
2. See Roger J. Williams, *op. cit.*
3. *Critique of the Social Democratic Program of Gotha.* (Letter to Bracke, May 5, 1875.)
4. This will be developed further in the chapters on the ethics of capitalism and of socialism.

CHAPTER TWENTY-SIX

1. Cf., for example, M. Cranston, *Freedom: A New Analysis* (New York, 1953) and Mortimer Adler, *The Idea of Freedom: A Dialectical Examination of the Conceptions of Freedom* (New York, 1958).
2. (University of Chicago Press, 1960.)
3. Bruno Leoni, *Freedom and the Law* (Princeton: Van Nostrand, 1961), p. 3.
4. For a very full list of references see F. A. Hayek, *The Constitution of Liberty*.
5. *Ibid.*, p. 19.
6. See Leoni, p. 4, and Hayek, *passim*.

CHAPTER TWENTY-SEVEN

1. *Dernières pensées* (Paris: Flammarion, 1913), p. 244. See also Ludwig von Mises, *Theory and History* (New Haven: Yale University Press, 1957), pp. 73-83; the same author's *The Ultimate Foundation of Economic Science* (Princeton: Van Nostrand, 1962), *passim*, and Moritz Schlick, *Problems of Ethics* (Prentice-Hall, 1939; Dover, 1962), Chapter VII.
2. Cf. Ludwig von Mises, *Theory and History*, pp. 77-78.
3. (New York: Harper & Bros, 1953), p. 75.
4. *Ibid.*, p. 77.
5. (Indianapolis: Bobbs-Merrill, 1953), pp. 120-121, 122, 124-125.
6. An excellent analysis of some of them only touched on here will be found in John Hospers, *Human Conduct* (New York: Harcourt, Brace & World, 1961), "Determinism and Free Will," Sec. 24, pp. 502-521.
7. The example is from Rashdall, *The Theory of Good and Evil*, II, 330.
8. Thomas Middleton.
9. Robert Herrick.
10. Shakespeare.
11. Mary Wortley Montague.
12. The Hitopadeśa, (c. 500) intro.
13. Martin Luther. Cf. H. L. Mencken, *A Dictionary of Quotations*.
14. Ludwig von Mises, *Theory and History*, p. 178.
15. *Ethics* (1677).
16. F. A. Hayek, *The Constitution of Liberty*, p. 73.
17. Henry Sidgwick, *The Methods of Ethics*, p. 53.
18. *Ibid.*, pp. 61-62.
19. David Hume, *Treatise of Human Nature* (1740), Book II, Part III, sec. II.
20. Thomas Hobbes, *Leviathan* (1651), Part 2, Chap. 21. (Many editions.)
21. Pp. 282, 278. Ayer's whole discussion of the subject is excellent. I am especially happy to call attention to it after my harsh criticisms of his moral positivism. Other excellent discussions of the determinism and free-will controversy, which arrive at a similar conclusion, can be found in Moritz Schlick, "When Is a Man Responsible?" *Problems of Ethics* (1931, English translation, 1939), Chap. VII; F. A. Hayek, *The Constitution of Liberty*, pp. 71-78; and John Hospers, "Moral Responsibility and Free Will," *Human Conduct*, Chap. 10. (The latter book contains an extensive bibliography on the subject.)

CHAPTER TWENTY-EIGHT

1. Paul Vinogradoff, *Common-Sense in Law* (Home University Library; New York: Henry Holt), pp. 61-62. I am here indebted to Vinogradoff's whole discussion of the nature of rights in positive law.
2. *Ibid.*, pp. 68-69.
3. *Ibid.*, p. 70.

4. A scholarly and illuminating history can be found in Leo Strauss, *Natural Right and History* (University of Chicago Press, 1953).
5. See George Santayana, *Dominations and Powers* (New York: Scribner's, 1951), p. 58n.
6. *The Theory of Good and Evil* (Oxford University Press, 1907), I, 227.
7. Justice Oliver Wendell Holmes, Jr., *The Common Law* (1881).
8. *Two Treatises of Civil Government* (1689), Book II, Chap. 2, sec. 6.
9. *Schenck v. United States*, 249 U.S. 52.

CHAPTER TWENTY-NINE

1. For the defense of this noun, see footnote 12, Chap. 22.
2. *The Free and Prosperous Commonwealth* (Princeton: Van Nostrand, 1962), p. 144.
3. *Essays, Literary, Moral, and Political* (1740), p. 198.
4. Professor Manley O. Hudson in *International Legislation*, I, xxxvi.
5. Appendix.
6. J. L. Brierly, *The Law of Nations* (5th ed.; Oxford: Clarendon Press, 1955), p. 316.
7. *Loc. cit.*
8. *International Law* (8th ed.), p. 65.
9. *Ibid.*, p. 322.
10. *The Law of Nations*, p. 317.
11. *R. v. Dudley and Stephens* (1884), 14 Q.B.D. 273.
12. *U.S. v. Holmes*, 1 Wallace Junior, I.
13. *Ibid.*, pp. 317-318.
14. He can find plenty of them in Bertrand Russell—and some excellent answers by Sydney Hook: cf. Hook's review of Russell's "Has Man A Future?" in the *New York Times* of Jan. 14, 1962.
15. "The Duty of the State," *Social Statics* (1850). Many editions.
16. *Little Essays Drawn from the Writings of George Santayana* (1920), p. 164.
17. Wilhelm Röpke, *International Order and Economic Integration* (original German ed., 1954; English translation, Dordrecht, Holland: D. Reidel Publishing Co., 1959), pp. 28-30.

CHAPTER THIRTY

1. Cf. *Human Action*, by Ludwig von Mises, a book on the principles of economics.
2. *Human Conduct*, by John Hospers, a book on the principles of ethics.
3. Cf. Ludwig von Mises, *Human Action, Socialism*, etc.
4. *The Wealth of Nations* (1776), Book I, Chap. 1. The phrase had already been used and the theme stated in a passage in Mandeville's *Fable of the Bees*, pt. ii (1729), dial. vi., p. 335.

The reader will notice a certain overlap and duplication in the quotations in this chapter from Adam Smith and Philip Wicksteed and those from the same authors in Chap. 6, "Social Cooperation." But I think these duplications are justified in the interests of emphasis and of saving the reader the inconvenience of turning back to that chapter to remind himself of the few sentences repeated here.

5. *Ibid.* (Cannon ed.), p. 12.
6. Ludwig von Mises, *Socialism: An Economic and Sociological Analysis* (English translation; Macmillan, 1932), p. 299.
7. Ludwig von Mises, *Human Action,* p. 144.
8. *The Wealth of Nations* (Cannon ed.) p. 18.
9. Ludwig von Mises, *Human Action,* p. 143.
10. *The Wealth of Nations* (Cannon ed.) I, 16.
11. *Ibid.,* I, 421.
12. See Murray N. Rothbard, *Man, Economy, and State* (Princeton: Van Nostrand; 1962), I, 440, footnote. See also *Ibid.,* I, 85-86.
13. Philip H. Wicksteed, *The Common Sense of Political Economy* (London: Macmillan; 1910), p. 158. The whole chapter on "Business and the Economic Nexus," from which this and later quotations are drawn, is a brilliant exposition that deserves the most careful study.
14. *Ibid.,* pp. 171, 172.
15. *Ibid.,* p. 180.
16. *Ibid.,* p. 174.
17. Cf. Israel M. Kirzner, *The Economic Point of View* (Princeton: Van Nostrand; 1960), p. 66.
18. See Professor Lionel Robbins's Introduction to the 1933 edition of Wicksteed's *Common Sense of Political Economy*: "Before Wicksteed wrote, it was still possible for intelligent men to give countenance to the belief that the whole structure of Economics depends upon the assumption of a world of economic men, each actuated by egocentric or hedonistic motives. . . . Wicksteed shattered this misconception once for all" (p. xxi).
19. Ludwig von Mises, *Human Action,* pp. 144-147.
20. Ludwig von Mises, *Socialism: An Economic and Sociological Analysis* (English translation; Macmillan, 1932), p. 432.
21. *Ibid.,* pp. 397-398.
22. E.g., Eugen von Böhm-Bawerk, *Karl Marx and the Close of His System* (1896); Ludwig von Mises, *Socialism* (1936) and *Human Action* (1949). Practically the whole of modern economic literature, in its acceptance of the marginal productivity theory of wages, is in effect a refutation of the Marxist exploitation theory, and a substantial acceptance of the conclusions of J. B. Clark.
23. *The Distribution of Wealth,* pp. 3-4.
24. *Ibid.,* p. 9.
25. The older economic textbooks (i.e., of the late nineteenth and early twentieth centuries) commonly devoted separate chapters or even separate sections to "Production" and "Distribution" respectively. This was misleading. Wealth is not first "produced" and then "distributed." This is a socialist misconception. If a farmer raises a crop by himself he gets the whole crop because he has produced it. It is not "distributed" to him;

it is merely not taken away from him. If he sells it on the market, he gets the monetary market value of the crop in exchange just as a worker gets the monetary market value for his labor.

26. For a fuller description of this process, see Henry Hazlitt, "How the Price System Works," *Economics In One Lesson* (Harper, 1947; MacFadden, 1962), Chap. XVI.

27. See especially the works of Ludwig von Mises, including his more popular *Planning for Freedom* (South Holland, Ill.: Libertarian Press; 1952), particularly the chapter, "Middle-of-the-Road Policy Leads to Socialism." I may refer interested readers also to my own *Economics In One Lesson*.

28. "Business and the Economic Nexus," *The Common Sense of Political Economy*, Chap. V, pp. 183-185.

29. *Man, Economy, and State* (Princeton: Van Nostrand; 1962), pp. 85-86.

30. "The Moral Element in Free Enterprise," in *The Spiritual and Moral Significance of Free Enterprise* (New York: National Association of Manufacturers), pp. 26-27.

31. *The Common Sense of Political Economy*, p. 154.

32. "The Moral Element in Free Enterprise," in *The Spiritual and Moral Significance of Free Enterprise* (New York: National Association of Manufacturers), pp. 32-33.

33. *Much Ado About Nothing*, Act IV, scene 1, line 219.

CHAPTER THIRTY-ONE

1. See especially Ludwig von Mises' essay "Middle-of-the-Road Policy Leads to Socialism," in his *Planning for Freedom* (South Holland, Ill.: Libertarian Press; 1952). Also the essay by Gustav Cassel, *From Protectionism Through Planned Economy to Dictatorship* (London: Cobden-Sanderson; 1934).

2. For scores of specific examples, see Henry Hazlitt, *Economics in One Lesson*.

3. *Looking Backward: 2000-1887*, Chap. 28. (Many editions.)

4. Ludwig von Mises, *Socialism*, p. 451.

5. And see Eugen Böhm-Bawerk, *Karl Marx and the Close of His System*; J. B. Clark, *The Distribution of Wealth*; and Ludwig von Mises, *Socialism*.

6. See the tremendously garrulous argument for this ideal in Bernard Shaw's *The Intelligent Woman's Guide to Socialism and Capitalism* (New York: Brentano's, 1928).

7. See Henry Hazlitt, *Time Will Run Back* (New Rochelle, N.Y.:Arlington House), pp. 88-93.

8. I related this history in an article in *Newsweek*, June 27, 1949.

9. The top U.S. rate until 1963.

10. See especially the chapters on Taxation and Social Security in F. A. Hayek's *The Constitution of Liberty*.

11. L. Garvin, *A Modern Introduction to Ethics*, p. 460.

12. F. A. Hayek, "The Moral Element in Free Enterprise," essay in symposium *The Spiritual and Moral Significance of Free Enterprise* (New York: National Association of Manufacturers, 1962), p. 31.
13. *Ibid.*, pp. 31-32.
14. Quoted by Max Eastman, *Reflections on the Failure of Socialism* (New York: Devon Adair, 1955), p. 83.
15. For that economic and war record, see Ludwig von Mises, *Omnipotent Government* (Yale University Press, 1944).
16. "The Religion of Immoralism," *Reflections on the Failure of Socialism* (New York: Devin-Adair, 1955), Chap. 7, p. 83.
17. *Ibid.*, p. 85.
18. *Ibid.*, p. 87.
19. *Ibid.*, pp. 87-88.
20. *Ibid.*, p. 88.

CHAPTER THIRTY-TWO

1. Fyodor Dostoyevsky, *The Brothers Karamazov* (1880), Part III, Book XI, Chap. VIII.
2. George Santayana, *Dominations and Powers* (1951), p. 156.
3. *Three Essays on Religion* (1874).
4. "The Dark Side of Religion," in *The Faith of a Liberal* (New York: Henry Holt, 1946), pp. 348-352.
5. *Ethics* (London, T. C. & E. C. Jack), pp. 92-93.
6. Exodus 21:24-25.
7. Matthew 5:38-39, 43-44.
8. John 13:34.
9. Exodus 21:2, 12, 17; 22:18.
10. We must remember, however, that the injunction to "love thy neighbor as thyself" occurs in the Old Testament (Leviticus 19:18) as well as in the New (Luke 10:27).
11. Mark 1:15.
12. The quotation is from Ludwig von Mises, *Socialism* (New York, Macmillan), pp. 413-414, but Mises is merely summarizing the views of such theologians as Harnack, Giessen, and Troeltsch.
13. George Santayana, *Dominations and Powers* (New York, Scribner's 1951), p. 157.
14. *Outlines of the History of Ethics* (1886, etc. 1949), pp. 141-142.
15. I refer the reader to many passages in the works of Charles Darwin, Herbert Spencer, E. P. Thompson, G. J. Romanes, Prince Kropotkin, C. Lloyd Morgan, W. L. Lindsay, E. L. Thorndike, Albert Schweitzer, R. M. Yerkes, H. Eliot Howard, W. C. Allee, F. Alverdes, Wolfgang Köhler, Konrad C. Lorenz, Julian Huxley, W. T. Hornaday, David Katz, C. R. Carpenter, William Morton Wheeler, and Joy Adamson. I believe that morality has at least a partly innate and instinctual basis, and that this has developed because of its survival value, both for the individual and for the species. I consider this, however, primarily a biological rather

than an ethical problem, and I shall not discuss it here. See the forthcoming book by Frances Kanes Hazlitt, *The Morality of Animals*.

16. This conclusion, I am happy to find, does not differ essentially from that of Stephen Toulmin: "Where there is a good moral reason for choosing one course of action rather than another, morality is not to be contradicted by religion. Ethics provides the *reasons* for choosing the 'right' course: religion helps us to put our *hearts* into it." *An Examination of the Place of Reason in Ethics* (Cambridge University Press, 1950), p. 219. The case is even more compactly summed up by William James: "Whether a God exist, or whether no God exist, in yon blue heaven above us bent, we form at any rate an ethical republic here below." "The Moral Philosopher and the Moral Life" (1891), in *Pragmatism and Other Essays* (Washington Square Press Book, 1963), p. 223.

CHAPTER THIRTY THREE

1. I venture to suggest this neologism not only to save syllables but to avoid ambiguity. It is confusing as well as cumbrous to refer to ethical systems as "teleological" or, simply, as "teleology." For *teleology* (from Greek *teleos*, an end, plus *logia*, science, doctrine, or theory of) traditionally means the belief that natural phenomena are determined not only by mechanical causes but by an over-all design or purpose in nature. The belief that *our* human acts or rules of action *ought to be* judged by the end or ends that they tend to bring about has no necessary connection with a "teleological" doctrine about Nature or the universe. *Teleotism*, *Teleotist*, *teleotic*, etc. are formed by dropping the *logy* and inserting a *t* for euphony.

2. Arthur O. Lovejoy, *The Thirteen Pragmatisms and Other Essays* (John Hopkins Press).

3. This is not only because it has developed some bad connotations, as a result of early confusions, or because it now covers such a wide variety of views, but because it has been from the beginning too cumbersome and unwieldy. (See note 9, Chap. 8). *Rule-utilitism* is a manageable description of a system, but *rule-ultilitarianism* is intolerable. *Utilitarian* and *Utilitarianism* are themselves, after all, deliberately invented words, and still comparative upstarts with only about a century and a half behind them. It is not presumptuous to suggest that they could usefully be shortened.

4. Except by Ludwig von Mises, who, unfortunately, has not written any work on ethics but has confined his remarks on ethical problems to brief passages in his great works on economics. Other writers, of whom Herbert Spencer was a notable example, explicitly and by that name recognized the need for "social cooperation," but did so only *parenthetically*, without giving it the central or *a* central place in their system.

APPENDIX

1. This was first published as a signed editorial of mine in *The Saturday Evening Post* of June 10, 1950. It is reprinted by special permission.

Index

(Numbers in parenthesis refer to footnotes)

Abbott, T. K., 372-373 (6,6)
Absolute, 152
Absolutism vs. relativism, 150-158
  See also Relativism
Accident, duties of, 190
Acton, Lord, 267
Act-utilitarianism, 60
Adamson, Joy, 385 (15)
Ad hoc utilitism, 60-61
Adler, Mortimer, 380 (1)
Agnostics, 353
Aid, mutual, 42, 365 (11)
Aims, focal, 135
Allee, W. C., 385 (15)
Altruism, 92-107, 313-315; and egoism, 92-107, 313-315, 356; and mutualism, 102-107, 313-315, 356
Alverdes, F., 385 (15)
Ames, 69, 369 (21)
Amos, 3
Anderson, Benjamin M., Jr., 166, 374 (7,13)
Angel, "neither a. nor beast," 106
Angels, society of, 157, 330
Animals, morality of, 303, 352, 386 (15)
Antoninus, Marcus Aurelius, 343
Appeasement, 299-300
A priori cognition, 250, 252-256
Aquinas, Thomas, 2, 63, 352
Aristocracy, moral, 200-201
Aristotle, 2, 3, 144, 218, 281, 344, 352, 358
Arnold, Matthew, 90
Asceticism, 46-48, 84, 207-222, 357
Athleticism, 47, 220
Atomic bomb. See Nuclear bomb
Attitude, 103, 291-293
Augustine, 2, 352

Austin, John, 81, 367 (2)
"Axioms," moral, 186
Ayer, Alfred J., 235-241, 277, 378 (25), 381 (21)

Babbitt, Irving, 217-218, 377 (14)
Bacon, Francis, 205
Baier, Kurt, ix, 123-127, 141-142, 366 (14), 371 (21), 373 (9)
Baumgardt, David, 363 (1), 370 (2)
Bebel, F. A., 388
Beccaria, C. B., 19
Becket, Thomas à, 345
Beethoven, 164
Beggar-my-neighbor policies, 289
Behaviorists, 169
Bell, Alexander Graham, 328
Bellamy, Edward, 327-329, 338
Beneficence, and benevolence, 86.
  See also Benevolence
Benevolence, 50, 176, 187, 250-251; and altruism, 92; and beneficence, 86; and Golden Rule, 250-251; negative efficient, 50, 84, 85; positive efficient, 50, 84, 86; and prudence, 81-91, 176; "self-evidence" of, 187
Bentham, Jeremy, viii, 4, 10, 12, 15-20, 28, 44-51, 53, 60, 63, 64, 66, 69, 81-91, 92, 95, 97-99, 111, 113, 175, 179, 181, 207-208, 218, 252-255, 285, 363 (2,1,2), 364 (11), 366 (12), 367 (1,2,9), 368 (9,5,8), 369 (23,1), 370 (1,2), 373 (13)
Berkeley, Bishop, 169
"Best thing to do, what is the?" 245-247
Better and worse (vs. absolutism and perfection), 154, 300

387

"Better this than that," 161
Bible, 91, 177, 347-351
Bill of Rights, 280-281
Blackstone, Sir William, 63
Body and mind, 270-272
Böhm-Bawerk, Eugen von, 170, 374 (11), 383 (22), 384 (5)
Borgias, 205
Bowring, Sir John, 19, 363 (1,2), 369 (1)
Bradford, Governor, 333-334
Bradley, F. H., 58-59, 148-149, 373 (13,3), 376 (15)
Brandt, Richard B., ix, 367 (2), 368 (18), 378 (29)
"Bourgeois," 301-302
Breathing spell, moral, 157
Brierly, J. L., 294-295, 382 (6)
Briffault, Robert, 177
Broad, C. D., 3
Buddha, 3, 200
Burke, Edmund, 80, 281, 307
Butler, Bishop, 26, 97-101, 120
Butler, Samuel, 45
Byron, Lord, 45

Caesar, 206
Calvin, 344
Cancer, 247
Capitalism: ethics of, 301-324; justice of, 315-318
Carlyle, Thomas, 17, 257
Carnap, Rudolph, 236-237
Carpenter, C. R., 385 (15)
Carritt, E. F., 113, 373 (13)
Cary, Joyce, 199
Cassel, Gustav, 384 (1)
Cassirer, E., 363 (4)
Categorical Imperative, 117, 143 ff., 358, 373 (13)
Catholics, Roman, 19, 212, 345
Causation vs. compulsion, 275-278
Celibacy, 144, 145-146, 202
Ceremony, 76-77
Chastity, 84-85, 177
Cheek, "turn the other," 177, 348, 350

Cheerfulness, 221
"Chemism," man as a, 232
Christ, Jesus, 3, 200, 343, 344, 348, 349, 350-351, 371 (19)
Christianity, 234, 252, 344-353 *passim*
Cicero, 205, 281
Circle, legislation as a, 66; law as a, 69
Circumstances, and duty, 118, 188-202 *passim*
Clark, John Bates, 315-316, 374 (7), 383 (22), 384 (5)
Class theory of ethics, 227-230
Coercion, 266-267. See also Freedom; Liberty
Cohen, Morris R., 236-237, 344-346, 349, 363 (5), 376 (2), 378 (10)
Collisions, avoidance of, 73-74, 356
Combination of labor. See Division of labor
Commandment, new, 9, 349-350
Commandments, Ten, 8, 59, 349
Commensurability: of ends, 131; of values, 173-174
Common Law, 9, 64-66, 181-183
Common-sense, morality of, 111-112, 354, 375 (11), 376 (16). See also Consensus morality.
Communism(ists), 288, 292, 295-296, 298-300, 301-324 *passim*, 325-341
Communist Manifesto, 302, 377 (5)
Comparability: of ends, 131; of values, 173-174
Comparative costs, 290
Competition, 303, 305-308, 315. See also Capitalism
Compulsion vs. causation, 275-278
Comte, Auguste, 237
Conflict: of duties, 148-149; between individuals, 356; of moral rules, 177-178
Confucius, 2, 3, 76-77, 200, 224, 251, 369 (1)
Conrad, Joseph, 218
Conscience, 7, 118, 176
Consciousness, 270-272
Consensus morality, 375 (11). See

INDEX

also Common-sense, morality of
Consequences: and acts, 177; consideration of, 176-177
Consideration: for others, 75; right to, 284-285
Consistency, as end in itself, 109
Constitution, U.S., 280-281
"Consumers' surplus," 374 (15)
Contract: moral, 186; social, 186
Cooley, C. H., 374 (7)
Cooperation, international, 288-300
Cooperation, social, 9, 13, 34-42, 174, 255, 288 ff., 303, 309-315, 356, 357, 359, 365 (12), *passim;* as heart of morality, 356, 359
Cooperatism, 103, 358-360
Copyright, 291
Costs: comparative, 290; as concept of "sacrifice," 114-116; opportunity c., 114. *See also* Sacrifice
Courage, 82, 296
Cranston, M., 380 (1)
Critique of Practical Reason, 3
Crusoe, Robinson, method, 379 (13)

Darwin, Charles, 200, 385 (15)
Dawson, Miles M., 369 (1)
Decalogue, 8
Democritus, 2, 344
Deontology, 16, 19, 81-91, 99, 363 (1,2,4)
Description vs. prescription, 11
Desire(s): 12, 21-24, 373 (4); and satisfaction, 32-33
Determinism, 269-278; activistic, 274; and fatalism, 272-274. *See also* Free Will
Dewey, John, 129-130
Discipline, 218, 366 (10)
Disciplinism, 47
Division of labor, 37-40, 303, 308-309, 356
"Do-gooders," 202
Dostoyevsky, Fyodor, 385 (1)
Dreiser, Theodore, 232-233
Dumont, Pierre E. L., 81
Duty (duties): of accident, 190; of circumstances, 118, 190-191; 188-202 *passim;* of consanguinity, 191; devotion to, 182; division and specialization of, 201; for duty's sake, 139-149, 358, 373 (13); as end-in-itself, 116; and interest, 99; limits of, 106-107, 117-121, 157, 190-193; to one's own talents, 198-200; prima facie, 142, 176, 184; of proximity, 191; of relation, 190-191; vs. risk, 110-112; and self-interest, 99; to speak the truth, 201; universal vs. special, 188-190; universality vs. particularity, 196-197; of vocation, 188-202; *passim*

Eastman, Max, 340-341, 363 (1), 385 (14)
Economics: and cooperation, 312; and Epicureanism, 312; and ethics, 175, 301, 312, 355, 365 (1); marginal utility, 175
Edison, Thomas, 216
Edwards, Paul, 239
Egaltruism, 102, 103
Egoism: 40, 91, 92-107, 313-315; and altruism, 92-107, 313-315, 356; ambiguous conception of, 125; defined, 101; ethical, 92; as inconsiderateness, 101; and mutualism, 102-107, 313-315, 356; psychological, 92
Emerson, R. W., 76, 129
Emotivism(ists), 241-246, 357-358, 379 (49)
Empiricism, 242-243
Employer, and employed, 314
Ends: intermediate, 138; kingdom of, 147; and means, 24-25, 128-138; as "pluralistic," 128; ultimate, 130, 134-135
Engels, Friedrich, 230, 338, 340, 377 (5)
Engineering, and ethics, 5, 245-246
Epicureans (ism), 2, 17, 131-132, 312, 364 (6)

Epicurus, 3, 17, 358, 359, 364 (6)
Equal distribution of income, 120, 317, 329-337
Equality (and Inequality), 251-255, 262-265; of income, 317, 329-337
Ethical skepticism, 223-247. *See also* Skepticism
Ethics: "absolute necessity of," 170; autonomous, 351, 358; and economics, 301, 355, 365 (1); everyday, 77; heroic, 77; and jurisprudence, 65-66; and language, 241-245; and law, 62-69; is not linguistics, 243-245; as a means, 34; and wisdom, 52
Ethics and Language, 241-243
Etiquette. *See* Manners
Eudaemonism, 21, 31-34, 358-359; psychological, 21, 31-34
"Every one to count for one," 251-255
Ewing, A. C., ix, 136, 137, 146, 176, 370 (5), 371 (8,10), 373 (11,13)
Exception, treating oneself as, 197, 355
Exceptions to rules, 72
"Exploitation" of worker, 315-316
"Eye for eye," 9, 177, 348

Falstaff, 237
Fatalism, 272-274
Felicitism, 359, 370 (1)
Feuerbach, Ludwig, 364 (11)
Fichte, 3, 137
Fitzgerald, Scott, 76
Flagellantism, 47
Focal aims, 135
Ford, Henry, 69, 216
Foreign aid, 191
Formalism, Kantian, 56
Four Freedoms, 282
France, Anatole, 66-68
Free Enterprise. *See* Capitalism
Free Markets, 303-305. *See also* Capitalism; Property
Free trade, 288-291

Free Will, 269-278. *See also* Determinism; Freedom
Freedom(s), 67, 70, 250, 266-268, 321-324; and coercion, 266-267; "four," 282; and justice, 248-249; and socialism, 325-326
Freud, Sigmund, 231
Freudian ethic, 231
Future vs. present, 18, 48-49

Galbraith, J. K., 373 (3)
Games, theory of, 308
Garvin, L., 384 (11)
General rules: how framed, 104-106; need for, 53-61, 354. *See also* Rules, need for general
Genius, duties of, 199
God, and ethics, 8, 63, 176, 342-353, 386 (16), *passim*
Goethe vs. golf, 175
Golden Rule, 105, 158, 224, 250-251; and converse G. R., 105-106; negative G. R., 158, 224, 251
Golf: and ethical theory, 3-4; and Goethe, 175
Good: as "indefinable," 178, 244; as "intuitively" known, 178; not a property, 171; "the," 130; as "unanalyzable," 244
Governments, role of, 289-291
Gray, Lord and Lady, 118-119
Greeks, 367 (2)
Grote, J., 116, 370 (6)
Grotius, 63
"Growth," as the moral end, 130

Hague Tribunal, 292
Hall, W. E., 294
Hamilton, Alexander, 339
Hammurabi, code of, 8
Happiness, 16, 20, 21-34; greatest, of the greatest number, 18, 19; Greatest H. Principle, 16, 45, 66, 90, 370 (1); and justice, 256-257; morality as art of maximizing, 16; vs. pleasure, 20; pursuit of, 281; and satisfac-

INDEX

tion, 21-34; and social cooperation, 356; and well-being, 24-26, 134, 358
Hare, R. M., 243
Harmony of interests, 313-314, 358
Haydn, J., 307
Hayek, F. A., ix, 59, 67, 192-193, 266, 322-323, 376 (14,1), 380 (4,6), 381 (16,21), 384 (10), 385 (12)
Hazlitt, Frances Kanes, 386 (15)
Hazlitt, Henry, 365 (1), 366 (11), 371 (11), 384 (26,7)
Hedonistic calculus, 18, 83, 173, 374 (16), 375 (19)
Hedonism, 15-20, 92, 358; ethical, 16, 31; psychological, 16, 21, 22, 31-32
Hegel, G. W. F., 3, 184-185, 373 (13)
Heraclitus, 2
Heroes, heroic ethics, 157, 372 (3), 373 (5)
Herrick, Robert, 381 (9)
Hindus, Milton, 377 (14)
Hobbes, Thomas, 92, 109, 180, 276-277, 381 (20)
Hobhouse, L. T., 177
Holmes, O. W., Justice, 285, 286, 382 (7)
Honor, "a word," 237
Hook, Sydney, 382 (14)
Hornaday, W. T., 385 (15)
Hospers, John, ix, 136-137, 364 (6,11,12), 367 (2), 368 (18), 372 (9,5), 373 (13), 376 (5), 381 (6,20), 382 (2)
Howard, H. Eliot, 385 (15)
Howard, John, 343
Hudson, Manley O., 382 (4)
Human rights: and property rights, 280; Universal Declaration of, 283. *See also* Rights
Hume, David, viii, 3, 53-60, 68, 70, 91, 150, 152, 170, 223, 259-260, 276, 290-291, 312, 317, 339, 366 (1), 367 (1,2,3,5,9), 369 (1), 370 (3), 372 (10), 374 (12), 380 (18), 381 (19)

Hutcheson, Francis, 19, 366 (1)
Huxley, Aldous, 135, 159
Huxley, Julian S., 271, 385 (15)
Huxley, Thomas H., 68
"Hysteron-proteron," 21, 26

Ideal law, 63, 206
"Ideal" Utilitarianism, 117, 130, 134, 372 (12)
Idealist, 240
Impartial observer (spectator), 104-106, 113, 118, 255
Imaginary constructions, 370 (1)
Imperative, Categorical, 117, 143 ff., 358, 373 (13)
Importance, judgments of, 237
Inconsiderateness, as essence of egoism, 101
Independence, Declaration of, 281
Individual, and society, 35, 104-106, 108-110, 313, 355
Inquisition, 344
Intentions, 90
Interdependence, of individuals, 313
International Court, 292-293
International ethics, 288-300
International law, 288-300, *passim*
"Inter-subjective" verification, 169
Intuition(ism) (ists), 9, 63, 176-187, 250, 253-255; and common-sense, 176-187
"Invisible hand," 310
Is and *ought*, 11, 13
Isaiah, 3

Jacobi, Friedrich H., 22
James, William, 212-217, 219, 220, 377 (8), 386 (16)
Janet, Paul, 376 (7)
Jefferson, Thomas, 281
Jellinek, 66, 368 (9)
Jenner, Edward, 200
Jerome, St., 211
Jesus, 3, 200, 343, 344, 348, 349, 350-351, 371 (19)
Jews, 8, 349

"Johnny and the Tiger," 293, 361-362
Jonson, Ben, 307
"Judge not," 350
Jurisdprudence, and ethics, 65-66, 355
Justice, 13, 53-54, 67-68, 103, 206, 248-261; Aquinas on, 352; and capitalism, 306, 316-318, 324; and competition, 306; and equality, 262-265, 335-337; and freedom, 248; and happiness, 256-257; as interest of the stronger, 224-225, 230; as a means, 259-261; *pereat mundus,* 313; "self-evidence" of, 187; "social," 317; and social cooperation, 257; and utility, 260-261
Justinian, Institutes of, 248

Kant, Immanuel, 3, 4, 62, 74, 113, 116, 117, 129-132, 137, 139-149, *passim;* 146, 150, 157, 196-197, 248-249, 358, 372 (6,6), 373 (9,13)
Kantian system, 56, 234, 313
Karamazov brothers, 342, 385 (1)
Katz, David, 385 (15)
Keynes, John Maynard, 49, 133, 366 (2,11)
Khrushchev, 340
Kindness, 75, 91, 104, 106, 350, 360
Kinsey, Alfred C., 231-232
Kirzner, Israel M., 383 (17)
"Know thyself," 202
Köhler, Wolfgang, 385 (15)
Kropotkin, Prince, 42, 365 (11), 385 (15)
Krutch, Joseph Wood, 271-272

Labor, division and combination of, 37-40, 303, 308-309, 356
Laissez faire, 289-290
Language, 9, 72, 178-180, 241-245, 355
Language of Morals, The, 243

Lao-tse, 3
LaPiere, Richard, 231
Law: and equality, 263-265; and ethics, 62-69, 180, 312, 355; and logic, 285; as a "minimum ethics," 66; Mosaic, 177; positive, 206; purpose of, 70; requirements of, 67. *See also* Common Law
Law of nature, 63, 203-206, 286, 376 (2). *See also* Natural Law
Lecky, W. E. H., 177, 208-212, 377 (4)
Legal rights. *See* Rights
Legislation and moral philosophy, 66
Leibnitz, 307
Lenin, 340-341
Leonardo da Vinci, 307
Leoni, Bruno, 251, 380 (3,6)
Leveler, and Socrates, 334-335
Liberalism, 288-291
Liberty, 249, 250, 266-268; and "Four Freedoms," 282-283; "highest political end," 267; and morality, 268. *See also* Freedom
Lincoln, Abraham, 200
Lindbergh, Charles, 200
Lindsay, W. L., 385 (15)
Linguistics, ethics is not, 243-245
Locke, John, 3, 21, 67, 70, 177, 281, 286, 364 (1)
Logical positivism(ists). *See* Positivism(ists)
Long-run, 13, 33, 44-52, 124-127, 354; vs. short-run, 44-52, 124-127; "we are all dead," 44, 49
Lorenz, Konrad C., 385 (15)
Love, 91, 350, 360; Christian, 104, 106; "one another," 9, 106, 349-350, 360; "thy neighbor," 348, 385 (10); "your enemies," 9, 348, 350
Lovejoy, Arthur O., 386 (2)
"Loving-kindness," 234
Luther, Martin, 381 (13)
Lying: when justified, 137; Kant's

INDEX

argument against, 143; universalizability, 145

Machlup, Fritz, 363 (5)
Maine, Sir Henry, 256, 376 (2)
Mandeville, Bernard de, 133, 225-226, 382 (4)
Mankind, and your neighbor, 193 ff.
Manners, 9; and morals, 75-80, 180, 355; as minor morals, 75; as petty sacrifices, 76
Manu, sacred law of, 8
Marginal: satisfaction, 175; utility, 175
Market economy. See Capitalism
Marshall, Alfred, 374 (15)
Martin, C. E., 231
Marx, Karl, 90, 194, 225, 227-230, 340, 377 (5), 380 (13)
Marxism. See Communism; Socialism
Mary, Queen, 344
Master morality, 144, 226-227
Materialism, 162, 228, 233, 269-273
Maugham, W. Somerset, 199, 233-235
Maxima and minima, 121, 371 (20)
"Maximization" ("maximize"), 27, 171, 174, 364 (7), passim
Mayo, H. B., 377 (6)
Meaning of Meaning, The, 244
Means: and ends, 24-25, 128-138, 221-222; exaltation of, over end, 247; "means-ends," 128; mistaking for ends, 139-143, 221-222, 247; treating others as, 146-147
Medicine, and ethics, 5
Melden, A. I., 372 (3), 373 (5), 376 (8)
Merit, as basis of distribution, 337
"Meta-ethical" problems, 244
Methods of ethics, 10, 243; empirical, 243; experimental, 243; imaginary constructions, 370 (1); not those of physics, 243; but of praxeology, 243; Robinson Crusoe, 379-380 (13); statistical, 243
Michelangelo, 164, 307
Middle-of-the-road systems, 325-326, 384 (27,1)
Middleton, Thomas, 381 (8)
"Might is right," 224-226, 230
Mill, James, 81
Mill, John Stuart, viii, ix, 28-29, 60, 81, 129, 132-133, 157, 175, 200, 202-206, 342-344, 353, 363 (5), 364 (11), 367 (2,9), 368 (9)
Mind and matter, 270-272
Minima and maxima, 121, 371 (20)
Minimum ethics, 66, 157
Mises, Ludwig von, viii-ix, 37, 114-115, 220-221, 290, 312-314, 320, 364 (11,4,7), 365 (1,2,10), 366 (3), 371 (12,14,1), 373 (1), 374 (5), 375 (18), 377 (3,3), 379 (41), 380 (14), 381 (1,2,14), 382 (1,3), 383 (6,7,9,19,20,22), 384 (27,1,4,5), 385 (15,12), 386 (4)
"Money-making," 216-217
Montague, Mary Wortley, 381 (11)
Moore, G. E., viii, 22, 29, 116, 132-133, 171, 244, 372 (3), 375 (6)
Moral aristocracy, 200-201
Moral contract, 186
Moral futurism, 230
Moral law, 165
Moral rights, 282, 286-287. See also Rights
Moral rules, how framed, 104-106. See also General Rules; Rules
Moral sense, 9, 176
Moral tradition, 164-165, 354, passim. See also Common-sense ethics; Morality
Morality: as art of maximizing happiness, 16, 83-84, 90; is autonomous, 351, 358; of common-sense, 111-112, 179-185, 354; as conduct each desires others to observe toward himself, 223; of each vs. of all, 156; as *the* end, 222; everyday, 77, 359; and lib-

erty, 268; and manners, 75-80; as a means, 133-135, 148, 157, 221-222, 354; necessity of, 170; objective and subjective, 162-165; and religion, 342-353, 386 (16); and self-interest, 123-127; sexual, 84, 177; as social, 164-165, 354; tradition of, 164-165
Morals and manners, 75-80
Morgan, C. Lloyd, 385 (15)
Moses, 4, 8, 9, 177, 344, 349
Mozart, 307
Mutual aid, 42
Mutualism, 92, 102-107, 313-315, 356, 359; defined, 102; as name for system, 103. *See also* Altruism; Egoism
Mystery of morals, 7-10

Nagel, Ernest, 378 (10)
Napoleon, 296
Natural Law, 62-64, 203-206, 376 (2). *See also* Law of Nature
Natural rights, 281-282
New Testament, 348-349, 350-351, 385 (10)
Newton, Sir Isaac, 307
Nietzsche, 3, 4, 73, 144, 181, 225, 226-227, 229, 365 (11)
Nihilism, 9. *See also* Skepticism
Nock, Albert Jay, 194, 376 (4)
Noncognitivism, 378 (29)
Non-conformists, 73
Nonfeasance, 111
Nonresistance, 297-300
Nowell-Smith, P. H., 243
Nuclear bomb, 288, 295-296, 298

Objectivism, 162-175 *passim*
Obligation: limits of, 106-107, 117-121, 190-193; and rights, 279-280, 282
Obligatory and optional ethics, 156-158
Occam's razor, 187
Ogden, C. K., 244
Ought and *is*, 11, 13
Old Testament, 52, 344, 347-350, 385 (10)

Optimum (optimific) act, 181
Optional and obligatory ethics, 156-158
"Oversoul," social, 165

Pacifism, 299-300
Pain, 20
Panphysicalism, 162, 233, 270-272
Paradox of virtues, 296
"Parliament of man," 292
Pascal, Blaise, 34, 118, 370 (6)
Pasteur, Louis, 200
Patent protection, 291
Paul (the Apostle), 3, 41
Perfect man. *See* Perfection
Perfect world. *See* Perfection
Perfection, 151-154, 300, 373 (4)
Perry, R. B., 170, 374 (10)
"Persuasive definitions," 242
Physics, 243, 374 (14)
"Pig philosophy," 17
Pilgrim Fathers, 332-334
Ping-pong vs. poetry, 28
Plato, 2, 3, 29, 281, 377 (1)
Pleasure, 15-20; abstract vs. specific, 30; as desired or valued state of consciousness, 174, 364 (11,12), 375 (18); "quality of," 28-31; "quantity of," 28-31; sensual, 32, 372 (12), 375 (19)
Poetry vs. pushpin, 28, 175
Poincaré, Henri, 269
Policemen, and soldiers, 297
Politeness. *See* Manners
Pollock, Sir Frederick, 369 (19)
Pomeroy, W. B., 231
Popper, Karl R., 236-237, 243, 363 (4), 374 (8), 377 (4), 379 (43)
Poor and rich, 317, 350
Positivism (ists), 162, 169, 181, 235-241, 247, 358, 378 (25)
Postal Union, 291, 293
Pound, Roscoe, ix, 69, 74, 248, 368 (1,6,9,10), 369 (20,5)
Poverty, 214-217
Practicality of ethics, 4
"Pragmatisms, Thirteen," 359

INDEX

Praxeology, 159
Precedent, importance of, 61, 64, 181-184
Predicament, our human, 127, 148
Predictability of actions, 60, 71; of law, 64
Preference, 173-174
Prescription vs. description, 11
Present vs. future, 18, 48-49
Priestley, Joseph, 19
Prima facie duties, 142, 176, 184, 286
Prima facie rights, 283-287
Principia Ethica, 244
Principle: acting on, 126; adherence to, 287
Private enterprise. See Capitalism
Private property. See Property (private)
"Profit," in morality, 115
Profit-and-loss system, 302. See also Capitalism
Property (private), 54, 249, 280, 303-305; in means of production, 304-305; wife as, 349. See also Rights; Capitalism
Protectionism, 289
Proverbs, Book of, 52
Proximity, principle of, 196
Prudence, 13, 50, 81-91, 176, 187; and benevolence, 50, 81-91, 92, 176; and egoism, 92; extra-regarding, 50, 84-85; "self-evidence" of, 187; self-regarding, 50, 84
Pseudo-rights, 282-283. See also Rights
"Public" opinion, 164
Punishment: preventive vs. retributive, 275; and responsibility, 277
Pushpin vs. poetry, 28, 175
Pythagoras, 2

Quixote, Don, 119

Rand, Ayn, 92
Rashdall, Hastings, 21, 31-32, 116, 117, 130, 134, 251-255, 284-285, 346-347, 363 (1), 364 (2), 372 (3,12), 373 (13), 374 (16), 375 (19,5), 376 (13,3,6,7,9), 381 (7)
Rate of interest, 50
Rationalism, 3
Reason: law of, 206; and natural law, 206
Red Cross, 291
"Refrain, will to," 217-218
Refraint, 377 (12)
Relativism, 66; vs. absolutism, 150-158. See also Absolutism
Relevance, moral, 196-197; judgments of, 237
Religion: and morality, 342-353, 358, 386 (16); utility of, 343-344
"Religion of Immoralism," 340-341
Renunciation, 220-221. See also Sacrifice; Self-Sacrifice
Reputation, 164-165
Responsibility: and determinism, 275-277; and freedom, 277; limits of, 106-107, 117-121, 190-193
Reversibility, of moral rules, 145
Ricardo, David, 290, 312
Rich and poor, 317, 350
Richards, I. A., 244
Rights, 279-287; Bill of, 280-281; to consideration, 284-285; imply obligations, 279-280
Risk and duty, 110-112
Robbins, Lionel, 383 (18)
Rockefeller, John D., 69
Röpke, Wilhelm, 299-300, 382 (17)
Romanes, G. J., 385 (15)
Romans, 205-206, 281
Roosevelt, Franklin D., 282-283
Ross, Sir David, ix, 118, 142, 176, 184, 286
Rothbard, Murray N., 320-321, 364 (7), 372 (19), 375 (18), 383 (12)
Rousseau, Jean-Jacques, 186, 194, 218
Rule, Golden. See Golden Rule
Rules: "follow unless," 184; how

framed, 104-106, 354; need for general, 53-61; 193. *See also* General rules

Rule-utilitarianism, 60, 367 (2), 386 (3)

Rule-utilitism, 60, 136, 354, 386 (3)

Russell, Bertrand, 22-24, 29, 132, 140, 142, 171, 181, 218, 306, 364 (5,6), 365 (9), 375 (6), 377 (14), 382 (14)

Russia, Soviet, 304, 318, 330, 337, 339, 340. *See also* Communism

Sabbath, 8, 349

Sacrifice(s), 90, 97, 108-127, 220-221, 357; as a "cost," 114-115; as instrumental, 116; as a means, 116; petty, 76; possible rule for, 113; prudential, 114; for sacrifice's sake, 113, 220-221; as temporary, 220

Saint(s), 34, 37, 157, 200, 208-212, 311, 321, 322, 345, 372 (3), 373 (5)

Saint-Simon, Comte de, 237

Samaritan, Good, 69, 121, 190

Sanctity, of moral rules, 96

Santayana, George, 22, 29-30, 161, 342, 351, 364 (10), 374 (4), 375 (6), 382 (5,16), 385 (2,13)

Sartre, Jean-Paul, 232

Satisfaction, 21-34, *passim;* and desire, 32-33; "maximization" of, 171; and happiness, 21-34, 354

Savage tribes, morality of, 72

Schiller, J. C. F. von, 140

Schlick, Moritz, 101, 237, 370 (4), 381 (21)

Schopenhauer, A., 2, 3, 373 (13)

Schumpeter, Joseph, 17, 364 (5)

Schweitzer, Albert, 3, 200, 368 (8), 385 (15)

Science: as determinist, 269; ethics as a, 4-6; as instrumental, 162, 247; as means, 162, 247; presupposes causation, 277; and value, 159-162, 247; "value-free," 160

Seeley, Sir John, 376 (6)

Self-defense, right of, 293-300

Self-denial, 221. *See also* Asceticism; Discipline; Sacrifice; Self-sacrifice

Self-discipline, 47, 217-221, 357

"Self-evidence," of moral maxims, 186-187

Self-interest, 40, 51, 123-127

Selfishness, 40, 101, 310-311, 315; as inconsiderateness, 101

Self-love, 97-100; and love of our neighbor, 100

"Self-perfection," 153-154, 222. *See also* Perfection

Self-preservation, "right of," 294-295

Self-restraint, 217-221, 357

Self-sacrifice, 77, 108-127, 220-221; as instrumental, 116; as a means, 116; not good in itself, 220-221; as temporary, 220. *See also* Sacrifice

Self-subordination, 117

Self-torture, cult of, 207-212

Sellars, Wilfred, 372 (9,5)

Sennholz, Mary, 363 (5)

Sensuality, 17-18

Servetus, 344

Sexual morality, 84, 177, 181, 219, 231-232

Shaftesbury, Lord, 3, 366 (1)

Shakespeare, 30, 164, 251, 307, 323, 376 (1), 381 (10)

Shared judgments vs. solipsistic, 168 ff.

Shaw, Bernard, 199, 384 (6)

Short-run. *See* Long-run

Sidgwick, Henry, viii, 150, 176, 179-180, 187, 250, 254, 352, 371-372 (2), 375 (2,11), 376 (16,2), 381 (17)

Skepticism, 9, 223-247; haphazard or random, 232-235

Smith, Adam, viii, 37-41, 56-57, 91, 110, 113, 118, 119, 290, 308-311, 368 (10), 370 (3), 383 (4)

INDEX

Smith, Sydney, 118-119
Social contract, 186
Social cooperation. *See* Cooperation
"Social justice," 317. *See also* Justice
Social mind, 165 ff.
Social objectivity, 165
Social value, 164 ff. *See also* Value
Socialism: vs. capitalism, 301-324, *passim;* as coercion, 337-340; and communism, 326; ethics of, 325-341; utopian, 326-329
Society, and individual, 35, 104-106, 108-110, 313, 355
Socrates, 2, 3, 27-29, 200, 224-225, 230, 334-335, 343
Soldiers, and policemen, 297
Solipsistic judgments vs. shared, 168 ff.
Spencer, Herbert, 1, 92-97, 113, 150-156, 177, 248-250, 253-254, 256-258, 297-298, 365 (11), 373 (1), 385 (15), 386 (4)
Spinoza, 3, 22, 200, 344
Stalin, 304, 341
Statistical theory of ethics, 232, 243
Stevenson, C. L., 135, 239, 241-243, 372 (13)
Stoics, 2, 3, 206
Strauss, Leo, 382 (4)
Stylites, St. Simeon, 210-211, 222
Subjectivism, 162-175, *passim*
Sumner, William Graham, 177
Supererogation, ethics of, 157
Superman, 144, 229
Sympathy, 75, 90-91, 104

Teleotism, 358, 368 (9), 386 (1)
Temperance, 18, 45, 85, 296
Ten Commandments, 8, 59, 349
Tennyson, Alfred Lord, 175, 292
Thompson, E. P., 385 (15)
Thomson, James, 118
Thorndike, E. L., 385 (15)
Thrasymachus, 181, 224-226, 228
Tiger, Johnny and the, 293, 361-362
Time discount, 50

Toulmin, Stephen, ix, 127, 170, 371 (23), 386 (16)
Traffic rules, and moral rules, 70-74, 183
Treason, 296
Trotsky, Leon, 339
Truthtelling, 79
Twain, Mark, 184
Twilight zone: of duty, 122; in solving problems, 371 (20)

Unanimity, 36, 357
Uneasiness, 21
United Nations, 283, 292-293, 294
Universalizability of moral rules, 143 ff., 196-197, 355-356, 373 (9); generality vs. specificity, 144; vs. particularity, 196, 355-356
Urmson, J. O., ix, 157, 372 (3), 373 (5), 376 (8)
Utilitarianism, 18, 56, 72, 132, 175, 179-180, 234, 286-287, 313, 330, 354, 358-359, 367-368 (9), 370 (1), 373 (13); act-, 60, 179; ad hoc utilitism, 60, 287, 359; "ideal," 117, 130, 134, 372 (12); naive, 72; rule-, 60, 359, 386 (3); rule-utilitism, 60, 287, 354, 386 (3)
Utilitism, 60, 287, 368 (9). *See also* Utilitarianism
Utility, principle of, 15

Valuation, all human action implies, 245
"Valuative," as substitute for "emotive," 379 (49). *See also* Value; Value-judgments; Value-words
Value(s), 25, 159-175; commensurability of, 173-174, 374 (16), 375 (19); comparability of, 173-174; "exchange-" vs. "use-," 170; of "gold" vs. "bread," 175; as "intrinsic," 162 ff.; judgments of, 159-162, 238 ff., 245-247, 357-358; marginal, 175; as measurable, 171-175; multifaceted

nature of, 169-171; not a "property," 170-171; as objective, 162 ff.; "paradox of," 175; quantification of, 173-174; as a relation, 162 ff.; as "relational predicate," 171, 374 (10); social, 164 ff.; as subjective, 162 ff.; "transvaluation of all," 182, 355

Value-judgments, 159-162, 238 ff., 245-247, 357-358, 379 (49)

Value-words, 237 ff., 245-247, and *passim*

Veblen, Thorstein, 97

Verdi, 307

Vinogradoff, Sir Paul, ix, 369 (4), 376 (2), 381 (1)

Virtue(s): and happiness, 24; as means, 133-135, 221-222; paradox of, 296; as positive, 218; as useful to others, 218

Vocation: choice of, 197-200; and circumstances, 188-202, 356, 376 (3); moral, 200

Voltaire, 154

Voluptuary's fallacy, 44-45

Wagner, Richard, 307
War, ethics of, 297-300
Washington, George, 200, 296, 343
Weber, Max, 159
Webster, Daniel, 294
Well-being and happiness, 24-26, 134
Wheeler, William Morton, 385 (15)
"Why should I (we) be moral?" 123-127
Wicksteed, Philip, 37, 40-41, 311-312, 313, 318-323, 373 (12), 383 (4,13,18)
Widgery, Alban G., 371 (2)
Wilde, Oscar, 73
"Will to refrain," 217-218
"Will to power," 227
Williams, Roger J., 380 (1,2)
Wilson, Mr. Justice, 63
Wisdom, and ethics, 52
Witch, "not suffer to live," 349
Wittgenstein, 237

Yerkes, R. M., 385 (15)

Zarathustra, 3